To Jane,
I hope you enjoy
reading about Marcellus
and its history. Best
wishes,
John Curtin

PUCKER STREET
The first 100 years

⪆⪅

THE VILLAGE OF MARCELLUS NEW YORK
ESTABLISHED 1853

John P. Curtin
June 24, 2003

BY JOHN P. CURTIN
EDITED BY JAMES C. QUINN

First Edition 2003
Published and Copyrighted © by the Board of Trustees of the Village of Marcellus for
The Marcellus Historical Society

Printed in Victoria, Canada

National Library of Canada Cataloguing in Publication Data

Curtin, John P., 1941-
    Pucker Street, the first 100 years : a history of the Village of
Marcellus / John P. Curtin.
Includes bibliographical references and index.
ISBN 1-55395-738-5
    1. Marcellus (N.Y.)--History. I. Title.
F129.M36C87 2003   974.7'65   C2003-900861-

TRAFFORD

This book was published *on-demand* in cooperation with Trafford Publishing.
On-demand publishing is a unique process and service of making a book available for retail sale to the public taking advantage of on-demand manufacturing and Internet marketing. **On-demand publishing** includes promotions, retail sales, manufacturing, order fulfilment, accounting and collecting royalties on behalf of the author.

Suite 6E, 2333 Government St., Victoria, B.C. V8T 4P4, CANADA
Phone   250-383-6864   Toll-free 1-888-232-4444 (Canada & US)
Fax   250-383-6804   E-mail sales@trafford.com
Web site www.trafford.com   TRAFFORD PUBLISHING IS A DIVISION OF TRAFFORD HOLDINGS LTD.
Trafford Catalogue #03-0101   www.trafford.com/robots/03-0101.html

10   9   8   7   6   5   4   3   2   1

About The Cover

The cover includes a pencil drawing completed by Margaret F. Parsons in 1840.
It is the oldest known illustration of the Village of Marcellus.
It was donated to the Marcellus Historical Society Museum Collection
by Pauline Parsons Docket.

The cover design is by Marcellus resident and graphic artist, Maribeth Powell.

ii

PUCKER STREET

The first 100 years

THE VILLAGE OF MARCELLUS NEW YORK
ESTABLISHED 1853

BY JOHN P. CURTIN
EDITED BY JAMES C. QUINN

First Edition 2003
Published and Copyrighted © by the Board of Trustees of the Village of Marcellus for
The Marcellus Historical Society

Dedication

To Maureen, always my welcome home

Preface

I am sure that people will first want to know why I decided to title this work about the history of the Village of Marcellus, "*Pucker Street*" and I begin by providing several reasons for this. I wanted to have a rather unusual name for the work, which would mark its unique character as a depiction of small town American life from the standpoint of a Village Trustee in 2003. I read a story about Marcellus Village in <u>Onondaga's Centennial,</u> which I have reprinted below, and that brief passage, helped me in my decision to name the work, *PUCKER STREET*.

"According to a credible story, Marcellus village was once nicknamed "Pucker Street." Mrs. Chloe Thomas, when a young woman, boarded at Rufus Lawrence's, and one day accompanied Adam Baker to town on horseback. Finishing her errands, she mounted her horse to return, but her escort was nowhere in sight, and she lustily called out "Ad-a-m!" At home she expressed her mortification of having to shout for "Adam right in the middle of Pucker Street," a term which so pleased the four Lawrence brothers that they mounted their horses and riding through the village shouted, "Hurrah for Pucker Street" <u>(Onondaga's Centennial</u> 650-651)

Another story that involves the name, Pucker Street, is taken from Kathryn C. Heffernan's book about Marcellus entitled, <u>Nine Mile Country</u>.

"In more recent years, Vic Lambdin, who drew historical cartoons for the Syracuse Herald, offered another version of the origin of the term in one of his sketches portraying historical aspects of Marcellus. His explanation claimed that Marcellus had so many Yale graduates among its early settlers that it was called 'Pucker Street,' which was early Americana for 'high hat'" (Heffernan 269).

Whatever the explanation, I hope that the name will help people remember that this little village in Central New York has a significant history, parts of which have already been told in one fashion or another and need not, after 150 years since its incorporation, be repeated.

I began doing the research for this book back in 1995, inspired in large part by a love for my home on First Street in the Village, where my wife and I have lived since 1971 and raised our children to adulthood.

I have also been motivated by an interest in family histories many of which have spanned the history of the village. My great grandfather, Michael Curtin, was just seventeen years old when he left Ireland in 1834. He first landed in Canada, then a part of the British Empire, and then traveled south, walking across the unguarded border into northern New York State. Within a few years, he married another Irish immigrant by the name of Johanna Gorman, and by 1846, settled in the Town of Marcellus, a place they would call home for the rest of their lives. In Pumpkin Hollow, they raised a family of eleven children, worked the land as well as a nearby quarry, and lived out their lives in unsophisticated fashion. When they died, they were buried on the hills overlooking the village that was part of their home, in graves marked by simple stones labeled Grandpa and Grandma.

As I studied the history of the community, I felt as if I was making a visit to the past, becoming immersed in the antebellum times of Michael Curtin and that of his contemporaries. As the story of the Village began to emerge, the lives of people long dead seemed more and more interesting, and as I continued to research and write, the

viii

world of succeeding generations unlocked a history that I found to be fascinating – the history of a small town in America, that is both common and unique.

What I have tried to do in this work is to provide the reader with a glimpse of the history of the Village of Marcellus from a slightly different perspective. I have primarily used the <u>Minutes of the Board of Trustees of the Village of Marcellus (1853-1953)</u> to help tell the story and throughout the book, those minutes are printed in a font that is different the rest of the narrative. While I hope that the narrative is interesting, I also know that reading a compilation of Board minutes will produce instant boredom. However, I also wanted this work to serve as a reference tool for those who might need to research items related to the history of the Village. To this end, I have tried to make the index as inclusive as possible and have cross-referenced many entries. As a Trustee of the Village, I was often at a loss trying to find information about government operations in the past and am hopeful that this work will assist future officers of the Village in their search for relative information.

I have also tried to incorporate a brief biographical sketch of some individuals who I have found to be of interest in the story of the Village. I feel that people make history, but they are also influenced by their circumstances, which in turn affects what they may or may not have done during the times in which they lived. Often, therefore, it is important to know something about individuals as well as their families in order to understand the times.

In addition, since it is one of the primary sources of information on the history of the community, I have made much use of *The Marcellus Observer* (1879-1953) in this work, copying whole articles and inserting a number of pictures from various editions of the paper. I am very much indebted to The Eagle Newspapers and its editor/publisher, Mr. Stewart Hancock, for permission to use both the stories and the pictures. In crediting the stories and the pictures in *The Marcellus Observer*, I have often used the initials "MO", rather than citing the entire name. I have done this mostly in the interest of layout and design.

Most of the photographs that are used in this work are from The Marcellus Historical Society collection and I am grateful to that group and particularly to its President, Mrs. Peg Nolan, for the assistance that she and other members of the society have provided in gathering these pictures and allowing me to use them. Since this work is being published and is copyrighted by the Board of Trustees of the Village of Marcellus, for the Marcellus Historical Society, any proceeds from the sale of this publication are earmarked for the benefit of that organization.

A number of individuals have been very helpful in my efforts and I would especially like to thank:
Dr. James Quinn, whose labors in editing this work have been immeasurable. In addition to editing, his insight provided me with a focus and a direction that, at the outset, was sorely lacking.
Maribeth Powell, whose skills and advice as a graphic artist were most appreciated as the book took final shape.

Martin and Dorothy Sennett, Peg Nolan and Jim Hettinger for their help in reading the rough drafts of the book and adding their thoughts, as well as making corrections when needed.

My fellow Board members, Fred Eisenberg, Bob Wilson, and Village Attorney, Jim Dwyer, whose encouragement and help at various stages was much appreciated.

Dawn Marshall, Gary and Elie March for their patience and understanding as I constantly interrupted the daily routine of their work in the Village Office.

Kathryn C. Heffernan, whose well-researched book, *Nine Mile Country*, was my handy reference and guide.

My wife, Maureen, my kids and grandkids, whose attention I often neglected while working on this book.

When I began, I had hoped to complete a work that encompassed the entire 150 years of the Village's history, in time for its sesquicentennial in 2003. I have not, however, been able to do this, narrowing the history to the first 100 years, 1853-1953. The remaining years, 1953 to 2003, might provide an interesting sequel to the story of the Village – a Volume II, perhaps – but that is for another time.

Writing and organizing this history has consumed much time and effort but to quote Jim Quinn, "it has been a labor of love, for the town we love so well."

X

Table of Contents

Chapter 1 - The Beginning

The Village of Marcellus is one of the oldest settlements in Central New York. It was incorporated as a Village on June 4, 1853 and in 2003 celebrates its 150th anniversary. The Village is part of the Town of Marcellus, one of the original towns of Onondaga County, with a history dating to 1794 and it included most of what now comprises the Towns of Skaneateles, Spafford, Otisco, Camillus, Van Buren, Elbridge, Geddes and Onondaga, as well as a part of Cayuga County. In time, the Town was reduced in area and today retains about one-third its original size.

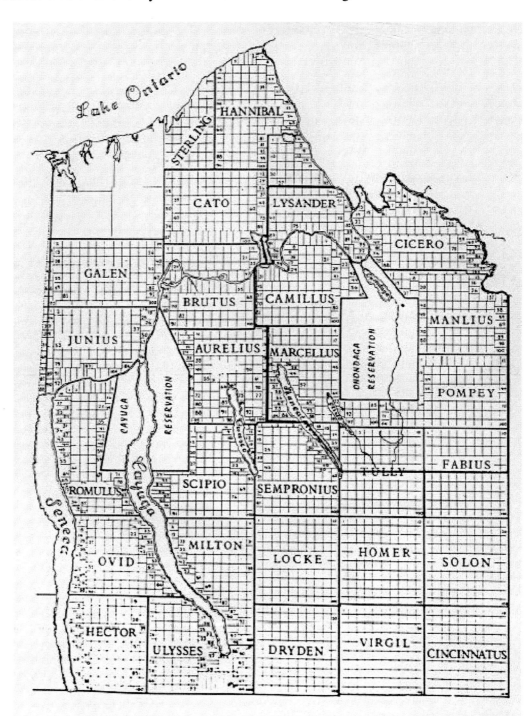

The Military Tract

Onondaga County, like other counties on the frontier of civilization at the time, was originally a military tract, land set aside by the government to be used as payment to Revolutionary War soldiers in recognition of their service in that war. Onondaga County was then divided into townships that were numbered rather than named, with Marcellus being known as Township Number Nine of the Military Tract. Later, proper names were desired, so the various townships were named after famous people, many of them ancient Greeks and Romans. Originally, as the maps point out, the Township of Marcellus covered considerably more territory than now, and " . . . contained one hundred lots of about six hundred twenty acres each and included all of the territory in the present Onondaga County south of the Seneca River, west of Onondaga Lake and Creek and north of the southern end of Otisco Lake and also parts of what are now Cayuga and Cortland Counties" (Heffernan 5).

By the early part of the 19th century, the creation of Cayuga and Cortland Counties would reduce the size of Onondaga County and with the establishment of the Towns of Onondaga, Camillus, Otisco Spafford and Skaneateles, the original area of the Town of Marcellus was reduced to its present size, about thirty-two of the original one hundred lots.

Most of the lots in the Military Tract were not settled by those to whom they had been granted but were sold to land speculators who in turn divided the land into smaller lots to be sold to settlers. The Village of Marcellus lies on parts of two of those thirty-two lots, numbers fifteen and twenty-four. Historians indicate that Lot 15 was granted to one Isaac Wheeler and that Abraham Tompkins drew Lot 24, but neither men settled the land having sold both parcels to Henry S. Platt, a Dutchess County farmer and land speculator (Heffernan 2).

Settlement

Marcellus, like most communities, developed at the crossroads of two major transportation routes: Nine Mile Creek and Seneca Turnpike. While abundant water and good soil in the area were significant attractions for farmers, the water power provided by

Nine Mile Creek, an outlet of Otisco Lake, was equally important, attracting a variety of individuals who built a diversity of mills (grist, saw, barley and woolen) on its banks. The products of these mills attracted even more individuals to the valley to work in the mills themselves, as well as provide other services for neighboring farmers.

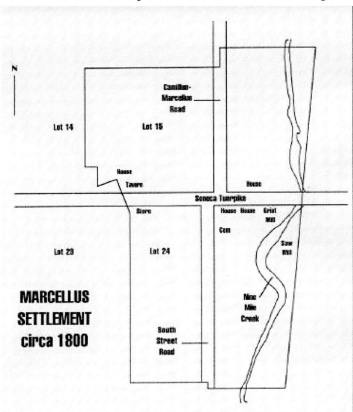

Following an old Indian trail, a primitive road had been opened across Onondaga County in the early 1790s and the first settlers came to Marcellus either on foot or horseback, following that old trail. Often, these pioneers found it easier to travel in the winter when sleighs could be used for transportation on the snow. Seneca Turnpike was an outgrowth of what came to be known as the Great Indian Trail, that stretched across the state and became a major highway for people moving from New England and the settled east to what was then the western frontier.

The settlement that came to be the Village of Marcellus was located on this main highway of east-west travel. Originally the road was almost a straight line through the Village, roughly the dividing line between lots fifteen and twenty-four, along what is now Slocombe (once Maiden Lane) Avenue, up the steep hill and across the property of what is now the Catholic Cemetery. About 1800, the State of New York decided to improve the highway and in the process changed the roadbed to reflect its present location on its way west out of the Village. This enabled both man and horse to avoid the steep climb, a winding and more gradual approach, east and west. This also encouraged the operation of more stagecoach lines on the turnpike helping to attract more settlers and promoting the area's development as a trading and manufacturing center.

Survey

During the first fifty years of its existence, the Town of Marcellus, although reduced in size by many partitions, would continue to attract people and industries at a rather steady pace. As these numbers increased, more people tended to concentrate in the valley that would become the Village, living closer and closer together, in contrast to their rural neighbors. The inhabitants soon began to realize the need for some sort of organization and it was out of this urgency that the Village would be incorporated in 1853. Before the incorporation could take place, however, a survey was necessary and this was completed by a Wheeler Truesdell, who used the terms "chains" and "links" in his review. The most common means of measurement at the time, a "chain" was a unit of length equal to sixty-six feet, and one hundred "links" made up a chain. Truesdell's original survey for the Corporation of the Village of Marcellus can be found in the

Corporation Book of Marcellus Village, secured at present in the safe of the Marcellus Village Office.

VILLAGE OF MARCELLUS
Original Corporation of Marcellus Village
Lots 15 & 24

Beginning on the West line of Lot 15, Marcellus, and at the North West corner of a farm once owned by Hiram Reed, thence South 21 chains and 96 links, thence East 3 chains and 29 links, thence South 4 chains and 50 links to the center of the Seneca Turnpike, thence North 74 V4° East 3 chains and 70 links, thence South 30 1/2° East 5 chains and 76 links, thence South 34 chains and 90 links, thence East 17 chains and 45 links to the center of South Street, thence along the center of said street South 1 chain and 49 links to the North line of the Slate Hill Road, thence along the North line of said road South 89° East 18 chains, thence North 3 1/4° East 71 chains and 62 links, thence West 20 chains and 24 links to the center of North Street, thence along the center of said street South 4 chains and 46 links, thence West 29 chains and 50 links to the place of beginning containing 282 16/100 acres of land.

Surveyed by Wheeler Treusdell,
1853

Boundaries

The original corporation comprised a little over 282 acres of land, about two-thirds the present size of the Village. The eastern and western boundaries of the Village have changed little since 1853. Nine Mile Creek is basically the eastern boundary of the Village, and the hills called the Lime Ledge mark off the western edge. On the north, the corporation line originally ended where, at present, the Chester S. Driver Middle School begins. A 1906 annexation added about seventy acres to the Village boundary including what we Marcellians commonly refer to today as Scotch Hill. On the south, the Village line has not changed very much in the last 150 years, a 1978 annexation adding about six acres of land to that border.

Petition and Incorporation

In April 1853, three prominent residents of the valley -- Samuel R. Ball, Nathan G. Hoyt and George N. Kennedy -- all of whom were representatives of a significant number of other individuals, petitioned the County of Onondaga for incorporation as a Village. The petition included a map and survey of the territory that they wished to incorporate, under the Incorporation of Villages Act, which was passed December 7, 1847 by the New York State Legislature. County Judge I. S. Spencer ruled that a special election was to be held within a given period of time and the electors of the defined territory would decide as to whether or not the Village was to be established.

29 Apr 1853 - "In the Matter of the Incorporation of Marcellus Village. At a court of sessions held at the Court house in the City of Syracuse in and for the County of Onondaga, on the 29th day of April 1853. Present - Hon. I. S. Spencer, County Judge and Associate Justice

". . . on reading and filing the petitions of Samuel R. Ball, Nathan G. Hoyt and George N. Kennedy, the map and survey of the territory therein embraced and proposed to be incorporated, the affidavit of Wheeler Truesdall duely verifying the same, a census of the resident population on said territory on the 14th day of March last, and the affidavit of Samuel R. Ball duely verifying the same . . . it is ordered that the following described territory ,that is to say, the same being situate on Lots number 15 8a 24 in the Town of Marcellus, once bounded and described as follows, . . . containing 282 19100 acres of land, be and the same is hereby incorporated as a village under the name of Marcellus, if the electors of said territory shall assent to said incorporation as provided by an act entitling an act to provide for the Incorporation of Villages passed December 7, 1847, and it is further ordered that Harry Fellows, Ira Bishop and James W. Herring, three of the inspectors of election in the Town of Marcellus, shall perform all the duties required of them by the provisions of the act aforesaid." (Minutes taken from the Corporation Book of the Village of Marcellus)

County Judge I. S. Spencer ruled that a special election was to be held within a given period of time and the electors of the defined territory would decide as to whether or not the Village was to be established. Fifty-one male, property owners voted on June 4, 1853, in the Public House of John Carpenter now known as The Alvord House. The vote was forty-one to ten in favor of incorporation and thus the Village of Marcellus was born.

4 Jun 1853 - "To the County Judge of Onondaga County. We the inspectors of election . . .hereby certify that an election was held on the 4th day of June 1853 at the house of John Carpenter in the village of Marcellus, and within the territory described, . . . the polls were open from about 10 o'clock in the forenoon until 4 o'clock in the afternoon of that day, . . . and the whole number of ballots voted was fifty one, and that of that number forty- one thereof had thereon the word yes, and ten had thereon the word no. Majority thirty one in favor of corporation."

Elections
With the approval of the voters to incorporate, the next step was the election of officers of the Village and in early July, again in John Carpenter's Public House, the day of election was set for July 23rd.

2 Jul 1853 - " . . . at the Public House kept by John Carpenter in said village on the 23d day of July instant, the following of ficers of said village will be then elected (viz) Five Trustees. Three Assessors. One Collector. One Treasurer. One Clerk. Three Street Commissioners. One Pound Master."

In that first election, a total of five trustees was chosen to represent the people of Marcellus, one of whom was selected as President and another as Vice President of the Village. The titles of Mayor and Deputy Mayor would not be used until the 20th Century. In addition, three (tax) assessors were elected, along with a Village Clerk, a Collector of Taxes, a Village Treasurer, three Street Commissioners and a Poundmaster. A Poundmaster was the individual responsible for gathering up any stray animals within the corporation limits and keeping them enclosed until they were either claimed or sold or destroyed. Over time, many of these offices would be either abolished (the poundmaster eventually became a dog warden) or combined into other positions (clerk, treasurer, collector of taxes). Still others would become appointed positions (street commissioners and fire wardens) or centralized and assumed by the Town of Marcellus government (assessors).

More on Elections
Beginning in 1853, elections would take place every year, continuing until the turn of the century, when elections would take place every two years. By 1968, elections every four years would be the norm. Election day was in March, just as it is today and in the beginning, until 1871, was the first Tuesday of the month. Later it would change to the third Tuesday of March, and it remains that way today.

Elections in the early years were generally held at a Public House, initially that of John Carpenter and later that of the Alvord Brothers when Carpenter sold out. Village Board Meetings were often held there as well. In later years, the meetings were sometimes held at the homes of various individuals, including those of the elected officials, or at local businesses, law firms, or the home of the village justice. After the Fire Engine House was built in 1889, elections and Village Board meetings would be held there, as they are today The regular Board Meetings were usually held every month at 7:00 p.m. and in the early years, these meetings were generally held on the first or second Tuesday of the Month, occasionally on Mondays or Wednesdays. There were also special meetings and public hearings held, just as they are today.

Most elections were not contested and, for the most part, few people voted in Village elections. There were a number of reasons for this, including some voting restrictions. A voter in the early years of the Village had to be male, a property owner and over 21 years of age, effectively excluding more than half of the population. Sometimes there was only one candidate for a position; many positions were uncontested, and there was little reason in the minds of Marcellians to vote for a position that went unchallenged. Most elected officials in the Village were not paid, contributing their time and their talents to the position as a matter of civic pride. This often meant that the only people who could afford to serve were those who were financially secure or those who not only had the time, but another job that would sustain this volunteer work. Because few people could afford the time, many positions in Village government went uncontested in the March elections each year.

Other times, there was little interest in the election because there were no serious issues that might attract a large voter turnout. Some elections did become challenged, however, a controversial issue bringing out an unusually large number of voters. Such an election occurred in 1953, at the time of the Village Centennial, when 465 ballots were cast in the largest voter turnout in Marcellus Village history. The issue of great concern that year was garbage pickup and the voters turned out in record numbers to voice their opinion, and confirming the now common expression that "all politics is local."

July 23, 1853

On July 23, 1853, in the Public House of John Carpenter, the voters would elected William J. Machan, Elijah Rowley, Isaac N. Soules, Isaac Bradley, and Daniel G. Coon as Trustees; A. H. Cowles, Chester Moses and J. Taylor as Assessors; Henry T. Kennedy as Village Clerk; Joseph Taylor as Collector of Taxes; G. N. Kennedy as Village Treasurer and J. G. B. White, Bishop N. Parsons and Nathan G. Hoyt as Street Commissioners. In addition, Avery Wilson was elected Poundmaster.

23 Jul 1853 - " . . . the whole number of votes given for the office of Trustee was two hundred and eighty three of which Isaac Bradley received forty seven, D. G. Coon received thirty two, Elijah Rowley received forty, W. J. Machan received forty nine, 1. N. Soules received thirty, Chester Moses received twenty four, Edmund Akin received ten, Sanford Dalliba received seven, A. H. Cowles received eight, Israel Parsons received sixteen, N. G. Hoyt received sixteen, G. N. Kennedy received two, George Reed one, and J. G. B. White received one. The whole number of votes given for the office of Street Commissioners was one hundred and seventy six: J. G. B. White received fifty seven, B. N. Parsons received forty, N. G. Hoyt received thirty seven, C. Moses, seventeen, George Reed, seventeen, A. Rockwell, eight. The whole number of votes given for assessor was one hundred and seventy one of which Chester Moses received thirty two, A. H. Cowles, thirty two, J. Taylor, forty two, C. S. Bennett, seventeen, B. N. Parsons, sixteen, W. J. Machan, sixteen, N. G. Hoyt, eight, S. R. Ball, eight. The whole number of votes given for the office of Clerk was fifty-seven of which H. G. Kennedy received thirty- five and C. W. Chase received twenty two. The whole number of votes given for the office of Collector was fifty six of which Joseph Taylor received fifty six. The whole number of votes taken for Treasurer was fifty seven of which G. H. Kennedy received thirty, S. R. Ball, seventeen, and J. W. Herring, two. The whole number of votes taken for Pound Master was fifty-seven of which Amery Wilson received fifty-seven."

The People

Those first elected officials of the Village comprised a group whose common interest was not only civic, but economic and social as well. Early U.S. and NY State census records, particularly those of 1850 and 1855, confirm not only those common interests but provide interesting background information as well.

The first President of the Village, selected by his fellow Trustees, was William J. Machan. He was a fairly wealthy man at the time, owner of the woolen mill factory that today lies in ruins at the end of Maple Street. Machan was also a family man, with a wife and three children, was forty-five years old at the time of his election and he had lived in Onondaga County all of his life.

The Vice President of the Village, again selected by his fellow Trustees, was Elijah Rowley. He was probably what might be termed a middle-class person today, a shoemaker by profession, with a wife and two children. Born in Vermont, he was forty-six yeas old at this time.

The other Trustees included forty year-old Isaac N. Soules, was a wagon maker, living with his wife and two children in the Village for about six years since his move from Madison County. Isaac Bradley, the largest vote getter in 1853, was in the insurance business and a fairly wealthy man with a wife and three children. He was born in Marcellus, the son of one of the first settlers of the community, and was thirty-five years old at the time. Daniel G. Coon, a future President of the Village himself, was the owner and operator of a distillery in Marcellus Falls. He was a family man, with a wife and two children and just thirty-nine years old. Born in Jefferson County, he had lived in Marcellus for about a dozen years and had a substantial income from his business enterprises.

Among the assessors was a physician, Alexander H. Cowles. Born in Connecticut, he was fifty-two years old and financially secure, a benefit for his wife and five children when he suddenly died in May 1854. Another of the assessors was Chester Moses. A prosperous businessman, he would eventually buy the woolen mill factory from William Machan, a venture that would later bankrupt him. The fifty-two year old Moses was born in Connecticut but had lived in Marcellus for over twenty years. He was also a family man, with a wife and three children at the time. Joseph Taylor, the third assessor and also the Collector of Taxes for the Village, was a wealthy farmer with a wife and two children. He was born in Connecticut and was sixty-five years old at the time of his election. He died the next year, in 1854.

The Clerk of the Village was Henry T. Kennedy, who was born in the community, a young man of thirty at the time. He was the Town and Village postmaster with a wife and one child. The Village Treasurer was George Nelson Kennedy, who was no relation to Henry. This Kennedy was a thirty-year old lawyer, married and wealthy. Born in Marcellus, he would eventually move to Syracuse where he enjoyed a distinguished career in state government and on the bench.

The street commissioners included Jeremiah G. B. White, a well-to-do hatter of fifty-seven years who had lived in the area for over thirty-five year, with a wife and two children. Another was Bishop N. Parsons, a wealthy clothier. Born in Massachusetts, he was sixty-five years old at the time, having lived in Marcellus for over thirty-five of those years. He, too, was a family man with a wife and two children. The third commissioner was Nathan G. Hoyt, a cabinet-maker as well as a local undertaker. He was well-off, financially, with a wife and six children. Forty-three years old at the time, Hoyt was another Marcellian who was born in Connecticut.

The Poundmaster was one Amory Wilson, also referred to as "Quaker" Wilson, an early penchant in our Village's history, it seems, for identifying people with certain name. Wilson was a nurseryman and to him is attributed the planting of cherry trees on what would soon be called Cherry (South) Street. He was also the local "bell ringer," a position probably of more importance to many in the Village than that of Poundmaster. He was a married man, born fifty-eight years before in Vermont, and through the years he would hold a number of positions in Village government.

Conclusion

From these brief descriptions, gleaned from census and other records, one can tell that the people in early Village government were, by and large, educated white men, mostly middle-aged, and most were financially secure. All were married and most had two or three children. Their occupations, while different, were typical of those who lived in a rural village that addressed the needs of local farmers. All were native born, largely of Anglo-Saxon background and while the New England connection, particularly Connecticut, was very strong, most were born in New York State. Although some would move from the community, east to Syracuse or west to the frontier, most would stay in Marcellus, live out their lives and be buried in the Village Cemetery.

It was during this same time period that America was experiencing the influx of group of immigrants quite different from the native born population, many settling in the valley of the Nine Mile. Although most would initially live beyond the corporation limits, primarily in places like Marcellus Falls and Pumpkin Hollow, these new settlers would impact the emerging Village of Marcellus. These immigrants were mostly Irish, overwhelmingly Catholic and poor, and their arrival in America aroused great suspicion and fear among some native born people who felt threatened by a people so different. Their fears would give rise, on the national level, to nativist groups such as the Know Nothing Party in 1853 and calls for immigration restrictions and quotas.

Most of these new arrivals in Marcellus were young, and most were needy. They brought their Catholic faith with them, along with a culture that was strange to earlier inhabitants. Many were uneducated peasants and while some might be able to farm rented land, others would take the meanest jobs to provide for their families, families that usually included many children. Some of these immigrants would move from the community, finding more opportunity in the west, but most would stay, live out their lives and be buried on the hills overlooking the Village.

As the history of the Village begins to unfold in the years ahead, the social interaction of different groups and individuals will not only enable civilization to grow and the economy to expand but American democracy to broaden its base in this place we call Marcellus, a microcosm of America itself.

Chapter 2 - Getting Organized

The Board of Trustees met in August of 1853, shortly after their election, to organize, pass a series of Village Ordinances and appoint people to fill positions in the Village administration.

4 Aug 1853 - " . . . meeting of the elected trustees . . . for the purpose of organizing themselves into a board . . .. the trustees then reported the . . . rules of ordinances to be adopted at their next meeting . . .. proceeded to appoint . . . persons to fill vacancies . . . adjourned to meet in the conference room of the Presbaterian (sic) Church on Thursday, August 11th 1853 at nine o'clock in the forenoon."

11 Aug 1853 - "Ordinances of the Village of Marcellus Prepared by the Trustees of Said Village."

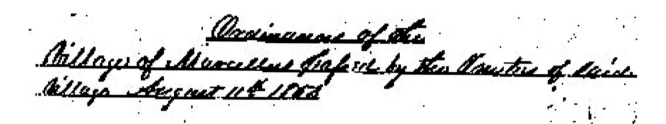

Village Ordinances

There were a total of 21 separate ordinances, or sections as they were called, enacted for all of the residents of Marcellus Village and they dealt with matters that parallel in many ways, the concerns of today's Village residents. The ordinances involved a range of problems: animals running at large, accumulating debris, snow removal, the firing of guns, fireworks, the building of fires, disturbing the peace, health regulations, public bathing or swimming, damage to public trees, disorderly houses and businesses, vagrancy, prostitution, liquor, billiard tables, games of chance, public exhibitions, damage to public streets, the public pound, lighted candles or lamps or cigars in a livery or barn, keeping ashes secure, chimney, boiler and furnace construction. A final ordinance, Number 21, called for the election, rather than the appointment, of three Fire Wardens, beginning with the election of 1854. Many of these ordinances, although somewhat modified in years since, are still applicable and serve as the basis of Village law today.

Taxes

Another matter was that of taxes. In order for the village government to operate and provide for its residents, the trustees would seek revenue from the village taxpayers. Often, this appeal would require, as it sometimes does today, a vote by the taxpayers themselves. The Trustees, in many cases, could only recommend that taxes be raised, the voters themselves deciding whether or not taxes would be imposed to pay for needed operations.

10 Sep 1853 - " . . . the Trustees recommended that " . . . taxes be raised . . . "

In September, 1853, taxpayers of the Village were asked to pay for the expense of incorporation, to purchase hooks and ladders, construct reservoirs, build a pound, lay new cross walks, publish the by laws, and to lay plank sidewalks.

11 Sep 1853 - " . . . We as Trustees would recommend such sums of money by a tax as will be necessary to defray the expenses of said incorporation for the past year in the following items and for the following purposes (viz):

"$30 - for procuring the incorporation of said village . . .

"$20 - for procuring the printing and record books . . .

"$15 - for compensation of the Clerk for last year . . .

"$25 - for compensation of the Trustees for last year . . .

. . . We would also recommend that a tax be raised from the taxable property in said incorporation to be expended in the following manner (to wit)

plank sidewalks to be laid . . .

$35 - for the purchasing hooks and ladders . . .

$20 - for two new cross walks . . .

$35 - for procuring the ground and erecting a pound in said village . . .

$210 - for constructing three reservoirs . . . "

In the vote that followed, some of these tax increases were approved by the voters, including the construction of new sidewalks, but the electorate chose neither to build reservoirs, nor build a pound, nor build new cross walks, nor purchase hooks and ladders. Not many taxpayers voted on these propositions, a total of seventeen, and on many issues it was a very close vote, nine to eight on several. Many of the issues voted down by the voters in 1853, however, would be revisited, and in future balloting would gain taxpayer approval.

The Early Years

On March 7, 1854, the residents of the Village would have another election of officers. This was in keeping with New York State Law, which, at that time, mandated annual village elections. In this second election in Marcellus Village history, the voters would again elect five trustees, three tax assessors, one collector of taxes, one treasurer, one clerk, and one pound master. In addition, the voters in this election chose three fire wardens, but the Board of Trustees now appointed street commissioners. In the election of 1854, a wealthy farmer by the name of Edmund Aiken became President of the Village, along with two holdovers from the previous year, Isaac Soules and Isaac Bradley. Aiken, forty years old and married, had been born in Connecticut but lived in Marcellus for almost 15 years.

Two new Trustees included Jeremiah G. B. White and Nathan G. Hoyt, both of whom had served as Street Commissioners in the previous year. Joseph Taylor was re-elected as Collector of Taxes, while George Kennedy remained as Village Treasurer and Henry Kennedy continued as Village Clerk.

In that election, Myron Mills, Sanford Dalliba and Edmund Aiken were the first elected Fire Wardens of the Village. Mills was a well-to-do farmer with a wife and family. He was in his mid sixties at the time and had lived in Marcellus for over thirty-five years. Dalliba was a wealthy merchant with a large family, and like Mills was born in Connecticut but had lived in the area for some time. He was in his late forties in 1854.

Sidewalks

During this second year, and continuing for a number of years to come, the major concern for officials of the Village was that of new sidewalks and crosswalks, the erection of a Village Pound a close second. In this second administration, the Board of

Trustees began to require that residents of the Village construct sidewalks in front of their properties, complete with specifications -- of hemlock, so many inches thick, appropriate grading. If a resident failed to construct the sidewalk, the Village would complete the task and then assess the owner.

Today, the Village maintains sidewalks in Marcellus and there is a regular maintenance program, which includes plowing during winter months. The sidewalk in front of a resident's home or in front of a business establishment is, in most cases, part of the Village right-of-way. There are restrictions today, including the prohibition of blacktopping any part of a Village sidewalk -- a fact that is sometimes overlooked when a resident's driveway is paved.

15 Apr 1854 - "MAIN STREET, . . . take notice that the owners of Lots on the North side of Main street in the village of Marcellus between the bridge and the west line of Caleb Gasper house lot and on the south side of said street between the east line of Edward Talbot house lot, and the west line of Caleb Cowles Jr house lot, are required to construct a plank side walk on the side of the street in front of their respective lots within 60 days from the service of this notice. Said side walks are to be built of new 2 inch hemlock plank laid parallel with said street five feet wide and thoroughly spiked to cross pieces of 4 by 4 scantling of the same materials laid 4 feet a part. The ground for the walks to be properly graded and walk laid under the superintendence of the Trustees or their agent, and if such owner shall refuse or neglect to construct such side walks as herby required thereon the said Trustees will proceed to construct the same and assess the expense of such construction upon the lots in front of which the same is made. By Order of the Trustees."

1855

In 1855, a new President of the Village, Lake I. Tefft, was selected. He was a physician by profession and owner of a brick house on North Street that would become a Village landmark. Today his home is known as the Stedman House and is a very good example of the style of architecture referred to as Greek Revival, with its massive front columns. Tefft was a married man, with a large income; fifty-eight years old at the time, he had lived in Marcellus for over thirty years. Elected along with him was Caleb Gasper, whose home is also a Village landmark today -- that of the Marcellus Free Library. Gasper's occupation is listed as "gentleman," which meant that he had enough money so that he did not have to work for a living. He was born in Connecticut about 1787, and had lived in Marcellus since the mid 1820s. In addition to Gasper, another "gentleman", James Herring, was elected to the Board. Born in Vermont, he was about 45 years old at the time, having come to Marcellus when he was quite young.

The new Village Board of Trustees would add revised sidewalk requirements and also stipulate that crosswalks be made of stone rather than hemlock, providing a significant improvement in longevity. There was also the issue of a village pound, which the voters had not yet approved for construction. Apparently, animals of all sorts were roaming unchecked throughout the Village, and the Pound Master, Amory Wilson, was in need of a place for their detention. A horticulturalist and nurseryman, Wilson, kept the animals he seized at his place of business and he eventually needed to have a pound erected to hold the animals. This issue, while significant at the time, did not have the urgency of sidewalks and would not be resolved for a number of years.

7 Apr 1855 - " . . . it was resolved that Mills and Phillips be chosen as a committee to enquire of E. Akin in regard to a village pound . . .. Gasper and Herring be chosen a committee to enquire about stone for cross walks . . .. all obstructions shall be kept from the side walks."

11 Apr 1855 - " . . . James W. Herring and Caleb Gasper be a committee to superintend the building of two new cross walks at the upper end of the village and be empowered to contract

with some person who will build such cross walks the best and cheapest for said incorporation. Said walks to be three feet wide of stone not less than five inches thick and such as will fully answer the purpose. Also another cross walk at the lower end of the village if there is sufficient funds for doing it."

18 Apr 1855 - " . . . to the inhabitants on Main and Factory Streets that the Trustees will meet on Tuesday, the first day of May next for the purpose of receiving proposals for furnishing plank and other necessary materials for side walks on said streets and laying the same. Also they will receive proposals for the making of gravel walks according to the votes of the electors of the incorporation."

Assessment - Taxes

As the demand for Village services increased, the Board of Trustees found it necessary to do what government often does when budgets must be met -- apportion new taxes. Not many houses existed in the Village at the time and those that did, were assessed a certain amount of money in order to pay for necessary projects, particularly sidewalks. The assessment of taxes in 1855, like today, was based on property value, and a reading of the tax rolls, and the map that follows, not only indicates some individual property wealth, but also tells something of occupation, location -- where these people of 150 years ago lived in the Village -- and other factors often overlooked in early village records. Starting at the northwest corner of Factory Street, what is today the corner of Maple and Orange Streets, where St. John's Episcopal Church now stands, the accompanying map and tax list provides a reference for property values of individual homeowners in 1855.

On the map that follows, some street names are different than those used today in the Village. North Street was often called the Camillus-Marcellus Road and South Street was often referred to as Cherry Street. Main Street was also referred to as Seneca Turnpike and occasionally as Genesee Street. By this time, Seneca Turnpike no longer followed a straight line west from the Village, the State of New York having altered the road some years before enabling wagon and horse to avoid a steep climb as they traveled west.

Factory Street included what we now know as Orange and Maple Streets, at the end of which, from both Main and North Streets was a woolen mill that employed many Village and Town of Marcellus residents. The factory built by Robert and Thomas Dyer in 1812 changed hands a number of times and in 1847 was destroyed by fire. In 1848, William J. Machan, the future President of the Village, rebuilt the mill and continued with the manufacture of woolens until 1855, when he sold the business to Chester Moses. The mill would continue to flourish until Moses died in 1870.

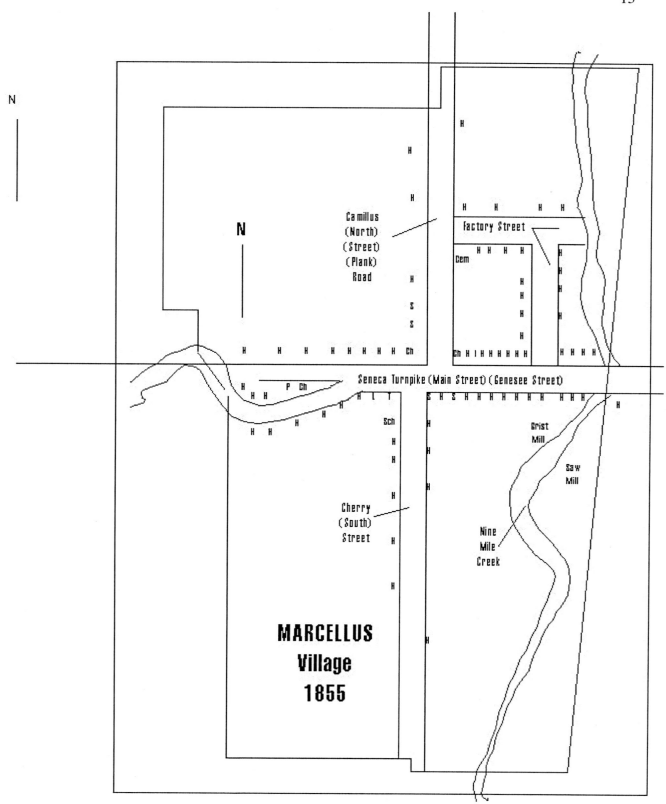

N

N

Camillus
(North)
(Street)
(Plank)
Road

Factory Street

Cem

Ch

Seneca Turnpike (Main Street) (Genesee Street)

P Ch

Sch

Cherry
(South)
Street

Grist
Mill

Saw
Mill

Nine
Mile
Creek

**MARCELLUS
Village
1855**

28 Jul 1855 - "List of taxes apportioned by the Trustees of the incorporation of the Village of Marcellus on the owners and corporations holding property thereon and upon the real estate lying inside the boundaries of said incorporation for the purpose of raising the sum of $332.73 laid and charged to said inhabitants . . . for the building of side walks:

Name of Inhabitants and Corporations	Location and Description of Lot	Amount
John Curtis	House lot on the north west corner of Factory street and west side of said street	$3.23
George Brown	House lot on the west side of Factory street and south of John Curtis	$11.55
E. W. Frost	House lot on the west side of Factory street and next south of George Brown	$15.41
Hezekiah Shepard	Three houses and lots on the west side of Factory street and north side of Main street beginning south of George Brown's house lot and terminating on the east line of Susan Chase house lot	$37.70
Susan Chase	House lot on the north side of Main street and next west of lot owned by H. Shepard	$4.77
B. F. Moses	Store and house lot on north side of Main street and next west of Susan Chase house lot	$14.30
E. Dorchester	Harnass shop lot on the north side of Main street and next west of B. F. Moses house lot	$4.81
Newton G. Case	Store and house lot on north side of Main street and next west of E. Dorchester harnass shop	$14.10
H. G. McGonegal	House lot on the north side of Main street and next west of N. G. Case store and house lot	$8.68
John Carpenter	Public house on the north side of Main street and next west of H. G. McGonegal house lot	$32.44
H. G. Kennedy	House lot on the north side of Main street and next west of John Carpenter's Public house	$4.84
Trustees of the Eastern Religious Society	House lot and Church lot on north side of Main street and east side of North street and next west of H. G. Kennedy's house lot	$28.36
Trustees of the Episcopal Church	Church lot on the west side of North street and north side of Main street and next west of the Presbeterian Church lot	$6.56
Addison Farnham	House lot on the north side of Main street and next west of the Episcopal Church lot	$11.53
Mrs. Mary Machan	House lot on the north side of Main street and next west of Addison Farnham house lot	$7.72
Alexander Mather	Shoe shop and house and lot on north side of Main street and next west of Mrs. Mary Machan house lot	$9.28
Caleb Gasper	House lot on north side of Main street and next west of Alexander Mather house lot	$9.64
Edmund Akin	Shoe shop, two shops and law office on south side of Main street and corner of Main and Cherry streets	$11.52
Rachel Newton	House lot on the south side of Main street and next east of Edmund Akin Law office	$7.59
Caleb Cowles Jr.	Drug store lot on south side of Main street and next east of Rachel Newton house lot	$5.88
J. G. B. White	House lot on south side of Main street and next east of Caleb Cowles Jr. Drug store lot	$14.20
Mrs. Jane Smith	House lot on south side of Main street and next east of J. G. B. White house lot	$10.38
Estate of A. H. Cowles	House lot on south side of Main street and next east of Mrs. Jane Smith house lot	$12.82
Nelson and Mrs. Palmer	House lot on south side of Main street and next east of the Estate of A. H. Cowles house lot	$11.97
Geo N. Kennedy	House lot south side of Main street and next east of Nelson & Mrs. Palmer house lot	$5.75
Samuel R. Ball	House lot on the south side of Main street and next	

| | east of G. N. Kennedy house lot | $9.94 |
| Moses Case | Store & House on south side of Main street and next east of S. R. Ball house lot | $17.05 |

Bills To Be Paid

The Village government also had its usual expenses, and, like today, a purchase order or invoice was needed, as well as the approval of the Board of Trustees, who would authorize the Treasurer of the Village to make payment. Often the amount claimed was quite small by today's standards, but in the 1850s, $10.00, for example, was a substantial amount of money.

14 Aug 1855 - " . . . the following bill was passed and amounts allowed and an order drawn on the Treasurer for the same:

No of Account	Names	Amount Claimed	Amount Allowed
No 1	Patrick Welch	$14.25	$14.25
No 2	Lake I. Tefft	$12.50	$12.50
No 3	H. G. Kennedy	$3.38	$3.38
No 4	Chase Cook	$16.45	$16.45
No 5	Joseph S. Platt	$110.57	$110.57

The issue of a village pound continued to be a predicament for officials who wondered how to enforce an animal ordinance without the money necessary for adequate facilities. In the fall of 1855 Alfred Rockwell resigned his position as pound master and it became necessary to appoint another, an early example of the transitory nature of some public service jobs.

1 Oct 1855 - " . . . Medad L. Lawrence was appointed Pound Master."

While the building of sidewalks was the responsibility of the Village resident, for which they were duly assessed, the building of crosswalks was the responsibility of the Village government, and the Board of Trustees would authorize this construction at the major intersection, where Main meets North and South Streets today.

24 Oct 1855 - " . . . if there are (sic) funds enough in the Treasury raised for building cross walks that the same be approximately in taking up and relaying the cross walk running now from Addison Farnham's house lot across the highway to Walker's and Rockwell's shop, and re-laid (sic) from the east of said Farnham's lot and Episcopal Church lot across the highway to the plank walk in front of the tin shop occupied by White & Smith."

24 Oct 1855 - "List of taxes apportioned by the Trustees of the incorporation of the Village of Marcellus on the owners and corporations holding property thereon and upon the real estate lying inside the boundaries of said incorporation for the purpose of raising the sum of $159.99 laid and charged to said inhabitants . . . for the building of side walks:

Name of Inhabitants and Corporations	Location and Description of Lot	Amount
Israel Parsons	House & lot on the north side of Main street and on the corner of Main and Factory street	$22.31
Jonathan G. Rowling	House & lot on north side of Main street and next east of Israel Parson's house lot	$1.72
Ira Bishop	House & lot on north side of Main street and next east of J. G. Rowling house lot	$12.78
C. S. Bennett	House & lot on north side of Main street and next east of Ira Bishop house lot	$1.80
Edward Talbot	House & lot on south side of Main street and next	

	west of Stone Mill	$20.29
Mrs. Taylor	House & lot on south side of Main street and next west of Edward Talbot house lot	$13.52
Moses Case	House & lot on south side of Main street and next of Mrs. Taylor's house lot	$9.59
William Wellington	House, shop & lot on the east side of Cherry street and next south of E. Akin's store lot	$11.27
Catholic Church	House & lot on south side of Main street and on the corner of Main & Cherry streets	$45.68
School District No. 2	House & lot on west side of Cherry street and next south of Catholic Church	$21__

4 Mar 1856 - " . . . Plank side walks on Genesee street have been completed, those on Cherry street as far south as the south bounds of the School house lot, those on Factory street the west side has been laid . . .. Gravel walks on Camillus street have been made with the exception of one lot that first north of Mr. Hooper's and owned by Hiram Reed."

Censure

In 1856, a new President of the Village, Stephen Cobb, was elected; he became a two-term executive when elected again in 1857. Before they left office, however, the outgoing Trustees passed a resolution that criticized Amory Wilson, for certain actions that he took as Collector of Village taxes. In reading the censure vote, it appears that Collector Wilson was, according to the Board of Trustees, somewhat negligent in his duties by not collecting the proper tax for a sidewalk assessment, perhaps an oversight. This censure vote would later be censured itself by the new administration and seems to indicate that, like today, personalities may have played a part in what might seem like a trivial matter today. At the time, however, and like today, a vote to censure was considered a severe reprimand, which a public servant would prefer be removed from public entry.

11 Mar 1856 - " . . . Resolved that the conduct of Amery Wilson, collector, as aforesaid in compromising and relinquishing as above small sums from certain ones and exacting and collecting full amounts of others, is in the opinion of this board highly censorable, unprecedented and ought not to be passed over in silence. Resolved that we leave the whole matter in regards to his oath of office and acting of official duty to be settled by his own conscience on such terms as he may best dictate. Resolved that the Trustees tender their entire approval to H. G. Kennedy for the faithful performance of his duty as clerk as well as for the neat and blotless manner in which he has kept the books. Resolved that we tender our thanks to the Treasurer, Dr. John H. Cowles for his promptness in the performance of his duties both as a dispensing and account office. Resolved that the foregoing preamble and resolutions be entered upon the Clerk's minutes."

The Pound, Again

Stephen Cobb was born in Marcellus in 1799. He was married with a large family, fairly prosperous as well as a Methodist Clergyman. When he died in 1875, having lived through virtually all of the history of the community, it was said that he was the oldest resident born in Marcellus. While he was President, Cobb's administration was as concerned about sidewalks and a village pound as those before him, and to a degree, action was taken on both issues. Lake Tefft, who had been elected Pound Master in 1856, and was the outgoing President of the Village, failed to qualify as Pound Master. This, in all probability, meant that he did not want the job, like several before him. The matter would soon be settled, however, when a replacement master was appointed and a new pound was built, removing stray animals from the Village center of the Village, and resolving an issue that must have been a serious concern for merchants and traders trying to conduct business.

16 April 1856 - " . . . the Committee in relative to pound matters reported in favor of removing Pound to J. B. Taylor's premises and Stephen Cobb of the Trustees was appointed for the purpose of removing the lumber of the old Pound to be constructing a new one on said Taylor's premises . . .. on motion of M. L. Mills a vote was passed in favor of building twenty rods of crosswalk and of raising sixty dollars for said purposes; after church, and on motion of John L. Smith, adjourned one week. "

1 May 1856 - " . . . John Fulmer was appointed Pound Master in the place of Lake I. Tefft who failed to qualify, and Stephen Cobb's bill of $3.96 audited for removing Pound, erecting new one . . .. "

Sidewalks, Again

The Board would also pass a number of resolutions at its June meeting regarding sidewalk construction, calling on the voters to approve or reject each of them in a July meeting. A reading of these minutes provides another picture of Marcellus residents in 1856 and where they lived in the Village at mid century.

20 June 1856 - " . . . resolved,

1st - that there be a plank sidewalk built 4 feet wide on the north side of the street leading from the woolen factory occupied by Chester Moses & Co. west to the Plank Road (North Street), the same to be laid on hemlock stringers not less than 3 x 4 inches

2nd - that a plank side walk be built in like manner beginning at the west end of Caleb Gasper's plank sidewalk on the north side of Main Street and running west to the east line of Benjamin Clark's land or village lot

3rd - that a plank side walk be built in like manner beginning at the southwest corner of the widow Sylvia Pierces' land or house lot and running north on the east side of the Plank Road to the north line of Lake I. Tefft's house lot

4th - that there be a plank side walk built in like manner, except it be seven feet wide from the south west corner of the Eastern Religious Society's Meeting House lot on the east side of the Plank Road Street and running north to the northwest corner of the burying ground

5th - that there be a good gravel walk built on the north side of Main Street from Cornell Crysler's office west to the northwest line of Joseph Phillip's house lot . . .

6th - that there be $24 raised of levied and raised by tax on the taxable inhabitants on property in the corporation for the purpose of building a stone crosswalk across Main Street and North Street opposite Caleb Cowles' house

7th - that there be $22 raised in like manner for building a stone crosswalk across Main Street opposite the widow E. Talbot's house

8th - that there be $10 raised in like manner for building a stone cross walk on Cherry Street opposite J. W. Herring's house

9th - that there be $12 raised in like manner for repairing the old crosswalks in the corporation

10th - that $20 be raised in like manner for defraying the incidental expenses of the corporation

11th - that $22 be raised in like manner for the purpose of paying H. T. Kennedy, ex clerk of the corporation

12th - that $7 be raised in like manner for the purpose of paying J. H. Cowles, ex treasurer of the corporation.

As previously mentioned, the elected Trustees were authorized to pass resolutions but these motions would then be referred to the electorate, which would then decide whether projects would be undertaken or taxes raised to pay for such. Only a few residents voted on the resolutions and the vote was quite close on almost all of them. This was direct democracy in action, and it was not uncommon for the voters to reject the decisions of their elected representatives, the Trustees.

19 Jul 1856 - " . . . meeting of the electors . . . at the House of Alvord Brothers . . . the object of the meeting being to vote on the twelve foregoing resolutions which were offered by the Trustees . . . and the following is the result.

The whole number of votes			was	for	against
1st resolution		20	8	12	
2nd	16	11	5		
3rd	17	9	8		
4th	20	11	9		
5th	18	12	6		
6th	17	10	7		
7th	19	11	8		
8th	16	8	8		
9th	19	11	8		
10th	17	10	7		
11th	18	12	6		
12th	18	11	7		

The voters authorized construction of several sidewalks and crosswalks, as well as the levying of taxes to pay the necessary expenses. A reading of the minutes from February 16th provides some indication as to the cost of sidewalk construction in 1857, as well as account for the reluctance of voters to invite more tax.

16 Feb 1857 - " . . . moved that Mrs. Machan's bill presented to her last year by the trustees for building plank side walks in front of her house be recorded which is as follows:

490 feet plank	9 1/2 per ft	4.77
55 ft stringers	"	.52
nails		.45
grading by trustees	1/4 day	.25
laying same		.94
grading by trustees	1/4 day	.31
incidental expenses in laying out and overseeing side walks		.27

The Censure Revisited

Having been in office for a year, the Cobb administration examined the censure vote passed against Amory Wilson by the previous administration, and issued a statement just before the March 3rd election, upholding Wilson's actions. His standing restored, Amory Wilson was a candidate for Clerk of the Village in 1857. He would be re-elected Clerk for the next fifteen years, a testament by the voters to his character and standing in the community.

20 Feb 1857 - " . . . we the undersigned trustees of the incorporated Village of Marcellus have examined some of the accounts of our predecessors in office and find amongst them one item charged for overseeing the building of side walks which is not a lawful charge and we have ample testimony that Lake I. Tefft was the one that made the charge and that he charged nearly all that had side walks to build with this item of overseeing them which we now to be unlawful and that James W. Herring and Caleb Gasper sanctioned the same and that they passed a vote of censure on the collector for not collecting it and passed another vote to have it recorded in the corporation Book and that after it was recorded Lake I. Tefft and J. W. Herring signed it as the records will show and that Caleb Gasper refused to sign it - and that they persuaded Joseph Phillips (who was not present at the time) to sign it. We also further state that when a man has been elevated to the station of president of an incorporated village and shall make an unlawful charge against the inhabitants there of and then pass a vote of censure on the collector for not collecting it and record it on the corporation Book as a breach of duty. We consider such a man as not having any moral principle and deserves the finger of scorn pointed against him by every law abiding citizen and those trustees who uphold such conduct are equally guilty, and we believe further that said tax would have been paid notwithstanding it was unlawful had not Lake I. Tefft been so arbitrary and domineering whilst laying down said side walk and upheld by said trustees."

President Cobb, Again

Elected to a second term in 1857, President Cobb continued to promote improved sidewalks and pay for village pound expenses during his administration.

3 Mar 1857 - " . . . we have also caused to be made a part of the plank walk leading from Caleb Gasper's plank walk to Benjamin Clark's lot and have had to wait for plank to build the remainder."

1 Jun 1857 - " . . . meeting of the trustees held at the office of J. H. Cowles . . . a majority of the trustees being present, motioned that Jonathan Rowlin's bill be allowed, . . . motioned that Medad Lawrence be appointed Pound master for the ensuring year, carried, adjourned."

13 Jul 1857 - " . . . Stephen Cobb and J. H. Cowles were appointed a committee to superintend the building of the gravel sidewalks on the north side of the old turnpike leading from the Methodist meeting house in said Village west along said road to Joseph Phillips west line of his door yard fence."

Daniel G. Coon
Village President
1858-1859
1874-1875
1878-1880

5 Feb 1858 - " . . . that Dorastus Holcomb's bill of six dollars for the use of ground for pound be allowed."

Election of 1858

On March 2, 1858, 10 individuals ran for the office of Trustee, and each of them received 12 votes. Because of this, five were chosen by lot from the list of ten. Two of the five that were chosen failed to qualify, and as a result, a special election was held on April 13, 1858 to elect two new Trustees. Daniel G. Coon and Seymour Warren were chosen as Trustees; Coon also would be chosen from the Board to be President of the Village. Coon was the owner of a local distillery and was in his early forties at the time. He was wealthy, married, and had several children at the time. Sidewalks would again dominate the Board's agenda during his term, and when asked to vote on a sidewalk for Cherry Street, the voters approved by a margin of eleven to one.

2 Mar 1858 - "By an act of statute laws of the State of New York it is provided that when two or more have an equal number of votes it should be determined by ballot and the following was the result which was drawn by the trustees: Stephen Cobb, Isaac Bradley, Alfred Venzia, Cornell Crysler, John Thompkins."

19 Mar 1858 - " . . . resolution for building a plank side walk on the west side of Cherry street . . . that part leading from George Reed's house lot north as far as the hay scales so as to admit of laying stone or gravel . . . "

Fighting Fires

A major concern for many living so close to one another in wooden structures in the Village was that of fire. It was also a concern of Village officials in 1858-59 and towards the end of the term, the Board of Trustees passed several resolutions that were designed to fight the ever-present threat of fire. The first motion called for incidental expenses paid, while the second and third resolutions provided that taxes be levied on property to purchase a fire engine and to build underground cisterns or reservoirs for storing water. On submission of the propositions to the voters, however, only the first resolution passed and it would be more than twenty years, and only after a series of disastrous fires, that the electorate of the Village agreed to invest in fire fighting expenses.

3 Feb 1859 - " . . . resolved 1st that $40 be raised by tax on the taxable property in said Village for incidental expenses, resolution 2d that one thousand dollars be raised in like manner to purchase an engine to extinguish fires in said Village, resolution 3d that $300 be raised in like manner to build reservoirs."

1 Mar 1859 - " . . . first resolution received 17 votes of which 12 had the word yes and five had the word no; the second resolution received 30 votes of which 26 had the word no and four had the word yes; the third resolution had 29 votes of which 18 had the word no and eleven the word yes . . .

The Village Pound

Cornell Crysler was chosen from the elected Trustees to serve as President of the Village in 1859. Crysler was a young man in his late twenties at the time, a lawyer, with a wife and three children. He was born in neighboring Cayuga County, and had lived in Marcellus for about five years.

With a large number of animals roaming at large throughout the Village, Crysler and the Board of Trustees began to offer bounties to those who would help keep the Village, including its sidewalks and crosswalks, clear of strays. By the summer of that year, Board resolution clearly defined the law regarding animals running at large throughout the Village and it appeared that some success was finally being achieved. The Trustees also granted more power to the Tax Collector, securing a more consistent source of income for the Village, and continued to promote more sidewalk improvement in the central Village. The Village was becoming more civilized, its development defined by improved administration and such enhancements as sidewalks.

11 May 1859 - " . . . that three cents be allowed to each person that drives any horse or cow or others cattle into the Pound within three months from date . . . resolved that the President be empowered to procure help to keep the cross walks clear during the summer . . . "

8 Aug 1859 - " . . . resolved that all cattle, horses, mules, sheep, goats, swine or geese or any such animals shall not be permitted to run at large in said village and if found running at large in said village and if found running at large as aforesaid or within any enclosure in said Village or within the bounds of said Village each and every such animal may be impounded in the common pound of said Village from whence they shall not be released until the owner or owners or some other person shall pay to the Pound Keeper the following Poundage fees for the use of said Village. Viz, for each sheep or goat twelve and a half cents, for each goose . . . six and one fourth cents and for all other animals named twenty five cents - any person violating the provisions of this section shall be subject to a penalty of not less than one nor more than five dollars. "

1 Feb 1860 - " To Stephen Cobb, Collector of Taxes in the incorporated Village of Marcellus, you are hereby commanded to collect the foregoing list of taxes of the owners of real estate described therein, . . . together with the percentage allowed by law for your fees - and in case any person upon whom such tax is imposed shall neglect or refuse to pay the same, you are to levy the same by distress and sale of the goods and chattels of the person or corporation so taxed in the same manner as warrants are issued by the boards of supervision."

1860

William Wellington's election as President of the Board of Trustees in 1860 seemed to signal a satisfaction with the status quo. Wellington was a local blacksmith, having lived in the area his entire life. He was in his late thirties at the time, married, and the father of a large number of children. A new face in Village government was Thomas DeCoudres, a local druggist. Born in New Jersey, DeCoudres was then 43 years old, with a wife and three children. The election total was just 17 votes in 1860, and the Board's preoccupation with proper grading and construction of the village sidewalks was again obvious.

10 Oct 1860 - " . . . the trustees all present agreed to inspect the sidewalks in said Village and found many places decayed in the planks which they ordered cleared out and filled with gravel and Alvord Brothers were ordered to raise their stone walk above the level of the ground so as to have the water run off and also to have the walk tip towards the south 1 1/2 inches so as to have the water run towards the ditch. Also ordered a gravel walk to be built on the north side of main street leading from the Methodist Meeting house west to Joseph Phillips house lot to the northwest corner after it was suitably graded. Also a gravel walk on the south side of said Street leading from Cornel Crysler to Guy Moses with suitable grading."

Conclusion

The map below shows the Village of Marcellus as it looked in 1860 and it has changed rather dramatically from its incorporation of just a few years earlier. As the1850s came to an end and the country moved towards Civil War, the Village of Marcellus hummed with activity, the center of exchange for local farmers and for those who served their needs. There were hotel keepers like the Alvord brothers, cabinet makers like Samuel Hooper, butchers like Addison Farnham, shoemakers like Alexander Mather, harness makers like Eliakim Dorchester, wagon makers like William Garnet, tinsmiths like William White, blacksmiths like Charles Lamb and carpenters like Addison Agar. Physicians like Israel Parsons and Franklin Bangs, druggists like Thomas DeCoudres, dentists like James Baker, lawyers like Fred Lyman and clergymen like John Tompkins provided professional services in the Village. There were others like the grocer, Thomas Herring, the merchant, Benjamin Moses and a cigar maker from Germany by the name of Henry Rochenberger were served the needs of the local community. Even women, domestics like Bridget Powell, milliners like Sarah Colton, dressmakers like Jane Whitney, and teachers like Harriet Smith, found work in the Village.

Churches and houses, factories and stores were built or rebuilt during this period. "Construction of some of the fine homes during this era reflected the fashion of the period in architecture, which was known as Greek Revival" (Heffernan 37). Distinguished by their splendid pillars and porches, such buildings as the Presbyterian Church, 14 East Main Street, and the North and Reed homes, give evidence of a history long past.

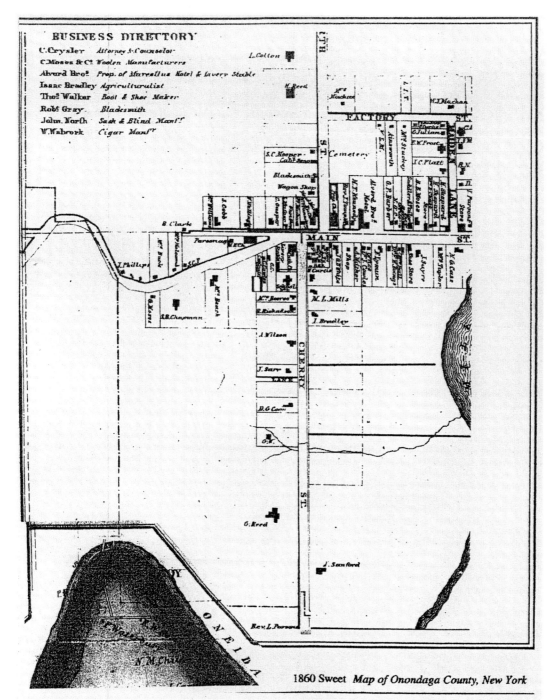

1860 Sweet *Map of Onondaga County, New York*

Travel into and out of the Village followed the old Native American trail that came to be called Seneca Turnpike, and more roads and streets would eventually be linked to this main east-west thoroughfare. Sidewalks and crosswalks, fine points that enhance a community, were being constructed to accommodate pedestrian traffic as well as to promote commercial interests. "The village at the time comprised little more than what is today known as 'uptown'" (Heffernan 39) but it had clearly become established as a commercial center.

The Village government that had been created felt a responsibility, since 1853, to create an atmosphere of civic pride. This included providing services for Village residents, particularly streets and sidewalks and an enclosure for stray animals, prerequisites, it would seem, for a developing community. The voters would reject other services, such as fire protection, but eventually this would become a fundamental part of Village government and its operations.

What had once been a gathering of several houses and a meeting place for itinerant travelers, was now a community defined by streets and sidewalks, and with the imposition of taxes, civilization had unquestionably extended into this frontier of Central New York. The population of the Village had grown from about 350 in 1853 to about 400 in 1860, a small but steady rise that would continue for the rest of the century, interrupted for a time during the 1860s by a bloodletting known as the Civil War.

●

Chapter 3 - Village Expansion

In 1861, the new President of the Village, Chester Moses, was the owner of the woolen mill on Factory Street. Moses had purchased the factory from William Machan about six years earlier and despite the threat of bankruptcy that might have destroyed the mill, Moses made the factory successful, ensuring many jobs for local residents. The mill's success in the 1860s can be attributed, not only to Moses' business skills, but also to the fact that his mill was a supplier of uniforms to the Union Army during the Civil War. In addition, despite the loss of many young men to the ranks of the army during the

conflict, Moses was also able to take advantage of the immigrant labor supply arriving from Europe, particularly Ireland, at the time.

The Village Clerk in the new administration was still Amory Wilson who was now being paid for keeping the sidewalks and crosswalks clear of snow during the winter. As more homes were being built and businesses expanding in the village, new walks would be needed, including one leading from the Moses mill on Factory, (what we know today as Maple) Street, as well as on the east side of the Marcellus-Camillus Road, what is termed North Street today. This business expansion seems to have also influenced the voters, who gave unanimous approval of these resolutions in the April balloting.

21 Mar 1861 - " . . . Chester Moses was chosen president for the ensuing years. Amery Wilson's account of $3, 5cts as Clerk and one dollar for cleaning off crosswalks was audited."

9 Apr 1861 - " . . . resolved that a gravel walk be built 4 feet wide on the south side of the street leading from the factory of Moses & Co. west to the road leading from the Marcellus village to Camillus Village." This resolution passed with voter approval, 17 - 0, on 2 May 1861.

12 Apr 1861 - " . . . that a gravel walk 4 feet wide be built in like manner from the Northwest corner of Lake I. Tefft's dooryard in said Village north on the east side of said road leading from

Marcellus Village to Camillus Village running North to the North line of the Corporation." This resolution passed with voter approval, 16 - 0, on 2 May 1861.

The Civil War

On April 12, 1861, the Army of the Confederacy fired on Fort Sumter and the war that had been brewing between the North and South for so long erupted. The community of Marcellus " . . . responded to the calls for troops and contributed its share to the support of the Union" (Heffernan 42), including units of the One Hundred Twenty-Second Regiment, New York State Volunteers. Lucius Moses who was the son of the mill owner, and would achieve the rank of Captain, organized company F of this volunteer regiment. Along with the 122nd, young men from Marcellus joined the 149th, the 185th and other infantry as well as artillery regiments and served on board Union naval vessels such as the *USS New Ironsides* and *USS Huntsville*. Over two hundred young men from Marcellus flocked to the colors during this bloody conflict and twenty perished in it.

Henry Fellows was just 24 years old when he was killed at the Battle of Malvern Hill in 1862. He is buried in the Village Cemetery, as is Aaron C. Gaylord who died in a Gettysburg hospital in 1863, his body brought home for burial. Anthony Coyne was one of those young Irishmen that the Know Nothings were so worried about. He died in the Wilderness in 1864 in defense of their right to express themselves. Joseph C. Jones, after whom a G.A.R. Post was named in Marcellus, died of wounds he received, also in the Wilderness, and was brought home for burial in Highland Cemetery. Some, like Charles Henry Sennett, did not return home. He was killed at Petersburg in 1865 and was buried on Robert E. Lee's front lawn – Arlington Cemetery. Most survived the war but were forever changed by it. Some moved from the community after the war and others, like Patrick Heenan, returned to Marcellus at the end of the fighting, lived out his life on First Street in the Village and died in 1931. Today he lies in a hillside grave in St. Francis Cemetery, overlooking the Village he called home.

Back Home

People in the community may have been far removed from the fighting during the war, but their lives and families had been disrupted by it. The community also suffered an outbreak " . . . of malignant diphtheria in 1861 and 1862 and an epidemic of malignant dysentery which caused a great number of deaths in 1865" (Heffernan 41) as well as a drought " . . . when crops in 1864 were injured by the drouth (sic) fully twenty-five per cent on an average" (Population Schedule for the Town of Marcellus 1865). Despite the rural nature of the community, the war also caused an increase in the cost of living, and comments listed in the New York State Census of 1865 note the following on the influence of the war upon prices:

E. Remarks on the influence of the war upon prices. What is the average monthly pay (including board) of farm laborers through the summer months? **$35.** What by the year? **$27.** What were these wages in 1860? **40 per cent less.** Has the price of farming lands increased since 1860? **Yes.** State the relative increase. **25 per cent.** How has the war affected the amount of debt between individuals? **Deepened it.** What effect has it had upon credit? **Diminished credit.** Has it tended to promote prompt payments? **It has.** How has it influenced the amount of crime? **Think it is diminished.** How has it influenced pauperism? **Increased it.** What other changes in the social condition of the people have you observed since 1860? **None.** (Population Schedule for the Town of Marcellus 1865)

With demand for their products at an all time high, however, some farmers and businessmen in Marcellus, which included " . . . one hotel, no wholesale stores, six retail stores, and three groceries" (Population Schedule for the Town of Marcellus, 1865) experienced a certain degree of prosperity during the war. This prosperity would also enable and encourage improvements to the Village infrastructure, primitive though it may seem by today's standards.

Streets Are Given Names

With the expansion of its network of sidewalks and streets, the Board of Trustees decided that names be officially designated for the major roads of the Village. In all probability, the residents already referred to them by these names, but the Board entry of February 11th, 1862 made the designation official for Main, Cherry, North, Orange and Factory Street in the Village.

11 Feb 1862 - "At a meeting of the trustees of Marcellus Village held at the drug store of Thomas DeCoudres in said Village, present C. Moses, T. DeCoudres and D. G. Coon. C. Moses presented an amount for work done on the cross walk at the north west corner of the burying ground of four dollars and fifty cents which was audited and allowed . . . moved and recorded that the streets of said village be recognized by the name indicated on the sign boards at the corners of said streets, viz the street running east and west shall be called main street - the street running south of main street shall be called Cherry street, the street running north from the Eastern Religious Societies meeting house shall be called North street, the street running north from main street to the factorys (sic) of C. Moses & Co. shall be called Orange street and the street running west from the factory of Moses & Co. to north street shall be called factory street. Adjourned."

Village Upkeep

During the war, a succession of civic-minded men was chosen to head Village government. John H. Cowles, the son of a former Village official, Alexander H. Cowles, succeeded Chester Moses in office, in 1862. Cowles was a young man, in his late

Joseph C. Platt
Village Trustee
1863-1865

twenties at the time, and a physician like his father; he would be elected President of the Village again in 1863 and relinquish the Presidency in 1864 to E. R. Howe who served for a single term. There were other newcomers to the Board of Trustees in these years, including such people as Joseph C. Platt, John L. Smith and Frederick A. Lyman. Like those who served before them, these individuals were usually family men and well off financially. Platt was a very wealthy farmer, whose farm in the southern end of the Village is part of Marcellus Park today. When he was elected, he was a man in his late fifties, with a wife and at least six children, and although he was born in Greene, NY, had lived in the Marcellus area for about twenty years. Frederick Lyman was a young lawyer, in his mid twenties who was born in the area, as was John L. Smith, who was a stove and tin dealer in his early 30s. As residents and as businessmen of the Village, all of these men were concerned about the upkeep of streets and sidewalks as well as providing the services they felt necessary for life in a small, but growing community. Some of the wooden sidewalks, which had been constructed in years past, were now starting to decay and it became necessary to replace them. The Village Pound continued to be a added expense for taxpayers but one that the Trustees felt essential to maintain.

15 Jun 1862 - " . . . the trustees report that the following walks will have to be rebuilt. Viz, from the south side of Wm. Wellington's lot on the east side of Cherry street from the school house lot north to Main Street. Also from the corner of Cherry and Main Streets east on the south side of Main Street to the east line of James C. Sayres house lot. Also from the southwest corner of Orange and Main Streets east to the north side of Main Street to the bridge or east line of the corporation. Also from the corner of Main and Orange Streets on the west side of Orange Street north to the corner on Factory Street. All of the above walks to be laid with two inch planks on three by four inch scantling and the plank to be laid crosswise. The walks on Main Street to be five feet wide. The other streets four feet wide. Also the following persons are to be notified to repair their walks: viz, M. L. Mills, Caroline Curtis, Catholic Church, N. G. Case. The Clerk is employed to notify the above owners of the same. The Clerk is also employed to repair the gravel walk from the southwest corner of the burying ground north to the lower gate and thence to the northwest corner."

21 Nov 1862 - " . . . it was ordered that Alexander Mather remove the stone out of the street that are in front of his house and that the Clerk inform him of the same."

3 Mar 1863 - "Resolution 6th - that when the Pound Master or others find cattle going at large within said Village and are driving them to the Pound and any person interfere to try to prevent the same, such person shall on conviction be liable to a fine not exceeding five dollars."

The upkeep of a village infrastructure is essential to good government and all too often can be ignored or delayed when more pressing issues take precedence. During the Civil War, Trustees of the Village continued to make necessary improvements to the roads and walks that residents and merchants found to be so important in a growing community, a lesson that succeeding officials of the government would hope to follow.

9 May 1863 - " . . . that the Clerk notify those having walks to build to built them within sixty days."

27 Feb 1864 - " . . . at a meeting of the trustees of Marcellus Village held at the office of John H. Cowles, . . . Amery Wilson presented his account for cleaning off the cross walks in said Village of one dollar and twenty five cents. Also for services as Clerk for the year past of two dollars and twenty five cents."

7 May 1864 - " . . . resolved that eighty dollars be raised to purchase stone and to repair the cross walks in said Village and keep them in order."

2 Mar 1865 - " . . . the trustees of the Village of Marcellus would most respectfully submit the following as their annual report, viz there remains in the treasury sixty seven cents of contingent fund and the crosswalk fund has all been expended and likewise the Pound fund. There was raised by tax in 1862 seventy dollars for funds to pay the expenses of said Village for the last three years and at the close of the fiscal year there will be wanting about twelve dollars for clerk fees and other expenses. It will be necessary to raise about $30 dollars for contingent funds and thirty for repairing crosswalks for the coming year, all of which is most respectfully submitted."

Census Figures

By 1865, the Village of Marcellus had changed somewhat and a Village Census taken in that year as well as Town of Marcellus and Onondaga County population figures provides some insight into the emerging community. The Village consisted of eighty-two households with a total population of four hundred-eighteen, about equally divided between men and women, a comparable figure in both the Town and County records.

21 Mar 1865 - " . . . the following is the census taken for the Village of Marcellus by Seth D. Gilbert in 1865, viz

Number of Dwellings		82
Number of Families		99
Population	418	
Males	200	
Females	218	
Native Voters		90
Naturalized Voters		19
Aliens		4
Over 21 and cannot read and write		3
Over 21 and can read only	2	
Owners of land		80

18 Feb 1866 - " Population of Marcellus 1866"   2,649

County of Onondaga	70,175
Number of Males	35,830
Number of Females	34,345

Of the Village figure, only ninety could vote, and the electorate returned Chester Moses to office as President for the next two years, 1865 and 1866, along with Irving Moses, his nephew of twenty-nine years and already a prosperous merchant supporting a wife and two young children. Thomas Walker, a local shoemaker in his late fifties, would also join Village government, as would Calvin G. Alvord a man in his early forties, who, together with his brothers, Warren and Charles, was proprietor of the public house that bore the family name. Walker was born in England in 1807 and had lived in Marcellus for almost 30 years while the Alvords, born in Saratoga had moved to Marcellus just prior to the Civil War. As local businessmen with families to support, they took an active role as Trustees of the Village, and both Walker's shop and the Alvord House became a meeting place for the Board of Trustees.

Postwar Reform

In the years after the Civil War, as veterans returned home to pursue peacetime activities, the people of Marcellus, like those throughout the country, experienced a moral uplifting that was reflected on the national level in the passage of Constitutional amendments that outlawed slavery and attempted to improve social conditions for the freedmen. On the local, as on the national level, throughout American history, reform has often been led and promoted by the churches and other religious elements in society. After the war, these institutions and individuals began once again to feel an obligation on their part to promote worthy causes and to protect or at least control moral behavior. Marcellus became known as the Village of Four Churches, one on each of four corners, and as antebellum reform movements gathered momentum in the postwar years, the churches and their congregations would again take the lead, as they had before the war, in such crusades as education, care for the needy, temperance, suffrage, immigrant re-settlement, and public health.

The Churches

The oldest of the buildings was the Presbyterian Church, its history dating back to 1803 and a wooden meetinghouse on the northeast corner of North and Main Streets. The Church and its long time pastors, Rev. Levi Parsons, who died in 1864 and Rev. John Thompkins, who died in 1866 had been instrumental in establishing the burial ground now known as the Village Cemetery on land to the north of the church in 1804 and the first Village school erected behind their meetinghouse in 1807. Later, two of their membership, Chester Moses and William Machan, both of whom were prominent in the community, " . . . took the leadership in erecting a new school building on the site of the present St. Francis Xavier parking lot, on what was then Cherry Street" (Heffernan 23). This school, built in 1846, would serve the village until 1891 when a new brick building was erected on West Main Street. In 1851, with the old meetinghouse badly in need of repair, the present Presbyterian Church was built.

The first Methodist Church building, erected in 1824, was of stone, on the hill immediately west of the Village where the present Catholic Cemetery is located. Seven years later that building was taken down and rebuilt on a site across the street from the present Methodist Church. This second building became too small for the congregation and so a third edifice was erected of brick in 1857 on the site of the present Church. When this third building burned in 1877, the present building was erected in 1878.

FIRST PRESBYTERIAN CHURCH
OF MARCELLUS
Building erected in 1851

ST. FRANCIS XAVIER
CATHOLIC CHURCH
Building erected in 1867

MARCELLUS METHODIST
CHURCH
Building erected in 1878

ST. JOHN'S EPISCOPAL
CHURCH
Building erected in 1881

The first Episcopal services in Marcellus were conducted in the village schoolhouse, north of the Presbyterian Church in 1824. Ten years later, in 1833, the construction of a wooden building on the northwest corner of Main and North Streets began to serve the congregation of St. John's Episcopal Church. Destroyed by fire in 1866, a new building was completed in February of 1870. This second building was also destroyed by fire in 1879 and a third Church was erected on the southwest corner Orange Street in 1881. By the 1920s, the building was in need of considerable repair, and in 1924, was moved to its present location on the corner of Orange and Maple Streets.

The first services of St. Francis Xavier Catholic Church were held in 1853 at the home of John McNally, but a growing population of Irish immigrants soon required much larger space. In 1854,

Deacon Rice's Tavern on the corner of South and Main Streets was purchased, serving as a place of worship until it was demolished and the site cleared for the construction of the present church in 1867, a moment in time that coincided with the arrival of even more immigrants, mostly Irish Catholics, to the community in the 1860s.

From Pool Tables to Mad Dogs

Inspired or perhaps driven by the churches, the Board of Trustees of the Village began to consider laws that, at first glance, might be viewed as social legislation. While the temperance movement and control over liquor consumption would become important considerations in years to come, the Trustees began to take seriously the Bible teaching and the Methodist credo that they were their "brothers' keepers." The Board viewed the licensing of billiard tables not only as a way to raise needed revenue but also as a way to indirectly control behavior in a public inn such as the Alvord House, pictured below. The Board was still concerned about what had been a major public safety concern for the past ten years – sidewalk improvement – and, apparently the problem of potholes, which we

tend to think is a more of a 20th century phenomenon, existed then in both the unpaved streets and sidewalks of the village.

22 Mar 1866 - " . . . Chester Moses and Thomas Walker were chosen a committee to settle with the Alvord Brothers for the billyard tables for the last three years."

10 Sep 1866 - " . . . that the side walks from Wm Salvage's lot to the corner of Orange Street on the north side of Main Street be repaved by filling the broken places with coal ashes."

13 Nov 1866 - " . . . the subject of the Billyard (sic) tables kept in the tavern by Alvord Brothers in said Village, moved and seconded that a tax of ten dollars be levied on the two tables for one year."

17 Mar 1867 - " . . . Jonathan Reed's account for clearing the snow from the side walks, $8.66, was allowed."

One public safety issue that neither the Trustees nor Village residents addressed at the time, however, was fire control, and a disastrous blaze in December 1866 destroyed the Episcopal Church on the corner of Main and North Streets. With little equipment to fight the fire, the small wooden building was completely destroyed. Church members began to construct a new edifice in 1869 on the same site but it would be a number of years before residents would agree to invest in adequate fire fighting equipment. Ironically, it was another fire at this same location in 1879 that finally convinced village inhabitants of this need.

James C. Sayre
Village Trustee
1867-1868

In the election of 1867, the new administration included, among others, Ira Bush, Seneca Hemingway and James C. Sayre. Sayre was not only a wealthy manufacturer supporting a large family, but he was also a master builder, responsible, it is thought, for constructing the Village school on Cherry Street in 1846 and the 1851 reconstruction of the Presbyterian Church. He would also open the first woolen mill, on the site of what is today the Lower Crown Mill in 1877.

An issue that this Board would confront was a threat to public health in the Village. Hydrophobia was most serious at the time, and with a great number of un-muzzled dogs running at large in the streets of the village, the Board authorized that they could be, and no doubt were, shot on sight.

23 Jan 1868 - " . . . the subject under consideration was mad dogs and it was resolved that the following bye law be added to the bye laws of our Village, viz section 22d, it shall not be lawful for any person owning a dog in the Village of Marcellus to suffer it to go at large in the limits of said Corporation without being securely muzzled, and it shall be lawful for any person to kill any dog found running at large in said Village without being so muzzled."

Today, the issue of animal control remains a concern and the Village employs a Dog Control Officer for this purpose. There are also Village ordinances today regarding dog control, including the provision that dogs must be leashed in the Village and that dog owners have a responsibility to pick up after their pet.

A Strange Election

Some elections were particularly interesting, especially the one that occurred in 1868. According to the Minutes of the Corporation, the Trustees who were elected on March 3rd "failed to qualify." The exact meaning of this phrase is ambiguous, for it could mean that an individual did not meet the requirements of the job or that the individual did not want the job, or simply that the individual did not attend the meetings. In any event, because of this, a special election was held a week after the regular election to fill four vacancies, with Chester Moses being the only Trustee who did "qualify." Those put into office at this special election on March 23, 1868 included William J. Machan, the former President, Harvey Sprague, Lauren Beach and Samuel Dady (also spelled Dada). Many of these same individuals would be re-elected in 1869 and serve in similar capacities. Beach was a 65-year-old farmer, while Dada, some 10 years younger, was a local craftsman. Dada's occupation was an interesting one, that of tallow chandler. His craft as a candle maker was certainly in great demand in those times before electricity changed America forever. Sprague was a miller, who also ran the local sawmill at the time. He was a middle-aged man with several children, and probably of moderate income.

The Board continued to license billiard tables at the Alvord House and this helped to bring in added revenue. This meant, of course, that taxes would not have to be raised as much, nor would the Trustees have to go to the voters to ask for a tax assessment increase. In addition, the Trustees, like those today, were often assigned a specific responsibility within the village government, acting as a sort of supervisor for separate departments, such as sidewalks or streets. It was the Trustee's responsibility then, to make sure that the Village was maintained in good repair. Later, such departments as water, lights, and fire would be added, as the services of local government expanded.

10 May 1868 - " . . . Samuel Dady was appointed a committee on sidewalks." . The Trustees also gave a license to the Alvord Brothers (Warren and Theodore) for and " . . . in consideration of ten dollars . . . do grant allow them to use two billyard tables now in their possession in said village for one year from first day of April 1868 at twelve o'clock at noon until the first day of April 1869 at the same time of day."

25 Feb 1869 - " At the last annual meeting there was remaining in the treasury, sixteen dollars and sixty five cents and there has been paid out as follows - paid Amery Wilson for Clerk fees, five dollars and twenty five cents - paid J. Reed for clearing sidewalks of snow, eight dollars. And then has been paid into the treasury as follows: received of Thomas Walker, justice, for fines the past year, twenty two dollars and fifty cents, and of Alvord Brothers for the right to use the billyard tables now in their possession ten dollars leaving a balance of thirty five dollars and ninety six cents on hand. There will be demands of about thirteen dollars at the close of the fiscal year, . . . "

22 May 1869 - special vote " . . . on repairing the walks in said Village where needed, . . . there were fifteen resolutions and each received fourteen votes."

End of the Decade

In the election of 1870, some new faces were added to the Board of Trustees, including three men who were all retired and wealthy farmers. They were Thomas Rhodes, who became President of the Village, Ira Bishop and Hiram Bronson. All of them were married men, with families, and either middle aged or becoming older. Elected along with them were some familiar faces, Samuel Dada and Samuel Hooper. In addition, a new role for local government officials began to evolve in 1870, as the Village of Marcellus started to issue liquor licenses. This would not only bring in additional revenue to local government but also add what was assumed to be necessary control over an expanding business in the Village. It also reflected the urge to reform that had been rekindled in the postwar years, and was a prelude to the temperance crusade soon to be launched.

30 Apr 1870 - " . . . Thomas Rhodes, Ira Bishop and Hiram Bronson were chosen as commissioners to grant licenses to those that deal in liquor."

Conclusion

The pictures below show the Village of Marcellus about 1870, looking east. During the previous ten years, the road over east hill brought more and more residents,

particularly immigrants from Ireland and England, to the town and village, and the valley began to fill up. The spires on the churches and the sloping roofs of both barns and houses give evidence of an active community and the picket fence in the foreground seems to delineate what would then be the Village incorporation line. As the decade of the 1860s came to an end, and the shadows of civil war lengthened, the residents of the Village of Marcellus looked ahead to a brighter future and the peaceful pursuit of everyday pleasures. With some 428 residents of the Village in 1870, there emerged a slight increase over the census of 1865 that represented about 18% of the Town of Marcellus population. The Marcellus community was still quite rural, with farming the overwhelming occupation of its inhabitants. However, the sustained influx of immigrants and the expansion of business and industry would bring changes that would continue to transform the community in the 1870s.

The Village was, as it is today, central to life in the community, the sanctified spot that acted as a magnet for the itinerant traveler on his way west, as well as a young couple like Charles H. DeCoudres and Georgia Platt, who following their marriage on August 25, 1870, settled into their home on Main Street and raised a family in the valley.

Chapter 4 - The 70s

Business and industrial growth, particularly of the mills along Nine Mile Creek, distinguished the period of the 1870s in Marcellus bringing changes to the Village and the services it provided. There was also a continued emphasis on social reform, some of it in reaction to the growing number of immigrants who settled in the area as well as an expansion and centralization of government that would more clearly define its role in the operation of the Village.

Re-incorporation

On July 25, 1871, the voters of the Village of Marcellus, in an attempt to both streamline local government as well as define its powers, agreed to re-incorporate the

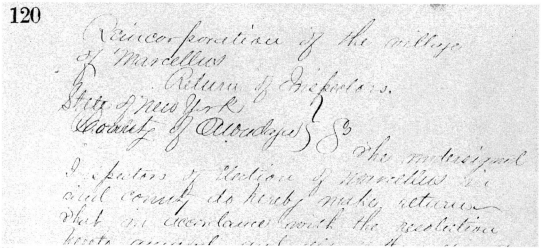

Village under new by-laws and to change the number of elected officials. This re-incorporation stipulated that another election be held within a month and on August 24, 1871, the voters would select a President, three Trustees, one Treasurer, and one Collector of Taxes. Ever since, the Board of Trustees has appointed the Village Clerk and fire wardens and would, until more recent times, assume the duties of the tax assessors. The voters also agreed to eliminate the pound master as an elected position in Village government, those duties also assumed by the Board or delegated to employees.

31 Jul 1871 - "... a special election was held at the Hotel of Alvord Brothers in said Village of Marcellus in said County on Tuesday, July 25th, 1871. That the polls of said election were opened ... at 12 o'clock noon and closed at 4 o'clock P.M. of that day. 'That the electors of said Village voted upon the following resolution, viz: Resolved that the Village of Marcellus be reincorporated under Chapter 291 of the Laws of 1870.' That at said election, 16 votes were cast, of which number, 16 had thereon the word, yes, and that none were deposited having thereon the word, no."

Election

At that election on August 24, 1871, the officers of the village were elected, some of them part of a new generation of Village residents, born in the community with more distant New England connections than their parents. The newly elected President of the Village was Lucius Moses, the son of the former Village President, Chester Moses. The younger Moses, however, declined to serve and nominated Oscar J. Brown, a young lawyer in his twenties, to carry out the duties of Village President, to which the rest of the Board agreed. Other elected Trustees included Albert Curtis, an older man and a very wealthy farmer, whose red brick home and extensive property on Orange Street gave evidence of his affluence. Another was Samuel Hooper, a cabinet manufacturer, and Jasper Hunt, a well to do farmer and mill owner, both of them family men as well as businessmen whose interest in the Village was considerable. From that time on, and into the 20th century, the elected Trustees would assume the duties of the tax assessors, a fact that would not be lost on the voters at election time. The new Treasurer was Irving Moses, a young grocery merchant with a wife and two children, and the Collector of Taxes was Stores M. Griffen, a middle-aged laborer, with a wife and six children

24 Aug 1871 – " . . . the following is a correct statement of the result of an election held in said Village of Marcellus on Thursday, August 24th, 1871. The whole number of votes cast for President was seventeen, of which number Lucius Moses received eleven and William J. Machan received six. The whole number of votes cast for Trustees was fifty-one of which number Albert Curtis received sixteen, Samuel Hooper received eleven, Jasper Hunt received eleven, James C. Sayre received six, . . . The whole number of votes cast for Treasurer was sixteen of which number Irving Moses received eleven votes, Oscar J. Brown received three and Amery Wilson received two votes. For the office of Collector, sixteen votes were cast of which number Stores M. Griffin received sixteen . . . ."

Police Protection

After they were sworn into office, the newly elected officials appointed Amery Wilson, who had been the elected Village Clerk since 1857, to that position for a period of one year. In addition, the 1871 Board of Trustees made other appointments, including the Street Commissioner, Thomas Rhodes and, for the first time, a Police Constable, in the person of Stores M. Griffin, the elected Tax Collector. The Board, sensing a need for a police presence in the Village, began to assume more responsibilities and provide more

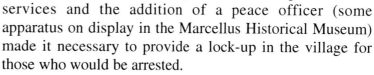

services and the addition of a peace officer (some apparatus on display in the Marcellus Historical Museum) made it necessary to provide a lock-up in the village for those who would be arrested.

Not only were there concerns about an increased crime rate in the Village, as well as the usual interest in sidewalk repair but also some complaints, in the form of petition, made by residents to the Board of Trustees against what was thought to be an excessive rate charge for the use of a farmer's hay scales. At the time, the Trustees seemed unsure about a response, but such complaints would later cause them to create a new position for Village government, that of Sealer of Weights and Measures, again redefining the role of government.

28 Aug 1871 - " . . . Amery Wilson was on motion elected Clerk, Thomas Rhodes Street Commissioner, Stores M. Griffin, Police Constable . . . Mr. Hooper was appointed a committee of one to notify all person in the Corporation whose sidewalks need repairing, to repair the same forthwith . . . "

23 Sep 1871 - ". . . President called the attention of the board to the condition of Orange Street. Mr. Curtis was instructed to fix the street, his bill to be paid from next year's highway tax. Moved that the walk around the cemetery be fixed and gravelled and that Mr. Curtis be instructed to do the same."

17 Jan 1872 - " . . . the President read a protest from citizens in relation to Mr. Reed's hay scales. Moved that the protest be placed on file, carried . . ."

36

Budget Finances

By the end of its term, the Trustees of the Village of Marcellus made a Financial Report to the residents, showing what expenses had been incurred during the past year, and what was to be expected in the next. There would be a noticeable increase in the budget for the Village, and an increase in the tax levy, which would bring some protest from village residents.

19 Mar 1872 - " . . . undersigned Trustees of the village do report as follows:

For clerk services	6.00
For cleaning sidewalks	12.00
For re-chartering the village	15.00

It is then "estimated that there will have to be raised for expenses the ensuring year:

For cleaning walks	12.00
For clerk services	10.00
For books rc (recording)	10.00
For lock up	25.00
For contingent expenses	50.00

which amounts we are of the opinion will be ample for the year, 1872."

The new budget called for a sizeable increase in the salary of the Village clerk, from $6.00 to $10.00 per year as well as the added expenses of a lock up and police service. Another item, which found its way into the Village budget, was that of contingency, an expense that covers the unexpected. It is commonly used by municipalities today to meet unanticipated costs, but was a recent innovation in the 1872 budget. When the Board, at its April 16th meeting levied a tax increase on village residents in order to meet the new budget, a number of complaints by the residents resulted.

8 May 1872 - " . . . the President laid before the board a statement that numerous complaints were made against the tax levy as being excessive. On motion, the vote of May 4th to adopt the report of the Committee on Taxes and Assessments was reconsidered. Ayes, Messrs. Curtis, Hunt and VanVranken. On motion, the report was sent back to the Committee with instructions to carry out the tax upon a basis of 1/6th of one per cent for highway purposes instead of 1/4th of one per cent as ordered April 16th 1872. Ayes Messrs. Hunt, Curtis and VanVranken."

Protest and Resignation

Protest over the tax levy apparently caused President Brown to abruptly resign his position three days after the May 8th meeting. The Committee on Taxes and Assessments had reconsidered the tax assessment and the three Trustees - - Jasper Hunt, Albert Curtis and John B. VanVranken - - agreed to the change, prompting, Brown's resignation and the appointment of Newton G. Case as President for the remainder of the year.

11 May 1872 - ". . . A communication was received from the President resigning his office to take effect from this date. On motion, the same was accepted. Newton G. Case was nominated for President to fill vacancy and on motion he was elected as President for the balance of the year."

1872

Newton G. Case was a dry goods grocery merchant, a fifty-five-year old married man with four children whose retail store on East Main Street, now known as the American Legion Building, served the interests of local farmers and Village residents. Trustees Hunt and Curtis who, along with John B. VanVranken, had been re-elected in 1872 appointed him to the office of President. VanVranken, a dealer in teasels, was about fifty years old at the time, married with four children. Teasels had been an important part of the local economy, a cash crop that many farmers in the area harvested. During the Civil War, a mechanical device was invented which out-performed the teasel in raising the nap on wool and while some small farmers were driven out of business, the demand for teasels remained high until the turn of the century, particularly with the local woolen mills of Marcellus. This is another indication, however, of the growing use of technology and an emerging mechanization, even on the farm.

Samuel Dada was elected Collector of Taxes in 1872 and he, along with the elected Treasurer, William B. White, would continue to be chosen for those positions for years to come. White, son of Jeremiah G. B. White a former Village Treasurer, was a local merchant and tinsmith and quite wealthy, much of it an inheritance, it would seem, from his father. The Village Clerk was Charles H. DeCoudres, son of a former Trustee,

Store of J. E. Woodbridge, Marcellus, N. Y.

Thomas DeCoudres. He was a young man in his twenties at the time, recently married and father of a young daughter. He was a merchant and worked as a clerk in his father's drug store on Main Street, a building which would change hands many times in the years ahead but is still distinguished today by its massive front pillars.

Temperance

Because, there was little control over the manufacture or distribution of alcohol, the era of state and federal regulation still some time distant, local governments, like the Village of Marcellus, chose to exercise control over liquor licenses for local establishments. This control was encouraged by the growth of the temperance movement in Marcellus: "Presbyterian records indicate the organization of a temperance society in 1873, and shortly after Frances Willard founded the Women's Christian Temperance Union in 1874, a local chapter was organized" (Heffernan 68). By granting a liquor license, the Trustees not only introduced some form of regulation, but also brought in revenue in the form of another tax. The cost of the license was small by today's standards, but so too were many of the wages, particularly that of the Village Clerk.

11 June 1872 - " . . . an application was made by Alvord Bros. of the Corporation of the village of Marcellus for a Hotel Liquor License which was granted on motion or Mr. Hunt. . . . An application was made by Thos. DeCoudres & Son of the Corporation of the Village of Marcellus for a Grocers Liquor License, which was granted on motion of Mr. Van Vranken. . . ."

11 Mar 1873 - "On motion, C. H. DeCoudres was allowed six dollars for services as Clerk during the present year . . . draft drawn on Treasurer for that amount and signed by the President . . . Clerk was directed to call the annual meeting of the electors for the election of officers at the House of Alvord Bros on Tuesday, March 18th 1873 and that he post the notices as required by law . . ."

1873 – More Regulation

By comparison with previous elections, the turnout of voters in March of 1873 was rather large – 87 votes, in contrast to the 31 cast in 1872. The faces of Village government, however, did not change much. Newton G. Case, who had been appointed President when Oscar Brown resigned, was returned to that office and the same Trustees chosen in 1872 – Albert Curtis, Jasper Hunt, and John B. VanVranken – would be reelected as well. Samuel Dada and William B. White would again serve as Collector and Treasurer respectively, and Charles H. DeCoudres would again be appointed Village Clerk.

Government rules and regulations continued to expand in the 1870s and the start of what we would call code enforcement in Marcellus today had part of its origin then. After the Civil War, the use of steam as a source of power found favor with a number of manufacturers and individuals, and the Board of Trustees of the Village, concerned about its safe use, would impose regulations within the corporation limits The Board was also interested in making sure that the annual fair was as successful as possible but limiting the use of retail stands on Village streets. The fairs often attracted strangers, as well as peddlers, some of whom were less than honest, requiring a police presence at times. During the winter months, clearing the sidewalks continued to be a major responsibility of Village government.

24 Jun 1873 - "Messrs. North & Coombs be allowed to place a steam boiler and engine on their premises subject to the approval of the Trustees as to safety when done."

9 Sep 1873 - "Motion made by Mr. VanVranken that no refreshment or retail stands of any kind be allowed in the streets of the corporation, Sep 16, 1873, the day of the Twin Fair. Carried. Ayes, Curtis, Hunt, VanVranken."

16 Mar 1874 - "Motion by Mr. Hunt that twelve and 50/100 dollars be paid Albert Curtis for scraping side walks and repairs to scraper, to date. Carried."

1874 – Weights and Measures

In March 1874, the election returned to office a former President, Daniel G. Coon. Elected along with him were Trustees James Johnston, Joseph Woodbridge, and Samuel Hooper. Johnston and Woodbridge were both older men, farmers, and like Hooper, were immigrants from the British Isles. Their origins seem to reflect not only the character of the Village of Marcellus at the time but also the fact that birthplace need not be a barrier to participation in government.

One of the first actions of this new Board was the appointment of a Sealer of Weights & Measures, a task that today, rests not with the Village, but with the County government. These Trustees also appointed an Excise Board from the Trustee membership, whose duty it was to impose a tax or fee on businesses that sold alcohol. It was, in a sense, an alcohol-licensing agency, a responsibility that now rests with the State government. Another responsibility, which is no longer a Village assignment, is that of tax assessing. In the past, the tax assessor was usually one or more of the Trustees of the Village, a job for which the Trustee was paid a nominal fee. This procedure continued until the Village decided to hire its own assessor. In recent years, however, this has changed again, and today, Village taxes are based on an assessment that is provided by the Town of Marcellus Assessor. The assessment used for determining the Town tax is also used for determining the Village tax.

21 Mar 1874 - "On motion, Amery Wilson was appointed Sealer of Weights & measures."

7 Apr 1874 - " . . . Board proceeded by ballot to elect an Excise Board for the present year, with the following result: Ballot No. 1. James Johnson rec'd 2 votes, Joseph Woodbridge rec'd 1, Samuel Hooper rec'd 1. Ballot No. 2, Joseph Woodbridge rec'd 3 votes, Samuel Hooper, 1."

2 Jun 1874 - "A bill was presented by James Johnston for two days work assessing at $2.00 per day. Amount $4, which on being put to vote was allowed."

The Economy

While the period of the 1870s on the national level has often been termed the "Gilded Age," a reference to the graft and corruption that was concealed by powerful businesses and the government, in Marcellus " . . . the economic picture . . . was marked by the growth and stabilization of industries which were to become the major sources of family income until well after World War II. Both skilled craftsmen and unskilled workers found employment in the paper and woolen industries, as the industries increased their production and expanded their markets" (Heffernan 44).

Harnessing the power of Nine Mile Creek, some of these factories had been started long before and were already profitable. However, the great impetus provided by the demands of the Civil War and the emerging industrialization of the nation in the postwar years caused them to expand even more. In Marcellus Falls, paper mills like those owned by John F. Jones and the Sherman Brothers, the distilleries of Olney and Coon as well as the Marcellus Woolen Mills on Factory Street brought both employment and a changing village scene. By 1874, two Irish immigrants, Michael Lawless and Dennis Tierney, having bought out what had been the Jones Paper Mill, expanded that business and added others. "In 1877, the sawmill which stood on the site of the lower Crown Mill was washed away. J. C. Sayre and a partner bought the property and . . . opened the first woolen mill on the site" (Heffernan 45).

Wages and Income

Immigrants would provide a cheap and abundant labor supply for the expanding mills, the wages for which were far from what would be considered a living wage today. Statistics from the New York State Census of 1875 provide some idea as to the estimated pay of hired laborers and mechanics, and are exclusive of living or board expenses.

NEW YORK STATE CENSUS
MISCELLANEOUS STATISTICS
FIRST AND SECOND ELECTION DISTRICTS
TOWN OF MARCELLUS
JUNE 1, 1875

Estimated average pay of Hired Laborers and Mechanics, exclusive of Board.

Occupation, not regular trade or requiring skilled labor	By the day	By the week	By the month
Common hand labor	$1.50		
Farm hands, hired by season or year	$2.00	$20.00	
Farm hands hired in Haying, Harvest	$2.00		
Women, common household work		$2.00	

Trades and occupations requiring skilled laborers	By the day	By the week	By the month
Carpenters and Joiners	$2.50		
Masons: Stone and Bricklayers		$3.00	
Shoemakers (journeymen)		$1.00	
Machinists	$2.50		
Moulders			
Blacksmiths	$2.00		
Painters and Glaziers	$2.00		
Printers			
Dressmakers	$1.00		
Sewing & other women's hand labor		$1.00	

Other hired persons not specified	By the day	By the week	By the month
Teamsters, with two horses	$4.00		
Male Teacher with public school			$100.00
Female Teacher			$25.00

With more workers, there was a greater demand for housing both inside and outside the corporation and this would lead not only to an expansion of streets and roads but also an increase in the services which village government would provide its residents.

Most people in the community were still farmers or worked at farm related jobs, the Village and its businesses still providing needed services. However, with the postwar increase in the production of cash crops, the role of the Village as a center for exchange and transportation of tobacco and teasels, apples and hay increased as well. By the middle of the decade, the Village of Marcellus had extended beyond its main corners, a rural village that was responding to the variety of changes taking place.

41

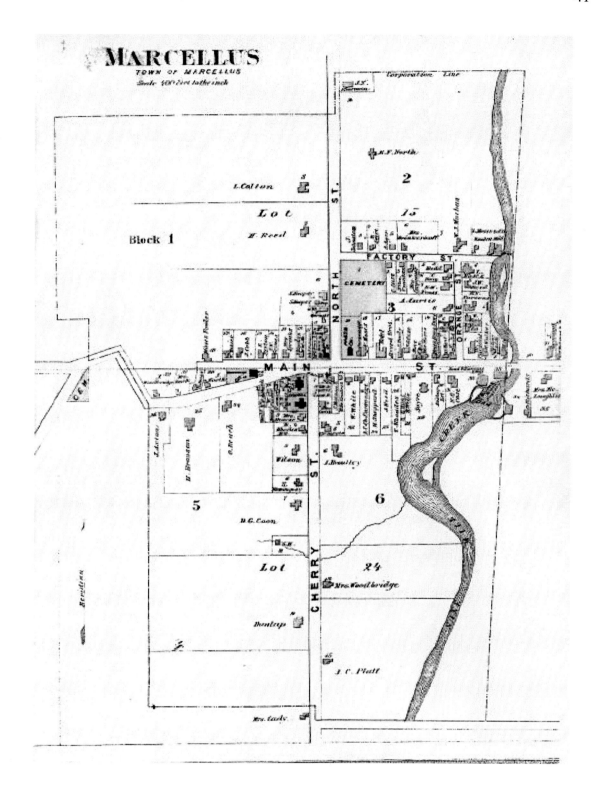

1875- Election

With the election of March 16, 1875, there came to the Presidency of the Village an individual who would serve seven terms in that office. Isaac N. Sherman was a well-to-do paper manufacturer and during his first three terms in office, a significant amount of road and sidewalk repair, as well as the enactment of new Village ordinances took place. Newcomers to the Board included Robert F. North, R. Warren Alvord, and James M.

Dunlap. North was a fifty-three-year old married farmer with a son, while Alvord, also in his fifties with a wife and two children, was a hotelkeeper and operated the now-famous public house with his brothers. Fifty-one-year old James Dunlap, too, was a farmer, with a wife and one child at the time.

Isaac N. Sherman
Village President
1875-1876-1877
1880
1881
1901-1902

6 Apr 1875 - " . . . committee on sidewalks with the request that they report at the next regular meeting."

13 Apr 1875 - " . . . need of new walk beginning at Albert Curtis' south line and to the corner of Main Street. Also repairs needed on Dr. Parsons', Mrs. Bishop's and Case & Sons on Main Street."

4 May 1875 - " . . . bill was presented by Simon Connelly for two days work on (South Street) sluice - amt - $3.00, which was accepted and draft ordered drawn on Treasurer for the amount. . . . bill was presented by Peter Mailey for $9.50 being for stone furnished, which was accepted and draft ordered drawn on highway fund for the amount. . ."

17 Aug 1875 - " . . . on motion of Mr. Alvord a draft was ordered drawn on the Treasurer for $4.71 in favor of John Dunn for improvements on foot of Main Street."

New Ordinances For the Village

During their years in office, the President and the Trustees initiated repair and maintenance of the Village infrastructure, particularly its roadwork and sidewalks. In addition, at a special meeting on March 1st, 1876, the Board of Trustees passed a resolution to create a new set of by-laws for the Village of Marcellus. The process was similar to writing a new Constitution and the resolutions included 20 rules or ordinances that replaced what laws had been in effect since the founding of the Village. The ordinances reflected many of the economic and social changes that had been taking place in the Village in recent years and were quite detailed as to what could or could not be done in the Village. The ordinances also provided penalties in the form of fines, from $5.00 to $25.00 and sometimes up to $100.00 per violation. The voters would ratify their approval by the Trustees later in the month.

1 Mar 1876 - special meeting " . . . at 7 o'clock p.m. for the purpose of passing such rules, ordinances and by laws as may be deemed necessary for the welfare and government of said village and to transact such other business as may be necessary."

Section 1st - a police constable of said village shall be annually appointed . . .

Section 2nd - no horses, cattle, mules, sheep goats, swine or geese shall be permitted to run at large . . . the owner . . . shall be liable to a penalty not exceeding ten dollars.

Section 3rd - no person shall place . . . any logs, timber, bot(tle), cask, stone, plank boards . . . in any street or alley . . . so as to incommode or obstruct the free passage or use thereof . . . nothing contained in this section shall prohibit merchants and others from placing goods and merchandise or household furniture on the sidewalks for the purpose of loading and unloading the same, provided it be done without any unreasonable delay.

Section 4th - every owner or occupant . . . shall during the winter season . . . keep the sidewalk . . . free from obstructions by snow and shall also at all times keep such sidewalks clean and free from all dirt, filth and weeds or other obstructions or encumbrances.

Section 5th - no person . . . shall . . . fire . . . any gun . . . crackers, rockets or squibs or throw or play with any fireballs, . . . fireworks, . . . or build any fire or fires in any of the public streets . . . or blow any horn . . . or make any improper noise which may disturb the peace or said village in the day or night time . . . the provisions of this ordinance shall not apply to the day which shall be celebrated as the anniversary of American Independence. . .

Section 6th - no person . . . shall bring, deposit or have within the limits of said Village any dead carcass or other unwholesome substance . . . on or about his or their premises . . . any putrid meat, fish, hides or skins . . . or any stagnant water . . .

Section 7th - it shall not be lawful for any person or corporation to . . . deposit . . . into any of the squares, streets, lanes of this Village, or the creek race or ponds or under any bridge or in any public place any dung, dead animals or putrid meat or fish or slops, dirty water or nuisance of any kind . . .

Section 8th - no person . . . in a state of partial or total nudity shall bathe or swim in any of the races, ponds, creeks or other public waters in the day time in said village. . . .

Section 9th - no person shall in anywise injure or destroy any shade tree or tie or hitch any team or horse or other animal to any shade tree planted along the streets or sidewalks in said village . . .

Section 10th - no person shall ride, drive, lead or place any horse or other animal upon the sidewalk . . .

Section 11th - no wagon maker, blacksmith, inn keeper . . . shall permit any wagon, carriage, cutter, sleigh, sled, cart or other vehicle to remain in the streets, in front of premises occupied by such person, detached from the animal . . . for a longer period not to exceed eight hours in succession . . .

Section 12th - no person . . . shall in anywise aid, promote or be engaged in any fight, riot, assault, breach of the peace disturbance or disorderly assemblage or shall keep or frequent any disorderly house . . . no person shall be guilty of drunkenness, indecent exposure of person or of any obscene or disorderly conduct in any of the streets or public places . . . no person shall procure any disorderly person or common prostitute to come into or remain in said Village . . .

Section 13th - no person shall sell or give away any wines or intoxicating drinks either by wholesale or retail in any street or square or vacant lot in said Village . . . forfeit the sum of not to exceed twenty-five dollars for each offense.

Section 14th - not be lawful for any person . . . to keep open for use any billiard table, nine or ten pin alley, or gun alley, shuffle board, E. O. table, Faro bank or any other instrument of gaming within said Village without having at the time a license from the Trustees to keep the same . . . penalty of twenty five dollars . . .

Section 15th - no person . . . shall exhibit for money any theatrical representations, feats of horsemanship, circus, caravan of animals or any animals or artificial curiosity or other shows . . . or performances for money . . . without having first obtained a license from the Trustees, and paying . . . not less than two dollars, nor more than twenty-five, at the discretion of the officers granting the license.

Section 16th - no person shall, without the written permission from a Trustee or Street Commissioner, dig or remove or carry away or cause the same to be done any stone, earth, sand or gravel from any public street, highway, lane or public square in this village; nor shall any person . . . deposit any coal ashes, stone or rubbish of any kind in any of the public streets of said village . . . ten dollars for each offense.

Section 17th - no person shall write, print, publish or post any obscene or indecent writing picture or print in said village and no person shall deface any post, wall, fence, building or other surface with any obscene or indecent mark, writing, picture or print . . .

Section 18th - not be lawful for any person to carry into any barn, stable or out building in said village any lighted cigar or smoking pipe or lighted candle or lamp not enclosed in a lantern in such manner as to endanger the safety of such barn, stable or out building, nor to deposit any wood ashes within ten feet of any building, fence or wooden structure in said village unless in a secure vessel or inclosure of iron, brick or stone . . . penalty not exceeding ten dollars.

Section 19th - no person . . . shall put up any stove pipe from any stove, boiler or furnace unless the same, when they pass through partitions, pass through earthen or metalic tubes and also be conducted into a chimney made of brick or stone unless when the Trustees shall deem it equally safe when otherwise put up to be certified under their hands . . . for every offense; forfeit five dollars and the further sum of one dollar for every twenty-four hours the same shall remain so put up.

Section 20th - hereafter there shall annually be elected in said village three fire wardens.

These new ordinances seem to illustrate part of what life was probably like in the Village of Marcellus in the 1870s. Some of them may seem quaint and picturesque, with

44

little relevance for today, while others are still quite applicable. Today Village ordinances in Marcellus are much more detailed and cover many dimensions of life, including, as they did in the 1870s, provisions regarding fire and police protection, sidewalks and trees, animal and noise control, junk and abandoned vehicles, as well as the licensing of businesses in the Village. The times may have changed, but certainly those rules governing life in the Village have merely been updated.

There was also, it appears, a desire on the part of the voters and the Trustees to have a voice in selecting the fire wardens. Because so many of the Village structures were made of wood, and residents lived in close proximity to one another, the fear of fire was a source of anxiety for many. A number of fires had already ravaged the Village in the 1860s and early 1870s, and little fire fighting apparatus had been approved for purchase. The apprehension was justified and it would seem that the vote for fire wardens was an attempt to sound that alarm.

21 Mar 1876 - " . . . for Fire Wardens, 96 votes were cast of which number
    Joseph Matteson   received 31
    E. V. Baker   received 30
    Isaac Bradley   received 31

Israel Parsons, M.D.
1821 – 1904

1876 - The Centennial

The centennial of the United States was 1876 and on the 4th of July, Dr. Israel Parsons, a physician who had served the community for many years, gave an address in the Presbyterian Church, a speech that was later published, in 1878. In his address, Dr. Parsons presented a history of the Town of Marcellus since its settlement up to that point in time, describing how the Village " . . . has become an object of pride to its inhabitants, and of admiration to strangers" (Parsons 106).

In the election of 1876, Isaac Sherman was returned to the Presidency of the Village, along with some of the same Trustees that had previously served. This Board continued to promote those elements of respect, which Dr. Parsons referenced in his address, including the establishment by ordinance of road widths and curb lines and the adoption of plans for laying sidewalks and planting shade trees along Village streets.

4 May 1876 - "Motion by Mr. VanVranken that the Chair appoint a time for the Board to meet with the Street Commissioner to establish the width of the road bed and designate the distance from the sidewalks that shade trees may be planted on the various streets."

16 May 1876 - Ordinances adopted by the board for laying sidewalks and planting trees. For example, " . . . on Cherry and North Sts. - curb stones to be eighteen feet from fence or line of

street - shade trees eleven feet from fence or line of street. . . . the street north of the Methodist Church leading west is to be called Maiden Lane and beginning where it intersects Main St. - the curbing to be twelve feet and trees nine feet from fence or line of street and to extend to northwest corner of lot owned and occupied by Worthy Rosier. . . . sidewalks on all streets but Main to be four feet wide and to be laid one foot from the fence or line of street. On Main St. sidewalks to be five feet wide and laid close to the fence."

Many merchants and shopkeepers looked with particular favor on the improved sidewalks of the Village. The streets of the Village were dirt roads at this time, and became paths of mud passable only by horse or wagon at times. The sidewalks and crosswalks of the Corporation, however, were made of planks or of stone or gravel, making passage more comfortable and convenient for both shoppers and shopkeepers. Throughout the year, the Board continued to insist that residents maintain this appealing characteristic of the Village and continued its own responsibility of clearing them of snow and ice in the winter months.

28 Aug 1876 - " . . . Clerk was ordered to serve a written notice on Johnathan Reed forbidding him to bridge the gutter in front of his roadway."

2 Oct 1876 - " . . . that a notice be served on the property owners beginning at Hiram Reed's south line and extending south on west side of North Street to Fulmer's plank walk, that they build suitable walk of either stone, plank or gravel."

11 Oct 1876 - " . . . a complaint having been entered of heaps of earth laying on North Street in front of the Cemetery, the same being a nuisance. The Clerk was ordered to notify the Trustees of the North Eastern Religious Society to remove the same . . . "

19 Mar 1877 - "The Board hereby finds that there is due James Woodbridge for scraping sidewalks up to this date, $21.00 and it is the only outstanding account against the corporation."

1877 – Fire

The March election of 1877 again returned Isaac Sherman to the Presidency along with some of the same Trustees. A newcomer was James Axton, a wealthy forty-year-old who had been born in England. He had a wife and child at the time and farmed a large tract of land on West Main Street near the bend. Across the road from Axton's home, on a wintry night in January 1877, the twenty-year-old Methodist Church was destroyed by fire. While " . . . the congregation immediately replaced it with the present structure which was dedicated in January of 1878 (Heffernan 56), the Village Fathers and residents seemed more concerned about highways and sidewalks than they did about fire fighting equipment. This was a concern that was too long delayed.

1 May 1877 - " . . . it was resolved . . . to furnish materials to pave the gutters on both sides of Main and Genesee Streets to the road running south from Main. It was left last year . . . to procure Mr. Galager of Syracuse or some other competent person to do stone paving under the inspection of the Road Commissioner."

3 Jul 1877 - " . . . that the Clerk notify William White, William Farmer, Diane Shepard and Jane Bishop to repair their sidewalks opposite their premises within the next 30 days . . . notify J. Parsons and Henry Wells to repair their sidewalks in front of their premises . . . that William J. Machan be instructed to gravel the walk in front of the Cemetery."

6 Nov 1877 - " . . . that the President is authorized to procure a scraper for the purpose of scraping the sidewalks."

3 Dec 1877 - " . . . that Albert Curtis be a committee of one to procure a man to scrape the sidewalks."

1 Jan 1878 - " . . . that a draft be drawn on the Treasurer for eight dollars and seventy five cents to pay Francis Baker for a snow scraper."

1878 – Village Lighting

The election of 1878 brought a familiar face back to the Presidency of the Village. Daniel G. Coon, who had served two previous terms as President was again elected to the office. James Johnston also was returned to office as Trustee, along with George Stocking and Jasper Hunt. Only Stocking was new to the Board. He was about fifty years old, married, the father of a grown daughter, and his occupation was unique to the Village -- that of a jeweler. One of the priorities of the Coon administration was the public lighting of village streets. This required not only the construction of lamps and lampposts but also providing oil for the lamps and paying for a lamp lighter, who, in the person of Michael Kennedy, was paid about $3.00 per month.

7 May 1878 - " . . . on motion of Geo Stocking, Jasper Hunt was appointed Committee to inquire the price of lamps. . . . to look after posts for the lamps."

3 Sep 1878 - " . . . order was drawn on the Treasurer in favor of C. McManus for $6.75 to pay for lamp hangings . . . in favor of James W. Reed for $3.07 to pay his bill for fluid (oil) . . . Mr. Coon's Bill for lamps for $48.75 . . . in favor of George Stocking for two dollars for labor lighting lamps, preparing post, . . . in favor of Jasper Hunt for $6.40 for money expended and labor . . . "

6 Nov 1878 - " . . . an order was ordered drawn on the Treasurer in favor of Geo Stocking for three dollars advanced to Michael Kennedy for lighting lamps."

3 Dec 1878 - " . . . in favor of White & Matteson for seventy five cents for repairing lamps . . . Jas Reed for oil to the amount of $4.00 . . . for $4.50 in favor of Michael Kennedy for lighting lamps . . . "

Today, Village lighting is, of course, provided by electricity and it is a service that is so taken for granted that residents know little about it or ignore the utility – until the lights go out in a thunderstorm. In 1878, while lamps on the streets would have imparted a faint view of the community at night, they also provided safer travel for the pedestrian and horseman as well as a sense of security for a shopkeeper like George Stocking who,  at the end of the business day, locked up his store on East Main Street and retired for the evening.

1879 - An Historic Year

Daniel Coon was returned to the Village Presidency for another term in the March 1879 election, as were most of those who had earlier served with him. The year would be an historic one for the Village of Marcellus, one that was both triumphant and tragic.

The Marcellus Observer

The year marked the successful start of a local newspaper, *The Marcellus Observer*, originally called *The Marcellus Weekly Observer*. It published its first issue on April 17, 1879 by Edmund J. Reed, a young man who had opened up a printing office on North Street some years earlier, and had been recognized by Dr. Parsons in his

Centennial Address of 1876: " . . . in the line of new business, we are glad to notice the Printing Office of Edmund Reed. Although small we must not 'despise the day of small things', Benjamin Franklin once began. The first printing office is a marked step in the elevation of a place. Its every business implies intelligence, and it also begets it. It is a great educator" (Parsons 107).

Edmund Reed was the twenty-one-year old son of Hiram Reed, a man who had farmed land on the Camillus Plank Road, North Street today, for the previous twenty years. Edmund Reed, however, had decided to embark on a career that was quite distinct from that of his father and he " . . . rode around the country soliciting subscriptions from the local residents, . . . began printing the first newspaper in his printing office on North Street" (Heffernan 223). It proved to be a great success in Village communication at the time but after a few years, Reed decided to sell his newspaper and tried his hand in other enterprises. Reed also served as Collector of Taxes for the Village of Marcellus in 1878 and 1879, collecting the property levy that was assessed by the Board of Trustees each year. Edmund Reed would also serve as President of the Village for a number of terms in the mid 1890s, his once fledgling business an established institution of the community by that time.

7 May 1879 - " . . . was resolved that the tax for the present year be one dollar on each thousand assessed and that one hundred and twenty five dollars of the amount raised be contingent fund."

Tragedy

There was also tragedy in that year, 1879: "On July 3, 1879, the worst fire in the history of the village consumed St. John's Episcopal Church on the corner of North and Main Street, a three story building to the north of the church, and a small store to the west of it. D. M. Fulmer owned the two latter buildings at the time. Fulmer rebuilt the present three-story block on the North Street site and a storekeeper, named Michael Sheehan, rebuilt on the Main Street site, in accordance with Village ordinances. A young lawyer, named William Gallup, who had moved into town about this time, purchased the corner site and built the block which still stands" (Heffernan 56). Discouraged as they were, the parishioners of the St. John's Church began to plan immediately for another church building. Another site was obtained, on the corner of Orange and Main Streets and in February 1881 the new Church building would be consecrated.

The Board dealt with another tragedy, and a first, that summer -- the death of a Trustee in office. Joseph Woodbridge died on August 29, 1879 at the age of fifty-three and the Board of Trustees, after passing a resolution of condolence, appointed his neighbor from across the road, James Axton, to take his place.

At the same Board meeting in September, the Trustees, concerned about the devastating fire in July, began to take an even greater interest in correcting any potential fire hazards in the Village. It was the start of what would become another major responsibility of the Village - more adequate fire protection.

2 Sep 1879 - A resolution of condolence, on the death of Trustee Joseph Woodbridge, of the corporation officers of Marcellus Village was adopted and published. " . . . James Axton was appointed trustee in the place of Joseph Woodbridge, deceased. . . . James Johnston was appointed by the President and Mr. Hunt to look after the defective chimneys in the corporation."

10 Sep 1879 - " . . . was resolved that a written notice be served on Michael Shean (owner of the new Main Street shop) to remove all obstructions from the side walk in front of his premises on the North side of Main Street."

Conclusion

Joseph Woodbridge was a twenty-five-year-old man when he came to America from England with his wife, Elizabeth, and a young daughter, Rhoda, in 1848. He settled in the rural community of Marcellus and began farming land on the main road leading west out of town, fathered another daughter and participated in the life of the community that he now called home. By the time Joseph Woodbridge died, thirty years later, the community where he had settled with his family had changed a great deal.

The Marcellus Weekly Observer
Thursday, September 4, 1879
Death Of An Esteemed Citizen

It is sadness that we have to chronicle the death of our esteemed townsman, Joseph Woodbridge, which occurred in this village Friday afternoon. Mr. Woodbridge had been suffering for about four weeks from a combination of diseases. He was born in England, in 1826, and in the year 1849 he removed to this town, where he has ever since resided, becoming one of our most respected citizens. He had no desire for having his name brought before the public, although he had served as a village trustee for several years, with entire satisfaction to the public. Mr. Woodbridge leaves a wife and two daughters to mourn the loss of a kind husband and a loving father.

When he first arrived, the community, in the words of Dr. Parsons, bore all the " . . . marks of a deserted or a discouraged village, that, even the full grown youths were really ashamed, and, in many instances, ignored the place of their nativity" (Parsons 106). The Erie Canal and the railroads had caused a mass exodus, mostly to the west, from the community that had once been a beehive of activity. Then began a period gradual recovery as " . . . a steady influx of Irish immigrants furnished farm laborers to the rural areas, coachmen and hired girls to the more prosperous families, and mill workers to the establishments along the creek" (Heffernan 28). The community was incorporated as a Village and began to assume more of the features of a civilized society, its sidewalks and streets, its laws and its lampposts attracting shoppers and shopkeepers, farmers and mechanics.

In the last ten years of his life, Joseph Woodbridge noticed that more and more men went to work in local factories rather than in nearby fields to farm. More and more of the people he met were immigrants, like him, looking for the opportunities that could be found in America. From his obituary, it appears that Joseph Woodbridge was a plain and humble man, a good husband and father, and a good citizen and that he had found opportunity in the place he called home. He was interred, far from the land of his birth, in a cemetery on North Street in a community that would continue to offer opportunity as it civilized itself through law and order and social interaction.

Chapter 5 - The 80s

Business expansion continued in the 1880s as James C. Sayre opened the first woolen mill on the site of an old saw mill that had washed away in 1877 and later became the Lower Crown Mill. In addition, the Powder Works along the Falls north of the Village were rebuilt following a devastating Thanksgiving Day fire that occurred in 1879. The Eagle Paper Mill of Lawless and Tierney continued to expand in Marcellus Falls and Edward Johnson started a pearl barley mill along the creek in 1882, the latter purchased, renamed and expanded under Allen V. Smith in the 1890s. The Moses mill in the Village, at the end of Factory Street would also witness reorganization and expansion beginning in 1886 and, south of the Village in Rose Hill, Frank B. Mills began his seed packaging and catalogue business in 1887. The next year, William Nightingale, an immigrant from England, opened up a mill south of the Village " . . . which served the local residents by grinding cattle feed, and graham and buckwheat flour, and also by making cider each fall" (Heffernan 50). The most notable changes to the Village in this decade, however, seemed to be social and political, as the community fashioned its social order and the Board of Trustees expanded services and centralized control over many of aspects of life in the Village.

Election

In a rather large voter turnout on March 16, 1880, Isaac Sherman was again returned to the Village Presidency, along with James Axton, Selah Bronson, and Charles H. DeCoudres. Axton was a returning Trustee, and DeCoudres had once served as Village Clerk, but this was Bronson's first term as a Village official. He was the twenty-eight-years old, unmarried at the time, and a miller by trade, the son of Hiram Bronson, who owned and farmed a large tract of land on the south side of West Main Street in the Village.

16 Mar 1880 " . . . at said election, 86 votes were cast for President of which

Isaac N. Sherman	received	54
Daniel G. Coon	received	31
Hiram Bronson		1

For Trustees, 257 votes were cast of which

James Axton	received	83
Charles H. DeCoudres	received	58
Selah Bronson	received	84
Thos Walker	received	2
Michael Shehan	received	27
Jasper Hunt	received	3

For Treasurer, 85 votes were cast of which

Wm. White	received	85

For Collector, 82 votes were cast of which

Jasper Hunt	received	52
Samuel Dady	received	30

Lighting, Permits and Hoops

The concerns of the Board continued to be an improvement in village lighting, as well as building and construction permits. This latter item was in response to the request of the Episcopal Society to rebuild its Church on the corner of Main and Orange Streets after the disastrous fire of 1879, the cornerstone for which was laid in September of 1880.

24 Mar 1880 - " . . . moved by S. M. Bronson that the President appoint a Committee of two to investigate the question of purchasing new lamps and disposing of the old ones . . . "

6 Apr 1880 - " . . . the application of N. G. Case for the Episcopal Society to use a part of Orange St for building materials for the Erection of a Church was granted subject to the approval of the trustees."

14 Apr 1880 - " . . . appoint a committee to procure 15 lamps and suitable posts for lighting the Village and have them located and put in proper shape for use, also to dispose of the old lamps."

There were also some complaints lodged with Village authorities that would cause the Board to prohibit ball playing in the streets as well as another critical of some boys in the Village who were "rolling hoops" and jeopardizing the safety of the residents. In more recent years, a relevant comparison might be made about young people who enjoy "skate boarding" causing some to criticize this activity at Village Board meetings.

7 May 1880 - " . . . resolved that the Clerk post a notice in some conspicuous place forbidding ball playing in the streets of the Corporation."

There were other matters in the Village that required police action that year. One incident had to do with illegal fishing (with a net and in violation of State Game Laws) in Nine Mile Creek and another with littering the streets of the village. An increased police presence brought about added expenses to the Village budget, but the people of Marcellus and the Trustees were interested in having this service provided.

7 May 1880 - " . . . J. M. Seymour, J.P. (Justice of the Peace), presented a bill for $9.80 costs in criminal cases against Maurice Donahue, Peter Maley, Wm Maley, Simon Conaly, Peter Devin & Jas Dolan & on motion of C. H. Decoudres was allowed and draft ordered drawn on the Treasurer for the same. Henry Jones, Police Constable, presented a bill for $2.00 for costs in serving warrant and mileage in the case of Corporation vs. Jas Dolan

During the summer of 1880, enumerators took the 10th Census of the United States and it indicated a growing Village and Town of Marcellus, with an outlook for even greater growth in the years ahead. There was also great excitement during the summer over the 8th Annual Town Fair that was held in mid-September. Fairs were a cause for much celebration in

---

The Marcellus Observer
Thursday, July 1 1880
The Census

The census for this town is completed and as we predicted a short time ago, there would be a slight increase over the census of 1875. The enumerators give the number of inhabitants at 2,715. In 1875 there were but 2,498, thus making a gain of 217 during the past years. In the village there are 490 persons, but as the corporation limits are quite too limited, the village had extended beyond and in reality there are about 700 inhabitants instead of the number that it is credited with. The prospect for the growth of the town is quite encouraging and we trust that by the next time the census is taken, there may be a still greater increase.

The Marcellus Observer
Thursday, September 9, 1880
Jottings About The Coming Fair

Only a week from tomorrow until the eighth annual fair. The Cornet Band will be in attendance and discourse numerous selections. . . . merchants and manufacturers should all make an exhibit of their goods. It is expected that many articles will be exhibited from the surrounding towns. For stands and eating booths application should be made at once to A. L. Brinkerhoff. A good day is all that is necessary and the people will be well repaid for a visit to the grounds. Extra precaution will be taken to guard against the work of the numerous swindlers who are always in attendance. The grounds selected by the committee are those of James Dunlap directly south of his residence. An excellent selection. Every member of the farmers' club is urgently requested to meet at the Alvord House, Saturday evening, to complete the final arrangements for the fair. Bring out your good horses, cattle, sheep, swine, poultry, fruit, grain, vegetables, farm implements, and in fact, anything. Everybody in town should take something.

19th century America and were an opportunity not only for having displays and exhibits but also for rural Americans to mix and mingle. 1880 was also an election year, and the Fair, like those today, was an opportunity for politicians to voice their opinions and meet the voting public.

7 Sep 1880 - " . . . it was ordered that Henry Jones, P. C. (Police Constable) notify the boys that they must stop rolling hoops in the corporation."

8 Dec 1880 - "complaints having been brought to the notice of the board of persons violating Section 7 of the Village ordinances by throwing coal ashes and other refuse in the streets. Jas Axten was ordered to notify the Police Constable to see that is was stopped."

As 1880 came to a close, Edmund Reed described in his paper some of the expanding Village charm and appeal when he commented " . . . in the evening, our Village looks quite city-like, when the street lamps are all lighted. Certainly it shows the interest our citizens take in the welfare of the place" (*The Marcellus Observer*, Nov 14, 1880).

1881 - Election

On March 15, 1881, Newton G. Case, the dry goods merchant who had previously served in Village government was again elected President. A new Trustee to the Board in that year was Simon Dodd, Jr. whose family had come to Marcellus by way of Massachusetts. Dodd was the son of Simon and Sarah Chandler Dodd, an Irish Catholic family, which had left Ireland in the 1830s to find work in England. Simon Jr. was born in Leeds, Yorkshire, England in 1839 and came to America with his parents and siblings just before the American Civil War. First settling in the town of Worcester, Massachusetts, the family would later, move to Marcellus, where Simon found work as a laborer in the Moses woolen on Factory Street. He was about forty years old at the time, with a wife and family and later in his career rose to become superintendent of the mills as well as President of the Village.

The Marcellus Observer
Thursday, April 21, 1881
Improve Your Place

As the Spring season comes around, it is necessary that many improvements should be made upon the buildings in our village. Some people go at this work in a business-like manner, and everything they do seems to add to the beauty of their property, while others are not so successful. A remark made by almost all strangers is, "how nice your village is kept up." This remark is true, for we think there is scarcely a village of this size that is found in as clean a condition as this. Never-the-less, there is much room for improvement, and every citizen should have pride enough to keep his property in ship shape order.

While the local paper urged residents to keep the Village tidy, the administration of President Case continued to promote better roads and lighting for the village and the appointment of Belus F. North as lamplighter seemed to be a job well suited to this former Civil War soldier. North, a most colorful character in Marcellus Village history, was responsible for re-mapping the Village Cemetery in the latter part of the 19th century and he took a special interest in the affairs of the G.A.R., an organization of Union veterans. The Board was also insistent that ball playing be prohibited from Village streets and the appointment of Stores Griffin as Police Constable to enforce this edict underscored the intent.

15 Mar 1881 - " . . . the poll of said election was opened at one o'clock p.m. & closed at sunset of that day . . . 73 votes were cast, . . . "

8 Apr 1881 - " . . . the salary of the street commissioners shall be at the rate of $1.50 per day . . . Belus F. North is appointed lamp lighter for the ensuing year."

10 May 1881 - " . . . it was moved that the Clerk be authorized to post three notices prohibiting any ball playing in any street of corporation. Motion prevailed."

26 May 1881 - " . . . Stores M. Griffin was appointed Police Constable for the ensuing year in place of A. W. Beach who refuses to qualify."

Idle Time

As fewer young people worked on the farms and more began to gather in the Village, residents and the Trustees became increasingly concerned about the idle time that so many young people seemed to have. Even the local paper printed advertisements that expressed this concern, about which all good citizens should beware.

The Marcellus Observer
Thursday, July 14, 1881
What Shall Be Done With The Boys?

This is the question of the hour. Enticed by the fascination of the game of pool, the boys are frequenting saloons, learning profanity, learning obscenity, learning to smoke, learning to drink and learning to gamble; and the boys' mothers think that this kind of education is what makes filial sons; the fathers think that it doesn't make their sons good providers; good citizens think that it is not a good way to learn the duties and obligations of citizenship; ministers think that it fails to make men of good morals and endangers their souls; and what the rest of the people think can only be judged by their indifference. We think that unless boys of eighteen or under are prohibited from entering the pool rooms, they will neither make good sons, nor good men, nor good citizens; nor will they be able to clothe themselves decently. We say keep them out of the pool rooms; send them over to Kent & Miller's, 18 and 20 South Salina where Spring Ulsterettes and Overcoats, Spring Suits and Walking Coats can be obtained at Lower Prices than anywhere else. Call and see what a magnificent stock they are displaying.

Apparently, times have not changed too much. There seems to be a similar lament today that the young have too much time on their hands. They do not frequent pool halls today as they may have in 1880, but mall walking is a common sight in many American cities, including nearby Syracuse, and the gathering of young people on the Main Street benches in Marcellus sometimes brings complaints from residents whose suspicions or fears are aroused by such congregation.

Politics As Usual

In the summer of 1881, Trustee Jasper Hunt died in office, and the Board would first appoint Dr. Franklin H. Bangs to the post. Later, however, Dr. Bangs refused to qualify and the Board would appoint former Trustee Albert Curtis to the post. The Board also became involved in a political brouhaha that spilled over in the next election. It seemed to stem from the decision of the Board to expend some funds for the grading of Factory (now Maple) Street, prompting a lawsuit from a former member of the Village Board. It is also another good example of how politics is really very local. The 1880s were a time of great political involvement throughout the country, especially on the local level and this illustrated how serious people were about politics at the time. An assassin mortally wounded President James Garfield in July of 1881 and his death in September caused many to both mourn his passing as well as promote an even greater interest in political involvement.

The Marcellus Observer
Thursday, September 22, 1881
Local News

Tuesday morning, groups of men could be seen here and there upon our streets all anxiously talking about the death of the president. The post office, Union School building, and many public and private buildings now wear emblems of respect to the nation's dead leader. In fact, a gloom of sadness hangs over each household

5 Jul 1881 - " . . . on motion of Simon Dodd, Mr. F. H. Bangs was nominated for Trustee in place of Jasper Hunt, Deceased. Motion carried."

9 Aug 1881 - " . . . on motion of Simon Dodd, Albert Curtis was appointed Trustee in place of Jasper Hunt, deceased. Franklin Bangs having been duly appointed and refused to qualify. Motion carried. Stocking & Dodd voting aye & Clerk was instructed to notify Mr. Curtis of his appointment."

7 Nov 1881 - " . . . resolved that the Clerk be instructed to notify James Johnston to remove the obstructions consisting of fences, posts, etc. from the highway in front of his premises on Factory street within thirty days from the date of this notice."

New Map of the Village
In January 1882, E. W. Coville did a new survey map of the Village of Marcellus. On the map, which is now displayed in the Village Hall Offices, the following streets are

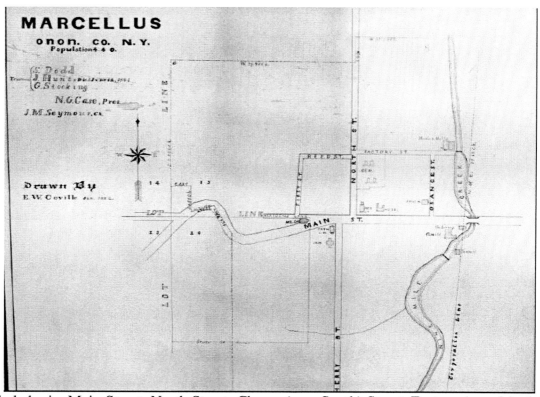

labeled, viz, Main Street, North Street, Cherry (now South) Street, Factory (now Maple) Street, Orange Street, Maidens Lane (now Slocombe Street), First Street and Reed Street. This also appears to be the order in which these streets were settled and occupied by the residents of the Village.

Old vs. New
That same month, a lawsuit was initiated against the Village by Mr. James Johnston, who lived on the northeast corner of Factory (Maple) and North Streets, across from the Village Cemetery. A decision of the Board ordering him to remove some obstructions from in front of his home so that the Village could grade the street on which he lived, prompted the lawsuit, and it also influenced the March elections, causing a rather large turnout of voters. The local editor urged that " . . . the welfare of our Village demands that the most desirable men should be elected in office. Men who have real estate and a desire for the general welfare of our town and will also be active in bringing lawless persons to the bar of justice" (MO 3/9/82). While these were prudent words for the voters

to heed, the election actually pitted the eastern (older) and western (newer) sections of the Village against each another in a battle (somewhat) for control of the Board of Trustees. In the end the old Board prevailed and the issue was resolved, but the election remains an interesting commentary on how seemingly minor quarrels can simmer into political contests.

The Marcellus Observer
Thursday, March 23, 1882
Charter Election

It has been many years since the interest in Charter Election had as firm a hold of the voters as it did this year. General improvement is the order of the day in this Village and as two tickets were in the field, each had their supporters. The old town officers constituted one ticket while the other was made up by numerous persons who were anxious that it should be elected. Both parties had carriages out to bring in the voters and the crowd around the poles resembled town meetings than it did the Village election. The principal cause of the strife seemed to be the manner in which the Board expended the funds last year in grading Factory Street, and thus causing a suit to be started. The people in the eastern part of the Village generally voted for the old board while those in the western part favored the new ticket. The old Board were elected by the following majority.

President N. G. Case, 19 maj.
Trustees, Curtis 10, Dodd 16, Stocking 17
Treasurer White 113
Collector Dady 114
Fire Wardens   Bradley 114, Fulmer 114, Walker 114
Whole number of votes cast was 115

---

3 Jan 1882 - " . . . whereas Mr. N. G. Case, President of the Corporation of the Village of Marcellus, having engaged Messrs. Lansing & Lyman as Counselors & attorneys in the action brought by James Johnston against officers of said corporation. Resolved that the action of Mr. Case in the above matter be and is hereby approved and that Messrs. Lansing & Lyman be the attorneys in the above mentioned action for the above named corporation."

21 Mar 1882 - " . . . at said election 115 votes were cast, ..."

Tax Assessment and Highway Construction

When the Trustees met in May, a tax assessment of $1.44 per $1000 not only helped to pay labor costs for construction as new streets, First and Reed were added to the growing village, but also for land on Factory Street so that it could be widened.

16 May 1882 - " . . . motion of Simon Dodd that the sale of tax for the ensuing year be one dollar & 44/100 on every one thousand dollars assessment."

5 Dec 1882 - " . . . bill of Maurice Dunn, . . . of Michael Curtin, . . . of John Connell, . . . for labor, on motion an order be drawn from highway fund, was carried."

18 Jan 1883 - " . . . that an order be drawn on the Treasurer from the contingent fund for seventy-five dollars for land for a three-rod road on Factory Street, on the south portion of land owned by James Johnson, according to deed given to corporation for the same."

Strange Election

The election of 1883 proved to be an interesting one in Village history. In that year, the President and three Trustees were elected, but "did not qualify", causing the old Board to continue in office. Its interest in sidewalks and roads remained its principal concern, and included the authorization of surveys for Cherry and North Streets in the Village, so as to establish ownership before any highway construction was begun.

20 Mar 1883 - " . . . at said election, 41 votes were cast for President, of which
Isaac N. Sherman   received 38
Dr. H. W. Post   received 2
N. G. Case   received 1
Whole number votes for Trustees was   125
S. N. Mogg   received 38
S. M. Bronson   received 42

John Keefe	received 41	
W. H. Galup	received 1	
Ward Hayden	received 2	
Michael Shehan	received 1	
Whole number for Treasurer was	42	
N. G. Case	received 42	
Whole number for Collector was	42	
Samuel Dada	received 42	
Whole number for Fire Warden was	126	
James Johnson	received 42	
Eli Newton	received 42	
F. H. Bangs	received 42	

3 Apr 1883 - " . . . Board met, on motion of the Clerk that the President & Trustees elected March 20 for the ensuing year, had each an(d) all of them refused and failed to qualify, and the old Board, not having any law or authority on the matter, resolved to procure counsel and instructions before making any judicial move."

7 May 1883 - " . . . that Simon Dodd Jr. be a committee of one to get notices printed to serve on property owners to have their walks repaired."

5 Jun 1883 - " . . . moved and seconded that the survey bill as made by E. W. Coville, Surveyor of North Street and Cherry Street, be placed on record. Carried . . .

Survey of Cherry St, Marcellus, May 17, 1883. Begin fifty links west of the store now occupied by J. F. DeCoudres and formerly occupied by Mires and Daliba in 1856 and set an iron stake at or near the south line of the Seneca Turnpike, ran thence south 34° west to the corporation line running west from Cherry St and set an iron stake in the center of Cherry St, change of needle, 3 1/2°

Survey of North St. Marcellus, May 17, 1883. Begin 50 links west of the northwest corner of the cemetery fence, run then south 15° west to the Seneca Turnpike and set an iron stake in the center of North St. at or near the north side of the Seneca Turnpike, thence north 15 minutes east to the corporation line running west from North St. and set an iron stake in center of the street, change of needle, 3 1/2°"E. W. Coville, Surveyor

Irish Immigrant Labor

With the surveys complete, Irish immigrants, whose labor was cheap but vital, did much of the construction work on these streets. Of those, whose highway labor bills were paid in July of 1883, every one was an immigrant from Ireland except John Gallup and Thomas Hackford who had come from England. Although most lived outside the corporation limits, and worked at other jobs, the Village provided extra work that would not only supplement a meager income but also support their families.

3 Jul 1883 - " . . . bills were considered and audited from Highway fund:
15.00	Anthony Flaherty	fifteen	dollars
14.00	Bernard Powell	fourteen	"
29.00	Michael Curtin	twenty nine	"
4.50	Patrick Joyce	four	dollars 50/100
3.75	Maurice Dunn	three	dollars 75/100
21.75	Thomas Hackford	twenty one	dollars 75/100
5.00	John Gallup	five	"
7.50	John Butler	seven	dollars 50/100
16.25	Karon McManus	sixteen	dollars 25/100

The foregoing bills were acted upon and ordered that they be paid from Highway fund."

Concerns Mount in 1883

As the Village of Marcellus grew and expanded in the 1880s, so too did its problems and concerns. Many residents became more concerned about health issues, such as an outbreak of cholera. It prompted widespread publication of ways for individuals to eliminate conditions that caused this disease and parallels efforts made by public health agencies today that alert people of preventive measures for 21st century epidemics.

The Marcellus Observer
Thursday, August 16, 1883
The Cholera

That the cholera may reach this country is a probability; that it may become a scourge is possible; that its terrors depend on bad sanitary conditions is certain. If you do not wish to have the cholera, live and eat like men; cleanse your house; remove and keep away garbage and pestilent odors; purify drains and privies and sewer pipes. Aid in enforcing wise health regulations throughout the town. A body kept from the weakening effect of vicious indulgences, intoxication, drugs, night carousing, grass or green food; and a mind kept hopeful and at peace and reasonably occupied are the best safeguards against epidemics. Cities are by no means the only unsanitary breeding places of pestilence. Villages have their nests; their undrained bogs; their damp cellars, in which water stands half the year; and villages have their holes where human beings are reduced by debauch, to become fit food for cholera, or any other plague. Let Marcellus clean up, not a superficial scour, a sort of holiday sweep up and polish, but a thoro' cleansing of the inside of the platter. One of the most disgraceful evidences of shiftlessness and utter disregard of law and order, to say nothing of decency, is the shameful condition of the street east of the Gallup block. Barrels, which were placed to receive the ashes and other refuse matter thrown out by the tenants of the building, were allowed to become full and run over, and some three or four weeks since were upset into the street by some unknown person, and there they have been allowed to stay until now, and none can say how much longer they will be countenanced. If the owner of the block has not sufficient regard for a neat and tidy appearance of his buildings and surroundings to remove the rubbish from the street, he should be compelled by the board of trustees to do so. Such a foul mess in the street is not only a potent agent in the breeding of pestilences, such as cholera, etc., but it is liable to and has already frightened several horses, nearly causing three or four runaways. It is a burning shame that our village officers allow such things to obstruct the street week after week. If they refuse or neglect to attend to such matters, the health officers should see to it, as such filth is sure to breed contagious diseases. We have a Board of Health; that board has rules - are they enforced? If the cholera comes, it will come soon. Let us be ready. Breathe pure air; eat right food; sleep regularly and behave yourself generally and there will be no danger. There is nothing more conducive to the evil dreaded however, than a state of alarm. Nurses in hospitals rarely catch contagious diseases, because familiarity with them removes anxiety. Being wisely prepared not to die, but to live, you can sit down or go about your work and have no fear.

Another service that citizens felt the Board should consider was that of fire protection and a petition to that effect was presented to the Trustees in mid July. Towards the end of the year a man who would serve many years in Village government would be appointed to fill a trustee vacancy. Sidney Slocombe's tenure in public service began in 1883 and when it ended a number of years later, a grateful Village would dedicate one of its streets in memory of his devoted public service.

17 July 1883 - "petition of citizens to Board asking that a public meeting be called in consideration the advisability of purchasing fire apparatus. Petition considered and the following resolution adopted: Resolved that a meeting in accordance with above petition be called at Hall Jul 27th... at 7 1/2 P.M. providing Mr. Hoae can be present."

11 Dec 1883 - " . . . petition of Albert Curtis offering his resignation, on motion of Simon Dodd, . . . the resignation be accepted, . . . moved by George Stocking that Sidney Slocombe be appointed to fill the vacancy . . . for balance of year."

Factory Street Becomes Maple Street

One of the last acts of the old Board was the changing of a familiar street. What had once been Factory Street, the home of the mills was now changed to the more placid Maple Street, a name that was appropriate for a growing residential area in the Village.

An article in *The Marcellus Observer* in February of 1884 gave testament to this image of an expanding Village, whose life force then and now is the creek that flows through.

The Marcellus Observer
Thursday, February 28, 1884
Marcellus Village Directory

The Village of Marcellus is healthfully and pleasantly located on Nine Mile Creek, the outlet of Otisco Lake. This creek furnishes a never-failing water power to the numerous factories that line its banks. These factories consist of two large woolen mills, three straw paper mills, a pearl barley mill, three flouring mills, and powder works, furniture factory and other manufacturing industries, which give employment to several hundred of the inhabitants. Ample shipping facilities are afforded by the Auburn branch of the New York Central railroad. A good macadamized road leads from the village to the depot. There are a number of excellent water privileges still unoccupied, which will be sold at reasonable prices, thus offering great inducements to capitalists to locate here. The Town of Marcellus has a population nearly 3,000, about 800 of whom live in the Village. There are four churches, a good Union School, commodious hotel and enterprising shopkeepers. Surrounding that village is a rich farming country. which makes Marcellus a market and trading town. Building and improvement are constantly going on.

---

4 Mar 1884 - " . . . petition from residents of Factory Street, . . . moved by Slocum that the petition changing the name of Factory Street to Maple Street. Motion Carried. Stocking, No, Slocum & Chairness, Aye."

1884 - New By-laws

Since its incorporation, the Village held election of officers every year. Beginning, however, in 1884, with a new set of by-laws approved by the voters, trustees were elected for two-year terms, although in some cases an individual might be elected for a single year in order to complete the term of vacated position. The President of the Village Board of Trustees, until 1927, continued to be elected every year and in 1884, the newly elected President was William H. Gallup. A local lawyer and a man of many interests, Gallup built a large residence on North Street for his wife and young family that is today the Norris Funeral Home and " . . . in partnership with Samuel Hooper, . . . built a furniture factory on the site of the present cement block building, just west of the creek on East Main Street" (Heffernan 58). He was also responsible for the construction of a new block of buildings at the corner of North and Main Streets, " . . . on the site vacated by the disastrous fire of 1879" (Heffernan 224). With Gallup's election, the Board made appointments and approved hitching posts, wells and ramps on Main Street, some of which are pictured below.

18 Mar 1884 - " . . . Polls of said election was opened at 2-30 P.M. and closed at six P.M., that at said election votes, . . ." a total of 97 votes were cast. " . . . votes for trustees for two years, . . . J. B. Van Vranken received 74, Edmund Reed received 79, . . . whole number of votes for trustees for one year, . . . Eli Newton received 97."

25 Mar 1884 - " . . . moved and seconded that Wm Hickman be appointed Police Constable for ensuing year."

6 May 1884 - " . . . resolved that the residents of the Village of Marcellus be allowed and are herby allowed to set hitching posts on the line of curb stones and that the wells & ramps on Main Street are with and by the consent of the Board of Trustees."

The Marcellus Observer
Thursday, July 1, 1884
FIRE
A Close Call For the Principle Part of the Village

Last Thursday at about 12:30 o'clock, some man, who was in James Saar's store, lighted his pipe and threw the burning match on the floor. Some new brooms were set on fire, and before it was discovered, a blaze several feet high went tearing through the rack which held the brooms. Robert Saar dashed what little water he had in the store on the fire, but it was not enough. He ran to the pump and brought enough water to quench the flames, but if the pump had been out of water, short of water, or farther away, the Gallup Block, James Hooper's buildings, M. Shehan's store and much other property could not have been saved. We cannot manage a fire in Marcellus too large for a pail or two of water. Will we ever have protection?

Fire Protection

The major concern, however, was about fire safety and this was again reinforced that summer when fire broke out in James Saar's store on Main Street and nearly caused another disaster in the Village. Along with the local paper calling for more protection, the fire that summer caused residents to approve three spending resolutions in a special election that August.

10 Jul 1884 - " . . . petition of taxable electors of Village of Marcellus requesting Board to call Special Election for the purpose of voting upon the question of raising money for the purchase of suitable apparatus for fire protection was presented to Board."

22 Jul 1884 - " . . . a Special Election of the Corporation of the Village of Marcellus be ordered to be held August 5th, 1884 for the purpose of submitting the foregoing resolutions to the electors of said Village to vote upon. . . . "

5 August 1884 - " . . . three separate resolutions were submitted to be voted upon, . . . the whole number of votes cast for Resolution No. One was fifty nine, of which forty three had the word Yes & sixteen had the word No. The whole number of votes cast for Resolution No. Two was fifty eight of which forty four had on the word Yes and fourteen had on the word No. The whole number of votes cast for Resolution Number Three was fifty nine of which forty five had on the word Yes, and fourteen had on the word No."

Three resolutions were submitted to the voters. The first dealt with the purchasing of a fire engine, the second the purchasing of a hose cart, and the third with the construction

Special Village Election.

Notice is hereby given that a Special Village Election will be held, in the village of Marcellus, N. Y., at the Alvord House, August, 5, 1884, for the purpose of voting upon the three following Resolutions. The polls of said election will be opened at 1 o'clock P. M. and close at sunset. All electors liable to be assessed for support of village in their own right or in name of their wife are entitled by law to vote at said election. By Order of Trustees,
J. M. SEYMOUR, CLERK.

RESOLUTION I.

Resolved, That the Trustees of the village of Marcellus cause to be raised by a general tax upon the taxable property in said village, liable to be assessed for taxes, the sum of twelve hundred dollars ($1,200) for the purpose of purchasing a Remington Horse Power Fire Engine and the necessary tools and implements for the same, and that the said amount be raised in four equal annual installments, with interest.

RESOLUTION II.

Resolved, That the Trustees of the village of Marcellus cause to be raised by a general tax upon the taxable property in said village, liable to be assessed for taxes, the sum of seven hundred and seventy-five dollars ($775) for the purpose of purchasing a hose cart and hose and necessary tools and implements for same, and that the said amount be raised in four equal annual installments, with interest.

RESOLUTION III.

Resolved, That the Trustees of the village of Marcellus cause to be raised by a general tax upon the taxable property in said village, liable to be assessed for taxes, the sum of two hundred and fifty dollars ($250) for the purpose of constructing and maintaining suitable reservoirs and cisterns and supplying them with water to be used at fires, and that the said amount be raised in four equal annual installments, with interest.

and maintenance of reservoirs and cisterns. All of them were approved, overwhelmingly.

Organization of the Fire Department

With the overwhelming approval of village residents, the Board of Trustees began to organize a Village Fire Department, authorize the purchase of fire equipment and build reservoirs. The Board of Trustees appointed a Fire Chief, Dr. Henry W. Post, as well as an Assistant Chief, Myron Whiting and approved a list of members of the Fire Company. Today, the number of assistant chiefs has expanded to three and the Chief continues to submit a list of members of the Department to the Village Board for approval each year.

28 Aug 1884 - " . . . we proceed in accordance with Statues made and provided to organize a fire company for the Village of Marcellus, . . . that Dr. Henry W. Post be appointed Chief of the Fire Department, . . . that Myron Whiting be appointed Assistant Chief of the Fire Department."

2 Sep 1884 - " . . . that the list of names submitted for members of Fire Engine Company and Hose Company be adopted & and the members be outfitted to notified to meet at Alvord House Sep 3d at 7 1/2 P.M. for the purpose of organizing. . . . that the first Person reaching Engine with team of Horses and Hitching on the alarm of fire receive five dollars & the second team three dollars & one dollar per hour for the second & each hour thereafter."

The Village Board also awarded the contract for building of fire reservoirs in the Village to Mark Dorchester. These underground reservoirs, or cisterns, were built in Village locations thought to be appropriate -- primarily near the Churches in the Village Center and as recently as 1997, several have been uncovered during reconstruction work on Main Street. The Village Board, similar to today, having received recommendations from the Fire Department for engine and equipment purchasers such as the request at left, authorized the appropriations. A license fee on every billiard and pool table kept and owned for public use in the Village would not only help to pay for these new appropriations but allow the Board to exercise some control over pool halls, a source of great concern for many parents and residents at the time.

5 Sep 1884 - " . . . this board accept the bid of Mark A. Dorchester for the building of reservoirs according to specifications, providing he will enter into contract satisfactory with this board and give bonds for the full and satisfactory completion, . . . "

17 Nov 1884 - " . . . bill of John Spaulding and Charles Raymond for cleaning Engine and Hose, amount of $8.75 & assigned to M. Shehan. . . . Bill of J. F. DeCoudres for Hose Jackets, amount of three dollars, . . . "

8 Jan 1885 - " . . . a license fee of ten dollars . . . be assessed upon each and every billiard and Pool table kept and owned for public use in Village of Marcellus in compliance with section fourteen of the ordinances . . . "

1885 – The Village Jail and Streets

The election of 1885, in which the Assistant Fire Chief, Myron Whiting, was elected President of the Village, seemed to exhibit the political power of the newly organized

Fire Department. Whiting was a man in his mid fifties at the time, a farmer with a wife and one child. His victory over Isaac Share was a close one, as were the votes for Trustee, won by R. Almon Julia. Those for Tax Collector, Treasurer, and Fire Wardens were equally close races. During Whiting's administration, the Village Board authorized the construction of a Village Jail, " . . . a small stone, ten-by-twelve-foot, lock-up, with an iron barred door, located in a space behind the present hardware store on North Street. Its most frequent inmates were the Saturday night over-indulgers who were arrested by the local constables, not for DWI, but for disturbing the peace. At a later date, two steel barred cells, each containing a cot, were installed in the fire house" (Heffernan 68). Today, the Marcellus Police Department maintains a small holding center in the former Engine House but it is used only for temporary detention before transportation to the Justice Center in nearby Syracuse. The Board appointed George Gilson as Village Policeman, a title that provided more authority and control than that of Constable and it also appointed special police and constables at times, such as celebrations, when more security was required.

The Board's interest in highway construction continued with the addition of First and Reed Streets to the expanding Village. Originally part of the Reed Farm, some of the land for these streets was in the Village and some in the Town of Marcellus. Although the streets appear to have been laid out and settled by residents in the 1870s and early 1880s, it was not until 1885 that a survey was completed and they would be deeded to the Village of Marcellus to be used as public highways.

17 Mar 1885 - " . . . at said election there were cast 102 votes for President of which

Isaac A. Share	received	45	
Myron M. Whiting	received	57	
(Total)		102	
The whole number cast for Trustee for two years was			102
Eli Newton	received	49	
R. Almon Julia	received	53	
(Total)		102	
The whole number cast for Collector was			101
Samuel Dady	received	47	
James Johnson	received	54	
(Total)		101	
The whole number cast for Treasurer was			102
W. T. Case	received	57	
N. G. Case	received	45	
(Total)		102	
The whole number cast for Fire Wardens			
I. Parsons	received	46	
F. H. Bangs	received	45	
W. L. Northway	received	46	
Selah Bronson	received	56	
Warren Alvord	received	57	
Michael Shehan	received	56	

14 Apr 1885 - " . . . that George Gilson be appointed Police Constable, . . . "

29 Jun 1885 - " . . . that George Gilson be appointed Village Policemen, . . . that Michael Kennedy be appointed special policeman, . . . that Chair appoint a committee to look for sights (sites) for lockup and expense of building the same, . . . that the board sanction the action of the Chief of Fire Department in hanging fire bell rope in church and the notice of 10.00 fine for ringing same except in case of fire."

1 Jul 1885 - " . . . George Hickman was appointed Police Constable for the Village and John Spaulding and George White special Police for July 4th."

4 Aug 1885 - " . . . that such measures be taken at once as shall change the boundary of North Street in said village so that the records of said road shall conform to the boundary as it is now used as a highway."

5 Dec 1885 - " . . . the clerk be instructed to provide a frame and glass for Village Map at an expense not to exceed two dollars . . . that a certain strip of land described in a certain deed a copy of same being added and on file in there records, dedicated to the Village of Marcellus, Onondaga County, NY by Martha J. Reed, Elpha C. Reed and Edmund Reed . . . for a public street be and is hereby accepted, . . . making the described strip of land a public street in said Village, subject in every way to the control of Village Trustees, . .

Copy of deed and description and Survey of the tract of land mentioned in the foregoing. This indenture made this 30th day of November, A. D. 1885 between Martha J. Reed, Elpha C. Reed and Edmund Reed unmarried of the Village of Marcellus, Onondaga County and State of New York of the first part, and the Village of Marcellus in the Town of Marcellus, County and State aforesaid of the second part, witnesseth, that the said parties of the first part convey and dedicate unto the said Village of of Marcellus all that tract or parcel of land situate and being part of Lot No. Fifteen in said Town of Marcellus and more particularly bounded and described as follows: beginning at the center of an Elm tree at the north east corner of a lot owned by John Keefe and on the west line of North Street in said Village of Marcellus running thence north 4 3⁄4° East 37 1⁄2 links to the center of the street herein described, thence North 86 3⁄4° west seven chains and sixty-one links, thence south 7 1⁄2° west ten chains 94 1⁄2 links to the north line of Maiden Lane Street. The same being a strip of land 49 1⁄2 feet wide, to be held and used by said Village of Marcellus as a public street and if not so used the same to revert to the said parties of the first part, their heirs or assigns. This conveyance is made by said first parties and accepted by said second party with the express understanding that nothing herein contained shall give any right or empower said Village of Marcellus or any of its officers or agents to, in any way or manner, molest, injure, destroy or remove the aforesaid mentioned Elm tree . . .

1886 - Committees

In 1886, William H. Gallup would be returned to the Presidency of the Village and when Trustee R. Almon Julia, who had been elected to a two-year term in 1885, resigned, Myron M. Whiting would be elected for a one-year term in order to fill that vacancy. James M. Dunlap and Charles Case were elected to two-year terms as Trustees, and the number of elected Fire Wardens would be reduced from three to two. After 1887, with the creation of the Marcellus Fire Department, and the appointment of a Fire Chief and Assistant Chief, the need for the position of Fire Wardens was eliminated.

2 Mar 1886 - " . . . resignation presented by R. A. Julia, Trustee, to the Board this day

10 Mar 1886 - " . . . Election of Officers for the Village of Marcellus, NY will be held at the Alvord House on March 16th, 1886. The Officers to be elected are a President, two Trustees for two years, one Trustee to fill vacancy, Treasurer, Collector and Two Fire

WILLIAM H. GALLUP
Hon. William H. Gallup, Syracuse, was born in Marcellus, May 27, 1858. His father, George Gallup, came from England to America in 1850, at the age of seventeen, and settled in Marcellus, where he was long a teasel merchant. He died February 1, 1882, and his wife s death occurred January 20, 1884. George Gallup was a citizen highly respected, influential and esteemed, and possessed sterling principles of head and heart, which his children inherited. William H. was educated in the schools of his native town, read law with Judge Vann in Syracuse, and was graduated and admitted from the Albany Law School in June, 1879. After practicing his profession three years in Marcellus, he succeeded to his father s business, which he still carries on. He was elected member of assembly in 1888 and 1889, his plurality in 89 being 2,015, the largest ever given to any candidate in that district. In 1892 he came to Syracuse and organized the Syracuse Improvement Co., with a capital of $120,000 and has since been its secretary, treasurer and general manager, making it emphatically successful. September 2, 1880, he married Emma Sweet of Marcellus and has two children, Mary and Bessie.

from Onondaga s Centennial, Gleanings of a Century, edited by Dwight H. Bruce, Volume II. The Boston History Company, Publishers, 1896, p. 66.

Wardens. The Polls of said Election will be opened at One O'Clock P.M. and close at Sun Set."

16 Mar 1886 - " . . . at said election there was cast 71 votes . . . "

Gallup, in his second term as President oversaw the addition of Reed Street to the Village highways as well as the construction of more sidewalks, some of it by laborers who earned $1.50 per day. Both highways and sidewalks had to meet Village specifications and occasionally there were complaints, like those from First Street residents who argued for sidewalks on their street.

President Gallup would also initiate the appointment of standing committees to oversee the various departments within Village government, a process that is still in use today. Generally, each of the Village Trustees was in charge of a Standing Committee, of which there were three in 1886. A year later, in 1887, another committee would be created for the Fire Department and in the early part of the 20th century, another would be added for water. Today, either the Mayor or one of the Trustees oversees the three major departments of Village government, Highways and Sewers, Police, and Fire.

27 Mar 1886 - " . . . President Gallup announced the following as the standing Committees for year 1886:
> Highways - Trustees Whiting and Case
> Sidewalks - Trustees Case and Dunlap
> Street Lights - Trustees Dunlap and Whiting

27 Mar 1886 - " . . . that day laborers be paid at the rate of one dollar and one half per day, . . . that the rate of tax for the ensuing year be three and 1/2, . . . that the sum of two hundred and fifty dollars together with Poll tax be for highway purposes, . . . "

13 Apr 1886 - " . . . resolved that the road bed and side walks on Reed Street & First Street be the same as on Orange and Factory Streets, viz, 24 foot Road Bed and 4 foot side walks."

2 Aug 1886 - " . . . the bill presented be allowed at its footing less the amount received from the Insurance money by said fire company."

7 Sep 1886 - " . . . complaint by James Woodbridge against Isaac Bradley & Almon Julia for defective walks on Cherry Street. Referred to Committee on side walks. . . . Petition of property-holders on First Street for side walk in front of premises occupied by John North."

The Village Board that year also authorized the Marcellus Fire Department to go to the assistance of those who needed help in the hamlet of Marcellus Falls -- the first expansion of Fire Department responsibilities beyond the Village limits.

11 Jan 1887 - " . . . resolution was offered and unanimously adopted. Resolved that in case of fire in any manufacturing establishment between Marcellus & Marcellus Falls or at Marcellus Falls, the Chief of Fire Department is hereby authorized to order out the First Department of Marcellus & go & assist at any such fire."

1887 – Sidewalks and Liability

Myron Whiting was returned to the office of President of the Village in 1887 and re-elected again in 1888. Trustee Charles Case, elected in 1886, resigned from his two-year term, and at the next general election (on March 15, 1887), Harvey Wells was elected to fill the vacancy. William H. Gallup, who had been President, was now elected to a two-year term as Trustee. Many of the same individuals who participated in Village government during the 1880s would rotate offices at election time, the position of President filled by an person who had previously been a Trustee, and vice versa. Being elected to local office at that time was viewed as a matter of civic pride rather than a stepping-stone to power and a non-paid elected position in local government was not very attractive to many, often resulting in a number of resignations.

8 Mar 1887 - " . . . the resignation of Charles Case as Trustee was duly presented and it was moved and seconded that the same be accepted."

15 Mar 1887 - " . . . the whole number of votes cast for trustee to fill vacancy was 65, of which Harvey Wells received 63 . . . Fire Wardens, James Woodbridge, 66 and Joseph Matteson, 66."

In order to modernize and renovate the Village, as well as prolong the lifespan of its sidewalks and prevent pedestrian accidents, a decision that walks would now be constructed using stone flagging or Portland cement or tar rather than wood was passed by the Trustees that spring. Today, Village sidewalks are constructed using only concrete materials and recent A.D.A. (Americans with Disabilities Act) regulations call for standard widths of five feet for all public walks of new, not repaired, construction.

23 Mar 1887 - " . . . moved by Gallup & seconded by Wells that John Dunlap be appointed Police Constable for the ensuing year."

11 May 1887 - " . . . Petition of Residents of First Street was called up from table. The following resolution was offered by Gallup: Resolved that in accordance with the papers contained in petition of residents of First Street, Marcellus, that all sidewalks to be built hereafter on said street, shall be composed of stone flagging, or Portland cement, or tar. Resolution was unanimously adopted."

The Village Board approved Fire Department appointments as well as that of John Dunlap as Police Constable in 1887. His employment included a new patrol -- preventing people from coasting or sledding down west hill (West Main Street today), the concern about liability applied not only to sidewalks but to public highways as well

23 Sep 1887 - " . . . that M. B. VanVranken be appointed Chief of Marcellus Fire Department, . . . that Joseph Matteson be appointed Asst. Chief of the Fire Department for the ensuing year."

11 Jan 1888 - " . . . resolution was offered by Mr. Wells & seconded by Dunlap. That the Clerk be directed to post three notices and published in the Observer, prohibiting coasting on highway on west hill in the corporation. Any person violating this resolution will be liable to a fine of five dollars."

The Marcellus Observer
Thursday, June 14, 1888
Local Items
-The new crossing at the junction of North and Reed Streets is a great improvement. Now for raising the grade of the adjoining side walks to a corresponding level.
-We are pleased to learn that Mr. J. M. Seymour, clerk of our village board, will go during this month to Trumansburg, to make arrangements direct with the quarry men at that place, for the furnishing of flagging for sidewalks in this village. From correspondence already had, it appears that this kind of sidewalk can be secured at so reasonable a price that it will be an inducement for all to use it. He will also endeavor to arrange for them to send persons to lay and complete the same.

1888 – Telegraph and Telephone

Whiting's return to the Presidency of the Village was accompanied by the election of J. B. VanVranken as Trustee, a position that he held for a number of terms in the past. The Board agreed to a rewriting of the Village Ordinances during this administration, and again insisted that sidewalks hereafter constructed on village streets to be built of flagstone, although it appears that some were still allowed to use planks for replacement walks. It also granted permission for the construction of telegraph and telephone lines along streets in the Village but the actual delivery of this service would be delayed for a number of years.

14 Mar 1888 - " . . . annual election of officers of the Village of Marcellus will be held at the Alvord House, March 20th, 1888. The Officers to be elected are a President, two Trustees for two years, a Collector & Treasurer."

7 Apr 1888 - " . . . moved and seconded that men working in Highway the ensuring year be paid twelve & 1/2 cents per hour."

11 Jun 1888 - " . . . moved by VanVranken and seconded by Gallup that the Chairman appoint a Committee of two to rewrite the Village ordinances, and that the Chairman of Board be the Chairman of the Committee."

11 Jul 1888 - " . . . in accordance with the petition signed by a majority of the residents and land owners of Orange Street in Village of Marcellus, it is hereby ordered that all side walks hereafter constructed on said street be built of flag stone."

1 Aug 1888 - " . . . that the American Telephone and Telegraph Company of New York be permitted to erect their lines and poles through Main Street and Maiden Lane of Marcellus Village, subject to the direction and satisfaction of the Board of Trustees."

Engine House

Fire was an ever-present danger in this Village, whose structures were made mostly of wood. Despite the fact that it was built of stone, and in spite of the new fire fighting equipment, the old grist mill erected about 1827 by Edward Talbot and Joseph Taylor on East Main Street was destroyed by fire in 1888. The Village Board and residents then decided to raise taxes, buy some property on Main Street and construct an Engine House for the fire equipment. A special vote in the fall of that year endorsed the resolutions for this new building that would not only serve the Fire Department, but also house the Village Offices, whose new official seal was approved by Village Trustees that year as well.

25 Sep 1888 - " . . . that the Trustees of the Village of Marcellus, . . . cause to be raised by a tax, . . . the sum of Five Hundred Dollars ($500), for the purpose of purchasing a lot of Mrs. Maggie A. Smith, on the north side of Main Street in said village, upon which to build an Engine House, . . . that the Trustees, . . . caused to be raised by general tax, . . .

the sum of One Thousand Dollars ($1000), for the purpose of building an Engine house, . . . a special election be held Oct 9th, 1888. Polls open at one o'clock P.M., close, sunset."

9 Oct 1888 - " . . . the whole number of votes cast for Resolution No. One was fifty nine of which thirty nine had on the word, yes, twenty had on the word, no. The whole number of votes cast for Resolution No. Two was fifty nine, of which thirty nine had on the word, yes, and twenty had on the word, no."

The vote to bond and build a fire engine house was as follows:

Resolution # 1	Resolution # 2
Yes - 39	Yes - 39
No - 20	No - 20
Total - 59	Total - 59

15 Oct 1888 - " . . . moved by Gallup that the seal hereby attached be the corporate seal of the Village of Marcellus."

Presidential Election Year

This was a national election year and the candidates included Grover Cleveland, the incumbent President, and the Republican challenger, Benjamin Harrison, grandson of the former President, William Henry Harrison. An interesting story in *The Syracuse Journal* that fall provides a glimpse into the politics of Marcellus at the time as well as forty years earlier, when the Republican Club was founded in the Town.

THEY VOTED FOR TIPPECANOE
And Will Vote for General Benjamin Harrison

Marcellus, N.Y., Oct 12 - Mr. Alfred Rockwell has collected the names of those who voted for General Harrison in 1840, and who will now vote for Benjamin Harrison in 1888, viz. -

J. C. Platt	Thomas Rhoades
A. L. Rockwell	J. H. Holcomb
C. P. Cornish	Orlando Beach
D. L. Beach	Dr. Davis
Chester Hilyer	Samuel Dady
T. P. Phillips	W. S. Walker
Isaac Bradley	Timothy Mills
Wm. J. Machin	D. S. Holcomb
Wm. Briggs	W. H. Holmes
J. G. Northrop	Wm. Barnett
Murray Day	

The ages of the above vary from 71 to 94 years of age. Mr. Rockwell cast his first vote in New York State in 1840, having emigrated from Connecticut in 1839. He with five others formed the first Republican club in Marcellus. It was done in the house now owned by H. Wells. The others were Col. Ira Bishop, J. G. B. White, Joseph Taylor, Myron L. Mills, Elijah Rowley. Messers. Mills and White had been Democrats and the balance, Whigs. All are now dead except Mr. Rockwell. The Whig majority in the town had varied from 30 to 40, but Gen. Fremont had a majority of 156. Mr. Rockwell has as keen an interest in politics as when in his youthful days and confidently expects the election of Harrison. - Syracuse Journal.

As the Trustees pushed ahead with the construction of the Engine House, the Firemen made plans to hold a special Fair that winter, the size of which required the appointment of special police for the week it was held.

The Marcellus Observer
Thursday, November 1, 1888
Local Items

-The trustees of the village are pushing forward the new engine house. It will be 26 by 36 feet with a ten feet square tower in one corner, and 55 feet high. Opposite the tower below, will be the trustees' room and the firemen's room on the second floor. Whitmore and Brill furnish the material, and lay the foundation. The rest of the work will be done by the day.

---

1 Feb 1889 - " . . . on request of the Chief of Fire Department that the following named members of Fire Co. be appointed Special Police to act as such during the week of the Firemen's Fair to be held from Feb 5th to Feb 9th, 1889: M. B. Van Vranken, Charles Case, Wm. Crysler, Sidney Slocum & E. H. Spinks. Moved by Van Vranken

& seconded by Wells that the above named gentlemen be appointed special police for the time mentioned & . . . take the oath of office."

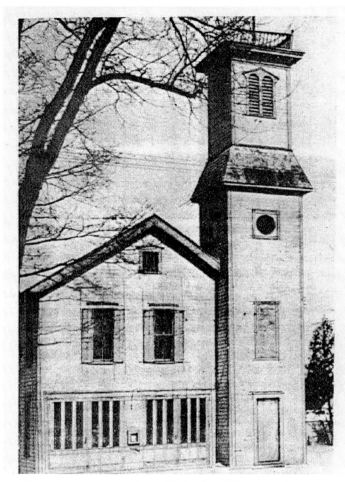

1889

In the election of 1889, a new President took over from Myron Whiting. His name was Simon Dodd, and his election was somewhat historic. This marked the first time that an Irish Catholic was elected President of the Marcellus Village government and it indicates, also, that the new immigrants were becoming more accepted in society.

Dodd's administration continued to insist on sidewalk construction and re-construction and it was also during his term that the Engine House would be completed. After the Fire Engine House was finished in the Spring of 1889, the Board of Trustees began to meet there, rather than in individual homes or businesses, and the Board continues to meet in the old Engine House today.

19 Mar 1889 - " . . . at said election there was cast 121 votes for President of which Simon Dodd received 101, James M. Dunlap received 19, and George Tibbits received 1."

23 Mar 1889 - " . . . that the Trustees room be located in the north east corner of the Engine House."

6 Apr 1889 - " . . . that James Axten by appointed Street Commissioner & his pay to be $1.75 per day for actual labor."

3 Jul 1889 - " . . . that an order be served on Dr. I. Parsons to build a new flag side walk from Main Street to the length of his premises on Orange Street, . . . that an order be served on Martin Dolan to build a five foot stone flag walk in front of his premises on Main Street, . . . that an order be served on Lydia W. Sayre to build a flag walk on part of the building occupied by (the) bakery, . . . that an order be served on the St. Francis Church to build a flag walk in part of this property on Main Street, the parsonage, . . . that an order be served on the Ellen Doyle Estate to build a five foot plank walk in front of said property on Main Street, . . . that an order be served on Mr. Hiram Coville and Edmund Reed that each build a five foot cement or flag walk in part of their . . . places on First Street. All of said walks to be built under the directions of (the) Board of Trustees."

22 Oct 1889 - " . . . that; M. B. VanVranken be appointed Chief of Marcellus Fire Department, for ensuing year and Joseph Matteson, Asst. Chief."

End of the 1880s

With the end of the decade of the 1880s, the Village of Marcellus could look back on another period of steady growth and this growth was particularly evident in Village government. Just as today's Village Clerk-Treasurer presents an annual statement at the end of the year, so too the Report of the Treasurer was significant 100 years ago as the decade of the 1880s drew to a close. It shows not only the receipts and expenditures, but also what the funds that had been set up for the fiscal year ending March 18, 1890. Today, the fiscal year for Marcellus Village extends from April 1st to March 31st, and there has been a great increase in government expenditure, but there has been little change to the classification of the funds themselves.

18 Mar 1890 - "Report of the Treasurer, showing balance on hand and receipts and expenditures for year ending March 18, 1890.

Highway Fund
Balance on Hand, March 19, 1889	$196.81
Received from Collector	$250.00
Received from Poll Tax	$98.00
(Total)	$544.81
Paid Out on Trustees' Orders	$401.63
Balance on Hand	$143.18

Contingent Fund
Balance on Hand, March 19, 1889	$148.54
Received from Collector	$259.20
(Total)	$407.74
Paid out on Trustees' Orders	$253.73
Balance on Hand	$154.01

Fire Department Fund
On Hand, March 19, 1889	$854.87
Received from Collector for bond	$556.25
Received from Collector	$350.00
Received from John Grimes for Plank	.94
(Total)	$1762.06
Paid out on Trustees' Orders	$1758.95
Balance on Hand	$3.31

J. M. Seymour, Clerk

Conclusion

Simon Dodd's election as President of the Village in 1889 was both a beginning and an end. It was the end of a decade, but also an end to some of the suspicions and fears that inhabitants harbored about these new Irish immigrants to the valley. It also coincided with an end to the total domination of the local market by agrarian interests and the emergence of the woolen industry as the prevailing element in the regional economy. So too, the size and responsibilities of Village government had changed, becoming more businesslike, and headquartered in its own office building rather than the cracker barrel atmosphere of a store or public house.

When Simon Dodd, Jr. left office in 1890, he moved to Rochester with his family where he started work in another woolen mill. He lived out his life in that city and died in 1915. His youngest daughter, Mary, who had been born in Marcellus just before her father's election as Village President, married a Rochester man by the name of Eisenberg and one of their three children was a son named William. In an ironic twist of fate, but also of some historic interest, William would have a son named Frederic who, over a century after Simon Dodd left office, was elected Mayor of the Village of Marcellus in 1992, reelected to his third term in 2002.

Chapter 6 - The 1890s

This decade witnessed the consolidation of the woolen mills in Marcellus and increased employment for

Workers – Upper Crown Mill – 1890s

both Village and Town of Marcellus residents. The Onondaga Woolen Mill started by James Sayre at the lower mill site was sold and reorganized, in 1882, as the Crown Mills Company. "In 1886, the Moses mill at the end of Maple Street, . . . was taken over by a stock company under the name of Marcellus Woolen Mills. Lucius Moses, son of the original owner, became president. Three years later the company consolidated with the Crown Mills Company" (Heffernan 45) and Edward Moir, later a figure in Village government, became the Superintendent of both mills. "Control of the Crown Mills Company eventually passed into the hands of Mr. Moir, and remained in the Moir family until the mills were closed" (Heffernan 45) in the 1960s. As the mills were enlarged, more labor was needed and a ready supply of immigrants, many of them from Moir's native Scotland was recruited, along with the children of earlier Irish immigrants. By the middle of the decade, " . . . these two mills constitute the principal life of the village" (Bruce 643).

Increased Government

As this industry and others in the area began to increase production and

> **The Marcellus Observer**
> **Thursday, March 13, 1890**
> **Crown Mills**
> **Absorb the Marcellus Woolen Company**
>
> The Marcellus Woolen Company has been absorbed by the Crown Mills and will be operated by that company under the superintendence of Mr. Moir.
>
> Mr. Moses becomes one of the Crown Mills stockholders so that his interest in Marcellus does not wholly cease. We understand the capital of the company will be increased to $150,000.
>
> The Marcellus Woolen Mill will have some repairs made in the shape of additions to the machinery and preparations for selling goods for the spring tradewhich opens in July. If anything opens up in the meantime to get work for the mill it will be taken advantage of, but it being a very dull season generally, the prospects for starting the mill before July are not good. Ultimately it is expected they will be run as constantly as the Crown mills and changes made as emergencies may require to meet the markets and demands of the times.

expand, so too did local government. In the 1890s, the Board of Trustees began to meet more often. Twice a month was not uncommon and the reason for this seems to coincide with an increased need for governmental services. Specifically, the decade witnessed the advent of more services such as electricity, water as well as railroad and other forms of transportation and this often required municipal regulation or approval by local government.

Election of 1890

The Board of Trustees elected in March of 1890 included Selah Bronson as President and his administration became absorbed, like previous ones, with the sidewalk issue. Throughout the latter part of the 19th century, and particularly in the late 1880s and 1890s, there were many orders issued by the Marcellus Board of Trustees to have village residents build sidewalks. There was an incentive to do this, since village residents were given rebates on

---

The Marcellus Observer
Thursday, March 20, 1890
Charter Election

The election of village officers which occurred Tuesday afternoon passed off very quietly there being no contest except for President of the village Board. The regular ticket was elected with the following ballot:

For President, Selah M. Bronson, 83

For Trustees, Isaac N. Sherman, 117

For Trustee, John E. Griffin, 115

For Collector, John N. Stearns,

TO . . . .

PLEASE TAKE NOTICE, That by virtue of a resolution and determination of the Board of Trustees of the Village of Marcellus, made at a meeting of the said Trustees, on the . . . . day of . . . . 189. . and by virtue of the statute in such case made and provided, you are hereby ordered and required, as owner (or occupant) of land situate in said village and on the . . . . side of . . . . bounded . . . . to make a sidewalk in front of said land so occupied (or owned) by you; and we have determined and do hereby determine and prescribe the manner of doing the same and the material to be used therein and the quality and kind of such material as follows, to -wit . . . . and you are hereby required to complete such improvement within 30 days from the date of the service of this order which is hereby determined a reasonable time within which to complete the same.

In witness whereof, we the aforesaid trustees of the village, have made and signed this order this . . . . . . .day of . . . . .189. .

. . . . TRUSTEES OF THE
. . . . VILLAGE
. . . . OF MARCELLUS

I . . . ., Clerk of the Village of Marcellus, hereby certify the foregoing to be a copy of an order made by the Trustees of the Village of Marcellus.

Dated, ... , 189. .

. . . . Clerk of said Village.

---

their tax assessments once the walk was completed. The value of the rebates depended on how much work was done. In 1894, for example, the rebate averaged about $3.00 per rod of sidewalk laid. A rod, another term for which was a perch, was a common measurement in the 19th century, and it meant about 16 1/2 feet or 5 1/2 yards. Quality sidewalks were a priority in the Village of Marcellus.

Appointments and Dogs

At the annual meeting that year, J. Fred DeCoudres was appointed Treasurer of the Village filling a vacancy caused by the refusal of W. B. White to serve, and later in the month, John Seymour, who had been Clerk for a number of years, resigned. Cary A. Roe, who had recently purchased and was editor of *The Marcellus Observer*, was appointed to succeed him. Owners were cautioned about a new dog law requiring registration and the Board of Trustees decided to lease out land in back of the Village Hall for gardening purposes, an interesting way to add revenue to the budget.

2 Apr 1890 - " . . . that J. Fred DeCoudres be appointed Treasurer for the ensuing year." . . . that J. M. Seymour be Clerk for the ensuing year, . . . that the Clerk's salary for the ensuing year be twenty dollars . . . " and " . . . the whole Board act as a body as assessors . . . "

16 Apr 1890 - " . . . J. M. Seymour offered his resignation as Clerk. Resignation accepted . . . C. A. Roe be appointed Clerk."

16 Apr 1890 - " . . . petition of property owners of Reed Street to provide for surface water on Street."

10 May 1890 - " . . . that the President be empowered to lease the grounds back of the Engine House for garden purposes, on a cash basis, . . . that dirt from the streets be sold for 15c per load."

14 May 1890 - " . . . that St. Francis Xavier's Church Society be directed to build a first quality, flag stone sidewalk, 4 feet in width on the east side of their premises on Cherry Street, from Main Street to the School House premises."

Taxes

In the 19th century, it was common practice to pay a poll tax, a levy that all adult males had to spend in order to vote. The tax in the 1890s was $1.00 per head but certain individuals were exempt by the Board of Trustees from paying the tax, including the volunteer firemen and those who were over the age of sixty, as in the case of Francis Baker.

2 Jul 1890 - " . . . that an order be drawn on contingent fund for $1.00 to reimburse Francis Baker for wrongfully collected poll tax."

The Trustees' concern about the cost of public progress might have been reflected in an 1890 editorial in *The Marcellus Observer*, which called for continued improvements, remaining in competition with neighboring communities, even at the expense of higher taxes.

The Marcellus Observer
Thursday, July 24, 1890
The Man-About-Town

I see that our neighboring villages are all on the move in the direction of waterworks, electric lights and other public improvements which are rapidly putting us in the shade. Baldwinsville and Jordan, with Elbridge near by have their waterworks and lights already in apple-pie order; Skaneateles has let the contract for her water system. Fayetteville and Manlius are surveying and figuring on systems for themselves and so on. Surely it is time that some move was made on our part looking in the same direction.

It might not be out of place to remark right here that we have natural facilities for such an enterprise second to none in the county. Why wouldn't it be a good idea for the corporation, for I believe in municipal ownership, to acquire by purchase, the stone mill property and install there an electric lighting plant? Arc lights upon our streets and incandescent lights in our residences would make Marcellus look a different village, while the revenue derived from the lighting of private property might pay the cost of the public street illumination.

A railroad from the village to the station has been in the minds of many for years, but the expense of building and operating a steam line has always been an insurmountable obstacle. The electric railroad requiring little grading and with power furnished the company by the corporation, from the electric lighting plant, would reduce the expense so much as to make the project feasible and at the same time add to the earnings and consequently reduce the cost to the village of the lighting system. The patronage of such a road would I believe be so ample to insure a handsome return on the investment to stockholders.

At the same time acquire the Knowles Spring on West Hill and construct there a sufficient reservoir for the storage of water both for public and private uses, allowing service pipes therefrom for private uses on the payment of proper annual rental. I understand that the outflow of these springs, if properly stored, would suffice for the whole village while their elevation would insure a pressure on the pipes which would make the service invaluable for street sprinkling and in case of fire. Should the supply from the springs at any time by chance run low, the matter would be easy of correction by the establishment of a pumping station in connection with the electric light plant on the Stone Mill property.

But, objects the chronic grumbler, our taxes are high enough and we have already ample protection against fire. True our taxes are high enough in proportion to the benefits derived from them, but would not the benefits of such a system out-balance the small increase which the outlay would entail? The very comfort derived from nicely sprinkled streets and freedom from dust, together with streets brilliantly lighted, should be compensation enough for anyone.

Theft and Taxes

An issue that confronted the Board that year was the theft of public property, specifically some village street lamps and the Trustees offered rewards for the arrest of the thieves. In the 21st century, the concern about streetlights is every bit as valid, although this involves more vandalism than theft. Streetlights in the Village of Marcellus today have, on several occasions, fallen victim, to air pellet and bb guns, and when apprehended, the vandals are often required to either make restitution or perform community service. Today, the Marcellus Police Department responds to acts of vandalism, but in the 1890s the Village did not have a paid police force to investigate or to make arrests. Sometimes the Board of Trustees appointed individuals for special police duties or hired a constable for certain circumstances, but raising village taxes to pay for a permanent policeman was hotly debated in the 1890s and would require a special vote in order in order to implement the position.

17 Sep 1890 - " . . . that C. A. Roe, Chas Case, Joseph Matteson and Myron Whiting be appointed Special Police for Firemen's Day."

8 Oct 1890 - " . . . that a reward of $15.00 be offered for information leading to the arrest and conviction of the parties who stole the lamp, . . . corner North and Reed Streets, Oct 4, 1890."

7 Jan 1891 - " . . . that bill of Jno A. Dunlap for $3.00 for constable services be paid from contingent funds."

Election of 1891

In the election of 1891, the voter turnout was so small that local residents, when asked 'why' by the editor of *The Marcellus Observer*, " . . . express surprise that no second ticket came into the field, even saying that they believe there should have been one, and yet to a man, when asked why they didn't start the movement, they reply, 'Oh! It's nothing to me, I'm satisfied' " (MO 3/19/91). It appears that times have not changed much in 100 years, in view of the fact that the turnout in Village elections in the 1990s was just as small and the reply by residents was often the same.

> **The Marcellus Observer**
> **Thursday, March 19, 1891**
> **Corporation Election**
>
> The old adage that "Competition is the spice of Business" was never better illustrated in its negative sense, than by the almost total lack of interest in the village election on Tuesday. The caucus which nominated the only ticket in the field was but a handful of men while of the one hundred and fifty or more in the village, only forty-one were sufficiently interested to go to the polls and vote. The ticket in the field looking, substantially to the placing of the old Board again in power, may have been so popular, as from last year's record it was known that matters were in safe hands, that no one cared to raise any opposition, while each trusted to others to cast sufficient ballots to elect them. The returns are as follows:
>
> | | | |
> |---|---|---|
> | Total number of votes cast | 41 | |
> | For President, W. H. Gallup | 39 | |
> | For Trustee, Selah M. Bronson | 39 | |
> | For Collector, John Evans, jr. | 39 | |
> | For Treasurer, J. F. DeCoudres | 40 | |
> | For President, George N. Tibbits | 1 | |
> | For Trustee, Jas. M. Harwood | 1 | |
> | For Collector, M. B. VanVranken | | 1 |
> | One ballot was wholly blank | | |

Controversy

There were some in 1891 who were not satisfied, however, included the Village lamplighter, Belus North, who resigned because of his low wages and William Julia who claimed that his sixty-two years entitled him to a poll tax exemption. Another resident called for the enforcement of Village ordinances against ball playing by young people on Village streets, a controversy that today could be applied to skateboarding or other youthful activities, not only on village streets, but on village sidewalks and on town and school property as well. The games have changed, but the conflicts between generations carry on.

8 Apr 1891 - " . . . the Treasurer be allowed a salary of $15.00 for the current year . . . "

13 May 1891 - " . . . informal discussion of resignation of B. F. North, as village lamplighter followed, . . . "

23 Jun 1891 - " . . . that a bill of $1.00 from Wm Julia assigned to C. A. Roe be paid from the contingent fund. This to refund a poll tax wrongfully assessed Mr. Julia being over age."

17 Jul 1891 - " . . . Hiram Coville appeared before the Board and entered a complaint against the prevailing practice of some young men of playing ball in the streets. Shortly before, while riding through Main St., a ball had descended into his carriage striking and badly splintering the back of the seat. He believed that if the ball had struck him he would have been seriously injured. The board thereupon ordered the posting of notices forbidding ball playing on the street in accordance with the existing ordinance."

Sidewalks, Again

As the village expanded, so too did the challenges and the local paper encouraged the Village Fathers to continue public improvements that helped to promote progress. The proper grading for all walks and streets in the Village and suppressing the unruly behavior that often occurred on Saturday and Sunday evenings, and to do this in spite of the "kickers," as the cynics were often called, were several of the difficulties facing President Gallup that summer.

To accomplish many of these tasks, however, the Board was required at that time, to obtain resident approval for large expenditures of money. Sometimes approval was denied by the voters, such as in October, when a vote for sidewalks was overwhelmingly rejected. The Village Board continued the practice of rewarding volunteer firemen for being first at a fire, but this small amount did not require a vote of the residents.

16 Sep 1891 - " . . . a bill presented by Ralph Stevens for the $5 reward for first team attached to engine at the time of W. H. Wright's fire, was upon motion, . . . ordered paid from the engine fund."

5 Nov 1891 - " . . . that the Trustees, . . . are . . . authorized to raise . . . taxes . . . the sum of $500, for the purpose of constructing the sidewalks in said village . . . at said election there were cast 43 ballots, of which 42 were against the resolution and one for the resolution."

Special School Meeting

Late in the year, residents did agree, however, to the construction of a new school building in the Village, one that would serve the Marcellus community for the next forty years. Plans drawn by the Board of Education to construct a new schoolhouse were published, and a special vote was planned for December 11, 1891 at Alvord Hall. Residents of School District No. 2, which was the Village, were urged by *The Marcellus Observer* to approve the decision of the Board of Education and " . . . that the necessary authority be granted them to take all needed steps for the speedy erection of the new building" (MO 11/26/91). Voters gave that approval, bonds were raised, property was purchased and in 1892 a new building was erected on West Main Street. The old wooden schoolhouse on Cherry Street School, which had served the community for the previous fifty years, was sold to St. Francis Xavier Church, torn down and the area eventually paved over for parking.

The Marcellus Observer
Thursday, May 21, 1891
The Man-About-Town

I hear that an engineer has been engaged to lay out the boundaries of North street, and to determine the grade for sidewalks on North street and other work of like nature in various parts of the village. This is as it should be. When walks are to be built and improvements made let them be made for all time, in accordance with some definite plan. It would not be a bad idea if a definite plan of grades, etc. could be made for the whole corporation and a map made of it. So that in making improvements there should be a definite ground to stand upon and to work to.

The Marcellus Observer
Thursday, June 18, 1891
The Man-About-Town

I am pleased to see the firm stand taken by the village authorities in the matter of suppressing the drunkenness and disorder which has become too common on Saturday and Sunday evenings. The prompt and vigorous enforcement of fines for violation of the ordinances will quickly put an end to the disgraceful scenes of the past week or two.

The Marcellus Observer
Thursday, August 6, 1891
The Man-About-Town

Although village improvements have progressed so far that to the unbiased, the value of the changes made is becoming apparent, some kickers still remain. One thinks that the course taken and the public spirit shown by the sympathizers with, and the promoters of the improvements is the very one to drive people away from town. He altogether fails to see that whatever tends to beautify a village tends to its welfare by encouraging those with good taste to locate there. Good sidewalks, nicely graded streets, good public buildings, including especially, well equipped and well ordered school buildings, all these help, not hinder, the growth and progress of any village.

74

> **The Marcellus Observer**
> **Thursday, November 26, 1891**
> **Now For A New School House**
>
> The plan of the Board is to take two and one-eighth acres out of the heart of the Roland Baker place, fronting nine rods on the street and extending back to Mr. Coon's land. It is proposed to place the new building about where the barn now stands, the latter being moved from the school property to the rear of the house as it now is. By suitable grading and that not of an expensive kind it is believed that the site can be made a most attractive one, while the size of the grounds will give abundant room for outdoor sports and exercises. Since the matter has become public, of course it has been the theme of conversation almost everywhere. Arguments for and against the eligibility of the site have been common. Among the chief points in its favor we hear that it contains about as much again ground as can be obtained elsewhere for the same money; that the soil is sandy and dry, not damp and breeding rheumatism, pneumonia, diphtheria or typhoid fever; that it is sheltered from the cold west and north-west winds; that it is on a well traveled street and one which does not drift, so the children will not be obliged to make paths for themselves after every storm; and last buy by no means least that it is nearer the center of the village and easier of access from east and west hills than any other lot..

Marcellus Union Free School

In 1893, six young women were the first to graduate from this new school, the first of over forty classes that followed. By 1937, when the last class graduated, a new school had been constructed and the old school was sold. It would be dismantled in 1939 and a private home, 27 West Main Street, was built on this site.

Safe and Seal

As the term for this Board came to an end, a decision was made for the purchase of a large safe to preserve Village records and that safe is still in use today, protecting many of the documents owned by the Marcellus Historical Society. In addition, a new seal of the Village of Marcellus would replace that which was adopted a few years earlier. It remains the stamp of the Village to this day.

19 Jan 1892 - " . . . because of the rooms being cold, an adjournment was taken to the clerk's office, where . . . business was transacted. . . . to purchase a suitable safe for preserving the Village Records from Fire."

5 Feb 1892 - " . . . that the Seal hereto appended, supercede the Seal of the Village as adopted October 15, 1888, and that the said annexed Seal be the Corporate Seal of the Village of Marcellus from this date."

Corporation Election

The year 1892 also saw the election of a man whose name had already become well known in the area. Edward Moir, as superintendent and later the owner of the Crown

**Edward Moir
Village President
1892-1894
1905-1909**

Woolen Mills, was elected to the first of six terms as the Village President. Edward Moir " . . . was born in . . . Scotland . . . in 1846. Ten years later he came with his parents to Canada . . . Before coming to Marcellus, he had received experience in the woolen industry in Galt and Waterloo, Ontario, and . . . became a recognized authority on the processing of wool and the manufacturing of woolens, as well as on tariff legislation . . . Under Moir's direction the Crown Mills operation flourished . . ." (Heffernan 45-46) and when he died in 1932, operation of the business passed to his son, John.

James E. Woodbridge, whose tenure in the Village government would last over 20 years, was elected Trustee in 1892 and J. George Hellganz was elected to the first of two terms as Tax Collector for the Village. Hellganz was a local cigar manufacturer who had emigrated from Germany in 1870. He was married to another immigrant, Jennie O'Grady, from Ireland by way of Canada, and they became the parents of nine children.

The local paper was " . . . pleased with the make up of the new Board believing the members to be representative men in the community, favorable to progress and the development of our business resources" (MO 3/17/92).

15 Mar 1892 - " . . . there was cast 60 ballots of which Edward Moir received 55, . . . "

Sidewalks

At its annual meeting, the new Board under President Moir, agreed to give the Clerk, Cary A. Roe, a pay raise, but the Treasurer continued to be paid an annual salary of $15.00. The Board also received a petition from First Street residents concerned about sidewalk and other improvements, a form of lobbying that is common today as well.

1 Apr 1892 - " . . . C. A. Roe was elected Clerk for the year at a salary of $30.00, . . . Treasurer J. F. DeCoudres, . . . be paid a salary of $15.00."

1 Apr 1892 - " . . . a petition of property holders on First Street was, . . . referred to the sidewalk committee with instructions to make early report. Petition as follows:

Marcellus, April 1, 1892

To the President and Board of Trustees of the Village of Marcellus.

We the undersigned respectfully request that some action be taken with reference to the sidewalk bordering the west side of the premises now occupied by Eli Newton, and repairs on the walk joining it on the north, in front of Edmund Reed's tenant house.

W. H. North

Henry Seynour

James Axten

Hiram Coville

Incorporation

By the summer, the Board had also taken note of the petition by the Marcellus Fire Department to incorporate and at its July meeting, the Trustees granted the volunteers this request. Today, the Department remains a legal corporation, subject to the oversight of the Village Board of Trustees. The Board also authorized the building of a coal storage addition to the Engine House and the purchase of a triangle for the Engine House. The coal storage addition has long since been renovated and incorporated into the present Village Offices and the triangle, once so vital as an alarm device, has been replaced by the purchase of individual pagers for each of the volunteers in the Marcellus Fire Department.

15 Jul 1892 - " . . . that the consent of the Board be and the same is hereby given to the proposed incorporation of the Marcellus Fire Department."

16 Sep 1892 - " . . . it was decided that an addition be built to Engine House, 12 x 16, suitable for coal storage."

4 Nov 1892 - " . . . it was ordered that a sum, not exceeding $15.00 be appropriated for the purchase of a triangle for the Engine House."

Increase in Crime

The Board of Trustees was also concerned that year about what seemed to be an increase in crime and what the local paper called "rowdyism." A small rural community like Marcellus was experiencing, it appears, a change that was reflective of the times. An economic downturn, later referred to as a depression, had taken place across the country, and the community was also experiencing the effects of a new national tariff, impacting exports from the local textile mills in Marcellus as well as employment for many of its residents. The community also attracted outsiders, tramps and peddlers, some of who were actually looking for work and others who needed to be looked after. The temperance movement also was gathering strength and some thought that crime was often fueled, in part, by alcohol consumption.

The Marcellus Observer
Thursday, July 21, 1892
Burglaries In Town

While surrounding towns have been suffering from petty burglaries to a considerable extent, Marcellus heretofore has escaped, but on Wednesday night last, two houses in town were entered and small sums taken. S. M. Bronson and Isaac Bradley were the sufferers. Both houses were entered through rear windows which were forced open. An entrance gained, the thieves made sure of safe exit by opening the outside doors leaving them open on their departure. At Mr. Bradley's they secured a little money from his clothing which they carried out doors for examination. It was not until the evening afterward that Mrs. Bradley discovered her gold watch missing, it not being in the accustomed place when she went to wind it. This loss she feels quite severely, the timepiece being a keepsake given her by George Ammerman, it having been left him by his mother. At Mr. Bronson's, the thieves obtained little beyond a small sum of money, about $20.00 overlooking watches and other valuables near by. The house as a whole was however thoroughly ransacked, bureau and book case drawers being pulled out, etc. Detectives have been looking into these cases but with little success.

There were some in the village who urged the appointment of a permanent policeman, although spending tax money for this purpose would require the approval of village residents in a special election. The village did its lock-up, but there was no full-time police force and the community often had to rely on county or state law enforcement agencies. Even today, the Marcellus Village Police Department, although it does employ one full-time officer, is largely a part-time force with coverage that is less than 24 hours per day. Some reliance on the Onondaga County Sheriff's Department and the New York State Police is still routine procedure in the Village.

Election of 1893

In one of the lowest voter turnouts in the Village's history, Edward Moir was re-elected to a second term in March of 1893, along with Selah Bronson as Trustee. A new Treasurer for Village government, however, was John N. Stearns replacing J. Fred Coudres, who was selling his business in Marcellus, and was moving to Syracuse. The office of Village Treasurer also was becoming far more complicated, and the Treasurer's Report had become more detailed and the disbursements more specific compared to earlier years.

18 Mar 1893 - " . . . a caucus for the nomination of village officers for the ensuing year was held Monday evening in the Board rooms in the Engine House. The small attendance would indicate either that the interest was likewise small or that it was taken for granted that the affairs of the villager were in good hands. After some informal discussion and much joking, the officers of the present year were re-nominated with the exception of Treasurer, the present incumbent, J. Fred DeCoudres, being about to leave town, not desiring the office longer."

Public Improvements

The Board of Trustees continued to be concerned about public improvements, particularly in regards to public sanitation, the cleaning of outhouses and the removal of wastewater in particular. There was also anxiety about public safety, the dangers, not only of overhanging tree limbs, but of street brawls and assaults as well.

8 May 1893 - "The Clerk was requested to . . . call attention of residents of the corporation generally, to the necessity in so far as it has not already been done, of thoroughly cleaning outhouses and removing decaying vegetable matter from their premises, also to the fact that in many cases trees overhanging the sidewalks and highways needed trimming."

17 Jul 1893 - " . . . it was ordered that the owners of the west Main street reservoir, Prof. M. I. Hunt and the Board of Education of the Union School be notified to take proper steps for caring

for the waste water from said reservoir, on their respective properties, and to prevent same from running in the highway."

The Marcellus Observer
Saturday, May 13, 1893
Local Improvements
Not Many New Buildings But Many Improvements On Old Ones
North, Orange, Main and Cherry Streets,
In Fact the Whole Village Interested

There is very little building going on here this   Spring thus far and but little contemplated as far as we know. S. C. Hooper has improved the appearance of his yard by a new fence, repaired his piazza and fitted over a room in his block for the Catholic Temperance Society. S. M. Bronson has fitted up a fine hall over the meat market by taking down all the partitions and rearranging. S. Slocombe has added a new awning in front of his store which will make it more comfortable, especially in the summer. Mrs. D. A. E. Cornish has enlarged her dining room and made more room over it by inclosing and raising up her east piazza. James Anderson has been newly painting his house. The Cash store has enlarged and improved their quarters. E. G. Rosser has been improving his kitchen, etc. Miss Jane Duggan has had a new piazza built to her house on Orange Street.

A number of improvements or additions are contemplated by the Crown Mills. The old Clements house on Cherry Street is undergoing a transformation by changes and removal, the main part being pushed back on to a new foundations, the rest torn away and when completed and the grounds graded, it will greatly improve the street. Now let public spirit assist in re-adjusting the Widow Curtis house and lot and the change would add still more to the street.

Mrs. A. S. Rhodes has made several improvements on her premises by changes in the kitchen and cellarway and reconstructing the barn floor, etc. Henry Jones recently made an addition to his barn. James Dunlap is preparing to build a new corn house, hog pen and shed. The new iron fence will soon be put in position around the old cemetery, which will add to the appearance of North Street. There may be many other changes that we have not noticed.

The Marcellus Observer
Saturday, October 14, 1893
Local Mention

Much adverse comment is heard on our streets regarding the general amount of drunkenness about the streets of late. Town and Village officials are hardly awake to their duty, it seems to us, to see that the laws are obeyed. The Village needs an efficient police officer.

The Marcellus Observer
Saturday, December 9, 1893
Local Mention

Considerable complaint comes to our ears regarding the considerable amount of sleigh riding which has been indulged in by our young people on the sidewalks of West Hill. The sidewalks, besides being rendered dangerous through the continual passing of sleds, are rendered so slippery as to be unsafe at any time for pedestrians. The place for "sliding down hill" is in the center of the highway, and the powers that be should be sure that protection to life and limb is ample.

While local residents were busy making improvements around their own homes and businesses, they also requested that Village government do something about the amount of drunkenness in Town and prevent young people from sliding down West Hill on the sidewalks. Sliding down the center of the road, before the advent of the advent of the automobile, was the proper course for the youngsters, said the paper at the time.

18 Dec 1893 - " . . . it was ordered that the Clerk post notices forbidding sliding down hill on the sidewalks within the corporation."

Temperance

Residents of Cherry Street who felt that the saloon in their neighborhood was both disorderly and a nuisance reflected the rising interest in and power of the temperance crusade in another petition to the Board. The Board followed up on this petition with a resolution that requested the Excise Board of the Town cancels the license of John O'Grady.

22 Feb 1894 - " . . . it was ordered that a petition by residents of Cherry Street and vicinity relating to the alleged disorderly saloon, kept by John O'Grady, be received. Petition as follows:

To the Board of Trustees, Village of Marcellus,

Dear Sirs:

We the undersigned, residents of Cherry St. and immediate vicinity of such, knowing that the establishment kept by John O'Grady on said street to be a nuisance and the surroundings of such, disgraceful to respectable people, we do hereby petition your honorable body to take some action in regard to this nuisance and that said nuisance may be abated and the offenders dealt with according to law.

C. E. Jones
V. H. Woodbridge
R. A. Baker
J. C. Perry
Francis Baker
J. M. Dunlap
H. S. Jones
D. D. F. Coon
C. C. Parsons
Emma Jones
Isaac Bradley
Mary Bradley
Sarah Bradley
Georgia DeCoudres
Maude DeCoudres
Mrs. L. Bicknell
Amelia Rhodes
D. A. E. Cornish
Mary E. Perry
Ida E. Seymour

Marcellus, N.Y., Dec 29, 1893

22 Feb 1894 - " . . . Upon resolution by Griffin, seconded by Bronson, the Clerk of the Board was instructed to submit a copy of said petition to the Excise Board of the Town for their information and action thereon.

The following resolution by Woodbridge, seconded by Bronson was also adopted, "Resolved that it is the sense and desire of the Board that the license of the said O'Grady should be cancelled by the Excise Board of the Town."

Sidewalk Petition

Since the residents of Cherry Street were able to petition the Board successfully, those on Reed Street followed with another appeal in March, asking the Trustees to make some sidewalk improvements. Upon resolution, the Board so ordered the owner of the property to make repairs, limiting its liability in case of accident.

8 Mar 1894 - " . . . it was ordered that petition by property owners on Reed Street be received for consideration.

Petition as follows:

To the Honorable Board of Trustees of the Village of Marcellus:

We the undersigned complain that since the sidewalk west of the big Elm Tree has been built or laid, the water backs upon our land more than usual and much to our damage and would hereby ask you to make some provision to get rid of the surface water in such way as you may think best. One sluice seems to have been stopped up by the filling in of the walk that formerly carried off much of the water. It is desirable that the matter secures your early attention.

J. H. Kelsey
A. Roe
Samuel Hooper
Fred O'Brien

8 Mar 1894 - " . . . Upon resolution by Griffin, seconded by Bronson, the Clerk was instructed to notify the Reed estate, and John Keefe that walks along their respective properties are not properly protected at the side and that the village will not assume liability for any damage to residents arising there from."

John E. Griffin

John E. Griffin, Marcellus, was born in Montezuma, Cayuga Co., April 2, 1865, a son of Stores M. and Lucy (Ebbon) Griffin. Mrs. Lucy (Ebbon) Griffin died in Marcellus May 9, 1891. Stores M. Griffin still resides in the village. John E. Griffin came to Marcellus with his parents, at the age of three years, where he was educated, and later began work in the woolen mills, serving as apprentice five years. He has since been employed by the Crown Mills, and has worked his way up in the woolen business until he now has charge of the wool sorting department in the Crown Mills. He takes a prominent part in politics, and ran for trustee of the village on a ticket pledged for general improvements, sidewalks, streets, etc. How well Mr. Griffin discharged his trust is shown by the fact that the sidewalks of Marcellus are superior to those found in any other place of equal size in the county. After serving four years as trustee, Mr. Griffin was elected in 1894 President of the Village.

From Onondaga's Centennial, Gleanings of a Century, edited by Dwight H. Bruce, Volume II. The Boston History Company, Publishers, 1896, p. 205.

Election of 1894

In 1894 there was a large turnout of voters and a rather close election in Marcellus Village for both the office of President and for one of the two Trustee positions that was being contested that year. John E. Griffin, who had been serving as a Trustee, was elected President of the Village by just four votes over Reuben R. Croxson; and Myon M. Whiting would beat out Isaac A. Share by just nine votes for Trustee. There did not seem to be any great issues that attracted such a large turnout of voters, although it seems that Griffin, a thirty-year resident of the village and working as he did for the Crown Mills Company, was being challenged by a relative newcomer to village politics. In addition to Whiting, whose his background in the Fire Department certainly helped him to win, James Anderson was also elected as a Trustee.

8 Mar 1894 - " . . . at said election there were 134 ballots of which Reuben R. Croxson for President received 63 and John E. Griffin for President received 67. . . . Myron M. Whiting for Trustee received 70 and Isaac A. Share for Trustee received 61."

Towards the end of the year, both Griffin and Anderson would resign as village officials. Griffin was replaced by the former editor/publisher of *The Marcellus Observer*, Cary A. Roe, and Anderson's position was taken over by Daniel

C. A. Roe.

Cary A. Roe

Cary A. Roe, editor and publisher of the Marcellus Observer and Camillus Enterprise is a son of Rev. Andrew Roe a prominent clergyman of the M. E. church and was born in Gouverneur N. Y., August 5, 1861 . . . Mr. Roe came to Marcellus, Onondaga County in 1887 and in March of that year purchased of the late A. de L. Rogers the Marcellus Observer of which he has since been the editor and proprietor. On January 1, 1894 he started the Camillus Enterprise, printing it at the Observer office but issuing from the village of Camillus. Mr. Roe is one of the ablest country editors in the county and has made his two papers powerful factors in the communities which they represent. The Observer especially under his energetic and business-like management ranks high among the leading weeklies of Onondaga. He is a Republican in politics, takes an active interest in local affairs and all worthy movements and served the village of Marcellus in 1894 as president. In June 1886, Mr. Roe married Mary L. daughter of Joseph Coats of Watkins, N. Y., and they have one son, Ralph Coats Roe.

From Onondaga's Centennial Gleanings of a Century, edited by Dwight H. Bruce, Volume II. The Boston History Company, Publishers, 1896, p. 209.

DeForest Coon, the son of Daniel G. Coon, a former Village President. Roe's appointment as Trustee left a vacancy in the office of Village Clerk, and the Board would fill this position with a young man by the name of Frank W. Knapp. He was a young lawyer who had just recently moved to Marcellus, and he became very involved in the life of the community. Knapp would remain Village Clerk for the next fifteen years and at the turn of the century, would initiate a number of public improvement projects for the Village.

Bills and Ball Playing

The administration continued to improve the sidewalks as well as maintain adequate street lighting, and was also concerned about the habit of young people playing ball in the streets of the village. By the end of the year, the Board of Trustees also decided to revise the village ordinances, a procedure which seems to take place every twenty years. Although approved in 1894, however, this revision would not take place for another four years.

1 Jun 1894 - " bills were presented and ordered paid:
C. H. Wright, for street lighting and repairs, $48.25
Michael Kennedy, labor, $9.27
William Duggan, labor, $5.25
Simon Connelly, labor, $5.25
C. A. Roe, printing and supplies, $19.25
C. E. Smith, janitor, $25.00
S. P. Pierce & Son, street lamps, $19.50
John Dunlap, labor, .30
John Dunn, labor, .30

" . . . that ball playing be prohibited in the streets of the village, according to the village ordinance forbidding the same."

24 Nov 1894 -" . . . President Griffin handed in his resignation as President of the Village."

1 Dec 1894 - " . . . the resignation of President Griffin was accepted, and C. A. Roe was chosen to fill vacancy for the unexpired term."

8 Dec 1894 - " . . . the resignation of James Anderson as trustee was accepted and D. D. F. Coon was chosen to fill the vacancy . . . " for the remainder of the term.

8 Dec 1894 - " . . . that the village ordinances be revised and copies furnished for each business place in the village."

Fire Department Requests

The struggle for control by the Fire Department over budgetary items was as much in evidence one hundred years ago as it is today. The Fire Department, like today's volunteers, had to make the Board of Trustees aware of equipment needs and in the 1890s the need was for more cisterns as well as fire nozzles and hoses. Today, the needs are somewhat similar although there is more fire equipment that has to be replaced or repaired and new technology requires updated apparatus. Another difference is that there is a need for medical supplies and equipment that did not exist one hundred years ago. In the present day in the Village of Marcellus, fire hydrants have replaced the need for cisterns, although in certain areas of the Town of Marcellus that are serviced by the Marcellus Fire Department, there is a need for what are called "dry hydrants." In all instances, in our day as well as in the 1890s, the Marcellus Fire Chief makes the Board of

Trustees aware of specific needs and prepares a budget that must have Board approval before purchase.

5 Mar 1895 - " . . . W. J. Matteson, Chief of the Fire Department, appeared before the Board and called their attention to the need of another cistern on Reed Street, a nozzle by means of which a small stream can be sprayed in case of a small fire in a room, and of five more lengths of hose."

Election of 1895

In 1895, President Roe decided not to run for re-election and the new head of village government had a familiar name. He was Edmund Reed, who had once served as a Trustee. In that same election, Charles J. Brown would be elected to a two-year term as Trustee, and Henry R. Jones was chosen as a Trustee to fill the one-year vacancy left by James Anderson's resignation. To the office of Tax Collector, a man by the name of Cassius A. Peck was elected, a position he would hold for several more terms. He was one of the local barbers in town, in his mid-forties, married and the father of two daughters.

19 Mar 1895 - " . . . at said election, there was cast 77 ballots, of which . . . Henry R. Jones, for Trustee to fill vacancy (1 year) received 71 . . . "

The Pathmaster
A pathmaster was a paid position. His job was to keep the paths of his area well marked and cleared of fallen trees and growing brush. The same was true for roads for cart or military travel. Some areas passed laws that held that anyone who had roads along or through his property had to keep them clear or be fined by the pathmaster. The pathmaster title gave way to the title of street commissioner or superintendent of highways and he became responsible for such maintenance. He had to keep brush from growing along the road so that branches did not hang into the roadway and he had to keep the ditches alongside the road clear as well. Sometimes he had to cut and lay small trees across muddy parts of a road or fill parts of the road with stone so that teams of horses, and later, autos, could pass. As Street Commissioner, he would often hire daily laborers to help complete these tasks, many of which were only seasonal jobs.

The Street Commissioner
Along with the sidewalks, maintaining village streets became a priority of the administration and it was delegated to the Street Commissioner, whose daily salary of $1.50 provides some evidence of what was the average wage at the time.

3 Apr 1895 - " . . . it was voted that Benjamin Powell act as Street Commissioner, and that his wages be fixed at $1.50 per day, and the laborers at $1.25 per day."

The Street Commissioner, who was Benjamin Powell at the time, was responsible for making sure that the village streets, which were not paved roads but muddy paths, were clear of debris and somewhat passable for both man and horse. This title replaced that of the pathmaster of earlier village days, although the responsibilities were quite similar, and it was now a full time position in Marcellus Village government.

Bicycle Riding

In the 1890s, bicycle riding had become very fashionable throughout the country and the Marcellus Village was no exception. The Board, however, was concerned about people riding bicycles on the sidewalks after dark, causing injury to pedestrians or themselves and imposed penalties for such infractions. The concern seems related in many ways to the issue of liability, whether it involved rolling hoops or playing ball on the village streets, or riding a bicycle or using a sled on the village sidewalks and it remains as valid today, with the arrival of rollerblades, skateboards, and snowmobiles.

7 Sep 1895 - " . . . it was voted to forbid the riding of bicycles after dark on the sidewalks in the village under a penaly of two dollars for each offense."

Invoices

At each Board meeting, the Trustees authorized the payment of bills, some of which were for part-time labor costs and others for materials and most of it, at this time, related to sidewalk or street repairs. Comparing the cost of painting the Village Hall can also be seen as another indication of wages and prices. In 1995, the Village Hall was painted at a total cost of over $2000. In 1895 that cost was $55 an amount that was taken from the Engine fund rather than general operating costs and was not paid until a final inspection in November.

19 Oct 1895 - " . . . following bills were accepted and ordered paid:
Simon Connelly, labor, $3.37
John Dunlap, labor, $5.25
J. N. Stearns & Co., supplier, $33.80
Martin Hogan, stone, $13.50
Michael Flood, labor, $3.50

19 Nov 1895 - " . . . The Board examined the painting of the Engine House and on motion by Whiting seconded by Brown the bill of $55 for painting the same was ordered paid."

Daniel De Forest Coon

Daniel De Forest Coon, Marcellus, was born in Marcellus, May 30, 1848, son of Daniel G. and Betsey C. Coon. Daniel was born September 5, 1814, in Adams, Jefferson Co., where he was educated and lived till 1841. He then moved to Skaneateles, and after one year to Marcellus. He rented for a few years a distillery at Marcellus Falls, forming a company composed of Norton, Parker, Coon & Olney, afterward buying out Norton and Parker. The firm of Cool & Olney did business for several years. Here he was located for nearly twenty-five years. Mr. Coon's business was a large one, and the distributing point of his product was Syracuse. After selling out his distillery he retired from active business and devoted his time to cultivating a fine homestead farm that he owned, on which he resided in the village of Marcellus until his death, March 4, 1893. He married in 1839 Betsey C., daughter of Zenas and Polly (Gore) Barney, of Gilford, Windham Co., Vt., where Mrs. Coon was born. Zenas Barney was a salesman by occupation and at the time of the gold excitement went to California, where he died. Mrs. Betsey C. Coon is still living on the family homestead and in good health. Our subject was educated in Marcellus and Cazenovia, and after leaving school went into the cheese business, then engaged in the drug business for two years, and then engaged in farming. Mr. Coon's farm consists of 130 acres under a good state of cultivation. He married April 6, 1871, Adelle Rhodes of Camillus, by whom he had two children, Bertha C., and Daniel Rhodes. Mrs. Coon died February 16, 1892. On October 3, 1895, he married Josephine Woodford of Marcellus.

From Onondaga's Centennial, Gleanings of a Century, edited by Dwight H. Bruce, Volume II. The Boston History Company, Publishers, 1896, pp. 203-204.

Election of 1896

Edmund Reed was elected to a second term in March of 1896 in a rather small turnout of voters, along with D. D. F. Coon, a local farmer and Eli Newton, an older man who worked in the woolen mill.

17 Mar 1896 - " . . . at said election there was cast twenty-two ballots . . . Edmund Reed, for President received 14 . . . "

During this term, the Village Board expanded its control over the operations of the Engine House and was as concerned as ever about bicycle riding within the corporation's limits.

29 Apr 1896 - " . . . Special meeting called to consider the matter of assuming the control and bearing the whole expense of running the Engine House. All the members of the Board were present, together with several members of the Fire Department. After considerable discussion it was resolved on motion by Coon, seconded by Brown that the village assume the entire control, and pay the expense of running the Engine House."

11 May 1896 - " . . . a number of citizens appeared before the Board and protested against the rapid riding of bicycles on the sidewalks and riding after dark. . . . that bicycle riding be restricted to six miles an hour within the corporate limits and that no riding be allowed after dark under a penalty of from $2 to $5 for each offense.

Peddlers

The primary issue of the day, however, was the concern over the influx of street peddlers into the village. The area businessmen would petition the Board of Trustees to impose license fees so as to restrict this activity by outsiders who threatened the livelihood of local merchants. Today, the issue of peddlers and licenses is just as valid, and village merchants continue to enjoy the protection of Village ordinance that requires seasonal or transient salesmen to apply for and obtain a license from the Village Office.

11 May 1896 - " . . . petition was presented signed by nearly all the merchants in the village, asking that a license fee be imposed on non-resident peddlers and traders. The questions was tabled until next meeting in order to get further information in the matter."

16 May 1896 - " . . . the following ordinance was passed in regard to licenses: No person shall hawk or peddle any merchandise, goods, or property of any description within the village of Marcellus, without having first obtained a license of the trustees of the village therefor, and having paid a fee not exceeding ten dollars for the same, under a penalty of five dollars for each offense, and each day or part thereof so employed without such license shall be considered a separate offense."

Resolutions and Contracts

The Village was saddened by the unexpected death of William H. Gallup. A native of Marcellus, he had been instrumental, as a businessman and as a Trustee and President, in the development of the Village. He had also been elected to the New York State Assembly and was a rising star in local politics. The Board of Trustees would pass a Resolution of Respect, a practice that is also common today, to honor the memory or the loss of a admired individual or to pay respect to a person or group for a noted achievement.

27 Jun 1896 - " . . . Resolved: That in the sudden and terrible death of the Hon. W. H. Gallup, the village of Marcellus received a great shock. Although removed from our village, we still considered him a townsman and as such mourn his loss. Born in our village and having grown up among us, we have seen his going out and coming in and thus have learned to know him thoroughly and well. He was very active in all that pertained to the good and welfare of our village, serving as Trustee and President for several terms. As a Member of the Assembly for two terms, he acquitted himself with honor. In his family relations both as husband and father his life might be taken as a model. Never was he so happy as when with his family. In the death of Mr. Gallup, the city of Syracuse has lost one of its brightest business men not only able but of the highest moral worth, and our little village joins its neighboring city in mourning his untimely end. To the bereaved wife and family we desire to lovingly tender our sincere sympathy with the assurance that we voice the sentiments of the entire community in this the great sorrow of their lives . . . "

14 Dec 1896 - " . . . the bids for scraping snow from the sidewalks were opened and the contract for the winter was given to Henry Kilcoyne at 90 cents a trip, his being the lowest bid."

16 Jan 1897 - " . . . the contract for supplying oil for the village was given to R. A. Julia at 8 1/2 cents per gallon, and the clerk was instructed to draw a contract to continue until January 1, 1898."

Election of 1897

In 1897, James Sarr was elected President of the Village of Marcellus. A carpenter by trade, Sarr was a man of many talents, and had already served in a number of positions, particularly on the School Board, before his election to Village office. Standing committees for streets and fire, lights and walks, employee appointments and salary schedules were made, along with street lamp and road material purchases at the annual meeting following the election.

29 Mar 1897 - " . . . F. W. Knapp was appointed clerk for the coming year, at the same salary as last year, or $25. There being a vacancy in the office of Treasurer, J. N. Stearns was appointed for the year at a salary of $10. There being a like vacancy in the office of Collector, C. A. Peck was appointed. John Dunlap was appointed street commissioner, his pay and that of the laborers to be the same as last year, or $1.50 and $1.25. . . . to purchase nine circular globe lamps to replace the old square lamps . . . . to look over the streets and draw in broken stone where needed."

James Sarr

James Sarr was born in Cayuga County, May 2, 1831, a son of William and Sarah (Van Waggoner) Sarr. William was born in 1803 in Sullivan County, went to Skaneateles in 1822, and from there to Otisco, later removing to Marcellus, where he died in 1882. His father, John, was a Revolutionary soldier. Our subject was educated in the public schools and at the age of fifteen came to Marcellus, where he learned the carpenter's trade, at which he worked for several years, then began building. He built the Methodist church at Marcellus, the Episcopal church (since burned), the large grist mills, located at the Falls, also the Crown Mills, a fine brick edifice which will rank among the largest in the county, and has also put up many structures in different parts of the county. After building for about twenty-five years, he retired and engaged in the sale of general merchandise, which he has followed for the past sixteen years, having the largest and oldest business in the town of Marcellus. Mr. Sarr has served on the School Board for sixteen years, and also as justice of the peace. He has been deeply interested in education and it was largely through his efforts that the new school building and high school department were established. The structure is a fine one, and the school is graded into eleven departments. Mr. Sarr's efforts in behalf of this school are highly appreciated by his townspeople, and he has been elected president of the Board of Trustees. He married first Alice Carr, and had four children: William H. Robert J. Frank L., and Nellie A. Mrs. Sarr died in 1885 and he married second Mrs. Julia Jackson.

From Onondaga's Centennial, Gleanings of a Century, edited by Dwight H. Bruce (Volume II). The Boston History Company, Publishers, 1896, pp. 210-211

Bicycle Riding Ordinances

There was considerable discussion about bicycle riding on Village sidewalks by this Board and ordinances were adopted early in the spring to regulate this activity. The laws probably seem quite antiquated today, but recent laws requiring children to wear bicycle helmets as well as the concern that many have about pedestrian safety seem to make them more current.

22 Apr 1897 - " . . . following ordinances were adopted in relation to riding bicycles on the side walk and the clerk was instructed to have fifty copies printed and posted in the village.

1. Every bicycle shall be provided with a bell, which shall be rung 20 yards before meeting or passing people.

2. Wheelmen when meeting or passing pedestrian should get off the walk unless the pedestrian waives his or her right by giving half the walk.

3. The speed shall not exceed eight miles an hour.

4. Wheelmen shall not ride lat4er than one half hour after sundown.

5. Wheelmen shall not ride on the south side of Maple street, or the west side of Orange street, or the south side of Main street west of the crosswalk by the Methodist church.

6. No riding on Sunday after nine o'clock A.M.

7. A fine of from one to ten dollars is imposed for a violation of any part of this ordinance."

Railway Transportation

An issue which seemed to occupy much conversation that year was the building of a short line railroad from the Marcellus Village to Marcellus Junction, on the Auburn branch of the New York Central Railroad, two miles to the north. There had been talk of this project for more than twenty years, but in the 1890s a railroad-building fever seemed to grip the country and several citizens of Marcellus decided that now was the time. "As a result, the Marcellus Electric Railroad Company was incorporated on June 4, 1897, with Edward Moir serving as president, Levi Mogg as vice-president, Edmund Reed as secretary, and John M. Seymour as treasurer. The sale of one hundred dollar shares quickly raised the proposed capital of sixty thousand dollars" (Heffernan, 71). The Village Board of Trustees gave its approval in July of that year and construction would

---

NOTICE

Notice is hereby given that the Marcellus Electric Railway Company has applied to the Board of Trustees of the Village of Marcellus, for its consent that the said Company may construct and operate a street surface railway, using electricity as a motive power on the following streets in the Village of Marcellus, viz:

Beginning in the north line of said Village, in North Street, running thence southerly to Main Street, thence beginning at the intersection of North Street, running easterly in Maple to the end thereof. Notice is hereby given that such application will be considered by said Board of Trustees, at a meeting appointed to be held in the Trustees Room in the Engine House in the Village of Marcellus on the 31st day of July, 1897, at 8 o'clock P.M."

---

begin the following year. It would not be until the turn of the century, however, before a number of issues were resolved, changes were made, and construction was completed.

31 Jul 1897 - " . . . the franchise asked for by said company was granted, . . ."

W.C.T.U.

Of equal concern to both the Board of Trustees and many citizens was the issue of temperance and the ladies of the Women's Christian Temperance Union, or W.C.T.U., organized a number of years earlier, wanted to place a fountain in the village as a symbol of their cause along with the argument that if men really wanted or needed a drink, water was available, free of charge. That fountain is on display today in the Marcellus Historical Society museum, a relic of the past but a very potent symbol in turn of the century Marcellus.

23 Aug 1897 - " . . . The ladies of the W. C. T. U. made application to the Board of Trustees for the privilege of erecting a fountain either in the center of Main Street opposite the store of Wm. B. White, or at the east end of the triangle in front of the M. E. Church, together with the privilege of digging up the street in laying pipe to said fountain and in carrying away the surplus. On motion by Brown, seconded by Newton, the application was granted."

Village Census

The Village of Marcellus was also directed by the State of New York to conduct a census of its inhabitants that year. Completed by the Village Clerk, the population of the

Village was listed as 600, 320 of who were females. There were 194 under the age of twenty-one and 406 were over the age of twenty-one, including all of the young men pictured below in their "iron derbies" on Christmas Eve, 1897.

13 Dec 1897 - " . . . that F. W. Knapp be appointed to take the enumeration of the inhabitants of the village under the law of 1896 and 1897 at $2.50 per day."

18 Jan 1898 - " . . . bills were accepted and ordered paid: . . . F. W. Knapp, for enumerating and copying names - $8.50. No objections having been made to the enumeration, the same was approved by the board and filed in the office of the Village Clerk. The total population of the Village is 600, of which 406 are over twenty-one years of age and 194 are under twenty-one."

Christmas Eve, 1897 – In Front of the Alvord House

Election of 1898

First elected in 1898 and re-elected to a number of terms thereafter, was a man by the name of Sidney Slocombe. Born in England in 1856, he came to Marcellus and America about twenty-five years earlier, married and raised a family of four children. A tinsmith by trade, Slocombe was in his early 40s when he was first elected. As President, he presided over a number of changes that took place in Marcellus Village and seemed to have gained the respect and admiration of virtually all its residents. Along with him and elected as Trustee was Arthur Drake, a dry goods merchant, in his early thirties and the father of three young children. John W. Scott was also elected as Trustee, a carpenter and machinist, and the father of two teenage sons.

Public Health and Safety

There was still the concern over public safety and health in the community, and during Slocombe's first term, the village would sell off the old stone lock-up and request, from the voters, the purchase new steel jail cages. In addition, a Village Board of Health, consisting of three men, was appointed, with power to enforce proper sanitation and impose penalties when necessary.

15 Mar 1898 - " . . . on the proposition: Shall $130 be raised by tax for the purchase of steel jail cages, 31 voted yes and five voted no, one voted blank."

13 Apr 1898 - " . . . the following persons were appointed a Board of Health for the village for the ensuing year: Henry S. Jones, Isaac A. Share, James Sarr. By resolution, the garden back of the Engine house was rented to George H. Smith for $3.00."

1 Jun 1898 - " . . . the stone lock-up was sold to R. A. Julia for $6.50. The following license fees were fixed by the board:
>　　　Fruit and merchandise - $3.00
>　　　Merchandise with horse - $5.00

Ordinances

This Board of Trustees would also adopt an entire new set of ordinances for the Village of Marcellus, codifying into a single set of regulations many of the resolutions and laws passed during earlier administrations. The ordinances that had been proposed four years earlier were now adopted and constituted Village law in 1898.

ORDINANCES OF THE VILLAGE OF MARCELLUS
ADOPTED BY THE TRUSTEES OF SAID VILLAGE, APRIL 13, 1898

SECTION 1. No person shall run or race any horse, or suffer his horse to run or race or drive at unnecessary or dangerous speed in any of the streets of said village, or leave or cause to be left horses untied or hitched for an unreasonable time in the streets or public places in said Village, or ride, drive, lead or place any horse or other animal upon the sidewalks in said village under a penalty not to exceed five dollars for each offense.

§ S. No person shall in any wise injure or destroy any shade trees, or tie or hitch any team or horse or other animal to any shade trees planted along the streets or sidewalks in said village. And any persons offending in any wise against the provisions of this ordinance shall forfeit to said village for each and every offense, a sum of not less than five nor more than twenty-five dollars.

§ 3. Every person who shall cut, mar or in any way mutilate any tree, shrub or flower, plant, fence, awning, sign, signboard, building, monument, or ornament of any description, in any of the streets, public grounds, or cemetery in said village, or who shall tear down any notice lawfully posted, shall forfeit a penalty not to exceed ten dollars.

§ 4. No person shall write, print, publish, or post any obscene, or indecent writing, picture, or print, in said village; and no person shall deface any post, wall, fence, building or other surface, with any obscene or indecent mark, writing, picture or print. Any person offending against the provisions of this section shall forfeit a penalty not less than five nor more than twenty-five dollars.

§ 5. Every person who shall sell any goods or merchandise by peddling from house to house, or in the public streets or public grounds of said village and every person who shall exhibit for money any theatrical representations, circus, or other shows, exhibitions, or performances, of any kind, without having first obtained a license therefore from the trustees, shall forfeit a penalty not to exceed ten dollars for each offense.

§ 6 No person shall, without the written permission from a trustee or street commissioner, dig or remove or carry away, or cause the same to be done, any stone, earth, sand or gravel, from any public street, highway, or lane in this village; nor shall any person, without such permission deposit any coal ashes, stone, or rubbish of any kind in any of the public streets or grounds of said village, or throw or deposit, or cause to be put or come upon any street, lane, creek, or pond, or under any bridge, or in any public place, any dung, dead animals, putrid meat, slops, brush, or refuse matter, or a nuisance of any kind under a penalty not to exceed ten dollars for each offence.

§ 7 No person or persons, or corporation shall bring, deposit or have with in the limits of said village, any dead carcass or other unwholesome substance, or any person or persons or corporation who shall have on or about his or their premises, any such substance or any putrid meat, fish, hides or skins of any kind, or any stagnant water may be required to destroy or remove the same. And any person or persons or corporation neglecting or refusing to remove or destroy such substance after a reasonable notice so to do, shall be liable to the penalty set forth at the end of this ordinance. And the trustees may abate any nuisance within said village injurious to the public health. Any person, company, or corporation offending in any wise against the provisions of this ordinance, shall forfeit to said village for each and every such offense, the sum of not less than one dollar or more than twenty-five dollars.

§ 8 All persons are forbidden to congregate or assemble on any steps or sidewalks within the limits of the corporation on Sunday, or to congregate upon the sidewalks or crosswalks of said village at any time in such manner as to obstruct the same; or to disturb the peace and quiet of said tillage by shouting or other improper noises under a penalty of not less than two dollars for each offense.

§ 9 No person shall place or cause to be placed, or keep or suffer to remain, any logs, timber, box, cask, stone, plank, boards or other articles in any street or alley so as to incommode or obstruct the free passage or use thereof; nor shall any person place any cask, box, plank, boards or other articles on, any sidewalks within the village. Any person offending against the provisions of this section or either of them, shall forfeit and pay a penalty of five dollars; and the further penalty of five dollars for every twenty-four hours that any street or sidewalk shall be so obstructed, but nothing contained in this section shall prohibit merchants and others from placing goods and merchandise or household furniture on the sidewalks for the purpose of loading and unloading the same, providing it be done with out any unnecessary delay.

§ 10 Every owner or occupant of any house or other buildings, and every owner or person entitled to the possession of any vacant lot, and, every person having the charge of any church or other public building in this village, shall during the winter season and during the time the snow shall continue on the ground, keep the sidewalks in front of such house, building or lot free from such obstructions by snow by nine o'clock a. m. and shall also at all times keep such sidewalks clean and free from all dirt, filth and weeds or other obstructions and incumbrances, and every person or persons neglecting to comply with this section shall forfeit and pay a penalty not exceeding five dollars for such neglect or refusal.

§ I1 No person or persons within said village, shall in any wise, aid, promote, or be engaged in any fight, riot, assault, breach of the peace, disturbance or disorderly assemblage; or shall keep, or frequent any disorderly house, disorderly grocery, house of assignation, or house of ill fame in said village. No person shall be guilty of drunkenness, indecent exposure of person, or of any obscene or disorderly conduct in any of the streets or public places in said village. And no person shall procure any disorderly person or common prostitute, to come into or remain in said village. Any person violating any of the provisions of this ordinance shall be liable to a penalty, for every such offense, of not less than five or more than fifty dollars.

§ 12 No person or persons shall, within said village, in any manner, fire or in any manner assist in firing any- gun or guns, whether large or small, crackers, rockets, or squibs, or throw or play with fire balls or any other fireworks charged with gunpowder or other explosive or highly inflammable materials, or build any fires in any of the public streets of village, or blow any horn or horns, or make any improper noise which may disturb the peace of said village in the day or night time. Provided that the provisions of this ordinance shall not apply to the day which shall be celebrated as the Anniversary of American Independence; also provided that the doings of said anniversary or day celebrated as such of any of the above forbidden acts, shall be strictly under the directions and regulations of the Trustees of said village, or either or any of them, and any persons who shall be guilty of violating any of the prohibitions in this section contained, and any person aiding or abetting such violations, shall for each offense, forfeit and pay a penalty not to exceed ten dollars.

§ 13 No person shall skate, ride, or slide upon any bob, sled, or board, upon any of the streets or sidewalks in said village under a penalty of not less than one nor more than five dollars for each offense.

§ 14 Any person who shall willfully give a false alarm of fire shall forfeit a penalty of two dollars for each offense.

§ 15 Ordinance pertaining to bicycle riding on the sidewalks in Marcellus village.

1. Every bicycle shall be provided with a bell which shall be rung 20 yards before meeting or passing people.

2. Wheelmen when meeting or passing pedestrian, should get off the walk unless the pedestrian waives his or her right by giving half the walk.

3. The speed shall not exceed eight miles an hour.

4. Wheelmen shall not ride later than one half hour after sundown.

5. Wheelmen shall not ride on the south side of Maple street, or the west side of Orange street, or the south side of Main street west of the crosswalk by the Methodist church.

6. No wheelman shall ride on the sidewalks on Sunday after nine o'clock A.M.

A fine of from one to ten dollars is imposed for a violation of any part of this ordinance.

All penalties for the violations for the foregoing ordinances shall be sued for and recovered in the name of the village of Marcellus.

	Sidney Slocombe, President
	Arthur E. Drake, Trustee
F. W. Knapp, Clerk	John W. Scott, Trustee

Another Franchise

In May, the Board approved a resolution granting a franchise to another company to construct another electric railway through the village. This second franchise, to the Syracuse, Skaneteles and Moravia Railroad Company, was in direct competition with the Marcellus Electric Railway Company, but it gave the Board of Trustees more supervisory control, not only over location of the rails and their construction in the Village. An additional control included a limit on the length of the contract or time in which the franchise was in effect.

May 13, 1989 - " . . . application having been made by the Syracuse, Skaneateles & Moravia Railroad Company for a franchise to cross certain streets in the Village, Resolved, That the Board of Trustees of the Village of Marcellus hereby grants to the said Syracuse, Skaneateles and Moravia Railroad Company the right to lay its tracks upon and across Main Street and Maple Street in said village at such places as the Board of Trustees may sanction, and to erect poles and string wires thereon to furnish electrical motive power for said railroad. Said tracks to be laid and poles erected under the supervision of the Board of Trustees. Said company shall keep the portion of said streets occupied by them in good repair at all times. Said franchise to be limited to two years unless the road is sooner constructed."

Village Curfew

The summer of 1898 was a somewhat disorderly one for the Village of Marcellus, as this article from *The Marcellus Observer* notes. There was no full time policeman on duty in the Village, but by August, the Board of Trustees, upset with some of the late-night behavior of young men on the Village streets, appointed John Griffin for the remainder of the year, relying on his presence to bring about some order. Towards the end of the year, the W.C.T.U. was demanding the enactment of a nighttime curfew, hoping this would bring an end to some of the unruly behavior. The Village trustees agreed that it was a good idea, but also indicated that there were no funds to enforce such a ruling.

18 Aug 1898 - " . . . to appoint John E. Griffin village policeman for the balance of the present year."

> **The Marcellus Observer**
> **Friday, June 10, 1898**
> **The Spectator**
> Some observant people in our village note with considerable interest that several of our convivial young men occupy some of their evenings in trying to work up to fever heat, the anti-license sentiment of our voters. They begin operations about 8 o'clock in the evening. Later they take the street and give a free concert, frequently resort between acts to the dens of Bacchus. That's right, boys, just whooper up and keep it up. Keep Father Renehan and Rev. Macnaughton and the Main street people awake nights and they will be all red hot and ready (when the time comes) to pitch into the battle for no-license, hoping thus to give our tired people a chance to get some sleep in the night time.

3 Nov 1898 - " . . . the following petition was read . . .
To the President and Board of the Village of Marcellus:
We the undersigned members of the Women's Christian Temperance Union, earnestly request that your honorable body, enact and enforce a law, that a curfew bell be rung every evening from May 1st to September 1sst at eight o'clock p.m. All other months (September 1st to May 1st) at seven-thirty o'clock p.m. and that all minors under sixteen (16) years of age shall not be allowed on the streets after said bell has been rung, unless with parent or guardian.
Signed: Mrs. Jennie Clark, Mrs. Isaac Share, Mrs. C. A. Peck, Mrs. A. M. Armstrong, Mrs. A. Roe, Mrs. Elizabeth Brooks, Mrs. A. Weaver, Mrs. Eli Newton, Mrs. Julia A. Richards, Mrs. McKenzie, Mrs. G. H. Smith, Marian L. Woodford, Mr. W. H. Wright, Mrs. Wm. Graham and Mrs. T. W. Rhodes, Secretary.

After considerable discussion pertaining to the petition, it was moved that the same be copied in the minutes of the meeting and that it is the sentiment of the board that a curfew ordinance, if properly enforced, would be a good thing for the village and the children thereof. But as no funds are available in the hands of the trustees to carry into effect such an ordinance at the present time, it would not be advisable to make such a rule with no means of enforcing the same. The sentiment of the board was further expressed to the effect that, if at the next annual village election, the electors of the village would vote for an appropriation to enable the board to engage an officer to see that law and order was maintained throughout the village, that the board would appoint such officer and see that law and order was maintained. . . . it was further resolved that all parties in the village using any gambling machines or devices of any nature be requested to remove the same, or some action would be taken to enforce the ordinance relating to them."

1899

On March 21, 1899, village elections took place, and the size of the Board of Trustees was reduced to three, a President and two Trustees. Arthur E. Drake, who had been elected to a one-year term in 1898, was now elected to a two-year term. Together with John W. Scott, a holdover from the 1898 election, and President-Elect Sidney Slocombe, the Village Board became the three-person arrangement that it retains today.

There was also a proposition on the ballot to pay for the services of a regular policeman. This proposition, however, was rejected by a close vote, 17 to 18, despite the urging of the local newspaper to approve it. The residents were not to be denied, however, and a petition was delivered to the Board of Trustees that demanded the hiring of a police officer, as well as raising taxes to pay for such a position. The Board responded to the petition of the voters and approved a resolution to raise such taxes and pay for a police officer.

21 Mar 1899 - " . . . on the proposition: Shall four hundred dollars be raised by tax for the purpose of paying for the service of a special policeman, thirty five ballots were cast, of which seventeen voted yes, and eighteen voted no, none voted blank."

7 Apr 1899 - " . . . a petition signed by more than half of the taxable voters of the village and requesting the board to employ a police constable for the ensuing year having been presented to the board it was moved and carried by unanimous vote that there be raised by taxation the sum of $400 for the purpose of employing a police constable for the ensuing year."

24 Apr 1899 - " . . . it was moved and carried that Edward T. Taylor be employed as police constable at $1.50 per day."

**The Marcellus Observer
Friday, March 3, 1899
The Spectator**

The annual charter election is rapidly approaching. The affairs of the present fiscal year in village circles are being rapidly closed up if, indeed, they are not already closed. The Spectator has for some years past had occasion to criticize, sometimes somewhat severely, the government or rather lack of government which has existed in the village. The present administration, however, has it seems to be, proved itself most painstaking, energetic and efficient in the maintenance of law and order. Disorder, it is true has existed to some extent, but not to the extent of previous years. President Slocombe has proved his executive abilities on several occasions, while Mr. Scott of the trustees has been a right royal co-worker. No better move can be made in the interest of the community than that these two men (Mr. Scott's term, I believe, covers another term) be retained in the public service. President Slocombe ought to be the unanimous choice of the caucus and have the unanimous . . ..

I understand that a proposition is to be submitted to the voters, to authorize the raising of $400 additional village funds this year, this amount or so much thereof as may be necessary, to be used to pay a regular village police officer for the coming year. Inasmuch as to this officer, according to the plans of the authorities, is to be given also the work of street lighting for which in the ordinary year $200 is available, it seems to me that so large a sum will not be necessary for this purpose as without doubt good men can be obtained in plenty for less than $600 a year. And yet believing that under an honest board and the clause 'so much thereof as may be necessary," there will be no needless expenditure of the people's funds. I hope to see the resolution and appropriation pass. Now is the time for order loving people to see to it that the means are placed in the hands of the authorities, by which order, so much desired, can be maintained. Give the Board the means to do. I believe that they will see to it that the work is well done.

Railway Construction

Meanwhile, construction by the Marcellus Electric Railway connecting the Village with Marcellus Junction had begun and with it, the Board " . . .granted a second franchise to the company . . . to run their tracks through the village from the north end of North Street, thence along Main Street to Cherry Street, and south to the end of Cherry Street" (Heffernan 71). The Company was also granted permission by New York State authorities to extend its line to Amber on Otisco Lake and there was also dialogue on extending the rails all the way to Homer and Cortland. The Company, however, was having construction problems with the rock formations at Marcellus Falls and by the turn of the century had only two miles of the roadbed had been completed.

13 May 1899 - " . . . the application of the Marcellus Electric Railway Company for a franchise through Main Street from the north end of North Street to the south end of Cherry Street and then south through Cherry Street was granted under restrictions as to construction of said road as the Board might hereafter see fit to impose."

Curfew Again

There were other ordinances passed by the Board that year including more restrictions on bicycle riding and ball playing, and the Village imposed a new schedule of licenses for merchants and vendors as well.

10 Jun 1899 - " . . . following ordinances were passed by the Board:
No person shall ride a bicycle on the sidewalks of the village with hands off the handle bars or feet off the pedals under a penalty of five dollars to stand committed until paid. No ball playing shall be had in the streets of the village under a penalty of two dollars.

10 Jun 1899 - " . . . the following schedule of licenses be imposed for Marcellus Village:
Dry goods, groceries, bake stuffs, house furnishing goods, stoves and hardware, clothing, $5.00
Fruits, vegetables, medicines, essences, jewelry, $3.00
Circuses and entertainments, $3.00 to $15.00 in the discretion of the Board."

Additionally, in July the Board responded to another petition to impose a curfew and unanimously approved this ordinance for those under the age of sixteen years. Curfews are often thought to be an immediate solution to the problem of youthful misbehavior, and there have been demands by residents in recent years to impose such restrictions. However, curfews generally are ineffective and police agencies spend much of their valuable time trying to enforce an ordinance that is all too often unenforceable. In addition, curfews are intended for those under the age of sixteen, while those over that age cause most of the misbehavior. After a while, both the police and the minors ignore a curfew, just as this law was in 1899 and beyond.

The Marcellus Observer
Friday, July 14, 1899
Almost An Epidemic
A dozen or more of the operatives in the upper mill are laid off from work and several are under the doctor's care, with typhoid fever or threatened with it. As the sickness seems to be confined to the employees of this mill, it is thought to proceed from the use of impure water. We understand the Board of Health is investigating the matter and it is not likely to spread much farther. We hear of no very alarming cases thus far and while some will have a run of the fever, it will probably be light in most instances. As the mill is now running on over time it is unfortunate for the mill as well as for the sick that so many should be taken ill at this juncture of affairs.

The Marcellus Observer
Friday, July 28, 1899
Notice
The water in the spring on the vacant lot on Maple street, having been analyzed and pronounced dangerous to health as drinking water, we hereby for the safety of community, forbid any further use of this water for that purpose, until corrected.
Board of Health Marcellus, July 28th, 1899

---

10 Jul 1899 - " . . . A numerously signed petition asking for the enactment of a curfew ordinance was presented to the Board. The following ordinance was passed by unanimous vote of the Board:
Resolved, That all minors under the age of sixteen years shall not be permitted on the streets later than 9 o'clock p.m., from April 15 to September 1st and from September 1st to April 15th not later than 8 o'clock p.m. unless attended by parents or guardian, or someone acceptable to them. For a violation of this ordinance a penalty of not to exceed five dollars is imposed."

Close of the Century

The summer of 1899 witnessed a near epidemic of typhoid fever in the Village, and the Board of Health was pressed to investigate and prevent its spread, thought to have originated from impure water.

As the 19th century was coming to an end, one of the oldest residents of the Village at the time, Isaac Bradley, penned a letter to *The Marcellus Observer* that summer which seemed to sum up what Marcellus had once been and what it had become in the last one hundred years. In his letter, Bradley, whose father was one of the founders of the community over a century earlier, commented that the valley of the Nine Mile Creek, once surrounded by forest, abounding in animals, and slightly inhabited, was transformed into a community by people who endured many deprivations and lacked many of the comforts that were to become so common. As if to remind his readers of the advance of history, Bradley concludes by saying: " . . . the close of the present century is seemingly uniting with another as the waters of rivulets, rivers and lakes, flowing onward, unite with the ocean" (MO 7/28/99).

Conclusion

Forty years after the close of the 19th century, a Marcellus Village Directory was discovered in the attic of the newspaper building and published in *The Marcellus Observer*. The Directory provided a glimpse into the past, listing the names of people and places that framed the Village so long ago. Some of the names remain part of the community today while others have passed into history.

The four churches of the Village still maintain their powerful presence, as do some organizations like the Morning Star Lodge. Others, however, like the Ancient Order of Hibernians and the International Order of Odd Fellows have long since disbanded or been merged into other units. Some of the businesses, remain, their names, with the lone exception of The Alvord House, however changed. There is still a barber in Marcellus, but no cigar maker advertises any more. Once there were three blacksmiths who made a living on Main Street, along with a harness maker and a livery stable operator. The 20th century would bring many changes to the valley of the Nine Mile, the older generation yielding to its children.

Village School on Cherry Street

Many of the children pictured above are the sons and daughters of those whose names were published in the 1899 Village Directory. As they gathered for this picture across the street from Isaac Bradley's house on Cherry Street at the start of the decade of the 1890s, these young people represented the future and, as the new century unfolded, would breath new life into the community they called home.

Chapter 7 - A New Century Dawns

The turn of the century caused many to ponder its meaning, to reflect on what had happened one hundred years previously and to anticipate what would occur next. It also appears to be no different from the speculation that happened as the 20th century gave way to the 21st.

Life in Marcellus certainly did change in the 1900s, both with the expansion of government services and with increased technology reaching the average citizen. As the century opened, Sidney Slocombe was again elected President of the Village, the boundaries of the corporation had not changed in fifty years, and there were few of the comforts which today we take so very much for granted. By the end of the decade, two railroads, electric lighting, a municipal water supply, and telephone hook-up would service Marcellus and an additional seventy acres of land, what is commonly referred to as Scotch Hill and Orchard Row, would be annexed to the Village, increasing in population from 589 residents to almost 1000.

> **The Marcellus Observer**
> **Friday, February 23, 1900**
> **One Hundred Years Ago**
> John Adams was president
> The seat of government was moved from Philadelphia to Washington
> War with France was imminent, but was averted.
> Louisiana extended from Canada to Mexico, and from the Mississippi to the Rockies.
> Florida was under Spanish dominion.
> The Hudson river had yet to see that famous first steamboat.
> Our great lakes were under British control.
> Slaves were imported from Africa.
> There wasn't a railroad in our land.
> Ditto telegraph.
> Ditto cable.
> Ditto electric lights. "Twas ye tallow dip that flourished.
> In fact, to make a long history short, it may as well be said that it would take much longer to tell the things they had not than those they had

Sidney Slocombe
Village President
1898-1901
1909-1910
1921-1922

> **Sidney Slocombe**
> Sidney Slocombe, Marcellus, was born in England, December 18, 1856, son of Samuel and Elizabeth Slocombe. Subject came to Marcellus in the spring of 1873, began as an apprentice and spent three and one-half years as an apprentice and journeyman at his trade of tinsmith. He then started in business in Marcellus for himself, and his business has gradually increased every year. He has a large store containing a fine line of stoves, agricultural implements and hardware, also has large storerooms in addition to his large store. Mr. Slocombe's trade is a large one and extends all through the town. He married Urena Nettleton, daughter of Samuel Stafford Nettleton, of Arnprior, province of Ontario, Canada. They have four children, Chester A., Blanche, Frederick S. and Mary E.
> From Onondaga's Centennial, Gleanings of a Century, edited by Dwight H. Bruce (Volume II), The Boston History Company, Publishers, 1896, p. 209.

Health Services

At the start of the year, the Village, seeing a need for expanded health services, made appointments to the Board of Health, in addition to the cost of providing a health officer for the Village. It also appears that the Village was somewhat lax in its payment for bills and services. The bills being paid in the year 1900 seem to indicate that there may have been a three-month backlog, particularly as they related to James Powell, who, as police, fire and street commissioner, was paid about

$1.50 per day, or about $45.00 per month. Today, village invoices are audited each month by a Village Trustee and paid on a monthly basis and unlike James Powell, Village employees today are paid every two weeks.

9 Mar 1900 - " . . . James Sarr, Henry S. Jones and Isaac Share were appointed a board of health for the ensuing year, and Dr. Israel Parsons, health officer."

25 Oct 1900 - " . . . following bills were accepted and ordered paid:

Jas Powell, service $48.10	R. A. Julia, supplies	$21.33
S. Slocombe, supplies $11.57	D. J. Chrisler, lumber	$5.94
F. W. Knapp, insurance $6.00	Jas Powell, service	$45.00
John English, stone $1.00	Jas Powell, service	$46.9

Railroad Controversy

Not surprisingly, the 19th century Village of Marcellus found itself in the midst of a controversy over the construction of a railroad through the village. The Board of Trustees had granted franchises to two competing companies, the Marcellus Electric Railroad and the Moravia and Skaneateles Railroad, hoping that they would be able to provide rail service for both passengers and freight through the Village. Moreover, because of friction between the two lines and with landowners along the way, as well as construction and financial troubles, the Board decided to rescind both of the charters that had earlier been granted. Additionally, although the railroads would eventually be constructed, the rails would not use village streets for a roadbed but would be laid to the east of the corporation boundaries.

The Marcellus Electric Railroad, had begun construction " . . . in 1898, with work beginning at the junction, now called Martisco, with the New York Central, . . . but ran into trouble when . . . workers encountered the rock formations at Marcellus Falls"

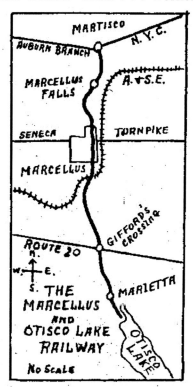

(Heffernan 71). It was not until 1901 that the rails finally reached the village limits, and when the Board of Trustees rescinded the franchises, the company began to secure rights of way along the east side of Nine Mile Creek, outside the corporation limits. Meanwhile, the Moravia and Skaneateles Railroad, also referred to as the Auburn & Syracuse Electric Company, intended to construct an electric trolley line from Skaneateles east, passing through Marcellus on its way to Syracuse. There was some initial opposition to this construction from the New York Central Railroad, with fears for the competition it would present to the Marcellus Railway, and for some individual property owners. Eventually the line would be built, but it too would skirt the Village limits. The new line actually " . . . proved to be a blessing in disguise as it fed the M & O.L. with passengers for Otisco Lake and provided a freight connection with the Solvay Process Company's Split Rock plant." (Palmer 5)

2 Mar 1901 - " . . . it was voted that the franchise granted to the Marcellus Electric Railroad Co., to build an electric road and light the village by electricity passed July 31, 1897, and covering North and Maple streets, and also the franchise granted to said company May 13, 1899, to pass through Main and

Cherry Streets, and also the franchise granted June 1, 1898 to the Skaneateles and Moravia electric road to cross Main and Maple Streets are hereby rescinded and declared null and void."

16 Mar 1901 - " . . . the resolution passed by this Board at its meeting of March 2d, 1901 rescinding certain franchises granted to the Marcellus Electric Railroad Company and to the Moravia and Skaneateles Railroad Company, be rescinded and the Marcellus Electric Railroad Company be directed to remove the rails and ties placed in the streets of Marcellus Village on March 10, and place the streets in as good a condition as before within ten days, under the supervision of the street commissioner of said village."

Election of 1901

A large turnout of voters in the election of 1901 was probably the outgrowth of the dispute over the electric railroad construction in Marcellus Village. In a rather close election, Isaac N. Sherman, owner of the large paper mill in the Falls, and a former President of the Village, narrowly defeated the village druggist and merchant, Arthur E. Drake, who had been a Trustee for several terms prior to this election. Also elected to a single term as Trustee was Isaac A. Share, a man in his mid-fifties who was employed at the woolen mill as a machinist.

19 Mar 1901 - " . . . at said election 138 ballots were cast, of which, For President, Arthur E. Drake received 56, Isaac N. Sherman received 58, Blank (were) 8, Spoiled (were) 16."

Consolidation

Isaac Sherman was now a man in his early sixties and could devote much more of his time to Village matters while his son, John R. Sherman, continued operations at the paper mill in the Falls. While he was in office (he would be reelected in 1902), the Board of Trustees would approve any early form of what today we refer to as consolidation of services, as the village and town combined into a single Board of Health. Today, that consolidation has taken on even larger proportions, in the form of the Onondaga County Health Department.

In addition, the Marcellus Fire Department increased in membership and having purchased new uniforms, not only attracted new volunteers who were approved by Board action, but proudly participated in some of the annual conventions that took place each year.

8 Apr 1901 - " . . . moved and carried that the Clerk write the State Board of Health to see if they approve the union of the town and village of Marcellus in one sanitary district with one Board of Health . . . . a poll tax of $1.00 for each male inhabitant between the ages of 21 and 70. . . . that the members of the Fire Department be required to appear before the Board of Trustees and be sworn in and that all members hereafter elected to the Department be sworn in before they are recognized as members."

22 Apr 1901 - " . . . the following members of the Fire Department were sworn in: P. J. Kelly, George Austin, Clement Wood, John Heenan, Talbot Case, Charlie Hellganz, Howard Spaulding, E. E. Wicks, John Coakley, James Robb, Eugene Johnson, Frank Van Hoesen, James Powell, Albert Taylor, Howard White, Arthur McKenzie, John Moir, Robert Shields, Wm. McKenzie, Chester Slocombe, Fred Griffing, Edmund Taylor, W. J. Matteson, Lew Scott.

The Marcellus Observer
Friday, July 5, 1901
New Uniforms

The new dress uniforms for the Marcellus Fire Department arrived Wednesday morning. For several years, the members of the department have looked forward to the time when sufficient funds could be raised for this purpose and their efforts have now been crowned with success so that the company can take its place in line at the County Firemen's annual convention, with the companies of other rival towns, turn out at home for annual inspection, etc. The company now consists of thirty-two members and it is said is in better condition than at any time during the last decade.

The boys have been doing some pretty good work in practice of late, and as the department has entered in the events of the Solvay Convention which occurs July 17, no doubt they will acquit themselves with credit to themselves and the village.

27 May 1901 - " . . . this Board appropriate to the Marcellus Fire Department the sum of $150, the same to be used by them in procuring uniforms. Of said sum, $83.75 to be paid from money carried over in Engine fund and the balance to be drawn from Contingent fund. Said appropriation is made in lieu of any demand by the department for Inspection Day."

The Marcellus Observer
Friday, July 26, 1901
Marcellus Fire Department

The following names constitute the present efficient corps of officers and members of the Marcellus Fire Department:

Chief - James Powell.
Assistant Chief - Edward Taylor.
Secretary - Louis W. Scott.

ENGINE COMPANY
Foreman - Geo. Austin.
Asst. Foreman - Eugene Wicks.
Jas. Robb, Frank VanHoesen, Wm. McKenzie, Fred T. Schoonmaker, Talbot Case, Chas. Helganz, Fred Schmidt, Louis W. Scott.

HOSE COMPANY
Foreman - Albert Taylor.
Asst. Foreman - Rollo Phillips.
Robert Shields, Howard Spaulding, George Dunlap, Arthur McKenzie, Howard White, W. J. Matteson, A. E. Drake, John Scott.

HOOK AND LADDER COMPANY
Foreman - Fred Griffing.
Asst. Foreman - John Coakley,
Clement Wood, P. J. Kelly, John Moir, Chester Slocombe, John Heenan, Edward Taylor, Bert Spinks, Howard Wright, James Hogan, James Powell.

Village Ordinance.

"No person shall keep a billard or pool room, bowling alley, shooting gallery or other similar place of amusement, or carry on any circus, theater, or other exhibitions or performances for money or hire, without having first obtained from the President of the village a license signed by him and countersigned by the Clerk of the village, permitting such amusements. Any person offending against the provisions of this ordinance, shall forfeit a penalty not to exceed $10 for each offense."

Board adjourned to meet the second Monday in March.   F. W. KNAPP, Clerk.
Dated, February 5, 1902.

Curfew and Census

While the W.C.T.U. was calling for exact enforcement of the curfew law, the State of New York called for another village census to be taken in 1902 and this reflected a slight increase in population in Marcellus over that of 1900.

13 Aug 1901 - " . . . communication was read from the W. C. T. U. asking for stricter enforcement of the curfew law. The matter was referred to the village policeman."

23 Dec 1901 - " . . . clerk was instructed to order the necessary blanks and to take an enumeration of the inhabitants of the village in the month of January as required by law."

Pool Room Ordinance

The continued request of some citizens to enforce more stringently the curfew law, caused Village residents, in 1902, to approve the creation of the office of Police Justice at the next election. Some also thought that pool halls or other such gathering places needed to be regulated more strictly, in the hope that such legislation might lead to the development of a more upright citizenry. One hundred years later, there are similar calls not only for curfews but also for the creation of wholesome amusement centers or gathering places for young people. The argument is very similar today – kids have nothing to do and appropriate diversions will keep them off the streets and away from undesirable gathering spots.

5 Feb 1902 - " . . . ordinance was duly published in the Marcellus Observer in the two issues preceding February 5, 1902, and the same was also posted in six places in said village."

Police Justice

The election of 1902 resulted in the reelection of Village President Sherman over John W. Scott, a former Trustee, who, though defeated in this election, would return to become President in 1903 and 1904. In that same election, another former Trustee, Charles J. Brown, would be elected to begin another tenure as a member of the Board, this time for eight years.

Voters approved overwhelmingly the position of Police Justice and in a special election about six weeks later. Edson Gillett was chosen to fill that position.

8 Mar 1902 - " . . . at said election, one hundred and six ballots were cast, of which, for President

Isaac N. Sherman received	60	
John W. Scott received	39	
Blank	3	
Spoiled	4	
(Total Vote)	106	

" . . . on questions submitted, Shall the office of Police Justice be established in Marcellus Village?

Yes	88
No	15
Spoiled	1
Blank	2
Total Vote	106

22 Apr 1902 - " . . . at special election, nine votes were cast, of which, for Police Justice:

Edson D. Gillett received	8
Blank	1
(Total Vote)	9

Police and Security

The summer of 1902 witnessed what had come to be an annual parade and inspection of the Fire Department. Village laborers, as usual, were hard at work doing their annual repair to village roads and sidewalks. There also was a rather large increase in the cost of part-time policemen during the month of June, reflecting the community's desire for more security during the summer months.

4 Jul 1902 - " . . . the Board expressed their hearty appreciation and commendation of the Marcellus Fire Department as witnessed in the parade and inspection drill of the 4th of July."

Clearly, security at the time was threatened by the danger of fire and disease. Sherman's Paper Mill suffered a loss due to fire in November of 1902 and another fire at Marcellus Falls in December, burned a boarding house to the ground. In January 1903, a second case of small pox broke out in the Town of Marcellus causing some schools to close

---

The Marcellus Observer
Friday, July 18, 1902
Proceedings of the Village Board
June 28, 1902

The following bills were accepted and . . . paid:

E. T. Taylor, police		$4.00
Howard Wright, police		$3.00
Rob. Whitmore, police		$3.00
John Spaulding, police		$5.60
P. Heenan, labor		$1.05
M. M. Whiting, labor	$3.50	
M. H. Spinks, labor	$3.50	
C. J. Brown, labor		$1.00
Marcellus Fire Dept Inspection		$50.00
Jas. Powell, police		$45.00

A petition was presented signed by numerous residents of Orange and Maple streets asking for a crosswalk from the sidewalk on the north side of Maple street to the corner of the sidewalk on Orange and Maple streets. By resolution, the street commissioner was authorized to put in a cement walk as asked for in the petition.

The Marcellus Observer
Friday, November 14, 1902
A Narrow Escape
Sherman's Paper Mill Suffers By Fire

———

Heroic Efforts of Employees and Others Succeed in Quelling the Flames Before serious Damage Was Done

The Marcellus Observer
Friday, January 9, 1903
A Second Case
Mrs. Lyle Carter Stricken with Small Pox

———

Precautionary Measures Taken by the Board of Education and the Board of Health

temporarily and the Board of Health to order the isolation of some half dozen persons. It would be a number of years before such fears would lessen, only to return in the 21st century, when the smallpox virus has become a biological weapon in the hands of terrorist groups.

The Marcellus Observer
Friday, October 16, 1903
Subscribers to Marcellus Telephone

The following is a list of the names of residents in the village and vicinity, as furnished by F. W. Knapp, who are subscribers to the Marcellus Telephone Co., and are or expect to be connected to the Central office in Edward Taylor's rooms in the Hooper Block.

20B Alvord, Warren, R., Hotel.
17A Baker, Chas. D., Residence.
17B Bishop, Charles, Residence.
14D Chase, Dr. J. M., Residence.
15C Chrisler, Dwight J., Residence.
19B Coon, D. DeForest, Residence.
14C Crown Mills No. 1, Office.
18C Crown Mills No. 2, Office.
11B Drake, Arthur E., General Store.
18A Drake, Arthur E., Residence.
11A Duggan, John, Saloon.
11D Elliot, Dr. James N. F., Residence.
15D Gallup, Emma S., Residence.
17C Hogan, James, Residence.
16D Hayes, William B., Residence.
16A Heenan, John T., Residence.
19A Jones, Henry S., Residence.
20C Jones, Chas. E., Residence.
11C Knapp, Frank W., Law Office.
12C Knapp, Frank W., Residence.
12D Kelly, Patrick J., Residence.
27 Kelly, John, Residence.
9A Kelly and Hogan, Shoe Store.
28 Lawless, M. J., Brick Paper Mill.
29 Lawless, M. J., Residence.
18B Moir, Edward, Residence.
21A Moak, Kassin, Residence.
20A Macnaughton, Rev. A. K., Res.
15A Mogg, Levi N., Residence.
13A Marcellus Railroad, Office.
17D Nightingale, Wm., Residence.
30 N..C.R.R. Sta., Freight Office.
22A Oatman, Lou, Residence.
31 Onondaga Paper Co., Office.
16B Rixon, Rev. H. L., Residence.
12B Roe, Cary A., Observer Office.
16B Roe, Cary A., Residence.
12A Roe, Rev. A., Residence.
32 Smith, Allen V., Barley Mill.
14A Smith, Allen V., Residence.
9B Schoonmaker, F. T., General Store.
14B Sherman, I. N., Paper Mill.
15B Sherman, J. R., Residence.
9C Williams, Fred, Store.
16C Walsh, T. F., Residence.
9D Weedon, F. W., Residence.
18D Weidman, Dr. C. E., Residence.
19C Woodbridge, J. E., Store.

Applications for instruments can be made to F. W. Knapp.

The Marcellus Observer
Friday, January 2, 1903
Fire At Marcellus Falls
Between 3 and 4 o'clock Wednesday morning, December 31, an alarm of fire was sounded by the whistle of the Onondaga Paper company's mill. It proved to be the Italian boarding house which soon burned to the ground with nearly all of its contents . . . A number of the boarders in the upper rooms barely escaped by jumping out of the windows. But for the timely warning of a little boy, his sister would have been burned as she was asleep when rescued.

1903 Brings Telephone Service to Marcellus

The beginning of the 20th century would not only witness an expanded rail service to Marcellus, but also the modern convenience of the telephone. One of the organizers of the Marcellus Telephone Company was Frank W. Knapp, " . . . a young lawyer who came to Marcellus from Tompkins County shortly after he was admitted to the bar. He bought the Gallup block on the corner of North and Main Streets, opened his law practice on the second floor, built the home at No. 2 Reed Avenue, and soon became involved in several projects for community improvement" (Heffernan 84). Early in 1903, the Village Board granted his company permission to set poles and string wires through the streets of Marcellus. The Village was also granted the right to use these poles for the installation of fire alarm fixtures, a concession that was very much appreciated by Marcellus residents. There were a number of informational meetings held and " . . . a committee was appointed to canvas the village to determine the approximate number of phones which could be placed in the village at an annual rental of $12.00" (MO 3/27/03). By the end of the year, the Marcellus Telephone Company, whose exchange was located in the Hooper Block building, at #7 North Street, numbered over 50 subscribers. This was a convenience which residents of Marcellus were eager to acquire and one that is so very common today. The advent of wireless telephone service to Village of Marcellus would take place about 100 years later, enhanced considerably by the erection, in 1998, of a large cellular tower on a hill overlooking the valley community.

7 Jan 1903 - " . . . that the Central New York Telephone and Telegraph Co. be given permission to set their poles and string their wires through the streets of Marcellus Village subject to the following restrictions:
    1st. That the poles shall be reasonably straight and subject to the approval of the Board of Trustees,
    2nd. That said poles shall be set at places designated by said Board of Trustees and if any dispute arises between said company and any abutting land owner as to where said poles shall be set, the same shall be referred to the Board of Trustees and their decision shall be final."

9 Feb 1903 - " . . . that in consideration therefore the said company agrees to paint and keep painted at reasonable intervals, all poles erected by them in said village, such color as such Board of Trustees may from time to time designate and also grants the said village a continuous right of way to support and carry the fire alarm fixtures upon any of the various poles erected, owned and occupied by said company in said village."

Project Bids

John W. Scott, a former Village Trustee, was elected President of the Board in 1903 and again in 1904. Neither election seemed to be very controversial in those years and the business of government seemed to involve the usual maintenance problems. Edson Gillett resigned his position as Police Justice, and the practice of bidding for government contracts became more common, even extending to such local matters as that of painting the Village Engine House. Today, New York State law requires such bidding practices, as well as the awarding of contracts to the lowest bidder. In the early years of the 20th century, there continued to be expanded rail service for the Village and this was enhanced by the construction of a new rail station just across the Main Street Bridge on what became known as Station Lane.

Trolley station at Marcellus

13 Apr 1903 - " . . . E. D. Gillett resigned his office as Police Justice and his resignation was accepted by the Board. It was moved and carried that Justice of the Peace A. E. Drake be designated to act as Police Justice during the vacancy in that office."

1 May 1903 - " . . . bids for painting the Engine House were opened and were as follows:

    J. E. Woodbridge $64.00
    C. H. Wright $79.50
    John Casey $95.00

It was moved and seconded that the contract be given to J. E. Woodbridge at the price bid."

The Marcellus Observer
Friday, October 2, 1903
Urgently Needed
Moderate Cost Dwellings for Rental in Marcellus

Once or twice previously we have noted in these columns the urgent need of more dwelling houses in Marcellus. The extensive additions of late made to the Crown Mills plant at both the upper and lower mills only accentuate the needs of the town along this line. Not a dwelling or part of one is obtainable, so far as we know, at any price. The large addition to the lower mill now approaching completion will call for additional help which must be imported and housed. A score of houses which could be rented at $6 to $8 per month would be quickly filled were they available . . ..

Marcellus as a village is thriving. It would do still better if it could have the modern comforts such as sister towns have, water works, sewers, electric lights and so on. It would seem that the time was ripe for the consideration of these things. In this connection the extension of the corporate lines of the village so that they should include the lower Crown Mill properties, and East hill up to "Dublin" and south to Slate hill, thereby bringing in considerable parts of the two railroad properties would be a step toward a solution of the whole problem. Why not have a "Greater Marcellus?"

A Greater Marcellus!

As the community expanded, there was some concern about having enough houses to rent in the Marcellus area by those who were employed in the local mills. With the additions recently made to the mill plants, and an expanding immigrant labor force, there was not only talk about more housing, but also a need, some thought, for an expansion of services in the Village, including postal delivery and even extention of the corporation's boundary limits.

Today, Marcellus is often referred to as a "bedroom community," with little need for the type of housing needed in a mill town. Housing, however, has increased in the 1990s,

---

The Marcellus Observer
Friday, January 15, 1904
Hardships of Villagers

The following letter written to the Post Standard by a resident of Marcellus village will be read with some interest by villagers:

There is one Postoffice Department scandal that has not, to my knowledge, been ventilated by the newspapers. Yet the facts are public property. Here they are:

If you live in a city or a village which meets certain prescribed qualifications, the government pays a man to bring our mail to your door from two to a half a dozen times a day, without cost to yourself.

If you live in a quiet country neighborhood your Uncle Samuel's employee delivers your mail daily, on condition that you provide a roadside box.

But if you live in a village too small for free delivery, you walk to the postoffice when you want your mail. For the privilege of taking this exercise your benevolent uncle charges you from 25 cents to $2 a year by way of box rent.

We cannot all live in Shepard Settlement or Syracuse. What have the people of those favored localities done for their country that they should be thus pampered by the government? Why should not the patriotic citizen of Fayetteville or Marcellus have his doorbell rung by the man in gray and save his box rent for car fares or foreign missions?

            Villager

---

especially in the number of multi-dwelling units for senior citizens, some of which were built on land formerly occupied by the mill itself. The village limits also expanded early in the century, and there are some today who are calling for another expansion of the village limits so as to include the Marcellus school complex.

9 Nov 1903 - " . . . petition signed by certain residents on First Street asking for a cross walk was read."

15 Mar 1904 - " . . . at said election, 9 ballots were cast, of which, for President, John W. Scott received 9."

Pool Halls and Chrisler Street

There was continued talk in the Village about issues of morality and the need for further regulation and promotion of virtue, especially as it related to the licensing of pool halls and the loitering of youth in the village. One hundred years later, that concern is still evident and residents wonder why youth have so little to do, urging that teen centers be created or that a curfew be imposed. The matter is one that defies quick solution, requiring the attention by each generation of parents and children, but never more so it seems than it did in the turn- of-the-century Marcellus.

> **The Marcellus Observer**
> **Friday, July 15, 1904**
> **Local Mention**
> The boy who haunts the streets after night fall without business or permission is cultivating a very dangerous habit. Any place where a boy has no business is a dangerous place for him, whether it is on the street, in the store or elsewhere. A boy that is all right, likes his home, friends, books or newspapers in preference to the class found on the streets without business. Business men of all kinds look upon a boy loafer as the dead beat of the future.

23 May 1904 - " . . . there appeared before the Board, Revs. Macnaughton, Rixon and Mott, in opposition to granting a license to C. A. Peck to run a pool room. Mr. Peck also appeared before the Board and stated his position in the matter and asked the Board to grant him a license. By resolution, the matter was laid on the table for two weeks."

6 Jun 1904 - " . . . petition was read signed by most of the ladies of the village asking that the Board refuse to grant a license to C. A. Peck. The petition was ordered filed. On motion made by Brown, seconded by Newton, the application of C. A. Peck for a pool room license was refused."

Main St. looking West, Marcellus, NY c1904

Mr. Peck was denied a pool hall permit, but the Villge Board did accept land for a new street that summer from Mr. and Mrs. Jonathan Chrisler and new housing would be constructed in that part of the Village.

11 Jul 1904 - " . . . that the deed made by Jonathan K. Chrisler and wife to the Village of Marcellus dated the 16th of June, 1904, and conveying to said Village what is now known as Chrisler Street in said Village, be accepted for highway purposes."

Fire Calls and Bicycles

In 1905, Edward Moir, the owner of the Crown Mills and former Village President, would again be elected to head the Village government. Along with him, Charles Dillon was elected as Trustee, a position he would hold for the next six years. Dillon and his wife Margaret were the children of Irish immigrants and as the century was unfolding were experiencing the upward social mobility that usually accompanied this next generation. He was a postal clerk in the Village at the time and the father of a growing family of six children.

As the Town of Marcellus expanded in the early years of the century, the Village Board was faced with the question of how the Village Fire Department should respond to fires outside the Village. In 1905, it was left to the discretion of the Fire Chief. Today, the Marcellus Fire Department responds not only to emergencies inside and outside the village but is also on call for mutual aid to fire departments in surrounding communities.

There was also a concern, in the beginning of the century, about bicycles on the sidewalks, similar to the issue of skateboards today and an ordinance was passed in 1905 to restrict bicycle use. In recent years, similar legislation was proposed to restrict skateboards on village streets but unlike 1905, no action was necessary because a skateboard facility was built in 2001 to accommodate these enthusiasts in Marcellus Park.

21 Mar 1905 - " . . . at said election, 48 ballots were cast, of which, for President, Edward Moir received 46

31 Mar 1905 - " . . . the question of taking fire apparatus to fires outside the Village be left to the Chief . . ."

30 Jun 1905 - " . . . complaint having been made to the Board in regard to a violation of the village ordinance pertaining to riding bicycles on the sidewalks, it was moved and carried that the village officer be instructed to use extreme vigilance in enforcing said ordinance, and that twelve copies of said ordinance be posted in conspicuous places in the village."

Village Water

One of the major concerns addressed by this Board was that of providing water for village residents. Although a number of years would pass before the matter was finalized, a committee was created in 1905 to draw up some plans and to search for a suitable source of water for Village residents.

10 Jul 1905 - " . . . moved and carried that four extra policemen be appointed and sworn in for Firemen's convention . . . . Edmund Reed appeared before the Board and asked for permission to run a water pipe in First and Reed Streets. The matter was laid over until the next meeting."

19 Dec 1905 - " . . . F. W. Knapp and C. J. Brown were appointed a committee to see what the springs known as Stuckney Springs could be obtained for . . .. that Geo. E. Smalley be employed to draw plans and specifications for water works and sewerage for Marcellus Village and the making of maps of the same as specified in his letter of Dec 8th to Mr. Main."

1 Feb 1906 - " . . . Mr. E. D. Smalley appeared before the Board and explained the maps prepared for the proposed system of water works and sewerage. It was moved and carried that said maps be placed on exhibition in the Engine House and that notice of the same be published in the Observer including the maps showing the proposed addition to the Village. It was moved and carried that the Clerk prepare the necessary petition for the signatures of the residents of the territory proposed to be annexed."

18 Feb 1906 - " . . . forward the plans for sewerage prepared by Mr. Smalley to State Commission of Health for their approval . . .. F. W. Knapp was authorized to obtain options on the Stuckney Springs on South Hill if possible."

An Extension of the Corporation of Marcellus Village Lot 15

Beginning at the Northeast corner of the original corporation of Marcellus Village, thence north 1500 feet to the north line of the Scotch Hill Road. Thence along the north line of said road north 83° west 300 feet. Thence along the north line of the same road north 61 1/2° west 550 feet to the east line of a road leading northerly to Marcellus Falls. Thence north 3° west 590 feet. Thence west 785 feet. Thence south 2640 feet to the north line of the original corporation of Marcellus Village. Thence east 325 feet to the center of North Street. Thence along the center of said street south 294 36/100 feet. Thence east 1335 84/100 feet to the place of beginning containing 70 acres of land.

Surveyed by E. D. Smalley, 1906

Scotch Hill Annexation

In 1906 Edward Moir was reelected as Village President. That year, a petition was presented to the Board of Trustees by residents north of the corporation line for annexation into the Village, including that area known today as the Lower Crown Mill property. Approved by a special vote of the residents, approximately 70 acres of land were annexed to the Village of Marcellus in 1906. There were some who questioned this annexation, arguing that the chief beneficiary was the Crown Woolen Mills, whose owner was also the President of the Village Board of Trustees. They argued that the addition of a water and sewer system as well as fire protection would be most beneficial for the area's largest employer, questioning whether the individual taxpayers of the Village should be burdened with extensive public works projects. There were others who claimed that in order for Marcellus to grow, annexation should be to the east, where there was already settlement and a trolley line, providing a larger taxable property for public works improvements. Still others argued that the addition of the lower Crown Mill property to the village would provide an even larger taxable base for such improvement. In the end, the vote total was 76, almost all of who were men, and 50 of those favored the northern annexation.

9 Apr 1906 - " . . . petition was presented to the Board asking for the annexation of certain territory lying to the north of the present boundaries of the Village, said petition being signed and duly verified by a majority of the voters in said territory, and who by a majority in value of the assessed valuation and accompanied by the consent of the members of the town board, living outside the Village. Resolved that a special election be called for April 24 from one to five o'clock p.m. to vote on the proposition of annexing the territory described in said petition. . . . Names of residents and qualified voters in said territory - Crown Mills, Edward Moir, Pres., Michael J. Thornton, Wm. Rutherford, Geo Austin & Anna Cone, Patrick Kilcoyne, William France, Michael Reynolds, Wm. Smith, James Bagguley, Wm. A. Gibson, Mrs. Anna Case, Phil Reynolds, Charles Arnold, G. S. Bigson, Charles Curtin, William Gibbon, E. L. Arnold, Wm. H. Sarr, John A. Shea, A. G. Rutherford."

NOTICE

"Shall the following described property be annexed to and form a part of the Village of Marcellus. Beginning at the N. E. corner of said village and then running north to the north line of Scotch Hill Road, thence westerly and northerly along said road and the valley road to a point opposite Crown Mills wool house, then west 785 feet, then south to the present village boundaries, then easterly along said north boundaries to place of beginning."

24 Apr 1906 - " . . . at the Special Election, . . . in accordance with the foregoing proposition, the whole number of votes cast was seventy-six (76), of which fifty voted yes for annexation and of which nineteen voted no against annexation, of which seven voted blank."

The vote to annex Scotch hill area to the Village Corporation. Vote was:

    Total   76
    Ayes   50
    No   19
    Blank   7

Water Works

By the end of the year, the question of annexation was no longer a topic of discussion but that of providing water for Village residents became a major issue: "At the turn of the century, Marcellus residents, both rural and village, were dependent on springs and wells for drinking water. Few homes boasted running water, and still fewer had bathrooms" (Heffernan 87. Many citizens wanted the convenience of a water works system as did local businesses and the Marcellus Fire Department, and the local paper reported a very spirited meeting in November, 1906 on the topic.

10 Dec 1906 " . . . J. Geo. Hellganz appeared before the Board and urged the establishing of a municipal water and electric light plant."

Electric Lights

Included in this discussion was that of providing electric lights for the Village and this too became a major topic. Some years earlier, Frank W. Knapp, who was also Village

---

The Marcellus Observer
Friday, November 16, 1906
Public Works Meeting
Rising Vote at Close Requests Trustees
To Call Election

The public meeting called last week Thursday evening in Alvord Hall by the Board of Trade for open discussion of having water works and sewers in Marcellus was well attended, fully two hundred being present. Some who spoke were requested to do so in advance, to prepare and present certain aspects of the question, and some who were known to object were also asked to be ready to speak.

P. J. Kelly of the fire department explained the condition of the existing fire protection equipment, 800 feet hose is available and some of it is not in the best condition. The department was about to ask, as their duty in properly protection against fire, for 800 feet of new hose. Also for five more cisterns to be built. Both would cost about $1,600. He timed the department the night of the Haster alarm and it was 15 minutes before the stream was ready.

The need of more cisterns is apparent when known that friction through 1,000 feet of hose makes a stream over two stories about impossible. Much property is menaced by the fact that, being located near a cistern, the heat if burning would make operating the pump engine impossible, such as the Methodist church and places opposite south the cistern being between the church and the south curb line; also the Presbyterian church and the row of stores across both Main and North streets. The raceway cistern near the Case residence was hardly accessible with brush growth. Mr. Kelly said he had talked with many fire chiefs from villages having water systems, and all were well pleased, the hydrants covered their town well, the people were no poorer and had the conveniences as well as perfect protection. This latter was the hope of the Fire Department, with the water system installed, and they were ready to do their share to secure it and their duty anyway.   . . .

Village President Edward Moir said the Village Board has been particular not to force this water and sewer question upon the people, preferring that the people should bring the issue and if major portion were found favorable, to submit the question to vote . . .. Mr. Moir was plain in saying that water and sewer conveniences must come from the pockets of the populace in one way or another and it was for them to decide whether or no they wanted it, for about $1,500 annually . . ..

E. D. Gillette said he was to speak on the effect water works might have on the business life of the community. .

Mr. Knapp confined his remarks to a definite reply to the question, "What Reduction in Insurance Rates might be expected if we have an effective fire department and water works system.

Clerk at the time, commissioned the building, on Nine Mile Creek, of " . . . a small electric generating plant at the site of Robert Baker's sawmill. With electricity generated from water power at Baker's dam, the plant made possible sixteen street lamps in the village, plus lights in some business places and homes" (Heffernan 84). Early in 1907, the Village Board granted a five-year franchise to Knapp to light the streets of the village.

11 Feb 1907 - " . . . an electric light franchise made by F. W. Knapp was taken up and the franchise was duly granted . . . said Board of Trustees hereby contracts with said Knapp to light the streets of said Village with arc lamps of an approved pattern and of least 1200 candle power for the term of five years, . . . said lamps to be lighted as soon at night as darkness may require and to continue until one a. m. and often six a.m. if so required by the Village Board. No lights to be turned on, on such moon light nights as the Village Board may think it unnecessary. Said Knapp agrees to furnish, install and keep in repair said lamps and light the streets of said village, placing said lamps where the Village Board may designate . . . "

Baker's Dam

In the years to come, this " . . . local source of power was becoming inadequate to meet the growing need and a line was extended to Camillus where power was obtained . . . from the first line bringing power from Niagara Falls into Central New York" (Heffernan 85). Knapp's venture, the Marcellus Lighting Company, was eventually merged with Empire Gas and Electric, a holding company and predecessor of the New York State Electric and Gas Company. This company continues to provide electric power to the Village today.

Other Concerns

The Board would also deal with other concerns that year, including Fire Department requests for new apparatus, enforcing fire code regulations and the trimming of trees in preparation for electric lighting. There were occasional liability claims against the Village for negligence, and similar to today, they usually involved the condition of a village street or sidewalk. There was also a concern about hydrophobia and the requirement by Trustees that dogs within the Village be muzzled.

1 Apr 1907 - " . . . P. J. Kelly appeared before the Board as a representative of the Fire Department, in advocacy of a chemical engine for the village. It was moved and carried that the Clerk write and get prices of such engines."

13 May 1907 - " . . . Resolved, that no person, partnership or corporation in Marcellus Village shall keep or store within fifty feet of any dwelling or other building within said Village more than five barrels of kerosene oil, gasoline, benzine, or other inflammable oils, without written permission from the Board of Trustees of said Village. For each violation of this ordinance, the offending party shall be liable to a fine of $10."

8 Jul 1907 - " . . . the street commissioner was given authority to trim such trees as were necessary to make the streets available for electric lighting."

11 Dec 1907 - " . . . the claim of John Spaulding for injury sustained in falling from bridge near his home on Cherry Street was compromised for the sum of $85.00"

The Marcellus Observer
Friday, October 12, 1907
Observer-ations
And now, Mr. Village, it becomes your deep and urgent responsibility to place a street light at the brow of that grade of walk at the east end of the Parsons property. No light is found from near the bridge to the one in front of Powell's and dark nights it is not possible to see a foot from one's nose up the incline and along the walk. Let somebody arrive in town with a friend on a dark night and if the darkness will not make one ashamed of their prided village, we miss our guess. Give us this light, even if you have to steal it from some less important spot.

13 Jan 1908 - " . . . Harold Spinks presented a claim against the Village for personal injury sustained in falling off the bridge on Cherry Street on Oct 12, 1907. The matter was laid over until the next meeting."

8 Feb 1908 - " . . . moved and carried that in view of the large number of dogs in the Village recently bitten by a mad dog, and in view of the fact that a number of those bitten have been taken with hydrophobia, it is requested that all owners of dogs thus bitten be requested to kill them immediately, and that all other dogs within the Village be muzzled until the further notice of the Board."

Village Water

The election of 1908 returned Edward Moir to the Village Presidency for another term, most of which was preoccupied with the issue of providing water for the residents of Marcellus. The issue was one that became very controversial, not only with village residents but also with members of the Board of Trustees as well. There were those who, being very suspicious of outside interests, favored using a local company for the construction project. Others, including Edward Moir, favored using Otisco Lake water rather than local springs, claiming that the water was better, especially for the washing process in the local woolen mills. Another faction argued that the amount of money bonded for the project was sufficient, while others claimed that the bonding would never be enough and should include sewer work as well as water works. "What good was water if there were no sewers?" many asked. Some claimed that the water pressure from Otisco Lake was not adequate for fighting fires nor for reaching the northern-most parts of the Village, while others maintained that local ponds had too much pressure. Some discussed the size of the water

The Marcellus Observer
Friday, April 24, 1908
Village Board Proceedings
It appears that the salary for police service and the care and lighting of lamps has been for years $1.50 per day, $45.00 a month, $540 per year, which amount has been in the annual budget. The police duties are from a reasonable hour in the forenoon to twelve o'clock at night, including watching for fires during those hours, care of the engine house and apparatus, filing, cleaning and lighting lamps, and ringing the village curfew bell. The salary for each duty has never been specified. So when electric lights were proposed it was understood that a saving would be effected by their use of the cost of oil and care, and this was estimated at $100 for oil and $340 for service, the $440 to apply toward the $840 for electric service. This would leave $200 for policing and care of engine house, and this amount was put in the last budget.
The electric lights were turned on November 1, yet since that time no cut has been made from the $540. The officer has added cleaning crosswalks to the duties. Following village election, the first meeting of the Board would have been held the second Monday in the month, but was not held until March 26, which President Moir could not attend, so at the meeting April 13 he placed himself on record as opposed to the action of the Board March 26 in continuing the policeman at the same salary.
There is a mistake somewhere, for no one expects pay for what they do not do, nor will the Village Board be able to pay $540 with $200 in the budget. So the matter will doubtless have reconsideration.

pipe, arguing the merits and cost of 6" vs. 8" sizes of cast iron. Still more thought that a local pond would eventually go dry, while the capacity of Otisco Lake would be dramatically increased when the State of New York authorized raising the dam to allow greater storage of water. The controversy led to some dramatic dissension between the President of the Village, Edward Moir, and the two trustees, Charles Dillon and Charles Brown. Throughout 1908, the issue found expression in weekly editions of *The Marcellus Observer*, each side claming their position as the proper one to follow.

Other Controversies

In addition to the dispute over a village water supply, there were other issues throughout the year. One was over the salary of the policeman, whose services would not be needed as often. The job of lamp lighter was eliminated when electric lights were turned on in 1907, and President Moir took exception when there was no change in the policeman's salary. One might also wonder if the previous November election results in the Town of Marcellus, when an entire slate of Democratic candidates, led by Patrick J. Kelly, was swept into office, had any effect on the Republican Moir. This was the first election of a Democratic ticket in 17 years and on that ticket was the Collector of Taxes, James Powell, who was also the village policeman at the time.

Another concern was that of allowing the young boys of the Village to use the back lot of the Engine Hall as a playground. At its first April meeting, the Board granted permission but two weeks later rescinded it.

13 Apr 1908 - " . . . Mr. Moir wished it noted in the minutes that he took exception to the action of the Board at the last meeting in engaging a policeman again at same salary as last year . . . moved and carried that the small boys of the village be allowed the use of the lot back of the engine house as a lot in which to play baseball."

29 Apr 1908 - " . . . the Board was called for the purpose of considering the matter of the Engine House lot. A petition was presented, protesting against the use of said lot for a ball ground. It was moved and carried that the boys be deprived of the right to play ball on back lot."

Village Water Works

The major concern of residents, however, continued to be that of providing water and the Board would, after considerable discussion begin to construct a water supply system that still operates today. There were many obstacles that had to be overcome, including the acquisition of a water supply as well as the actual construction of water pipes throughout the village. In addition, overcoming some of the local opposition was a major undertaking of the Board of Trustees. Eventually, a special election was held in the summer of 1908, when the residents of the village would vote to bond themselves for the construction of the system. It would continue to meet legal, engineering, construction and other obstacles throughout the year, and not until 1909 was the project finally completed.

11 May 1908 - " . . . Mr. Geo. M. Bailey for the Suburban Water Company appeared before the Board and made application for permission to lay and maintain water pipes through certain streets of the Village."

14 May 1908 - " . . . After considerable discussion of and participation in by numerous citizens of the Village, the application of said Suburban Water Company to lay pipes in Cherry, Main and North Streets was granted."

28 Jul 1908 - " . . . special election held at the Engine House in Marcellus Village, on the 28th of July, 1908, from 1 to 5 o'clock p.m., the following proposition was submitted: Resolved, that the Village of Marcellus, N.Y. bond itself for the sum of $25,000 and the proceeds of the same or

such part thereof as shall be necessary to be used for the purpose of establishing for said Village and the inhabitants thereof, a suitable supply of pure and wholesome water, as provided by Article VIII of the Village Laws. On said Resolution, one hundred and forty three votes were cast, of which eighty-eight voted yes, and forty three voted no, and twelve voted blanks."

25 Aug 1908 - " . . . moved by Dillon, seconded by Brown that a contract be entered into between this Board and Edson Brothers of Phelps, N.Y. to the effect that said Edson Bros. shall be engaged to draw off the water from Rockwell's pond and to employ such help as they may wish in doing so, and to do such other work as they may be directed to do by the Engineer in charge, and all work done shall be under the direction of engineer in charge. Dillon & Brown voted yes, Moir voted no. It was moved by Dillon and seconded by Brown that the attorneys for the Village secure permission of owners of pond and of the people below to draw off the water."

Village Reservoir

Selecting and obtaining the source of the water supply continued to be controversial, as were the attempts on the part of the Village to obtain easements for the laying of pipe. This issue of eminent domain, or public acquisition of private property remains controversial today and often results in situations that seem to pit government against private citizens. In recent years, attempts to obtain easements for the reconstruction and drainage of Reed Street met opposition from some residents and proving to be too costly resulted in a change in engineering designs.

21 Sep 1908 - " . . . whereas the Board of Trustees with their engineer, Mr. Bowman, have investigated many sources of supply of water, to wit, Otisco Lake, springs on Edmund Reed's farm, the Alvord Springs, and the Rockwell Springs, and said Rockwell Springs is a good, sufficient, and proper supply of water in said Village, it is there resolved, that the plans herein specified are hereby approved and the Rockwell Springs as the source of supply hereby accepted and approved . . . "

9 Nov 1908 - " . . . that the action of the Village Attorneys in making settlement with Mary Whitmore for $65.00 for right of way across her premises be approved by this Board. A contract was presented by Auburn and Syracuse R.R. Co. granting permission to lay water pipes under their tracks."

9 Nov 1908 - " . . . that an arc lamp be located near the bridge leading to East Hill, provided the Marcellus & Otisco Lake R.R. Co. pay over half the expense thereof."

17 Nov 1908 - " . . . whereas, the Board of Trustees have been unable to acquire the interest of Edward A. Cornwell in and to and the outlet of 'Rockwell's Pond' and the reason that said Cornwell asks a price largely in excess of the value of said interest and for that reason, it will be necessary to acquire said interest by condemnation, it is hereby Resolved, that the attorneys for the Board of Trustees be and they are hereby empowered and directed to offer said Cornwell the sum of three hundred dollars for his interest in and to the water of said stream of water, and in case the same is not accepted by said Cornwell, that said attorneys are hereby directed and empowered to commence condemnation proceedings to acquire the same as provided by law . . "

Water Question In The Courts

The debate over the village water supply continued throughout the fall and winter of 1908-09. The two Trustees, Charles Dillon and Charles Brown were determined to proceed with the project, the bonding for which had been authorized by the July vote of the village residents. The President of the Village, Edward Moir, was as determined to prevent its completion, refusing to sign the bond notes, and left the village when it came time for him to do so. The Trustees traveled to New York City, where Moir was located, to request his signature on the bond notes, but he refused. The issue finally ended in court, where Moir argued that he did have to sign the notes, challenging the July ballot, with the argument that the vote should be declared void since the 57 women who cast their ballots in that election did not have the right to vote on such matters. The controversy found much expression in the local newspaper, with both sides making arguments for their positions. This controversy even caused the contractor, the Edson Brothers, to cease operations until the matter was resolved. At the end of January 1909, the court ruled in Moir's favor, stating that women did not have the right to vote on such matters as loans. The issue would be resolved only with the election of a new President in March and another vote on the bonding issue in April. In those elections, the residents of the village turned to a former President, Sidney Slocombe, and vindicated the efforts of Chas Dillon by reelecting him as Trustee. The voters also reaffirmed their desire to finish not only the construction of the water works project but indebt themselves as well. The vote did not include the women of the village this time.

19 Dec 1908 - " . . . letter was read from the Engineer for the Board stating that Edson Bros had abandoned the contract or ceased work under the same . . .. Resolved that said Engineer be and is hereby empowered and directed to set hydrants, complete laying pipe at the corner of North and Main Streets and closing the same with the stop valve across the creek near Nightingale's, lay the pipe at the connection of the 6" and 8" conduits north of Whitmore's, setting the reducing valve and connections and building the valve box at Whitmore's, excavate the 10" flow off and do such necessary work at the pond as he thinks proper for the protection thereof. It is further resolved that said Engineer be and is hereby empowered to employ such help as may be necessary for the proper performance of the work specified."

1909-Water Works , Finally

With Sidney Slocombe as the new President of the Village, and Charles Dillon reelected as Trustee, the Board of Trustees proceeded to finalize the construction of the water works project. At its annual meeting, Charles E. Jones was appointed to replace the

The Marcellus Observer
Friday, January 29, 1909
Board Decision Upheld

A hearing was made in Rochester last Friday before the Appellate Division in the matter of Justice Andrews having decided that President Moir need not sign the Marcellus water bonds, which was carried up and decision is made Wednesday, sustaining the decision . . . if bonds, when signed, would be void because of defects in the proceedings authorizing their issuance, the writ should not be granted.

The votes of women should not be received. They only vote on the question as to whether a village shall be incorporated (sec. 12), and also upon a proposition to raise money by tax or assessment or for the dissolution of the village (sec. 41). The proposition to loan does not come within any of these classes of cases.

It is time now to call a halt on law. The taxpayers should get together, adjust this difference, get the bills from the attorneys to date, hire at fixed sum some one in law to study and report a way out, and build a good water system. Mr. Moir is quoted as stating that it is not law he seeks, but a legal and satisfactory system of water.

In view of this, voicing the sentiment of many citizens as expressed to us, we assume in their behalf, and of any other so minded, to appoint the night of Monday next, Feb. 1, at which time there will be a discussion of water system to date, and toward completing it without further legal cost. This issue closes our third year and we have never tried to run anything but the paper, so please do not infer we do now, except to avoid delaying such a meeting until after another issue. So if you are favorable, come out and we'll turn on the lights; if not, they will stay dark - and the costs will go merrily on.

The Marcellus Observer
Friday, February 26, 1909
A New President Nominated

A red hot caucus was held at Alvord Hall, Marcellus, Wednesday night . . .. On the first ballot 187 votes were cast, of which Sidney Slocombe had 117 and Edward Moir 70. The next for trustee gave Charles Dillon 123 and Rollin M. Stone 61. For treasurer J. E. Woodbridge had 104 and Austin C. Marble 57. For collector Clarence C. Woodford was given 95 and Eugene Seymour 52 . . . It was a water fight, the majority sentiment being to elect a village president who would sign the water bonds, Mr. Moir having refused to do so, as generally know.

long-time Clerk of the Village, Frank W. Knapp, and James Powell was rehired as policeman and street commissioner.

On April 1, 1909, the Board authorized the calling of a special election, to be held two weeks hence, to establish a system of water works and to bond the village for a figure not exceeding $25,000 to pay for the construction of the system. The voters approved rather overwhelmingly. In May, the Board of Trustees would negotiate for the acquisition of Rockwell Pond and in June another vote was taken authorizing the expenditure of an additional $7,000 to complete the water works. Again, the response of the voters was an overwhelming "yes."

16 Mar 1909 - " . . . at said election, eighty-five ballots were cast of which for President, Sidney Slocombe received 85, for Trustee, Charles Dillon received 85 . . . "

22 Mar 1909 - " . . . Charles E. Jones was appointed clerk for the ensuing year at a salary of $25, . . . the lot in the rear of the engine house was rented to George H. Smith for one year . . . James Powell was engaged as policeman and street overseer for the ensuing year at salary same as previous year."

1 Apr 1909 - " . . . a special election for and is hereby called . . . for the 14th day of April, 1909, at which election, the following proposition shall be and is hereby submitted to the qualified voters of said Village. Resolved, that there be established a system of water works for supplying the Village of Marcellus and its inhabitants with water, at an expense not exceeding the sum of $25,000 and that said Village borrow upon its bonds not exceeding the sum of $25,000 for the construction and maintenance thereof, said bonds to mature $1,000 annually commencing in the year 1914, and that an annual tax be and is hereby levied sufficient to pay the interest and maturing principal thereof."

14 Apr 1909 - " . . . whole number of ballots actually voted were 72. Number of ballots blank were 8, number of ballots yes were 50, number of ballots no were 14. Total number accounted for by us, are 72."

11 May 1909 - " . . . the President of this Board . . . is hereby empowered to effect a settlement with E. A. Cornwell for the liquidation of the riparian rights, titles and interest in the overflow of

Rockwell Springs, so called, at a price not to exceed the sum of twelve hundred and fifty

Marcellus is on the map. Electric lights, municipal water, what next? Tuesday, the municipal water pipes were filled with Rockwell pond water, the valves being opened for the first, and Wednesday night an informal test was made.

Tuesday night late, a stream was turned on near the Alvord House and thrown easily over the house, also at the school. Wednesday night about six, a single stream was put two feet or better higher than the top of the cross on the Catholic church. About 7:30, Officer Powell tapped the Presbyterian church bell as if for fire and several fire department members ran from the hotel steps to the engine house, where others waited, five men drew the hose cart to the hydrant in front of Coyne's barber shop made the connection, and water left the nozzle in less than four minutes. A second hose was also attached to the Powell House hydrant and both played together, throwing streams to the tops of the trees. A gauge had been set in Matteson's hardware which showed about 106 pounds, with one stream on this showed 87 and with two 63 pounds. All this with the reducing valve on.

There is no water in the reservoir, just the natural flow, enough to just cover the intake pipes. Other formal tests will be made when the reservoir is full, with the electric valve open, as in time of fire and when the systems of village pipes is complete, none being laid except on Cherry and Main streets. Tuesday, President Slocombe applied a test gauge at Schanzle's which showed 122 pounds pressure, and after the reducing valve was on, about 100.

The injunction was settled Saturday with E. A. Cornwell, paying him $1,000 as originally asked by him and $250 additional, his attorney's fee for the fight brought about by the refusal to pay, the thousand as he asked for at first.

($1,250.00) dollars. . . . to close the negotiations pending for the purchase of the riparian rights of the owners of Rockwell Pond and to have deeds executed for the same, . . . to proceed with the work of completing the retaining wall and . . . cribbing at the reservoir of the Village Water Supply and put the reservoir in condition for holding its full capacity of water."

14 Jun 1909 - " . . . whereas this Board has found that the sum of seven thousand ($7,000) dollars additional to the money already borrowed will be required to complete said system of water works, . . . a special election . . . called and held . . . on the 29th day of June, 1909 . . . "

29 Jun 1909 - " . . . whole number ballots actually counted were 53, whole number ballots actually blank were 3, whole number ballots actually yes were 43, whole number of ballots actually no were 7, whole number ballots actually accounted for by us were 53."

Total   53
Blank   3
Yes   43
No   7

Automobiles

It would seem that no concerns other than the water works faced the Board during those years, but by the summer of 1909 there were other issues. One was the growing popularity of the automobile that caused the Board to enact legislation regulating its speed on village streets.

7 Jul 1909 - " . . . no person shall drive or cause to be driven any automobile on any street of the Village of Marcellus faster than the rate of eight miles per hour; under a penalty of a fine of $10 or imprisonment for ten days for the first offence and a fine of $50 or imprisonment for sixty days for each subsequent offence, or both. . . . no person shall operate a motor cycle upon any sidewalk, upon any street of the Village of Marcellus under penalty of $10 fine or 10 days imprisonment for the first offense and a fine of $50 or sixty days imprisonment for each subsequent offence."

Orchard Street

In the fall of 1909, the Board of Trustees was asked by the Crown Mill Company to accept, as a village street, the street known as Orchard Row. On this street lived many residents whose employment was at the nearby Crown Mills, and the petition to accept the street also included a request to buy water mains for the street.

11 Oct 1909 - " . . . petition of the Crown Mill Co. asking the Board of Trustees to accept as Village Street the street known as Orchard Row and deed of same accompanying same presented

by John M. Moir, Treas. of said company . . . motion by Dillon, seconded by Brown, the petition was granted and the street known as Orchard Row accepted as a Village street. . . . Mr. Moir then . . . asked the Village to buy water mains in said street and that should the Village be without sufficient money to pipe said street, the Crown Mills would loan the Village the amount required and they be reimbursed by allowance for same on their taxes in two annual installments."

The Village Clock

Earlier that summer, Mr. And Mrs. George Case donated a large four-dial clock that was placed in the Methodist Church steeple. Later, lights on the faces illuminating it at night were added by donations from community residents and the Board of Trustees agreed at its October meeting to pay for the lighting of three of those dials. The Church later donated the clock to the Village, and the Village continues maintenance of the clock to this day. After almost 100 years, however, this Village landmark had weathered many storms and by 2002, the faces of the clock were badly deteriorated. With some very generous contributions by the Marcellus Olde Home Days Committee and Marcellus Historical Society, the Village Clock was restored, numbers made of copper replacing those made of wood and installed so long ago by Edgar Bartlett.

11 Oct 1909 - " . . . a communication from Edgar Bartlett, caretaker of the Town Clock, stating he was soliciting funds for the installation of one electric light over one of the dials of same, that he had Mr. Knapp's offer to furnish electricity for one light gratis and that he would light the other three dials for the sum of $12.00 per year. On motion by Brown, seconded by Dillon, the Board of Trustees assumes the lighting of the three dials at the expense of $12.00 annually."

New Fire Equipment

By December, the Fire Department requested and would be authorized to purchase new hose, some of which was needed to withstand the intense pressure that the new water works system had produced. Additionally, in the new year, the Board would authorize Officer Powell to complete a daily investigation of the electric lights in the Village, and to notify the Board of any that were not illuminated.

13 Dec 1909 - " . . . contract and agreement made . . . between the Eureka Fire Hose Company of New Jersey, . . . and the Village of Marcellus, . . . party of the first part hereby agrees to furnish the party of the second part, in good order, 300 feet of their Red Cross Brand of fire hose coupled complete, two and one half inches internal diameter, and capable of standing a pressure of 400 pounds per square inch, when delivered at 90 cents per foot."

12 Jan 1910 - " . . . meeting of the Board of Trustees of the Village of Marcellus held on above date at residence of Trustee Dillon, he being ill, all members present . . .. Resolved that Officer Powell be instructed to make a daily investigation of the electric lights of the Village during the ensuing month and make a report at the next regular meeting of this board of what lamps are not lighted, the date of same and the hour each day the power is turned on, and that a deduction of 50 cents for each lamp not lighted for each and every night same are not lighted will be made from bill for lighting the Village streets."

A New Struggle

By the end of the decade, the electric lights of the village of Marcellus seemed to be illuminating the start of a new struggle among residents. The issue was that of prohibition, and it was one that would last for two decades, with far reaching effects, not only in Marcellus, but also throughout the United States. One of the symbols of that struggle was the saloon and probably the most famous landmark in the Village of Marcellus was the then-one hundred-year-old building known as the Alvord House. Built about 1815, the Alvord House had already had a long history and had been the scene of

numerous assemblies and a place where the residents often expressed opinions and voted for or against any number of propositions. Until the Engine House was built in 1889, it hosted the monthly meetings of the Village Board of Trustees. By 1920, the Alvord House was dry, a victim of a struggle between those whose views seemed never to be reconciled.

A Man For All Seasons

As Marcellus entered the 20th century, several men seemed to be foremost in the community, and one of them was Frank W. Knapp. When he arrived in the community in 1894, he opened up a law office in a building that he bought on the corner of North and Main Streets. From that time, until his death 45 years later, Frank W. Knapp was involved in virtually every project that was undertaken in the Village at the time. He organized the telephone company and the electric company, was responsible for building several homes in the Village and had a special interest in the success of the local library. He served as Village Clerk for almost fifteen years, was involved in his church and other community organizations and seemed to embody the energy and the enthusiasm of the early 20th century. He was " . . . a man ahead of his time, one with great vision" (Heffernan 84), who loved his adopted community and served it well. When the community needed a "man for all seasons," Frank W. Knapp came forward, and his ambition became a legacy for future generations.

Chapter 8 - A Peaceful Village in 1910

By the start of the next decade, the issue of the water works seemed to have been resolved and Sidney Slocombe, like Cincinatus of old, went back to his business as a tinsmith. A grocer by trade, the newly elected President of the Village in 1910 was Fred A. Thompson and he would be reelected several times thereafter. Thompson was apparently well liked by the voters and at his death in 1921, the eulogies made much mention of the concern he had for his adopted village. Elected along with Thompson was

North Side of Main Street, Marcellus, N. Y.

F. T. Schoonmaker, a merchant like Thompson, who would hold a single term as Village Trustee. With a new Village Board, it did not seem that there was much of the rancor that had been evident in earlier years. The normal operations of village government were

---

The Marcellus Observer
Friday, March 18, 1910
Powell Has Broken Nose
With Taylor, They Hold Up City Horse Thief and Have Run and Scrimmage

The home of heroes. That's Marcellus. They only await the opportunity. When Andy Carnegie hears of us there'll be a library. And in it we'll have a complete set of those Diamond Dick's and Wild Wests, with local doings down to date. The opportunity came by wire. Last week Tuesday, James Powell went in the Bell telephone office to answer a call, which told him to be on the watch for a young man with a stolen rig. He then turned into Main street and told Albert Taylor about it, Taylor and Burt Hickman had both noticed the rig pass, the horse seemed worn out, and was then passing the M. E. church. Powell and Taylor hurried across lots near the creamery and when there saw the horse had fallen and the driver trying to unhitch. They offered to help and finally Powell told the fellow he was under arrest and they brought him cross lots. . . When back of Sарr's he plugged Jim one, jumped away and ran south. They chased, got him down, and in the scrimmage he kicked officer Powell in the face breaking his nose. City officials were advised by phone and came in an auto for him. Powell went there to appear Friday. They gave up trying to unhitch the horse, being worn out and covered it. Here First-Aid-to-the Injured Tom Wilson came to the rescue, rubbing the old horse, applied something in a long black bottle, it did the bizness and the horse was drawn to Walsh's stables where it is all right now. Tug saved the horse, and is looking for $2.

---

conducted with little quarrel. The water system was expanded and Village officials were

appeared including Officer Powell, whose altercation with a horse thief made headlines in the local newspaper.

The Marcellus Observer
Friday, April 15, 1910
To Boom Fire Department
Rousing Gathering Held and Call Issued by Trustees for Meeting April 18

A rousing meeting of firemen and citizens met with the new board of trustees on their call Monday night in the engine house, new life was infused in the local fire department and a call issued for a department meeting next Monday night. . . .

Chief Howard Wright was called on. He said there was lack of interest, failure of good turnout for practice, dues and fines had not been laid or paid, officers inactive, meetings not held. He criticised the former board for buying apparatus without consulting the department, . . .

James Armstrong . . . felt something lacking for an efficient department. Officers should command and men would follow the right leader. Such organization needed constant individual effort.

P. J. Kelly said the organization lacked many things. . . . Drilling had not been carried out, rules not enforced, tendency for few to do the work, a squad haul trucks to the fire and department members along the walk or running empty handed to watch the fire and see the fun. Reorganization might be wise, to stir up the inactive members.

W. J. Matteson said nothing could be done with laws, rules and fines, that interest would awaken members.

Fred O'Brien said the department lacked a certain dignity, which meant discipline, recognition of the authority of officials. Rules are lax, members of taxpayers gave way to youthful interest, resulting in none at all. It had of late resolved into uniforms, parades and a good time rather than work and sense of duty. Meeting were as necessary as practice and equipment. Many members were beyond the sound of the fire bell, in the country or removed from town. The roster would show much deadwood.

A. E. Drake told of similar conditions in the past, believing them to come every so often, and needing, as now, a stirring up.

Trustee Schoonmaker . . .volunteering to become an active member of a new organization. . . . Chief Wright thought this incorporation obsolete unless renewed every few years, which had not been done.

F. W. Knapp thought that a small department, drilled and active, with the present water system and no need of engine nor pumping, would be adequate to handle any ordinary fire, while if large, volunteers would be found to assist. . . .

Deciding that every encouragement should be offered present members of the department, and in fact, as stated, no thought is held to take from the department's hands any authority, but simply to inspire it to better work, conclusion was reached that Chief Wright should issue call for a special meeting to be held next Monday night, April 18, at 8:00 o'clock. . . . The rules adopted long since that members should be dropped upon failure to attend a special meeting called by the Chief will be enforced. So a full attendance is imperative, and from this it is expected that the Marcellus Fire Department, which has a long and admirable record, will take to itself a new lease of life.

---

15 Mar 1910 - " . . . at said election thirty three (33) ballots were cast, of which, for President, Fred A. Thompson received thirty-three, . . . "

22 Mar 1910 - " . . . James Powell was appointed Village Officer, Water Superintendent and Street Commissioner at the salary of $700, $400 of which to be paid from Village funds and $300 from the Water funds."

22 Mar 1910 - " . . . there being no nominations presented for the appointment of Chief and Assistant Chiefs of the Fire Department, the Clerk was instructed to request firemen to submit nominations . . ."

12 Apr 1910 - " . . . F. W. Knapp made formal application for tapping the water main to supply the property known as the Beehive . . . was duly granted."

Dissension in Fire Department

There was some concern, however, in the ranks of the firemen. The department had nominated no one for Chief and Assistant Chiefs and there were many grievances, some directed at the Board, others at the firemen. Meetings to express concern and revive interest in the Fire Department were held and by the end of April, the "Firemen Take On New Life" (MO 4/22/10)

Village House Cleaning and Census Forms

As spring came to Marcellus in 1910, the census takers were out in force, completing their work for the 1910 federal enumeration and there was also some concern expressed in the local paper about the need for improving the looks of the Village, including the need for a bank, a ballpark and a public library. The

Board of Trustees responded to the residents' requests and throughout the rest of the year approved a number of resolutions that would promote local improvement. The dirt streets were still in need of paving and some residents had to be reminded to pay their water bills, trim their grass and hedges and repair the sidewalks. However, the local Civics Club placed waste cans on Village streets and a prominent place in the Village center was selected for the W.C.T.U. fountain.

23 Apr 1910 - " . . . the Supt. of Water was instructed to shut off the water from the premises of Ella A. Peck on Monday, . . . if all arrears were not paid on that date. . . . the Board then reviewed to Main Street to select site for fountain and on motion by Schoonmaker, seconded by Dillon the same be placed in the center of Knapp Block on Main Street."

9 May 1910 - " . . . the Civics Club requested permission to place on the Village streets cans for collection of waste paper, etc. and for locations for same, and President appointed Trustee Schoonmaker as Committee on same."

13 May 1910 - " . . . John E. Griffen appeared before the Board asking consideration from the Board for a public playground and after general discussion, on motion by Dillon, seconded by Schoonmaker, the sum of $50.00 was voted applied thereto."

13 Jun 1910 - " . . . take proper steps to have grass bordering on the walks of Cherry Street mown, to investigate the feasibility of the removal of the hedges on property of Mrs. Sarah Beach on West Main St., also the repairs of sidewalk adjacent to the property of Sarah D. Baker on Cherry St., and the English property on Main St. . . . to investigate suitable fence to surround the reservoir. . . . to place a For Sale ad in the Syracuse Post Standard and the Rochester Democrat-Chronicle describing the Fire Engine now offered for sale by this Board."

The Marcellus Observer
Friday, April 8, 1910
Village House Cleaning

This is the time of year when one's thoughts turn toward house cleaning and the general improvement of one's home, and it seems an appropriate time for thinking what we can do to improve the looks of our village. "God made the country, but man made the town," so if our town is not beautiful and attractive we have only ourselves to blame. It is said the reason the streets of Holland are so clean is because every person sweeps in front of his own door, so let us each ask ourselves whether we are doing all we can to make our homes and our business places attractive.

Have we any unsightly sheds or buildings on our premises that should be torn down - buildings that are an eyesore to our neighbors? Are thee alleys provided behind all the stores, so that delivery wagons can load and unload at the rear door and not obstruct the sidewalks? One merchant at least keeps a beautiful green parking in front of his store and allows no driving on it. Why couldn't the others do so? Certainly Uncle Sam could afford to pay for keeping the postoffice corner in good condition.

A much-needed fountain for man and beast was purchased by the W.C.T.U. last fall, and the Village Board was asked to set it up. Most towns would be glad of a gift of that kind and thank the donors. Our fountain is still waiting a change to show how useful and ornamental it can be. The Civics Club has taken a step forward and purchased trash cans, which will be placed in convenient localities so that papers, banana skins and other trash can be deposited in them and not be thrown upon the streets. Will the parents and teachers please impress upon the children the need of their cooperation in the use of the cans? When the autos were speeding through our village last Sunday, raising a perfect cloud of dust, the need of street sprinkling was again made apparent. Why can't a sprinkler be brought and the streets sprinkled, now that we have plenty of water, and a slight tax, say a dollar a year, be levied on each family? If would certainly be worth that for the comfort we would get out of it. If we want our village to grow we must make it the most attractive village in this part of the state then perhaps someone would give us a park, a town hall and a public library.

A Library and a Bank

The demand for a public library grew and a July 1st editorial in *The Marcellus Observer* that summer argued, " . . . the value of a library to a community cannot be over estimated. In addition to being a matter of great convenience, it exerts an influence for culture and refinement and keeps young people off the streets by affording them a pleasant place in which to spend an evening" (MO 7/1/10). It would be several more years, however, before the Marcellus Free Library was established. In October of 1910, the First National Bank of Marcellus opened for business. Owned and operated by local businessmen and community leaders, it would help to provide many services for the

developing community of Marcellus, its businesses, and its residents.

Complaints

The fall also witnessed a revival of what was referred to as hoodlumism and calls for stricter enforcement of the curfew laws for those under the age of sixteen. The use of shaving cream by today's youth seems to have replaced the whitewash that was used by the youth of 90 years ago, and that might be considered a welcome change, environmentally.

There were also complaints made to the Board about the dumping of garbage on village streets and the littering that remains a problem today. The Village Highway Department maintains a street/sidewalk sweeper for such purpose and there is a village clean-up held in the spring of each year. Nevertheless, an all too familiar problem for the Village administration is the refuse that is sometimes left in front of an apartment when a tenant decides to move or is evicted. This is one of the reasons why the Village employs a building inspector, whose duty it is to enforce the uniform code for fire and sanitary safety.

The Marcellus Observer
Friday, November 4, 1910
Halloween Hoodlumism

We do not honestly believe there is a village in the United States where such lawlessness could be carried out and go unpunished as was done here Monday night. The police protection is simply nil. Hoodlums care no more for our officers of the law than for a gentle south wind. Even a group of respectable onlookers stood and laughed. We have quit long since "criticizing" the trustees. Their proceedings go unpublished, with all comment. But the whitewashing of Morton's nice carriage is the limit.

Trustee Dillon was out and Peter Egan sworn in, but Officer Powell needs to make arrests thru the year to win.

The Marcellus Observer
Friday, November 11 1910
Snow Plows

The village board will receive sealed bids for plowing the snow from the sidewalks in the corporation during the coming winter. The board prefer that two plows and two horses be sued, that the walks may be cleaned in time for the people working in the mills. This can only be done by one plow going to the lower end of the village and one in the middle and upper end. Please bid on the early trip and also on what succeeding trips are necessary.

Chas. Dillon, Committee

The Marcellus Observer
Friday, November 11, 1910
Census Returns

The population of the incorporated villages of the county for the last three censuses follows:

	1910	1900	1890
Baldwinsville	3,054	2,992	3,040
Camillus	763	567	487
Eastwood	810	...	...
East Syracuse	3,274	...	...
Elbridge	462	549	693
Fabius	344	387	312
Fayetteville	1,481	1,304	1,410
Jordan	978	1,118	1,271
Liverpool	1,389	1,133	1,284
Manlius	1,322	1,219	942
Marcellus	917	589	563
Solvay	5,139	3,493	...
Skaneateles	1,615	1,495	1,359
Tully	551	574	498

The Village administration also found itself in some minor litigation in 1910 involving claims for damages received. That also rings familiar tunes today. In recent years, claims have been made against the Village for such damages as sewer back-ups, cracked sidewalks, and blown automobile tires. In 1910, the Marcellus Telephone Exchange also offered the use of its telephone lines for notifying the Fire Station in case of fire, a practice similar in some respects to calling 911 today.

19 Dec 1910 - " . . . complaint having been made regarding tenants in Parsons Block dumping refuse in gutters. Officer Power was instructed to request Dr. Parsons to have same stopped."

28 Dec 1910 - " . . . to consider a claim for damages by Daniel Conroy for injuries received by being thrown from his wagon by reason of obstructions in the highway in front of resident of Louis W. Scott on North Street on or about Oct. 1st, 1910. The Board, after questioning Commissioner Powell and W. F. Malay (the quarryman) as to the cause of the obstruction, passed the following resolution. Resolved, that the President be instructed to inform Mr. Malay that the Board of Trustees considered him alone to blame for the accident to Mr. Conroy and if Mr. Conroy sued the Village, this Board would hold both Mr. Scott and Mr. Malay responsible therefor."

9 Jan 1911 - " . . . in view of the fact that continuous service is now given at the Marcellus Telephone Exchange, F. W. Knapp hereby offers the . . . use of the telephone lines in notifying the Central Station in case of fire . . .. the offer, . . . is hereby accepted and this Board hereby offers the sum of $1.00 to the operator of the Exchange for receiving the alarm causing the fire bell to be rung and notifying the firemen of the location of the fire. The said sum to be paid by the owner of the property on fire."

Census Returns

By the end of the year, the census returns of the villages and towns of Onondaga County were published. "Of the villages of the county all show gains in the last decade except Elbridge, Jordan, Fabius and Tully. Skaneateles shows 1,615 against 1,495 in 1900, a gain of about 8 per cent. Both Marcellus and Camillus show nice gains, due, doubtless, to their thriving manufacturing interest," stated *The Marcellus Observer* in November of that year. 1910 appeared to have been a good year for people in Marcellus reflecting the optimism of the national progressive movement at the time. Prices for goods were lower than they were in 1875 and wages were higher. Attempts to improve social and economic conditions could be seen in the demands for a public library, parks, playgrounds and even a W.C.T.U. fountain. 1911 would witness more of this same commitment to improving the quality of life in a small American town in Central New York.

Trees and Streets

In the Village election of 1911, voter turnout numbered only 27 and Fred H. Thompson was returned for a second term. Frank H. Gillette was elected to replace the retiring Charles Dillon as Trustee. There was concern about the trimming of trees on village streets but even more interest about the condition of the streets themselves, particularly Main, North and Cherry (South) Streets. Working with Marcellus Town

Supervisor Patrick J. Kelly, the Village Board approved the construction of a state highway through the Village along those streets, part of what is known as Route 174 today.

10 Apr 1911 - " . . . there being many trees on the streets of the Village needing trimming by reason of their branches hanging too closely to the sidewalks as well as depriving the street of the best results of the electric lights, be it Resolved, that property owners on whose premises are trees that need trimming, that they be notified to have said trees properly trimmed on or before a given date and should they fail to comply with said notice the work will be done by the Village and the expense thereof charged to the property owners and that the same trimming shall be under the supervision of the Sidewalk Committee."

8 May 1911 - " . . . Supervisor Kelly offered some numbers regarding the petition to be presented by the Village for the construction of State highway through the Village, through North, Main and Cherry Streets, that there was probability of obtaining the same in 1912, and asking the Board to take necessary steps to procure said improved highway."

Loitering, Bicycles and Sidewalks

The Board was still concerned about loitering on village streets and the safety of pedestrians on the sidewalks and made a concerted effort to enforce the village ordinances regarding these matters. The local paper echoed these sentiments in both cartoon and editorial fashion, especially during the summer months when pranks and mischief were more common. Similar sentiments exist today. There are many who deplore the gathering of young people on street corners and the disregard that some skateboarders have for those who use the sidewalks. They argue that the Village Board takes action against those who seem to pose a threat or interfere with their sense of security and well-being. In response, Village government would not only enforce the law but today it has also sought to involve more residents in such organizations as Neighborhood Watch and has also enlisted the support of the Town Recreation Department and other groups so as to meet what has become a rather serious problem with so many young people in our society today - lack of parental guidance and an apathy that can often lead to restlessness and trouble.

Board of Health and King Booze

The Marcellus Observer
Friday, May 12 1911
Board of Trustees

All persons are forbidden to congregate or assembly on any steps, sidewalk, or in doorways within the limits of the corporation, or to congregate upon the sidewalks of said village at any time in such a manner as to obstruct the same; or to disturb the peace or quiet of said village by shouting or other improper noise, under a penalty of not to exceed ten dollars for each offense.

Ordinance pertaining to bicycle riding on sidewalks in Marcellus village:
1. Every bicycle shall be provided with a bell, which shall be rung 20 yards before meeting or passing people.
2. Wheelmen when meeting a passing pedestrian shall get off from the walk, unless the pedestrian waives his or her right by giving half the walk.
3. The speed shall not exceed eight miles an hour.
4. Wheelmen shall not ride later than one-half hour after sundown.
5. Wheelemen shall not ride on the south side of Maple street, or the west side of orange street, or the south side of Main street west of the cross walk by the M. E. church.
6. No wheelman shall ride on the sidewalk on Sunday after 9 0'clock a.m.
All penalties for the violation of the foregoing ordinances shall be sued for and recovered in the name of the Village of Marcellus.

The Marcellus Observer
Friday, May 26 1911
Enforcing the Ordinances

Three arrests for violation of the recently published village ordinance and appearance before Justice Coon were made Tuesday afternoon, each fined $5 on their plea of guilty, and fines paid. President Thompson, trustee Schoonmaker, clerk Jones, officer Powell, and several residents interested in law and order were present. It is very evident that there is "something doing" in our erstwhile decent village. Other arrests are to follow for the same offense, and there are various other offenses to be investigated covered by the ordinance.

Village President Thompson would like to have a talk with all those who ride bicycles, about the enforcing of the village bicycle ordinance. He will be glad to explain, if you will call at the store. A full understanding is desired before action is taken against anyone, saving some unpleasantness; but it is to be understood that the law is to be enforced. Unless you understand it and mean to comply, it is best to see him. Those who ride on walks, without bells, feeling the walks are theirs as much as pedestrians, are wrong. It is a privilege, not a right. Unless all can understand and comply with the ordinance it may result in another, that they must ride in the road instead of on the walk - that is, be excluded entirely from the smoother riding. Several report being nearly run down and all are alive to this question.

As part of a continuing effort to improve the health of Village residents, the Board of Trustees would appoint Dr. C. E. Weidman as its Health Officer and reappoint members to the Board of Health for the Village, an agency whose duties are now fulfilled at the county rather than the village level.

9 Oct 1911 - " . . . Dr. C. E. Weidman was appointed Health Officer for the Village for a full term and H. S. Jones was appointed a member of the Board of Health for a term of three years, term to expire at the fiscal year, 1914. The Board of Health now consisting of Martin Hogan Jr., term expires 1912; Geo. H. Smith, term expires 1913; H. S. Jones, term expires 1914; C. E. Weidman, Health Officer."

No issue provoked more heated discussion and sentiment, however, than the Temperance Movement. The voters of the town would again be asked, as they had two years earlier, to vote on four excise questions regarding the licensing and regulation of alcohol and the local paper was filled with arguments pro and con. The vote at the end was summarized by the a report in *The Marcellus Observer* entitled "King Booze Wins." The forces of temperance were far from dead, however, and the issue would be brought up again and again until Marcellus finally went dry in 1914.

Good Roads and Reservoir Fence

The year began with a concerted effort by the Village Board to improve the roads through the Village of Marcellus and early in the year approved the construction of a state highway through the Village. The construction of roads was very heavy work in those days when most of the road workers were Italian immigrants and " . . . were openly referred to in the press as 'dagoes' or 'guineas'" (Heffernan 83), a reflection of Nativist attitudes that a generation earlier were directed at the Irish immigrants who settled in the area. That year also would see the construction of a fence around the village water reservoir, an enclosure that would not be replaced until 1998.

23 Jan 1912 - " . . . meeting . . . to consider the plans of additional pavement on Main Street to be constructed when the State road is being built through the Village, via North, Main and Cherry Streets."

8 Mar 1912 - " . . . whereas the State Commission on Highways has prepared plans, specifications and estimate of cost for the improvement of said Village Street, to be known as the Marietta-Marcellus County Highway, . . . that the excess cost to be borne by the Village is $1,038.94."

11 Mar 1912 - " . . . clerk reported correspondence with Knox Fence Co. relative to fence for reservoir, also contract duly signed by Fence Co. received and the same was accepted with the words "with scroll" inserted in description of gates, . . . "

Election of 1912

The 1912 election produced a large voter turnout, fashioned it would seem by the popularity of the candidates as well as the temperance issue. In that election, long-time Trustee Charles Dillon was defeated in his bid to become President of the Village by the incumbent Fred A. Thompson. A new term also witnessed the removal of a long-time Village employee. James Powell, who had been the Village Constable, as well as the highway, fire, and water superintendent, was not rehired, a victim, it appears of both budget considerations and local politics, and one which would be regretted by the middle of the summer.

The Marcellus Observer
Friday, April 19, 1912
Communication

I wish to ask our board of trustees or village president to publish in the paper their reason for not employing a police officer. Are we to go without the protection of a village officer or policeman, without street patrol, watching for fires, all the various duties which should be performed?

A Taxpayer

---

19 Mar 1912 - " . . . the whole number of votes cast at said election was two hundred seventeen (217), of which, for President Charles Dillon received ninety-one, Fred A. Thompson received one hundred twenty-three, blank were three; for Trustee for two years, Dwight C. Baker received ninety-eight, James E. Woodbridge received one hundred seventeen, blank were two. . . . "

1 Apr 1912 - " . . . motion by Mr. Thompson, seconded by Woodbridge it was voted to dispense with the services of James Powell as policeman . . . Gillett voting no."

Water Use and Curfew Bell

The Village Board encouraged residents to use all of the water they wanted so as to keep the water running freely (to keep it from becoming stale, was the argument), but many, who felt that its free and unrestricted use was a burden on the taxpayer, would later criticize this. The Board allowed some of the residents to construct their own sewer system on First and Reed Streets, but again was criticized because this action only

---

The Marcellus Observer
Friday, April 19, 1912
Notice To Water Consumers

The Village Trustees have decided to allow every family who has water connections to use all the water they wish during the year 1912 for house, lawn or street for the low sum of $5 per year. In using the water freely you will avoid using the stale water that stands in the pipe leading from the main pipe to the house and the water will always be fresh and good to drink

The Marcellus Observer
Friday, June 28, 1912
Village Affairs

Attention has been directed to the increasing use of the village water, especially from the public fire hydrants, and for private purposes. . . .

Naturally, Marcellus water is for Marcellus people, yet its free and unrestricted use, with or without authority, and especially in cases where its use should result in a just revenue to lessen the burden of the taxpayers, is not permitted by law in Marcellus . . .

This freedom and carelessness in the use of public property has no doubt grown out of the need for running the water to keep it in good condition . . . but neither the village president nor any of the village officers has the power intrusted to him by law to give away a public commodity for which bonds have been issued and regular rules and rates determined.

The Marcellus Observer
Friday, April 19, 1912
The Curfew Enforced

From April 1 to October 1, the time for the curfew bell to ring is 9 P.M. If the Presbyterian bell does not right at this time the clock will strike 9, and will notify boys and girls under 16 years of age that it is their duty to go home and the duty of their parents to see that they are home for the night. If children disobey the curfew ordinance the Village Trustees will understand by this that their parents wish to pay a fine of $5 for disobeying the law. It is now the duty of the parents to see that their children obey the village ordinance.

The Marcellus Observer
Friday, April 19, 1912
Observer --Ations

We recall that Mr. Moir advocated strongly throughout the water agitation in favor of building sewers together with the laying of piping for the water system, someway, to satisfy the certain demand. His arguments were tabooed. Today people find the absolute need of sewage to the extent that residents along First and Reed streets are making plans to build a sewer, with septic tank, the cost to be shared jointly. Thus it comes about, and will in all the future, that those well able will build and have the advantages of sewerage. The general public will not be so favored. Those of us who are not able to build our own will still depend on the long distance telephones.

While recalling, we also remember that Mr. Moir held that retaining Officer Powell was an unwise financial burden to the village, but in this he was opposed by Trustees Dillon and Brown.

---

benefited those who were able to afford it. The Board stressed the issue of curfew enforcement and by July found it necessary to hire a new policeman, Ephraim Spinks, to enforce the ordinances. Additionally, Charles E. Jones, a local undertaker who had served as Village Clerk for a number of terms, resigned. Howard White would be appointed to that position and would remain Village Clerk for the rest of the decade. A five-year contract with Frank W. Knapp for lighting the village streets was approved and this found much favor with local residents.

2 May 1912 - " . . . it was voted to post the Village reservoir against fishing, . . . it was voted to employ Bert Chapman as watchman at the reservoir during the month of May at $2.00 per month."

13 May 1912 - " . . . petition presented by F. W. Knapp in behalf of residents of First and Reed Streets asking permission to construct, maintain and operate a sewer in First Street, extending from Maiden Lane to Reed Street, . . . "

8 Jul 1912 - " . . . resignation of C. E. Jones as Clerk be accepted. Carried. Moved by Gillett that Howard Wright be employed as clerk for the balance of year. Carried."

23 Jul 1912 - " . . . motion made by Woodbridge that Ephraim Spinks be engaged as policeman and to do other work as required."

11 Nov 1912 - " . . . Mr. Knapp being present, submitted for the approval of the Board a contract for lighting the Village streets for a term of five years, extending from Dec. 1, 1912 to Dec. 1, 1917. After reading the contract, it was decided to accept the same and same was signed by Mr. Knapp and all members of the Board."

1913 - Street Signs and Petitions

In 1913, the Village Board engaged the services of Edgar Bartlett to make signs for the Village streets and also encouraged " . . . numbering houses in a thorough and systematic manner at a small expense. It is hoped that every house owner will avail himself of this opportunity and have his house numbered. When houses are properly numbered you have a directory that will direct. The Village Board is very much in favor of this work being done" (MO 2/21/13). While the Board received some congratulations in the press about its handling of many village affairs, it also received several petitions from village residents to correct some problems. The number of chickens and other fowl that were allowed to run at large throughout the Village annoyed some people and the Board responded with an ordinance that would order this practice stopped. As recently as 2001, the Village Board was again requested to have this ordinance enforced when a resident was found to be in violation.

The Marcellus Observer
Friday, January 17, 1913
Petition
A petition was handed the Board, as follows:
"We, the undersigned, annoyed as we have been by the chickens and fowls of our neighbors trespassing on our premises, petition your honorable Board to take such action as may be within your power to compel the people in the village who own hens to keep them on their own premises . . .

13 Jan 1913 - " . . . it was decided that Edgar Bartlett be engaged to make street signs of the streets of the Village and to post the same at the corners."

6 Feb 1913 - " . . . that the owners of fowls be restrained from allowed same to run at large in the highways and other public places in accordance with section 90 of the Village laws."

> **The Marcellus Observer**
> **Friday, February 21, 1913**
> **Village Affairs Looking Up — At Good Lights and Many Other Things**
> Marcellus has never been lighted so satisfactorily as now, and we congratulate the Village Board on their study as to cost, location, kind of lamp, ect., with Mr. Knapp. For the present service costs practically the same as before, with twice the number of lamps. . . . The village is lighted perfectly, one may say, still a few changes will be made to further improve when poles, etc., will make this possible. . .
> While on the subject of village affairs, every taxpayer should observe the care given the village hall, or engine house. Mr. Spinks has everything spick and span there, like a good housekeeper, and when the trustees meet the place is fit for more callers than they ever receive. . . . Crosswalks are looked after, as inspector of our village highways he has been efficient, his care of the water duties are well done. In this connection, the water is better, due to flushing at ends and the freedom given patrons of liberally using the water . . . And have you observed (by not observing) that the streets are clear of standers? Do you recall the former conditions, or ever give thought to comparison? It is notable, and the youth generally enjoy respect of these bettered conditions, helpful to all concerned.
> One of the big benefits to our water system, too, which people do not see, we mention while before us, the building of the wire fence around the reservoir. It is said to be excellent in all respects, built right, durable and one of those permanent improvements at minimum cost which is not on the surface. And before leaving Mr. Spinks' work, there is little or no drunkenness seen on our streets. This is a thing in which the hotel men will take satisfaction with all other good citizens and the present regime has effectively given such characters as indulge in this kind of thing to understand that it will not go unpunished in our well governed village. . . .
> The above are but a few of the many activities of which we have meant to tell some time past. Board members are always present, on time, and the business at hand is done with attention to detail, expeditiously and in harmony. They are accomplishing effectively for the good of the place. One such unnoticed action is, they have ordered signs to be placed at all intersections, giving names of streets. As stated, such good work is common, and we regret our failure to inform the public as fully as we should.

Another petition called for the creation of a village justice which would help " . . . to relieve the town justice of the burden of village trials, and . . . better care of all village laws, their enforcement and proper meting out of justice to those who would fail to obey village ordinances" (MO 3/17/13). This petition would find immediate favor with the Board of Trustees and in the March election that year, the voters approved the position. Fred Thompson would again be elected Village President and Edmund Reed would be elected as Trustee.

5 Mar 1913 - " . . . petition of the residents of the Village of Marcellus to create the office of Police Justice was received and a motion was made . . . to submit the same to the electors at the annual village election."

18 Mar 1913 - voters approved the position of Police Justice. In the next general election, Horace M. Stone was elected Police Justice.

Business Expansion

Business activity in the Village of Marcellus also began to expand at this time. Phillip A. Schanzle, who had established a bakery on West Main Street in 1903, moved his business next door when Levi Parsons decided to buy the building and move it to clear the site for another building. Parsons requested permission of the Village Trustees to move the building along village streets to a site on the south line of the village and erected a cement block building that would later house the "old theater" and still stands in the center of the village today. Schanzle, meanwhile, expanded his bakery, added other businesses and remained in business until his death in 1940.

23 Mar 1913 - " . . . L. E. Parsons requested permission to move the building now used by P. A. Schanzle as a bakery, through Cherry St. to the south line of the Village. Permission was granted provided that moving of building should not unduly interfere with traffic; also that Mr. Parsons shall be liable for all damage resulting therefrom."

Street and Road Work

The Trustees met a number of times that spring with engineers to plan for the state highway construction along North and South Streets which would take place in the months ahead, including use of the famous "Malley's quarry" curbstone.

The Marcellus Observer
Friday, April 16, 1913
Board of Trustees

Special meeting to decide as to rate for water used in constructing the new State highway through the village . . .

John L. Curtin presented a blue print of the new highway to be constructed through North, Main and Cherry streets and considered with the Board various points regarding grades, care of water, culverts, etc.

The Marcellus Observer
Friday, April 23, 1913
Village Affairs

The Marcellus Village Board planned at their last meeting to notify about ten property owners that sidewalk flagging must be made level, up heaved by frost of tree roots. The members gave careful consideration with Engineer Curtin as to conditions of the proposed street and roadwork, and the care of water.

The Marcellus Observer
Friday, August 15, 1913
The Curbing Fever Catching

The liberality of property owners all about the corner of Main and North streets to adopt the plan while it is timely of placing the Malley curbing is highly commendable . . . .

Old Home Day Planning

There was considerable concern that summer with Fourth of July activities and the appointment of special policemen to enforce the noise ordinances of the Village. That summer also marked the planning of an Old Home Week for the Marcellus community, to be held in the summer of 1914 when the County Firemen's Convention likewise was scheduled to be in town.

3 Jul 1913 - " . . . special meeting . . . to choose officers to keep quiet and peace of the Village during the night and day of the 4th. This meeting is called at the request of residents that there be no fires and no cannon be fired. President Thompson appointed Geo. Austin, Edgar Bartlett, Edward Quigley, Howard Spaulding and Colden Austin. The above named persons were duly sworn in as special police by Justice Coon."

The Marcellus Observer
Friday, August 8, 1913
Why Not An "Old Home" Week?

Right now, if ever, is the ripe time to begin a movement for an "Old Home Week" for Marcellus. With plans even this early under way for the County Firemen's Convention to be held here next year, with our village improvements in the building of the State road through the two longest streets, with the curbing setting this off to advantage around the corners of these streets, many new structures finished in the past few years and others under way, with many notable changes and betterments, all the kind of thing of which the locality may well be proud and which friends and relatives from away will be interested in paying us a visit to see, Why Not?

We offer this suggestion. The firemen, as such, are going to have their hands full with the convention work. But to fully recognize their leadership in planning, let them, at their earliest meeting, name a committee of business men, from their own active ranks or outside, as a nucleus of this Old Home Week movement. The two activities can then go hand in hand. Advertising of the one can include the other. And in the year to come everybody from far and near will be able to learn that an Old Home Week is under way, and they can make plans to be here. Next winter we'll be sleeping. Next spring will be too late to give the long advance invitation. Let's DO IT NOW!

Unpaved to Paved

By the fall of 1913, North and South (Cherry) Streets were paved with macadam, although there was some concern about Levi Parsons moving his building along the new

state road. The dirt roads of the past were gradually giving way to hardened surfaces of an expanding village.

4 Oct 1913 - " . . . communication was received from Guy B. Dickinson regarding the moving of the old bakery. As the road was not yet accepted by the State, Mr. Dickinson objected to this building being moved over the new road. After a discussion, . . . L. E. Parsons was forbidden to move the building into the highway until he has made satisfactory arrangements with the state road contractor, freeing the Village from all damages resulting from the moving of said building."

Marcellus Votes Dry

In the fall election of 1913, the " . . . unremitting warfare of the temperance advocates continued, . . . and Marcellus was finally voted dry in November . . . " (Heffernan 101). That vote called for prohibition in the Town of Marcellus but it would not take place until October 1, 1914 and the year to come would witness one of the biggest events in the history of the Village - an Old Home Days Celebration that attracted thousands of people to the sleepy village.

1914 - Village Expansion Continues

1914 would see the Village expand as Reed Street was extended to the west, up the hill to the Turnpike, Edmund Reed presenting a plan and deed to the Village Board for

this purpose. Construction of a number of homes on the hill would soon follow, some of which were part of a contiguous block of the craftsman style residences in Marcellus, such as this house to the left. The craftsman style, popular in the United States from about 1905 to 1930, and this house displays " . . . features in its full-length front porch, wide overhanging eaves with exposed rafter tails and purlins, and in the use of both single and clapboard siding" (Elliot 4), the style of this house on the Reed tract. This is also an example of some prefabricated housing in Marcellus. Many of the homes on this block of Reed Street were assembled in a factory and then constructed on site and evidence of this is seen in the similar features that each house shares, including the foundation material and siding. Interestingly, one of the few remaining parcels of buildable land in the village is on upper Reed Street, subdivided in 1997 for the purpose of new home construction.

The Reed Street hill also provided a safe course for those youngsters who wished to try out the new sleds and coasters they received for Christmas in 1913, since sledding on West Hill was absolutely forbidden by the Village Board of Trustees. "Officer Spinks has been instructed to strictly prohibit coasting on High School hill, but the Village Board will provide a sled way down the new hill of Reed street for use of our youth." (MO 1/2/14)

7 Jan 1914 - " . . . that the Village Clerk, Howard White, be appointed Registrar of Vital Statistics."

12 Feb 1914 - " . . . Edmund Reed presented a deed to the Board for land upon which he is making an extension of Reed St. After a discussion, it was decided to accept the same . . . "

> **The Marcellus Observer**
> **Friday, March 6, 1914**
> **Severe March Blizzard**
> **The Worst Storm of the Winter and Greatest in Several Years**
> A snowstorm, accompanied by a stiff wind from the north, set in about 10 a.m. Sunday and continued without intermission until 10 o'clock Monday morning, a period of 24 hours. It was the most severe blizzard of the winter and the worst storm since March 1902, . . .
> The streets in this village and the roads in the country were badly drifted . . .
> Mail service during the storm called for vigor. Monday routes did not start, for that day everybody shoveled snow . . ..
> Miss Godfrey of the school faculty, . . . was the only teacher to brave the storm and reach the building . . ..
> The officers of the fire department, authorized by the village trustees, have engaged two teams to stand in harness and placed two firemen on duty, night and day, at the engine house, to act promptly in case of fire

Winter of 1914

The youth of 1914 might have enjoyed the wintry weather, but for many in Marcellus, one of the worst storms in recent years arrived in early March, closing roads, shutting down the trolley, schools and mail service and causing concern among Village officials that fire hydrants should be kept open.

Election of 1914

Earlier in the year, a lengthy letter to the editor in *The Marcellus Observer* made comment as to how village affairs should have been conducted in the year just past. Included in this list was a litany of complaints about how the village water rates should have been made, about the dangers that existed from trees that were too large and watering troughs poorly located, about neglected sidewalks, about unkempt premises and poorly lit streets. Village President Thompson responded a week later, answering, word-for-word and in detail each of the allegations made by an individual who had signed his name as "A Subscriber." Today, of course, anonymous letters to the editor are not published and people are held accountable for their statements. Such letters may have been enough, however, to discourage Mr. Thompson from running again. Although nominated for the job, he it appears did not wish to continue and in the March election that year, Frank H. Gillette was chosen as Village President in a rather large voter turnout. Gillette was a man in his early forties who worked in the local creamery, married and the father of a young daughter and had already served as Trustee in an earlier term. Elbert W. Coville was also elected as Trustee in 1914. A man in his early sixties, Coville was not only a farmer, but also noted for his surveying abilities, having drawn, at the Board's request, several maps of the Village. In addition, the office of Police Justice, created a year earlier, was filled by the election of Horace M. Stone to that position.

> **The Marcellus Observer**
> **Friday, March27, 1914**
> **The Marcellus Free Library**
> The Marcellus Free Library was formally opened to the public on Saturday, March 21st, and a large number of interested townspeople availed themselves of the opportunity of visiting the Library room and inspecting the books and progress made.
>
> **The Marcellus Observer**
> **Friday, April 3, 1914**
> **The Marcellus Free Library**
> The Library, which was closed on account of the Scarlet Fever, is now open for the circulation of books and the use of the Reading Room.

17 Mar 1914 - " . . . the whole number of votes cast at said election was ninety six (96) of which for President for one year, F. H. Gillette received sixty one (61), F. A. Thompson received twenty-nine (29) spoiled were five (5), blank were one (1). . . . for Police Justice, H. M. Stone received seventy-two (71). . . ."

Marcellus Free Library

Additionally, the Marcellus Free Library opened that month, in the offices adjoining those of Frank W. Knapp over the Post Office and a few days later had to be promptly closed by Village officials because of an outbreak of scarlet fever in the community.

23 Mar 1914 - " . . . that E. H. Spinks call on all cases of quarantine and furnish all supplies as required by law."

Water Rates and Residency

Following the annual assembly of the Board of Trustees on March 23, 1914, a special meeting was called to revise rates for the village water system, in response to complaints that some had not been paying their fair share. The revision not only increased water rates but would also, following another special meeting, implement the use of water meters to determine what those charges should be.

25 Mar 1914 - " . . . that the present water rates, with the exception of meter rates be rescinded. . . . that the following rates for use of water be adopted . . .. "

House, 1 faucet only	$5.00
House, Bath, etc.	$7.00
Stores, 1 faucet	$5.00
Stores, 2 or more faucets	$7.00
Barn, 1 faucet, 1 horse or cow	$3.00
Barn, 1 faucet, 2 or more horses or cows	$5.00
Barn, 2 or more faucets	$6.00
Motors	$1.00
Sill faucets	$1.00

Water used for hotels and commercial purpose to be metered. Dwellings, stores or offices in single building to be charged at separate rate, namely each dwelling or store or office to be charged the same as though in separate buildings. For each family in any block or apt. supplied with water from fixture connected with water system, $5.00. The Board reserves the right to place meters in any or all parts of the system at any time it may be deemed necessary or to make any changes in the above rates."

7 Apr 1914 - " . . . that previous meter rates be changed as follows:

At least $7.00 per annum must be paid for each family supplied who will be allowed 3,600 cubic feet of water; any excess to be paid for at the rate made by quantity used, as per established rate shown by semi-annual consumption.

1900 or less cubic feet	17 cents per 100'
1900 to 2400, inclusive lump sum	$3.70
2400 to 6000, "	13 cents per 100'
6000 to 8300, "	$7.80
8300 to 14,400, "	9 cents per 100'
14,400 to 17,700, "	$12.95
17,700 to 21,00, "	5 1/2 cents per 100'
21,000 to 27,300, "	$14.70
27,300 to 40,000, "	5 1/2 cents per 100'
40,000 to 57,100, "	$22.00

The above classification is in addition to flat rates adopted by the Board at a meeting held on March 25, 1914. All consumers may have their choice as to which rate they will have. All bills for water for the current half year will be mailed to consumers at flat rates unless notice that meter rates are preferred is given to the Clerk on or before April 15, 1914."

Today water rates are also determined by usage and the Village's primary means of financing the annual costs of owning and operating its water system is through revenues derived *via* user charges and credited to a Water Fund. Should the revenues not meet the expenditures required to own and operate the system, the Village must draw upon its taxing and assessment authority and meet the balance through its General Fund. Marcellus residents are billed quarterly for their water usage. As of 2002, a descending rate block schedule of water rates are charged by the Village as follows:

Minimum Charge (5,000 gallons) $16.00 per quarter

Next 8,000 gallons	$2.12 per 1000 gallons
Next 16,000 gallons	$2.59 per 1000 gallons
Next 561,000 gallons	$1.90 per 1000 gallons
Over 600,000 gallons	$1.67 per 1000 gallons

Residency

Another issue arose early in the administration of President Gillette concerning the question of village employees maintaining residence in the village with the stipulation that Commissioner Spinks would be appointed to his position provided that he live in the Village. That issue has been of some concern in recent years, not only for the Village of Marcellus but also for the City of Syracuse and for other governmental agencies in Onondaga County. While there are those who claim that employees who are also residents might become more involved in the community, there are also those who argue that employment should be based on merit and qualifications rather than on residency. Members of the Village Board as well as members of the Planning and Zoning Boards must be residents of the Village, but the law, at present, does not require other Village employees to have their homes in the Village. This is a concern that is not easily resolved.

> **The Marcellus Observer**
> **Friday, April 3, 1914**
> **Make Some Day a "Clean-Up Day."**
> Why should not all of our citizens join heartily in the growing crusade against dirt and disorder that is being waged in many cities and villages of the State, by having a special day or days set apart for a general spring "clean-up"? . . . Our trustees of recent years have evinced commendable pride in keeping the village streets clean, the dust laid, the yards and parks neat and attractive. A united effort by all our citizens to have back yards, as well as the more conspicuous front lawns, made spick and span before the advent of warm weather and summer visitors, would make our lovely village still more attractive.

21 Apr 1914 - " . . . that E. H. Spinks be appointed Street Commissioner for the coming year at his present salary, provided that he move into the Village."

Clean Up -Fix Up

As spring came to the Village, there was call for a general clean-up of the Village, much of it, it seems, in anticipation of the up-coming Old Home Week celebration planned for the summer. There was some hope expressed that there would be road and street improvements as well, particularly on Main Street, which remained a dirt road and a quagmire of mud when it rained. The Town Supervisor at the time was Patrick Kelly and, ever since his election in 1907, it appears that one of his goals was general road improvement, particularly to the State roads that crossed the Village. Some work had already been completed on the corner of North and South (Cherry) streets, but Main Street remained a dirt highway. Unfortunately, the issue would not be forcefully addressed until after the Old Home Week celebration.

> **The Marcellus Observer**
> **Friday, May 8 1914**
> **Our "East Side" Improvement**
> There is talk, or hope, new hope, of some way making sluices to convey ditch water down the hill on Main street in Marcellus toward the stone bridge and to the creek, and so cover them up as to level the entire section, make more attractive this entrance to "our fair city" and benefit the village generally. A start is made, Edw. Rosser is building a sluice for his driveway, of cement, square, large and very high, which will be covered over, making the drive almost level. Such work has been withheld in hope of this entire stretch being raised to a higher grade level with the railroad tracks on the east and nearly as high as the top at the Parsons-Case properties. Such work observed elsewhere proves that this job well done would not detract in the least way from the Williams property nor that on the north side, with proper plans and finish.
> This is one of Supervisor Kelly's ambitions and it will doubtless remain until he can carry it through. We have not spoken to him of it recently. The sluice matter is an idea expressed in connection with "slicking up" for Old Home Week.

8 Jun 1914 - " . . . the question of a new road from the end of the State road east on Main Street was then taken up and after some talk as to plans, it was decided best to call on the Town Board at its next meeting in regard to using the town road machinery."

Come Back For Old Home Week

From May through July, every issue of *The Marcellus Observer* would headline an article devoted to the planning that was being done for the Old Home Week Celebration. " . . . The executive committee in charge of planning the event . . . sent invitations to former residents to 'come home' and join in the festivities, which were to begin on Tuesday, July 21, and continue through Saturday, July 25, along with the Wednesday and

Committee members snapped on the morning of July 4th 1914. Back row, left to right, Secretary John Stewart, Treasurer John E. Griffin, President J. C. Parsons, Frank D. Powell, James Hogan. Front row, Edward J. Dillon, P. J. Kelly, David J. Lawless
- *The Marcellus Observer – July 10. 1914*

Thursday activities of the Onondaga County Firemen's Association. Lawns were trimmed, fences and hydrants painted, and streets decorated . . . " (Heffernan 99). Beginning with an alumni banquet and continuing with speeches, an old time ball game, dinners, contests, exhibits, church services and receptions, a monster parade would conclude the celebration on Saturday, July 25th. The Village Board was concerned, as usual, with safety and authorized more security for the event, " . . . described in the press, as the 'greatest week in the history of the village'" (Heffernan 99).

13 Jul 1914 - " . . . that the President be instructed to engage two detectives for Thursday and Saturday of Old Home Week provided that detectives are not furnished by the Sheriff's Office."

It was a week not soon forgotten, especially the first day of the celebration when a big windstorm took down the Liberty Pole in front of the Alvord House. The Village and its residents became host to thousands of visitors and despite some rain, the festivities were very successful, generating an enormous amount of local pride and patriotism. The patriotism of these Marcellians would be put to an even sterner test a month later when war broke out in Europe.

In 1994, when the Town of Marcellus observed its bicentennial anniversary, the Old Home Day celebrations were revived, and they continue to energize some of the enthusiasm and local pride promoted by those Marcellians of 1914.

The Marcellus Observer
Friday, August 14, 1914
Marcellus' New Block & Hall
"Parsons' Hall" and Block In Progress-Hall to be 36x80, for Public Use-Two Stores, Lodge Room, Cellar Under All

The Marcellus Observer
Friday, Sept. 11, 1914
Good Roads
The Marcellus village board met Wednesday night especially to consider with Supervisor Kelly as to beginning the new highway on Main street from in front of the Presbyterian church, where it joins the former new road, to the crossing in front of the Powell House, at Orange street. This work will be a continuation of the present street construction the entire length of North and South streets and around the Busy Corner. . . Among features of the plans, the Alvord House scales will conform with the new grade, which is lower than at present, and will be moved back a little. Also the broken liberty pole will be taken down.

The Guns of August

In August of 1914, the world was shattered by the start of a great war overseas. The people of the United States were glad that the war was "over there", although *The Post-Standard* urged the people of Marcellus to " . . . subscribe now and you will be sure to get all news of the war in Europe - news that is reliable" (MO 8/7/14).

The people in Marcellus, however, were more interested in the news about the building and road construction that was being promoted in their Village in the late summer

---

The Marcellus Observer
Friday, Sept 18, 1914
Raise The Bridge Grade Now
Rare Opportunity for Village Board to Make This Long-Planned Improvement at Great Saving.
The Marcellus Board of Trustees have before them this moment a way to give the village its greatest improvement, to fill and grade Main street near Nine Mile Creek stone bridge. This ugly low spot can be made a fit approach to our village at less cost today than ever again. Decision must be reached at once . . . . . Mr. Gillett, Mr. Reed, Mr. Coville, what do you say? Call a conference with Supervisor Kelly and the Town Board. Let us have this. NOW.

and fall of 1914. Levi Parsons began excavating for his new building on Main Street, a two-story structure that would include room for stores, lodge rooms and a public hall. There was also street construction on North and South Streets, as well as talk of reconstructing Main Street east to the bridge.

9 Sep 1914 - " . . . for the purpose of considering . . . the building of the new road from the end of the State road east on Main St. to the Powell House."

The local paper also called for the Trustees to fill and grade the low spot at the Nine Mile Creek stone bridge, an entrance to the Village that was in considerable need of repair.

The Marcellus Observer
Friday, Sept 18, 1914
"A Hot Time In The Old Town"
October 1st is eventful. On that date, Marcellus and Onondaga townships go "dry". Many other towns begin a journey across the hot sands, as the shriners say, on that date, if the ballots said so in their section.

The Marcellus Observer
Friday, Oct 30, 1914
Border Saloon Vigorously Opposed
Gleason & Tierney opened a saloon Saturday just over the Marcellus town line . . . Feeling is exceedingly strong against this establishing of a country saloon, isolated from all control or possible criticism, such as naturally governs in a neighborhood. The public is aroused and great interest is manifested among good citizens.

Marcellus Goes Dry

On October 1, 1914, the Town of Marcellus went "dry," as directed by the vote of the previous November. This was a high watermark in the local temperance movement, but it was by no means an end to the struggle by the Anti-Saloon forces. The neighboring towns of Camillus and Skaneateles were still "wet" and those who wanted a drink often visited saloons in those towns. Some enterprising proprietors even decided to move their business just across the town line, and continue to operate with full license.

Meanwhile, there was still some concern in the Village about the rowdyism of some juveniles who, charged with some pranks that were judged to be malicious acts, ended up in the newly created village police court. Others felt that the police authorities were more concerned with " . . . hauling a young fellow up to the Koop than having to deal with a man who was lyeing on the Grass on Main Street dead drunk" (MO 10/16/14).

Austin C. Marble

Village Tragedy

In November 1914, Austin C. Marble, who had first been elected as Village Treasurer in 1912, replacing the long-time Treasurer, James Woodbridge, died suddenly at the age of thirty-five, shocking Village residents. The full-page picture and obituary that graced the December 4th edition of *The Marcellus Observer* gave evidence of the great respect this young man generated in the community. He had worked in his father's drug store on Main Street, and left a wife and young daughter to mourn his passing. To many, this young man represented all that was good and wholesome in the community, a future that was suddenly extinguished. To his position, Varnum S. Kenyon was appointed on December 14, 1914, the beginning of a forty-year period of public service by this individual to the Village, serving in a variety of capacities, as Treasurer, Trustee and Mayor, from 1914 to 1953.

14 Dec 1914 - " . . . motion made by Reed, seconded by Coville that Mr. Kenyon be appointed Village Treasurer for the balance of the term."

Conclusion

When the decade began, the issue of the water works had been resolved but that of temperance was gaining momentum. In five years, the main roads in the Village had been paved, the reservoir had been fenced, and a public library and bank had been established. There were complaints about chickens on the loose, bicycles on the sidewalks and boys out after curfew. The community came together, however, for a great celebration in 1914, a celebration that was "dry" but thoroughly enjoyed by thousands and ranked as one of the greatest events in the history of the Village. A month later, the world entered a great conflict that, although it captured the interest of most people in the community, seemed quite distant, almost unimportant to them. They, like most Americans, thought that the conflict would be over quickly and felt secure behind their ocean walls. The next five years would end that naiveté and, like the death of Austin Marble, destroy innocence and a wholesomeness that had been nurtured for so long.

Chapter 9 – Into the 20th Century

When the new year arrived, Europe was actively engaged in a great conflict. Most Americans wanted to avoid involvement in a war that was none of their concern, but they

---

The Marcellus Observer
Friday, Feb. 26, 1915
Rumored That It Will Bid For The American Trade
Mystery Surrounding New Structures at Split Rock Now Believed to Be Solved - Small Army of Laborers Now at Work

There has been much speculation for the last month of six weeks as to the purposes of the large buildings now being erected at Split Rock by the Solvay Process Company. There are three buildings, one of which is about 90x140 feet, another about 60x150 feet, and a smaller one, about 20x60 feet. For several months a small army of workmen have been employed on the new buildings, some of which are still a long way from completion. The number from Syracuse is so great, that a special car, night and morning has been necessary for their transportation. Of this large number, no one seems to know anything about the structures. As some of the workmen pout it, they get their pay regularly and don't care about what the buildings are to be used for.

It is now learned from what seems to be a reliable source that the Solvay Company intends to engage in the manufacture of dyes for the American trade.

The Marcellus Observer
Friday, April 2, 1915
Village Affairs

Marcellus voters indicated their confidence, and their desire for proven and efficient service by casting a total of 71 votes, as against the usual disinterested dozen to twenty, and elected for president, F. A. Thompson and for trustee, Edmund Reed, with 67 votes, 4 spoiled. Mr. Thompson served several terms before the last one, which has been satisfactorily filled by Frank H. Gillett. Mr. Reed is re-elected. Perhaps no one in town has made so full a study of public affairs and needs, finances, etc. as has Mr. Reed. Vernon S. Kenyon of the First National Bank is chosen treasurer, so our accounts are in good hands and money too, and Clarence M. Woodford can be relied on to get it in and turn it over properly. Village affairs are in good hands. Now, good people don't stand back and kick. If you want anything done, know something wrong, step right forward and tell the whole truth and nothing but the truth, to Mr. Thompson, and watch him keep things right. And when you complain, be ready to stand back of it. If complaint in writing is required, sign your name and give the matter you moral support. The kickers usually want to shift the responsibility.

---

were interested in continuing to trade with both sides in the conflict. The mills of Marcellus produced material for uniforms and in nearby Split Rock, several large buildings were being constructed, supposedly for the manufacture of dyes for the American trade. A number of Marcellians would soon find employment at the Split Rock facilities, which, we now know, were being built for the manufacture of explosives.

1915

In the Village of Marcellus, however, the horrors of war seemed quite distant although there was an appeal by the Belgian Relief Committee " . . . to those in Marcellus who may wish to contribute toward the purchase of food . . . to be sent to the starving women and children of war-stricken Belgium . . . " (MO 2/26/15). In the 1915 election, former Village President, Fred Thompson, was returned to serve another term, a voter turnout that reflected much confidence in the leadership chosen.

16 Mar 1915 - " . . . the whole number of votes cast at said election was seventy (of which) for President for one year, F. A. Thompson received sixty-seven (67) . . . "

Streets and Sidewalks and Speed

Protecting the reservoir and improving Village streets were issues again addressed by the Board of Trustees. The Board appointed a watchman for the pond and it also announced that it " . . . knows of places where good clean ashes are wanted" to be dumped . . . (MO 4/16/15), as fill for the dirt roads. Maple, formerly Factory, street would be filled with broken stone and made much smoother, prompting some to drive too fast and the Board to pass speed ordinances for the Village.

10 May 1915 - " . . . motion was made by Reed, seconded by Coville that Bert Chapman be engaged to care for pond at $1.00 per month. Carried."

17 May 1915 - " . . . the Board of Trustees . . . do hereby ordain and order that:

1. No person, association or corporation or employee or agent thereof shall operate or drive or cause to be operated or driven a motor vehicle over, along, upon or across the streets or highways of the Village of Marcellus, N.Y., at a speed greater than one mile in four minutes . . .. No person shall operate on any street or highway in said village any motor vehicle with cut-out open or muffler released.

2. That any violation of this ordinance shall be deemed and constitute a misdemeanor, and upon conviction thereof, the person or persons so convicted shall be liable to a fine of not less then ten dollars or more than fifty dollars or imprisonment for one day for each dollar of fine unpaid.

3. This ordinance shall take effect on the 25th day of May, 1915."

Tax Rates & Divided Highways

There was some protest over the village tax rate, although it was lower than the previous year and *The Marcellus Observer* was quick to mention that with improvements often call for an increase in taxes.

The Village Board also made a decision about maintaining some of the highways that were shared with the Town, a division that continues to this day on West Main Street and Scotch Hill Road. The Board continued to maintain its interest in improving sidewalks in the Village, raising the grade on Main Street following the new construction there. This same sidewalk will soon be re-graded so as to conform to the guidelines established by the Americans with Disabilities Act (ADA), eliminating trip hazards, making business entrances handicap accessible and adding more green space to beautify the area.

14 Jun 1915 - " . . . motion was made by Coville that on West Hill and Scotch Hill where the corporation boundary passes along the center of the highway, to divide this portion of the highway into two equal parts by a transverse line, one part to be maintained by the village and the town board to be asked to maintain the remaining part."

23 Jun 1915 - " . . . to establish a grade for a five foot (walk) in width, from the Marcellus Hardware Co.'s walk to a point connecting the walk of F. W. Knapp . . .. permission was given the said Schanzle, Parsons and Blake to raise their walks . . . . "

The Marcellus Observer
Friday, July 2, 1915
Some Census Figures
Dealing With Towns and Wards in the First Assembly District

The following . . . show . . . population of the various towns and wards in the First Assembly District of Onondaga County.

	1915	1910
Camillus		3,031 2,642
Cicero		2,679 2,475
Clay	2,661	2,431
Elbridge		3,039 2,980
Geddes		9,471 5,959
Lysander	4,628	4,509
Marcellus	2,927	2,826
Otisco		1,005 1,066
Salina		3,208 3,980
Skaneateles		4,619 4,274
Spafford		1,082 1,064
Van Buren	2,410	3,200
First ward	5,970	6,182
Second ward	6,983	7,015
Third ward	9,446	8.401

The total population of the district is 67,841, showing a gain of 3,784 in the past five years. Only three towns in the district show a decrease . . . Three of the city wards show a decrease, while one shows a handsome increase. Only two towns in the district - Geddes and Lysander - exceed Skaneateles in population, which has gained 345 inhabitants in the past five years.

Census Figures and A Flag Pole

The results of the New York State Census of 1915 were completed by the summer of 1915 and despite some initial fear that Marcellians were under-counted, there was an increase of just over 100 people in the Town. There was also much discussion about the need for Marcellus to purchase and erect a new flagpole, replacing that which was destroyed a year earlier. A meeting to discuss the purchase of a new steel pole was held at Parsons Hall on July 6th and the local G.A.R. Commander, Edward V. Baker, led the campaign to raise money for this project.

Safety Concerns

Safety was and continues to be a major concern of the Village Board and the increased use of gasoline and other combustibles would cause the Trustees, in the summer of 1915, to pass legislation regulating their use and storage in the community. Today, the regulations involving the handling and use of such materials are even more stringent and State agencies such as the Departments of Environmental Conservation and Transportation add more force to local ordinances. The Board also posted a reward for those who damaged

North Side of West Main Street – c1915

public property, in particular the public drinking fountain on Main Street, which was apparently tampered with, on a regular basis, by the youngsters of the village. In August, meetings between village officials within the County began, the start of what today are often labeled intermunicipal consortiums. These meetings, like those of today, try to address some of the similar concerns that officials face in their respective communities.

12 Jul 1915 - " . . . the question of the gasoline tank in front of the Marcellus Hardware Co.'s store was brought up and after some little discussion it was decided to withhold permission to place same until the matter can be looked into. In the meantime, the Clerk is to write Mr. Cuddeback, forbidding further work in setting the tank."

Special Meeting of the Board of Trustees
July 14, 1915
Village Ordinance
BE IT ORDAINED, Section 1. No person shall place or store, or cause or allow to be placed or stored upon any sidewalk, crosswalk, or in any street or alley in the village, any cask, tank, barrel, box or other contained or receptacle containing gun powder, gun powder, nitro-glycerin, dynamite, petroleum, gasoline, benzene, naphtha, kerosene, oil or other explosives. In no case shall any of the articles mentioned herein be allowed on any sidewalk, crosswalk or in any street or alley or in front of any building in the village a longer time than shall be required for immediate shipment or delay of same, or after sunset. Any person violating this ordinance shall be liable to a penalty of $25.00 and any violation . . . shall constitute disorderly conduct, and such person so violating . . . a disorderly person.

The Marcellus Observer
Friday, July 16, 1915
Village Ordinance
A reward of five dollars ($5.00) is offered for information leading to the arrest and conviction of any person guilty of violating section three of the village ordinances, which is as follows:
Sec. 3. Every person who shall cut, mar or in any way mutilate any tree, shrub or flower, plant, fence, awning, sign, signboard, building, monument or ornament of any description, in any of the streets, public grounds or cemetery of said village, or who shall tear down any notice lawfully posted, shall forfeit a penalty not to exceed ten dollars.
Attention is especially called to the above section in regard to the various drinking fountains about the village, which have been tampered with a good deal of late.

---

14 Jul 1915 - " . . . for the purpose of passing an ordinance in regard to the storing of gasoline, naphtha, etc."

9 Aug 1915 - " . . . invitation was received from the Board of Trustees of Skaneateles to attend a conference of village officers of Onondaga County . . .. invitation was accepted with thanks and as many as can will try to attend."

The Marcellus Observer
Friday, October 15, 1915
Exercise In Marcellus
Next Friday 2:00 P.M.
On Flag Pole Raising
The committee in charge of preparing exercises and a suitable and enjoyable program in connection with the new steel flagpole in Marcellus met Thursday afternoon and set the date for Friday of next week, Oct. 22, at 2 o'clock. Horace M. Stone will make the address of the day, the Marcellus quartet will sing, school children will give exercises, with other program numbers, given in Alvord House square; in Alvord hall in case of rain.

There were other complaints to the Board and in the press about juveniles and the " . . . danger of the roller coaster wagons that are being run around town on the sidewalks by the boys who shout, 'Get out of the way, you 'old fool!' . . . " (MO 9/3/15). The concern of residents of Maiden (Slocombe Ave today) Lane, however, was that more street lighting needed to be provided in that area.

11 Oct 1915 - " . . . petition was received from several residents of Maiden Lane requesting a street light at the head of that street. No action was taken."

Flag Pole Raising

By the fall of 1915, the campaign to raise a new flagpole had met with success and in early October, it was erected in front of what was then called Alvord House Square. At the same time, the Marcellus Board of Education had also bought a new flagpole for the front of the school and a ceremony on October 22, 1915 dedicating and commemorating both events was held.

The Marcellus Observer
Friday, October 15, 1915
Firemanic

Marcellus firemen held a red-hot meeting in the engine house Wednesday night of great importance to every resident. For it means protection to property.

Village President Thompson called a firemen's meeting and but 7 came. Another call was made and 18 attended. It is his duty to maintain a fire department in the village. He wanted to ask local firemen where they stood. Meetings have not been held, interest flagged. No officers were elected last annual meeting, so few present and old officers held over. Inspections have not been carried out according to custom.

The firemen's contention was that $50 was to be paid by village officials in their treasury each year which had not always been done. They claim they have to ask for it, "beg for it." Last year, the village finally gave over $100 to the Old Home Week fund as applying toward firemen's money, thus to help out the county convention in their behalf. So this has deprived the fire department. Mr. Thompson held that the $50 annually was granted on condition that an annual inspection day be held, this to defray expenses of a showing of the department to the village residents. This is done in other villages, used to be held here, in some form or other. Failing in this, the $50 was not earned.

We look in the village laws and do not find any provision made for such a $50 payment. It may be a by-law or a 'custom', precedent.

It is stated that such item when awarded has been used by firemen for a trip away from home or some purpose not local as intended. Firemen have the argument that they buy their own uniforms, devote time and effort, ruin clothes at fires, all that. There is urgent need of harmony in the fold.

The upshot of the matter and meeting was that formal election of new officers was held, as follows: History repeats itself, that the fire department hopes to take on renewed interest, activity, attend meetings, drills, etc, etc. Will the boys take hold?

Fire Protection

Of special concern for Village officials and residents at this same time was the issue of fire protection and the reluctance of some firemen to volunteer because of a dispute with the Village over a contribution to the Fire Department's Fund. This issue is very much a concern of the Fire Department today and there are contrasting opinions held by many. Some argue making payments to volunteer organizations such as the Fire Department violates the very nature of the organization, while others contend that certain amenities need to be extended to such groups in order to keep up membership and interest. Rather than making monetary contributions to the Fire Department, some would express the opinion that incentives such as a Service Awards Program should be initiated and that this would help sustain membership. Others think that volunteer fire organizations will not be able to maintain members and that it is only a matter of time before a paid professional fire department is the norm for many suburban communities like Marcellus. What is certain is the fact that the cost of maintaining a volunteer fire department will continue to increase. New York State requires much more intensive training for volunteers than ever before and the cost of vehicles and equipment has risen to even greater heights, again because of more stringent regulations by the State. Today, the Marcellus Fire Department and its Ambulance Volunteer Service responds to all sorts of crises. Many of these emergencies are of a medical nature and the demands of this type of rescue have made it necessary to hire a full time paid staff of paramedics. This is perhaps a portend of what is to come.

November Elections

The November elections of 1915 again centered on the issue of prohibition and in particular the question of license. The license question on the ballot had four parts and asked the voters if a license could be granted to dispense alcohol in (1) saloons, (2) stores, (3) by druggists, or in (4) hotels. In each case the voters rejected the idea of license and Marcellus voted itself "dry" for another four years. It also seems that the license issue carried over into the election for supervisor, as Patrick J. Kelly was defeated in his re-election bid, as were many of the Democratic candidates for office throughout

The Marcellus Observer
Friday, Nov. 5, 1915
Comments On Election

Mr. Kelly suffers the inevitable with others who serve to the best that is in them and find the dear public ruthlessly unappreciative. He was first elected in 1907, so has served four terms of two years each, during which time he has also been Assemblyman one term.

Prayer meetings Wednesday night had as topics for at least a portion of the hour general thanksgiving and praise service for the outcome of election in favor of no-license. Where would such expressions of gratitude, thanksgiving and joy have been held had the questions gone the other way?

The Marcellus Observer
Friday, Nov. 12, 1915
Prohibition in Onondaga County

Four towns in Onondaga county - Manlius, Van Buren, Tully and Spafford - voted from wet to dry Tuesday. This gives ten dry towns in he county - Marcellus, Fabius, Pompey, Lafayette, Onondaga and Otisco, having gone dry two years ago. The combined population of the dry towns is 27, 149. Nine towns in the county are wet - Lysander, Clay, Geddes, Cicero, Dewitt, Salina, Elbridge, Camillus and Skaneateles, with a combined population of 35,000. Thus more than half the towns of the county are dry, and about three-sevenths of the country population live in dry towns. In Tuesday's voting the drys gained four towns from the wets, while the latter failed to gain a single town from the drys.

The Marcellus Observer
Friday, Jan 21, 1916
Population Of Villages
Of Onondaga County
Solvay the Largest - Skaneateles
Ranks Fifth in the List of Fifteen
Incorporated

Statistics show that Solvay is the largest village in Central New York. It also has the largest population of aliens, who exceed 25 per cent.

East Syracuse is the second largest in Onondaga county, while Baldwinsville is third. Camillus is next to Solvay in he percentage of aliens to citizens.

The population of the incorporated villages of Onondaga county and the number of aliens at the time of the census was taken are given as follows:

	Alien	Total.
Baldwinsville	45	3,220
Camillus	160	840
East Syracuse	296	3.839
Eastwood	13	777
Elbridge	2	475
Fabius	...	340
Fayetteville	62	1,779
Jordan	6	1,063
Liverpool	11	1,591
Manlius	131	1,304
Marcellus	86	991
Minoa	76	668
Skaneateles	61	1,768
Solvay	1,432	5,886
Tully	16	559

the township. Marked, as many of them were, with a "wet" Catholic and immigrant label, the Democratic Party candidates met defeat not just in Marcellus but also throughout the county, reflecting a cultural bias among voters in their choice of candidates. In addition to Marcellus, four other towns in Onondaga County voted to become dry, including Manlius, Van Buren, Tully and Spafford.

The issue of women suffrage was also on the ballot in many towns, including Marcellus. The vote was very close in both Marcellus and Skaneateles, but it appears that only voters in the Town of Camillus approved the amendment that granted women the right to vote in local elections. By 1917, this right was approved throughout the State of New York and in 1919 a constitutional amendment would certify this on the national level.

1916

Early in the year, The Marcellus Observer would publish some interesting statistics regarding the population of villages in Onondaga County, including the number of alien residents. This might be reflection, perhaps, of the concern that some Americans had at that time about immigration and the fact that Europe was involved in a conflict that most Americans wanted to avoid.

In Marcellus, the Village continued its day-to-day operations, making appointments and recommending a budget for the new Board of Trustees that was selected on March 21st that year. Elmer P. Clark was chosen to replace Fred Thompson as President of the Village and E. W. Coville was re-elected to a second two-year term.

15 Jan 1916 - " . . . accept the resignation of Dr. Weidman to take effect Jan. 19, 1916 and appoint Dr. Parsons as health officer . . . that the nomination of P. J. Kelly as fire chief be accepted . . . that E. H. Spinks be appointed as policeman for the remainder of the present term of the board."

13 Mar 1916 - " . . . that the following be recommended to the new Board of Trustees as a tax budget for the coming year:

Highway Fund	$2000.00
Contingent Fund	$1000.00
Lighting Fund	$1140.00
Hydrant Fund	$1350.00
Firemen Fund	$100.00

Tribute to a Veteran

March was also witness to some heavy snowfall as well as the death of one of its

E. V. Baker

MO Mar 31, 1916

more notable citizens, Edward V. Baker Sr. A Civil War veteran, as well as town and county official, Baker had been very instrumental in raising funds for the erection of the Village flag pole the previous year. A tribute to all of the veterans and to the generosity of the entire community, the flag flew at half-mast on the day of his funeral.

In a move that would seem to promote both membership and training for junior fire fighters, the Marcellus Fire Chief, Patrick Kelly, asked that the Village Board allow the Boy Scouts to be instructed in the use of fire apparatus and equipment. The new Board also established a tax rate of $11.00 per thousand to fund the new budget.

10 Apr 1916 - " . . . P. J. Kelly, representing the Boy Scouts, asked permission of the Board for the boy scouts to use such of the fire apparatus as many seem suitable to the persons in charge of the scouts for the purpose of teaching the boys the use of hose, ladders, etc. No formal action was taken further than individual consent."

12 May 1916 - " . . . that the tax rate of eleven dollars per thousand be levied on the present assessment. Carried."

Tree Trimming

Spring brought a renewed interest in cleaning the village streets and ditches, as well as concerns about some

---

The Marcellus Observer
Friday, May 19, 1916
Home News

Streets have been cleaned all over the village the past week, ditches, etc., under Officer Spinks with several men. The village bought a new scraper, small and serviceable, from P. J. Kelly, but it has not yet arrived.

The Marcellus Observer
Friday, June 2, 1916
Little Visitor With The Editor

Dr. M. W. Sullivan trimmed two trees in front of his place, the corner property at the big tree in Marcellus. . . .
James Pilot is giving attention to the fine big tree in front of his home, trimming dead limbs. . . . Fred O'Brien had a tree taken down this spring between his house and Thompson's. It shaded the room undesirably and was not well located . . . Edmund Reed has given much attention and labor to the great trees about his place this spring. G. L. Amerman, Mrs. Oatman, others have engaged men to treat trees thus to preserve them both from sentiment and for shade. Thus, Marcellus has had its share of tree doctors

trees that needed trimming. particularly a rather large elm that grew on the corner of North and Reed streets. This tree may have dated back to the very early history of the village and it as well as other trees were the subject of some debate, as homeowners and village board members wrangled over whose responsibility this was. Today, the Village of Marcellus is responsible for trimming those trees that grow in what is commonly referred to as the village right-of-way -- the space between the road and the sidewalk. In the early 20th century, the issue of responsibility was not as clear-cut but like today, many residents at that time were concerned about trees that were trimmed without consideration for sentiment or aesthetics. Conservation was a major concern for Americans in the early 20th century, and local arborists wanted to maintain and protect village trees.

12 Jun 1916 - " . . . Dr. Sullivan appeared before the Board in regard to the elm tree (on corner of Reed and North Streets) with a contract for fixing the tree and requested the Board to accept the contract as to have the tree cut down . . .. decided to donate the sum of $25.00 for the benefit of the baseball field . . .. decided to take out an insurance policy for the employees of the village . . . . resignation of H. M. Stone as Police Justice was presented . . .. "

James E. Woodbridge

10 Jul 1916 - " . . . after some discussion it was decided the Board visit the tree before deciding in regard to it."

The Marcellus Observer
Friday, July 14, 1916
False Fire Alarm; $25 Reward
A false alarm of f ire sounded on the Presbyterian church bell in Marcellus at 2:30 a.m. Sunday morning, only a few taps, but it brought out a large group of firemen and citizens. President Clark wishes to compliment the men upon this quick and good response to the alarm, as much so as if it had been a fire.
There is a village ordinance that the person sounding a false alarm of fire in any way is guilty of a misdemeanor and subject to heavy fine and imprisonment. The same ordinance also provides a reward of $25 for information leading to the apprehension of the guilty party. President Clark wishes to emphasize that this reward holds good in this instance and urges that it will be promptly paid for such information relative to the alarm of Sunday night. He also indicates that the village will go to the limit in punishing the guilty party.

Resignation and Reorganization

That summer witnessed the resignation of Horace M. Stone as Police Justice, a position newly created in the village and to which, the Justice of the Peace at the time, Frank H. Gillett, was appointed. James E. Woodbridge, a former and long time Village official (Treasurer and Trustee) died that summer and the Fire Department conducted a reorganization that seemed to create more interest in what was termed "firemanic spirit" among members. Village President Elmer Clark was " . . . faithful in attending these meetings as any fireman, . . . " (MO 6/9/16) helping to bring about a reorganization of the association that would be satisfactory to all. False fire alarms also made headlines that summer as well as an announcement of a reward leading to the arrest of those responsible. Today, false fire alarms do not seem to be as prevalent as they once were and a more common problem is the frequency of alarms that are set off by malfunctioning equipment in a home that has been wired with an alarm system.

Infantile Paralysis

Early in August, the community of Marcellus was inflicted with an epidemic of infantile paralysis or polio and officials in the town and village as well as the school were quick to respond with public announcements and the ordering of quarantine. Apparently the epidemic began in communities to the east of Marcellus and spread rather rapidly, especially among the young. Citizens were called upon to notify the local health officer of any new folks in town, traveling salesmen were refused licenses and precautions were urged to safeguard drinking water and public establishments. Finally both the village and town boards ordered quarantine and the schools in the community were closed until further notice. Although there were some who thought that this might have been an over-reaction to poliomyelitis hysteria, there were others who claimed that such action was necessary to prevent its spread. By the end of September, the children were back in school and the polio plague seemed to have run its course.

The Marcellus Observer
Friday, Aug. 11, 1916
Infantile Paralysis

This epidemic is spread more or less through most of the counties east of us and is rapidly approaching our community, and to circumvent this dreaded disease the State Sanitary Commission at Albany has sent out warnings and suggestions for meeting the emergency . . . The law provides that all children coming in our midst from infected districts, even for a short stay, must necessarily submit to quarantine for a specified time. And it also provides that it is the duty of every resident knowing of any such visitors to notify the local health officer, Dr. J. C. Parsons, of the circumstances, when prompt action will be taken.

The Marcellus Observer
Friday, Aug. 25, 1916
Quarantine!

At a meeting held Monday night, the following quarantine notice was passed by a joint meeting of Marcellus town board and village trustees, with Health Officer Parsons. They also urged the usual, or more than usual, vigilance on the part of the Health Officer toward his inspection and demand that property owners clean up possible sources of contagion or unhealthy conditions in town or village.

First - All persons of the age of sixteen (16) years or under who shall enter this Town or Village after the date above stated, August 21st, 1916, shall be placed under quarantine for at least two weeks from the time of such arrival . . .

Second - All persons of the age of sixteen (16) years or under who shall after the above date, August 21st, 1916, leave this Village or Town and go into an affected district, shall, upon their return, be subjected to a quarantine for at least two weeks from the date of their return . . .

Resolved, and it is hereby further resolved, that any parent or guardian who shall break either of these above sections of this resolution, shall and will be subject to the full penalty of the law . . .

The Marcellus Observer
Friday, Sept. 1, 1916
Poliomyelitis vs. Other Infectious Diseases
Town Board Meets School Trustees

They passed this resolution: "District schools in Marcellus township shall remain closed until Monday, Sept. 18th." . . . By order of the Board of Health, the primary departments in all the Sunday schools in Marcellus village are closed until further notice.

Marcellus Board of Education decided not to open school until Monday, September 11.

We are asked to suggest that Sunday schools be closed as well as other gatherings of children. And that while at it, the party says, close the churches a month to be safe.

The Marcellus Observer
Friday, Sept. 22, 1916
When The Children GoBack To School

As the paralysis plague nears the end of its 1916 career of frightfulness and the rigors of quarantine begin to relax with health boards recovering from the hysteria that has made so much discomfort and contributed in no small measure to the public distress of this memorable season, there is need of special alertness against the dangers of too swift reaction on the part of citizens who have been panic-stricken. Cooler weather, even if it may not control the mysterious contagion, will increase powers of resistance, while the close of the vacation period and the resumption of routine the agencies of germ dissemination are restrained.

The school authorities are arranging for every precaution; and parents must do their part

Post Office Robbed

No sooner had the polio epidemic subsided than a rash of post office robberies occurred in the area. In early November, the Marcellus Post Office was robbed, and the local paper indicated that " . . . this is the fourth time Marcellus has had such callers. Other village post offices all about are robbed. They do not touch banks, jewelers, and protected safes. But Uncle Sam, supposed to have the best talent in the land, has none. And these fellows seem to know it. These days of auto bandits our money is easily taken. For this is the public purse" (MO 11/10/16).

November Election

More astonishing than the robbery at the post office, however, were the results of the Presidential election that November. In a race that featured the New York Governor, Charles Evans Hughes, running against the President, Woodrow Wilson, many thought that the war in Europe played a very important part. Wilson campaigned on the slogan that he would continue to keep America out of a foreign conflict and the results of the election seemed to favor that stance. Americans in sleepy little villages like Marcellus were more concerned with local issues, like the extension of Reed Street, leaking water mains, new fire fighting equipment and the question of who was going to pay for the publishing and printing of public health matters. The European conflict seemed to echo a past that their ancestors had long ago forgotten and repudiated when they emigrated to the United States. Little did most of them realize that within six months, their children would be drafted to fight in a war that was 3000 miles away from the corner of Main and North Streets in Marcellus.

13 Nov 1916 - " . . . the grade of Reed Street Extension, as surveyed by Chas Ogle, C. E. and graded by Edmund Reed, be and is hereby accepted and adopted as the official grade for said Reed St. to the west line of property now owned by W. H. Wright."

The Marcellus Observer
Friday, Nov. 17, 1916
Board of Trustees

Marcellus village board met Monday night, President Clark, Trustees Coville and Reed, Clerk White, Mr. Spinks reported on various matters.

Certain improved conditions were discussed on the new Reed street, grades, etc., and the board seemed to understand that Mr. Reed was taking best care of the street and such portions as are to be done there other than by property owners.

Thomas Smith has reported some time past a leakage of water near his place by the bridge, which, while on the wrong side of the road and not near the water main, still may be a leak in the main. This is to be looked after.

Payment for needed publishing and printing of public health matters, paralysis, quarantine, etc., authorized by a joint meeting of town and village officials, might be payable by both, but the village board felt this justly a town charge, and named Mr. Reed to arrange with Supervisor Stone and the town board that it be accepted as such. The amount is $22.75, covering the year.

The Marcellus Observer
Friday, Dec. 18, 1916
From Marcellus Village President

To the Editor:

Is Marcellus fully equipped with fire fighting apparatus that the advanced ideas of the present time demands? Our hydrant facilities have been tried out to quite a satisfactory conclusion, but in view of the universal use of chemical appliances used in all the cities and the rapidly increasing number of these machines coming into use in the villages, the question arises, is Marcellus fully prepared to fight fire as it should be.

In Syracuse the chemical engine is always the one that begins work first, and usually succeeds in putting out over 50 per cent of the fires, and with much less damage to buildings and contents. Chemical compounds can be forced into burning buildings much quicker than water. Persons who have seen the work they do are highly pleased with results. A 50-gallon tank mounted on wheels would cost something less than $300. Two 35-gallon tanks placed on one vehicle could be procured for about $500. The taxpayers of the village are invited to make some comment on the question in the next issue of The Observer. It is confidently hoped that there will be a general response.

E. P. CLARK

Community Christmas Tree

As 1916 came to a close, the community of Marcellus began a tradition that

> **The Marcellus Observer**
> **Friday, Dec. 29, 1916**
> **Community Christmas Tree**
> **A Grand Success - Exercises Witnessed By Several Hundred People**
>
> Marcellus made her first Christmas tree a success despite handicaps. It was bitter cold, beyond the possibility of comfort, though many braved the wintry chill when the church bells rang at 6:45, and the corner was well filled to enjoy the program. The tree was a blaze of tinsel and colored lights and the center of attention.
>
> Young people planning to take part in the singing gathered promptly in the Presbyterian church . . . . The carols sung were well done, the public interest aroused to the desire spirit and future Yuletides such plans will be again carried out.
>
> The tree was lighted all night before Christmas and each evening of holiday week. This made its most pleasing feature. Bad weather washed the coloring off and Kelly and Thornton will need Ed. Bartlett to apply some red and green paint to the whitened globes. But all had much satisfaction by the effort.

MO Dec 29, 1917

continues to this day. It was decided to display a community Christmas tree, followed by a variety of activities and a program in which many members of the community took part. The village was putting out the lights on an old year and making resolutions for a new one. No doubt at the top of that list of resolutions was the promise and the hope that America would continue to stay out of the war overseas and that their boys would stay "down on the farm". They would be disappointed and 1917 would be a year filled with news of the war and our entrance into it. Marcellus and America would lose its innocence in the muddy trenches of France and Belgium.

1917

In the meantime, village residents were as concerned as ever with the often mundane and everyday occurrences in a small rural community. Dr. Ell Walsh's house on First Street was saved from destruction by fire in early January, a bucket brigade of neighbors responding to the alarm. This may have been the inspiration for the Board of Trustees to install another fire signal at the north end of town. There was also news that three new garages were to be built on North Street, a response, it appears to the growing interest and use of the automobile even in rural communities. In addition, the Marcellus Free Library would find a new home

> **The Marcellus Observer**
> **Friday, Jan. 5, 1917**
> **Bucket Brigade Beats Firemen To It.**
>
> **The Marcellus Observer**
> **Friday, Jan. 19, 1917**
> **Three Garages For Marcellus**
>
> **The Marcellus Observer**
> **Friday, Jan. 25, 1917**
> **Marcellus Library Opening**
>
> **The Marcellus Observer**
> **Friday, Feb. 9, 1917**
> **Liquor Seizure At Alvord House**

over the First National Bank on Main Street and news that beer and liquor were being stored and sold in Marcellus brought out the detectives who would make raids on local establishments.

12 Feb 1917 - " . . . that the Village purchase a fire signal to be placed at the north end of the town."

Election and the Effects of War

On Election Day, March 20th, the vote of just 16 men confirmed the re-election of Elmer P. Clark as Village President, along with the election of Ward Curtis as Trustee. One of the first acts that the new Board of Trustees took at its annual meeting in April was the adoption of a resolution supporting the decision of President Wilson when he asked Congress for a declaration of war against Germany on April 1st.

The patriotic fervor also carried over into meetings of the Marcellus firemen, who

---

The Marcellus Observer
Friday, April 13, 1917
Board of Trustees

Whereas: we realize the momentous crisis in which the Government of the United States has been forced by the aggressions of a hostile foreign power, therefore be it

Resolved, That we uphold President Wilson in the firm stand he is taking to protect the lives and property of our citizens and safeguarding the dignity, honor and freedom so dear to the American people, and which has been jealously fostered since the foundation of the Republic, and further, we firmly believe that the President's resolute action will be a benefaction to the civilized world.

The Marcellus Observer
Friday, May 4, 1917
Pro Patria

Monday night, April 30, there was one of the best turnouts that the firemen have had in years. P. J. Kelly made a very fine speech on the subject of raising a sufficient sum to buy uniforms for the firemen in order that they might make a neat appearance on all occasions . . .

Mr. Kelly read a communication from Governor Whitman calling on all civic bodies of men to organize a "Home Defense Military League," the government to supply rifles, ammunition and more or less uniforms. All who were present had an opportunity to vote on the proposition and were unanimous in accepting the opportunity to protect home property. The State government will send a man once a week to drill the men and supervise their target practice.

The Marcellus Observer
Friday, May 11, 1917
High Cost of Living

This is the contribution of Mrs. Wm. H. Lavey, written for The Marcellus Free Library Bazaar and read by her the opening night.

Food-stuff is going higher
   I'll tell you the reason why
Most of our sons and daughters
   The city life want to try.
If our boys do stay at home
   They don't want to work the farm;
They're looking up a place to go
   On the screen they find the charm.
And the girls are just as bad,
   They want to be on the go;
Or else are taking basket ball,
   Or waiting for a beau.
So that leaves us old folks
   On the farm to grub and hoe,
While the young folks auto-ride,
   Where to we never know.
So we old ones have concluded
   We will not work so hard,
And it is "up to" you young people
   To till your own back yard.
Then some of our old-time farmers
   Are getting auto crazy,
And will be as bad as young folks
   But I hope not quite as lazy.
So you see it don't leave many
   On farms to do the tilling
That's what makes the cry we hear
   About the High Cost of Living
If I ever get an auto
   I'll get it for the farm,
It must do the work in the house
   And all the chores at the barn
It must saw the wood, milk the cows,
   Skim the milk and churn,
Not run around the country
   Just it's gasoline to burn.
Good night, all young people,
   Come with us, lend a hand
We'll raise onions and potatoes
   We will call it the Venture Band.

---

enthusiastically supported the raising and arming of a home defense league for protection of home and property. In addition, "Marcellus women contributed heavily to the war effort on the home front. In May . . . a branch of the American Fund for the French Wounded was organized. A committee . . . supervised the making of all kinds of towels, shirts, pajamas and hospital supplies . . . the same committee organized the Marcellus Soldiers Comfort League, which raised money to outfit Marcellus servicemen with sweaters, socks, helmets, scarves, wristlets and toilet articles" (Heffernan 97).

High Cost of Living

Not all were as enthusiastic, however, particularly farmers throughout the country, and including those in Marcellus. While the federal government, in response to the demand for food supplies, urged them to produce more than they had in the past, it also imposed price controls on certain farm products, limiting their income and extending their working hours. Many farmers responded with a demand for a shorter workday and for a lifting of the controls that had been imposed. Others thought that the farmers were not being patriotic causing the farmers to respond that they were doing all of the work while others, particularly " . . . the politicians and ministers, who do nothing, shout patriotism the loudest and hardest" (MO 5/11/17).

More Than Just Memorial Day

The Memorial Day celebration had added significance in 1917 and by early June, *The Marcellus Observer* would publish a now famous cartoon of Uncle Sam marching off to Europe to make the world safe for democracy. The entire community of Marcellus seemed galvanized for the war effort as citizens were urged to donate to a war chest - " . . . the ladies are out. Cough up!" (MO 8/10/17). They were urged to ration such things as butter and sugar and to limit the amount of meat and bread they consumed. The residents of the community became accustomed to wheatless Mondays and porkless Thursdays, all in an effort to do their part to win the war. For the young men of the village, the war would become even more personal as the government imposed a military

MO Jun 22, 1917

Memorial Day Gives Added Significance As Country Meets Another Crisis

Memorial Day observance in Marcellus was by far the largest and best in ten years or more at least, due to general participation of citizens. They responded cordially to the call issued by The Citizens Committee to take part in the parade and program and each man who took his place in the ranks is, to be thanked and congratulated . . . . the Veteran Comrades of Joseph Jones Post, G.A.R. must have had hearts filled with pride at the recognition given of their Memorial Day, 1917, when we again face the condition whey they faced in '61.

The parade formed promptly and proceeded to the school building to meet pupils and teachers, who joined them and all marched down Main street to the junction of Orange, turning there and counter marching to the Methodist church . . . . Much hand clapping was heard along the line of march by spectators.

The program was carried out in pleasing detail before an audience which completely filled the church . . . The address of Mr. Stone was given undivided attention, his every word plainly heard, forceful and fitting. The male quartet sang twice, Messers. Frost, Jones, Murray and McNair. The girls quartet were Ruth Dunlop, Frances Jones, Jeanette Waite and Helen Uttley. Paul Curtin delivered the Gettysburg Address of the immortal Lincoln. Grade 2 gave a fine flag drill. Ideal weather prevailed, the great change from that which has prevailed in the past, stirring all to real enjoyment of the beautiful day . . . .

The Marcellus Observer
Friday, Aug 10, 1917
Marcellus To The Front - As Usual

Brother Keegan went to Syracuse and staid in the Mizpah to be first before the Draft Board. Billy Muldoon and John Stewart had breakfast and a cigar, and walked down past the MizPAH. Keegan came out of the hotel five steps at a time to be No. 1 on the registration. Billy Muldoon was No. 1 and our friend Keegan was No. 15. Skaneateles always was behind Marcellus anyway. Mr. Shotwell showed up later. E. Pluribus Unum. Erin go braugh!

draft, the first since the Civil War. Shortly after war was declared, all young men between the ages of 21 and 31 were required to register for the draft, and in early August 1917, numbers were selected by drawing in a national lottery. Not all of those drafted would serve in combat and many would be exempted from service for a variety of reasons, but there were " . . . few flat footed farmers or failing hearts among our class of resident youth, . . . " (MO 8/10/17). The entire community was called upon to assist in the war effort and the New York State Fair in September encouraged all to attend so that they could learn how to help.

148

Irvin R. Webber	Marcellus
Chas. R. Wilson	Marcellus
Francis N. Casey	Marcellus
Ernest J. Marsh	Marcellus
Henry T. Martens	Marcellus
Arthur Hickman	Marcellus
Norman C. Buffan	Marcellus
Chas. L. Garvey	Marcellus
Wm. S. Spaulding	Marcellus
Roy A. Curtis	Marcellus
Wm. C. Thornton	Marcellus
Wm. E. Heenan	Marcellus
Fred'k O. Watkins	Marcellus
John B. Keegan	Marcellus
J. Went'h Chapman	Marcellus
Wm. F. Muldoon	Marcellus
H. G. Kennedy	Marcellus Falls
Wilmar Bunt	Marcellus
Pat'k F. Waters	Marcellus
Dr. M. W. Sullivan	Marcellus
John D. Johnson	Marcellus
Robert E. Muldoon	Marcellus
James Franco	Marcellus
Emmett L. McNally	Marcellus
Wm. J. Kelley	Marcellus
Wm. C. Curtin	Marcellus
John Moslo	Marcellus
Theodore Leader	Marcellus
J. C. Parsons Jr.	Marcellus
Albert Griffin	Marcellus
Joseph Furgal	Marcellus
A. D. Ammerman	Marcellus
J. G. Nightingale	Marcellus
James E. Walsh	Marcellus
Wm. E. Engler	Marcellus
John L. O'Shea	Marcellus
Glenn C. Lindsley	Marcellus
Wm. V. Share	Marcellus
Louis Edw Haster	Marcellus
James Puffet	Marcellus R.D.
Wm. J. Lennon	Marcellus R.D.
H. T. Lanning	Marcellus R.D.
Jas. D. Murphy	Marcellus R.D.
E. H. Williams	Marcellus R.D.
R. E. McNally	Marcellus R.D.
Wm. J. Gray	Marcellus R.D.
A. A. Schram	Marcellus R.D.
Austin Vinton	Marcellus R.D.
F. H. Albring	Marcellus R.D.
Fred R. Cooper	Marcellus R.D.
L. S. Giles	Marcellus Falls
John R. Haney	Marcellus Falls
Edward Letson	Marcellus Falls

wartime measure to conserve electricity). It is interesting to note that Village residents

The Marcellus Observer
Friday, Aug. 17, 1917
Song For the "Bit" Done At Home
The following poem, written by an employee of the New York Telephone, . . . will afford inspiration to those whose duty keeps them away from the firing line. It is not very spectacular - having to keep the wheels running at home so the soldiers at the front will have food and warmth and wherewithal to fight - so a poem on that side of the question is welcome:

DOING OUR BIT
By George H. Esler
We may not sound the bugle call,
We may not beat the drum,
We may not fly above the clouds,
Or hear the bullets hum.

We may not fight beneath the flag,
We may not charge the foe,
We may not help poor farm lands thrive,
As "Soldiers of the Hoe."

We may not sail the mighty deep,
A-hunting for the U's,
We may not play a hero's part
Or figure in the news.

But we may serve our Uncle Sam,
And we may serve him well,
If we but do our little bit,
As workers of the "Bell."

Village Matters

Meanwhile, the business of village government continued. The matter of insurance for village employees was discussed and this continues to be a concern for both employees and the Trustees of the Village today. In 1917, insurance involved compensation for those employees who might be injured on the job, and the cost was, even relatively speaking, a small amount. Today, insurance for Village employees is a large item in the budget, is very costly, and involves not just unemployment compensation, but health, dental, and vision care for employees as well.

Because the Board of Trustees was aware of the growing use of automobiles in the community, the placing of more traffic signs throughout the Village was authorized. Rockwell Pond, the source of Village water supply, continued to be regularly inspected, as it is today. There was also inquiry made about the Village Clock and the reasons why the clock faces were not lighted at night (a

continue to inquire about both the lighting of the clock faces and the accuracy of the time registered.

The war was ever present, however, and the Crown Mills, the largest employer in the Village, having large government orders to fill, made some desperate appeal for workers not only in the Village but also throughout the community.

14 Jul 1917 - " . . . matter of compensation insurance covering village employees was brought up and after some discussion a motion was made . . . that the policy as presented by H. M. Stone be accepted . . . also that the bill of $50.00 for the same be paid."

12 Aug 1917 - " . . . the question of signs to read 'Keep to Right' to be placed at the corner of North and Main, also Main and South Sts. was brought up, and on motion by Curtis, Mr. Clark was empowered to procure two signs as soon as possible."

The Marcellus Observer
Friday, Aug. 31, 1917
Crown Mills In Need of Help
Marcellus Principal Industry Appeals To Public For Workers In This Time of Country's Need. Greatly Handicapped By Lack of Help. Offer Good Opportunities

Crown Mills, Marcellus are in greatest need of help. They have a Want Ad in this paper, have advertised in trade journals, made inquiry at milling centers, and accepted all workers available who seek employment between various milling towns, . . .

Offer is made to teach such new hands trades in the mill, at good wages. Spinners are the special demand at present. They make good wages . . .
Marcellus' greatest industry is serving Uncle Sam, by making cloth for soldiers. Help is in greatest demand. They need, must have, helpers. If anyone can apply for a position, let him visit Crown Mills at once and learn what he may do. Here is a way to do that bit. . . .

The Marcellus Observer
Friday, Sept. 21, 1917
Rockwell Pond Inspection

The regular inspection of the Marcellus Village water supply was made last Saturday by Commissioner Masters and "Village Engineer" Howard Clark. The Rockwell Pond and its surroundings were inspected and a sample of the water was properly taken to be forwarded to the State Board of Health at Albany for its examination. In spite of the fact that the season has not been a dry one, and that little water has been consumed for sprinkling lawns during the summer, the reservoir is not overflowing, though the supply is ample for all general use and for emergency in case of fire.

Our "High Lights" Burn Low

Considerable and frequent inquiry has been made of the Village President and others as to why the four faces of the village clock are no longer lighted at night.

"I Can't Vote
Neither Can Ma
If the Town goes Wet
Blame it on Pa!"

MO Nov 1, 1917

November Elections

The 1917 election was again a contest between the "wets" and the "drys." A petition from those who favored the licensing of alcohol was gathered, as well as published in the paper, and the question would again be put to the town voters in November. The forces of prohibition continued to be very adamant in their attempt to preserve and continue the "no-license policy" approved by the voters in 1913 and they too gathered a petition that was published in *The Marcellus Observer*. The issue also carried over into the vote for women suffrage in New York State, some indicating that "license" might win because women could not vote. The results of the election proved to be a victory for both the forces of prohibition and women suffrage in New York State, although the latter seemed somewhat close in the Town of Marcellus and nearby communities. So, too, the neighboring towns of Elbridge, Camillus and Skaneateles finally went "dry." The 1917 decisions for "no-license" and suffrage for women seemed to be a prelude for the 18th and 19th Amendments to the United States Constitution, enacted within just a few years of the New York vote.

The Village Board of Trustees, in what appears to be another attempt at consolidation and recognizing the problems inherent in trying to prevent the spread of infectious disease, asked the State Commission of Health to combine the health districts of the Village and the Town into one district. Since that time, all health districts in the villages and towns of the County have been combined into one Onondaga County Department of Health.

**The Marcellus Observer
Friday, Dec. 20, 1917
Marcellus High School Will Have Program To Day, For The Former Pupils Who Are Now Pupils of Uncle Sam**
Honor Roll
Lt. Com'r W. J. Giles
Frederick H. Hyatt
Robert Muldoon
Charles Wilson
Will Heenan
Will Bennett
Louis O'Shea
Ambrose Welch
Harold Dillon
Roy Edwards
Francis Casey
Ray Haney
Vernon Woodford
Emmet McNally
John Keegan
Wm. Kelly
George Brow
Ralph Share
Frank Ward
Carlton Egan
Thomas Egan
Joseph Egan
Edward Egan
Thomas Callahan
Harry Matteson
John Reagan
Matthew Connell
Michael Conroy
George Leach
Robert Muldoon

---

10 Dec 1917 - " . . . that this Board of Trustees of the Village of Marcellus respectfully requests the State Commission of Health to combine the Village of Marcellus and the Town of Marcellus into one health district, to be known as a consolidated health district."

1918

As 1918 began, the war in Europe would enlist more young men from Marcellus and school programs would honor those former pupils. In addition, boys at the high school between the ages of 16 and 19 were

---

**The Marcellus Observer
Friday, Jan. 17, 1918
All Local Industries Close**
Crown Mills, Marcellus, closes the present five days, and will do so each Monday, in accordance with the new order.
Garfield makes it plain in current dispatches that congestion of freights, that is, of the product of industries, blocks the movement of coal. The cart ahead of the horse, temporarily. All must stand still until the primary article, coal, with which to keep warm, to move freight, to drive ships transporting troops, are supplied.
Garfield also emphasizes the fact that seaboard terminals are congested beyond description.

**The Marcellus Observer
Friday, Feb. 7, 1918
The Flour Limitation Order**
Local dealers receive the following formal instructions as to the sale of flour: . . .
(This is for the purpose of preventing hoarding by individuals, which is against the law.) . . .

---

encouraged to enroll for military training and a U.S. Service Flag was displayed, with new stars added as young men entered the service. The war dominated much of the news of 1918, as Marcellians were urged to buy bonds, support the efforts of the YMCA, and learn both to conserve some precious food items as well as be faithful to war production efforts on the farm and in the factory.

1918 Inductees

Election

The voter turnout for Village elections was high in 1918, reflecting, perhaps, the fact that New York State had granted the right to vote to women in 1917. Edward V. Baker Jr. was elected rather overwhelmingly as Village President, the other votes cast for persons who had not actively sought the office. A new five-year contract for lighting the village streets was presented and approved but the major efforts of both the village and town seemed to be that of promoting the sale of war bonds. The town was divided into almost 30 districts and workers solicited Liberty Loan subscriptions in a carefully laid-out plan that encouraged all to participate.

19 Mar 1918 - " . . . that the whole number of votes cast at said election was:
    For President for one year
    E. V. Baker   received 105
    R. P. Smith   received   5
    F. A. Thompson   received   1

8 Apr 1918 - " . . . F. W. Knapp presented a five year contract for lighting the streets of the Village and on motion . . . the same was accepted. A Street light being needed in Maiden Lane, a motion was made . . . that a 100 Watt lamp be placed in this street."

Spring of 1918

By May, a new batch of Marcellus boys was sent off to Europe and while some would rally to see them off, others would raise money for the Marcellus Soldier's Comfort League by performing dramas in Parsons Hall.

The Marcellus Observer
Friday, May 2, 1918
Marcellus Sees The Sendoff

The Marcellus contingent along with the Syracuse boys and others left the D. L. & W. depot Monday about 11:30 a.m. for Camp Dix. Quite a number of our friends from the village, from fifty to about one hundred, were in to see the boys off . . .. The boys from the village were James Haney, Louis Thornton, Tolman Spaulding, Harry Welsh, Raymond Hunt, and Frank Williams . . . When this war is over such of us as may be left will meet our boys on their return and if ever there was a jubilee on earth we will have one then . . ..

The Marcellus Observer
Friday, May 2, 1918
The drama, "Twixt Love and Money"

. . . presented by members of St. Francis Xavier's church of Marcellus, was most cleverly portrayed before appreciate audiences . . . The drama is a sparkling story of New England life, teeming with humor, mingled with tragedy and pathos. It tells, the story of the struggle of a young man's heart, torn by conflicting emotions of love for a poor girl and the fear of the loss of wealth, which he must sacrifice to attain his heart's desire. Charles Riley as the young man played a difficult part with remarkable skill . . .. Miss Mary Curtin as the girl whom he loved handled the most difficult part with the skill of an artist . . . Thomas Reynolds as her adopted father, a blind veteran, . . . Wilson Knapp as an enterprising promoter of a new hotel scheme, . . . Miss Eileen Newell as his fiancée, won the hearts of all, . . . James Hogan, sr., the rich uncle, . . . M. J. Thornton as the scheming friend of the young nephew . . . The rheumatic fisherman, . . . was played by P. J. Kelly . . .. Mrs. M. J. Thornton as his wife, kept the audience in an uproar of laughter . . . The young sailor, . . . was admirably impersonated by James Hogan . . . Paul Curtin as his brother Bill was excellent in portraying the down East twang and drawling speech of a young fisherman. The net proceeds are not known as yet, but maybe well over $200, to aid the good purposes.

At its May meeting, the Village Board decided to raise salaries, and that spring also witnessed a horrible trolley wreck near Split Rock that injured many Marcellus men who were employed at that war munitions plant.

The Marcellus Observer
Thursday, May 23, 1918

AWFUL TROLLEY WRECK NEAR SPLIT ROCK INJURES 50

Friday morning, May 24, the trolley car leaving Marcellus at 6:45 for Split Rock, eastbound, collided with two loaded gondola coal cars and the power car attached to them at the east end, around a curve 1/4 mile or more east of Olney Crossing, down the grade toward The Rock, causing a frightful wreck, killing one man of the 80 odd men packed on the car . . .. Edward C. Lewis was killed, instantly it is presumed . . .. Louis Powell is probably the worst injured of any. Upward of 20 Marcellus men are in Syracuse hospitals . . ..

The Marcellus Observer
Thursday, July 4, 1918

Fire and Explosion at Split Rock; Two Marcellus Men Heroic Victims.

C. Homer Wright and Andrew Dunn of Marcellus met tragic death and John H. King (he later died) lies in critical condition, victims with scores of others of an explosion and great fire at Split Rock, Tuesday, July 2. . . . It is said the history of Syracuse and vicinity records no such calamity

A pall prevails in our entire section. Sentiment prevails that these men were as truly heroes of the great fight for Freedom as are they of the battle front.

13 May 1918 - " . . . the salary of the Village Clerk; was raised from $25.00 to $40.00 per year . . .. the salary of the Treasurer be raised from $30.00 to $50.00 per year . . . carried."

Split Rock Again

A little more than a month later, another tragedy occurred at Split Rock. On Tuesday night, July 2, 1918, a terrific explosion and fire took place at the munitions plant where three Marcellus men -- Andrew Dunn, Clarence Wright, and John King -- lost their lives, victims and heroes in another way of the struggle going on in Europe at the time.

The tragedy would cause the postponement of some summer fund-raising events and probably made the war seem much closer to Marcellus than previously comprehended. Throughout the summer, the Board of Trustees continued to address village concerns, making a variety of appointments and providing needed services. In addition, a joint meeting of the town and village boards would end the quarantine imposed some months earlier

> **The Marcellus Observer**
> **Wednesday, Oct 23, 1918**
> **Board Raise Quarantine**
> A joint meeting of town and village boards was held Friday night in Marcellus and the following resolution passed: Resolved that the prohibition placed upon all public gatherings in the Town of Marcellus including schools and churches be lifted at 12 o'clock midnight, Saturday October 26, 1918.

15 Jul 1918 - " . . . John Stewart and Jas Powell were chosen as delegates to represent the Marcellus Fire Dept at the county convention at East Syracuse, Wed. July 24, 1918."

12 Aug 1918 - " . . . the office of Registrar of Vital Statistics being vacant, the Clerk was appointed to succeed himself . . . "

9 Sep 1918 - " . . . the health officer of the Town was appointed as health officer for the Village . . .. the question of using copper sulphate in the pond was next brought up . . . On advice from Dr. Parsons, a motion was made by Scott that the health officer secure information in regard to the purchase and use of copper sulphate."

End of the War

By the fall of 1918, the addition of fresh American troops to the Allied cause earlier in the year would cause Germany to ask for an armistice and in early November, demonstrations were held both in Syracuse and in Marcellus that would celebrate an end

> **The Marcellus Observer**
> **Wednesday, Nov 6, 1918**
> # PEACE ?
> Demonstrations were held in the city and all our villages, Thursday that WAR HAD CEASED. Flag raising, bells ringing, parades and general thanksgiving prevailed with inspiring spirit of patriotism.
> Word came over Crown Mills special wire that firing would cease at 2 p.m. John Daye and Miss Austin phoned Rev. Frost, he rushed out and began pulling the church bell, while they hastened to the Episcopal bell and the din did not cease till dusk and later.
> Principal Ruland found study nil as the bells were heard and youth returned with reason. Pupils were formed in line, teachers, flag bearers in the midst, led by Kenneth Spaulding and Geo. Black with a bas drum, and proceeding to the liberty pole, where the big flag had been raised, and here in a great circle, under Old Glory, they sang America, gave the Salute to the Flag and sang the National Anthem, then closing up, with a rousing cheer they were dismissed.

Pvt. Ralph Share

Pvt. Thomas Dunn

to the hostilities. There was also sadness, however, for the families of those ten young men who were killed in action or died in the service of the country. Two of these young heroes, Pvt. Ralph Share and Pvt. Thomas Dunn, would be pictured in *The Marcellus Observer* just a few days after the armistice was signed on November 11, 1918. Others were still missing in action, while others would succumb to their wounds within a few weeks. For Marcellus, " . . . out of an estimated population of three thousand people, nearly one hundred and thirty enlisted or drafted men went to the various fields of instruction or military camps. Of these about one hundred and ten were sooner or later engaged in active service, and before the close of the war, ten per cent had lost their lives on the battlefield or died from causes connected with the war. This was a larger percentage than fell to the lot of any other town in Onondaga County . . . They came back, those who could . . and quietly took their place again in the familiar life as citizens who had done that which they were called to do and who were willing to let the work speak for itself . . ." (Davenport 7-8). The end of the war had brought many changes to the world, to the United States, and to the community of Marcellus. The village was at peace, but it was just waking up to a new world.

1919

The year, which saw the end of the decade, began with a surprise resignation of the Village President. Edward V. Baker, having been elected in 1918, had to resign because his job was relocated out of town. To that position, Charles E. Jones was appointed and to which office, after having served for several months, he would also be elected in March.

The Marcellus Observer
Wednesday, Jan 1, 1919
Home News

Shall we get up a petition for better movies in town? Who would sign it? Who wouldn't, that likes to go to the movies?

A Little Pick At The Pictures

To the Editor:

Through your weekly paper, I would like to criticize our moving pictures here in town. Now we all know that 22 cents is a lot of money to pay for the pleasure of seeing the movies for an hour. I for one feel we are not getting our money's worth. I also know the pictures the last two weeks are not fit for my kiddies or anybody else's to see and further more a child of 6 to 10 cannot understand them and that is all the recreation our children get in this town.

Now it may not be the fault of Mr. Parsons as these pictures may not be his choice, but I am sure if he would ask his children which they would rather see, A Western picture of The Hooded Terror, they would choose the former. The Hooded Terror is much like the stories in our Monthly Magazines, it comes in installments. Now I as well as my children like to see the movies every Saturday night but where you take three children in and have them come home and all they could understand was where the heroine or hero was knifed and not have that clear, one begins to think the best thing he can do is stay at home with his children.

---

13 Jan 1919 - " . . . E. V. Baker have(ing) been taken from town on business, his resignation as President of the Village was presented, to take effect at once . . . that C. E. Jones be appointed to fill this vacancy for the balance of the year."

The Marcellus Observer
Wednesday, Jan 15, 1919
Jones Is Village President

At a regular meeting of Marcellus Village Board held Monday evening, Jan 13, the resignation of E. V. Baker as president was accepted, and the Board appointed Charles E. Jones to fill the vacancy.

Mr. Baker has accepted a position in Detroit, Mich., thus making the action necessary. We believe the appointment of Mr. Jones to be a good thing for the Village at this time, as he is well qualified to look after our interests.

FOUR MARCELLUS PLACES PLUNDERED BY BURGLARS

Marcellus is on the map again. Big, bold Burglars! Oo-Oo-Oo! Early Wednesday morning, . . . along comes an auto filled with men. They set one to watch, forced open the M. T. Smith Store, . . . The Marcellus Hardware store was on their calling list, . . . They went through a window in the new Jordan market, . . . They then went to the post office . . . Who's next?

---

10 Feb 1919 - " . . . John Spaulding was engaged as policeman."

18 Mar 1919 - " . . . that the whole number of votes cast at said election was: For President for one year   Charles E. Jones   received 16

Culture Wars

There was also some concern, as the year began, that the movies being shown at the local picture house (Parsons Hall) were not as wholesome as they should probably have been. This seems to be a good example of the social reaction of many Marcellians to the war recently concluded. Many people wanted a return to normalcy, to the way things used to be and the changes that they were now witnessing were an outgrowth, many

---

The Marcellus Observer
Wednesday, Jan 15, 1919

Knocked Out In The Thirty-sixth Round!
Local Villages Beat Uncle Same To It!

The champ is champ no longer. Slow music and black horses for old John Barleycorn. It took some years to do the deed, but it's did at last. After January, 1920, our great nation will be absolutely dry. Not one wet spot. Our villages may be proud of the fact that they were among the leaders in the greatest movement in the history of the world. The prayers of countless mothers and little children have been answered. Sons and fathers from overseas will come home to a nation purified and clean, safe from the tyranny of the 'booze barons" safe from the yoke under which Columbia has labored these many years. 'Praise God from Whom All Blessings flow.'

The Marcellus Observer
Wednesday, February 19, 1919
Old Land Mark Gone

The old "elm tree" as it has been called many generations in Marcellus, has been leveled at last. No one in Marcellus knows the exact age of this, the greatgrandfather of all elm trees in Onondaga county. Probably a sapling when the redskins roamed over this section, a tender young forest king in the days of our first settlers, the old elm' had grown to be a menace to public safety, and it was thought best to cut it down.

Could the old tree have spoken what tales it could have told of old-time lovers, who whispered their vows under its boughs. Of the little children of by-gone years, whose gleeful voices rose to the topmost leafy branch as they built their doll houses and chased Indians, and had their childish quarrels and made up and grew to be men and women. Long ago those children have gone to their last sleep, and now their children's children, aye, it may be their children's children's children, are watching with round eyes as the old elm' is laid low. We have bent our ear close to the ancient trunk and whispered, 'Old tree, tell us a story'. But he only tossed his branches in the wind, and hugged his secrets to bosom, and so much of the history of old Marcellus is gone with the "old tree'.

---

thought, of that conflict in Europe. Many did not like what seemed to be happening and public opinion turned against things that were different or would threaten what had been before the war. There would be an increase in cultural animosities as public opinion began to turn against unions, minorities, immigrants, and city dwellers, all of who seemed to be associated with change and a threat to the old rural ways. The earlier cultural war between wets and drys was renewed as the 18th Amendment to the United States Constitution was approved and it again pitted those who lived in the rural areas (usually dry) against those who lived in the cities (usually wet). Anything out of the ordinary, such as a series of burglaries that occurred in the Village in early January, might be associated with an increase in lawlessness and another indication of how futile the war effort had been. Even the felling of an old elm tree on the corner of North and Reed Streets early in February seemed to evoke a feeling that the past was being destroyed and that the future had little to offer. A feeling that was both reactionary and isolationist would persist into the 1920s and even found expression in the emergence of a Ku Klux Klan group in Marcellus in the middle of that decade.

Memorial Welcome

The citizens of Marcellus were also concerned that their soldier heroes be welcomed

home and that a fitting monument be erected to the memory of those who had fallen in service. Committees were organized, reports were made and fund drives were begun to pay tribute to the past. At its annual meeting in April, the new Board of Trustees, headed by President Jones, made appointments and granted permission for the school to install its own sewer system. As Memorial Day, 1919, rolled around, an invitation went out from President Jones asking all veterans to help celebrate a true day of remembrance for the Village.

20 Mar 1919 - " . . . J. H. Weidman gave a report of the Committee for welcoming the soldiers home. Nothing definite was decided on and the same committee was continued. H. M. Stone and Father Melich were appointed as part of the committee for arranging the first welcome for the soldiers."

4 Apr 1919 - " . . . that F. J. Uttley be appointed Registrar of Vital Statistics . . . . from Jan 7, 1919 to Jan 7, 1922, a term of 4 years . . . . that the petition of the Board of Education asking permission to lay a sewer in West Main St. and to cross South St., . . . be granted . . . "

Summer Activity

As summer approached, and street construction in the Village began, the Board approved an increase in pay for some workers, wages that had been frozen, as had many prices, during the war. The cost of cutting the elm tree was also presented to the Board and the concerns that some had about the danger of coasting on West Hill sidewalks led to that prohibition. The biggest event of the summer, however, was the Welcome Home Celebration, which was held in honor of the soldier boys on Saturday, July 19, 1919.

3 Jun 1919 - " . . . that the Village Street laborers be paid an advance of 2 1/2 cents per hour, raising the former price of .35 cents to .37 1/2 cents per hour."

9 Jun 1919 - " . . . a bill presented by Dr. Sullivan for removal of elm tree at corner of North and Reed St. itemized and totaling $91.00 was placed in the hands of Trustee Curtis for investigation and future action."

24 Jun 1919 - " . . . in view of the danger of coasting down West Hill on sidewalk, it was deemed necessary to adopt some prohibiting measures. Whereupon Curtis moved that all persons be forbidden coasting on West Hill sidewalk, north side, with bicycles, carts, wagons, roller coasters, sleds or any other rolling or sliding device. Motion seconded by Scott and carried."

14 Jul 1919 - " . . . that the Village donate $25.00 to the Welcome Home Committee (to welcome the men in the U.S. service just returning from the European war)."

The Marcellus Observer
Wednesday, July 16, 1919

MARCELLUS HONORS HER SERVICE MEN
Saturday, July 19, at 2 p.m., All Men of Uncle Sam's Service are Requested to Meet at the Engine House as Guests, Autos and Mounted Escort. Ball Game. Banquet at 6:30

Heroes all, is the title by which Marcellus will greet her veterans of the world war when on Saturday, citizens will extend formal Welcome Home to her honored soldiers.

Hon. William Nottingham will give the speech of welcome at the banquet given at 6:30, other speakers whom all will wish to hear being Edward C. Knapp in the response, he having just returned from France, "mayor elect" Capt. Harry Farmer, who will tell of experiences in war, W. J. Shotwell, chairman of the draft board, Prof James Shea, and Rev. Howard McDowell in a tribute or eulogy to the departed heroes.

Banquet tables will be laid for seating 400 in Parsons Hall, each soldier having been sent three tickets . . .. The banquet will be the most inspiring occasion ever held in Marcellus . . ..

Events of the day will be of surprising and entertaining character. Auburn Band will arrive at 2 p.m. A mounted cavalcade is planned and all horsemen of the section are invited to join, under Marshall Stone. This and other features of the parade are in care of F. T. Schoonmaker, who urges all riders to turn out. He also urges all to decorate autos and show the boys something than those French boxcars in this parade in their honor . . ..

Decorating of all homes and places is most important, and this is the urgency given to Roy P. Smith, who wishes in our columns to invite all to do so, emphasizing the need. And get something read to wave, flowers to throw, act the way you did the day the 'Peace bells rang', let the boys known where the homes are which they help to preserve.

A ball game at 3:30, Amber vs. Marcellus on the school grounds. Later a reception is set on the Presbyterian lawn, where everybody may meet and "glad hand" the boys.

Welcome Home - By Rev. Walter E. Cook

"Never will Marcellus forget the memorable day when the soldier boys of this town and vicinity were accorded the jubilant and enthusiastic welcome which loving and grateful hearts had planned so long. It was a day of days . . .. The boys were congratulated, honored, feted and feasted. Proud we were of those boys? Yes! But pride does not express the joy and admiration and love which broke loose from pent up hearts when those boys marched shoulder to shoulder down Main Street and gave us a brief, vivid, painful though fleeting reminder of those long, dark days which tried the hearts of men and nations, and then we remembered that it was all over, and the boys were home to stay, and simultaneously the thrill of it, and the realization of it, found unmistakable expression in the alternate cheers and tears and the tears and cheers of the devoted people of Marcellus. . . . It was an ideal day for celebration. The town was literally clothed in patriotic dress. Flags and colors floated from every house . . . crowds gathered in the street and the long to be remembered Welcome Home ended with an outdoor dance on the new asphalt pavement in front of the post office. The Auburn band furnished spirited music, while lad and lassie, old and young, made merry in the very exuberance of joy, and all Marcellus looked on" (Davenport 43-46).

Village Business

The summer of 1919 also saw the installation of a new fire siren for the Village, the sound of which causes some concern among residents even today, almost 90 years later. Trustee Lewis Scott would also resign from his post that summer because of a move out of town, and was replaced by Howard I. Clark for the remainder of that term.

13 Aug 1919 - " . . . meeting called for the purpose of establishing a fire alarm signal code . . . . that the following code of signals be adopted and put to practical use."

8 Sep 1919 - " . . . Trustee Scott, who recently removed to Clyde, N.Y., sent in his resignation, which was accepted."

As the summer began to fade into fall, so too the memory of the Great War became a little more distant. November elections in 1919 brought no local surprises, and people in Marcellus not only had much for which to be grateful at Christmas that year but they, like all Americans were being challenged by some new realities. The movie presented at Parsons Hall on Christmas night was entitled "Beauty Proof", a shooting mystery about a Northwest Mounted policeman who surrenders to the love of a girl he had arrested. Is a man always right in performing his sworn duty? they asked. The war had made many people uncertain.

Conclusion

Much had happened since the war broke out in Europe and its effect on small town America was profound. While they had hoped to stay isolated, removed from the conflict, Americans still wanted to carry on trade with both sides and the mills of Marcellus and nearby Split Rock employed many men and women in continuing this commerce. In the summer of 1916, the residents of Marcellus were faced with an outbreak of polio that threatened the isolation they had enjoyed for so long, an isolation that was permanently shattered when America entered the war in 1917. Small towns throughout the country, filled with patriotic fervor, sent their youth over there, confident that it would soon be finished. There were some government controls over production on the farm and factory, but there was no rationing, the people willing to sacrifice and do without, for the duration of the war. The 18th Amendment was viewed as a wartime measure to help conserve grains and the 19th as acknowledgment of the role that women played in helping win the war. When the "war to end war" ended, many Americans were convinced that a permanent peace was now possible and they wanted to retreat to the small towns that had been their splendid solitude prior to 1917. The years ahead would be very anxious ones for communities like Marcellus. As the cities grew, urban ideas began to overwhelm rural America causing both confusion and suspicion. The roaring decade ahead brought much prosperity, even for those in the country, but it was somewhat deafening for those who sought sanctuary in a memory.

Chapter 10 – The 1920s

The year began, as do all new years, with high hopes and resolutions. The 1920s would witness a terrific increase in the amount of product advertisement, encouraging people to buy and spend more. Even rural areas like Marcellus would be subjected to the

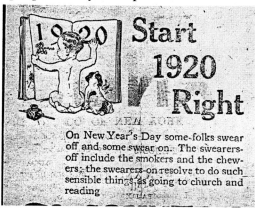

On New Year's Day some folks swear off and some swear on. The swearers-off include the smokers and the chewers; the swearers-on resolve to do such sensible things as going to church and reading

> **The Marcellus Observer**
> **Wednesday, February 25, 1920**
> **CLARK FOR MARCELLUS TRUSTEE**
> "Steve" Hunt lacked only one dollar of being made trustee of Marcellus village, he failed to buy one more vote, getting but 11 while Howard I. Clark had 12. The latter will succeed L.W. Scott, who has moved from town. Charles E. Jones was renominated for village president, Ward R. Curtis for trustee, V. S. Kenyon, treasurer, C. M. Woodford, Collector.

appeal of retailers, particularly in the local newspaper, to participate in what was to become a roaring economy.

Election

At the Village Caucus in February, the incumbents were re-nominated and there was a rather large turnout of voters in March, the challengers receiving a substantial number of votes. The ratification of the 19th Amendment to the U.S. Constitution, granting women, nationwide, the right to vote to, may have been a factor in this large turnout.

16 Mar 1920 - " . . . that there were, between the hours of 1 p.m. and 5 p.m., two hundred (200) ballots cast:

For President
Charles E. Jones	Received	114
Sidney H. Slocombe	Received	76
Stephen H. Hunt	Received	1
Fred A. Thompson	Received	1
Spoiled		6
Blank		2
	200	

For Trustee
Howard I. Clarke	Received	101
Stephen H. Hunt	Received	92
Blank		1
Spoiled		6
	200	

Safety and Clean Up

The Board began to address several concerns in the Village. One was the fact that automobiles, and there were an increasing number of them, were being parked on sidewalks, affecting the safety of pedestrians. Today, the issue might still be considered a concern, but it occurs more often in the winter when cars are parked on sidewalks or on village rights-of-way during the snow plowing season. Another matter in 1920 was the fact that some milk producers and distributors were not complying with state laws, a concern that is not as significant for today's Board since there are few vendors, other than ice cream trucks, licensed to distribute within the village.

15 Apr 1920 - " . . . the question of parking autos and placing signs for protection of sidewalks for pedestrians on West Main St. was mentioned but left for future decision."

22 Apr 1920 - " . . . Health Officer Dr. J. C. Parsons was in attendance for the purpose of discussing the production and distribution of milk or cream within the limits of the Village. Some procedures had not complied with state laws, and it was thought necessary to find some means whereby compliance would be made compulsory . . .. that cards be permitted to the effect that no license would be granted until application was made and stables, etc. be found up to sanitary requirements. The cards were to be sent to each individual . . . the sanitary condition of barber shops, as well as their customs, was discussed, but did not consider any action necessary."

The Marcellus Observer
Wednesday, April 21, 1920
CLEAN-UP WEEK BEGINS MONDAY

Our Village President is in receipt of the following: "During the long severe winter, it is inevitable that a great deal of filth and rubbish should accumulate since conditions have been such that its proper disposal has often been difficult or even impossible. With the melting snow, a large amount of decaying animal and vegetable matter has been left, often in conspicuous places where it is likely to become a nuisance.

"It is therefore particularly desirable that a special effort be made by health authorities to have all accumulations of filth and rubbish destroyed. That such action may be general throughout the State. April 26 is designated as clean-up week."

In accordance with these suggestions, the Village board has designated the week of April 26, as clean-up week, by householders.

Hearty co-operation of our people has marked past cleanup weeks and it is believed there will be no exception to the rule this year.

The Board also addressed the issue of village clean up, with another appeal by the Village President for residents to join in what was now becoming, and remains today, an annual rite of Spring in the Village of Marcellus. Young and old alike answered the clean-up call throughout the decade, including this lass, Marie Hickman, standing in front of her father's house on a spring day in the early 1920s.

The Summer of 1920

As the summer began in 1920, the Village Board reacted to some of the changes that were taking place. With the war over, tax laws changed and the assessments were to be adjusted to reflect that fact. The Board also began to enact laws, 15 in all, to govern traffic, speeding and other operations related to motor vehicles in the Village limits, another indication of the growing number and influence of automobiles in the "roaring 20s".

14 Jun 1920 - " . . . on account of a change in the tax laws of 1919, the following resolution was presented: Resolved: that all taxes paid upon assessments of the 1920 assessment roll of the Village of Marcellus be refunded and all taxes remaining unpaid at this date be canceled in accordance with the Article 16 of Sec. 352 of the tax law of New York State."

12 Aug 1920 - " . . . to consider the enactment of Village ordinances relating to traffic and speeding of all kinds of vehicles within the Village limits. . . . were adopted with none dissenting."

Resolved: That the following ordinances be adopted by the Board as ordinances of the Village of Marcellus and that the clerk cause the same to be posted and published according to law:

Sec. 1. . . .

Sec. 2 No person shall operate a motor vehicle. . . on any public highway in the village of Marcellus at a greater rate than one mile in four minutes; nor . . . any vehicle drawn by horse or horses . . . at a rate of speed faster than 8 miles per hour, or when rounding a corner faster than 5 miles per hour. . . . Every person violating any of the provisions . . . shall forfeit and pay a penalty of one hundred dollars . . .

Sec. 3. . . .

Sec. 4 Every bicycle, automobile or motorcycle driven in any street, highway, . . . of the village of Marcellus shall be equipped with a horn, bell or some other signal . . .

Sec. 5 No person shall ride or drive any vehicle on the sidewalk of the village, nor drive any vehicle with the hands off the guiding apparatus. . .

Sec. 6 Any vehicle meeting another shall reasonably turn and pass to the right.

. . . the foregoing is a true copy of an ordinance adopted by the Board of Trustees of the village of Marcellus on August 12th, 1920.

The Marcellus Observer
Wednesday, July 21, 1920
Villages Sign For Next Year

Community Chatauqua, Inc., have contracts signed by Marcellus, Jordan and Camillus for a return next year . . .

The Marcellus Observer
Wednesday, September 29, 1920
Raid Nets 21 Gallons Of Rye

The Alvord House, Marcellus, was raided last Thursday, Sep 23, at midnight by a force of Federal agents and Deputy Sheriff Hoffmire . . . They found and confiscated 21 gallons of whiskey, kept in jugs in a little outbuilding adjoining an acetylene lighting plant. . . .

The Marcellus Observer
Wednesday, November 3, 1920
To Sell Railroad Next Week

Next Wednesday, Nov. 10, at ten o'clock in front of the Court House, The Marcellus & Otisco Lake Ry. Co., will be sold "bag and baggage" at auction . . . .

The Marcellus Observer
Wednesday, December 15, 1920
Marcellus Has Another Fire

Monday evening, about 8:30, Donald Scott was the first to discover a rope of fire from the pole in front of Dwight Baker's house to the tree in front of I. A. Share's home. An alarm of fire was set in to central and soon the fire apparatus was on hand but by that time the fire was about out. I. A. Share is still using kerosene light.

The Marcellus Observer
Wednesday, December 22, 1920
Unemployment

The army of unemployed has been steadily increasing. The immigration of people seeking work has reached new high marks. Within the past few weeks, the increase in crime in many cities has been as steadily increasing.

The troubles we read about are found to a certain extent in our own town and village. They are unemployed people . . .

A continued interest in adult education was evident that summer as the Chatauqua movement, a series of public lectures given each year in that New York town, attracted much upstate interest. In addition, police agencies, local and national, seemed to step up enforcement of the Volstead Act, which was passed to enforce prohibition, by raiding several places thought to be selling illegal spirits and removing it from the premises.

The Fall of 1920

By the fall, it appeared that the M. & O. L. Railway would not long survive. Reorganized a year before, the railroad company continued to fall on hard times and did not generate enough revenue to justify operation. The firemen were busy, however, patrolling during Halloween and fighting fires that continued to be a concern for Village residents. Electricity was replacing kerosene as the principal means of lighting, but the technology was not as perfected as it would eventually become and defective wiring was a concern that both residents and the Village Board would discuss.

8 Nov 1920 - " . . . that the Board make some formal recognition of the work rendered by patrolling Halloween Eve by the firemen . . . that $100.00 be placed in the hands of James Powell, Treasurer of the Fire Department, for the benefit of that organization. Motion carried."

9 Nov 1920 - " . . . meeting . . . to consider the condition of the electric wiring of the town as to its safety or hazard, as several fires had occurred recently on account of faulty or defective wires . . . a committee of three was appointed to wait on the Underwriters Bureau of Syracuse and secure a competent person to inspect the wiring system exhaustively and make report to the proper officials."

29 Nov 1920 - " . . . the trimming of the lower branches of the trees throughout the Village which were a menace to wires and an obstruction to the electric lights and in other ways were objectionable."

As the year ended, the issue of unemployment overshadowed the holidays, particularly in industrial jobs such as those at the woolen mills in Marcellus or the cutlery in Camillus. With the war over, the demand for many American made products declined, as did the demand in European markets for American farm goods. It may have been the start of the "roaring 20's, but in rural America, times were not booming.

> **The Marcellus Observer**
> **Wednesday, January 26, 1921**
> **Home Capital Buys Railroad**
> The Marcellus & Otisco Ry was bought for $65,000 Thursday, Jan. 27, by local capital from the Philadelphia bank . . . The road will resume operation at once probably Saturday - Just as soon as they can fill the engine with water.

1921

In the new year, it appeared that local businessmen, Frank W. Knapp among them, would be able to purchase the M. & O. L. Railway, despite the fact that some of the rails had been taken up near Marietta. By the end of January, the road resumed operations, but there was concern as to how long it could sustain itself financially.

Women in Politics

Village elections were held on March 15th, and in a light turnout of voters (37 in all), Sidney Slocombe was again elected President along with Patrick J. Kilcoyne as Trustee and V.S. Kenyon as Treasurer. Clarence M. Woodford, who had first been elected Collector of Taxes in 1908 decided not to run for that office. His wife, Mrs. Minnie Woodford, was elected Collector of Taxes by the voters, the first woman to become officially involved in Marcellus Village government.

14 Feb 1921 - " . . . the Village Board voted to pay one half the expense incurred in repairs on the piano owned and controlled by the Fire Department and housed in the fire department rooms."

> **The Marcellus Observer**
> **Wednesday, April 13, 1921**
> **Will Hold Bazaar May 4, 5, and 6**
> For some years past Marcellus Fire Department has not been represented at the County Conventions either by Company or delegates, for lack of suitable uniforms to parade.
> During the war the boys were patient as money was needed more by Uncle Sam to equip and take care of the boys that he wanted. But that is ended and our village wants to again be represented at conventions.
> Every other village in the county has a Uniformed Company. Our village is as good as any. Our boys are better, because they are Our Boys and we are proud of them . . .

28 Mar 1921 - " . . . that the following names, Edward Dillon, P. J. Kilcoyne, Howard Wright and John Keegan be placed on the exempt list of Firemen and certifications of membership be issued to each."

Interest in the Marcellus Fire Department continued to be a concern for the Village Board and in April, the Village Board and the Firemen met to plan for a major event -- a bazaar to raise funds for Fire Department uniforms. The community was very proud of its firemen and "Marcellus Against the World" was an expression that seemed to convey the attitude of many that their boys were as good as any.

Continuing Issues

The issue of Daylight Savings, a carryover from the war years, was again a topic of discussion in the Village. The Village Board decided to do away with the services of Bert Chapman as caretaker of the Village Reservoir and it also sent notices to those who were violating Village speed limits. To recognize Memorial Day in 1921, the flag poles in the Village (at the school and in front of the Alvord House) received new coats of paint and the cemeteries were again flagged, a grand total of 126 according to *The Marcellus Observer* of June 1, 1921. In addition, George Amerman made a suggestion that military record keeping should receive more attention and that there should be more suitable plots and diagrams for the three cemeteries to more suitably recognize our solider-dead. With the memory of the Great War still fresh in many peoples' minds, Marcellians assiduously

The Marcellus Observer Wednesday, April 27, 1921 "Save Daylight" Monday	The Marcellus Observer Wed, June 1, 1921 Do Full Honors To Comrades	The Marcellus Observer Wednesday, June 1, 1921 A Memorial Day Suggestion
Crown Mills, Marcellus, announce that they will operate on new time from Monday, May 2. This follows the desire of their workers, and this time is accepted as governing other local affairs to the extent that it will be generally adopted. . . . The trolley is ahead the hour, city workers must go by this time and meals must be fixed to favor the poor housewife. So the school, churches and Ed Bartlett's town clock will all get up earlier Monday morning.	Painting the poles, both the big Liberty Pole at The Alvord House and the one at the School, was one way Marcellus took to celebrate Memorial Day. These were done last Friday, an Auburn man engaged by the school, and while he was here Aaron Waldron raised $12 to do the big pole. The bottom, ten feet or more, is painted red, all that above black. One authority, asked why black, said the town is dry.	. . . Provision is made for regularly recording and keeping an enumeration of the living voters of the town and the other vital statistics. It would seem that some such provision should be made for the Honored Dead! It may be that the county or government provide proper forms and stationery for these required records. In the writer's opinion it would be wise also to have suitable plots and diagrams made for the three cemeteries. These should be properly drawn to scale, lettered and mounted on permanent linen mounts . . .

continued to embrace duty toward country and self in the years that followed.

9 May 1921 - " . . . pay Bert Chapman, caretaker of Rockwell Springs, to May 21 - 14 months - and to give notice that his services will not be required after that date, May 21, 1921 and also to inform him that a dead calf was found in close proximity to the reservoir and exposed to the elements . . . send notice to Charles Gallinger that he had been violating the speed laws of the Village and that he must cease driving automobile any faster, within the Village limit, than the prescribed statues allow."

The Marcellus Observer Wednesday, August 17, 1921 "Reed Avenue Petitioners
The action of the Village Board in naming Reed Avenue was done by granting the request of the following petitioners who signed such a petition: F. W. Knapp, Mrs. Kasson Moak, Mrs. P. J. Kelly, Chas. M. Dye, Mrs. James Hogan, James Lanning. J. B. Parsons, Mrs. Bray, Mrs. Cuddeback, Mrs. Emily Gray, Hugh Woodford, Charles Dillon, Mrs. Chas. Dillon, Thomas Hogan, Mrs. Thomas Hogan, Hugh Adams, Mrs. Hugh Adams, Hugh Oliver, Mrs. B. Marshfield, Miss Brooks, Miss Sherwood, Mrs. Ethel Marble

Reed Street vs. Reed Avenue

One of the topics of discussion for the Village Board that summer was a petition by some residents of Reed Street to change the name to Reed Avenue and the Board allowed the change as long as the petitioners bore whatever expenses were incurred. It is not known if the residents thought that this change would reflect a more dignified name, but the change continued to cause some confusion for the next 70 years. This became particularly significant when Onondaga County adopted the 9-1-1 emergency system in 1988 and calls to that agency were made more scrambled by the mix-up in names. In 1992 the Village Board, headed by Mayor Martin Sennett, passed a resolution to name the entire road as Reed Street, ending the confusion. The legal names of the properties involved, however, may still be subject to some mix-up especially when sales of homes on that street take place.

8 Aug 1921 - " . . . that the petition of the residents of Reed Street, to have the name of Reed Street changed to Reed Avenue, be granted. . . . on condition that the names of the petitioners be published in Marcellus Observer and whatever expense was incurred thereby, if any, is to be borne by the aforesaid petitioners in such publication."

The Marcellus Observer
Wednesday, September 14, 1921
Marcellus Firemen's Big Day
The Field Day held on Labor Day under the auspices of Marcellus Fire Department was in every way a thorough success, and much credit is due the boys for the able manner in which they handled the immense crowds with no accidents to mar the pleasure of the day and no officer of the law necessary to preserve order. So that only satisfied, happy visitors wended their way homeward, well pleased with the cordial manner with which they were treated by their hosts, the Firemen.

Labor Day, 1921

In September, the Marcellus Fire Department held its annual inspection and field day on Labor Day, attended and enjoyed by large crowds of Marcellians. The Village Board also made a contribution to the Fire Department that month, an annual donation that continues to this day but somewhat more than the $100 made in 1921. The Board also received some complaints about unsanitary conditions in some areas of the Village and that too remains a concern for local government. Today, there are more stringent codes governing such conditions as well as a codes officer who is employed by the Village to enforce the ordinances. Nevertheless, the problem of unlicensed vehicles, litter and unkempt yards is one that continues to receive notice and complaint.

The Marcellus Observer
Wednesday, September 14, 1921
F. A. Thompson
In the death of Fred A. Thompson on September 7th, Marcellus lost one of its most useful and honored citizens, one who nearly 40 years had held a conspicuous place in the business and general community life of the village . . .. Although Mr. Thompson put the ideal of service into his business with much satisfaction to both customers and employees, he by no means confined the exercise of that ideal to his own concerns. In all that ministered to the general welfare of the community, he found time and energy to become an active participant, giving himself with fearlessness and fidelity to every cause that sought to promote moral and social betterment. For several years he held the office of Village President, giving to his administration a vigorous activity and resoluteness or endeavor that had always for its aim the improvement of local conditions . . .. The passing of such men as Fred Thompson leaves a place which is not readily filled, for they are the real assets of the community to which they belong, and the community is the poorer for their loss. We can only be thankful that we have known him and have had the loyal service of such a man here, and show our appreciation, by seeking as best we may, to maintain the serviceful spirit of which he was so loyal and courageous an exponent.

---

6 Sep 1921 - " . . . that an order for $100.00, the annual donation to the Fire Department, be drawn in the name of the Fire Department Treasurer, James Powell . . . complaint was read from the National Economy Grocery Store in regard to the bad condition of the rear premises of neighboring houses. The complaint referred to bad odors and unsanitary conditions and requested than an abatement of the condition might be effected"

1921 witnessed the passing of Fred A. Thompson, who had not only served the Village as President, but performed many other civic duties and conducted a successful business in the Village as well. His obituary in September went on to extol his many virtues and the esteem in which the Marcellus community held him.

1922 - Wages

The year began with an admonition from National City Bank that the high wages demanded by workers were retarding economic revival following the war. How serious this problem was in Marcellus remains unclear, but it does indicate a national concern that would reach even into rural communities. It also reflects the fact that some significant economic forces were at work in the nation, a depression having begun in mid 1921 with recovery still six months away. It was obvious that the effects of the Great War would reach into even the smallest communities.

The Village Board reacting to a letter from the State of New York would purchase a new safe to protect and preserve village records, including election results that

---

The Marcellus Observer
Wednesday, January 4, 1922
High Wages Retard Revival

In estimating the outlook for 1922, it is necessary to consider the causes of the depression and inquire to what extent they have been removed or are likely to be overcome. The rapid decline of the European demand for our products is one of the causes . . .

The principal factor in the depression is within the control of the American people. It is unbalanced relationship between the prices of farm and other primary products and the prices of manufactured goods, transportation service and various other products and services. . . .

In large part the situation is chargeable to the action of organized labor in clinging to the wartime wage rates. Raw materials and foodstuffs have had a great decline at wholesale markets and consumers the cost of handling and manufacturing has not decline in like proportions. The effect is to obstruct the distribution of goods and throw millions of wage earners out of employment at the same time keeping up the cost of living on the entire wage-earning population. There is no gain, but a great loss, to the wage earners as a class.

---

next month. Candidates for office in 1922 include Charles F. Jones for President and Howard I. Clark for Trustee. In addition, the March 21st election reflected the fact that women were more politically active now, as Mrs. Alice M. Wright was elected Collector of Taxes and Miss Helen L. Austin was elected Village Treasurer. *The Marcellus Observer*, as if to remind its readers, noted " . . . Camillus did not follow suit with other villages by naming a woman to hold office" (MO 3/15/22).

13 Feb 1922 - " . . . letter from James Sullivan of the Division of Archives and History of New york State was placed before the Board for their consideration and disposal. The letter stated that the safe containing the Village records was not of sufficient capacity to hold the records now under the control of the Village Officials. It recommended immediate action on the part of the Board to secure a new safe or other fireproof protection sufficient for accumulated records. The State laws make it obligatory for all Villages, Towns and Cities to make proper provisions and protection from loss by fire or other means."

21 Mar 1922 - " . . . the polls were open between the hours of 1 p.m. and 5 p.m., also that there were 22 ballots cast of which:

        For President
        Charles E. Jones   Received   22

        For Trustee
        Howard I. Clarke   Received   19
        Scattering   2
        Blank   _1_
                                       22

        For Treasurer
        Helen L. Austin   Received   22

        For Collector
        Alice M. Wright   Received   21
        Blank   _1_
                                       22

At the April 4th meeting, however, Miss Helen L. Austin resigned from her newly elected position as treasurer, citing the fact that she could not continue to fulfill her duties. J. Fred Woodbridge would be appointed to take her position as Village Treasurer, continuing to hold that position for the next forty years.

Petitions and Memorials

One of the first issues confronting the new Board in 1922 was a petition by Marcellus business for all night electric lighting. The Board granted this request but tabled a motion to provide a night watchman. The Board also discussed a proposal for a memorial " . . . to the men who gave their lives in service during the war" (Heffernan 98).

10 Apr 1922 - " . . . W. S. Spaulding, representing the business tax payers of Marcellus, presented two petitions signed by fifteen of the business men of the Village. The petition relating to all night service for electric lighting was considered favorably . . . The request in the petition of the business men for a night watchman was by common consent laid on the table."

9 May 1922 - " . . . President Jones presented a movement on part of Village Improvement Society to have a memorial placed somewhere in the Village to the soldiers of the World War who died in the service. The matter of place for location was discussed, but final decision was left for future deliberation."

> **The Marcellus Observer**
> **Wednesday, May 31, 1922**
> **Memorial Day Holds Its Own**
> . . . The Comrades and Ladies of the G. A. R. regret very much that the younger portion of the community barring, the children, showed so little interest in the proper observance of the Day which means for them a reunited and prosperous homeland, made possible only y its brave defenders who fell in battle and their comrades who, one by one, are answering the last roll call. . .

As Memorial Day rolled around and the Great War was still fresh in the minds of many, there was some concern noted in the paper by the members of the Grand Army of the Republic, an association of Union Veterans of the Civil War, that the younger generation did not seem as interested in the day's observance. Perhaps this is a typical response of those too young to have known the horrors of war. At the time, the 20s were a time to enjoy life, and the young would experience all too soon their own war, an even more horrible conflict that some would call an extension of the Great War of 1914-18.

In June, the Village Board was presented with a petition signed by many residents who opposed the opening in the Village of a hot-dog and soft drink stand, the forerunner it appears of what we would know as the fast-food business of today. "The petitioners were concerned that Robert Whitfield's business on the corner of North and Orchard Streets "would bring noise and confusion to the neighborhood. The petitioners were informed that they had no legal recourse for preventing a person from opening a legal business on his own property" (Heffernan 94). Today, the opening of a business is governed by a series of codes and zoning laws that must bear the scrutiny of not only the Village Planning Board, but also of public hearings if a variance is necessary.

16 Jun 1922 - " . . . meeting was called at the request of residents of the North side to protest against the erection of a building for the sale of soft drinks and other things usually dispensed at such summer stands, just below nor north side of what is called the White Bridge, by Robert C. Whitfield. A petition containing thirty-five names of residents of the community was presented to the Board claiming it would be unsightly, dangerous to travelers, obstructing the highway, disturbing the peace of the neighborhood and other objectionable features such as being open late hours and on Sunday and questionable as to some things that might be sold on the premises. The petitioners desired that the Village do what it could to prevent the carrying out of Mr. Whitfield's project. Atty Stone (H. M.) was present and was called on to present the legal aspect of the

situation. . . . There were no Village laws by which the Board could interfere with the plans of Mr. Whitfield in building and establishing a place of business where he has already begun."

James J. Renehan

June marked the celebration of and reception to honor Rev. James Renehan's 50 years in the Roman Catholic priesthood. Pastor of St. Francis Xavier Church in the Village for almost half a century, Fr. Renehan had witnessed much of the early history of the Village, beginning with his appointment in 1879. In failing health, he is shown in this photo from *The Marcellus Observer* along with some of the priests who assisted him in those years. (From left to right: Rev. Edw. J. Mellick, Rev. Henry Curtin, Fr. Renehan, Rev. J. Frank Kelly, Rev. Paul L. Hemmer).

The summer of '22 saw the expansion of the powers of the Village Board in relation to the inspection of public assembly halls and the licensing of billiard tables and halls. Some of this was necessary for safety reasons of course, but it might also be considered another example of the expansion of government. Many, morally objectionable to some, questioned billiard and pool halls, and as with prohibition, thought that legislation would be able to enforce morality in the 20's.

10 Jul 1922 - " . . . A notice from the State Industrial Commissioner, Henry D. Sayer, in relation to inspection of public assembly halls and one from the State Tax Commission in regard to licensing billiard tables in public houses and the 1922 law relating to the same which goes into effect Sept 1 . . . "

14 Aug 1922 - " . . . blanks sent by the Bureau of Stamps and Licenses from State Tax Commission were ordered by the Board to be sent to the proprietors or operators of billiard halls located in Village limits. Said blanks are to be used by said proprietors or operators to get the privilege of running billiard tables at the license fee of $5.00 per table each year, beginning Sept. 1, 1922."

Highways and Memorials

The Board that summer became involved in making improvements to Main Street in the Village as Onondaga County began to rebuild and repave Seneca Turnpike from Dublin (Road) Street, through the Village and beyond Highland Cemetery towards Skaneateles. In addition, Scotch Hill Road from North Street to Sheehan's Crossing was to be repaved, both of these improvements reflecting, not only a progressive community, but the continuing influence that automobiles were having even in the small communities like Marcellus.

> **The Marcellus Observer**
> **Wednesday, August 2, 1922**
> **New County Highway Makes**
> **Great Civic Improvement**
> **To Marcellus' Main Street**
> Marcellus village is to gain one of the greatest steps in her progress by the construction during the forthcoming weeks of the strip of modern highway to be built by the county connecting the present county road at the junction of Dublin street and Seneca turnpike on East Hill, Marcellus, with Skaneateles, by way of Highland Cemetery and Thorne schoolhouse beyond the Gulf. It is not the road due west.
> Marcellus village will thus gain by that portion passing through the corporation.

The Board listened to the local Comfort League Committee, whose involvement in the war years was recited and which organization now wanted to disband. One of its last activities was securing a bronze tablet recognizing those who were killed or who died in service during the Great War. Thus, work on the memorial continued, although a place for it was still a year or more away. The Board also purchased the new safe, as required by the State to secure important documents, a safe that is now used by the Marcellus Historical Society to preserve some of its important artifacts and documents.

25 Jul 1922 - " . . . special meeting . . . for the purpose of arranging plans with representatives of County Highway Department for constructing an 18 foot wide concrete pavement through the limits of the Village. The said road being a continuation of County road outside Village limits. Also the addition of Scotch Hill Road from North St. to Sheehan's Crossing."

14 Aug 1922 - " . . . Mrs. F. T. Schoonmaker, a member of the local Comfort League Committee came before the Board and gave a condensed history of its work to the present time and stated what was yet to be done before disbanding, an object they desired to attain. The League was originally organized to furnish necessities and comforts to those bearing arms in the World War. The recital of what was undertaken and accomplished during those tense years was of much interest and worthy of record. Among the notable things performed was the securing of a bronze tablet on which was cast the names of all who were killed or died in service from Marcellus. Mrs. Schoonmaker requested the Village to secure a suitable place for the erection of the tablet. It was necessary to this before the organization could finish its work, dissolve, and become a thing of the past."

9 Oct 1922 - " . . . Mr. June and President of the Syracuse Office Furnishing Co. were present and showed varieties of Art-Metal Model Safes. The Board selected one designated as Art-Metal 73 with dimensions: width 24 7/8 inches, height 66 3/4 inches, depth 28 1/2 inches outside measure, as the one suitable for the present needs of the Village and gave orders for its immediate installation in the office of Village Clerk. Cost of safe, $257.20, 2% off for cash.

"When the frost is on the punkin"

"Frost on the Pumpkin"

The November elections in the County produced no surprises that year and America seemed to be rolling along with advertisements that encouraged travel and the auto industry enjoying immense popularity. While the farmers complained of " . . . the watering troughs taken away and the sheds done away with - no place to water their horses or tie them" (MO, 11/8/22), the Marcellus Fire Department in petitioning the Village for new motorized equipment, " . . . voted something of an ultimatum addressed to the Village Board, and named a committee to wait on the Board . . . a formal demand for motorized apparatus" (MO 12/13/22)). This issue would await the meeting of a new Board of Trustees and a new year.

County Championship

The year did end on an update note, however, as Marcellus High School was recognized for having won the County Football Championship, beating Skaneateles in its last game and winning some notoriety for the community and a newly formed organization called the Onondaga School Athletic Association. Today, high schools throughout the area compete with one another in a league that had its roots in this organization. This photo pictures some of the young men of Marcellus in 1922 and hangs

today in the Village Hall, in the office of the Village Clerk, a good reminder of our history and our roots.

(From left to right-Lower Row: Spaulding, Phillips, Wicks, Shafer, Woodford. Second row: Gustin, Helfer, Horsington, mascot; Clark, captain; Hyatt. Back Row: Irving Noakes, Coach; Speich, Welch, Parsons, manager, McLaren, O'Shea, Helfer, principal).

1923 – Village Business

It was hoped that the spirit embraced in this newspaper picture from the last week of December 1922 would carry over into the new year. The year began with the Trustees approving a new street lighting contract for the Village in early January and the approval of bills, including taxes levied against the Village water supply by the Town of Marcellus. There was also a petition presented to the Board asking residents to bond for the purpose of motorized fire equipment. A vote on this proposition as well as the Village elections was held on March 20th. James G. McNair was elected President of the Village Corporation and he was re-elected a number of times throughout the 1920s, including the first President to be elected to a two-year term in 1927. In addition to McNair, John Spaulding was elected Trustee, while J. Fred Woodbridge and Mrs. Alice M. Wright were re-elected as Treasurer and Collector respectively. The bonding proposition, however, went down to defeat by a rather large margin of the taxpayers who voted. It seems that the size of the bond may have alarmed the voters, since a later vote on a smaller amount received voter approval.

8 Jan 1923 - " . . . Kilcoyne moved that the 5 year contract for street lighting with F. W. Knapp (manager) beginning Apr 10, 1922 and ending Apr 10, 1927 be accepted and signed by the proper officials."

20 Feb 1923 - " . . . petition . . . requesting the Village to

---

The Marcellus Observer - Wednesday, February 21, 1923
Vote On Motor Apparatus

Marcellus needs motorized fire apparatus, according to sentiment sounded, following agitation for a long time past. This sentiment was expressed when a petition was passed, and 27 signatures were obtained of men who are taxpayers mostly about the business section and including Mr. Moir of Crown Mill. This petition requests a vote at the regular village election on raising funds, $5,000 to buy fire equipment. The petition was considered by the Village Board Tuesday night and the question will be submitted to taxpayers in March.

bond itself for the sum of $5000.00, . . . by submitting to ballot on next election day . . . for the purpose of securing adequate chemical fire extinguishing apparatus . . . placed before the Board"

The Marcellus Observer
Wednesday, March 21, 1923
"No" Vote On Fire Equipment

Marcellus votes totaled 73 Tuesday, and of this number McNair had 63, Spaulding 58, Woodbridge 61, and Mrs. Wright 65. We told Mrs. Wright she ran ahead of her ticket, but just like these "new women" voters, she didn't know what the compliment meant. The proposition for bonding $5,000 for fire apparatus, was voted down, 47 no to 17 yes.

---

20 Mar 1923 - " . . . the number of ballots cast for the proposition of bonding the Village for $5000.00 to secure fire extinguishing apparatus was as follows:

Ballots containing the word   Yes   17
Ballots containing the word   No   47
Blank   2
Total   66

New Clerk and New Housing

One of the first acts of the new Board, following the election, was the appointment of a new Village Clerk, Charles Dillon, who would hold this position for the next five years. In addition, a committee was appointed to advise Board members on important issues. It appears that government was becoming more specialized in the Village and the issues, which in the past would be easily considered and voted on by ordinary citizens, were becoming too complicated, requiring both legal and engineering consultants.

The Marcellus Observer
Wednesday, March 28, 1923
Crown Mill To Build
Six Houses This Summer

William F. Maley has just taken contract with crown Mills for excavating, stonework, and furnishing six cellars, to be left in condition for the carpenters.

This means the assurance of six more house for Marcellus this fall, or earlier. The building will be done on the property across the creek.

---

26 Mar 1923 - " . . . that Chas Dillon be appointed Clerk for coming year . . . that an advisory committee be appointed of five representative citizens to confer with Board on any matter of importance that may arise in the conduct of Village affairs. The following men selected to act in that capacity - Edward Taylor, John Moir, F. W. Knapp, James Powell and Dwight Chrisler."

New Housing

In the Spring, new housing was being built in the Village on Scotch Hill Road and there was additional discussion about the placement of the memorial boulder in the Village Center. There was hope that the stone might be placed in time for the Memorial Day celebration that year, but working out the details involved some legality and other considerations that delayed the decision. *The Marcellus Observer* commented, "Only four Civil War Veterans still remain alive of all the old "Boys in Blue," who fought in the great struggle to preserve the Federal Union. The four will probably be at the exercise" (MO 5/16/23)

The Marcellus Observer - Wednesday, April 18, 1923
Site For Memorial Boulder

To the Editor: Let the Monument be placed on the green in front of the M. E. church - an ideal location, for all time to come.

The Marcellus Observer - Wednesday, May 9, 1923
In Memory Of Our Soldiers

The hope was expressed that the new stone or boulder in memory of Marcellus World war heroes might be set at the point of the Methodist lawn and dedicated on this Memorial Day. But it appears the legal aspects cannot be cleared up so quickly and the formality can hardly be arranged. The Official Board of the Methodist church have formally passed favorably upon giving a lease of this spot to the village, in return for certain things, which include a walk, care of curbing, suitable cement work surrounding the monument. Etc. These details are in the hands of Attorney Stone.   . . . and can hardly be perfected within the time to May 30. All will be completed this summer, and some formalities may then be anticipated for another Memorial Day . . . .

New Map and Survey

That same month, Prof. E. L. Black of Marcellus High School presented a new map and survey of Marcellus. This new design indicated how far the Marcellus community extended beyond the center of the Village, and suggesting that future activities should consider such data in any planning that was considered.

> **The Marcellus Observer**
> **Wednesday, May 16, 1923**
> **The Marcellus Community**
> As a community, Marcellus is much larger than the confines of the Township boundary lines. All of Marcellus Township and portions from the Towns of Camillus, Onondaga, Otisco, Spafford, Skaneateles, and possibly of Elbridge, are located in such relation to Marcellus Village that it is a natural center of a Community.

Marcellus merchants also joined other nearby villages in agreeing to close their stores at 6 p.m., four nights a week, a move, it appears to be, towards the progressive attitude of fewer working hours and more rest and recreation for workers. It also helped that in this period of recession, fewer hours would mean less pay and more businesses might survive with a smaller payroll, causing *The Marcellus Observer* to comment, "Hail to Marcellus! Hail to all progressivism!" (MO 5/16/23).

On-Going Issues

At the end of May, the Marcellus Fire Department played host to officials from the County Voluntary Firemen's Association as well as local officials, and Village President McNair presented certificates of exemption to several long-time firemen. These exemptions absolved the recipients from having to pay certain taxes -- an idea that has recently been revived as an inducement for volunteer fire departments today. In recent years the number of individuals who volunteer for local fire departments has fallen dramatically across New York, and there is movement in the State Legislature to promote such innovative strategies for recruiting new and retaining present members.

That same month, Edmund Reed, a former Village President and the founder of *The Marcellus Observer*, died. Reed was eulogized for his conspicuous public career, not only as editor and publisher but also as Town Supervisor and Village President, Director of the local bank and for his many other enterprises.

In June, the Board met to listen to complaints about unsanitary conditions related to septic tanks and cesspools in some neighborhoods. This would portend an on-going concern about the lack of sanitary sewers in the Village and the growing demand that something be done to correct the situation. Even today, it seems, an issue such as sewage disposal is usually ignored or taken for granted until there is a back-up or break in the pipeline. One of the major responsibilities of local government, it might be noted, is to make sure that the infrastructure remains healthy, often requiring the expenditure of public funds in advance of problems.

19 Jun 1923 - " . . . special meeting for the purpose of hearing the complaints in regard to the overflow of septic tanks and cesspools onto the Parsons' property . . . resolved to notify the Trustees of the I. O. O. F. Building to clean out the cesspool of that building as its overflow ran in the Parsons' property. Also to again notify Messrs. Knapp and Amidon to clean out their septic tank which overflows into the cellar of the Parsons Building and in case they do not, the Village Board will shut the water off their buildings."

Fire Department Winners

In July, the Marcellus Fire Department sent representatives to the County Firemen's Convention in Brewerton and they came home winners of the hose race and other competitions. Today, the young men of the Marcellus Fire Department still compete in

MO 7/25/23

contests with other fire departments, enjoying a rivalry that promotes both fellowship in and association with a brotherhood that links common interests and the volunteer spirit throughout the County.

Left to right, top row: Giles Case, Howard Leach, Gordon Hickman, Harold Powell, George Morgan, John Head, James Hogan, John Shay, Arthur Schanzle. Bottom row: Paul Curtin, Clem Armstrong, Enric Hackford, John Scott, Bob Stewart, Joseph Thornton.

Death of Harding

The country, as well as the Marcellus community was shocked in early August with the death of President Harding, the first President since Zachary Taylor to die in office of natural causes. *The Marcellus Observer* noted that " . . . his end was hastened by the bitter onslaughts of enemies within as well as without his own party. Coolidge, a cool-headed, calculating, silent, though able and just man, we predict will soon boss the party much the same as did Wilson, and if successful in domestic and foreign policies in the next 18 months, he will surely be renominated and reelected" (MO 8/22/23).

The Marcellus Observer
Wednesday, August 1, 1923
President Harding Died Thursday, Aug. 1
at 7:30 p.m In San Francisco
A good man has passed on.
That is the greatest tribute we can pay him.
A man who loved his God and his country, and strove to do his duty faithfully.

The Marcellus Observer
Wednesday, November 7, 1923
Halloween
To the Editor:
"Children and fools" says an old remark "tell the truth as they learn it at home."
You get a good deal of a kid's home atmosphere by the line of his talk and the way he behaves . . ..
The spirit of boyhood is in every boy. They have got to have their fun, and everybody expects it. But they do not expect a crowd of boys to beak all bounds and do vicious and malicious acts as they did last week . . ..
It was the children and fools who wrote the mean things on placards and windows. Nobody cares for that for it does not break any of the commandments. Rather it is instructive, for it carries a clue of the sentiment that is back of the writer's thought - they are simply reporting the opinion of the Family Circle that discusses and arraigns the folks of the village. The damaging inclinations of the mischievous must be curbed. Give the boys the nightlife of the town, if they will use it right on such occasions, as the spirit moves them to do things. But let the Village Board appoint patrolmen to keep them within bounds, and collect evidence in case they become unreasonable and overstep the line of decency.

Disturbance

In the Fall of 1923, perhaps in reaction to the death of Harding as well as the fear and suspicion that had been grown after the war, much of the country, even rural communities like Marcellus, experienced an outbreak of disturbance and disorder. In Marcellus, local merchants complained loudly to the Village Board about unruly people and acts, asking that special police be assigned to handle the situation. Some malicious acts that occurred during Halloween that year were also disturbing to residents of the community, many people placing the blame on those who seemed to preach hateful things at home and failed to provide proper guidance for the young.

30 Oct 1923 - " . . . a petition from C. H. Fuller and others was received complaining of people congregating in front of stores and other buildings, obstructing the sidewalk, using vile language, breaking windows and other disorderly acts, and asking the Board to take some action in the matter . . .. that the President appoint a special policeman to act for one month from date, from 7 p.m. to 11 p.m."

The Ku Klux Klan

The 1920's were a period of great change in America and groups, such as the Ku Klux Klan, found fertile ground for practicing their brand of hate-filled patriotism in rural areas especially. In September of 1921, the State of Oklahoma was put under martial law because of terrorist activities

Syracuse Post Standard Magazine
August 25, 1963
The Fiery Cross Burned Here
The KKK in Onondaga
by Robert R. Haggart

Forty years ago, bands of white robed Ku Klux Klansmen burned burlap and bailing wire crosses on the hillsides of Onondaga County and chanted mysterious and secret rites in Syracuse meeting halls . . . On Sunday, Dec. 21, 1923, residents of the Village of Marcellus looked out their windows and saw a huge glow to the south. When curious residents followed the glow they found an enormous cross 40 feet high and burning brightly . . ..

by the KKK, which had become a powerful force in politics throughout the Midwest. In the East, even in Central New York, "the fiery cross burned". Marcellus itself was not immune from such activity, as residents of the Village found out just before Christmas, 1923. While the original KKK was usually associated with the South and a lingering hatred of blacks, the focus of the hate group in the 20s was directed more at immigrants, who were usually Catholic, lived in the cities and were often labeled "wet". As America became more urban, less white, less Protestant and less Anglo, many in rural communities, which were traditionally "dry", felt that profound changes were taking place, ones that would adversely affect them, their children and their children's children. It was a fearful time for many who saw the foundations of the country being challenged by these new forces and this alarm often carried over into expressions of hostility.

The Third Alarm

In mid October, the Marcellus Fire Department sponsored the showing of a movie called "The Third Alarm" as a fund raiser for the 1924 County Firemen's Convention, which was to take place in Marcellus the next July. The benefit was successful in October and the Firemen decided to show the picture again on

"The Third Alarm"

At Parsons Hall, Matinee, 3:45 Night, 7:45

Tuesday, October 16th

Let's Go.

The most stupendous exhibition of twentieth century realism ever flung upon the screen.—

A colossal drama of the heart and soul of America that glorifies and immortalizes the firemen of the nation and their loyal wives, sons and daughters!

Its very flames will burn an everlasting impress on your soul!

This thrilling picture is put on under the auspices and for the benefit of the

Marcellus Fire Department

Matinee—admission	20c
" children under 12 years if accompanied by an adult of his or her family will be admitted for	10c
Night—Admission	30c
" Children under 12 years	20c

December 4th. Hailed as a "colossal drama of the heart and soul of America," its very title suggested that America should glory in such people as its firemen, ordinary men from ordinary families who respond when a call for help is made. Although many Americans had become disillusioned by the last war and by the materialism of modern life, expressed so often by the authors and artists of the 20s, the spirit and optimism of a small town in Central New York seemed to be well demonstrated at Parsons Hall in Marcellus as the year came to an end.

1924

As 1924 began, the children returned to school following the holidays and some people in Marcellus, like so many today, traveled to Florida to spend the winter months. Meanwhile, there were others who complained about snow removal and water bills as well as some interest revived for purchasing motorized equipment for the Fire Department.

> **The Marcellus Observer**
> **Wednesday, January 9, 1924**
> **Beautiful Florida**
> So many northern people go south to spend the winter months that the subject is of widespread interest in the upper country of the United States, every section without exception having its representatives enjoying balmy southern winters.
>
> **The Marcellus Observer**
> **Wednesday, February 27, 1924**
> **. . . Birdie Told This To Me**
> people that live on Bradley place would appreciate a visit from the snowplow

12 Feb 1924 -" . . . President McNair instructed the Clerk to write to F. G. Oakley, 44 Central Ave, Buffalo, inviting him to come and give us a demonstration of his fire apparatus in the new picture."

10 Mar 1924 -" . . . Trustee Clark explained that as he was not doing only a fraction of the business in his creamery as formerly, he thought his water for his creamery should be cut down. He explained that he owed $10 for the present half year and on buying this he asked the board to consider the bill for the creamery paid until Oct. 1, 1924. This was agreed to by the board."

Elections and Appointments

In March, James McNair was again elected President of the Corporation, along with Varnum S. Kenyon as Trustee and incumbents Wright and Woodbridge as Collector and Treasurer.

18 Mar 1924 - " . . . the polls were open between the hours of 1 p.m. and 5 p.m., . . . that the whole number of votes cast at said election were 22:

Votes cast as follows:

For President one year	James G. McNair		21
Trustee for 2 years	V. S. Kenyon	21	
Treasurer for one year	J. Fred Woodbridge		22
Collector for one year	Alice M. Wright		22

Official Newspaper

Following that election, one of the first acts of the new Board was the designation of an official paper, a requirement of Village Law that had not been addressed until now. At its meeting on April 14, 1924, the Board of Trustees *designated The Marcellus Observer* as its official paper, an act repeated every year since, for the last 80 years.

Church Moved

After returning from a meeting of the Village Board on April 28th, Trustee John Spaulding died unexpectedly. He had been an active member of the community, not only as a Trustee and Fireman but also as an Onondaga County Deputy Sheriff and Village watchman. At its next meeting, the Board appointed James Parsons to complete the two-year term to which Spaulding had been elected in 1923. The Board also approved a permit for St. John's Episcopal Church to move the building from the corner of Main and Orange Streets one block north to the corner of Maple and Orange Streets. "By this time, the church, built in 1881, was in need of extensive repairs. The congregation faced an important decision. Should they build a new church . . . or should they move the old church to a new location and repair it? The second choice was determined to be less costly. Accordingly, . . . St. John's Church was moved almost the entire length of Orange Street by team and wagon and situated at its present location"(Heffernan 188).

12 May 1924 - " . . . a permit was granted to St. John's Episcopal Church to move and transport the Church from its present site to the corner of Orange St. . . . a vacancy occurring in the Board by the death of Trustee Spaulding, James Parsons was duly appointed to fill the position."

Bicycles, Poppy Sales and the Band

May brought out the sun and also some complaints that bicycles were being used on the sidewalks, threatening the safety of pedestrians and the Fire Department published a lengthy article in the paper thanking the community for its generous support -- a prelude to the big convention that was to be held in the summer. The American Legion also conducted its 3rd annual poppy sale drive to benefit the veterans and own needs.

> **The Marcellus Observer**
> **Wednesday, May 14, 1924**
> **Wear A Poppy**
> The Third Annual Poppy drive for the Veterans' Mountain Camp will take place during the week beginning Friday, May 23, and ending on memorial Day, May 30. The poppys are to be sold at a minimum of 10c, the entire proceeds to be turned over to them. The Veterans Mountain Camp is a home for those veterans who cannot prove that their ailment is the result of their service, and who cannot, therefore, get any Government aid.

In June, *The Marcellus Observer* mentioned that a " . . . goodly bit of praise should be given the newly organized Marcellus Band for adding so much enjoyment to the community . . . We are proud to think that Marcellus once more has a band and hope and believe it will equal the famous Marcellus Band of twenty years ago" (MO 6/18/24).

Busses and the Convention

July's Village Board meeting noted a complaint from the railroad company regarding bus service in Marcellus, a indication perhaps of how threatening this form of transportation was to the rail lines.

> **The Marcellus Observer**
> **Wednesday, July 16, 1924**
> ### A Right Royal Welcome Awaits County Firemen
>
> **The Marcellus Observer**
> **Wednesday, July 23, 1924**
> **Welcome To Our City**
> Saturday night a bunch of "rough necks" came driving thru Marcellus on their way to the city.
>
> **The Marcellus Observer**
> **Wednesday, July 30, 1924**
> **Convention Ends in Blaze Of Glory**
> Marcellus Surpasses Her long Standing Reputation For Hospitality.
> Convention Fully Up To Mark, If Not Excelling.

7 Jul 1924 - " . . . a communication from the Vice President and General Manager of the Auburn & Syracuse Electric R.R. objecting to the granting of a permit or franchise by the Board for the operation of a bus or busses between Marcellus and Syracuse or other points on the line of the Auburn & Syracuse R.R. was received and ordered placed on file."

The bus service, however, had been added to accommodate the number of people who would attend the annual County Firemen's Convention later that month. Large crowds came to Marcellus and were entertained with a ballgame, parade, drills, hose races and water fights as well as dinners provided by the local churches. The Village Board was quick to appoint a special deputy for the event, especially for the " . . . rough necks who came driving thru Marcellus . . . " (MO 7/23/24). *The Marcellus Observer*, noting how times had changed since the last convention in Marcellus, remarked, " . . . the Firemen's Convention (was) held in Marcellus ten years ago, . . . The world moves fast. It was a decade previous to that when Marcellus had the Convention. They fed the guests in a tent, visitors drove Dobbin instead of Lizzie. The trolley had just been built" (MO, 7/23/24). The convention was a big success, a tribute to the firemen and the convention committee, whose picture shows them in uniform, in front of St. Francis Xavier Church rectory.

Convention Committee: Front row, left to right: George May, Dan McLaren, Arthur Wilson, Clem Armstrong, Enric Hackford. Second Row: Giles Case, Dick May, John Shay, Leon Gustin, P. J. Kelly, William Rumsey.

21 Jul 1924 - " . . . that Timothy Sheehan be appointed a special deputy and have charge of the parking of automobiles on Thursday, July 24, 1924 . . . the Clerk was requested to write to the Syracuse Water Dept and ask their advise as to the use of some preparation to use in the Village reservoir to prevent the disagreeable taste of the water."

Calls For Sewers

That summer, there was renewed interest in a sewer system for the Village and the Board of Trustees began to address more seriously the concern at its meetings in August. It was an issue that would involve many more meetings and several more years of effort before being implemented in the 1930s.

11 Aug 1924 - " . . . several citizens, interested in a sewer system for the Village, attended the meeting."

25 Aug 1924 - " . . . that the Village Board of Trustees be authorized to ascertain an estimate of the cost of a sewer system by employing a competent engineer and to report the result at a future meeting."

An Indian Summer

The autumn of 1924 was, what is still often referred to as, an "Indian Summer," and very well described by Cora A. Marshfield in an October issue of *The Marcellus Observer*.

The minutes of a Village Board meeting in December seemed to echo some of those same

---

The Marcellus Observer
Wednesday, October 15, 1924
Indian Summer
(By C. A. Marshfield)

Can anything be more beautiful than the days of early fall? Cold, frosty nights, crisp, sparkling in mornings, warm, hazy days. Blue, blue skies, with here and there a lazy white cloud floating along. Scarlet and gold, brown and deep wine, the trees clothe the peaceful hillsides with a colorful splendor. The little valley towns doze in the sunshine, while the smoke from the children's bonfires rise like incense to the gods of the harvest day.

"The frost is on the   punkin, and the fodder's in the shock" and the apples lie under the trees in heaps of red and yellow. Bare, stubbly fields lie rimed with frost at dawn and glorified with gold under the noonday sun. Voices of children at play float on the still air. Over all broods peace, golden fruitful peace. And yet a feeling akin to sadness is in the air. The brief summer is over, birds have flown, flowers are dying. We are getting nearer the cold and snows of winter. Like our own existence, bright and gay for such a brief spell, then life's autumn steals o'er the hills and we lie down beneath the leaves for a long, long sleep. But, oh, glorious hope! As the flowers sleep for a season to bloom again in the spring, so will our resurrection come on that joyful Easter Day.

178

sentiments, as the Trustees extended sympathies to fellow Board member, V. S. Kenyon, whose daughter died just before the Christmas holiday season.

9 Dec 1924 - " . . . whereas in the providence of Almighty God, death has taken from our midst Nettie Kenyon, beloved daughter of our esteemed fellow member, Mr. V. S. Kenyon, be it resolved by the Board of Trustees of the Village of Marcellus, that our earnest sympathy be extended to the bereaved father, mother and brother of the deceased."

Like autumn, life can be brief, but there is always hope and a new beginning – a resounding echo that seems to ring again and again in the history of the valley.

Conclusion

This postcard encapsulates Marcellus in the early 1920s. This was the age of the automobile and all that it represented – personal freedom, travel, development of suburbs,

jobs – a mobility that had profound effects on peoples' lives. Before the automobile, most people lived out their lives working at home or at a local job and died in the community in which they had been born. The effect of the automobile on the younger generation of the 20s was especially significant. Many of them were in a hurry to enjoy all that was offered by the roaring consumerism of the times and some took exception to the slower pace that was more common in rural America. A clash of cultures had emerged and it was one that would continue to find expression throughout the rest of the decade.

Chapter 11 – Prosperity Before Depression

The rest of the 1920s would include prosperity for some, but not for many farmers who were almost invisible to city dwellers. While there were some notable changes in the Village of Marcellus, including street expansion and new housing, there was much agitation for a sewer system and garbage collection. The radio brought news and advertising even to rural Marcellus, but it also combined with motion pictures to introduce urban ways to the country, lifestyles that would continue to threaten tradition.

1925

In early January 1925, a new motorized fire truck arrived in Marcellus and the salesman provided a demonstration of its effectiveness. Purchased by the firemen, the truck would eventually be outfitted with equipment approved by the voters in the March elections that followed. The Board of Trustees approved a proposition to submit such a vote to the voters in mid February and in early March, the firemen entertained the Board at a dinner, perhaps in gratitude for or in anticipation of the March 17th vote on the fire equipment.

> **The Marcellus Observer**
> **Wednesday, January 7, 1925**
> **New Motor Fire Truck Arrives**
> The long anticipated and much needed fire truck arrived in Marcellus last week, and is ready when it is needed, right by the door in the engine house. It is painted a beautiful bright, shiny red, and the metal on it shines with silver.
> It was given public exhibition Monday about noon or a little later. The salesman was demonstrator, and he certainly was a "demon." The way he drove that red truck around corners and between telephone poles was an education in itself. The truck is a decided acquisition for our town, and the fire laddies are to be complimented on their purchase.

> **The Marcellus Observer**
> **Wednesday, March 4, 1925**
> **Trustees & Vets As Guests**
> Marcellus firemen plan to entertain the members of the Village Board and the exempt firemen at their next monthly business meeting to be held Monday night, March 9, at the rooms in the Engine House.

16 Feb 1925 - " . . . that the following proposition be submitted to the electors of Marcellus Village at the next annual election to be held on the 17th day of March, 1925:

"Shall the Trustees of the Village of Marcellus, Onondaga County, New York, be authorized to borrow from its Bonds, Certificates of Indebtedness, or other obligations, . . . the sum of three thousand dollars ($3000.00) for the purpose of purchasing certain fire equipment and apparatus to be used for the prevention of and protection against fire within said Village, . . . That said money thus derived . . . to be used as aforesaid for the purchase of fire equipment and apparatus described as follows: One American LaFrance, Type Two Combination Hose and Chemical Engine Mounted on Brockway Torpedo Chassis."

In addition to the proposition, voters in the Village of Marcellus would again cast ballots for President McNair and Trustee Parsons as well as return J. Fred Woodbridge and Alice M. Wright to the offices of Treasurer and Collector respectively.

17 Mar 1925 - " . . . total number of votes cast on the proposition to bond the Village for $3000.00 for chemical engine was 38.
Number of Votes for proposition was 34
Number of Votes against proposition was 4

Death of Fr. Renehan

Rev. James J. Renehan

March also witnessed the death of Fr. James Renehan, the long time pastor of St. Francis Xavier Church in the Village. Organized in 1854, " . . . the congregation grew under Fr. Renehan's ministrations from less than a few hundreds to nearly 1,000 . . . born in Cullyhanna, Ireland, . . . he came to

Marcellus, becoming pastor Nov. 24, 1879 . . . All his early years he traveled our country roads ministering as spiritual guide to parishioners. He served a church at Onondaga Hill, eight miles distant, and the Otisco church, fourteen miles distant as out-missions, in connection with his parish work in Marcellus. He was a good executive, promoting the material ends of his church, the having had many elaborate additions of much cost. A parochial resident was built twelve years ago, aggregating some $30,000, and during the last year of his pastorate in 1924, a Parish Hall was built for $25,000. These simply mark the loyalty of his people to him as leader and he appreciated their effort" (MO 3/18/25).

Taxes, Signs, Sidewalks, Daylight Saving

The new pastor at St. Francis Xavier Church, the Rev. Thomas Driscoll, would also distinguish himself in the Village, making an appearance before the Village Board to request a tax exemption for the parish residence. The issue of tax exemption for houses of worship has generally met with approval by most governmental units, but that on a residence, owned by a church, was becoming and remains to this day, a somewhat controversial topic of discussion. Tax exemption for the rectory of St. Francis Xavier initially met the approval of the Trustees, but at a later meeting, this decision was reversed. Like today, the issue of tax assessment on property (residential or commercial) that is owned by a religious or non-profit organization results in controversial discussion and sometimes ends up in litigation.

In addition to this concern, the Trustees ordered new street signs and continued to promote, by means of rebate, the construction of sidewalks in the Village, particularly in those areas where new residential building was taking place. The Board also approved the adoption of Daylight Savings Time and noted a report in its minutes that " . . . the New York State Census of 1925 credited a population of 1110, consisting of 1062 citizens and 48 aliens to the incorporated Village of Marcellus, N.Y." (Minutes of the Board of Trustees, May 19, 1925)

The Marcellus Observer
Wednesday June 10, 1925
Daylight Savings Monday
At a regular meeting of the Village Board held in the Engine House June 9, the following resolution as adopted:
That the Village of Marcellus will go on Daylight Saving time Monday, June 15, 1925, until September 15, 1925.
Effective Sunday at 12, midnight.
By Order of Village Board

5 May 1925 - " . . . Rev. Father Driscoll appeared before the Board in regard to the assessment of the Rectory of St. Francis Xavier Parish. He presented decision of law in favor of the exemption from tax. The assessor took the question under consideration until the next regular meeting."

12 May 1925 - " . . . . that the Parish House of St. Francis Xavier Parish be exempt from the Village taxation.. . . that the Board order street signs for the Village. That the sidewalk on the property of Chas Curtin be accepted and a rebate of $18.00 be allowed, 60% of the cost ($30.00)."

19 May 1925 - " . . . that the resolution . . . exempting the dwelling house of the Pastor of St. Francis Xavier Parish, be rescinded."

9 Jun 1925 - " . . . that the Village adopt Daylight Savings Time, to commence on Monday, June 15, and notice to be published in the Marcellus Observer."

Turnpikes, Streets, Expansion

A most interesting development occurred in June, with the announcement that plans were being devised by the State of New York to connect by turnpike the area known as Onondaga Hill with the Village of Marcellus. At the time, roads up East Hill only extended to Town Line Road, and the turnpike from Onondaga Hill was to extend only to Card's Corner. This new construction, clearly showing the extraordinary influence and use of the automobile, would, as the Marcellus Observer commented, "put Marcellus village on a Continental Turnpike."

The Marcellus Observer
Wednesday June 17, 1925
Marcellus On A "Pike"

"Col. Greene's Map" is a plan for building roads over the State in a comprehensive manner, designed to build arteries or thoroughfares connectedly rather than in a haphazard way, leaving unfinished gaps. The long-distance, through traveler will thus find his pikes finished, and these can be used locally as they may serve.

Supervisor Spaulding of Marcellus saw one of the Col. Greene Maps, and observed that this showed proposed construction all the way from Onondaga Hill to Marcellus. He saw reason to wonder at this, for it had been understood and assented to that this highway would be built from Onondaga Hill to Card's Corner only. Here it would connect with the former county road north to Split Rock, and construction would continue south through scenic Freida's Gulf to Cedarvale, thence to a point south of Navarino village, turn toward the Will Amidon place, to the Dunfee's corner, turn and go down to the Otisco Lake Road.

Grading was actually begun at Onondaga Hill this week by the State forces, and it is fully understood that this plan is to build this State Highway directly east and west to Marcellus village. Supervisor Spaulding is in fact informed that this is the present undertaking. So - Hurrah for Col. Greene!

Marcellus Town has built town roads in sections different years up East Hill to Town Line road, some three miles, and this is accepted by out traffic as reasonably good. But this will be junked with the proposed work . . . This big newer project will put Marcellus village on a Continental Turnpike. Watch us shoot!

There was also discussion in the Village about opening up the Reed Avenue extension street to West Hill, much of this in anticipation of more building lots and expansion of streets into what had once been farmland.

The Marcellus Observer
Wednesday June 24, 1925
The Inquiring Reporter

Do you advise proceeding for an opening of the Reed Avenue extension street to West Hill now, instead of waiting until further building is done there?

Prof. Ernest Black - What need is there to open it now? There is an opening there now and in case of heavy traffic they can go down through there anyway. It would be best to wait until Mrs. Reed has sold her building lots and has her park ready to open, then would be the time.

Rev. Gustin - I think they ought to open it because it would cut off a lot of traffic around the hill, but the merchants would not be in favor of it.

Kenneth Spaulding - No, there's no sense in opening it now. The time for that is when there is something to recompense an opening.

Prof. Helfer - Yes, I think that a town ought to provide good roads ahead of time. I would advise proper street planning for future growth . . . the village is sure to grow.

The Marcellus Observer
Wednesday June 24, 1925
Village Improvements

We who "belong" don't realize so much what the neighbors are doing as the occasional visitor notices.

A man came to town the other day and took a walk around town, and when he came back he said: "Well, the old place looks good to me. There have been many changes for the better. Houses are all in good repair and nicely painted, lawns and gutters are smooth and well kept, and it looks like every man is trying to make his place outshine his neighbor's efforts. And that's what makes a spotless Town. And your sidewalks - It is a pleasure to walk on them, for they are mostly so good.

Plans were being devised for dividing up what was left of the Reed Farm into building lots and streets and a map of the proposal was presented to the Village Board by Mrs. Hattie Reed in mid July. Much discussion and questioning would follow for another year, but it was clear that the Village of Marcellus was growing, not only evidenced by the 1925 census, but also by the number of building lots that were planned for the northwest part of the corporation.

14 Jul 1925 - " . . . Mrs. Hattie Reed appeared before the Board and presented a map of her farm which showed it cut up into building lots and streets. The map was made by a civil engineer and is a fine piece of work. Mrs. Reed explained it to the Board in a very efficient manner. The proposed streets were named on the map and she told what she proposed to do. The members of the Board studied the map carefully and gave careful attention to Mrs. Reed's

explanations. As the question of adopting it is of such magnitude, they put it off for further consideration until some future meeting."

Not only was the Village of Marcellus growing, but visitors were also impressed with improvements that were taking place in the community as well as the pride that seemed to be reflected in maintaining a positive image. The visitor to small-town Marcellus seemed to enjoy his stay.

An Attractive Village

July marked the publication of some interesting comment as to how to make Marcellus Village more attractive to visitors, the general public and perhaps to new businesses. Interestingly, some of the suggestions mentioned almost 80 years ago are discussed today. Some of the ideas, such as flower gardens and an attractive green space on the Methodist Church point have been adopted, maintained by the Village Highway crew and the Marcellus Garden Club. Other ideas, such as improving building facades are

---

The Marcellus Observer
Wednesday July 8, 1925
The Inquiring Reporter

What can you suggest toward making Marcellus strikingly attractive to the passing automobilist, to make them remember the place and keep it on the map of their memory?

C.H. Fuller - What I would suggest is a nice ornamental drinking fountain on the Methodist church point. That would be something to make it attractive and would serve a good purpose for the tourist.

Floyd Abrams - There is nothing that will make a town more attractive than will a beautiful flower garden. By making flower gardens in front of their homes, and keeping them beautiful, our town will be remembered by the tourist. If I was driving through a town and saw a flower garden, I would remember that scene. There is nothing that will impress the human mind more than nature's beautiful works.

Aaron Waldron - I would think that new, good-looking buildings would make them remember the town. Our good streets will also remain in their memorys. A general improvement would also be a good idea.

W. J. Matteson - A memorial to the boys who served in the late war, with a list of names of all from the Town of Marcellus, headed by those who gave their all, suitably lighted, so it could be plainly seen at night paced on the point of the green in front of the M. E. Church. An ornamental fence to enclose the whole green would be an attractive suggestion. Or a park of green in front of the church with a suitable Memorial to our boys.

And speaking about that new band stand and where to put it; And how to beautify Marcellus let's leave the Methodist out for once and ask why the Presbyterian sheds could not be removed and a park made that would run back of the parsonage and a nice driveway around to Main Street thru the park. Then bandstand would have a real home and the nice lawn parties for the church could use the bandstand for a stand or tables, etc. The good farmers of the Presbyterian church could supply the parsonage with garden supplies and everybody would be enjoying the Presbyterian Park.

---

encouraged, promoted by the Planning Board and in some cases paid for, in part by county agencies such as the Community Development Council. In recent years, the Board of Trustees has been instrumental in encouraging the Chamber of Commerce in the revitalization of our downtown or village center.

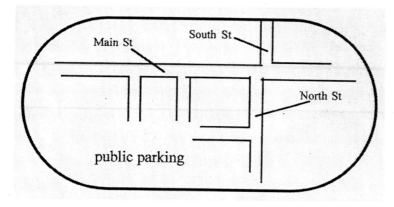

Parking

Another idea, which dates back to the 1920s that has had some promotion in recent years, is the establishment of public parking in the rear of Main Street businesses. Entrance to and exit from this parking from two directions, both Main and North Streets, is an idea that is presently being discussed by the Board of Trustees. It would seem to be a long-term solution to what has been an on-going concern for many years - creating more public parking and helping to make a business more accessible to the driving public. The idea might also be considered for the south side of Main Street, provided proper easements can be secured for entrance to and exit from both Main and South Streets.

On-Going Village Business

During the summer the Village, as usual, experienced some street and sewer line repairs and in early September, the Village Board voted to rescind Daylight Savings and return to Standard time. For many years, the issue had been and would remain a steady debate, appreciated by many and criticized by those who favored " . . . the God-given Rural Hill time that the sun and the moon regulates" (MO 7/8/25). It also seemed to be but another example of the divide that widened the gap between people in the1920s.

8 Sep 1925 - " . . . that Daylight Savings Ordinance be rescinded and that Standard time be returned, on Monday, Sept 14, 1925, at 2 a.m. instead of Tuesday, Sept 15."

The firemen responded to the alarms, even if they were false and by the end of October, " . . . the State troopers were in town, . . . and as a consequence, Halloween pranks were not so extensively indulged in this years as the village has enjoyed the past few years" (MO 11/4/25).

As winter descended on the Village in 1925, the Board prepared for its arrival by authorizing the purchase of a new snowplow for the sidewalks. The practice of plowing Village sidewalks continues to this day, and is something to which the residents have become quite accustomed as the LaRose war wagon makes its rounds long before many of them are awake on a wintry morning.

LaRose War Wagon

10 Nov 1925 - " . . . that the Clerk be authorized to write to firms in Utica and Clayton, N.Y. for prices on snow plows."

9 Dec 1925 - " . . . that the Clerk be authorized to buy one, No. 1, 5 foot sidewalk snow plow, price $85.00 of the Julian Scholl Co, N.Y. City . . . be authorized to order one Frink Snow Plow, V Type, of John Barga of Syracuse and to forward the order to the President for his signature."

1926 - Expansion of Governmental Powers

In January 1926 the Village Board appointed Mrs. Fred Uttley as Register of Vital Statistics for the Village, a position that no longer exists at the Village level. Today, a Bureau of Vital Statistics is maintained by the County of Onondaga and registration of births, deaths and marriages are filed with that agency. In the 20's, however, in rural Marcellus, most people were not only born at home, they also died from the home and registration of such statistics required the services of a local authority.

12 Jan 1926 - " . . . the Board appointed Mrs. Fred J. Uttley, Registrar of Vital Statistics for the Village of Marcellus."

By 1926, with the growing use of automobiles, it also became apparent to local government officials that the enactment of an ordinance regulating the storage, sale and distribution of gasoline and other volatile fuels was necessary. Accordingly, the

> **ORDINANCE**
>
> At a regular meeting of the Board of Trustees of the Village of Marcellus, N.Y., held on the 2nd day of March, 1926, be it ORDAINED:
>
> Section 1. That o person, firm, co-partnership, corporation or party shall keep, use, store or manufacture within the limits of the Village of Marcellus any gun powder, dynamite, gasoline, benzene, kerosene, crude oil, earth or rock oil, or any products therefrom, or any inflammable volatile fluid or explosives in quantity exceeding five(5) galls until he, it or they shall have first obtained a permit and license for such purpose from the Board of Trustees os said Village . . .
>
> Section 2. All applications for permits or licenses to keep, use, manufacture or sell such inflammable volatile fluid or explosives must be made in writing to the President of said Village in such detail as he shall prescribe and containing such information so he shall require, and the President of such Village on receipt of application, shall make or cause to be made an inspection of the premises proposed to be be used for the consumption, manufacture, storage or sale and the means of distribution of such inflammable materials and explosives, . . .

Trustees, at their meeting in early March, enacted such legislation, anticipating the construction of fueling stations in the Village as well as bringing about increased regulation as well as enforcement of codes to protect the general public and private property.

2 Mar 1926 - " . . . an ordinance regulating the storage, sale and distribution of gasoline, benzene, gun powder and other explosives within the Village limits."

Election

The March elections in 1926 produced no surprises as James McNair and Varnum Kenyon were returned to office as President and Trustee, in one of the lowest recorded votes in Village history. Just eleven people voted on March 16th, an indication it seems, that residents were satisfied with the efforts of the incumbents in the past as well as their desire to maintain the status quo in Village government. It might also be indicative of the fact that there were few controversial issues at the time or concerns that in earlier balloting might have attracted more of the electorate. This was also the last time that the election of the Village President would be for a single year. In later elections, the term would cover two years, as had been the case for Trustees since 1884.

Board Action

One of the first actions of the new Board was the consideration of new auditing books, so as to comply with suggestions made by the State Auditor. Even today, the accounting books of the Village Clerk-Treasurer of Marcellus are subject to the annual review of state inspectors, an examination that is not only good accounting but a review that provides some very helpful suggestions from expert professionals and keeps local government abreast of current accounting practices.

25 Mar 1926 - " . . . special meeting . . . for the purpose of discussing the new form of books required to comply with the suggestions of the Auditor of the State Dept who recently audited our Village accounts. . . . notify by letter Miss Mildred Case and Mrs. Marble that the empty ice cream barrier which they store in front of their respective places and leave there days at a time, are a nuisance which the Board wishes them to abate."

The Board also received a delegation of local citizens who were complaining about the actions of some youth, congregating in front of their stores and becoming disorderly and annoying to their customers and asking that there be an increased police presence in the Village. In 1999, local residents brought similar complaints to the Board of Trustees in an attempt to deal with youth who were congregating on Main Street and displaying an attitude and acting in a manner that seemed to threaten them. Their complaints were well received and led to the creation of a Neighborhood Watch Committee by the Board of Trustees as well as an increase in the number of hours that the police would patrol. By the summer of 2001, juvenile crime and the number of complaints brought by residents to the Board had dropped dramatically. The Neighborhood Watch group, however, continues to meet every month, conscious of the fact that complacency can often lead to unsettling conditions.

13 Apr 1926 - " . . . delegation of citizens consisting of L. E. Parsons, P. H. Schanzle, Miss Mildred Case and C. H. Fuller, appeared before the Board and advocated several things and wanted the Board to take action thereon. One of the complaints was boys congregating before their places of business, being noisy and disorderly and making it unpleasant for customers coming in and out of the sores. Another was a request for a policeman on the P. O. corner and for him to control the walk in front of the stores on the north side of the street. They also spoke against the changes of times this coming summer. A friendly discussion of the questions presented took place and the result was that the two first questions were held over for future consideration and the President said he would have a straw vote taken on the question of changing times."

Daylight Savings, Dog Licenses and Arbor Day

In other action that spring, and again in reaction to the concerns of residents and some businessmen of the community, the Board would survey the Village as regards Daylight Savings time, voting to rescind the resolution of a year earlier. The Board also notified the Town of the need for dogs to be licensed in the Village and would encourage the school children to participate in an expanded Arbor Day celebration. Some of the 8,000 trees planted in May of 1926 have since reached full maturity and mark a truly memorable occasion. In recent years, the Village Board, particularly after the storms of 1998 caused enormous damage, became very concerned about the planting of trees on Village streets, setting aside reforestation money in the budget as well as sponsoring local Boy Scouts who conducted a survey of village trees and created a database of information for possible use in future plantings.

> **The Marcellus Observer**
> **Wednesday May 12, 1926**
> **A Memorable Day**
>
> One of the most memorable happenings for Marcellus occurred Friday, May 7, when 8,000 trees were planted by the pupils of the grade, high and Ag schools. An organized corps of willing workers placed a living monument that will carry the day down in the history of reforestation and conservation of the forests . . . Those who were engaged in setting out these trees on this occasion will live to see the results of their labor handed down to coming generations as showing what can be done by cooperation and a singleness of purpose that accomplishes so much in the lives of all. It was a most spectacular sight when this army of young Americans headed by a drummer, marched up the road, showing the "Spirit of '76" is still alive.
>
> These were set out as we told last issue, just south of Otisco Crossing, a mile or so from the village line. Other places have been set, Gowland's land, back of Dr. Parsons' home, near the Stone woods, etc.

5 May 1926 " . . . moved and seconded that the sum of $5.00 be paid to Christine McNair and Mary Stone, each, for canvassing the village on Daylight Savings vote."

11 May 1926 - " . . . motion was made and carried that the resolution of 1925 in regard to Daylight Savings Time be rescinded."

8 Jun 1926 - " . . . notify the Town Board that all dogs in the Village of Marcellus that are without tags or dog licenses be taken care of."

Road Extensions and Filing Stations

By July, the Village Board decided that the northern extension of First Street along with the western extension of Reed Ave should be surveyed for the purpose of

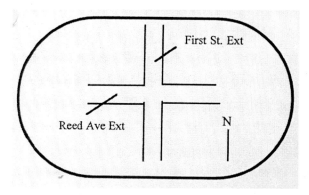

establishing a grade for those roads, and in anticipation of adding them to the list of Village streets. In addition the Board was presented with an application for a permit and plans for erecting a gasoline filling station on the Hackford property, at the intersection of South Street and Slate Hill Road in the Village. Both of these actions continue to reflect the expanding influence of the automobile in the 1920s, even in small-town America. The extensions of First Street and Reed Avenue would mean additional home construction in the Village and filing stations would not only increase business in the Village, it would also lead to an expansion of government into areas that were still quite new. By September, the Village Board also decided to install illuminating entrance signs to the Village, again reflecting a growing number of visitors to the Village, mostly by means of automobile.

13 Jul 1926 - " . . . that E. H. Coville be authorized to survey the extension of First Street on Mrs. Hattie Reed's lot for the purpose of establishing a grade for the proposed extension and also to complete the survey of the grade of the west end of Reed Ave."

20 Jul 1926 - " . . . the Standard Oil Company of New York hereby makes application for a permit to erect upon the property of Arthur A. Hackford and Clara A. Hackford, situated at the north east corner of the intersection of South Street and Slate Hill Road in the Village of Marcellus, N.Y., a 9 x 17 frame building for gasoline filling station purposes, as shown by certain plans and specifications annexed hereto and made a part of this application."

14 Sep 1926 - " . . . to install ten fixture, reflector lamps, etc., . . . for the purpose of illuminating entrance signs to the Village at the following points:

2 at Village Line	South Street
2 at Village Line	North Street
2 at Village Line	Scotch Hill
2 at Village Line	East Main Street
2 at Village Line	West Main Street

The Marcellus Observer
Wednesday Sept. 22, 1926
Little Visit with the Editor
The Knapp Block, upper floor formerly used many years by the Masons, has been partitioned and made over into two modern living apartments or "flat," with all conveniences, most pleasant and attractive. The one fronting Main Street is occupied by Mr. and Mrs. John Johnstone and son William; the other with living room windows facing on North Street, but quite as good view of the Busy Corner, is taken by Mr. and Mrs. Leon Bishop. Miss Louise Palmer has the corner front room for her Beauty Parlor, . . . and Attorney Knapp has his office in the same two rooms as before. The lower (sic) floor of the Knapp Block is occupied, as for many years, by the Post office, by Marble's Pharmacy, and on the North Street side by the combined telephone and electric lighting offices.

Apartments & Businesses on Main Street
Several other changes in the Village occurred that Fall, as the Knapp Block on the corner of North and Main Streets was transformed into a combination of apartment dwellings on the second floor while several

businesses occupied the first, including the telephone company, electric company and post office. Telephone service in particular expanded in the Marcellus community in the 1920's as the Finger Lakes Telephone Company took over the local business, with "... a corps of operators, ... comprise Miss Cora Garvey, Chief Operator, Mrs. Cora Marshfield, Miss Irene Muldoon and Miss Mary McAvoy, while the heavy work, from 9 o'clock into the night hours to 7 a.m. is capably and pleasantly done by Stephen H. Haney, who is also 'dean' - they sometimes call it 'deacon' of the force" (MO 9/22/26).

The Marcellus Observer
Wednesday, October 6, 1926
Celebrate 125th Anniversary
Marcellus Presbyterian Church Will Commemorate Origin In 1801 With Special Services

On Oct. 13, 1801, eighteen inhabitants of the Village of Marcellus, gathered to perfect a religious organization. Being of different faiths, they called themselves the "Church of Christ." The following May they voted to build a church edifice. This building was completed in 1803, standing on the site occupied by the present Presbyterian Church. Although there were other church organizations in existence, Marcellus could boast of the first church building in Onondaga County. In fact, it was a matter of renown that it was the only church between New Hartford, near Utica, and the Pacific Ocean.

Church Celebration -"Busy Corner"

The end of the year witnessed the 125th anniversary of the founding of the Presbyterian Church in the Village of Marcellus and the congregation still meets today, in the oldest church edifice in Onondaga County. Founded in 1801 by a small number of residents of the Village of Marcellus, the congregation and the building have remained an integral part of the village and community for over 200 years.

The Village Board also authorized the installation of flashing lights at the Main Street intersections in an attempt to more carefully regulate traffic at what was known as the "busy corner." The Board also heard again from Mrs. Hattie Reed, regarding the First Street extension and plans for development in that area, an issue that would be decided at a future meeting.

11 Nov 1926 - "... that the Marcellus Lighting Co. be instructed to install 3 way flash lights - one at the intersection of South and Main Streets and one at the intersection of North and Main Streets."

14 Dec 1926 - "... Mrs. Hattie Reed appeared before the Board and requested said Board to accept the extension of First Street which she is developing. After discussion, the Board decided to consider her application and decide at a future meeting."

Radio

One of the more desirable Christmas items on many people's wish list in 1926 was widely advertised, and that was a radio. Like the movies, radio was altering American life, even in small town Marcellus. It sold American consumer products, broadcast news reports almost immediately, and entertained Americans in a variety of ways. Much like television today, radio not only became a big business causing significant change, but it became a very familiar item in American homes. Even Marcellians could buy "on time" but if that weren't possible in 1926, joining a Christmas Club would satisfy that desire in 1927.

1927 – Plight of Farmers

While the 1920s were a booming time for many, this financial security rested on a shaky foundation and excluded from this general prosperity were many of the nation's farmers, as expressed in this 1927 political cartoon in *The Marcellus Observer*. Signs of economic trouble, which would become more evident as the year advanced, started to appear that year as other industries began to share some of the difficult times with farmers. In the Village, some changes were being discussed in Albany concerning Village Law, and the Board of Trustees voted to send President McNair as a delegate to the deliberations.

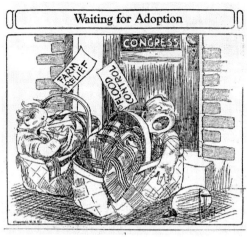
Waiting for Adoption

8 Feb 1927 - " . . . a notice from John V. Williams of the Legislative Committee on Villages was received giving notice of a joint hearing of the committee on Feb. 16, 1927 at the Senate Chamber at Albany and inviting a representative to be sent from this Village to consider and discuss proposed changes in the present Village law. After discussion, it was thought it would be well for the Village to have a representative at this meeting. It was moved by Kenyon and seconded by McNair that President McNair be appointed as the delegate to go."

Streets and Sidewalks

The Board approved the extension of First Street north to a street drawn as Reed Parkway and while many residents approved of this street expansion, some complained of the poor conditions of Village sidewalks, a grievance that continues to this day and usually during the winter months. The Village, it seems, has always had a significant walking population and, for the most part, the sidewalks are and have been well maintained. Some residents have even written letters that commend the Village for its well-maintained sidewalks. There are a

> **The Marcellus Observer**
> **Wednesday February 23, 1927**
> **Since The Flood**
>
> To the Editor:
> A poor foot-walking pedestrienne would respectfully ask why our village roads are so much better than our side-walks. While the roads are wide and smooth and clean, the side-walks are regular canyons of slush or a glare of ice. Don't we pay taxes enough to entitle us to a safe place to walk?
> ---TRUDIE

number of occasions, however, when complaints are received from residents and visitors alike that a fall has taken place and that the poor condition of the sidewalks is to blame. Today, the Village Board is very much aware of this concern and has an on-going replacement plan for Village sidewalks. It also enforces a "no parking" ban by automobiles on sidewalks, plows those sidewalks in the winter months and urges residents to notify the Village of sidewalks that present a safety hazard to pedestrians.

8 Feb 1927 - the Village Board would approve the " . . . extension of First Street in a northerly direction to a street drawn as Reed Parkway . . . "

Election Results

Beginning in 1927, the President of the Village Corporation would be elected for a two-year term, rather than the single year term that had been used since Village incorporation in 1854. The first person elected to this two-year term was James G. McNair, who had been the incumbent executive since 1923. In addition, James B.

Parsons would be re-elected as Trustee and J. Fred Woodbridge and Alice M. Wright would be re-elected as Treasurer and Collector respectively. McNair would go on to win another two-year term in 1929.

15 Mar 1927 - " . . . the total number of votes cast was 20
James G. McNair   received 19 votes   for President   for 2 years
James B. Parsons   received 19 votes   for Trustee   for 2 years
J. Fred Woodbridge   received 20 votes   for Treasurer   for one year
Alice M. Wright   received 20 votes   for Collector   for one year

Spring Comments

Some interesting comment in the local paper and at Village Board meetings reflected

The Marcellus Observer
Wednesday, April 13, 1927
The Ghost

. . . The new semaphore on Main Street will be a boon to the village during the summer traffic. Several smash-ups have occurred at that corner. Another bad corner is at the foot of Scotch Hill. . .
. . . Officer Hackford grabbed a few youths the other night that were making sport of running across the road in front of approaching cars. A pedestrian may have the right of way but folks should remember that a driver also has rights. Mr. Hackford did the proper thing in lecturing the offenders.

a bustling community that spring. A Go-To-Church Campaign reflected an increasing attendance at services and " . . . a real interest in church going, even in competition of the radio and automobile" (MO 4/13/27). While some residents were happy to see a new semaphore, similar to the one pictured here, installed on Main Street, others complained about the restlessness of youth.

The Marcellus Observer
Wednesday April 13, 1927
Home News

Parsons Hall will have an entrance of new design after work done this week by Mr. Parsons. Cement laid with an incline from the sidewalk well into the foyer, or corridor, will permit bringing the doors nearly out to the front of the building, leaving separate entrances for the two stores, Fuller's jewelry, and Miss Case. While tending to general improvement, we have Mr. Parson's word for it, but assume to say the provision is mainly to make it so that a crowd of youthful time-killers will not have the former enclosure as a hang out. Instead, we presume, they will now have to stand out on the walk and obstruct it. The village has bought a new scraper for the roads, but it needs also a scraper to clear the sidewalks at certain hours.

Parsons Hall

While some questioned its reasoning, Parsons Hall received a new entrance that spring – one that seemed to accommodate ease of entrance and one of the few businesses on that part of Main Street which did not present a major handicap for people with disabilities. Interestingly, that part of Main Street has always presented some major difficulty for people with handicaps, limiting access to residences and businesses. In 2003, some 75 years after Parsons Hall was redesigned, the sidewalks on that part of Main Street will be reconstructed so that all places will be handicap accessible. This will be made possible by Federal Transportation grant money for which the Board of Trustees made successful application in 2000.

Few residents showed up in May 1927 to voice complaints about tax assessment and later that month, the Village Board examined the draft of a new set of Village Ordinances, complying with the requirements newly imposed by the State of New York.

3 May 1927 - " . . . the Board met as a Board of Assessors to hear complaints . . . But few came and no complaints made."

10 May 1927 - " . . . hereby resolved that a draft of the new Village Laws be presented to the Village Board of the Village of Marcellus, N.Y. and a set of suitable ordinances for said Village not later than Aug. 15, 1927 for approval of said Village Board and that Horace M. Stone be employed for that purpose."

The Memorial Boulder

With the Memorial Boulder in place, Marcellus paid full honor to its veterans as well as the soldier heroes of all wars on May 30, 1927. Beginning with special church services, the celebration included music, and a parade as well as speeches and a cemetery ceremony. The honor is repeated every year and to the boulder have been added the soldier heroes of wars that have been fought since, including World War II, Korea, Vietnam and the Persian Gulf Conflict. The stone is also appropriately set on what might be termed the Village Green, a point of land in the Village that has come to symbolize its center and its focus.

The Reed Tract

By the summer of 1927, an extensive building development was started in Marcellus entitled the Reed Farm Tract. The project, begun by Mrs. Hattie Reed, called for the

---

The Marcellus Observer
Wednesday June 1, 1927
The Vision Of A Woman Materializes
Mrs. Hattie Daboll Reed Of Marcellus Develops Reed Farm Tract As new Residential Section. The Survey is Completed And Map Made As Shown By F. J. Schnauber, C.E., And Lots Are Now On Sale

What will perhaps be the most extensive building lot project ever undertaken in Marcellus is about to be launched by Mrs. Hattie D. Reed, owner of Reed Farm Tract, the title she gives to the enterprise.

The possibilities and attractiveness of this parcel of land, which lies directly behind, north and west of the present Reed Homestead, has probably never occurred to those who have not walked over the property.

Entering the Tract by a newly acquired roadway directly opposite the   Chrisler office, one immediately encounters Reed Parkway Drive, which will be a wide, roomy street with a series of grassy landscaped parks in its center, extending to the extreme west end of the property.

Connecting with this main drive are to be three new streets: First Street (continuing the present street of the same name); Second Street; and Highland Drive, on the upper or western side. The new Second Street will enter the present Reed Street just west of the former James Parsons' house - or six houses west from First Street - and Highland Drive will come out just below the new Mrs. Whaley home and opposite the Benj. Leggett property. This gives four convenient entrances to Mrs. Reed's development.

Parallel with Reed Parkway and the present Reed Street will   lie new Meadow Street, connecting the new streets midway.

---

development of a new residential section in the northwest quadrant of the Village of Marcellus, including the sale of over 130 building lots and construction of new roads which would connect with existing Village streets. Eventually, many of these lots were sold and residences were built, thus increasing the size of the Village. Other lots were not sold, for a variety of reasons, some of the related to concerns about proper drainage. Nor

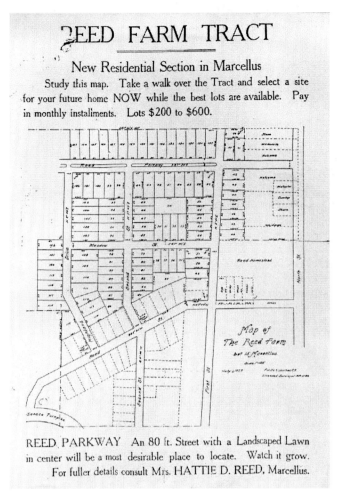

REED FARM TRACT

New Residential Section in Marcellus

Study this map. Take a walk over the Tract and select a site for your future home NOW while the best lots are available. Pay in monthly installments. Lots $200 to $600.

REED PARKWAY An 80 ft. Street with a Landscaped Lawn in center will be a most desirable place to locate. Watch it grow. For fuller details consult Mrs. HATTIE D. REED, Marcellus.

would homes be built on what would eventually became property of the Marcellus School District and today is a large expanse of open green space in front of the Driver Middle School. It is also interesting to note that the corporation limits include this green space, ending at the steps of the school.

In addition, several streets were laid out, looping the quadrant and extending the reach of Village government as well as its responsibilities. One of these, Reed Parkway, remains a very wide road largely because the landscaped island parks in its center were never built. Other streets, such as Highland, Second and Meadow, were built, but they were not connected to Reed Street as originally envisioned, drainage concerns again being a major consideration. The project, however, did attract many people and families to Marcellus and " . . .

to stand at the extreme west end of (Reed) Parkway Drive and look toward the east, north and south, one is presented with what is veritably a birds eye view of the beautiful Marcellus valley and the eastern hills . . .. a picture that one must travel far to equal" (MO 6/1/27). Today, that view remains unspoiled, and homes in the area continue to appreciate in value.

New Map and Payments Due

A Firemen's Parade in July celebrated their success at the Convention that summer and in August, E. W. Coville presented a new map of the Village to the Board of Trustees. Because of the many changes that had recently occurred, Mr. Coville had been authorized by the Board to plot a new map of the Village, incorporating those changes and updating that which he had designed in 1906. The Board also made note of taxes in arrears, authorizing their collection, as well as a payment that was due on the soldier memorial.

9 Aug 1927 - " . . . Mr. Coville presented the map of the Village which he was authorized to make and it was accepted by the Board. Mrs. Alice M. Wright appeared before the Board with her books - receipts and etc. received as Village Collector. Her report was accepted and showed $9,325.32 collected and $205.50 due. The Clerk was instructed to give the Tax Roll to Treasurer for collection of the taxes in arrears."

19 Aug 1927 - " . . . a communication from Mr. J. H. Weidman in regard to a payment due on the memorial to deceased soldiers of the World War was presented by the Clerk and upon motion, was laid on the table for the present."

Water Supply

In the fall, the Village Board received an application from the Onondaga Water Supply Company requesting a right of way under the sidewalk at the White Bridge on North Street. An interesting side note is that today the Onondaga County Water Authority (OCWA) still maintains a water main at this location and on occasion, the Village of Marcellus, when its own reservoir is low, requests connection to this main so as to maintain an adequate water supply for its residents.

11 Oct 1927 - " . . . application . . . by the Onondaga Water Supply Co. and asking a right of way under the sidewalk to connect their main at the White Bridge on North Street."

Fire Prevention

There were also some significant discussions that fall on fire prevention, what ordinary residents could do to prevent fires and the question of whether or not the Village

---

The Marcellus Observer - Wednesday October 19, 1927
More On Fire Prevention – Facts About Local Dep't

Do you ever stop and consider how few serious fires we have had in our community in five years? Marcellus Fire Dep't has responded to 31 alarms since the delivery of the new truck in February, 1925, ten of which were for fires outside the corporation limits. Only three of four of these fires have resulted in at all serious damage to property, and these few were from inadequate supplies of water, combustible material being housed in the building, or distance from Marcellus. In cases where the fire got beyond control, the men bent their efforts to save adjoining property, and in each instance succeeded.

The question of whether the apparatus should go beyond the village limits is always a delicate one to cope with. A man may live just over the line and still we couldn't stand by and see his house burn down. Yet the farmer two or three miles away feels that he deserves the same consideration. While the truck is miles away, who protects the village - its owner? One-third of our fires have been outside the village line.

Hay stacks and barns filled with hay and grain are hopeless fires, where even an abundant supply of water would do little or no good. You will recall the many serious fires in our territory back a few years. Do you ever wonder why so few serious ones occur now? Quicker response and faster and more efficient apparatus, as well as quick fire reports by telephone, the siren, etc., are the answer.

---

fire apparatus should go beyond the limits of the corporation in order to fight fires. The Marcellus Fire Department still promotes an aggressive fire prevention program in the local schools and the question of fire apparatus going beyond the village limits has also been addressed. Today, the Town of Marcellus contracts with the Village of Marcellus, the owner of the Fire Department, for fire protection. This resulted in an increase in the number of volunteers needed to fight fires as well as an increase in fire apparatus, housing, equipment and supplies. This also necessitated a comparable rise in taxes as well as a concern each year as to what the cost of the fire contract would be. The cost of the fire contract each year is based on the assessed valuation of the Village and the Town. Because the assessed valuation in the Town represents about 75% of the total, the Town then pays the lion's share of the fire budget. The Village, which owns the Fire Department, makes most of the decisions about its operations, yet it pays less than 25% of the budget. Therein lies the crux of the dispute each year during talks about the fire budget and the contract.

First National Bank, Marcellus

The Bank and Ben Hur

In October, the First National Bank of Marcellus celebrated its 17th anniversary with additions to its new bank building in the heart of the Village. Begun in 1910 by several merchants as well as professional and businessmen and women, the institution prospered in the Village and provided much needed services to local residents. "In building the new Bank it was provided that the Free Library be also included, and a financial arrangement was entered into by which the Library has a permanent home on the upper floor" (MO 10/19/27). Today, although the Library now has its own home, the

---

The Marcellus Observer - Wednesday November 30, 1927
Advertising Does It All

The fact that Marcellus' folk are interested in Radio is evidenced by the report of sales from the R.P. Smith and Son Store at Marcellus. According to Mr. Smith the Radio season begins with the World's Series games in late September, or early October, and continues until after Easter.

The sale and installation of 25 radio sets since Oct. 1 in a village the size of Marcellus is considered an excellent record by the manufactures of the radio that Mr. Smith sells. The firm does not consider that the Christmas sales are yet begun, and look for a greatly increased business at the Yuletide season.

The Marcellus Observer - Wednesday November 30, 1927
Ben Hur Here Dec. 8, 9, & 10

Parsons Hall, Marcellus, announces two quite unusual attractions for next week, which should make an appeal to the usual patron and as well to those who do not regularly see the movies, and must admit that they come to us at home exactly as good as the ones they may attend on those trips to the city.

Wednesday night comes The Road to Romance, with Ramón Novarro. He is also the star in Ben Hur, . . . the wonder production begins in Parsons Hall, Thursday, Dec 8, and continues Friday night, Saturday matinee and night. Making, you see, of Marcellus a place right up with the big burghs, a picture house running every night. Beat it if you can.

---

old bank building accommodates the government offices of the Town of Marcellus, a fitting use for a structure that continues to serve the community so well. There was also much anticipation in the community about the arrival at Parsons Hall of a much heralded movie production entitled "Ben Hur." As with radio, the movies were changing American life styles and movie audiences in "up town Marcellus" were excited by what they saw on the screen.

Christmas Lights and Tree

As 1927 came to an end, the Village Board ordered the streetlights to be kept on through the night, perhaps in anticipation of more Christmas shopping. There was some criticism that there were too few decorations on Main Street that year. A community tree, however, was displayed during the season, and a Christmas festival was also held that many Marcellians found to be a unique opportunity to get together and celebrate the peace that existed in 1927.

13 Dec 1927 - " . . . that the street lights be turned on at 5 p.m. and left on until 7 a.m. each day until further notice from the Board."

1928 - Advice and Lights

The year began with some fatherly advice being dispensed by the Village President to the community 's youth, upset as he was with some of the misdeeds being committed in the Village. Like many young people throughout the country in the 1920s,

---

The Marcellus Observer
Wednesday December 14, 1927
Rovin' With Roy

Shame, Marcellus! shame, Camillus, Jordan and Elbridge! You let your little sister village of Skaneateles beat you to it on decorations. For a week past old "Skinny" has been decked out in all the glory befitting the holiday season. Every lamp post on Genesee Street has been transformed into a bank of evergreen, with small American flags arranged around the top.

The Marcellus Observer
Wednesday December 21, 1927
Community Tree Ablaze

A large Christmas tree has been placed on the Presbyterian Church lawn in preparation to the Christmas festival Saturday night. All plans have been laid and it is expected the entire village will turn out. To take part in this Yuletide event . . . .. gives us an opportunity to get together, both Catholic and Protestant, to celebrate the birth of One whom we both call King.

194

The Marcellus Observer
Wednesday January 4, 1928
Youth Given Some Fatherly Advise

Village President James McNair acted the true role of "Village Father" Thursday night, when he called about a dozen boys to the Engine House and gave them sound warning and advice regarding some depredations that have been going on for some time. "You boys could be arrested," Mr. McNair said, "but I don't want to see it. I want the boys to have all the liberties possible, but we must have order. It is in our power to enforce the Curfew Law, but that, I believe, has its evils, also." Complaints have been coming in recently in larger numbers than before regarding boys committing petty mis-deeds and causing trouble. The Village Board wants the youth of Marcellus to have a good time, but they claim that rowdyism and property destruction must cease. If advice cannot bring about the change there still remains access to the law.

The Marcellus Observer
Wednesday January 4, 1928
The Ghost

Just why, ask the merchants on the South Side of Main Street, is the ice and slush allowed to collect and lay there while the other side is free from such nuisance. Some say that folks deter from crossing the road because of the water that lays there on soft days. Anyway we have been folks picking their way cross and jumping.

it appears that youngsters in Marcellus were challenging the authority of their elders and expressing themselves in ways that were unheard of in earlier generations. Young people were spending less time at home, enjoying more freedoms and older people were shocked by what they saw, and by the boldness of youth, which often bordered on disrespect for the law. Not only were merchants disturbed by the loitering of young people, some were also upset with the conditions of the streets and sidewalks during the winter months. A new street did open up into the Hackford Tract, attracting potential home buyers to the Village and in mid

The Marcellus Observer - Wednesday January 18, 1928
Hackford Tract - Fine Homes

With the completion of another new home on his land, Arthur Hackford, Marcellus builder, announces his Tract officially open to prospective home buyers. The home now nearing completion is the fifth to be erected on the Hackford Tract since it was stacked out. The new street that is opened east from South Street (and as yet unnamed) is generally conceded to be a "coming" proposition. Mr. Hackford has installed a modern sewer, with connections for every lot on the Tract. Trees have been set out on both sides of the street, and with the coming of spring the drive will be improved . . .

With the growing ease of transportation, commuting of former city folks is becoming more general. The villages are attracting more people every year, and such plots of ground as local Marcellus people are offering should prove a source of interest to prospective citizens.

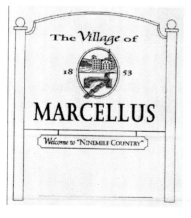

January " . . . Marcellus stood agape, . . . as Philip Wilson of Marcellus Lighting Company did acrobatic stunts on the face of the Town Clock, . . . (which) received needed new lights and reflectors . . . Everyone breathed a sign of relief when the first light was completed" (MO 1/18/28). New lights were also set at the entrances to the Village, warning drivers of the posted speed limit. It was also noted that a sign of welcome to the Village might also be added to the posting, an invitation that is evident today when one enters the community. There are plans, headed by Trustee Robert J. Wilson, to make these signs even more special as the Village approaches its 150th anniversary in 2003.

The Marcellus Observer -Wednesday January 25, 1928
Rovin' With Roy

The Marcellus Trustees had 2 spotlights set at the various village entrances with the intention that it would strike upon the "speed limit" phrase inscribed on the board. . . This wording could be made to include a cheery welcome, and all done in lettering to invite admiration.

Changes Take Place

Early in February the firemen began to test the fire siren every week, a custom that continued for some time, usually on Saturdays, to make sure that the signal system was in working order. February also marked the notice of a Village caucus in preparation for the March elections, a special vote that reflected some changes that had occurred in Village law. A most interesting article in the local paper not only encouraged people to vote in that election, it also wrote about the changing times that had and would continue to occur. These changes were favored by some and were feared by others, another example of how the 1920s were an unsettling time and how change was reaching into even the smallest towns.

Some significant changes occurred in Village government at this time, some in order to comply with State law. Titles were

---

The Marcellus Observer - Wednesday February 22, 1928
Rovin' With Roy

Did you ever fell like this? One of the best things a fellow can have is civic pride, and the man without it must feel queer. Civic pride is getting out to caucus, voting at election, nominating who you want for office, even if he loses and continually boosting for improvements. If your town needs a new fire apparatus, boost for it. The old schoolhouse that served you may not serve your children. Boost for a better one. Things are changing every day. Where are the hitching posts and water troughs of yesterday? Gone. Gas stations and parking signs stand in their place. The old buggy is the exception rather than the rule. One hardly dares think of the tomorrow when traffic is transferred to the air or when ribbons of concrete 100 feet wide stretch from coast to coast. We must change our ideas in keeping with progress. Yesterday's program is obsolete. Boost for today's!

---

changed, elected positions became salaried, offices were abolished or combined with others, and the number of persons on the Village Board was in a state of flux for about a year. These changes did not do much to prevent some from complaining about public officials and how little gets accomplished by those elected to office. This, it seems, has become magnified in recent years as well. Encouraging people to run for public office by offering salaries, as was done in 1928, seemed to be a good idea, but it also encouraged

The Marcellus Observer
Wednesday March 7, 1928
Rovin' With Roy

A member of the Board of Trustees in one our villages aid, "It's terrible, the knockers that a man in public life has to put up with. We do what we see we ought to do, but really, we cannot see everything. What we don't see, folks knock us for missing. If folks would cooperate and come right up to Board meetings and spout to us about their grievances we would be glad to attend to them. But instead, they knock us at the grocery, in church at Men's Club, to the tourist and salesman - in fact to everyone but ourselves. To us they are pleasantness itself, never a word of kick or suggestion. How much smoother things would be if WE were told instead of outsiders.

those who complain with little or no suggestion for improvement. Often referred to as "knockers," they can be found in every community and they often discourage good people from participating in public life.

14 Feb 1928 - the title of President of the Village Board changed to that of Mayor.

13 Mar 1928 - " . . . the Board completed the auditing of the books of the Treasurer and Clerk. It was along job but the Board was pleased to find that not a single error was found. The books are kept in the latest form approved the State Comptroller so that no complaint should be found by a State Auditor . . . that the Village Board be paid a salary for 1928 as follows: Mayor - $300 and Trustees - $200. Motion carried."

In other changes that took place in 1928, the office of Collector of Taxes was abolished and combined with that of Village Treasurer. The voters would no longer elect individuals to either of these offices, and the position of Treasurer-Collector would become an appointed one. At its annual meeting in April, J. Fred Woodbridge would be appointed to the job and he would continue to hold this position for the next forty years. There was also a requirement in the March 20th election of that year to elect two additional Trustees so as to comply with State law. Thus, there would now be five members of the Village Board (President, now called Mayor + four Trustees). Those held over from the election of 1927 included President James G. McNair and Trustee James B. Parsons, and those elected in 1928 included Trustees Varnum S. Kenyon, Frank H. Gillett and John H. Weidman.

20 Mar 1928 - " . . . total number of votes cast was as follows:

21 votes was cast	for V. S. Kenyon	for Trustee	for 2 years
21 votes was cast	for Frank H. Gillett	for Trustee	for 2 years
20 votes was cast	for J. H. Weidman	for Trustee	for 1 year
Spoiled ballot was 1			

2 Apr 1928 - " . . . that J. Fred Woodbridge be appointed Treasurer-Collector for the coming year. Motion carried."

9 Apr 1928 - " . . . that the salaries of the Clerk, Treasurer and Road Commissioner remain the same as last year, viz.: Clerk, $120 per annum, Treasurer, $120 (per annum), and Road Commissioner, $1200 per annum."

The Marcellus Observer
Wednesday April 18, 1928
The Spirit Of Service

Fifty years ago! To those who remember it seems but yesterday, but to us who have not reached the half-century milestone, it seems time immemorial.

Fifty years ago, April 17, Edmund Reed, then a very young man, turned out the first issue of The Observer, on a little hand press, in a building on the old Reed homestead.

The Observer and the Cemetery

April 17th marked the 50th anniversary of founding of *The Marcellus Observer* by Edmund Reed and a memorable editorial by Roy A. Gallinger paid tribute to the pioneering spirit of the first publisher of that paper. Another article in the same issue by Elizabeth Chapman relayed an inspiring story of the Village Cemetery, also paying tribute to the early pioneers of the community and of the need to care for its upkeep. Maintaining the village cemetery and preserving its stones and heritage remains a concern today.

The Marcellus Observer - Wednesday April 25, 1928
Fireman Keep Eagle Eye On Apparatus

The Marcellus Observer - Wednesday June 6, 1928
Fire Ladies Organize To Help Fire "Laddies"

Marcellus is expected to carry home the bacon, . . . if the enthusiasm of the newly organized Ladies Auxiliary to the Marcellus Fire Department is any criterion . . . .

Officers of the newly formed Ladies Club were elected as follows:

Mrs. Mable Wickham
Mrs. Jennie Hunt
Mrs. Stella McLaren
Miss Lucy Case

A committee consisting of Mrs. Cora Marshfield, Miss Fanny Wilson and Mrs. Frank Seymour was appointed to draft a set of by-laws for approval at the next regular meeting, . . . June 16.

The Ladies Organize

Of concern to the firemen in the spring of 1928 was the apparatus used to fight fires, and to many women of the community, the organization of an auxiliary to the Marcellus Fire Department seemed to exhibit their growing influence in the 1920s. Not all were flappers, nor did all bob their hair, but they did want to experience the new freedom and the new opportunities that the 19th Amendment to the Constitution had spawned. A concern of the Board of Trustees was the existence of a slaughterhouse in the Village, an unsanitary condition that had to be remedied. Local merchants were concerned about business and again agreed to close their stores on Wednesdays at noon through the summer months, signing an agreement to that effect. Marcellus also " . . . paid homage to the memory of the Boys in Blue and Khaki with fitting services on Memorial Day" (MO 5/30/28)

The Marcellus Observer
Wednesday June 6, 1928
This Will Make Us Look Like A Million

Agitation is on foot to widen Main Street, Marcellus, between North Street and the beginning of Slocombe Street on the North side, and in front of the stores on the south side of the street. Moving the curb back four feet on each side of the street would give eight feet more for traffic.

If this procedure is carried thru, it would eliminate much of the danger and congestion on busy nights. It is also suggested that the corners be cut back, as is being done in other villages, and thus do much to alleviate the traffic problem in Marcellus.

And while the Village Fathers and property owners are considering these betterments, they should likewise look over North Street. The Odd Fellows have a nicely cemented front walk, but it is out so far; there remains, though not so cemented, the similar width both at the corner Knapp Block and The Observer frontage. "Squint" your eye on a line with the row of trees in front of Pilot's and Gillett's, and see if it would not be fine to set a new curb in line with these trees from the corner.

---

14 May 1928 - " . . . Clerk reported on conditions he found at the slaughter house on the property of Mrs. Thomas Walsh. Moved by Weidman and seconded by Kenyon that the Clerk notify Mrs. Walsh that the waste of water at the slaughter house must be eliminated and the overflow pipe which discharges a stream into the brook, be taken out."

Traffic, Parking and the Pond

Traffic congestion and parking in the Village was another issue that drew the attention of many people. There was a call for widening streets, for installing and moving curbs, for parking ordinances, and for laying new sidewalks. The Board also visited Rockwell Pond, concerned about the purity of the village water supply and ordered that steps be taken to clean the reservoir and reconstitute its design.

The Marcellus Observer - Wednesday June 13, 1928
"No Parking" Need Not Drive You Away

They are prohibiting all parking in the business section of Marcellus. At first thought this may seem a hardship, but if properly carried out will inconvenience no one . . . It is the habitual parker, who uses the main street for a day and night garage, that the ordinance is aimed at. Cars are left parked while owners go to the movies, or even to the city.

Our Village Fathers

The contract for laying sidewalks in Marcellus has been awarded to Levi Parsons. Mr. Parsons will start immediately on several stretches of walk in the village. The moving of the curb on Main Street to allow more freedom in traffic at the Busy Corner has been indefinitely postponed . .

Plans to give Marcellus more and purer water are embodied in a decision made by the Village Board at a meeting this week . . .

It was decided, . . . to close the second reservoir entirely until it could be cleaned and connected permanently with the first. This would give us an abundant supply of pure water, to the village, the spring in the second reservoir being better than that in the first . . .

---

11 Jun 1928 - " . . . a resolution . . . ordering No Parking signs as follows: On the North side of Main Street from the Postoffice corner to the west line of the P. A. Schanzle property, and from the Postoffice corner fifty feet north west side of North Street. On the south side of Main Street from the Corner Store to the east line of the R. P. Smith property, and from the Corner Store fifty feet south on the east side of South Street . . . several members of the Board having visited Rockwell Pond previous to the meeting, it was decided that something ought to be done to insure a pure water supply for the Village. Having found the West Reservoir very low and the East Reservoir very dirty on the surface, they reported same to the meeting . . . that the East Reservoir be cleaned out and a wall built at the east end which would provide an additional supply of pure water to run into the existing reservoir."

The Marcellus Observer - Wednesday July 11, 1928
Careful, Speeders!

State Troopers are watching traffic in the vicinity of Marcellus around 5 o'clock in the afternoon when campers go through. Some of the lake sojourners seem to forget that there is a speed limit in our town, and in their haste to reach the cooling breezes of Otisco Lake, are apt to speed a little dangerously. We like the outside traffic, but must raise a warning finger at times.

Early morning speeding, while not so dangerous, is getting to be quite a habit also. We don't like to see a fellow late for work, but if it continues we fear that someone may complain, and that will be stopped also. It may pay to drive a little carefully.

The Marcellus Observer - Wednesday July 25, 1928
The Great Need Of A Park – A Suggestion

A man came into this office Tuesday and suggested that an Old Home Day be held in Marcellus. The idea was very acceptable and one we had thought on many, many times, but in our conversation, the old question arose regarding a spot in which to hold the festivities. Marcellus is without a park. We can have no such home coming day without a speaker. No speaker likes to "do his stuff" on a paved street, on a mid-summer day, harassed by passing cars. It is absolutely necessary to have quiet and shade.

How much better the band concerts would sound and be enjoyed if there was a park in which to hold them. The band is knocking around from pillar to post, anxious to please but handicapped by conditions.

Marcellus has an ideal spot for a park and children's playground, but apparently has overlooked it. A grove of trees, not too thick, a stream of water and grass. Away from the arteries of travel, this natural amphitheater has the most possibilities of any spot we know of in any town. The plot lies in the present Hackford tract. Entrances could be made from three streets. The grounds could be improved, drained, and artistic bridges built across the creek effectively. Flowerbeds, walks and drives could be laid out, and the result would be a beautiful, quiet park equal to the best. The shallow water would make it ideal for children's bathing, and of course swings and other paraphernalia could be installed.

We need such a place and soon spots like this will be turned into building lots and sold piecemeal, ruining forever our chance for this kind of improvement.

Where in Marcellus is there another place for a park? We welcome suggestions. Other towns have natural groves which have been turned into beauty spots, so why not our own town.

It will be only a matter of time when another street will be built from Main Street through to the Slate Hill Road, paralleling South Street. This will pass our suggested tract. We advise a little thought by far seeing citizens regarding this thing, and would like to hear other suggestions

Summer and the Park

The 4th of July was "safe and sane" according to *The Marcellus Observer*, although " . . . the night of the 3rd, several boys attempted to burn a shack they had hauled from somewhere, and deposited in Main Street . . . Early July 4th, just after daybreak, a crowd of youngsters who had 'slept out' somewhere in a tent or shanty, began to throw giant crackers under porches and on lawns to disturb the sleeping populace. Firecracker racket was kept up all day, but no serious burns were reported. Some beautiful displays of fireworks took place at night, at several village homes, children, for the most part, participating" (MO 7/4/28). Perhaps because he felt the Village was more secure, Mayor McNair authorized the removal of the Village lockup that summer, but more likely it was an order from the State mandating that this be done. As more and more people visited Otisco Lake in the summer, there was more concern about some who posed a threat to the safety of residents as they sped through the Village.

23 Jul 1928 - " . . . Mayor McNair read communication from State Commission of Correction regarding removal of the Village Lockup and ordering same removal."

Much discussion took place that summer over the idea of an Old Home Day celebration and where to hold such an event. The proposed location for a community park to hold such festivities was in the Hackford tract, an ideal spot thought many, for concerts, picnics and playgrounds, and its natural beauty and easy accessibility by means of Village streets. Eventually this plot of land would become the Marcellus Town Park, and today it is used not only for the Olde Home Days Celebration each year but for a variety of public functions as well, by individuals and groups who enjoy its scenic beauty and well kept grounds. It is truly a jewel in the midst of the community, a pastoral scene in a village setting, reflective of attempts by other communities to bring the country into the city and a reminder of the past as well. The Village incorporation line runs through the park, embracing almost all of Nine Mile Creek as it meanders through the park.

A Resignation and a New School Year

In mid August, Charles Dillon, who had been Village Clerk since 1923 and had also been a Trustee for a number of years at the turn of the century, resigned from office due to poor health. To that position was appointed Charles E. Jones, a local undertaker in his mid-fifties at the time who would devote ten years of service in this new position.

The Marcellus Observer Wednesday August 22, 1928 School Opens Sept. 4; Marcellus Faculty	
Marcellus High School will open September fourth with the following staff of teachers:	
J. M. Molyneaux, Principal	Science
Flora W. Smith, Preceptress	Drawing
Elizabeth Slattery	French, Latin
Mary Rodgers	English
Virginia Treptau	German, History
Eunice Burnett	Music
Raymond R. Jansen	Agriculture
Emma R. Avins	Science
Milford A. Campbell	Mathematics
May Chrisler Edwards	Librarian
Helen Byrne	English
Arthur Hyatt	Physical Education
Elizabeth Wicks	English
Marguerite Pendergast	8th Grade
Ida M. Banning	7th Grade
Agnes Pearsall	6th Grade
Florence A. Robinson	5th Grade
Elizabeth Donovan	4th Grade
K. Belle Hackford	3rd Grade
Nellie E. Leggett	2nd Grade
Katherine W. Kenyon	1st Grade

13 Aug 1928 - " . . . the resignation of Chas Dillon as Clerk of Village be accepted, due to the state of his health and that a letter of regret be drafted and sent to Mr. Dillon. There being no objection, Mayor McNair appointed Charles E. Jones to fill the unexpired term of Mr. Dillon."

A new school year began on September 4th and an interesting addition to the local paper also began to appear in the weekly gunwad. Entitled the *High School Speedometer*, it appealed to all who were interested in school activities with articles written by the students themselves. It also reflected an attempt to channel the activity of the young, whose growing influence in society and the economy was much stronger than that of their parents had been at a similar age. Like newspapers today, readers are often more interested in the local news as well as what is happening with local people and *The Marcellus Observer* tapped into this curiosity in 1928. People also enjoy reading about accomplishments and the success of young people and the paper was an excellent opportunity to exhibit this aspect of human nature as well.

Remodeling the Engine House

The Firemen, who elected a new set of officers at its annual meeting in September, discussed the "remodeling of the Engine House to suit present day needs. The present quarters . . . somewhat unfitted to an up-to-date Dep't. No toilet accommodations . . . available, and the remodeling of the upper rooms would better fit social activities of the men and women of the village . . . The need is apparent to visitors at the Engine House, ... more than to village folks. The accommodations in most other towns are better than those in Marcellus . . . equipped with brick structures to house the motor apparatus . . . if the building was improved and a few modern conveniences put in, it would serve for many years longer, and help to beautify the village" (MO 9/12/28).

Halloween and the November Election

The end of October brought out the annual celebration of Halloween by the youth of the village. "A rather amusing trick this year was to put Hoover signs on the homes of avowed Smith men, and Smith signs where Hoover reign" (MO 10/31/28). The Presidential campaign and election of 1928 was one that caused many Americans to take sides, a battle between what had been and what was happening. Herbert Hoover represented big business, rural America, Protestantism and prohibition, while Al Smith was a champion of the city workers, and urban areas. Combining this with his Roman Catholic religion and his opposition to prohibition, Smith was like a lightning rod for many, particularly in the rural communities. Hoover won an overwhelming victory throughout the country, including a plurality of almost two to one in the Town of Marcellus. His smile was one of great confidence and most people had every reason to believe that the prosperity of the 1920s would continue. Perhaps this confidence helped prompt the Village Board to contribute Village funds to the Village Library that November.

12 Nov 1928 - "... this Board donate ... the amount of $200.00 to the Village Library."

The Spirit of the Season

As the Yuletide season approached, people in the community felt secure and positive. They had elected a man in whom they had great confidence and the spirit of the season enveloped them. "Someone . . . suggested that a rink be flooded for the use of children and grownups alike . . . there glows and glistens a Christmas tree full of shining colorful lights, so that all who pass may see and admire . . . How cheerful to the cold and tired traveler to see a beautifully lighted tree in the public square . . . giving a very seasonable appearance" (MO 12/19/28). This euphoria, however, would give way to depression in 1929.

1929 - Go Forward or Fall Short

The last year of the decade would prove to be a disastrous one in our nation's history but the year began, even in Marcellus, on a swell of optimism, with many people convinced that the good times and social progress would go on forever. This was quite evident from a lengthy editorial printed in the local paper urging local residents to be progressive in their thinking and to reject the old ways, now relegated to the days of the horse and buggy. The automobile had altered thinking all over the world and even the smallest towns had better move ahead or be forever left in the dust of the past, according to the editor. The paper urged that a sewer system be installed in the Village, that garbage collection be enacted, and that curbing, parks, and playgrounds be addressed. It was felt that lights should be used to decorate Main Street and a Chamber of Commerce should be set up to promote the community and its merits.

Eventually, many of these concerns would be addressed in the Village of Marcellus, but it would take time, and there were many who were opposed to any action that might lead to a rise in taxes or an expansion of governmental powers. Similar opposition remains evident today, moderated somewhat by the use of state or federal grants rather than local taxes to upgrade village streets, sidewalks and the sewer plant. Despite these improvements, there are those who remain opposed and long for a return to what had been. They are often deaf to logic and like the farmer described in the following story, are waiting to be coaxed or dragged into the 21st century.

The Chain Store

Another concern for a small town in the 1920s was the arrival of large chain stores, which took a substantial share of business from the home merchant. The local paper, in

> **The Marcellus Observer - Wednesday January 16, 1929**
> **There's Only One Way – Time To Go Forward**
>
> Two men stood on the Postoffice corner. One a business man of the newer type, who believes in progress and the other a retired farmer. The farmer came to the village ten years ago with his little "roll" and lives contentedly on it.
>
> "What we need," the young business man was saying, " is a series of ornamental lights along both sides of Main Street; we need to cut those curbs back to make better corners, and we want a sewer system.
>
> "Oh, the devil," snapped the farmer, "our taxes are enough now, what good are ornamental lights? Cesspools were used before you were born, so why burden the taxpayers with a sewer tax for years to come?"
>
> Here are portrayed the two types of citizen. One the active, progressive type, full of civic pride, and the other the contented man who prefers to stay in the same rut regardless of whether his town grows or not. As long as the axes are kept down he is satisfied. He it was who fought against the new school building, but is proud of it now. But for such as he, the sewer, garbage collection, park, playgrounds, bandstand, might have been instituted long ago.
>
> Let us leave the two men standing on the corner and place ourselves in the shoes of a city man who desires to move into a country town. What does he ask? He first inquires if our town has lights. Yes, we say proudly and good water too. Sewers? No. Garbage collection? No. Chamber of Commerce? No.
>
> We point proudly to our fire department, our band, our school and churches, our bank, but the city man shakes his head. Another town attracts him. Our town loses a good citizen - and a thousand dollars of business the nest year.
>
> Fifty years ago a few hitching posts, a general store - and a dingy post office, a church and saloon constituted a town. But in those days there was little or no travel. Folks drove to town Saturday nights, and on circus days. The city was a day's travel away; cotton, calico and gingham were good enough anyway. The "Chamber of Commerce" sat nightly around the chunk stove in the store and munched crackers and prunes, or tried their luck at squirting tobacco juice at the bagoon ten feet away.
>
> With the coming of the automobile the world woke up. The cities first, and now the towns are drowsily stretching themselves and coming to life.
>
> On the postoffice corners of a thousand towns are sanding the prototypes of the two men mentioned in the beginning of this article. One boosting, pushing, ADVERTISING; the other settling back against the breeching - waiting to be dragged, coaxed or better still - kicked. And shouting "keep the taxes down."
>
> What shall we do? Shall we let our sister towns take our share of new citizens with the resultant rise in property values, or shall we get together as one gigantic Citizens' Civic League and boost for the very best there is - and get it. It is the survival of the fittest! If we fall short, we are lost.

another edition, stated that " . . . it is very probable that the chain store is here to stay . . . Home merchants . . . must fight back . . . must brighten up, clean up, keep his stock sold up, and be courteous, . . . be civic minded. He must push, push, push, and boost, boost, boost. To him, his town must be the best place on earth - it must be the best town in the best state in the best country on God's footstool. The local merchant is the backbone of the community and on him rests the future of his town" (MO 1/23/29). Today, the Village of Marcellus is largely a bedroom community, and many local merchants have a difficult time competing with large retail stores that offer lower prices and a greater variety of merchandise. Many businesses have left the community while many others struggle to maintain a visible presence. This is a scene repeated all too often in small town America today and one which defies immediate solution. In Marcellus, a Chamber of Commerce has met with some success in recent years but all too often this organization has depended on the interests and efforts of a few business people rather than most. For all to be successful, all must be active, as those home merchant of Marcellus were urged in 1929.

Fire At Midnight

The winter of 1929 witnessed a devastating fire in the Village of Marcellus. In mid February, " . . . just after midnight, the siren sounded, telling the countryside that the beautiful Masonic Temple, . . . was belching forth flame and smoke from its attic floor.

The Marcellus Observer
Wednesday February 13, 1929
"Go Ahead" Board Tells The Firemen
New Apparatus Is in Prospect, Masonic Fire
Proves The Great Need. Close Inquiry To Be Made
Into Cost of Pumper

More efficient apparatus with which to battle future fires was requested by Marcellus firemen at a special meeting of the Village Board Wednesday night. The shortage of proper ladders at the Masonic blaze and possibilities of further incapacitation should a fire break out in a larger building, prompted the Dep't to act at once.

Giles N. Case, spokesman for the Firemen, stated that a pumper would be necessary to meet demands of a modern village where water conditions, . . . exists . . .. At present, the only hope for protection in a large fire lies in the generosity of neighboring villages loaning a pumper, and the possibility of its arriving too late.

Mayor James McNair assured the committee that they could expect full co-operation from the board, and instructed them to get estimates on the necessary equipment, and the question will be submitted to voters at a Special Election at the earliest date.

The firemen, roused from their slumbers, hastily donned clothing and raced out into the darkness toward the east section of the village, which was brightly lighted by the flare of the burning building . . . The entire ceiling and roof . . . burned away; one looks up into the open sky, a pitiful scene . . . Cause is not known . . . The structure was old, historic, built over 100 years ago, known locally as the Talbot-Case homestead. (The) Masons bought it for a Temple in 1926, making large outlay toward a model gathering place" (MO 2/13/29). The devastation of this fire prompted Board members to approve the request for more and up-to-date fire apparatus, including ladders and a pumper, a request that would be put to the voters in a special election. In addition to this proposition, " . . . a petition was presented to the Village Board asking that an appropriation of $250 be made for the Marcellus Band, to be used to further concerts during the summer" (MO 2/20/29).

McNair For Mayor, Other Propositions

Also in February, there was a " . . . desire to do away with two members of the Marcellus Village Board, and to get along with the two remaining and the Mayor . . . James B. Parsons and J. Hynds Weidman will have no successors. The election ballot . . . only for Mayor, and for the band proposal" (MO 2/27/29). James McNair was nominated to serve another two-year term as Mayor, and along with Varnum S. Kenyon and Frank H. Gillett would constitute the Board of Trustees following the March elections. That three-person structure remains intact today, although the terms of office have changed from two to four years. The voters in that election also approved the band proposition.

23 Feb 1929 - " . . . Meeting of the electors of the Village of Marcellus, in caucus, . . . Mr. E. V. Baker . . . spoke relative to the number of persons constituting the Board of Trustees, which at the present time consists of four members, and recommended that said Board be reduced to two members . . . The report of the committee was that . . . a unanimous choice was for a Board of two Trustees. Mayor James G. McNair was then nominated for the office of Mayor for the term of two years. As a result of the above sentiment of the caucus, there were no nominations made for Trustees, as the unexpired terms of V. S. Kenyon and Frank H. Gillett constituted a complete Board."

19 Mar 1929 - " . . . whole number of votes cast for Mayor was 13, of which James G. McNair received 13 votes. The following proposition submitted to the taxpayers at the annual election: 'Shall the Village of Marcellus employ the Marcellus Band for band concerts to be held between June First and September Fifteenth, annually, at an expense of not exceeding the sum of two hundred and fifty ($250.00) dollars.' The whole number of votes cast on said proposition was 12, of which 11 were recorded 'yes' and one (1) 'no'."

> ### The Marcellus Observer
> ### Wednesday February 27, 1929
> ### Some Figures And Facts About Sewers
>
> To the Editor: --
>
> As a member of the Marcellus Village Board for the past five years and Village Treasurer ten years previous to that, I naturally have been much interested in the arguments put forth regarding sewers and fire equipment which have come up from time to time.
>
> While I do not wish to dwell on past history, the proper time to have had sewers was at the time the water system was put in. At that time it would have cost approximately half the cost to-day and would be at least half paid for at the present time. Of course, the argument then was the same as the present: "Can the village stand the bond issue?" That same argument will be put up 10 or 20 years from to-day....
>
> First: ... It will cost anywhere from $50 to $100 to build new cess pools or tanks and this item must be paid for immediately ... whereas if it were in a bond issue for a sewer system, this cost would spread over a longer period of years and also the fact that the individual has the same condition confronting him every ten or twelve years, while with a sewer system, this is entirely done away with. ...
>
> Second: With regard to financing, ... As I figure the proposition, it will be necessary to raise the tax rte $7.00 per thousand and only for the first ten years, as at the end of that period our water bonds will be fully paid off ...
>
> Third: It is only a matter of time when the State Health Department will compel and force the village to install a sewer system

> ### The Marcellus Observer - Wednesday April 3, 1929
> ### Ode To Spring
>
> There are tasks we like and tasks we loathe, and task we must espouse;
> but of all the tasks that get our goat the worst is cleaning house.
> We start it in the cellar and end it at the roof,
> with so many complications that most drive a fellow goof.
> Two hours straight we beat the rug, that graced the parlor floor,
> and then we scrub the old back stairs till hands and knees are sore.
> Washing windows, painting sash, taking down the stove,
> when we know we should be fishing in some shady little cove.
> Here I end this little wail, for I hear the wifie call --
> Come! Take this mop and take this pail and clean the upstairs hall."

> ### The Marcellus Observer - Wednesday May 1, 1929
> ### Rovin' With Roy
>
> Jim Dillon and his men have filled up a lot of holes in the pavements in Marcellus village. We may have a few rough spots in our village roads, but Main Street, Marcellus is much more pleasant to drive on than Main Street in Skaneateles. One can at least keep his teeth in place.

> ### The Marcellus Observer - Wednesday May 15, 1929
> ### Plans For Sewer Discussed By Board
>
> Plans for the installing of a municipal sewer system were discussed by the Village Board of Marcellus ... the system is to be in two units and will take care of the entire village in a proper manner ... Petitions have been circulated ... the sewer system is much needed to make Marcellus a town to attract new homeseekers ...

Some Facts About Sewers

An issue that would continue to gain interest and promote discussion in 1929 was that regarding sewers. An article written by V. S. Kenyon, a member of the Board of Trustees, to *The Marcellus Observer*, noted some interesting facts that he wished to impress on the reading public of the Village. He also had some concerns about fire equipment, arguing that "the modern equipment manufactured nowadays means that quick response to fires saves considerable damage . . . the better our fire-fighting equipment, the better our individual homes are protected and the cheaper our insurance rates" (MO 2/27/29).

Ode To Spring

As April descended on the Village in 1929, residents were reminded of the need for Spring cleaning and the Board of Trustees requested that " . . . any citizen report immediately to any member of the Board any street light that may be extinguished, in order that it may be restored promptly" (MO 4/3/29). The Board also authorized the village crew to complete roadwork and accepted a petition from residents of the Village requesting the installation of a sewer system.

13 May 1929 - " . . . a petition signed by ninety-six property owners requesting the installation of an adequate sewer system and disposal plant for the Village was presented by Mr. F. W. Knapp, and on motion by Mr. Gillett seconded by Mr. McNair, the petition was accepted, ordered filed and that the Board act in accordance therewith."

The Marcellus Observer
Wednesday May 15, 1929
O'Hara Bus Lines May Extend
To Marcellus

M. J. O'Hara , of the firm, . . . who own and operate the Syracuse-Camillus Bus Lines, . . . was in Marcellus last week . . . to see if he could get permission from the Village and Town of Marcellus to extend their Bus Line through to the Village of Marcellus in case the trolley line discontinues doing business. . . . They would run by the way of Marcellus Falls, and would guarantee to give satisfactory service.

The Village Mayor and Town Supervisor also entertained a visit from a representative of a bus line seeking permission to extend its service in the event that the trolley line discontinued, as it would in 1935.

An Old Home Day?

In June, the community again considered an old home day celebration but there were questions of when and where, as well as how to finance the event. The Olde Home Days Celebration that have been held in recent years seem to have resolved most of these questions and through the efforts of a number of interested volunteers the festivities have been quite successful. The response of the community to this now annual event has been most positive and has achieved what those in 1929 hoped it would be, " . . . a day when former residents may return to native haunts and meet others who have moved away, besides the friends who still remain in town . . . A parade of officials, firemen, school children and fraternal orders, with floats and music . . . Flags and bunting . . . emphasize the welcome . . . a day which would be enjoyed and remembered . . . of renewing old friendships and the undeniable boost that such an affair would give to Marcellus" (MO 6/5/29).

Vendors In the Village

The Village Board was also concerned that summer about the number of " . . . non-resident vendors of vegetables, brooms, hosiery, extracts, bead, men's suits, vacuum cleaners, and other necessities of life . . . Wandering merchants . . . taking business away from village merchants . . . inferior goods at lower prices, with short weights and measures . . . " (MO 6/12/29). As a result, the Board raised the license fee for such vendors to $25, indicating that this did not apply to the local farmer who raised his own produce, and encouraged housewives to ask the peddler to show his license.

10 Jun 1929 - " . . . that all peddlers and hucksters license fees be increased from ($5.00) five dollars to twenty five dollars ($25.00)."

Summer in the Village

It was hoped that July 4th would be safe and sane and while " . . . some towns have curbed their youth from indulging too strenuously in the racket making material, . . . so far our Village Fathers have been lenient" (MO 6/26/29). It was an issue about which many residents continued to be concerned, throughout the summer.

Bids for the new road "down East Hill" from Card's Corner to the Village of Marcellus would be opened that summer as well, a tribute to the efforts and persistence of Town Supervisor William S. Spaudling. With the opening of this road, traffic would no longer be diverted south at Card's Corner but move directly west, in which path lay the Village of Marcellus, its merchants and businesses. Seneca Turnpike, as it is known today, is the major highway linking Marcellus residents with their jobs in Syracuse, as well as one connecting travelers from Syracuse to Skaneateles and points west. In the aftermath of its construction, Cedarvale and Howlett Hill Roads became less traveled, depriving communities in those areas of commercial traffic.

Street business was also an issue with the Village Board that summer. It appointed a new street commissioner and was somewhat alarmed about the danger that seemed to exist for pedestrians on the North Street bridge. That concern is still evident today. A foot bridge does allow pedestrians, mostly school children, to cross with some degree of safety, but only on the east side of the highway. In 2004, it is hoped that a new bridge will be in place, on both sides of which will be a pedestrian pathway, built by New York State's Department of Transportation.

The Marcellus Observer - Wednesday, July 3, 1929
Boys Burn Awning At Marble's Pharmacy

A lighted firecracker ignited the awning of the Marble Pharmacy, Marcellus, Monday evening, causing no little consternation and endangering the whole block. It was extinguished before harm was done, other than a large hole in the awning. Later in the evening, boys tore the awning into shreds, making repairs impossible, thus adding further injury to that already done. A new awning will have to be purchased to replace the ruined property. Public sentiment is reaching the boiling point regarding the depredations of boys and young men on Main Street evenings and late at night. Property is being destroyed, sidewalks littered and passers-by insulted. Upon one occasion thievery from an out of town car was reported. Women refrain from going to the stores and movies in the evening because the crowd of rowdies who infest our business section. The name of the village is being blackened by the insults and indecent language which is brazenly hurled at, or is audible to occupants of passing cars. Owners of business places are becoming disgusted with the state of affairs, and will no doubt ask for protection and peace. It is the duty of the authorities to see that the situation is remedied, and at once.

The Marcellus Observer - Wednesday July 17, 1929
Cement Road This Fall, Marcellus To Card's Corner,
Supervisor Spaulding Assures Bids

Supervisor W. S. Spaulding has been persistent in his effort to obtain construction of the highway "down East Hill, might be one way to put it; from Card's Corner to Marcellus village, four miles, of concrete . . . This is mighty good news for Marcellus village. With that new road south from Cards Corner naturally diverting city driving to the lake, and country trading going this route to the city, Marcellus village was to an extent "off the map." We were about to meet the inevitable situation brought to many communities by road building; some are favored as others lose . . . Those out for a ride are as apt to find this route as any . . . To local drivers it will provide an "air line" route to Syracuse, though hilly, and winding in places.

---

12 Aug 1929 - " . . . subject of appointment of a Street Commissioner in place of Thos. McAvoy who is incapacitated by reason of illness, it was on motion by Mr. Gillett supported by Mr. Kenyon that William Kilcoyne be engaged as such commissioner. The matter of danger to pedestrian traffic over the White Bridge by reason of heavy automobile traffic was discussed and the Clerk was instructed to confer with the County Commissioner of Highways relative to the elimination of the danger to pedestrians by the erection of a foot bridge thereat and to ascertain upon whom the responsibility rests."

The Marcellus Observer
Wednesday September 11, 1929
Local Burglaries Need Official Action

The confectionary stand of M. Kulba, at the foot of Scotch hill, Marcellus, was entered by thieves sometime Wednesday night and money and merchandise to the amount of $75 taken, besides wanton destruction of property . . . That same night the thieves entered five private homes in the village but took no booty except a roast of beef from the refrigerator at the home of Frank Knapp. Other homes entered were those of Arthur Robinson, Dwight Chrisler, John R. Malcolm and George York

---

Dogs, Burglaries, Goblins

Unlicensed dogs captured some attention in September, but a concern about burglaries in the community was more noticed. The Board responded by adding more officers to the night patrol. In recent years, reacting to residents' concern about youthful gatherings, the Board has likewise found it necessary to add more hours to the police patrol. Reducing the hours when the offenses lessened also seems to be part of what is and has been a pattern common in many small communities.

> **The Marcellus Observer**
> **Wednesday October 23, 1929**
> **Halloween Goblins Gambol Thursday**
>
> If you hear a cabbage crash against your door next Thursday night, while you are reading the latest edition of the Gunwad, don't be sore, but just hope that it is big enough for dinner the next day . . .
>
> If we may be allowed to advise, a few little acts of thoughtlessness may be omitted from the night's celebration. First, find out where the elderly folks live, who are liable to be severely frightened and then leave them alone . . . Another place to steer clear of is the home with a new baby in, especially babies just lately arrived . . . Don't use paint on porches or clapboard. This is nothing short of a crime, . . . defacing property
>
> Don't steal, even if it is Hallowe'en. You can be held for stealing . . . just the same as any other night. Don't break windows or screen doors. Don't tear off porch rails . . . And last, be careful of fires . . . bonfires are dangerous . . . Hallowe'en is a grand occasion for the youth, but nothing is more disgusting than to see full grown men (?) going around in herds destroying property and causing all sorts of trouble. The sight is seen every year in small towns, where police protection is limited, and nothing pleases the public more than to see such rowdies jugged and forced to spend the night in the calaboose. Police are watching for this type rather than the innocent little tick-tacker.

13 Sep 1929 - " . . . in view of the many recent petty burglaries in the Village, it was on motion by Mr. Gillett, seconded by Mr. Kenyon to employ four officers to patrol the streets of the Village from 9:00 p.m. to 3:00 a.m. - two each night, alternating their labor, to terminate at the pleasure of this Board."

14 Oct 1929 - " . . . the Clerk was instructed to advise Mr. Hackford to suspend police operations Oct. 15, 1929, until further notice."

This suspension of police action before Halloween may have been somewhat premature, since there were " . . . a lot of goblins in town champing at the bit waiting for the signal to go . . . " (MO 10/23/29). It is also interesting to note that, like 1929, there are today some who celebrate Halloween in a manner that is unacceptable, defacing property and frightening those who are somewhat defenseless. Often they are much too old for this annual rite of passage and, as in 1929, travel in herds or packs, exhibiting the mentality of a mob. Such individuals offend the public and the effort of law enforcement to curb their behavior is always welcome.

The Crash

While Marcellians were reading the article on Halloween in *The Marcellus Observer*, brokers in New York City were watching prices as they dropped sharply on the stock market. The plunge continued the next day, and October 24, 1929 has been known as "Black Thursday" ever since. Huge blocks of stock continued to be dumped on the market by investors who tried to get whatever they could. This was the first stage of what would become the Great Depression of the 1930s -- hard times that farmers had experienced for some time now and which were about to get worse for many others. The editor of the local paper seemed to forecast those hard times when he asked: "What is getting into the community? I counted seven bills of sale within a radius of ten miles. An auction in the fall is unusual, to say the least, but seven held within a space of two weeks is more so" (MO 10/30/29).

> **The Marcellus Observer**
> **Wednesday November 13, 1929**
> **FIREMEN APPEAL FOR PUMPER**
> **AS GREAT NEED**
>
> **The Marcellus Observer**
> **Wednesday December 11, 1929**
> **GET OUT YOUR SKATES - RINK ALMOST READY**

Life As Usual

November elections in Marcellus and the surrounding area did not seem to be affected by the events of October, however. Republicans continued to score big wins and life went on as usual. The Marcellus Firemen made a great appeal to the taxpayers of the community to support the purchase of a new pumper and there was much agitation to create a " . . . first class skating rink for children and hockey players of the

area . . . it will keep the children off the creek, which is claimed to be dangerous in spots. It will also give good winter sport to the village, and aid in putting us on the sport map" (MO 11/13/29). With money raised by contributions, the ice rink was ready in December, and one newspaper ad suggested that skates might be a sensible gift for a boy that Christmas. The spirit of the season was alive in local stores and the pending disaster of depression did not seem to dampen yuletide spending.

As Christmas and a new decade loomed, the local editor commented: " . . . Darkness has just begun to fall and the tree on the church lawn is showing up with a beauty peculiar to Christmas. Folks, laden with packages, are hurrying home to enjoy the thrill of Christmas Eve. It makes a fellow wonder how many poor families will be without Christmas this year. Some will suffer rather than to make their wants known, while others will spend foolishly and lavishly. The real Christmas would be to help the other fellow first, and then enjoy your turkey knowing that you had done a few good turns. After all, that is what Christmas is for" (MO 12/25/29). In the 1930s, there would be many more people in need of help and the lavish spending and good times of the 1920s would be but a memory.

Conclusion

The 1920s have been given many labels, including the Age of the Radio. By the end of 1929, Roy P. Smith and Son of Marcellus had finished " . . . the year with a radio business of $19,291.60 . . .a total of 109 new radio sets . . . since last Christmas . . . installed in the homes of satisfied customers . . ." (MO 12/25/29). For a rural community like Marcellus, that was probably a remarkable accomplishment. Radio allowed news and ideas to spread more quickly, narrowing some of the distance that separated urban and rural communities. It also brought the world beyond the "busy corner" much closer, a threat to privacy for some, a welcome change for others. For all of them, the 1930s would be a test of their resolve.

Chapter 12 – The 1930s

Many remember the 1930s as a period of business failure and economic hard times. Although Marcellus would experience many of the symptoms of depression, there was not the devastating crash that occurred in many other communities in New York and pervasively in the United States. The mills of Marcellus were fiscally sound and employment remained steady: " . . . though the mills may have reduced their work schedules, local tradition says they never fired anyone, so workers were able to earn some income, and prices were declining" (Heffernan 105). In addition, since Marcellus was still a farming community, food was largely available and people were able to find work on local farms. Some farmers even began to expand operations, including the Mulroy Dairy which, in 1930, operating out of a new plant on West Main Street in the Village, ". . . was the first local dairy to deliver milk in bottles with patented sanitary tops, . . ." (Heffernan 110). At the same time, some new business ventures were started, including a dining room that Robert Whitfield added to his ice cream stand on North Street in 1930. The Village itself continued to be a major employer for individuals and businesses that provided services for people in the surrounding countryside, like George Hickman whose market on the corner of Main and South Streets provided meats and groceries and Steven Hunt who operated a grocery and general store in one of the oldest buildings in the Village at 19 East Main Street" (Heffernan 113-114)

The Marcellus Observer
Wednesday January 15, 1930
Villages Unite In Agitation To Maintain A. & S. Trolley Road

Small hope was held for the continuation of the Auburn & Syracuse line at a meeting held in Skaneateles Wednesday evening, attended by residents of Auburn, Marcellus and Skaneateles, many of whom depend upon the trolley for means of transportation to their business places . . ..

The Marcellus Observer
Wednesday March 12, 1930
Should It Not Be Slocombe Street?

Was the street in Marcellus, west from Main, passing First - up "Piety Hill" - named for Sidney Slocombe? Then why is "Slocum Street" on the sign at First Street instead of Slocombe Street? When the street signs were order, who gave this name by mistake to the maker of the signs? We printers call it "copy". Who made the "copy" for the sign job and spelled Slocombe, "cum?"

Dr. Aumock wanted printing done with directions on it, "Corner of Slocum Street." We wanted to make the change to Slocombe, but he said if anybody was looking for him they would see the sign Slocum; he had no acquaintance with the man after whom the name was taken. Just now Fred Slocombe has an ad to rent the house he inherited from his father. We will print the ad: "To Rent, the Slocombe House on Slocum Street, inquire of F. S. Slocombe." Why not Reide Street, or Bradlee Place? The cost will be very small to correct this and do definite honor to our departed friend, instead of this half honor. He did his work well, we all know; mistakes were not in his accomplishments. Let us follow his good example.

From Trolley Road to Bus Line

As the year began, residents of Marcellus and other communities were concerned about the loss of the Auburn and Syracuse Trolley line as a means of transportation. A victim not only of hard times, but of increased dependence on and preference for the automobile, the A & S would eventually pass into history, its rails removed and sold for scrap. Throughout the year, there would much discussion and agitation for the addition of a bus service for the community, including a direct line to Syracuse over the hills. The Village government was also concerned about transportation issues as well, including the construction of a foot bridge for pedestrians over Nine Mile Creek at the north end of the Village, as well as some safety issues, including the installation of new fire hydrants on Main Street. The appointment of Village officials and a criticism about a street sign honoring the memory of former Village President Sidney Slocombe also faced the Board just before the March election that year.

23 Jan 1930 - " ... Mayor McNair was designated to confer with the Onondaga Water Service Corporation relative to the installation of two hydrants from their conduit, one on South Street and one on North Street as near the corners of Main Street as practical, as an auxiliary water supply for any emergency that might arise, as an additional water supply in case of fire in the business section. ... was also empowered to confer with State Engineer ... regarding construction of a foot bridge at the bridge known as the White Bridge in this Village which is under State control as a hazardous condition to pedestrians existed at that point . . . was also empowered to procure two dozen chains for the assembly room up stairs in the Firemen's rooms."

10 Feb 1930 - " ... the term of office of Mrs. Addie Uttley as Registrar of Vital Statistics for the Village Health district having expired, she was again appointed . . . term expiring Dec. 31, 1933."

23 Feb 1930 - " ... Mr. H. M. Stone made . . . remarks relative to the abandonment of trolley transportation and cautioned the citizens relative to the granting of franchises to bus companies."

Large Voter Turnout
On Tuesday, March 18, 1930, in one of the largest voter turnouts in Village history,

---

The Marcellus Observer - Wednesday March 12, 1930
Vote Tuesday
Show your colors on election day by going to the polls and casting your vote. Let the candidates see that you are in favor of them whether there is a chance of his being defeated or not. Nothing inspires a candidate to want to work, like a good-sized vote on election day. Get the voting habit and trot over to the polls and mark a ballot.

The Marcellus Observer - Wednesday, March 19, 1930
Kenyon And Hunt Are New Trustees
A prancing team of "dark horses" appeared upon the horizon early Tuesday morning, and consternation reigned in the ranks of the Marcellus candidates a few hours before the polls opened for voting. The two candidates, S. H. Hunt and C. A. Spade, for Village Trustees, were chosen at the caucus and, as is usual in Village elections, supposed themselves to be the only men in the field for the office. Early Tuesday morning, it became apparent there were others when it became whispered around that V. S. Kenyon and Frank Gillett, outgoing Trustees, were again seeking the office on an independent ticket. When the polls opened at 1 o'clock, the voters began to come, mute evidence that both parties had been working. Instead of the election board putting in the afternoon smoking cigars and swapping yarns, they were kept busy with the voters. When the final curtain was drawn, a total of 289 votes had been cast, in contrast with the 13 vote landslide that swept Mayor MacNair into office last year. For the first time in history, candidates got out on the street and spoke to friends and others for support. When the box was opened, it was found that Mr. Hunt received the highest, or 134 votes, Mr. Spade, 110; Mr. Kenyon, 114; and Mr. Gillett, 91. That put Hunt and Kenyon in as Trustees for two and one years respectively. Two ballots went blank and 5 spoiled. Mr. Kenyon has been a member of the Board of Trustees for a period of 16 years. His name was not brought up at the caucus, although Mr. Gillett received 10 votes to Mr. Hunt's 24. Mr. Spade's nomination was unanimous. Upon the urging of his friends, Mr. Kenyon became the "dark horse" and won.

The Marcellus Observer - Wednesday, March 26, 1930
Election Will Stand – All in Favor, Say 'Aye'
The election will probably stand. Although there is still some dissension to the validity of it, the Citizens party are understood to have withdrawn all objections to it, and to allow the candidates to take their seats, in accordance with the report of the election board. The story is too well known in Marcellus to make repeating necessary. Briefly, S. H. Hunt and C. A. Spade were candidates for election to the board for two years and one year respectively. The morning of election day, V. S. Kenyon and Frank Gillett, outgoing Trustees, made an independent drive for election, resulting in Mr. Kenyon getting 114 votes to Mr. Spade's 110. The election board announced Mr. Kenyon's election along with Mr. Hunt's. The Board took into consideration the avowed contest and made formal determination before the start of the balloting that the two candidates receiving the highest number of votes should be declared by them elected. Friends of Mr. Spade immediately protested on the grounds that while ballots marked for him were specifically for a term of one year, Mr. Kenyon's were marked for both two years and one year, and most with no term written. This, they declare, gives the election to Mr. Spade on the strictly one year basis. The shoe pinches just there. While Kenyon received the majority, the Spade men declare that Kenyon's votes were mixed as to term and therefore will not hold for a total. Whether further steps will be taken in the matter is not known. Both men are popular in the Village and both lay claim to the election. Both are conscientious . . . and in all probability, Mr. Spade will withdraw and allow the veteran Trustee, Mr. Kenyon, to resume his seat.

Varnum Kenyon was returned to serve another year as Trustee and Steven H. Hunt was elected to a full two-year term as Trustee. The election may have been a reflection of the times and a desire on the part of many to participate more fully in the electoral process, as urged by the paper, rather than accept the status quo as in previous years. As the local paper mentioned at the time, both parties were out working the polls and the voters. The election results were also contested that year, on the grounds, it appears, of some technicalities. In the end, there were no changes, but this contest did set the stage for an even greater voter turnout in 1931. The election of a Democrat as Mayor, the first in its history, reflected a national voting trend and a reaction to the policies of the Hoover Republicans.

18 Mar 1930 - " . . . at such election the total number of votes cast were 248.
   That 137 votes were cast for Stephen H. Hunt for the term of two years.
   That 110 votes were cast for Calvin A. Spade for the term of one year.
   That 114 votes were cast for V. S. Kenyon for the term of one year.
   That 91 votes were cast for F. H. Gillett for the term of one year.
   That 2 votes were blank. That 11 votes were spoiled.
   That 1 vote was cast for Arthur Hackford.
   That 1 vote was cast for James Powell.

Bus Proposal

Following the election, the concern of residents and Board members turned to the issue of bus service for the community. A public hearing was held in early April to consider the applications of several companies that wished to provide that service and following some lively discussion, the Board would eventually grant a five-year franchise to the Cayuga Omnibus Corporation. The Auburn-Syracuse Trolley had its last run on April 15, 1930. "For nearly three decades the trolley . . . served the towns faithfully . . . Buses will start operating as soon as the trolley quits, so the towns are assured of continuous service" (MO 4/9/30).

The Marcellus Observer
Wednesday, April 30, 1930
New Parking Order For Marcellus

Garage men this week received notice from the Village that parking of cars in front of their places of business was prohibited in the future. This action was found necessary because of bus service and the anticipation of summer traffic. Some of our garages have been using the street as a day and night parking place for used autos, it is this that the Board objects to.

The Marcellus Observer
Wednesday, April 30, 1930
New Crosswalks

Cement cross walks are being laid this week at the entrance of Bradley Terrace and of the Hackford Tract. A number of men from the Village force are engaged in the work. With a few exceptions Marcellus is well supplied with walks, and the roads are in good condition. With the laying of the new sewer system our Village will be up-to-the-minute as a residential community and a good place for commuters to live and enjoy life.

17 Apr 1930 - " ... meeting ... for the purpose of consideration of granting permission and consent to the Cayuga Omnibus Corporation for the operation of busses in and through the Village of Marcellus, supplanting the Auburn and Syracuse Electric Railway which is now abandoned. After careful consideration of the matter, it was moved ... that said permission and consent be granted as per the terms and agreements set forth in the contract herewith filed ... permission and consent .. shall be held ... for a term of five (5) years from the date of the issuance of the Certification."

Parking and Crosswalks

Soon after granting the bus franchise, the Board of Trustees began to consider new parking restrictions and authorized the laying of new crosswalks in the Village. As a community, whose population had increased about 20% in the last decade, the Village of Marcellus had attracted a number of new residents as well as visitors. Some visitors, however, during these economic times, such as hucksters and peddlers, were not especially welcomed and the Board reacted to their presence by increasing the cost of their permits by an extraordinary 600%. The Village Board would also engaged the services of Arthur Wilson as Village Attorney, anticipating the need for legal advice regarding conditions at the village reservoir and construction of a sewer system for the Village.

21 Apr 1930 - " ... a report of the Supt. of the Census for this district shows Marcellus population as 1183, as compared with 989 of 1920, a gain of about 20%. ... the Clerk was directed to notify all garage owners to remove all parked cars from the streets and that from this date they be ordered to keep all cars off the sidewalks and out of the highways. ... that hucksters and peddlers license be raised from $25.00, the present amount, to $150.00."

12 May 1930 - " ... Mr. Arthur W. Wilson was engaged as Village Attorney at annual salary of $250.00."

9 Jun 1930 - " ... communication from the State Dept of Health relative to the report of the Sanitation Director advising recommendation to alter conditions at the reservoir ... and Clerk was instructed to advise the Dept that the matter was under consideration - that of purchasing land surrounding the reservoir or installation of chlorination."

> **The Marcellus Observer**
> **Wednesday, July 16, 1930**
> **Village Finances**
> Marcellus village has an assessed valuation in 1930 of real property, $633,400.00; personal, $11,600.00; special franchise, $24,150.00; total, $669,150.00. The Village budget is: general, $6,544.70; streets, $2,500.00; lighting, $3,00,00; total, $12,044.70. Tax rate, $18.00.

Village finances were published that summer, including a donation to the Fire Department to help defray expenses to the summer convention, along with the budget figures and the tax rate. Compared with today's Village property assessment of over $54 million and a Village budget of over $600,000, these 1930 figures bear little resemblance, but are interesting to note.

7 Jul 1930 - " ... it was decided to hold an inspection of the Fire Department on Tuesday, July 8, at 7:30 p.m. ... it was voted to grant the Fire Department One Hundred and Fifty Dollars ($150.00) to defray the expense of a band and other expenses to the Onondaga County Fireman's Convention at East Syracuse, July 18."

A World Record!
Summer was again a time for the Band and Fire Department to display and parade at

> **The Marcellus Observer - Wednesday, July 16, 1930**
> **THE TWO BIKE BOYS SET RECORD 225 HOURS, STOP WEDNESDAY MIDNIGHT**
> Marcellus has captured a world's record! Marcellus smiled a week ago when two boys began on an endurance bicycle ride. To-day that same Marcellus is cheering with a pride that comes once in a lifetime. The two youthful heroes, Stanley Bartlett, 15, son of Mr. and Mrs. Edgar Bartlett, and Martin Sennett, son of Mrs. James Dillon, have done what they said they would do, breaking the then-existing record for endurance bicycle riding. It was no easy task . . . A few minutes after 10, a crowd of citizens had gathered on the sidewalks laden with firecrackers and other noisemakers, donated by Newell Bros. and C. W. Jones. The minutes rolled slowly. Men held their watches in their hands - two minutes, three, four, five minutes. THE WORLD'S RECORD WAS BROKEN! Then came the din. Fireworks, auto sirens, yelling of hundreds of voices, rockets - cheering. A huge bonfire burst out in the public square fed by boxes and barrels from behind every store in town. The street shone like day. Enthusiastic autoists formed a parade and drove the streets, continually blowing horns and cheering. Others drove cars on the sidewalks until the Mayor, fearing accidents, advised them to keep in the road. The engine House was thrown open, and the siren sang out into the cool night air. Firemen answered the alarm, only to join with the merrymakers around the bonfire. Residents, aroused, came to the corners from all directions. Far into the night this was kept up. It was long after midnight when the crowd began to leave the scene, but in time the streets became quiet and the citizenry returned to their homes. Still later on in the night, long after the cheering throng had found the warm comfort of their beds, a silent form crept out to the middle of the deserted street. Soon a boy on a bicycle appeared and as he reached the other threw his leg deftly over the crossbar. His companion slid into the saddle and turned the wheel into South Street. The cheering was gone, burnt firecrackers lay in the lonely street - but Marty Sennett turned his boyish face to the silent stars and rode into the night..

the annual convention, and it was also an exciting one for Marcellus as two teenage boys captured the fascination of the community, another reflection of the times. Not unlike "Shipwreck Kelly" and his flagpole sitting, Stanley Bartlett and Martin Sennett, the latter a future mayor of the Village, broke the bicycle endurance record of 107 hours, riding for over 225 hours. The community turned out on the evening of July 7, 1930 to celebrate their success and that of the faithful companions who followed the two record holders, including Martin's brother Eddie Sennett, who did much of the night riding. In the midst of hard times, the youngsters of 1930 seemed to brighten the community and bring it together in a festive celebration that all welcomed that summer.

East Hill Open

There was additional excitement that summer as word spread and the paper published information that the new road over East Hill would soon be opened for traffic. In the next issue of *The Marcellus Observer*, however, a retraction was made. The road was not to be opened for another four weeks, the paper having misinterpreted the

---

The Marcellus Observer - Wednesday, August 20, 1930
East Hill Road Open Next Thursday

Announcement is made that the road over East Hill, Marcellus, will be opened to traffic next Thursday. This will be heralded with joy by the farmers who have bumped the ruts on that road for the past year in getting to and from Marcellus. The road, which is something over four miles long, is from Marcellus to Card's Corners. It is the original Seneca Turnpike and will probably always be called that. Many of the steeper hills have been cut down and the hollows built up, until former residents who may drive over the new road would scarcely know the place.

The grading was begun late last fall, and left in bad condition all winter. The redeeming feature is that now the road is finished, just that much earlier. But they were certainly martyrs to a good cause for one long stretch. Completion of this road will open the shortest route of any between Marcellus and Syracuse. It enters Syracuse at Elmwood. It will undoubtedly get the heaviest of the travel between these two points, the Howlett Hill being somewhat rough in places.

The road was built by Provo Brothers, who have faithfully met all of the conditions of the contract. The road is built of first class materials and under excellent supervision. Supervisor W. S. Spaulding of Marcellus was instrumental in getting the road built.

---

contractors. The road, once opened, would prove to be a major thoroughfare for people and freight into and out of the Village of Marcellus and would also be welcomed by those young entrepreneurs selling lemonade to thirsty travelers along the way.

Along the Concrete

New Appointments and New Ordinances

Following the resignation of Dr. Parsons as Village Health Officer in August, the Village Board appointed Dr. J. H. Walsh to replace him. The Board, reacting to concerns about health issues, also published some remarks in the local paper regarding the purity of the village water supply. In reassuring residents of the quality of the village reservoir, the Board was also reacting to some concerns that the New York State Health Department had forwarded a few months earlier, including chlorination of the water. The Village Board also began to consider and then adopt an entire new set of laws for the Village. The ordinances, 51 in all, seemed to cover all aspects of life in the Village, and set penalties for violations of each. Today's Village Ordinances have been updated from 1930 and they are somewhat less descriptive, but they are similar in that they still make reference to many of those aspects of life which residents of the community deem important - noise, pollution, zoning and traffic - quality of life issues that distinguish an organized community.

26 Aug 1930 - " ... communication from Dr. J. C. Parsons resigning as Village Health Officer, to take effect Sept 1, 1930, and the same accepted.

2 Sep 1930 - " ... that Dr. J. H. Walsh be appointed Village Health Officer to replace Dr. J. C. Parsons ... "

8 Sep 1930 - "BE IT ORDAINED, that the following Ordinances to be known as the General Ordinances of the Village of Marcellus be and the same herby are adopted and enacted . . . "

The Marcellus Observer - Wednesday, September 17, 1930
New Ordinances For Marcellus Village

There are " divers(e) laws and ordinances" in the successful running of a village and we are printing this week those of Marcellus. These ordinances were adopted only after much discussion and if carried out will make for a better village.

There is one section devoted to peddlers, which should be read by the housewife . .   . Another section devoted to bonfires and defacing trees and poles should be digested by the small boy, who has a hatchet and handful of matches. And about bicycles. And of groups standing on sidewalks or in doorways. If you wish to hold a parade, telephone the Mayor first . . . And again, don't run the red light . . . One more will bear mentioning. If you drive an ox or a goat to town, don't drive him on the walk, and when you get here be sure to tie the goat fast. Let them take the ox, but for heaven's sake, don't let them get your goat.

The Marcellus Observer - Wednesday, September 17, 1930
Drink 'Er Down. It's As Pure As Driven Snow

Our water supply is pure.   This is assured by a member of the Village Board of Marcellus. If the consumers of Rockwell Springs water could understand how the pond is arranged they would plainly see how impossible it is for contamination of any sort to enter the pond . . . Plans are under way to purchase the watershed to the pond . . . A Chlorinator has been discussed but not found practical for Marcellus water reservoir. Residents are urged to visit the source of the water supply for the village and see for themselves the sanitary manner in which the water is taken care of. In the near future, a high fence is to be erected around the pond . . . for future safety.

Kids and Dogs

October not only brought a change in the weather, but a reminder to keep dogs quarantined and some complaints about youngsters causing a fuss at the water fountain in the village on their way home from school. Perhaps this was a reason for appointing William Kilcoyne as a police officer, a position he would hold throughout the winter.

The Marcellus Observer - Wednesday, October 1, 1930
Our Village Fathers

To the Village Board:

There is considerable disturbance and nuisance caused by the young people squirting water from the fountain in front of the postoffice. They should be made to come home from school without loitering around the street. The water scares the children, they scream and run all over. A solution would be to shut off the fountain, or put a cap on the stream so they couldn't fuss with it. This matter affects the business section of the village, also tourists passing thru.

A Victim

The Marcellus Observer - Wednesday, October 1, 1930
Keep Dogs Locked Up Quarantine Still On

The dog quarantine in the Town of Marcellus and Camillus is still in force. If your dog roams around at night, he is just as liable to be shot as he was when the edict first went into force.

The Marcellus Observer - Wednesday, November 19, 1930
Sewers Next

Marcellus has long contemplated, or anticipated, with, a sewer system. This is to be considered at a formal public hearing, legally called, on Thursday night, Dec. 4. Seed notice. Advancement waits upon such a needed municipal demand. And the echo answers: "what of garbage disposal?" It behooves all property owners to attend the meeting, or forever after keep their peace.

10 Nov 1930 - " ... William Kilcoyne was appointed police officer from Nov 1, 1930 to April 1st, 1931, at an additional salary of $12.50 per month."

Election Results and Sewers

Election returns were not reported in the local paper that November, and instead, the editor mentioned, " . . . we stick to our guns and give you all we can of good home news" (MO 11/5/30). This attitude, in Republican Marcellus, may have been a reaction to the election of Franklin Roosevelt, the Democratic candidate, as Governor of New York and a poor showing by the dry vote in 1930. The election was also a sign that voters were concerned about the economy, an issue that would continue to dominate politics throughout the decade. While discussing state and national politics, village residents were also concerned with a more local issue, that of a municipal sewer system. By early December, a public hearing was held on the proposition to construct such a system. Most seemed to favor the question.

4 Dec 1930 - " ... The Board of Trustees of the Village of Marcellus convened on above date for the purpose of granting a hearing of the property owners of the Village on the proposition constructing a sewer system in and for the Village. ... The discussion which ensued revealed strong sentiment in favor the question ... "

The Marcellus Observer
Wednesday, December 10, 1930
Town To Pay For Village Fire Service
The custom of our modern fire fighting apparatus going outside corporate limits on call to cope with farm fires is a moot question. Solvay established a fixed charge of $10 per mile for the apparatus and $1 an hour for each fireman. Called for fires in the Town of Camillus, this made up $104 and bill was sent to Camillus Town Board . . . Solvay also has a bill against the Town of Onondaga.

The Marcellus Observer
Wednesday, December 24, 1930
Decorations A Great Success
The St. Francis Church Parochial House Awarded First Prize; The James Welsh New Home Second Prize. Honorable Mention Given Many Others; Highest Praise Given To All, For As A Whole Marcellus Shone Resplendent - Beautiful. Decorative Proposal A Great Success. Excel it Next Year.

Payments and Prizes

The idea of the Fire Department going outside the limits of the Village to fight fires would again be questioned, some suggesting that a fixed charge be levied against the Town for each mile traveled and each fireman utilized, as was now being done in Camillus. While the legality of this idea would be challenged, most would later agree to an arrangement that would satisfy the interests of both the Village and the Town of Marcellus, an arrangement that even today often requires some intense negotiation and compromise.

While the Town would eventually pay for fire service, other payments were being made that December to those businesses and residences that were judged to have the best Christmas decorations; and " . . . among other diversions of the holiday season the picture show will have its appeal, . . . now conducting talkies in Parsons Hall, Marcellus" (MO 12/17/30). The end of the year also included a large Christmas Party for " . . . about 750 school children, parents and friends crowded into the auditorium of Marcellus High School . . . The program given by the school children was especially delightful . . . and the most wonderful part of the evening came when a distant jingle of sleigh bells told that someone was on the roof of the building . . .. Santa lacked the proverbial preponderance of what is known as 'bay window,' but we must remember that we are in the midst of a depression period, and Santa has had to curtail himself on food, as have we common folks . . . " (MO 12/24/30). By now, depression was a fact of life in Marcellus but it did not dampen life itself.

1931

Shortly after the new year began, the head of the President's Emergency Committee for Unemployment Relief, estimated that there were between 4,000,000 and 5,000,000 people unemployed nationwide. Marcellus, however, " . . . was fortunate, in that public works and construction projects brought relief and some business to the community. In 1931, the state began grading for the construction of the Cherry Valley Turnpike between Skaneateles and Cazenovia. From then, until completion of the project in 1934, construction workers were needed, and those who came from any distance were housed in bunkhouses along the route, and no doubt spent some of their earnings locally. The Cherry Valley construction also brought a new source of business to the M. & O. L., business much needed for the maintenance of its financial stability" (Heffernan 106).

Sewers and School

The Village Board of Marcellus was also concerned about a construction and a public works project that would not only offer employment but rid the community of a long-standing problem. Following a public hearing in December of 1930, the Board authorized its attorney, Arthur Wilson, to obtain estimates on the cost of constructing a sanitary sewer system and disposal plant, in the Village, " . . . the probable life of said improvement . . . 40 years" (MO 2/25/31). Armed with these figures, the Trustees approved a bond

The Marcellus Observer
Wednesday, January 28, 1931
Sewage Vote Upon At March Election
About 30 people attended the meeting called by the Village Board to discuss the proposed sewer project Thursday night.
The installing of sewers in Marcellus will entail a bond issue of about $75,000 and the question will be decided at the March election. The sewer proposition has been talked for several years and engineers employed to survey the town. It is now brought to a head and is to be settled by vote.

resolution for $75,000, a proposition that would then be put before the voters in the March election that year. In addition, the Board would give final approval for the Cayuga Bus Company to operate in the Village. It also denied the request of the High School Principal to utilize the services of the Village Police Officer as a Truant Office for the School District, a mix of education and municipal law that was perhaps an overlapping of jurisdictions. The use of police agencies by a School District is not unheard of, however, and it is a common practice today for schools to contract with local law enforcement for a variety of services. Patrolling school grounds during an after school event or monitoring traffic during school dismissals are common services. In recent years, some school districts have begun to include the cost of a police information officer in their budgets. In such instances, a professionally trained police officer is then assigned to a school building, not only providing needed security but also serving as a laison between the school and local government. In the Village of Marcellus today, the school campus no longer lies within the corporation's boundaries as it did in 1931, resulting in a loss of the police service upon which it once depended. Today, it is necessary for a separate contract to be negotiated between the Village and the School District in order for the Marcellus Police to extend its presence on that campus, although Village taxpayers do pay for a school crossing guard on North Street.

13 Jan 1931 - " ... Attorney Wilson reported he had obtained estimates on the cost of the sewer construction as per plans of Glenn D. Holmes, Engineer, as follows:

Mondo Construction Co.	$65,000
D. D. Murray	$75,000
J. Park Bailey	$70,000 to $76,000
C. J. Hookway	$71,000

20 Jan 1931 - " . . . the application of the Cayuga Omnibus Corporation for a franchise for the operation of busses through East Main Street was taken up and on motion by Mr. Hunt, the permission and consent was granted. Mayor McNair and Trustee Hunt voting in the affirmative, with no negative votes."

29 Jan 1931 - " . . . Mayor McNair submitted the estimates of the several contractors for the construction of sewer system showing the necessity for a bond issue of $75,000 for the system with an approximate increase of an average of about $4.50 per thousand dollars of assessment for a term of forty years."

The Marcellus Observer
Wednesday, March 11, 1931
Sewers Will Be Voted Upon In Marcellus

Next Tuesday is to be decided whether or not sewers will be installed in the streets of Marcellus. It is a question of utmost importance to the voters. There are many opinions regarding this proposition. Without a doubt, and according to Town and Village officials, sewers will have to come, just as the electric light and water system came over a score of years ago. The question merely resolves itself into one of time; whether we can afford to do this job now or later.

The estimated cost if $75,000. The village has already been surveyed, and plans drawn, but it is up to the people to say when the job shall begin - now or in the future.

Harry Masters: I am in favor of sewers. Anything that will improve the village suits me.

L.S. Parsons: I am in favor of the sewers and believe they are needed at this time.

J. C. Pilot: Although the sewer proposition does not effect me, I will vote for the best interest of the town.

W. S. Conley: Everybody wants the sewers. No town can be progressive without our modern methods. I endorse the proposition.

F. W. Knapp: I am strong for the Sewer proposal, as I am for a bigger and better Marcellus; all these good things go hand in hand.

F. H. Gillett: I think sewers would be for the best interest of the Village, and as we will have to come to it 'eventually, why not now?'

Hugh Woodford: I think the sewers are needed. We have our own system on Reed Street, but I think there are other sections of the village which really y need a sewer system. . . .

Mrs. H. D. Reed: I favor that sewer proposition, but suggest that the work be done as economically as efficiency will permit. I also suggest that when the streets are torn up that some provision be made for taking care of the slush and water that accumulates at the four corners at certain seasons.

C. W. Jones: I am very much in favor of sewers, but not at the present time. I think the taxpayers have about all they can do, in this time of depression, to meet the present obligations and to build the sewer later on would be better. However, I will gladly do my share toward the betterment of my town.

P. A. Schanzle: I shall vote for sewers, positively. I am provided for in this respect, but others are not. The cost of survey was necessary to get an estimate on the job. If laws change this would be obsolete a few years later and a loss. Right now is a buyers' market, contractors will bid low to keep busy, the same work a few years later will cost much more, I believe, Do it now.

---

9 Feb 1931 - " . . . said resolution calling for a bond issue of $75,000 for the construction of a sanitary sewer system for the Village be submitted to the property holders for approval at the annual village election, to be held on the 17th day of March, 1931."

9 Feb 1931 - " . . . Prof. Molyneaux appeared before the Board asking if objections would be made to the appointment of William Kilcoyne as Truant Officer for the School Dist. No. 2 and after discussion it was the consensus of opinion that it was not advisable."

9 Mar 1931 - " . . . advise the state Dept of Health that steps were being taken and plans made to correct the unsatisfactory conditions existing at the Municipal Reservoir, at as early a date as weather conditions would permit."

The Election

A week before the election, a number of residents were asked in an opinion poll conducted by *The Marcellus Observer* whether or not they approved of the proposition to install a sewer system in the Village. In the election that followed on March 17th, the voters not only approved the project but also elected a new Mayor. Michael J. Thornton became the first Democrat elected as Mayor of Marcellus in its history, even though he ran on what was termed the Citizens Party ticket. The election of Thornton, the son of Irish immigrants and a life-long Democrat seemed to be another example of just how disenchanted the voters had become with the state of the economy. Thornton would become a very popular Mayor, re-elected to three more two-year terms in the 1930s.

17 Mar 1931 - " ... that at such election the total number of votes cast for the office of Mayor was 290. That 222 votes were cast for Michael J. Thornton for such office . . . That at such election the total number of votes cast for the office of Trustee for two years was 290. That 249 votes were cast for Varnum S. Kenyon for such office . . . That at such election the total number of votes cast upon the proposition to construct a sanitary sewer system and disposal plant was 185.

That the number of votes for such proposition was 107
That the number of votes against such proposition was 76
Blank 1
Spoiled 1

The Marcellus Observer - Wednesday, March 18, 1931
How's Election? Here's How It Is

Marcellus election resulted in the carrying of the Citizens' ticket without noticeable opposition. Michael J. Thornton was elected Mayor with 222 votes and V. S. Kenyon, Trustee on 249 ballots. These men were nominated at the caucus. The sewer proposition was carried 107 to 76, showing that it was generally wanted. Many who did not need the sewer, having independent systems, voted for it in a public hearted way. Work on this project will start as soon as possible. The cost . . . around $75,000.

Now Garbage Pickup and Ornamental Lights

No sooner had the voters given their approval than rights-of-way were secured for the sewer lines, an engineer appointed and bids for the project were advertised and awarded. The new Board that met in April was also greeted with another request from the residents - a petition to begin garbage collection in the Village. It appears that rather than stumble through the misery of depression, these stalwart citizens were moving ahead with one project after another, bowed but hardly broken by the times. As spring descended in 1931, this optimistic attitude was reflected in the ornamental lights that decorated the Village and in the urging by many to fix up and paint up, and promote the community's merchants and business interests.

19 Mar 1931 - " ... Mr. Holmes, . . . was directed to prepare lines of the sewer system through private rights of way for the purpose of negotiation with the owners and Mr. Wilson was empowered to enter into said negotiations with the property owners for the purpose of procuring the same. . . . Mr. Holmes and Mr. Wilson were also directed to prepare for and advertise for bids for the sewer construction."

13 Apr 1931 - " . . . some petitions signed by several property owners asking the Board to make provision in their annual budget for the collection of garbage, ashes and refuse. Owing to rumor that additional petitions are to be presented, the matter was laid on the table until the next regular meeting."

28 Apr 1931 - " . . . it was voted that Mr. Glen D. Holmes be engaged as supervising Engineer for the construction of the sewer system."

30 Apr 1931 - " . . . met . . . for the purpose of canvassing proposals for the construction of the sewer system . . . "

1 Jun 1931 - " . . . the Village Treasurer is hereby authorized to sign orders for the payment of an easement over . . . property . . . to be used for a sewer system to constructed . . . that said contract for the construction of said sanitary sewage system and disposal plant be awarded to Street Brothers Construction Co. Inc. of Syracuse, New York, for the sum of $56,990.75, which is the amount of their bid."

8 Jun 1931 - " . . . Attorney Wilson reported that rights of way for the sewer had been obtained and papers passed on the following: Marcellus and Otisco Co., Mrs. Ellen Wilson, Robert C. Whitfield, R. M. Stone and James H. Stone, Albertus and Charles Arnold, James Stalker, James G. McNair, Wesley I. McKenzie, John W. Keegan and D. J. Chrisler, Mary Kennedy."

218

The Marcellus Observer - Wednesday, May 20, 1931
Town Will Grow If Everyone Boosts

New ornamental lights, thirty in number, will adorn the village of Marcellus when plans now being put in force are carried out. Red stakes on Main, North and South Streets mark the location of the lights. This is in keeping with other towns and villages, and marks a forward step in the progress of the town. The sewer project, upon which bids are being received, is another worthy move toward a better and more inviting village. This is now assured.

To become rather pointed, it seems to this writer that one of the crying needs in the main street in our village is paint. There are a few buildings in the center of the town that would look a lot better if adorned with a coat of some colorful paint. A bright looking business section gives the town the appearance of being lively, and in these days when optimism is needed we want to keep up a proper spirit. Our village is naturally pretty with its shaded lawns and pleasant streets. City people are taking more and more to the villages because the villages offer purer air, better living conditions and more quiet. It is now but a matter of minutes to get to either of the cities near us. We must make the village inviting if we are to get the people, and if we ge the people, it means increased business for the merchant and the bank. One complaint made shows the need of a night policeman to keep order in the center of the village. With the coming of summer this need becomes more urgent. Residents near the center of the village tell that there are nights when sleep is almost impossible due to the noise of the boys and young men who sit on the steps and carouse until morning. This seems almost unnecessary. A policeman on the street, such as Skaneateles has in John Conway, might go far in controlling this menace. Instead of talking against your town, talk for it. You can say more for the place than against, and it sounds better. Once a knocker and you will always be known as a knocker, so get behind the band wagon and push.

The Marcellus Observer - Wednesday, June 17, 1931
A Suggested Plan For Village Beautification

A good citizen noticed our comment in a former issue about public parks, and he pays us an interesting visit to state his opinion on parks. With us all, he laments, is sorry there is dearth of parks in our lovely village. He is however sincere in his theory that we could strikingly beautify our common center in all three directions with some united planning and painstaking effort. He cites the Roy P. Smith & son grass plot between the walk and curb, and claims there is no possible reason why this same grass plot plan could not be provided all the way to South Street corner. This would mean of course that autos would not drive inside the curb, and this would mean a sacrifice on the party of many.

Again, . . . see the P. A.   Schanzle plot. Continue on this side, . . . to North Street at the   Postoffice corner. Why not? Schanzle, we understand, would still further improve his pleasing ornamental plot with a costly fencing material, but he hesitates doing this lest the Board carry out a plan to widen Main Street. It is 56 feet now, and wider than many similar situations. Sentiment to widen here should be sounded out, not done disastrously.

Look down Main Street, all the way from North Street, with the Presbyterian lawn and space to the curb, way down to Orange Street, there is possibility of developing this curb-to-walk grass -plot-plan. And the same on the opposite side, east from Smith & Son's.

The park-grass-plot might extend down North Street to the Gillett Garage anyway. But here comes in the I.O.O.F. Temple cement frontage. The mail would need to be carried a few steps. The Observer has a plot to offer toward this end. Great oaks from little acorns grow.

Streets and Curbs, Gas and Water

During the summer months, the Village Board would be asked to accept Reed Parkway and Second Street as village highways and it also received requests from several companies to lay gas mains in the Village.

A most interesting suggestion made to the Board came from the local editor -- a plan to beautify the village by adding "green space" to that area between the street and the sidewalk and prohibiting automobiles from parking there. Today that area is known as the village right-of-way and is the grassy public park suggested back in 1931. In addition, the Board of Trustees and its Planning Board have, in recent years, made much progress in adding more "green space" to this area, from curb to sidewalk on Main Street. They have also been effective in reducing both the width of some streets and the speed of traffic through the Village.

It was also suggested in the paper that residents " . . . do their part in curtailing the waste of water at this season of the year. Rockwell Springs reservoir, . . . is dropping at the rate of an inch a day, . . ." (MO 7/1/31)

13 Jul 1931 - " . . . Mrs. H. D. Reed appeared before the Board petitioning for the acceptance of a deed of the highway within the Village limits known as Reed Parkway. After much discussion, it was voted on motion by Mr. Kenyon, seconded by Mr. Hunt that said street be accepted, extending from intersection of said street with North Street to what is known as Second Street designated on maps of the Reed Tract. This being acceptable, it was so voted . . . "

24 Aug 1931 - " . . . Mr. O. E. Benson of the Associated Gas and Electric Co. appeared before the Board and requested for the company a franchise for laying gas mains in the Village, but no action was taken."

Local Businesses

Despite the depression, there were some local businesses that were thriving and the local paper began to publish a series of articles in 1931 that each week highlighted a certain one. Stories about the Mulroy Dairy on West Main Street, Kenyon's Hatchery on East Main Street, and the James Stone farm on North Street were chronicled that year and there were a host of smaller businesses that advertised their services and products in the paper as well.

MO Sep 16, 1931

Fire Protection

There was continued interest in the issue of fire protection for those outside the village boundaries. Some who lived outside the limits of the corporation expected fire protection while those who lived in the Village wondered why they should bear the entire financial burden, including the cost of new apparatus. The Board did take over the financial responsibility of the incorporated department, relieving individual members of that charge, but it was fearful of taking on more financial obligations, such as a new pumper, when sewer bonds and reservoir improvements had to be paid. It was a situation that would not be resolved any time soon.

The Marcellus Observer - Wednesday, October 7, 1931
Will Non-Villagers Buy Fire Apparatus?

. . . All you farmers outside the corporations have no hesitancy in accepting help at your fires; you rely on this, fully expect the response to your call. Buy why should you have this service, gratis? . . .

The village should give complete protection to the corporate taxpayers. But if his house burns while the apparatus is out in the country for a non-taxpayer, who meets his loss? This has come to be a serious menace . . .

To-day, for years back Marcellus has needed a pumper. It can't, or don't dare, buy one, with water system bonds being paid, new school, new sewers. Must the firemen go in again to provide to save our lives and properties? Well why not let these outsiders do something, incorporate a fire district, bond and buy, and let the village house it. Operate it, use it in any need?

No, this will not amount to a thing. The "poor farmer" will not do for himself any quicker than will the "rich villager." But both ought. And just now, for ten years, with these bonds and buildings, it is up to the outlying farmer to come across.

220

November Discontent

Emboldened by some earlier victories, both local and state, the Democrats in Marcellus presented a strong slate of candidates for Town office that November. The contest would be a heated one and spokesmen for both sides were quick to point out the reasons why their candidates should be elected. In the end, the Republicans would prevail

---

The Marcellus Observer - Wednesday, October 28, 1931
To The Voters Of The Town Of Marcellus

Primary politics is that branch of government which deals with the prosperity, peace and safety of the community, the hand sin which power is placed, and the development of its resources, and treatment of the measures necessary for meeting the movements.

The Democratic party stands flatly for all these principals. The old, worn-out arguments of full dinner pails, humming wheels, prosperity for all, that has been shouted for years, apparently are not holding water to-day.

The Democrat ticket in Marcellus has been made up of citizens who are fighting for the principles outlined above, and for cooperation and economy for the people of the township and county. You voters all know what the results are showing under Ring politics. (Autocratic Rule.)

What we desire to-day is a rule by representatives of the people, which stands for service, economy, cooperation and prosperity, and we believe the people on the Democratic ticket stand for all these principles.

Vote for a Straight Democratic Ticket on Election Day.   COMMITTEE

---

but the contest again illustrated the frustration of people, even on the local level, with the state of the economy. "Widespread disillusionment with politics, prompted in part by the seeming inability of the federal government to end the Depression was reflected in the year's hit musical comedy, *Of Thee I Sing*, . . . a sharp but good natured satire on presidential politics. The show opened . . . in New York City on Dec. 26 and ran for 441 performances. When the show won the Pulitzer Prize for drama the next year, it was the first musical ever to be so honored." (Carruth 719). The people of Marcellus were not as discontented as many in the nation, and few probably traveled to New York after Christmas to see the hit comedy. There was, however, a concern that politics as usual was not working and that change was necessary. 1932 would witness that transformation.

1932

In 1932, economic conditions, which had already been poor for a number of years for farmers, including those in Marcellus, would become worse as the price of milk began

---

The Marcellus Observer - Wednesday, January 20, 1932
Rovin' With Roy

. . . Milk, $1 for 100 pounds. That is what Mr. Farmer gets this month. A fraction over 2 cents a quart. A year ago he received over 6 cents a quart for the same liquid. Albert Thompson sold a nice veal calf Saturday for $1.50 and was offered $6 for three sheep. Just a small part of their real worth. Who gets the profit from the milk and other farm products that the farmer is forced to sell at such low prices? Does it cost the city milk peddler 10 or 12 cents a quart to market the milk? Thousands of heads of cabbage are rotting in the fields this winter because the farmer, in many instances, would actually lose money if he harvested them. And folks are starving for food in the midst of plenty. The farmers raise enough food and are capable of raising more food than the world needs, but you cannot expect the farmer to be Santa Claus all the time.

The Marcellus Observer - Wednesday, February 3, 1932
Clothing, Assistance, Mot Urgently Needed

Again there is a call in Marcellus and vicinity for clothes for children and women, and money. About 40 children have been given clothes, besides the grown ups, given by the kindness of our townspeople, and given out through Welfare Officer, Frank Griffing, assisted by Mrs. Griffing to those in need. A lady said the other day, "I cannot imagine anyone here without a coat or clothes." Well, that lady has not looked around very much or inquired into the situation. Many people do not realize what there is to be done or could be done if there were clothes and money to do with.

We thank all those who have given, and hope   others will give, as there is need now.   Children without mittens, shoes, etc. Please leave your donations at the Griffing and Curtis store, or at Frank Griffing's resident on South Street.

to drop dramatically. Some farmers even allowed their crops to rot in the fields rather than harvest them since they would probably lose money by doing so. Hard times were also evident from the cry for help in Marcellus for more clothing and money for needy children and women, evidence that the depression was worsening.

Stephen H. Hunt
Village Trustee
1930-1944

Interestingly, the winter of 1931-32 had been one of the mildest on record, with high temperatures and little snowfall. March, however, came in like the proverbial lion that year and early in the month, dumped a great amount of snow and caused much disruption, " . . . the worst snow since 1925 . . . One remarked that the milk was worth a dollar a bottle that day" (MO 3/9/32). It would be another 70 years, the winter of 2001-2002, before Marcellus would experience a season as mild as that which allowed young men like Ed Dillon and Jim McMahon to play golf every month that winter.

Any snow that came melted rather quickly, in time for voters to go to the polls that year and re-elect Steven Hunt as Village Trustee. First elected in 1930, Hunt was a local grocer and following his re-election, the Board met the next day at his store where they enjoyed a lunch of " . . . limburger sandwiches, Spanish onion, sardines, smoked herrings, coffee, etc" (MO 3/16/32), a depression meal if ever there was one.

Gas Mains and Sewers

The new Board would act on the requests it had received to lay gas mains in the Village and in March, the Empire Gas and Electric was granted this franchise, a license that continues to this day. The Board also received a report on the completed sewer system in the Village and passed a resolution that authorized property owners to hook up to the new system, but only after the connections were examined and approved by the Village Inspector.

The Marcellus Observer
Wednesday, April 20, 1932
Engineer's Report On Marcellus
Sewerage System
A sanitary sewerage system and sewage treatment plant have just been completed in the Village of Marcellus. This makes Marcellus one of the most modern and up-to-date villages in Onondaga County. It has boasted an excellent water system, an efficient volunteer fire department, and improved streets. Now it can point with pride to the fact that its sanitary facilities are the equal of any village of its size in the State or County.

14 Mar 1932 - " . . . the Clerk was instructed to advise the Empire Gas and Electric Co. that this Board would grant a franchise to said Empire Gas and Electric Co. . . . "

18 Apr 1932 - " . . . whereas numerous property owners in said Village are about to make house connections to said sewerage system, and whereas it is necessary for the proper care, protection and maintenance of said sewerage system and treatment plant to see that all house connections are properly made, . . . be it resolved that before any house connections are made, . . . all such connections be passed upon and approved by the Village Inspector, and be it further resolved that all house connections must be approved by the Village Inspector before the trench or ditch is filled in, and in case the property owner fails to get the approval of the Inspector before the trench or ditch is filled in, then the Inspector shall be authorized to cause the trench to reopened and connection approved by him. The cost of such reopening shall be borne by the property owner making the connection, and . . . that William Kilcoyne be and he hereby is appointed Village Inspector."

The Marcellus Observer
Wednesday, May 25, 1932
Wednesday Closing To Start Soon

Marcellus stores will . . . close Wednesday afternoons until the week before Labor Day.

The Wednesday closing gives the clerks and proprietors a short respite each week during the warm summer months. It gives them a chance to catch up on garden work and other duties around the home, or to take a ride into the country and forget the troubles brought about by the depressing times.

It is hoped that customers will cooperate with the merchants and get their shopping done before noon of Wednesday.

The Marcellus Observer - Wednesday, May 25, 1932
Marcellus Streets Being Repaired

Street Brothers, contractors, are repaving the streets of Marcellus which were torn up by the recent sewer construction. In accordance with the contract, the sewer contractor is obliged to replace four feet of each street thus torn up. The Village Board engaged the Street Brothers' firm to make a complete job of it and finish the remaining 14 feet.

About four inches of stone is lad on the road. Then hot Tarvia is forced into the stone by air pressure. This is again covered with a light layer of stone and rolled hard. When the mass cools it hardens into a solid pavement. Later, a thin coating of Tarvia is spread on, making the road waterproof.

The Marcellus Observer - Wednesday, July 6, 1932
Rain Prevents Injuries In Fourth Celebration

No serious Fourth of July casualties were reported from this area. The pouring rain that visited us . . . may have had a part in dampening the ardor of Young America. . . . inclination toward the banning of fireworks . . . The city of Syracuse . . . awaiting an ordinance . . . which would forever bar the sale or using of fireworks, . . . it would only be a short time before the movement would spread to the villages.

Daylights Saving and Wednesday Closing

Spring also brought about the seasonal battle over daylight saving time. Many merchants, mostly those in the cities, favored this old wartime measure and during the depression, being able to stay open longer and conduct more business made sense. For those in rural communities, especially farmers, there was no great advantage and they were opposed to it. In their own words, " . . . noses kept to the grindstone until sunset . . . We toilers leave our machines or desks at six o'clock . . . hurry home to hear Amos an' Andy. They come on an hour earlier now. As we pelt up the steps and crash in we hear the theme song, but it is the signing off tune - and daylight saving has worked another hardship" (MO 4/27/32).

Many merchants in Marcellus, however, were like Steve Hunt whose store on East Main Street (shown here, but demolished in 1999) would close early on Wednesday afternoons, allowing workers to enjoy a break from routine during the summer, to relax, perhaps spending time with family or in other activities. This battle also seems to be another indication that the struggle between urban and rural, so prevalent in the 1920s, was still being waged, even during the Depression. Some in the rural areas thought that the Depression itself was a result of the country's increasing trend towards urbanization and industrialization.

Streets, Fireworks, Drainage

In addition to those roads being reconstructed as a result of the sewer project, the Village Board's budget for fiscal 1932 made provision for street repair that summer. The 4th of July passed rather quietly that summer, unlike some of those in years past. The rain may have dampened the festivities, but the mood in the country did not prompt celebration in 1932. When federal troops drove the Bonus Army out of Washington at the point of bayonet that summer, the mood of the country was dark and depressing.

The Board did pass an ordinance, which remains in effect to this day, requesting residents not to throw dead grass or rubbish into the streets. In order to prevent storm drains from being choked with debris, that same admonition is still requested of residents every summer.

9 May 1932 - " . . . the following budget for the Village expenses for the ensuing year was submitted by Mr. Kenyon and being seconded by Mr. Hunt, its adoption was voted.

Assessed Valuation	$764,000.00
Tax Rate	$20.00 per $1000
Light Fund	$3,800.00
Street Fund	$8,000.00
General Fund	$3,488.00
Total	$15,288.00

11 Jul 1932 - " . . . the Clerk was directed to publish notices in the Marcellus Observer requesting property owners to desist from throwing dead grass and other rubbish into the gutters of the street to avoid clogging of the catch basins."

Water Mains, Busses and Peddlers

Summer is always the time for repairs, and the highway crew fixed a major water main break that summer along what is today Platt Road. The complexity of the problem can be seen in this picture showing William Kilcoyne and James Powell at work on the repair. There was also another urgent plea for help for the needy, especially for clothing as well as an appeal to the community to hire the unemployed. "There are . . . many men who would like work of any kind. Any householder or farmer who can use a man will confer a favor on some worthy person by calling Frank Griffing, Welfare Officer, at Marcellus and telling their wants. Mr. Griffing has a waiting list of good men who are willing to work for a fair wage at any kind of labor" (MO 7/20/32)

The Marcellus Observer - Wednesday, July 20, 1932
Break In Water Main
A four inch water main on the Hackford Tract broke last week necessitating several days' work in digging up and repairing. The main developed a slight crack and started a stream running down the road, which was almost immediately lined with miniature dams and lakes by the delighted children in that locality. William Kilcoyne and his gang dug until the break was located and then James Powell made the repair. The break was under a sidewalk . . . difficult to reach.

Because of the damage done to their property, the Presbyterian Society presented a petition to the Board that summer, objecting to the busses stopping on the corner of North and Main Streets. Today, it is along this same corner that the busses continue to stop, the problem apparently having been successfully addressed.

The Board also addressed the issue of peddlers in the village, passing an ordinance that reduced the license fee enacted two years earlier, but, still wanting to protect the business interests of local merchants, enforced more rigid regulations.

224

The Marcellus Observer
Wednesday, August 24, 1932
New Peddler Ruling Advanced By Board

Two years ago a rumpus was raised in Marcellus Village Board regarding the rights of outside peddlers who seemed to be infringing upon the rights of the village merchants, the merchants claiming that they pay taxes and support the home institutions. At this time the Board incorporate an ordinance into the Village calling for a $10 a day fee from each peddler, or $150 a year. At a meeting of the Board July 11, 1932, Trustee S. H. Hunt offered a resolution lowering the fee to $5 a day or $100 a year. A peddler caught without the proper credentials, however, can be collared and held on a charge of disorderly conduct and fined $25 . . .

11 Jul 1932 - " . . . RESOLVED, . . . no person shall truck, peddle or sell . . . in any of the streets or elsewhere in the Village without having obtained a license therefor; the fees or such license shall be . . . Any person who shall violate any of the provisions of this shall be liable to a penalty of Twenty-five Dollars ($25.00). . . . any violation . . . shall constitute disorderly conduct . . . ."

8 Aug 1932 -" . . . a communication presented by the Presbyterian Society objecting to the stopping of busses along their curb and after discussion, the Clerk was directed to confer with the Cayuga Bus Corporation and see if arrangement could be made for designation of another side."

Thieves and Burglars

One of the most popular songs of 1932 was "Brother, Can You Spare A Dime," but some people were more interested in stealing than in begging. Hard times often brings about an increase in theft and there was no exception to this in Marcellus that fall: "Chicken thieves are thought to be responsible for a fire which completed destroyed the barns of Arthur Hackford, Marcellus, . . . The loss, estimated at around $5,000, was only partly covered by insurance" (MO 9/7/32). In addition, "Burglars visited Marcellus . . . and successfully looted three stores, getting away with a haul of around $192 . . . the men entered the Community Store first, . . . From there they entered the basement of the Thornton Bros. store . . . the burglars got into the Market Basket Store . . . . It is thought by some that the robbers who worked in Marcellus are the same men who made a haul in Camillus recently, the mode of entrance being the same . . . " (MO 9/21/32).

November Election

By October, the presidential candidates for both major parties had been chosen, the election this year proving to be a referendum on the Hoover's administration handling of the depression. Franklin Roosevelt, the Governor of New York and Democratic candidate for President, called for a "new deal" for the American people in his acceptance speech that summer in Chicago. While Roosevelt's campaign speeches were well received in urban areas, in rural Marcellus the local editor called him a "medicine man . . . swinging about the country exactly like the old time peddler of quack medicines, . . . offer(ing) a

The Marcellus Observer - Wednesday, November 9, 1932
Election Is Most Interesting

One of the most exciting of elections has just passed into history, an election which ushered the Democratic party into power, not only in Washington, but in many state and county offices.

Next to the presidential vote, the fight for the Assembly seat proved to be the most interesting to local voters. Fred E. MacCollum, Democrat, was pitted against the present incumbant, Hon. Horace M. Stone and made an unusually good run, although he final count gave the election to Stone.

The Marcellus Observer - Wednesday, November 9, 1932
Rovin' With Roy

Now that election is over and the cigars all smoked up we can get down to business, wondering what the future has in store for us. A few Republicans roamed the streets Wednesday morning, but for the most part the folks we talked to were Democrats. Seems funny, too, because the villages were full of G.O.P. adherants election day. I was one myself, and have walked up like a man and paid the ice cream soda bet to the stenog next door. We are not holding any post-mortems, but are just hitching up the old belt a couple of holes more and hoping for the best.

mysterious panacea, a new palm of life, which he claims is a cure for all the economic ills of the American farmer" (MO 10/19/32). If FDR had campaigned in Marcellus, one wonders would he have been required to pay the same fee levied against other peddlers?

Halloween, like the 4th of July, passed quietly that year, " . . . one of the least exciting . . . in many years . . . in Marcellus . . . The goblins consisted almost entirely of younger boys and children and the depredations were of a minor or childish character. No real serious damage . . . reported" (MO 11/2/32). A week later, on November 8, 1932, Franklin D. Roosevelt was elected President of the United States in a landslide victory over the incumbent Republican candidate, Herbert Hoover. In addition, the Democrats took control of both house of Congress, a majority that was so large as to indicate widespread discontent with Republican fiscal and monetary policies. The local Republican candidates were generally elected to office, but had faced serious challenges.

The Marcellus Observer - Wed, Nov 30, 1932
Boys Destroy Flags On Memorial Stone
. . . Please - in the name of decency - show your respect for the soldiers of Marcellus by leaving the Memorial Boulder alone.

The Marcellus Observer - Wed, Dec 28, 1932
Darkened Streets Cause Hardships
Complaint is made that Marcellus Village lights are turned off too early in the morning. The time of shutting off the lights varies from 6 to 6:30 a.m., which, at the present season, is still part of the night.
Residents who go to work at an early hour find that the darkened streets constitute a hazard due to passing trucks or ice-covered sidewalks. It is suggested that the lights be turned on later each night and shut off later each morning until the daylight gets back to its spring and summer schedule.

Rovin' With Roy
Here it is the end of 1932. It has been a great old year. Full of dark sports, stumbling blocks, brambles, financial storms and all manner of scary things. Some folks have gone hungry while others lived in the lap of luxury. Call it hectic if you will. If you happen to be sitting at home New Year's Eve, tip back in the old armchair, stick your feet on the stove and go back over the year. True, it has been tough, but can't you recall some bright moments - a few occasions that stand out as being brighter than the rest? Sometimes the bright spots outweigh the gloom. They will if you'll let them. Anyway, the old year has pulled his cloak tighter around him, yanked the ear-lappers down, and has departed to the Land of Oblivion. We will never see him again - and who wants to.

A few days later, Armistice Day was again celebrated, reminded by the local paper that " . . . on the striking of the eleventh hour on this eleventh day of the eleventh month, our whole land is called to observe two minutes of absolute silence" (MO 11/9/32). A sad commentary to this celebration was recorded a few weeks later when " . . . complaints were made of boys who persist in breaking the little flags off the monument and otherwise deface it" (MO 11/30/32). Even today, one wonders why such acts of vandalism occur. Perhaps acting out of frustration or displaying a sense of hostility toward the adult world and its symbols, explains why youngsters in recent years have desecrated local cemetery monuments and have found satisfaction in overturning community flower gardens. To be sure, these problems are not as serious as those in some communities, where shootings and deadly violence has become more evident. Nevertheless, it is an issue that often defies solution, reaching into even the most innocent communities.

December Lights

The end of the year as well as the community were brightened with the lights of Christmas, although there were complaints that the village lights were turned off too early for some. By the end of 1932, most people were content to see the old year pass, although they were unsure as to what the new year would bring. A new President had been elected, but he would not take office until March. What had he meant by a "New Deal"? What changes would he propose for the American people? A great many people were uncertain, trusting a man disabled by polio to lead a nation paralyzed by depression.

1933

While FDR had been elected President in November, he was not to take office until March, with President Hoover remaining in office in a "lame duck" administration. This would be rectified by the adoption of the 20th Amendment to the Constitution, changing the inauguration from March 4th to January 20th, but not in time for the Depression to deepen. In responding to the mood of the voters, Congress also passed the 21st Amendment effectively repealing the 18th amendment, ending prohibition and returning liquor control to the states. Few had thought that an amendment would ever be repealed, while others took solace in the argument that "if beer can come back, so too can the country."

> **The Marcellus Observer**
> **Wednesday, January 25, 1933**
> **Firemen's Play For Community Benefit**
> A play, "The Blue Bat" is to be put on by the Marcellus Firemen, Thursday and Friday, Feb. 16-17, at Marcellus School Auditorium for benefit of the needy of the community, . . .
>
> **The Marcellus Observer**
> **Wednesday, February 22, 1933**
> **Firemen's Play Nets Money For Charity**
> . . . The proceeds of the play have not been reported, but it is known that a good sized check will be given over to those who have charge of the charity work in the village . . .

Locally, in an attempt to offset some of the cost associated with electricity, the Village Board was considering the idea of establishing a municipal electric lighting plant for residents, and the Firemen responded to the needs of the community by sponsoring a benefit play that realized a generous return for charity work in the community.

9 Jan 1933 - " . . . a good number of citizens present listened to a proposition presented by Mr. Cramer representing the McIntosh-Seymnour Co. relative to establishing a municipal electric lighting plant. Mr. Cramer advised the Company would make a survey and submit the proposition to their attorneys for opinion as to the feasibility of such plant."

Panic

The mood of the country grew even more gloomy and ominous when an attempt was made on the life of the President-elect in February of 1933. By inauguration day, much of the country was in a state of panic, with banks closing and unemployment continuing to soar. Following his inauguration, the President asked for and received broad powers to deal with the effects of the Depression. He declared a "bank holiday" throughout the nation, closing all banks, including the First National Bank in Marcellus, and effectively halting a run on banks by worried depositors. After Congress passed the Emergency Banking Act, all banks " . . . were to remain closed until inspection found them to be in sound condition. The First National found itself unable to meet the requirements for reopening" (Heffernan 230) until August of 1933 and the Board was forced to find another bank to act as a depository of Village funds.

Municipal Lighting and Election

Beginning in March and lasting until June, the 73rd Congress met in special session and passed a great deal of legislation that would change America forever. In that same month, the Board of Trustees met and, in a series of hearings, listened to and discussed the advantages and disadvantages of installing a municipal electric lighting plant in the Village. Because the issue would have major implications for residents of the Village, the Board decided to put the question to the voters in the election that March. In a rather large turnout, Michael Thornton would be returned to office for another two-year term as Mayor, and Varnum Kenyon would be re-elected as Trustee. In addition, the voters

---

The Marcellus Observer - Wednesday, March 1, 1933
Editor's Chat
Much agitation is rife in Marcellus regarding the purchase of a municipal lighting plant and many arguments are given, some in support and some against the proposal.

The Marcellus Observer - Wednesday, March 15, 1933
Do We Really Want A Municipal Electric Plant In Marcellus

The Marcellus Observer - Wednesday, March 15, 1933
Taxpayer Sets Forth Advantages of Municipal Plant

---

agreed, by a large majority, to establish a municipal lighting system. Although this proposition was not binding,, it did authorize the Board " . . . to apply to the Public Service Commission for a permit to operate a plant" (MO 3/22/33)

21 Mar 1933 - " . . . the total number of votes cast for the office of Mayor was 250. That 234 votes were cast for Michael J. Thornton for such office . . . the total number of votes cast for the office of Trustee for two years was 250. That 209 votes were cast for V. S. Kenyon for such office . . . the total number of votes cast upon the proposition to establish a municipal lighting system was 164. That the number of votes cast for such proposition was 133. That the number of votes cast against such proposition was 27. Blank (were) 4."

3 Apr 1933 - " . . . Resolved that owing to the closing of the First National Bank of Marcellus, N.Y. due to the national bank holiday, the Lincoln National Bank and First Co. of Syracuse be, and is hereby designated, as temporary depository for Village funds."

The Marcellus Observer
Wednesday, April 12, 1933
What? No Beer?

The band did not turn out to celebrate the return of beer to our fair village last Friday night. In the first place there was no celebration and in the next place there was little or no beer to rejoice over. Those whose tongues had been handing out since Christmas in anticipation of a big schooner of 3.2 stuff went to bed with that same tongue hanging out a little farther, and just a little more parched.

And what is more, beer will, no doubt, be scarce for several weeks. It takes time to get into shape, so lovers of the cup that cheers will either have to take pot luck or start another batch of their own. A few places have some real beer on tap, however, and are hoping fore the best (?).

Drys are watching with interest the outcome of the reopening of the beer kegs. Church and temperance organizations have asserted that they will not stand for any law violations and do not intend to allow conditions to revert to those manifest in "the good old days." It is not expected that such conditions would exist under the present law prohibiting the saloon.

Local Option and Historic Markers

With the end of prohibition, and control of alcohol returned to the states, New York responded by repealing the statute regarding liquor enforcement and allowing all communities to be wet. The legislature would then pass a law that provided for the re-establishment of the right of individual communities to remain dry if they chose to do so in an election called for that purpose. Beer did return and Marcellus became a "wet" town once again but " . . . the most-talked of question in town is regarding the opening of the bank. No one seems to know the answer - exactly - but those who should be in the know are firm in their conviction that it won't be long now before business will be going on as usual . . . " (MO 4/12/33).

In the meantime, as plans were made for West Hill Road to be repaired that summer, more work was found for those who were unemployed locally. In addition a project was begun, encouraged by the State of New York in which a series of historic markers were created and placed throughout the state. Not only did this provide work for unemployed artists and historians, it also promoted an interest in local history that continues to this day. Today, in the Village of Marcellus there are a number of historic markers dating back to the1930s and 1940s that not only recount the past, but also serve to enhance the community and promote its historic image.

228

One such marker is in front of the Presbyterian Church, proudly recounting the fact that this was the site of the first church edifice in Onondaga County. In 1933, however, Church Trustees complained to the Board about offensive conditions on their property produced by bus traffic.

8 May 1933 - " . . . communication from the Board of Trustees of the Presbyterian Church relative to the unsightly conditions existing on corner of North and Main Streets and abutting Church property caused by existing bus stops . . ."

Memorial Day, Beer and the Bank

The Memorial Day speech that year again promoted the history of our nation and the liberties enjoyed by Americans throughout the past. The speech that year, however, also seemed to include an attack on the policies of the administration in Washington. "The Revolution of 1776 gave us political freedom; the Civil War struck off the shackles of human slavery - but are we 100% free politically when a super-government by autocratic groups of seekers subvert the very officers elected to govern?" (MO 5/31/33), said Prof. P.M. Helfer in his address that year. Many in the country thought that the New Deal legislation was not only a radical departure from traditional government, but the beginning of the end of political liberties and that government programs would destroy the freedom of the American people by substituting governmental control for free enterprise.

By June, however, government controls from Washington were being lifted somewhat in Marcellus and other communities. Towns throughout the state were allowed to vote on local option, which was " . . . specifically provided in article VI of the alcoholic beverage control law, passed at the last session of the (New York) legislature and signed by Gov. Lehman on April 12" (MO 6/14/33). The law called for local option questions to be put to the voters at any general election, following the filing of petition of names requesting the same, a appeal that was successful in neighboring towns such as Tully, but not in the Town of Marcellus. In addition, the plan for reorganization of the First National Bank in Marcellus was prepared and approved by authorities in Washington. William Spaulding, the Bank President, " . . . went to Washington, D.C., accompanied by Frank Knapp, Horace Stone and Reverend Thomas Driscoll . . . the group was able to arrange for a reorganization and opening of a new bank. Depositors of record prior to the closing were able to recover their holdings. However, stockholders in the original bank lost their investment" (Heffernan 230). The news in late July was exploded across the headlines of the local paper and was met with great relief by residents of the community.

The Marcellus Observer - Wednesday, July 26, 1933

MARCELLUS BANK HOLIDAY IS OVER

The Marcellus Observer - Wednesday, August 2, 1933
Marcellus Bank Resumes Business After Holiday
Banking Public Cheered By Accomplishment of Bank Officials. New Officers Elected

August first, 1933, marked an epoch in the history of Marcellus; for on that day the bank again threw open its doors to the business public and thus did much to speed up the business of the town . . .

With the opening of the bank local business has shown a marked acceleration. Many who had ordered new cars just prior to the bank holiday are renewing the orders and accepting delivery. The fact that the bank is again doing business has allayed the fears of those who looked upon the cloudy side of the affair during the months of inconvenience. Business at the bank has been at a high point all the week and it shows much promise for the future.

Fireworks and a Milk Strike

The summer of 1933 produced other fireworks in Marcellus, one of which involved a discussion and then a ban on the sale of such explosives in the Village. Following the lead of the City of Syracuse, villages and towns throughout the County began to pass ordinances banning the sale of fireworks, arguing that they were not only a nuisance but dangerous for the public, particularly youngsters.

14 Aug 1933 - " . . . communication from the Marcellus Exchange Club requesting the passage of an ordinance forbidding the manufacture, sale and use of fireworks within the Village limits was read . . . Ordinance #53 was offered . . . resolution was adopted . . . "

Another explosive issue that summer was a major strike by some farmers whose anger with low milk prices resulted in conflict. Throughout the county and the country,

---

The Marcellus Observer - Wednesday, August 9, 1933

COUNTY IN GRIP OF HUGE MILK STRIKE

Local Farmers Take Law In Own Hands In Unprecedented Warfare Against Low Prices. Many Milk Cans Dumped By Embittered Producers Who Gather At All Roads To Waylay Trucks.

The die has been cast! Onondaga County, west of Syracuse, has thrown down the gauntlet and has entered the ranks of the milk strikers to fight to the last ditch for what they term their rights. Although rumblings of war have been heard in this vicinity for a few days past, the first actual movement took place Wednesday at Card's Corners, four miles east of Marcellus. Five trucks were mounted and the contents of the cans deposited in the ditch, although no violence was used toward the drivers. The cans were then replaced in the truck and the driver allowed to proceed. Wednesday morning the trucks of John Shay, Philip Vile, Michael Geiss and Lester Marshfield were held up and unloaded . . . .

230

dairy farmers, arguing that scarcity of their product would lead to an increase in prices, refused to sell their milk and tried to prevent other farmers from shipping theirs as well. In Marcellus, this became particularly meaningful because of the abundance of dairy farms and there was not only a dumping of milk, but some arrests as well. Interestingly, the Roosevelt administration was using this very logic, scarcity, to combat low prices. By paying farmers to plow under millions of acres of cotton or by paying them to slaughter millions of piglets, the New Deal encouraged a cutback in production by farmers.

Buy and Conserve

While the New Deal paid some farmers not to grow certain crops or otherwise dealt with the issue of over-production, the pressure on consumers in many communities was

All Roads Lead To Our Town!
Buy In September And BUY AMERICAN

> **The Marcellus Observer**
> **Wednesday, November 8, 1933**
> **Marcellus Village Notice**
> Owing to the low water level in the Municipal reservoir which is far below normal, the consumers of Village water are urged to conserve in its use as far as possible. A dangerous condition exists should we be faced with a serious fire, and extra precautions should be exercised at this time. This condition can be relieved if our supply is conserved. Consumers are urged to have all dripping faucets repacked, and all leaking connections repaired to eliminate all unnecessary waste. We request your cooperation. By Order Board of Trustees

to buy "locally" and "American". The Village Board urged local residents to conserve water, nature's way it appears, to bring about a scarcity of its own that fall.

9 Oct 1933 - " . . . Clerk was instructed to publish in the Marcellus Observer a notice requesting the households of the Village to conserve the water supply, owing to the low level of water in the reservoir and that all non-residents are prohibited from drawing water from the Village water supply."

Firemen's Bazaar and Red Cross Help

In November, elections in Marcellus produced " . . . a Republican landslide . . . when the township voted on State, County and Town officers" (MO 11/8/33), a local reaction perhaps to the New Deal. That same month, the Marcellus firemen staged a bazaar for the benefit of their convention fund, attracting a great many people from nearby towns and cities as well as local residents. "The Annual Firemen's Convention so dear to the heart of a volunteer fireman, is to be held in Marcellus next July and it is for this that the bazaar is held" (MO 11/8/33).

> **The Marcellus Observer - Wednesday, November 22, 1933**
> **Red Cross Deserves Help Of Community**
> In conjunction with the Red Cross membership drive which has been in progress since Nov. 11, Syracuse chapter officials have revealed data which shows the services rendered unfortunate and poverty-stricken families in the Towns of Marcellus and Onondaga.
> Needy residents of Marcellus received more than 21,000 pounds of government consigned flour from the county Red Cross during 1933, . . . Articles of clothing distributed in that township during the year totaled 1,937 . . . Six school children who were in need of dental care were taken care of . . . These figures are but a sketch of the work being done throughout Onondaga county by the Red Cross organization . . .

America was still in the midst of depression as Thanksgiving arrived on the 30th of November that year. President Roosevelt in his Proclamation urged Americans to " . . . hold clear the goal of mutual help in time of prosperity as in time of adversity" (MO

11/22/33) and the Red Cross responded to this challenge, providing relief to the poor, the sick and the hungry throughout the County, including many in Marcellus.

Yuletide Burglary

The village tree was again set in place that Christmas, " . . . the Empire Gas and Electric Company . . . tendering its usual Christmas gift to the communities by trimming and lighting the various trees . . . " (MO 12/20/33). News of a burglary at the high school, just before the holiday, may have shocked the community but it might also seem to be another indication of how desperate some had become during these hard times. School officials may also have wished that the funds had been deposited in the local bank, safe and guaranteed, after January 1, 1934, by the Federal Deposit Insurance Corporation.

The Marcellus Observer - Wednesday, December 20, 1933
Burglars Rob Safe In Marcellus High School
Using a jimmy to pry open the rear door of Marcellus High School, burglars made their way to the office of the school, wrecked the safe and made away with $75.

The Marcellus Observer - Wednesday, December 27, 1933
Bank Deposits To Be Insured After Jan. 1
The local bank along with all the banks in Syracuse will be insured under the federal plan for the guaranty of bank deposits, which goes into effect on Jan. 1.

1934 – Terrific Cold Spell

The year began with a meeting of a newly organized Chamber of Commerce, a group which was " . . . organized for the purpose of community welfare and to weld a stronger bond between those who conduct the town business" (MO 1/3/34). One of the first actions of the group was to send a committee to the Board asking for more controls over the licensing of peddlers in the Village.

8 Jan 1934 - " . . . a committee from the Chamber of Commerce requested an amendment to Ordinance No. 48, . . . to be amended to include the word "soliciting', and on motion . . . it was voted to so amend said ordinance . . . "

The Marcellus Observer - Wednesday, January 3, 1934
B-R-R-R-R!
The coldest snap in 38 years visited this part of the country last Friday when the thermometer dropped to 40 degrees below zero in some sections up to 20 degrees in others. Nearly every car owner had trouble, even those who had warm garages and garage men were kept busy all . . . day . . .

One thing that neither they, nor anyone else could control, however, was the weather and throughout the county, record cold snaps would continue throughout January and February that year. The extreme cold even taxed the printing facilities of the local newspaper, causing *The Observer* to publish " . . . a diminutive edition . . . on a job press, . . . without doubt, the smallest weekly newspaper in this community" (MO 2/7/34)

CWA, and a Sales Tax

Because many thought that the federal government was providing handouts to people too lazy to work, there was an attempt by the New Dealers to set up a program that would provide work, and such an agency was the Civil Works Administration or CWA. An attempt to find work, even for women in Marcellus, was made, although often the jobs became what were termed "boondoggles" or "make-work" temporary projects.

One idea that would become permanent and successful, at least for local government, was the enactment of a sales tax, receipts from which would be used by cities and villages to fund municipal operations. Even today, receipts from sales tax in Onondaga County are returned to local governments in a formula that is based, for the most part, on population. For Marcellus, that figure approximated $5,500 in 1934 and by fiscal year 2003 had risen to almost $300,000.

The Marcellus Observer - Wednesday, January 10, 1934
Marcellus To Find CWA Work For Women

An effort is being made to find projects for work for women who need employment in the county under the C.W.A. Any local women who need employment should register at once under the C.W.A., at Frank Griffing's. Opportunity for teachers, nurses, clerical workers, house keepers, for women who can sew, for women who want training in library work, or any others are being created . . . We all hope something good for Marcellus will come out of this new project.

The Marcellus Observer - Wednesday, January 24, 1934
Sales Tax Would Net Considerable Revenue

At a meeting of Mayors and Mayors-elect held in Syracuse, Dec. 7, 1933, it was proposed that a bill be enacted levying a 2% sales tax, a portion going to the municipalities. Following are the estimated amounts which would be returned to Syracuse and surrounding villages under the proposed tax.

	Population	Amount		Population	Amount	
Syracuse	209,326	$1,674,608	Marcellus	1,083	$5,415	
Jordan	1,145	5,725	Camillus	1,036		5,180
Elbridge	452	2,260	Skaneateles	1,882	9,410	

Hatchery Fire

In February, during one of the coldest days on record, a fire " . . . destroyed the barn and hatchery of V. S. Kenyon with a loss of around $5,000 . . . The frigid temperature of 40 degrees below zero hampered the firemen, freezing the hose and causing much discomfort" (MO 2/7/34).

Library and Playground

The winter of 1934 also witnessed the campaign for two major projects in Marcellus. The Marcellus Library had purchased the Ernest Smith property (originally the Caleb Gasper home) on Main Street next to the Engine House, and in the process of remodeling the structure for use as a library facility. This remodeling would take another few months and in June, the Marcellus Library would have its own permanent home. Another effort was that of building a

---

The Marcellus Observer
Wednesday, February 14, 1934
Unprecedented Cold Snap Visits Community

. . . Old timers shake their heads sagely when asked about records of other years. None have known it to be so cold. It was, without doubt, the coldest spell of weather in over half a century, if not more.

The Marcellus Observer
Wednesday, February 28, 1934
Marcellus Library Nearing Completion

Work on the new Marcellus Library is rapidly drawing to a finish. In about three more weeks the work is expected to be done and the building ready for occupancy.

The Marcellus Observer
Wednesday, February 28, 1934
Playground For Marcellus Children

With the increasing traffic through Marcellus the need of a playground for children has become more apparent. During the summer months, when children are free from school duties, the smaller tots must play in the streets or be confined in a more or less uninteresting backyard. This, according to modern thought, is not conducive to mental and physical health. There is on foot in Marcellus a movement to fit up a playground for local youngsters, away from the dangers of traffic and rough play. No definite plans have been laid but are soon to be discussed.

The Marcellus Observer
Wednesday, March 21, 1934
Hunt Reelected As Village Trustee

Stephen H. Hunt won the election of trustees for two years for the Village of Marcellus. Although only 14 votes were cast, it showed that the voters were sure of his re-election. Mr. Hunt has served faithfully in the past and still enjoys the confidence of the local citizens.

Mr. Hunt was at one time chief of Marcellus Fire Department and is placed on all important committees in the civic life of the village. Since coming to Marcellus from Navarino some years ago he has become one of the leading business men of the community, and his election to his present as village trustee is a source of gratification to his friends.

The Marcellus Observer
Wednesday, April 25, 1934
Marcellus Municipal Playground Hoped For

A committee, consisting of the following five members: Rev. Harold Gosnell, chairman, assisted by William Spaulding, William Thornton, Carl Peterson and Arthur Wilson, has been formed to organize plans for a Municipal Playground in Marcellus.

The proposed location is in the rear of the new library building on Main Street. Something to interest everybody is the aim of the committee. For this reason it is planned to put in 2 tennis courts, sand boxes, horseshoe pitching grounds, swings, slides, and perhaps a shuffle board. If we are to do this, however, the project will depend upon the cooperation of the entire community. It would certainly be for the greater safety of children to have a place to play which was out of the reach of automobiles and state roads. Also, it will build up a community spirit if a center such as this can be provided at which old and young alike might meet for recreational purposes.

Let's all put out shoulders together and see that this thing is done. Can we depend on your support?

playground for village children, an attempt, perhaps, to not only provide a safe area of play for the children, but also to promote a spirit in the community in the midst of hard times.

Sales Tax, An Election and the Playground

The issue of the sales tax in New York State moved slightly beyond the talking stage, and more details were now being discussed about what was termed the Merrill Tax Plan. Today, it is interesting to note, cash sales and farm products are not exempt from sales tax as they were in 1934. In addition, the sales tax of 2% in 1934 has risen to a total of 7% in Onondaga County today. Of that figure, 4% is levied and collected for the State of New

The Marcellus Observer -
Wednesday, March 7, 1934
Sales Tax Revenue To Benefit Community

A great deal is being said in regard to the so-called Merrill Tax Plan, which in brief proposes to levy a 2% Sales Tax on all retail sales of merchandise and of services, except wages and salaries, and to rebate 90% of the taxes so raised to the cities, towns, villages and school districts, to be applied to the reduction of any bonded debts and where the existing bonded debts have been satisfied the amount to be used for the reduction of the real estate taxes . . . It would exempt all cash sales below five cents and all farm products produced in the state when sold at retail by the farmer who produced it in the state. This is done because the tax on such sales would produce a nuisance tax and the cost of collection would approximate the tax to be collected . . .

York while 3% is collected by Onondaga County and distributed locally.

On March 20, 1934, Stephen H. Hunt, facing no opposition, was returned to office for a third two-year term in a very low turnout of voters. The push for a village playground continued to gain momentum that Spring and its location behind the Marcellus Library seemed to be an ideal choice, offering recreation for both young and old alike.

Board Issues

When spring arrived, the Village Board decided that the Engine House needed to be repaired and authorized that the building be shingled and painted. It also took up the question of peddlers again, receiving complaints that " . . . an excessive number of peddlers, claiming to be incapacitated, have visited . . . of late . . . violating the peddling ordinance now in force in the village . . . Many dollars . . . taken from local stores every week by out-of-town peddlers who pay no taxes, and who, in many cases, work upon the sympathies of the kindly country villager" (MO 5/23/34). The Board also found it again necessary to warn residents that the water in the Village Reservoir was very low and that they should conserve as much as possible.

14 May 1934 - " . . . Mr. Kenyon moved that the Engine House be shingled and painted, seconded by Mr. Hunt and was duly carried . . . "

Old Glory
ITS 158th BIRTHDAY

What flower is this that greets the morn,
Its hues from Heaven so freshly born?
With burning star and flaming band
It kindles all the sunset land;
O tell us what its name may be—
Is this the flower of liberty?
It is the banner of the free,
The starry flower of liberty.
—Oliver Wendell Holmes.

Marcellus
Bids You
WELCOME

PROGRAM

Thirty-Sixth
Annual Convention
Of The
Onondaga County Firemen's Association
Wednesday and Thursday,
July 11 and 12, 1934

Fireworks and Firemen

June meant "no more pencils, no more books, no more teachers' sassy looks" and the local editor published a scathing article that caused him to " . . . wonder if kids hate school like many did in the days of the rod and dunce cap? . . . (and) teachers . . . were well versed in punishing" (MO 6/20/34). The end of school meant summer and the Fourth of July, minus some of the fireworks that had been outlawed by the Village Board. Celebration was not outlawed, however, and the annual Firemen's Convention was held in Marcellus, complete with a parade, prizes, dinners and contests that attracted thousands. The Board also made sure that visiting firemen were not inconvenienced, and authorized that toilets be built in the Engine House just prior to the big day.

The Marcellus Observer - Wednesday, June 27, 1934
Fireworks Scarce As Fourth Draws Near

Fourth of July in Marcellus will be a quiet affair if the ordinance enacted by the Village Fathers last year is regarded - and there is every indication that the Board proposes to enforce it.

Although this may seem like tough news to the small boy the ordinance has teeth in it . . . The damage done by dangerous fireworks in the past cannot be estimated. Fire and death have followed in the wake of the Fourth of July since the days of our grandfathers, but it has been just recently that agitation has been made on the subject.

The Marcellus Observer - Wednesday, July 11, 1934
The Heroic Firemen

The work of a village fireman is often grossly underestimated. The fireman receives no pay, yet he is ready at a moment's notice to place his life in danger for the good and safety of the community. Without him the villager would live in constant fear of that dread enemy - fire. With a group of 20 or 30 fine, active young men and an efficient fire fighting apparatus ready to answer the frightened call of a home stricken by the Demon Fire, the village rests in a peace it far too often fails to appreciate.

No stone should be left unturned to aid this vigilant organization. If better tools are needed to meet the requirements of modern firefighting, the men should have them. It is better that a fire engine stand in the bar fire years unused, than for a village to be without such an engine when the occasion arises when one is sorely needed. Welcome, Firemen, to our beautiful village. You represent a cause we are bound to respect and for which we are profoundly grateful. You are our guests and the key is in your hands.

9 Jul 1934 - " . . . the necessity of toilets in the building being imperative . . . it was voted unanimously to install same on the ground floor by enacting an addition in rear of tower for same and the toilets installed at once."

Village and Real Fathers

While the Village Fathers contended with local affairs, like a traffic light at Main and Orange Streets, " . . . resurfacing some of the streets in the village . . . (and) water in the village reservoir . . . still at a low level . . . " (MO 7/18/34), other dads were watching their sons join the Civilian Conservation Corps (CCC), a New Deal agency which employed over 2,000,000 young men in conservation work throughout the nation. The

---

The Marcellus Observer - Wednesday, July 4, 1934
Rovin' With Roy

It isn't the easiest thing in the world for homeloving boys to leave the pleasant surroundings of the old town and join the CCC. Many of our boys have served in this branch and others are leaving this week. Thursday Billy Spaulding and Jimmie Owens shook hands with their friends and started on this new experience, after a busy term at school. It is not easy for a lad to give up the prospects of a vacation on the lake or in the woods, for the discipline of a CCC Camp, but there is a lesson to be learned in this branch of work that cannot be found lying on the grass and watching the clouds sail by. There is a contact with other young men and a change to use the good qualities of character instilled into him by patient parents. The CCC Camp is an education that will have a big bearing on the future of e young men experienced it.

CCC not only provided employment for young men in a most worthwhile cause, but also mandated that a portion of the wages that they received be sent home to help the family. A popular program, it temporarily removed a potentially explosive element from growing in urban areas - unemployed young men, with nothing to do.

23 Jul 1934 - " . . . it was voted to place a traffic light at the intersection of Main and Orange Streets to avoid some of the speeding in Main Street."

The Marcellus Observer
Wednesday, August 22, 1934
Marcellus Water To Be Increased By 45,000,000 Gallons

A preliminary gesture to increase the supply of water to Marcellus is being made this week in the removing of the pipe from the surface water pond directly in back of Rockwell reservoir, preparatory to raising the dam . . .

The Village Board also intends to raise the present dam two feet or more enlarging the reservoir capacity by 45,000,000 gallons of water. This should do away with all danger of shortage.

Water Protection and Roads Opened

The year began with some severe wintry conditions, and by the summer brought searing heat and drought conditions throughout the country, including parts of New York State. The Village Board responded to this threat by increasing the supply of water in the reservoir and, later in the year, purchasing more land surrounding the pond to provide additional protection of the watershed. The summer also saw the opening of the new Cherry Valley Turnpike, " . . . the last link in the new federal transcontinental highway from Boston to Seattle . . . (and) the road between the center of Marcellus village and the Cherry Valley Turnpike . . . " (MO 8/29/34), closed for several weeks of resurfacing. Seventy years later, in 2003, South Street, from the center of the Village to the corporation would again be resurfaced and this time with both drainage pipes and granite curbing, prolonging the life of what is and has been a major access road into the community.

22 Oct 1934 - " . . . that a certain plot of land adjoining the south line of the Municipal Reservoir, containing approximately two acres, be purchased of William Raymond at the price of three hundred dollars ($300.00), as a further protection of the watershed of said reservoir."

236

Governor's Visit and Guernsey's Drug Store

One of the most exciting events to take place that year in Marcellus was the visit of Governor, a short campaign stop on his way to Syracuse. Probably of greater significance for most residents was the sale of Marble's Drug Store to LeRoy Guernsey, who would maintain the business for the next thirty-three years. "To supplement his income from the sale of patent medicines and sick room supplies, Guernsey installed an ice cream machine. His soda fountain, with its marble counter and marble top tables, became a sort of social center" (Heffernan 108). Recently, concern about a drug store in the Village again became paramount when the local pharmacy suddenly closed its doors in 1999. Not until 2002 did another pharmacist reopen what is today the Main Street Pharmacy of Marcellus. It is most welcome in the Village and one that Marcellians hope will remain as long as did Mr. Guernsey.

MO Nov 21, 1934

Thanksgiving and Local Option

Although times were still hard, Thanksgiving was celebrated in Marcellus, residents giving thanks for what they had. There were others who wanted to give voters the right to vote " . . . on local option in connection with the liquor question, permitting the communities of the State to vote on this question" (MO 11/28/34). Petitions were circulated throughout the community and, in 1935 the residents would answer the issue of wet or dry.

A New Start

The local hardware store urged people to buy and give useful gifts that Christmas

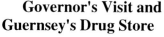

and as they said goodbye to 1934, there was hope among many residents that the Depression was coming to an end - that in the new year, the economy would be revitalized and prosperity would return in 1935. A new start, however, was still distant.

MO Dec 21, 1934

Conclusion

The Great Depression was now five years old and in spite of misfortune, the people of the community were still very hopeful. In the years since the crash, the Village had

The Marcellus Observer
Wednesday, December 26, 1934
Goodbye, Old Year

The old year is closing. A year ago we welcomed with hope and good-will the year which today is grasping for breath. Many hailed the coming of the new year with the hope that perhaps it would bring more prosperity than the year that had just faded over the hill. To others it meant a chance for new endeavor; a hope that someway, somewhere, there might be a new start.

actually seen some noted improvements, including a new bus service, improved roads both within and accessing the Village, a sewer system and a new code of ordinances.

One of the most significant accomplishments at this time was the acquisition, in 1934, of a permanent home for the Marcellus Free Library. First built about 1811, the house on Slocombe Avenue was once the home of Caleb and Fanny Gasper, perhaps " . . . a wedding gift from Major Martin Cosset to his daughter and her husband" (MO 7/25/34). In that house they had raised four children and watched as much of the early history of the Village appeared outside their front windows. The children grew up and moved on, the parents eventually succumbing to old age and passing on themselves in the 1870s. They were buried in the Village Cemetery and their

house changed ownership a number of times. In the midst of the Depression, the house became the property of the Marcellus Free Library. Since then, the front windows at #2 Slocombe Avenue have continued to watch as the history of the Village comes into view each day. The building serves not only as a reminder of the past but as a tribute to those civic-minded people of the 1930s who, in the midst of widespread foreclosure, helped to make a permanent home possible for the Marcellus Library.

Chapter 13 – The Depression Continues

The Depression continued throughout the rest of the1930s, but the Village and community responded with a resilience born of long tradition. A number of public works projects, particularly the construction of a new school, as well as private business expansion, kept many employed in the community. In addition, the pride of the community swelled with the arrival of a new fire truck and the dedication of Marcellus Park, even as the clouds of war began to gather once again overseas.

1935

Early in 1935, residents and the Trustees became quite concerned about the village water supply, following a report to the Board by an engineer who inspected the pond. The inspector recommended construction of a standpipe for storing water in or near the Village and he also recommended that consumer meters be installed, thereby decreasing unnecessary consumption by village residents. Another recommendation was that the Village hook up the Otisco water supply in case of emergency. It would take some time, but all of these recommendations would eventually be implemented, although not all at once.

14 Jan 1935 - " . . . in accordance with a request of the Board to Mr. J. H. Weidman to make an inspection of the Village water supply, owing to the low level of the reservoir, and also as to the probabilities of obtaining additional supply, Mr. Weidman submitted his report recommending immediate steps for conservation of present supply and to seek additional supply if possible . . .. moved that water from several adjacent springs which could be made available for additional supply be analyzed to ascertain if they were free from impurities and an engineer be employed to secure the necessary surveys appertaining thereto."

The Marcellus Observer
Wednesday January 16, 1935
Interest Lags On Liquor Question

Apparently apathetic are the advocates of the dry cause in this community if the recent poll conducted by this paper can be taken as a criterion.

A ballot appeared in the paper for a run of four weeks and although it caused considerable comment in both wet and dry circles, the response was not as great as would be expected. Less than 50 votes were cast in favor of local option while not a single wet vote is recorded . . .

This lethargy seems widespread over the country. Some think that due to the depression drinkers and non-drinkers alike are more interested in getting a living than they are in discussing the liquor question.

"Wet" or "Dry"

There was not too much interest expressed, however, in the liquor question. Ballots were printed and petitions circulated but they generated no

---

The Marcellus Observer - Wednesday January 23, 1935
Villages To Share In ABC Tax Funds

According to a new provision of the law, town supervisors must pay to the villages in the town a percentage of the funds received from the state liquor tax fees, the amount to be based upon the proportion of the population that each village may have.

Onondaga County's share in the alcoholic beverage tax collections for the fourth quarter of 1934 is $101,212.52. This is divided among the 19 towns, and subsequently a portion contributed to each of the 15 villages.

---

more than fifty responses in favor of a vote on local option. As a result, the question of whether a community was to be "wet" or "dry" was not to be answered in a vote, and liquor in Marcellus, it seemed, was here to stay. Apparently, people were not interested in discussing the issue any more, but more interested in finding a job. In addition, the new state liquor tax brought in revenue to operate local town government, some of which had to be shared with the Villages.

Still Need For Relief

Despite the gains that seem to have been made in 1934, there were still a great many who needed assistance in these hard times. County relief rolls continued to swell and need for relief was acute, particularly for dependent mothers and children, as well as the elderly, all of whom were unable to work. In Marcellus, the local paper sponsored a charity ball that not only raised money but also raised hopes as the community came together in a spirit of neighbor helping neighbor.

> **The Marcellus Observer**
> **Wednesday, February 20, 1935**
> **County Relief Load Is Much Higher**
> The number of cases on the county relief rolls, including veterans, was 11% higher in January than in December, . . . The total is an all time high.
>
> **The Marcellus Observer**
> **Wednesday March 6, 1935**
> **Charity Ball Is Huge Success. Welfare Gets Funds For Work**
> With the goal of $100 reached, the Charity Ball, sponsored by The Observer for the benefit of the Marcellus Welfare League, went off in great shape last Monday night . . .
> The reaction to the Charity Ball is very favorable and there is talk of making it an annual affair . . .The grand march, led by Mayor and Mrs. Michael Thornton, brought back memories of the good old days when every dance started off with the grand march . . .

Thornton Again Elected

Perhaps no person in Marcellus better symbolized the spirit of the 1930s than the Mayor, Michael J. Thornton. First elected in 1931, this son of Irish immigrants from Galway seemed to

Michael J. Thornton
1873-1965
Mayor – 1931-1939

represent a spirit of strength and endurance during those hard times. Just as FDR and Governor Lehman seemed to symbolize leadership on the national and state level, so too did Mike Thornton command that image locally. The first Democrat ever elected Mayor of the Village, the 59-year-old Thornton had been a long time employee of the Crown Mill, beginning at the age of 12 in 1885. First elected in 1931, he would go on to be re-elected for three more two-year terms and his years in office are often associated with significant achievements. Just as FDR had his "New Deal" and Herbert Lehman his "Little New Deal" in New York, Thornton's administration was associated with public works projects, most notably, construction of a sewer system for the Village. Thornton's election and re-elections were often uncontested and that in 1935 was no exception. The Village Board, to which both Thornton and Varnum S. Kenyon as Trustee had been re-elected, would again relate to the typical concerns of streets, parking, and paying the bills. There was again a suggestion of transforming the space between the sidewalk and curb into lawn as a way of beautifying the village, a practice that continues to this day.

19 Mar 1935 - " . . . the whole number of votes cast was eighty-two (82). The number of votes cast for Michael J. Thornton for Mayor for two years was 78."

Thumbnail Sketches

Throughout the months of April and May, the paper published a series of thumbnail sketches or short histories of local people, usually businessmen whose prominence in the community was not only interesting to readers, but also encouraged residents to buy

---

The Marcellus Observer - Wednesday March 27, 1935
Streets Look Fine

Street Commissioner William Kilcoyne and his assistants have brushed up Marcellus until it looks like a real town. These faithful servants are every busy, and ever conscientious, taking a great interest in seeing that the village is presentable at all times.

The Marcellus Observer - Wednesday March 27, 1935
Where Could They Park?

It is suggested that the space between the sidewalk and curb in front of the stores on the south side of Main Street, Marcellus, be transformed into a lawn, with flower gardens placed at intervals. This arrangement could extend as far down and including the Masonic Temple if the expense were not too great, and would be a thing of beauty to the eyes of passing motorists. Marcellus is not blessed with many exceptionally beautiful business buildings and a bright spot of flowers in the center of the town would be an asset.

The Marcellus Observer
Thumbnail Sketches

Allan L. Palmer
Hardware, Marcellus

Earl M. Bush
Dodge-Plymouth Sales

Leroy Guernsey - Druggist

Fred J. Uttley
Undertaker-Justice of the Peace

Carl S. Webb
Meat Market Proprietor

William Thornton
Groceries and Provisions

Dr. M. Wallace Sullivan
Veterinarian, Marcellus

Philip A. Schanzle - Baker

Morris H. Mulroy
Farmer, Milk Dealer

Albert Davenport
Construction Foreman, Historian

Rev. Harry Stubbs
Pastor, Marcellus Methodist Church

Stephen H. Hunt
Merchant, Village Official

"D.D.F." Coon - Iceman

---

locally. Their biographies seemed to convey an image of success, of young men who had done well and whose accomplishments in these hard times should be advertised.

The community was also shocked that spring with the death of Charles E. Jones, a local undertaker who had been successful in business as well as active in civic and church affairs. Jones had served as Village President in 1919 and 1920 and as Village Clerk since 1928. With his death, the Board decided to merge the offices of Clerk and Treasurer, a position that remains combined today. J. Fred Woodbridge would be appointed to this position, and he continued to serve as Clerk or Treasurer or both until he died in 1963.

13 May 1935 - " . . . by reason of the death of the Clerk, Chas. E. Jones, the offices of Clerk and Treasurer be combined and that the acting Clerk and Treasurer, J. F. Woodbridge, be appointed to the combined offices at a salary of $350.00 per annum. The Clerk was instructed to write Resolutions of Respect on the death of Charles E. Jones."

Fires and Trees

The community was also shocked with two fires that occurred that spring. In mid May, "Marcellus firemen battled a stubborn fire at Marcellus High School . . . saving the building with a comparatively small property loss" (MO 5/15/35). Firemen, however, were unable to save the Marietta Hotel as flames devoured the century-old landmark building that had served as a hotel and " . . . at one time was an important stopping place on the old stage route which led over from Skaneateles, . . . through Marietta and off . . . to the southern tier" (MO 5/29/35).

While fire continued to threaten the community, the Village Board aided by local boy scouts decided that the Village reservoir needed more protection and in a remarkable display of volunteerism, planted thousands of trees along the south side of the pond. Today those trees have reached immense proportion and continue to serve not only as protection for the Village water supply but as a reminder of the exceptional efforts of the Boy Scouts in 1935 and the wise decisions made about guarding a valuable asset.

The Marcellus Observer - Wednesday March 15, 1935
Boy Scouts Set Trees On Reservoir Bank
The land on the south side of the Marcellus reservoir, cleared of timber the past winter, was reforested last week with 4 year old Norway spruce . . . Trustee Stephen H. Hunt suggested . . . that the reservoir land ought to be set out to trees for the sake of conserving water, preventing erosion, and beautifying the reservoir site . . . in a couple of hours some two thousand trees had been set out in rows about five feet apart, parallel to the bank of the reservoir. Trees in the rows were set six feet apart. It is expected that n about ten years the trees will have attained a sufficient height to make the plantation take on the appearance of a young forest.

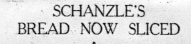

SCHANZLE'S BREAD NOW SLICED

—§—

Due to popular demand Schanzle's Peerless Bread is available sliced and unsliced.

We have installed a new modern GELLMAN slicer and now offer this service at no extra cost to the customer.

Watch For The Red Bakery Truck

We appreciate the patronage of the community and ask for its continuance

P. A. SCHANZLE
MARCELLUS, N. Y.

The Marcellus Observer
Wednesday June 12, 1935
Master Meter To Record Water Flow
Marcellus water was turned off Wednesday from 9 o'clock in the morning until around 6 at night due to the installing of a master meter at the reservoir.

Peddlers and Pig Pens

Amid complaints about a pigpen in the Village, June witnessed the arrival of the itinerant peddler to Marcellus, and with it more complaints to the Board about those who " . . . take orders and do not sell directly to the customers" (MO 6/5/35). Schanzle's Bakery, meanwhile, announced the arrival of a new bread slicer, and the Village Board authorized the installation of a new master meter to the Village water supply system, hoping to determine the amount of water needed for daily consumption as well as reduce waste. In 1935, " . . . the average per capita water consumption is between 85 and 100 gallons a day. At this ratio, . . . Marcellus would need approximately 100,000 gallons a day" (MO 6/12/35). By 2002, per capita water consumption has not changed radically and averages about 110 gallons a day. The amount of water consumed per day in the entire village, however, has doubled in the last 70 years to about 200,000 gallons. This is a decided increase from 1935 and can be attributed largely to the increased need for water at the Village Waste Water Treat Plant as well as increased use by commercial interests and an expansion of Village water to areas in the Town of Marcellus.

10 Jun 1935 - " . . . the Clerk write Dr. Walsh, requesting him to investigate the complaint of William Gray relative to the Hackford pig pen . . . that William Herron representing the National Meter Co. be authorized to install an 8" master meter in the water supply system."

Fires Beyond the Village

Following the devastating fire at the Marietta House in May, some began to ask questions about fire protection and the need to fight fires beyond the village limits. This would lead many to ask if it was time for the Fire Department to provide protection beyond the Village and for the Town to begin providing that service to farmers and others who lived in the rural areas of the community. In 1937 a contract was negotiated between the Village and the Town that would provide that protection.

> **The Marcellus Observer - Wednesday June 12, 1935**
> **The Farmer And The Fire Department**
> Although we may not realize it, we are entering upon a new era as regards fire protection. Up to a few years ago organized fire protection was confined to the four boundary lines of the village and if a house or barn took fire outside of these lines the farmer lost his buildings. This was, and still is, because the fire apparatus was owned by the village and could not be taken outside of the corporation. This ruling is sometimes loosened up a bit in cases where the local fire department could be of real use in the saving of buildings . . . The time has come when farmers as well as village residents are demanding fire protection, and they should have it . . . It is time that town boards took the matter into consideration. Some plan must be worked out which will enable the township to own efficient and modern apparatus for use both in village and country. Cisterns and catch basins must be placed in strategic spots around the community for use in time of need or some other method must be planned to supply water with which to fight country fires. This may seem a far cry, but it is bound to come. Even now village firemen are talking of extra equipment for use at country fires. The firemen are willing to help . . . but they are handicapped. They have no tools but their bare hands.

Bus Service and a Paint Job

In July, the Village Board approved a five-year extension of the franchise granted the Cayuga Bus Company, a service that received almost universal praise from residents, businessmen and government officials. In August, the Board also authorized the shingling and painting of the Engine House. This was completed in September, much to the satisfaction of the firemen who elected new officers and again spoke of the need for more modern equipment to deal with country fires.

> **The Marcellus Observer**
> **Wednesday July 23, 1935**
> **Cayuga Buses To Run For Another 5 Years**
> Absolute satisfaction was the element which weighed most in the granting of an additional five-year franchise to the Cayuga Omnibus Corporation to operate buses through the town and village of Marcellus at a hearing held here last Tuesday night.
> It has not been easy sledding for the bus company during ht past five years. Encountering the depression at the very outset the company was forced to take a severe loss due to the closing of Syracuse factories, . . . Notwithstanding this, the buses maintained an almost perfect schedule . . .

> **The Marcellus Observer**
> **Wednesday September 11, 1935**
> **Marcellus Village Hall Has New Coat**
> A new coat of shingles is being laid on the village hall this week by C. A. Spade and men. In addition to this new doors are installed, making it possible to get the truck out in shorter time . . .

> **The Marcellus Observer**
> **Wednesday September 11, 1935**
> **Marcellus Firemen Elect Officers**
> At the annual meeting of Marcellus Fire Department . . . Enric A. Hackford, present chief, was reelected to serve another year. This makes his third term as chief.
> The record of the year . . . shows that the local firemen have answer 14 alarms and fought at least five disastrous fires . . . Marcellus firemen are not equipped to combat country fires.

24 Jul 1935 - " . . . resolution extending the franchise of the Cayuga Omnibus Corp. . . . was duly adopted

12 Aug 1935 - " . . . that C. A. Spade be employed to shingle and paint the Engine House and install overhead doors - he to furnish all materials." Total cost for this was $716.99.

30 Sep 1935 - " . . . it was voted to increase the water rates on Marcellus High School to $100 per year."

A New Park

The fall of 1935 brought some very significant news to the community. The County Board of Supervisors notified the Board of Trustees that it had been awarded a grant to purchase land in the southeast portion of the village to be used as a park. When a park was first suggested back in the 1920s, there were those who argued that it was a useless piece of pastureland that it would be a waste of money, and that it might attract undesirables to the town. Now with funds provided, useless land would be reclaimed in

> **The Marcellus Observer - Wednesday, October 9, 1935**
> **Marcellus Village Gets $2,500 For Park**
>
> News has reached us that a grant of $2,500 has been made to the Village of Marcellus by the Board of Supervisors, through Supervisor Arthur W. Wilson, to be used for the purchase of 30 acres of land to the south east of the village, to be used as a park.
>
> The land to be purchased stretches to the north from the bridge on the Slate Hill road, known as the Platt Bridge and terminates at Main Street in the village. The land is comparatively flat with possibilities of athletic courts, walks, swimming pool, and flower beds. There are several streets through which entrances can be made.
>
> It is not known when the work on the park will be started, but it will probably be a relief   job which will take many men from the town rolls.

> **The Marcellus Observer - Wednesday, October 9, 1935**
> **New Park Project In Marcellus To Mark Forward Step For Town**
> **Supervisor Sees Possibilities For Reclaiming Useless Land. Park To Include Playgrounds For Both Adults and Children. Work On Project May Start Soon**
>
> The new proposed 30 acre park for Marcellus will mean the fulfillment of a long felt wish of the residents of our otherwise pretty village.
>
> Through the efforts of Supervisor Arthur W. Wilson, the park is about to become a reality. Mr. Wilson conceived the idea of using the waste land stretching from the former Platt farm on the south, to the point known to Marcellus boys for years as the "Fall In", (near the M. and O. L. property) on the north. This land is comparatively flat and with a little draining can be transformed from a mosquito and snake breeding swamp into a piece of beauty.
>
> According to real estate men, the acquisition of the park will raise the value of property in that section of the town and village, and may stimulate building on the streets forming entrances to the park. This factor was taken into consideration in making the drive for the money with which to purchase the land.
>
> When completed, the park will be a county charge, and will be paid for and maintained by the county and not by the village and town. Whether or not it will be a relief job is not known at this time, but there is a possibility that Marcellus relief rolls will contain less names during the time the work on the park is being done.
>
> Marcellus has long needed a park. Children have been forced into the streets because no adequate playground and supervised recreation, and Marcellus children can be assured of all year round sports, as the hills bordered the proposed park will make coasting possible for the smaller children. The natural layout of the land makes possible tennis courts and many other interesting recreational features for both children and adults.
>
> The property included in the park project has been used as pasture for many years, and has been poor pasture at that. The lower end, near Main Street, has been a useless swamp, covered with dank weeds and brush. In the summer it was always unpenetrable, due to the swampland and undergrowth. The continued roar of the old falls, coupled with the dismal jungle-like appearance, has made the spot one to be avoided. Clouds of mosquitoes, hatched in the dark recesses of the swamp, infested the village on the warm summer nights. The park project will do away with this nuisance.

the Village for recreational activity for adults and children as well as relief work provided for the unemployed. Almost seventy years later, the park is a jewel in our midst, maintained with great care over the years and has provided enormous benefits to village and town residents alike.

A New School

In addition to this grant, the Federal Government awarded a large sum of money to Marcellus to aid in the construction of a new centralized school. For the rest of the year, the major subject of conversation was the school project and, following a vote on October 29, 1935, residents from six surrounding towns agreed to consolidate their school

districts, " . . . to unite and build a central school large enough to offer students a more

---

The Marcellus Observer
Wednesday, October 3, 1935
Town To Vote On Centralized School Plan Next Tuesday
Votes To Decide Whether Future School Children Shall Follow Footsteps of Forebears,
Or Go Modern. Present School Overcrowded Due to Rural Students
Next Tuesday, . . . the people of this community will have a chance to vote upon perhaps the most
important question that has ever been brought before them, namely the centralization of our schools.

---

comprehensive program of studies, health services and activities " (Heffernan 208). In a
later vote residents approved two propositions, which would fund the acquisition of a site
at the northern end of the Village and construction of a new grade and high school
building on that site. " . . . A few voters wanted the school built on the Horsington
property on East Hill and others on South Street, near the new proposed park . . . " (MO
11/20/35). The approved site occupied most of what was known as the Stone farm, and
in contrast to the school on West Main Street, this site was outside Village limits. The
decision, for both the school district and the village, changed forever the responsibilities
of each entity. No longer a village school, the centralized district assumed more
responsibility, its relationship with Village government diminished considerably.

The Marcellus Observer - Wednesday October 9, 1935
MARCELLUS GRANTED $238,500
Federal Government Gives Huge Sum For Centralization Of Schools
Centralization To Make Possible Larger Educational Facilities To Rural Scholars. Credit Due
Marcellus School Board For Accomplishment
Marcellus has been given an outright gift of $238,500 to aid in the construction of a new school. This
is the largest grant made in the United States to a community smaller than a third class city. It is one
of the most fortunate things that has ever come to this community, and the district in this village has
invited the surrounding districts to join them in a new Central School district and participate in the
good fortune.

The Marcellus Observer - Wednesday, October 30, 1935
953 VOTE ON CENTRALIZATION
FOUR-TO-ONE VOTE DECIDES SCHOOL QUESTION FOR MARCELLUS AND VICINITY

The Marcellus Observer - Wednesday, November 13, 1935
Voters To Decide On School Site Tuesday
Board Offers Two Propositions
. . . The site chosen to be voted upon is at the north end of the village, taking in a large portion of the
Stone farm . . .

The Marcellus Observer - Wednesday, November 20, 1935
New School On Reed Parkway Finds Favor of Local Residents

Happy New Year

As the local editor wished all in the community a joyful New Year, he also
expressed his joy in being able " . . . to chronicle the bright events of the countryside, . .
." (MO 12/25/35) and the year had seen several. Despite lingering hard times, the
community remained resilient and residents could point with pride to the future, a future
that would include better schooling for the young and a place for them and their children
to enjoy the bounty of nature's beauty within easy walking distance of Main Street.

1936

The year began with some cold and forbidding weather that persisted throughout the winter, drifting snow tying up traffic, closing schools and hampering the delivery of mail. By March, because of the massive weight of the ice pressing against it, even the dam at Otisco Lake was threatened. What was additionally threatening, in what appeared to be a cold but peaceful Village, was an outbreak of scarlet fever in February. The epidemic eventually came under control but it also pointed out the importance of a local health officer for the community. Contagious diseases and the use of quarantines may seem like relics of the past, but terrorist activity in the United States in the 21st century have caused many in the health community to be more concerned, their vigilance even more focused, like that of Doc Walsh in 1936.

The Marcellus Observer - Wednesday, February 26, 1936
Epidemic In Marcellus Under Control
In the past week the community has been threatened with an epidemic of scarlet fever, but at present it appears to be well under control, due to the vigilance and systematic treatment of the problem by our local health officer, Dr. Walsh. . . . the community has been threatened with the disease at different times in the last few years. On one occasion, the school authorities became alarmed, . . . the county health officer, . . . advised that the worst possible procedure would be to close the school for the health officer would then have no method of checking up on new cases and thus preventing the spread of the disease. Since that time, it has been the policy of the school authorities to cooperate with the local health officer in this way to prevent the spread of the disease with the result that the epidemic has been suppressed at the very beginning. Up until now there have been nine causes in this community affecting only four families. At this date all known contacts are under quarantine, thus protecting the community should they come down with the disease.

Election

Following a total of twelve votes cast on March 17, 1936, Stephen H. Hunt was re-elected as Trustee for another term, a vote that was probably more indicative of voter satisfaction than of apathy.

17 Mar 1936 - " . . . the total number of votes cast for . . . Trustee was 12 . . . 12 votes were cast for Stephen H. Hunt . .

Construction and Approvals

Excavation began on the new Marcellus Central School, and the use of local labor did help to reduce the unemployment rate in the community. However, a time extension for completion was necessary due to the   weather, the work " . . . progressing slowly because of mud conditions . . .. The school . . . is scheduled to be ready for occupancy by December 15 . . . but with the extension of time granted, it will undoubtedly be a few months after that date before the opening day will be celebrated" (MO 3/11/36). Additionally, the Village Board was concerned about the impact of the new school on the

246

Village water supply and urged that measures be taken by the school district to find an alternate source of water for the new school.

25 Mar 1936 - " . . . whereas the present supply of Village water is limited at certain seasons of the year and at the present time only about one half of the water consumers are connected with the Village sewer system, a still greater load will be put on the water system as more residents are connected to the sewer system, it would seem unwise for the Village to assume the additional burden of supplying the new school with water at this time, therefore, Be it resolved that this Board grant permission to the Board of Education of Central School District No. 1, Towns of Marcellus, Skaneateles, Camillus, Onondaga, Spafford and Otisco, Onondaga County, N.Y. to purchase its water supply from the New York water Service Corporation."

The Marcellus Observer - Thursday, May 7, 1936
Theater In Marcellus Open After Remodeling
Modernized Picture House Has Latest Cooling
Facilities. Large Crowds Attend Reopening
Marcellus Theatre, which as been closed for several weeks for remodeling, has been reopened and patrons of the theatre are enjoying up-to-date pictures and sound effects in a modern picture house.
The floor of the theatre has been raised at the back and two ramp approaches lead to the main floor. Those entering will walk down carpeted aisles and sit in new, modern theatre seats. The former darkness of the house is done away with by the new indirect lighting system.
The old stage, which as been the scene of many amateur performances in other days, has been taken away and a new screen placed further back towards the north. With the latest improved Western Electric wide-range sound the Marcellus theatre equals anything of its kind in Central New York . . . A Marcellus girl, Miss Margaret Fenner, is cashier . . .

The Park & Theater

When spring arrived, work began on the new Marcellus Park and by May, band concerts were begun. In addition, the local theater re-opened that month, attracting large crowds of moviegoers. In 1936, " . . . movies enjoyed their most prosperous year since the Depression, even though four out of five films were called financial failures by their producers" (Carruth 744).

Lights and Water

At its May meeting, the Board considered a new license for the Empire Gas and Electric Company, which " . . . was granted a twenty-year franchise to service Marcellus provided they changed the current from twenty-five to sixty cycle" (Heffernan 115). This change in cycle would mean improved lighting and cause appliances and motors to work more efficiently. It also meant that electrical motors in village homes, such as washers, water pumps, refrigerators, gas pumps and oil burners, would have to be changed over to 60 cycles, giving evidence of a growing dependence on electricity and the need to upgrade such service. Combined with a rate reduction that took place in January, residents of the village would now be provided with more efficient service as well as a lower cost, a reflection, perhaps, of the growing influence of the Rural Electrification Administration established by President Roosevelt in 1935.

25 May 1936 - " . . . meeting . . . for the purpose of considering a new franchise to the Empire Gas and Electric Co. . . . carried."

In June, the Board acted upon recommendations made earlier that water meters be purchased and installed in all Village homes and businesses. This not only provided a greater degree of efficiency but also tended to limit waste and over consumption. Water rates, which previous to this were basely solely on the number of faucets and virtually standard for all regardless of usage, were now based on consumption. Not only was metering a more equitable distribution of the cost of providing the service, but it tended to lessen the threat that seemed to emerge every year -- not enough water in the village reservoir. Throughout the summer, water consumption dropped dramatically, reinforcing and further validating the decision to meter water in the village.

Today, water is still metered in the Village of Marcellus and if drought threatens or if the natural springs in the pond do not sufficiently recover in a given year, a back-up system is in place. That system allows the Village to switch immediately to the water pumped by the Onondaga County Water Authority from Otisco Lake. In recent years, this back-up system has been used rather frequently, a sign perhaps that the Village Reservoir, after almost 100 years of use, is no longer as active as it once was.

29 Jun 1936 - " . . . that water meters, sufficient to meter all services, be purchased from the National Water Co., the said company to supervise installation and furnish billing system."

Business Changes

By 1936, there had been and would continue to be a number of changes in the business community of Marcellus. In 1934, " . . . George Hickman II had vacated the old market at 4 East Main Street and moved his meat market and grocery business to the remodeled barn behind his home at 10 First Street" (Heffernan 113). Two years later, in March of 1936, George Walsh took over the former Hickman store and operated a market at that location for the next twenty years. The store next door, on the corner of Main and South Streets, also received some notable publicity when it was remodeled and then reopened for business in June of 1936. The store and the corner have been such an integral part of the community for so long that a litany of its occupants reads like a history of the village.

The Marcellus Observer - Thursday, June 11, 1936
Story Of Corner Store Recalls Memories Of Other Days
Early Marcellus Merchants Carry On In Old Historic Building.
Failure And Success Mark Trial Of Long List Of Tenants

It was something over a hundred years ago that Thomas J. Field, one of the early merchants of Marcellus looked at the site of the present Corner Store and saw possibilities. The village was still young and was not much more than a trading post in the wilderness. There is a possibility that as Mr. Field looked at the corner site from the armchair of the tavern across the street (the site of the present Catholic Church) he had visions of a thriving town. Marcellus was the main stem from Albany to Buffalo - the age-old Seneca Turnpike - and it might some day develop into a flourishing business.

Thomas J. Field purchased the land and built the store. Rough timbers were hauled from the woods and hewn into shape for the framework. When the store was finally opened, it was a wonderful addition to the town and was the center of trade for the farming community . . . The store remained unchanged for over 100 years. Old pictures show the same architecture as that of a few months ago. The present store is modern in every respect, a monument to the aggressiveness of present day businessmen. The old order is past and gone and new era has come. What would or ancestors of a century ago think, were they to return and seen the changes of today?

248

Today, the corner and the store retain that same visible presence in the Village, accommodating commercial business on the ground level and living quarters on the second floor.

The School and the Professor

In June, one of the last commencements at the old high school on West Main Street took place, the largest graduating class in its history. That same month, Charles Dillon, a former teacher at the Falls School, as well as a former Trustee and Clerk of the Village died at the age of 81. Long active in community affairs, Dillon had been instrumental, at the turn of the century, in helping establish electric

> **The Marcellus Observer - Thursday, June 25, 1936**
> **Marcellus Graduates Largest Class In School History**
>
> **The Marcellus Observer - Thursday, June 25, 1936**
> **Former Village Clerk Dies At Marcellus Home**
> Charles Dillon, 81, former clerk of Marcellus died at his home, June 18 . . .
> Mr. Dillon has long been connected with the life of his home village of Marcellus. For several years, he taught the Falls school and many local residents attest to his knowledge and kindly firmness . . . long be remembered as one of the leading citizens of the town.

lighting, a village water system, as well as the 1906 Village annexation. Meanwhile, construction on the new school continued, despite the heat, labeled " . . .the greatest in the history of Central New York . . . unparalleled in local history . . ." (MO 7/9/36), causing some workmen to be overcome and forced to leave the job. Beginning in January and continuing into July, it was a year marked by many extremes of temperature.

Firemen and Dedications

While water consumption by residents continued to drop during the summer, the

> **The Marcellus Observer - Thursday, August 13, 1936**
> **Marcellus Firemen Avert Devastating Fire On East Hill**
>
> **The Marcellus Observer - Thursday, August 13, 1936**
> **Firemen To Have New Truck Equipment**
> Several lengths of hose, new white rubber boots, helmets to replace the old rubber hats and several other articles of truck equipment have been virtually promised to the Marcellus Fire Department by the Village Board this week.
>
> **The Marcellus Observer - Thursday, August 27, 1936**
> **Marcellus Park Opening To Be Held Sunday**
> Prominent Men To Give Addresses At Opening Of Beauty Spot of Village. Supervisor Wilson Praised On Accomplishment. Neighboring Villages Invited.

Arthur W. Wilson

firemen found continued use for it, battling a fire on East Hill in August. The Village Board also agreed, that summer, to provide more equipment to the firemen, in anticipation perhaps of expanding fire protection to areas beyond the village.

The new Marcellus Park would also be completed in the summer of 1936 and dedicated in a ceremony that rightly acclaimed the efforts of Town Supervisor Arthur Wilson in this achievement.

September seemed to be a month for dedications and by mid month, the corner stone was laid at the new Marcellus school. A few days later, another ceremony took place in the old village cemetery " . . . when about 200 descendants and friends gathered to do homage to the 47 Revolutionary soldiers buried within the confines . . . " (MO 9/24/36). A memorial tablet, bearing the names of the soldiers lying there, more than in any other cemetery in Onondaga County, was unveiled by the Daughters of the American Revolution in a ceremony that also marked the 160th anniversary of the American Revolution.

> **The Marcellus Observer**
> **Thursday, October 1, 1936**
> **E.A.E.P. Activities**
> " . . . adult education classes, sponsored by village and community groups, . . . part of county-wide program of adult ed and recreation activities . . . "
>
> **The Marcellus Observer**
> **Thursday, October 6, 1936**
> **CHECK THE WATER LEAKS**
> Notwithstanding the fact that water is now metered to Marcellus homes, many householders are running up considerable water bills according to the report given to the Village Board this week. The condition is caused by leaking faucets. One local house had a record of over 300,000 gallons or about enough water to run the entire village a week.

> **The Marcellus Observer**
> **Thursday, November 5, 1936**
> **Marcellus Loses In Local Option Battle**
> **Wets Win In Contest To Eliminate Sale of Liquor**
> By approximately 2 to 1, Marcellus lost the drive for local option at the polls Tuesday. The town was the only one in the county placing the question before the people at this election . . .
> The loss of the election this year makes it necessary for the drys to wait three years before presenting the question again . . .
>
> **The Marcellus Observer**
> **Thursday, November 5, 1936**
> **Stone Defeat Big Surprise To Voters of Both parties**
> **Veteran Legislator's Loss To Democratic Candidate Not Expected**
> Fighting against the combined opposition of the governor and upstate propaganda, Horace M. Stone met defeat at the polls Tuesday by a total of 11,914 votes. Mr. Stone was a candidate for state senator and was arrayed against Francis L. McElroy, Democrat, who carried the city of Syracuse. Stone carried the towns by nearly 6,000, but not enough to offset the combined Democratic and Labor vote of his opponent in the city.

Village Leaks

October brought some adult education classes to the community as well as a warning for village water users to check the faucets in their homes for leaks. The latter is a reminder that is still valid for today's residents, many of whom find themselves with inordinate utility bills because toilets are constantly running. Many property owners, particularly those who own and rent multiple dwellings in the village are often faced with this difficulty and look to the Village Board for redress. Unfortunately, the Board often cannot do much to forgive a debt that is usually incurred because of neglect or ignorance.

November Elections

In November, elections were to be held on national, state and local levels and, anticipating that, local "drys" printed sample ballots and petitions in the paper so as to force a local option vote. It did not happen, nor did the Republican candidate for President win. In fact, few Republicans won, not even on the local level. Horace Stone, first elected to the New York Assembly in 1922, was now the Republican candidate for the New York State Senate and he was defeated, as FDR was swept into office for another term as President, a landslide victory that included huge majorities for the Democrats in both houses of Congress as well.

A New Truck and a New Theater

As the year came to an end, a petition that gained much favor with the residents was one circulated by the firemen, asking for financial assistance to purchase a new truck. "The Village Board . . . expressed a willingness to purchase new fire fighting apparatus for use in both village and country, providing the Town Board . . . cooperate by paying a part of the cost and . . . establish a fire protection district . . . (MO 12/3/36), an issue resolved in 1937.

250

Christmas in 1936 witnessed the lighting of the Village clock as well as the re-opening of the local movie house in Marcellus, with appropriate seasonal showings.

14 Dec 1936 - " . . . that the Village enter into a contract with the Empire Gas & Electric Co. to light the Village clock at a flat rate of $75.00 per year."

Village residents also participated in another house Christmas decoration contest that year, a somewhat simple, yet meaningful expression by people in a small community. They were still able to find joy in the midst of hard times in America and peace at a time when aggressor nations in Europe were becoming increasingly lawless. The new year would continue to challenge their optimism.

1937

In the new year, there were a growing number of Americans who were still very concerned about the far-reaching effects of the New Deal, in particular that workers in the country must now subscribe to the requirements of the social security law, beginning January 1, 1937. Franklin Roosevelt was inaugurated as President for a second term on January 20, 1937, as required by the 20th Amendment and opposition to his programs seemed to increase throughout the year.

By mid January, on a more local note, the Marcellus firemen finalized plans for the new fire apparatus, having received approval from the town that it would pay "rent" on the truck after the Village purchase. The establishment of a fire protection district was the

next step and by mid February, several hearings were held so that taxpayers could voice their opinions on that issue as well as the truck purchase.

The Vote

Village elections in 1937 called for the selection of a Mayor and a Trustee and most people expected the incumbent Michael Thornton and Varnum Kenyon to be renominated. In February, however, Varnum Kenyon resigned as Trustee, stating that he would not be a candidate at the March election. Kenyon had served as a village trustee since 1924 and had taken an active role in a number of different projects. Thornton was renominated for Mayor and the new nominee for Trustee would be Leonard Norris, a retired farmer, who moved to Reed Street in the Village and became active in the trucking business. When elections took place on March 16, 1937, voters not only returned Thornton to office and elected Norris as Trustee, but also by a vote of 15 to 1, approved the purchase of a new fire truck. The vote is not recorded in the Village minutes but newspaper headlines seem to indicate overwhelming approval by residents for this test of village-town collaboration.

Leonard Norris
Village Trustee
1937-1945

It's Time

When the new Board met in April, it approved a contract for the purchase of a 600-gallon pumper for the fire department, also reminding several residents that it was time to hook up to the village sanitary sewer system. Although the modernized system had been installed some time earlier, the Board realized that some residents might need more time before assuming the expense of connecting to the sewer system. By the end of the decade, most of the residences in the village were linked to the municipal sewer system, one that drained into a septic tank, near the present treatment plant, before eventually emptying into Nine Mile Creek. Today, there remains a single property in the village that has never been connected to the village sewer system and it is a concern that has never been adequately addressed.

The Marcellus Observer - Thurs, April 22, 1937
Time To Spruce Up

The last few weeks of winter are usually pretty dirty. The melting snow shows up the dirt and makes the world look in need of a bath. So spring is a time to clean up and make things look new again

The Marcellus Observer - Thurs, May 13, 1937
Residents Notified To Connect Sewers

Several homeowners in the center of the town have received orders from the Village Board to make connections with the village sewer system before July 1. The reason for this order is said to be the increasing nuisance made by the old system where it discharges in the vicinity of the new school building. Most of the individual lines in the effected area discharge directly or indirectly into a large tank situated on the former Hooper property at the rear of the Pilot Garage or into another such tank near the school site. These tanks are constantly the cause of trouble and frequent digging is made to keep the lines free.

Some of the homes on Reed Street have sewer lines which eventually discharge into a system of land tile. This system has been overflowing at times and has been the source of considerable trouble to property owners on upper First Street and on lower Reed Parkway. This is temporarily taken care of through diverting the flow at a point further up the hill.

The sewer system was installed five years ago at considerable cost to the village. The Village Board expects that eventually all homes will be connected, but are not officially ordering connections made where the sewage is disposed of without causing a nuisance or unsanitary condition. The Board expects, however, that all new homes will be connected and older ones as soon as conditions permit. In some cases, connections with the main sewer entail considerable expenses, such as in causes where paving must be removed and relaid. These conditions were anticipated when the sewer was installed and connection outlets were left at the best possible location for each home. Homeowners in the area affected by this order of the Village Board are urged to comply as quickly as possible, thus hoping to do away with the present unsanitary condition.

The Marcellus Observer - Thurs, June 3, 1937
Addition Planned On Engine House
Building To Be Ready For Arrival
Of New Truck June 10

Excavating operations are going on at the rear of the Marcellus Engine House preparatory to building an annex to house the new village road truck and other equipment. With the coming of the new fire truck, voted upon last March, the present lower room of the Engine House will be used for both fire trucks. To make the floor safe, a new concrete floor is being installed . . . firemen plan to use the new fire truck at all fires and to keep the old chemical truck ready for emergency. The new truck will answer country fires as well as village fires . . . The new plan of village-rural fire protection is watched with interest by other communities and may be followed if the Marcellus experiment is successful . . .

12 Apr 1937 - " . . . a contract in the amount of $6996.75 with the Sanford Motor Truck Co. for the purchase of one 600 gallon pumper to built in accordance with specifications furnished was duly executed."

12 Apr 1937 - " . . . the Clerk was instructed to notify the following householders to connect with the Village Sewer System by July 1st, 1937: James C. Pilot, Walter H. Kellogg Est., L. E. Mowry, Jessie G. Parsons (Block), F. H. Gillett, Marian Woodford, J. H. Weidman (Res.), Thomas Collard, Hattie Marshfield, Bertha Whaley, Roy P. Smith (Reed Ave.), Crown Mills (Reed Ave.), Sarah Wright Estate (Reed Ave.), E. T. Taylor, Alex R. Smith, Wm. McFarlane, Effie Carroll, W. D. Snyder."

10 May 1937 - " . . . that the following be notified to connect with the Village sewers by July 1, 1937: James Lanning, Patrick Kilcoyne, Mary Kennedy, Wm. Rutherford Est., E. N. Engler, Giles Case."

Engine House and School House

In anticipation of the arrival of the new vehicle, the firemen requested and received permission from the Village Board to construct an addition to the Engine House. This addition would allow both fire trucks to be housed, ready for any emergency in the village or town.

The old Marcellus High School also witnessed its last graduation that June, as thirty-nine students received diplomas from the principal, Mr. Molyneux, who was also resigning because of a disagreement with the school board. The new school would be ready for a September opening and the old school on West Main Street would be closed, 45 years after it first opened in 1892. It had served the

The Marcellus Observer
Thursday, June 24, 1937
Marcellus Central Graduates Last
Class From Old School
39 Pupils Receive Diplomas From
Principal

community well, having graduated over 600

students and it enjoyed the reputation of being the only village high school in Onondaga County at the time to be credited by the Middle States Association of Colleges and Secondary Schools.

Insurance Rates and Water Rates

The Marcellus Observer
Thursday, July 1, 1937
New $7,000 Fire Fighting Machine Delivered
Village Accepts New Fire Truck

By the end of the month, the new truck had arrived and at a July Board meeting, the Trustees approved an insurance policy on the Sanford Pumper and also allowed the firemen to display the new apparatus at the convention that summer.

14 Jul 1937 - " . . . that public liability, property damage, collision, fire and theft insurance be taken on the Sanford Pumper . . .. that $50.00 be advanced to the Marcellus Band to apply against their contract . . . . that the Fire Department be granted permission to take the Sanford Pumper to the Convention at Jamesville."

The Trustees also, because the new metering system had been so efficient and a majority of residents had kept within the allotted amount, voted " . . . to allow each user of water 2000 gallons additional per quarter or a total of 12,000 gallons a quarter, at the basic rate of $2 for that amount of water" (MO 7/15/37). By comparison, today's water rates are not as generous -- a minimum charge of 5,000 gallons per quarter is $16.00, with incremental cost for added usage.

Fire Protection

With the arrival of the new fire truck, parking near the fire barn became a problem and residents were asked to observe the parking laws so as not to hamper the firemen as they exited the Engine House. A similar condition exists today in front of the Village Hall and again residents find it difficult to park in this area, which is quite congested at times. Shoppers, churchgoers and library patrons vie with police vehicles for the limited places that are available for parking in this area.

In August the firemen conducted a demonstration of the new Sanford Pumper, reassuring residents and government officials that the community would have adequate protection. The demonstration may also have been an attempt to influence a public hearing, held later in August that would discuss a contract between the village and town providing fire protection in the town. By mid September, a five year contract was approved by the Trustees, at a cost to the Town of $900 annually, a figure that has risen dramatically over the years.

With the new contract, however, a problem soon developed in fighting town fires and that was the number of drivers who tried to reach a fire before the volunteers, blocking roads or otherwise interfering with the ability of the firemen to reach the scene. Today, Fire Police keep the roads unobstructed and re-route traffic when necessary, insuring a quick and safe response to emergencies.

The Marcellus Observer - Thursday, July 22, 1937
Cars Near Fire Barn Menace To Safety

Movie patrons and local shoppers who park cars in the immediate vicinity of the Marcellus Engine House are frowned upon these days by the village fathers.

The Marcellus Observer - Thursday, August 5, 1937
Pumper Throws Five Streams Over Village Flagpole In Test
Large Crowd Witnesses First Demonstration
Town and Village Sure of Sufficient Fire Protection

The Marcellus Observer - Thursday, August 5, 1937
Notice

Notice is hereby given that a public hearing will be held at the Engine House . . . on August 11, 1937 . . . for the purpose of considering a proposed contract . . . between the Village of Marcellus and the Town Board of the Town of Marcellus for providing fire protection to the property located in the Town of Marcellus within the limits of the fire protection district heretofore formed . . .The contract proposed to be entered into . . . for a five year period.

The Marcellus Observer - Thurs, August 12, 1937
Firemen Request Open Road Enroute To Fires

Considerable difficulty was encountered last Monday when the new fire truck sought to answer the alarm from the home of Arthur Woodford in Pleasant Valley, due to autoists who tried to reach the fire ahead of the truck. The drivers of these cars, overzealous in their anxiety to reach the fire; first blockaded the road to such an extent that at one time the truck was forced almost to a dead stop . . . The department urgently requests any driver . . . in the path of the truck to pull over as far as possible . . . give the firemen a chance to do their duty unhampered by needless interference.

13 Sep 1937 - " . . . a contract with the Town of Marcellus, executed August 12th, providing for fire protection within the Town for a period of five years, for the annual sum of $900.00 was duly approved."

Village Optimism

Although there were indications of a new recession late in the summer of 1937,

The Marcellus Observer - Thursday, August 26, 1937
Village Now In Good Shape And Appearance

Roads in the village are now in ship shape condition. The job of resurfacing and repairing has been completed . . . Marcellus now presents a pleasing appearance . . . good roads, inviting streets, newly painted and remodeled homes, several new houses, neat stores and a new school make the village stand out from others. The village is noted in the county as being free from rowdyism, little or no police service being necessary. Several new residents have expressed their pleasure at becoming associated with Marcellus people, claiming that local folks are most democratic and agreeable.

The Marcellus Observer - Thursday, August 26, 1937
New Marcellus School Ready To Receive Pupils September 7

The Marcellus Observer - Thursday, September 23, 1937
Success Marks First Village Gathering At Park Last Saturday
Perfect Weather Draws Large Crowd Of Neighbors To Grounds

residents in Marcellus seemed to be optimistic about their village, its image, and its many attractions. They seemed to be especially proud of their new school, which opened its doors in September. The community's optimism was also on display at the first annual

Village Picnic that month in Marcellus Park. It was an event that would bring together young and old, village and rural folks, in " . . . a program so full of fun that no one can afford to miss (it) . . . free to all and no one . . . asked to contribute in any way . . . unlike the popular brand of Old Home Days, it will not be used as a money making proposition" (MO 9/9/37).

The Marcellus Observer
Thursday, October 7, 1937
Along Main Street
STREET SCENES AT NIGHT: C. W. Jones closes his store-The picture at the theatre ends, and the crowd goes home-The Drug Store closes its door-The window of the Light Company office stays lighted all night-The traffic light blinks red, green, amber-The water in the fountain in front of the Post Office gurgles on and on-The last bus leaves for Auburn at 12:45-The clock keeps her vigil all night long-What a haven of peace and quietness-The town sleeps.
MOVIE OF THE MONTH: If you want to see the best picture of 1937, don't fail to see "The Lost Horizon," adapted from the book by James Hilton . . .
OTHER GOOD MOVIES: "Topper" for many good laughs and some trick photography: "Stella Dallas," the tale of mother love: "The Good Earth," the story of the farmer in China: "Dead End," dealing with the social problems of New York's lower east side: "Thin Ice," , , , "The Prisoner of Zenda," . . . "The Big City," . . .

The Marcellus Observer
Thursday, October 28, 1937
Hallowe'en Carnival And Theater Party For Children Friday Night

The Marcellus Observer
Thursday, December 30, 1937
Wading Pool In Park Ready For Summer
Good times are in store for local youngsters in the Marcellus Park. The wading pool at the park is completed and will be ready for business when the park opens for the summer. The new rustic fence has been installed at the park adding greatly to the beauty of the scene . . .

The Marcellus Observer
Thursday, January 20, 1938
Death of Dr. C. E. Weidman Comes As Shock To Community

Beloved Physician Suffers Collapse Due To Continued Work

Practiced 58 Years

Dr. Weidman Held Warm Place In Hearts Of Rich And Poor

The community seemed to be at peace that fall, despite the gathering clouds of war in Europe and Asia. The scenes along Main Street echoed quiet. People enjoyed simple pleasures, going to the movies, celebrating the dedication of their new school, or hosting a Halloween party for the children of the village, the latter a tradition that continues to this day. There were still concerns about unemployment and the needy, and another Charity Ball to benefit the Welfare League served as a reminder of that. When fire swept through the Tuscarora Club in November, people were reminded of a threat that was especially frightful in the winter and when school children were immunized against diphtheria in December, the community was reminded of another threat to their safety. Yet, their optimism seemed to prevail. As homeowners decorated for Christmas and the firemen remodeled new rooms in the Engine House, people were already looking forward to summer, when the new wading pool would be open in the park for their children to enjoy.

1938

January's weather included a real cold snap " . . . when the mercury took a nose dive, reaching a new low for this year of 20° below zero . . . not as intense as the now famous cold spell of 1934, when, on February 14th, the thermometer dropped to an unheard of low of 44 below. It will be remembered that at that time water pipes froze in the streets. Many stream and hot water plants were rendered useless and plenty of real suffering was the result" (MO 1/13/38) In addition to the weather, the death of Dr. Charles E. Weidman that month was another jolt to the community. A physician for almost 60 years, Dr. Weidman, who had

C. W. Weidman
Village Health Officer

also served local government as the Village Health Officer for a number of years, was very much respected throughout the area, " . . . probably the best known man in the community" (MO 1/20/38).

Coon's Pond

Another person whose death that winter was mourned by the community was that of Daniel DeForest Coon. Known as the Village Ice Man, " . . . in 1899 he built a dam across the brook on his property and for 25 years supplied the village with ice from that source" (MO 2/3/38). Coon's Pond, as it came to be called, would remain a fixture in the village for the next 100 years, serving not only as a supplier of ice but also as a skating rink for village youngsters. It also acted as a retention basin for the great amount of water that rushed down from the surrounding hills every spring. By the end of the 20th century, however, the pond had become a serious threat to the health and safety of nearby residents. Water in the pond was estimated to be about a million gallons and eight feet deep, with no fencing to protect against accidental drowning. It also served as a breeding ground in the spring and summer for mosquitoes and other insects -- a public health menace, particularly in view of recent outbreaks of the West Nile Virus. In 2001, the Village Board authorized the reconstruction of the area, and with the addition of new piping, Coon's Pond was drained, the dangers eliminated along with a little bit of Village history.

Main Street

Another concern that had existed for many years was that of traffic congestion. As the number of cars increased in the age of the automobile, so too did the need for more

---

The Marcellus Observer - Thursday, February 24, 1938
Widen Main Street
An Open Letter To The People of Marcellus

For several years residents have watched traffic through the center of the village, especially on busy days and evenings, and have marveled at the dexterity of drivers in plotting automobiles through the jam of parked cars. Few accidents have been reported, although there have been a number of minor clashes, resulting in bent fenders and ruffled tempers.

Many suggestions have been made to remedy this condition, and the consensus of opinion seems to lie in a plan for widening Main Street in the common center. Conditions in front of the Corner Store have become so dangerous that these merchants have requested the Village Board to widen the curve in front of the store, making more road room for cars turning into or out of South Street.

While this work is being done it would be a fine plan to allow the Village to continue the widening of the street on both sides, . . .

---

parking in small communities like Marcellus. There were many suggestions, one of which was to widen Main Street to eliminate the jam of parked cars and allow for a freer movement of automobile traffic. By the end of the 20th century, however, traffic through the village center was moving at a dangerously fast pace and plans were made to narrow Main Street. With the installation of new curbing, drainage and green space in the late 1990s, not only was speed on this military road reduced but more systematic parking space made available as well as street beautification.

An Election and A Broadcast

March saw the re-election of Stephen Hunt as Trustee, " . . . 20 votes were cast, Mr. Hunt receiving every one" (MO 3/17/38), as well as the appearance of Mayor Michael Thornton on a local radio broadcast, asked by station WSYR to say a few words about the Village of Marcellus. Mayor Thornton's message, while not quite like a fireside chat by FDR, gave a brief history of the community and urged listeners that if they " . . . want a nice village to live in, you will make no mistake if you locate in Marcellus" (MO 3/17/38). While the Mayor spoke eloquently about the many attractions of the village, the local paper printed a work written by the late Elizabeth Chapman which told of the old historic homes in the village, and a newspaper editorial urged the local community to preserve its historical landmarks as well as the stories associated with them. To its great credit, the Marcellus Historical Society, established in 1960, has been able to gather and preserve much information about the community. Unfortunately, some of those historic spots, which the preservationists of the 1930s urged be maintained, have since been destroyed, and concrete memories of the past often buried with them.

> **The Marcellus Observer**
> **Thursday, March 24, 1938**
> **Beauty Of Marcellus Fades As Architecture Changes**
>
> **The Marcellus Observer**
> **Thursday, March 31, 1938**
> **Preserve The Landmarks**
>
> **The Marcellus Observer**
> **Thursday, April 7, 1938**
> **This 'n' That**
>
> Lower North Street is getting more and more like the "rocky road to Dublin." It was never a good road at its best, but now seems to be much the worse for wear.
> . . . What a fine thing it would be if we all could install curbing through the village. Good curbed streets are an asset and add to the beauty of the village.
>
> **The Marcellus Observer**
> **Thursday, May 12, 1938**
> **This 'n' That**
>
> . . . the Village Board is going to place a rubbish can or two at strategic points in the common center. When you finish that bag of popcorn or cheerio don't throw the wrapper into the street. Drop it into the can. Nothing looks worse on the street than papers strewn around. Help keep your village in such shape that you will be proud to show Aunt Mary and Uncle Jim around the next time they are here.

Suggestions For The Village

Early in April, the Village Board listened to complaints about the condition of lower North Street and the need for more curbing throughout the village. It also approved the new officers for the Marcellus Fire Department and heard from residents on a variety of other topics. One suggestion was for a Village Flower, " . . . as the lilac is to Rochester, another flower would be to our town" (MO 4/28/38). Another concern, persisting to this day, was that of village trash receptacles. The Village continues to maintain such containers, although in the 21st century the concern is that many who live outside the Village often use these receptacles as a place to dump their household garbage. Monitoring this has been difficult in recent years because this illegal dumping of trash is done at night by those who wish to avoid paying for garbage pickup at their residences out of the Village.

11 Apr 1938 - " . . . the following officers for the Fire Department were confirmed: Chief - Clayton Edgerton, 1st Asst. Chief - Albert Palen, 2nd Asst. Chief - Lester Norris."

The Village Board was faced with another problem that remains a concern today -- that of tree infestation by insects. In the 1930s, a problem with tent caterpillars was met

---

The Marcellus Observer
Thursday, May 12, 1938
This 'n' That

More and more readers are asking what is to be done with the bandstand. It is apparent that it must be moved, but where? The band built the stand with their own money and they should have a say in the matter. Many have suggested a small village park in the rear of the fire hall and library, but it is doubtful whether money is plentiful enough to do that just now. Such a park and playground would be a wonderful thing but we must let the Village Fathers decide...

The Marcellus Observer
Thursday, May 26, 1938
Band Question Arouses Village
Band Halts Preparations For Summer Concerts Until Location Decided

At a recent meeting of Marcellus Band it was decided to stop rehearsals until it could be definitely ascertained where the bandstand was to be placed. The controversy seems to have arisen because of the indecision as to the final location of the bandstand. The band strongly objects to locating the bandstand in Marcellus Park because of the mosquitoes which infest that section at night. The band claims that it would be uncomfortable for both band members and audience and would result in failure.

Main Street merchants are strongly for having the bandstand placed somewhere in upper Main Street claiming that the band brings the farmers into town on Friday nights. To take this stand elsewhere would result in loss of trade, something that few merchants can afford at present . . . Unless some move is made to support the band, there will probably be no summer concerts.

---

by having village trees sprayed to prevent foliage from being destroyed. In later years, many Village trees would be infected with and destroyed by Dutch Elm disease. Today Village trees remain a consideration, and an inventory of trees is regularly updated, thanks in large part to the work of local Boy Scouts and help from the New York State Dept of Environmental Conservation.

28 May 1938 - " . . . in view of the destruction of foliage by tent caterpillars, a contract was entered into between Jerome J. Krick and this Board, whereby Mr. Krick agrees to spray all trees in the Village between the sidewalk and gutter for the sum of $300.00"

The Bandstand

No issue seemed to be of greater concern that spring than that of the bandstand, forced to relocate because a new garage was being built in the Village center. While some wanted the stand relocated in Marcellus Park, others thought that mosquitoes at night would cause much discomfort at that site. The merchants wanted the band to perform in the common center, perhaps in a new park behind the Village Hall and Library. The Village Fathers argued that there was no money to create such a playground, and eventually a home in the Park was found.

The Summer

The school year ended in June, the community very proud that their " . . . children can leave school as well equipped as city children, something unheard of a few years ago" (MO 6/30/38). One of those youngsters was Frank Kelly, a young man who found the summer to be an exciting challenge. In July, he was elected Mayor of Boys' State, a unique program, still sponsored by the American Legion, which fostered active participation by the young in government.

The summer also witnessed the first band performance in Marcellus Park, a park that was promised lights, enabling " . . . visitors to spend more hours there. It will also increase the attendance at the band concerts" (MO 8/4/38). The band also planned to broadcast an August performance over the radio, but technical difficulties prevented that from happening.

> **The Marcellus Observer - Thursday, July 14, 1938**
> **Marcellus Boy Mayor In "Boys' State" City**
> Frank Kelly, son of Mr. and Mrs. John Kelly of Marcellus was elected Mayor of Bennett City, Clancy County at Empire Boys' State Tuesday. The Boys' State, a unique plan of the American Legion, is composed of boys from all over the state. Located on the fairgrounds, the state elects its own officials, punishes its own violators and carries on its business in exactly the same manner that the business of a large municipality is carried on. Observers claim that the youths take more interest in voting than their elders . . .
>
> **The Marcellus Observer - Thursday, July 21, 1938**
> **Band To Hold First Concert Sunday**
>
> **The Marcellus Observer - Thursday, August 4, 1938**
> **Board Promises Lights For Park**
>
> **The Marcellus Observer - Thursday, August 11, 1938**
> **Marcellus Band To Broadcast Program**

The Fall

School would reopen in September and the Village Board was presented that month with a request from the Fire Department to install and maintain a new fire hydrant to protect the lower or northern part of the Village, including the lower Crown Mills property.

2 Sep 1938 - " . . . Fire Department filed a petition requesting that the Village Board to have a hydrant installed on the New York Water Service Corp. pipeline at the lower Crown Mill.

To the Members of the Board of the Village of Marcellus

At a meeting of the Marcellus Fire Department held September first, the matter of adequate water supply for the lower end of the Village was taken up and whereas this department feels that because of the numerous times when the water in the mill pond is too low to permit the use of the pumper and for the better protection to property located in the north end of the Village, that the Board cause to have installed and maintained a hydrant on the suburban water line directly opposite the lower Crown Mills."

The Fire Department also went to Skaneateles that Labor Day and " . . . walked off with the honors in the . . . Parade, . . . and . . . in the water fight later in the afternoon" (MO 9/8/38). The 2nd annual Village Picnic was planned for September 17th, but it rained, and rained, and rained, canceling the event for that year.

> ## 2nd Annual
> ## VILLAGE PICNIC AT MARCELLUS PARK
> ## SATURDAY, SEPTEMBER 17
>
> **The Marcellus Observer - Thursday, September 22, 1938**
> **Rain Prevents Villagers From Holding Annual Frolic**
> Band Plays Farewell To Summer" In Shelter of Village Hall. Hope For Better Weather Next Time.

Reactions To Danger

The weather, however, did not seem to affect international events as the world moved closer to war in 1938. The local editor warned of the growing Hitler menace, who,

260

" . . . unless his demands are met by October first, . . . will march to war. . . . unless the powers of the world toady to him, . . . he will cover over across the railroad tracks and show them. . . . the ego that now has the warlord in its grasp grows stronger. . . . We must have peace. The world wants peace. No one wants to go through what the world went through 20 years ago. So the will of this seeming madman must be appeased. His terms must be met by October first. But will they?" (MO 9/29/38).

While the threat of war continued, that of fire in the Marcellus community had been reduced significantly in the year, from seventeen in 1937 to three in 1938. The fire prevention program launched by the volunteers, which included fire extinguisher recharging and additional promotion during the Halloween carnival that had now become somewhat traditional in the Village, had met with much success.

The Marcellus Observer
Thursday, October 6, 1938
Small Number Of Fires Laid To Prevention Program
Marcellus Holds Number of Local Fire To Three. Makes Record.

The Marcellus Observer
Thursday, October 20, 1938
Firemen To Recharge Extinguishers Free

The Marcellus Observer
Thursday, October 27, 1938
Firemen Ready For Halloween Fair

The Marcellus Observer
Thursday, October 27, 1938
Vote Early

Owing to the many issues to be voted on this year, it is important that as many as can get out early and go to the polls. Polls open at 6 a.m. and voting is normally slow until 10:30. If more voters go between these hours, it would facilitate matters for those who cannot go early. Voters are urged to cooperate by voting as soon after 6 a.m. as possible.

Voting machines are being placed in the bank, at the Corner Store where voters ma go before election and in the polling place at Marietta, stay (sic) and receive any information they desire regarding the machines. Competent instructors will be placed in each of the above locations.

Read the amendments in the daily paper, find out what you want to know about the voting machine and then ---

Vote early.

The Village Board also responded to a danger involving traffic and children going to school. It authorized the moving of a traffic light to the corner of North Street and Reed Parkway for use during school hours. Despite the fact that a 20 mph speed limit is in effect during school hours today, it is still a concern for many parents and Village Police try to maintain a visible presence from 6 a.m. to 3 p.m.

10 Oct 1938 - " . . . the matter of moving the traffic light at Main and Orange Streets to North and Reed Parkway for use during school hour was brought up and the Clerk was instructed

to get in touch with Mr. Benson in regard to the matter."

Elections and Appointments

Residents were urged to vote early in the November elections, taking care that they not only learn about the issues and candidates, but that they also familiarize themselves fully with the new voting machines which had only been in use for a year. Shortly after the election, Arthur W. Wilson, the Town Supervisor, surprised many in the community by resigning that office. Appointed to the office of the District Attorney, Wilson was succeeded by Morris H. Mulroy as Town Supervisor, a position he would hold for a number of years to come.

The Marcellus Observer - Thursday, December 1, 1938
Mulroy Appointed Supervisor As Wilson Gets D.A. Post
Appointment Comes As Surprise To Marcellus.
Mulroy Logical Choice As Successor

Arthur W. Wilson tendered his resignation as Supervisor of the town of Marcellus Monday night following his appointment to the district attorney's office as 6th assistant district attorney.

Mr. Wilson's resignation came as a surprise to the townsfolk and members of the town board. The board immediately appointed Morris H. Mulroy to fill out the unexpired term of Mr. Wilson. Mr. Mulroy opposed Mr. Wilson at the primaries in 1937.

Mr. Wilson was elected to the post of supervisor in 1933, . . . He succeeded W. S. Spaulding, . . . Mr. Wilson has been instrumental in getting many improvements for his town, the foremost being the new Marcellus Park.

The Marcellus Observer
Thursday, December 22, 1938
"Useful Citizen" Contest Closing
The Nominees

Dr. Joseph H. Walsh	Health Officer
John H. Moir	Crown Mills
Horace M. Stone	Attorney
Leroy Guernsey	Pharmacist
William Gray	Furniture Repairs
George Impson	Grocery Clerk
William Kilcoyne	Village Caretaker
Dr. Russell Lowell	Physician

The Marcellus Observer
Thursday, January 19, 1939
"My Hills"
by Mrs. Cora A. Marshfield

These are my hills, o'er them I walk,
Of them I dream, to them I talk.
Within their arms the village lies,
Their tops reach up to the skies.
Spring's tender green, lush summertime,
In beauty clothe these hills of mine.

When Autumn spills her colors bright,
Or winter draws her mantle white,
Their beauty fills my heart with bliss,
There is no beauty quite like this.
I long to stop the hands of time,
So lovely are these hills of mine.

Sometimes I've watched with misted eyes,
Aurora from her bed arise.
Or paused a moment on some crest,
To see the day die in the west,
And known, that from the birth of time,
The calm, majestic hills are mine.

Someday, I shall lie down to rest,
Safe folded 'neath the earth's soft breast,
None shall disturb me where I lie,
I shall not mark the birds that fly.
But I shall keep one thing apart,
A secret, deep within my heart,
Thru winding reels of endless time,
The hills I love shall still be mine.

Most Useful Citizen

The local paper sponsored an interesting contest, entitled "The Most Useful Citizen", in November and December. The nominees, although all were men, seemed to reflect the job diversity that was Marcellus in 1938, including William Kilcoyne, a long-time Village employee. Each year he would erect the Village Christmas tree, a symbol of the peace that all hoped would continue, despite the spectrum of war that loomed large in the world. A Pulitzer Prize winner in 1938 was the play, *Our Town*. Through the innovative voice of the Stage Manager controlling the dialogue, the play by Thornton Wilder analyzed how residents of a small New England village in 1901 lived and died, undisturbed by many of the changes taking place. It was, in some ways representative of many small towns in America, including Marcellus in 1938. The new year, however, would bring changes that would be very unsettling to America and the world.

1939 - A Decisive Year

This was a momentous year for America and the world, the end of a decade, a time when many significant events took place that would forever alter the lives of people even in small town Marcellus. Hard times would start to ease and employment rose, as European nations began to rearm. The United States wanted to remain free of conflict, but its factories would warehouse the world with any needed materials.

Love of Community

In literary circles, many Americans enjoyed the historical novels of Steinbeck and Faulkner while moviegoers thrilled to such motion pictures as *Gone With the Wind*. The people of Marcellus, like all Americans, seemed to be looking to the past for inspiration and to ordinary heroes like Doc Walsh who was the winner of the "Most Useful Citizen" contest that January. Mrs. Cora Marshfield's poem, "My Hills," seemed to reflect a love of community, a permanence, that was quite singular, almost possessive.

The women of the community, like their predecessors, continued to promote civic pride and, in an open letter to the Village Board, urged that a number of projects be undertaken to improve conditions in the village. In addition, the ladies of the D.A.R. sought and received permission from the Board to erect a number of memorial tablets throughout the Village, commemorating the historical events that helped to fashion the community's past. Many of these tablets are still visible today in the Village center.

> **The Marcellus Observer**
> **Thursday, February 2, 1939**
> **Study Club Ladies Advocate Many Village Improvements**
> **Open Letter Sets Forth Program Of Worthwhile Projects**
> At a recent meeting of the Marcellus Study Club, one of the subjects for discussion was Village Improvements. The following were suggested: --
> . . . removal of two or three trees on South Street, which are in dangerous condition.
> Setting trees where several have been cut . . .
> Spraying trees early in the spring . . .
> . . . work done on sidewalks . . .
> . . . sand walks in front of homes . . .
> Setting back of curb . . .
> A parking zone, with lines marked . . .
> Another street light on First and another on Maple Streets
> . . . weeds being cut and burned on vacant lots
> A little park back of the Engine House . . .
> Street along creek to Marcellus Park.
> A street from Main to Bradley.
> Garbage and ash collection.
> Not allow trucks . . . to run through town with cut-outs open . . .

7 Mar 1939 - " . . . application having been made . . . on behalf of . . . General Asa Danforth Chapter, D. A. R., permission to erect certain memorials and tablets in and about the Town of Marcellus, New York, for the purpose of commemorating certain historical events . . . it is hereby resolved that . . . the General Asa Danforth Chapter, D.A.R., be . . . given the right and permission of erecting the following tablets and insignia at the following places . . .

1. First Tavern kept by Deacon Samuel Rice - 1797 - First Church services were held - also first town meeting. (The Catholic Church now stands here).

2. Site of the First Methodist Church (where the Catholic Cemetery now is).

3. First Sawmill owned by Judge Bradley and Deacon Samuel Rice (where the old Stone Mill stood - 1796).

4. Site of the first frame house - 1797 - built by Dr. Elnathan Beach, Revolutionary Soldier, first physician, kept first store, was first Postmaster and first Sheriff. (This stood in the rear at right - west of the establishment where Jones, Uttley & Norris now stands).

5. Old hotel kept by Dr. Bildad Beach - entertained LaFayette in 1824. (Where the Alvord House now is).

6. Home of Major Ruben Humphrey - first county judge. Later the home of Dr. Israel Parsons for over 70 years.

7. First Presbyterian Church - built 1803 - present one built in 1851.

8. Tablet erected by General Asa Danforth Chapter, D. A. R., to 47 Revolutionary soldiers buried in this cemetery.

9. Birthplace of Erminnie Platt Smith - Onondaga County's most famous woman - daughter of Joseph Platt. She was mineralogist, geologist and anthropologist. (Place now owned by Mr. John Moir).

Election Change

When village elections took place on March 21st, a new mayor would replace Michael Thornton who had decided to retire after eight years of service. In one of the largest elections in many years, Leonard Norris was re-elected as Trustee and William S. Spaulding was elected Mayor. Spaulding, who had already served as Marcellus Town Supervisor for ten years (1923-33), was, at the time, President of the First National Bank of Marcellus. He and his wife and family lived on Bradley Street in the Village and his election as Mayor would be repeated in 1941, and again, in 1943. During his terms in

William S. Spaulding
Village Mayor
1939-1945

> The Marcellus Observer
> Thursday, April 6, 1939
> Road Condition Brings
> Wave Of Complaints
> Bad Spot On North Street
> Draws Fire Of Taxpayers.
> Village And County Cannot
> Repair State Property.

office, a number of notable changes would take place in the Village of Marcellus, complimenting the many accomplishments of his predecessor.

21 Mar 1939 - " . . . that the total number of votes cast was 203. . . that William S. Spaulding received 187 votes for the office of Mayor for two years . . . that Leonard Norris received 145 votes for the office of Trustee for two years."

A New Administration

In April, the new administration not only appointed J. F. Woodbridge to another term as Clerk-Treasurer, and approved the new budget but it also heard complaints about the continually deteriorating condition of lower North Street as well as the congestion resulting from private automobiles using the bus stops as parking places. While the latter issue would be quickly addressed " . . . the village board, having designated official bus stops, requested car owners to refrain from using these stops as parking places" (MO, 4/6/39), that of lower North Street would require more time and effort because the road was a state highway, not subject to village nor county maintenance. The road remains a state highway to this day and continues to be a source of discussion between the village and the state over maintenance issues.

Another issue tackled by the new administration was that of daylight savings time. It had been a concern of residents for many years and controversy over it had not been fully resolved. Consequently, a " . . . referendum was decided upon at a special meeting of the village board called by Mayor W. S. Spaulding . . . " (MO 4/27/39), the residents approving the decision overwhelmingly.

3 Apr 1939 - " . . . that J. F. Woodbridge be appointed Clerk and Treasurer for a term of two years, salary to be determined at the next meeting."

14 Apr 1939 - " . . . the budget for the year, 1939, a copy of which is annexed thereto, was duly adopted and a public hearing thereon appointed for May 28th at 7:30 p.m."

27 Apr 1939 - " . . . the ballots on the Daylight Saving referendum were counted with the following results: Total number of votes - 558.   For - 482, Against - 76. It was regularly moved, seconded and carried that Daylight Saving Time be adopted, to become effective at 2:00 o'clock a.m., April 30th."

Alvord House Fire

At the end of April " . . . the Village was turned into turmoil . . . the historic Alvord House was in flames . . . It looked as if the old wooden structure, . . . was . . . doomed to destruction" (MO 4/30/39). The firemen, however, were successful in putting out the fire before permanent damage was sustained and with repairs made, the Alvord House continued to operate as the oldest business in town.

Ash Pickup

One of the reasons for the large turnout of village voters in 1939 appears to have been the desire by many residents for ash and garbage pickup and the Village Board early in its administration would face this issue. Throughout the years, there were those who felt that providing services were not the responsibilities of local government, but individual obligations and many were also concerned about a rise in taxes to cover these expenses. These attitudes, of course, remain very commonplace today. As Marcellus expanded, however, and additional services such as water and sewer came to be assumed by the Village, there were those who thought that garbage collection should be added to this list. At the time most residents burned coal as fuel, the ashes from which had to be collected from the cellar and discarded. Because this was somewhat labor-intensive and could be expensive, the Board solicited bids for the job, one for ashes at the back door and another for ashes taken from the cellar.

1 May 1939 - " . . . the following bids for ashes and garbage removal were received:

Bid	From Back Door	Ashes From Cellars
Melville R. Corp	$1500.00	$1800.00
Eugene Crysler	$1000.00	$1400.00
Francis Rosa	$1850.00	$4150.00
James Wood	$1400.00	$1800.00

. . . that Melville Corp be awarded the contract for removing ashes from the cellars and the garbage from the back doors for one year from May 15, at annual price of $1800."

Traffic, Peddlers, and Worms

With the arrival of spring, an increased amount of traffic apparently threatened the safety of youngsters walking to school on First Street. Consequently, the Village Board authorized the removal of the traffic signal at Main and Orange Streets and its placement at the intersection of First Street and Reed Avenue. School traffic on First Street has, it appears, always been heavy and today, residents still voice their concern. As recent as 2001, the Village Board, reacting to a petition by residents in the area, authorized the establishment of a 25 mph speed limit on First Street in order to protect the many students who walk to school, as well as the children living, on that street.

> **The Marcellus Observer - Thursday, May 18, 1939**
> **Marcellus – On Parade**
> The peddler ordinance has been passed. This is bound to keep a lot more business in town, where it should be kept. Every time you buy a loaf of bread, a magazine or any other product from an unlicensed peddler you are shortening up the business of some merchant.
> Some of the peddlers will get licenses. Others will attempt to bootleg. Still others will work under the guise of taking orders. Housewives are earnestly requested to cooperate with the village authorities, by reporting any peddler without a license. With these out of the way, the legitimate vendor, whether he be local or an outsider, will have a chance to make a living.
> A $25 license fee means only a fraction over 8 cents for each working day. Think of what your local merchant is paying in rent, salaries and other expenses. Yet we only ask the peddler for 8 cents a day. He should pay it.
>
> **The Marcellus Observer - Thursday, May 18, 1939**
> **Village Board Begins Worm Pest Battle**
> **Spraying Completed on All Trees.**
> **Hope For Complete Eradication**

8 May 1939 - " . . . that the traffic signal at the corner of Main and Orange Sts. be moved to the intersection of First Street and Reed Avenue."

Another question, addressed by the Village Board in the spring of 1939, was that of an ordinance regarding peddlers selling their goods within the village limits. This seems to have been a concern of Marcellus businessmen ever since the village was incorporated and the problem became even more serious for them during the depression of the 1930's. Again, the Village Board, following a public hearing, passed a law to regulate itinerant peddlers in an attempt to protect local businesses from outside competitors.

18 May 1939 - " . . . adopted at a meeting of the Board of Trustees of the Village of Marcellus, . . . and the same shall become of full force and effect on the first day of June, 1939, in the following manner, to wit: No persons shall truck, hawk, vend, peddle, solicit orders, or otherwise solicit or sell any goods, wares, merchandise or other commodities excepting meats, fish, fruits and farm produce sold by farmers or other persons producing the same, in any of the streets or public places or by going from house to house in the Village without having obtained a license thereof; the fees for such license shall be as follows: For every foot or pack peddler, $5.00 per day. For peddling from wagon or truck or from a temporary stand, wagon, automobile or truck, $5.00 per day, or $25.00 per year. Any person who shall violate any provisions of this ordinance shall be liable to a penalty of Twenty-five Dollars ($25.00)."

Spring not only brought out the peddlers, but it also hatched the worms that infested Village trees. The Board responded by having " . . . all trees on the village streets . . . thoroughly sprayed, and many homeowners . . . engaged the company to treat trees inside of the curb line" (MO 5/18/39), hoping for a worm free summer.

Memorial Day Color Guard, including Ambrose Welch, George Harkola, David Cooper and Lewis O'Shea

Memorial Day and Old Home Day Plans

While the firemen made plans for a big Marcellus Old Home Day in the summer, "Marcellus observed Memorial Day with one of the village's most colorful parades" (MO 6/1/39). Also, as the school year was coming to an end, the community was reminded of how vulnerable they and their children were to an outbreak of smallpox -- at the time a dreaded fear. No public clinic was thought to be necessary, but Dr. Walsh advised " . . . all adults to be vaccinated by their own family physicians for protection against an epidemic" (MO, 6/8/39).

> **The Marcellus Observer - Thursday, June 8, 1939**
> ### Marcellus Vaccinates 660 Pupils And Teachers
> **Public Clinic Unnecessary At Present Time**
> Vaccinating 660 against small pox, Marcellus Central School officials are confident that the school is fully protected in case an outbreak of occurs in the community. Included in the wholesale immunization were pupils, teachers, and even the janitors at the school . . .

Revival of Old Home Celebration

In an attempt to revive old memories, reunite old friends, as well as celebrate the heritage of the community, the Marcellus firemen early in the year mapped out plans for an Old Home Celebration for the summer of 1939. Scheduled for July 2nd, 3rd and 4th, the committee wanted the event to be one of the biggest affairs in local history. Many, remembering the 1914 celebration with over 10,000 visitors as the most significant, wanted the 25th anniversary of that event to be as memorable and as well-attended. Invitations were sent out to fire departments, drum corps units, fraternal and other organizations, businesses and church groups as well as old time residents, urging their participation. A history booklet, detailing the community's past, was prepared by Henry

Phillips and a number of different events, including a big parade on the 4th of July, planned. It was a great success, attracting thousands of visitors to the biggest celebration in the village since 1914.

The Marcellus Observer
Thursday, July 6, 1939
Celebration Draws 5000 To Marcellus For Holiday
Firemen Have Success In Initial Venture
Torrid Heat Does Not Deter Crowds From Watching Events

Village Business

Business of the Board continued that summer, extending the contract of the Empire Gas and Electric Company for another twenty years in the village. It also listened to suggestions from residents " . . . that the flagpole be moved to the monument point and a cannon be secured and planted in front of the boulder. Would that not be a pretty picture to those entering the village from the east? . . . that it is possible to provide more water for the village by a little expenditure at the reservoir, . . . in case the village grows . . . " (MO 7/27/39). This latter concern was heightened that summer when a water shortage forced the closing of the Crown Mills for a time, and temporary unemployment for its 300 workers, 95% of whom lived in Marcellus.

The Marcellus Observer
Thursday, August 3, 1939
Water Shortage Forces Crown Mills Shut-Down
Merchants Face Serious Loss In Trade
The closing of the Crown Mills Thursday noon, due to the lack of water will, if continued, mean a loss of thousands of dollars each week to Marcellus merchants. The mills are shut down until sufficient water can be obtained with which to operate. . . .

The Marcellus Observer
Thursday, September 14, 1939
North Street To Be Widened And Surfaced
Work on the North Street road project in Marcellus has started. At first it was planned to widen and repave only the lower end of the street, but later developments indicate that the whole street , from the village line to the Pilot-Chevrolet Company garage will be widened.
Word of the change in plans came Wednesday through Mayor W. S. Spaulding, who has been working for some time on the matter. North Street is state property and does not come under the authority or supervision of the village board. The board, however, has brought considerable pressure to bear in the state highway department with the result that the whole street will be improved. This thoroughfare will make a pleasing entrance to the village from the north.

---

10 Jul 1939 - " . . . granted right . . . to the Empire Gas and Electric Co., its successors and assigns, for the term of twenty years, to erect and maintain poles, lines, wires, . . . and to suspend wires, . . . for the purpose of conducting electricity."

By September, the Crown Mills were back in operation and another issue had developed -- what to do with the old village school building on West Main Street. At a meeting of voters on September 1st, "The Paul Construction Company of Syracuse was granted permission to purchase the old school property for $2500 . . . The Paul concern will dismantle part of the building and remodel the remaining portion into an apartment" (MO 9/7/39).

Remodeling also took place on North Street, a road that was in desperate need of repair and a project that required the combined efforts of Mayor Spaulding and Supervisor Mulroy in order to complete it.

War In Europe

While local issues seemed to dominate the news in Marcellus that September, the residents were also shocked with the sudden invasion of Poland by Hitler's armies and the start of what was to become the greatest war in human history. Marcellians, like most Americans in 1939, desperately wanted to stay out of what was thought to be another

European conflict, not realizing how quickly the war would spread and, like a fire out of control, reach America. An interesting parallel likens instructions to the Marcellus Fire Department in 1939 not to answers calls beyond the Town limits without permission, and an attempt to remain forever local.

> **The Marcellus Observer**
> **Thursday, September 7, 1939**
> **This Time, Keep Out!**
> The saddest day for the human race in a quarter century dawned September 1st, when, with bomb-shell suddenness, Hitler abruptly ended the diplomatic exchanges which an anxious world has been following and attacked Poland by land and air and sea, . . . True to their commitments to defend Poland, England and France silenced the doubting cynics by entering into a state of war with Germany. Momentous developments are announced almost hourly. . . .
> That we never again will fight in a European war, no matter how great the blandishments or how alluring the catchwords, and will make war only to protect tour own land from invasion, seems rightly to be our almost unanimous national attitude.

11 Sep 1939 - " . . . the Clerk was instructed to advise the Fire Department not to answer calls to points outside the Town of Marcellus without permission from the Mayor, or, in his absence, a Trustee, and then only when assistance has been asked for by a responsible official of a neighboring community."

Peace At Home

From the headlines a month later, it would appear that all was well with the world and with Marcellus in particular, on the verge of a boom and an ideal place for people to live. Local government continued to operate, calling for a new ordinance and the appointment of inspectors to check all public buildings for fire hazards. Such an inspection, it might be noted, is still completed each year by order of the Village Board. The Board also appointed Doc Walsh to another term as Health Officer and gave

> **The Marcellus Observer**
> **Thursday, October 12, 1939**
> **Marcellus Ready For Growth, Experts Say**
> **Ideal Location Attracts Urban Residents**
> **House Shortage Is Handicap**
> **Many Who Desire Rural Homes Look Toward Marcellus As Desirable Place to Live**

Park Street its name that month.

10 Oct 1939 - " . . . that the ordinance relative to the appointment of a Board of Fire Inspectors, a copy of which is attached hereto, be submitted to a Public Hearing to be held October 23, 1939. . . . Dr. J. H. Walsh was appointed Health Officer for the regular term ending October 22, 1943 . . ."

Supervisor Morris Mulroy

23 Oct 1939 - " . . . the rest of the street running east from South Street through what is known as the Hackford Tract, to the Onondaga County Park, petitioned the Village Board that the street be named Park Street. The petition was granted and the Street so named."

The Township Votes and the Village Decorates

In an "off year" election that November, "Marcellus made a clean sweep for the Republican ticket . . . Supervisor Morris H. Mulroy . . . nominated by the Republicans and endorsed by the Democrats, . . . was sure of election. The popular supervisor got practically all of the votes " (MO 11/9/39).

As the holidays approached, the Village would " . . . show forth the Christmas spirit. Homes . . . decorated, lights . . . ablaze in a riot of color . . . " (MO 12/7/39) and the Village Board appointed two fire marshals, with " . . . authority to enter and inspect all public buildings in the village, . . ." (MO 12/14/39).

11 Dec 1939 - " . . . that Richard V. May and Albert Palen be and hereby are appointed Fire Inspectors under the ordinance adopted October 23rd."

MO Dec 21, 1939

A big tree decorated the village square that December and in the background stands the Marcellus Methodist Church. Earlier that year, the American Methodist Church had reunited after 109 years of division, a Declaration of Union unifying millions of American Methodists. By the end 1939, declarations of war, unfortunately, seemed to be more common.

Conclusion

The 1930s had brought many changes to the community -- the construction of a new central school one of the most noteworthy. The old Main Street school had served the community well, as had the Cherry Street school in the previous century. The decade had also tested the inhabitants of the Village and they responded with the resilience that seems to be native to the community. In the years ahead the new generation, including those graduating from the new school, would have their own fortitude tested -- in the fires of combat overseas.

Chapter 14 – From Depression To War

Those who grew up or lived through the decade will always remember the 1940s as the "war years" and a time when the nation's leaders asked for and received universal sacrifice and undivided loyalty from its citizens. In the community of Marcellus, over 350 young men and women enlisted or were drafted into military service, while their parents planted victory gardens and younger siblings became involved in scrap drives. Ration stamps, war stamps, and bond drives became common, and would remain almost routine until the war was won in 1945. Following on the heels of the Depression, the war was another anxious time for many citizens, but it also seemed to strengthen their character and reinforce their determination once again.

John M. Moir
1876-1971

1940

The year began with the announcement that John M. Moir, in recognition of the hundreds of jobs, which he provided for town residents, was voted the Most Useful Citizen in Marcellus. "The vote was an expression of gratitude to Mr. Moir by the hundreds of employees of the mills and others who saw the far-reaching effects of his contribution to local prosperity" (MO 1/4/40). It might also be mentioned that John Moir was what might be termed the "kingmaker in local politics" in the years before and after World War II. Few individuals ever came to power in the Village of Marcellus without the approval of this man. Because he employed so many in his Crown Mills and because he was involved in so many community activities,

Moir was undoubtedly an influence maker and the "power behind the throne" when important decisions were made in local matters.

Local News

Other local news welcomed the arrival of new buses to service the community and

New Style Cayuga Bus

MO Jan 11, 1940

plans made early in January to fight the scourge of the times, infantile paralysis, " . . . thru the March of Dimes and balls and entertainments to be held in Syracuse and throughout the county . . . to fight this cursed disease . . ." (MO 1/18/40).

By February, fire inspection of public buildings was ready to start and the Village Board made it clear that " . . . private homes do not come under the survey. The inspection takes in business blocks and no home will be entered. Homeowners are asked to do what they can in their own homes to lessen the possibility of fire" (MO 2/15/40). A similar condition exists today in the village, in that single and two family homes are not subject to inspection. Multiple

King Winter Has Last Fling

TAKE A GOOD LOOK for a few months from now you will forget that Main Street, Marcellus, ever looked like this.

MO Feb 22, 1940

dwellings, however, as well as places of public assembly and businesses are inspected each year by the village-appointed codes inspectors. In addition to fire inspectors, the Village Board in 1940 approved fire department membership for men living outside the corporation limits, a step that dramatically improved the ability of the department to fight fires and also gave testimony to the fact that fire and its prevention knows no geographic limits.

23 Feb 1940 - " . . . that the Fire Department be authorized to accept into membership, persons residing within the Town Fire District, but outside of the Village limits, such authorization to be retroactive. The forty-five members of the Department present were then sworn in."

Parking and Park Street

By the end of February, the community was digging out from a series of snowstorms

The Marcellus Observer
Thursday, February 29, 1940
Parked Cars Near Engine House Bring
Complaints From Firemen
Crash Narrowly Averted As Truck Swerves
Out of Fire Barn

The Marcellus Observer
Thursday, March 7, 1940
Local Readers Suggest Name For New
Street
Street Leading To Park Should Be Labeled
"Park Street"

that closed schools, snarled traffic, crushed barns and dampened local business. The weather was also a problem for the firemen trying to respond to local emergencies but an even greater concern was the number of cars that parked in front of or near the engine house. Almost in spite of "no parking" signs, drivers continued to leave their cars unattended for great lengths of time, a parking situation that remains somewhat confounding to this day. A situation that was corrected however was that at the village reservoir, the New York State Department of Health recommending purchase of additional land and fencing to protect the public water supply and its watershed. Another entrance into Marcellus Park was also being considered and one resident suggested that the name for this new street should be "Park Street." The Village Board eventually adopted the name but the road is not used as an entrance to the Park by automobiles today and is actually a dead-end for vehicular traffic.

16 Mar 1940 - " . . . communication from the New York State Department of Health regarding the public water supply serving the Village of Marcellus recommending that the Village purchase or obtain control of the side of the hill between the Chapman barn and the reservoir so that manure from the barn can be stored on the slope away from the reservoir . . . glad to note the construction of fencing along the south side and part of the east end of the reservoir so that there now remains only a small section along the north side of the swampy area to be completed. It was noted that the fence along the road had apparently been damaged and . . . that necessary repairs be made . . . that the water was of satisfactory sanitary condition at the time the sample was taken."

Records Preserved

Following the re-election of Stephen Hunt as Trustee, one of the first orders of business for the new Village Board was to react to a letter from the State Education Department regarding the preservation of public records. Known as the Public Records Law, this state mandate calls for the proper care of public records in fire-resistant rooms or safes and allows for the disposal of records only after a careful analysis and documentation has been made using its very strict guidelines. Updated throughout the years, the Public Records Law remains a primary responsibility of the Village Board and its Village Clerk. Other responsibilities for the new Board that April included the re-appointment of William Kilcoyne as " Mr. Everything" for the Village and the re-enactment of daylight savings time, the latter a controversial decision once again in 1940.

19 Mar 1940 - " . . . that the total number of votes cast was ten. For Stephen H. Hunt, Trustee for two years, ten."

1 Apr 1940 - " . . . communication from the New York State Education Department, Division of Archives and History regarding the proper care and preservation of the public records filed in the office of the Village Clerk is one of the primary responsibilities of that office. Such responsibility, however, is shared by the members of the Village Board of Trustees . . . "

8 Apr 1940 - " . . . that William Kilcoyne be paid $100 per month as Street Commissioner and $20 per month as policeman, said police duties subject to discontinuance during the winter months . . . whereas the referendum held April 27, 1939 indicated that a large majority favored the Daylight Savings Time and its adoption during the summer of 1939 met with general approval, now, therefore, be it resolved that Daylight Saving Time shall be the official time for the Village of Marcellus, from 2:00 o'clock a.m. on the last Sunday in April until 2:00 o'clock a.m. on the last Sunday in September of each year until such time as this resolution may be revoked or amended."

> The Marcellus Observer
> Thursday, April 18, 1940
> Parking Of Cars Over Curb Lines Stirs
> Ire of Merchants; Demand Seen For
> Widening of Main Street

M. & O.L. and Main Street

That spring brought about the further dismemberment of the M. & O.L. Railroad, as officials of that company, claiming that there was not enough business to keep operating, filed papers with the Interstate Commerce Commission to abandon the road from Marcellus to Otisco Lake, a distance of almost 7 miles. "If the road is cut to the desired 2.84 miles, it will probably be the country's shortest railroad" (MO 4/11/40).

As the railroad was being dismantled, the automobile was stirring controversy on Main Street, with drivers parking their cars wherever they could find room, including far over the curb line, even on to the sidewalks. Parking in the Village was a problem that the

Ray Haney, John Rogers, George Harcola, William Richards, Robert Muldoon

Board would have to address, but the response only seemed to be temporary and it remains a concern for the Board today.

The Marcellus Observer
Thurs, May 2, 1940
A Village Flower!
What .Do You Think?

Poppy Reminder

As in previous years, there was talk about a village flower and the local paper again encouraged letters on the subject. With the arrival of May and the annual Memorial Day parade, the poppies sold by the American Legion seemed to be the choice of many that spring. The poppies not only reminded the community of sacrifices made in the past but also caused many to wonder about the future -- if America could stay out of the war that had by now engulfed much of the world.

The Marcellus Observer
Thursday, May 2, 1940
Fresh Air Children To Arrive
July 16

The Marcellus Observer, June 6, 1940

The Marcellus Observer, June 27, 1940

School's Out

June saw summer vacation and trips to the old swimming hole as well as the work of the Fresh Air Children committee for Marcellus, " . . . getting homes for as many tenement children as possible . . . into the country . . . to give them brief respite from the sultry pavements and treeless surroundings" (MO 6/6/40). It was a peaceful summer for most young people in 1940, many of whom would soon be diving into foxholes or flying fighter planes. The vitality of the community, however, was well depicted by the "Spirit of Marcellus" as residents of the Village and Town prepared to welcome back visitors for the annual Old Home Day celebration in July. "No stone has been left unturned in making this a grand occasion. Even the weather has been taken care of. The committee has actually taken out insurance . . . If it rains, the insurance company will reimburse the firemen for losses incurred by an untimely visit of Junius Pluv . . ." (MO 7/4/40).

Bus Garage, Sidewalks and Second Street

That summer also marked school board consideration and then approval of a proposition to build a bus garage on the Marcellus Central School campus while the Village Board set about to improve village sidewalks, replacing those made of slate and stone with new concrete. The Board also received an offer from Lloyd and Ruth Cummings to dedicate a portion of the Reed tract for a new street to be named Second Street. In addition, the Trustees continued to receive complaints, particularly from merchants, about the parking on Main Street.

The Marcellus Observer - Thursday, July 11, 1940
New Bus Garbage Decided upon At Meeting Tuesday

Voters of Marcellus Central School District . . . elected to erect a bus garage on the school property at a cost not to exceed $22,000. The meeting also voted to purchase four buses, . . .

The bus garage will be erected on the school property, between the school building and North St. The building will be one story high and will be built so that the top of the roof will be slightly below the elevation of North St. Thus, the building will in no way cut off the view of the school, nor be conspicuous in any manner. The garage will be 70 by 74 feet and will have space for 12 busses, an office and storeroom. A trained mechanic will be engaged to take charge of the plant . . .

The Marcellus Observer - Thursday, July 25, 1940
New Sidewalks For Main Street

Take a good look at those slippery, uneven slate and stone sidewalks which have been one of the no-so-nice things about Marcellus for many years. Take a good look at them so that you will remember their faults and appreciate the new concrete walks that Irv Christensen and his men are now laying.

The project is a part of an extended program by which Marcellus plans to improve the walks all over the village. Each year a certain sum of money will be spent for this purpose.

At the present time the walks along both sides of Main Street from the North Street corner to the Orange Street corner are being put in. . . .

The Marcellus Observer - Thursday, August 15, 1940
Business Hurt By Parking, Say Marcellus Merchants

Considerable dissatisfaction is found among Main Street merchants this week regarding the parking conditions in that area during rush hours, . . . business is seriously handicapped at times because of customers' inability to find parking space . . .

The Marcellus Observer - Thursday, September 12, 1940
"Second St." Is Now On Village Map

. . . one block above First St. . . . The new street is in the fastest growing section of the village and fills a need for village expansion. New homes are springing up in and around Reed Parkway and Second Street is a welcome addition . . .

---

12 Aug 1940 - " . . . the Board . . . accept the offer of Lloyd Cummings and Ruth R. Cummings to dedicate to the Village of Marcellus the portion of Second Street described . . .''

War's Effects

By September, the war in Europe was becoming quite desperate for Britain and its Allies. Hitler's forces had overrun most of Western Europe and launched a battle against Britain, standing alone against the forces of Nazism. President Roosevelt authorized the Destroyers For Bases Agreement with Britain, and Congress passed the Selective Service Act, the first peacetime draft in the nation's history, requiring all men between the ages of 20 and 36 to register.

Back home in Marcellus, a local group of women met to organize a "Bundles for Britain" society. "The work . . . all voluntary and . . . for the benefit of the English soldiers who are badly in need of warm sweaters, socks, etc. . . . to help the brave English people who are going through so much to uphold their ideals and save their country from ruin" (MO 9/19/40). In addition a local draft board was named, including Horace M.

**The Marcellus Observer
Thursday, September 19, 1940
"Bundles For Britain" Aim Of Local Group**

**The Marcellus Observer
Thursday, September 26, 1940
Local Draft Board Named**

**The Marcellus Observer
Thursday, October 17, 1940
First To Register For Draft**

To Jimmy Quinn of Reed St. goes the proud distinction of having been the first to register for the draft.

Jimmy, a Mottville boy by birth, but a Marcellian by adoption, hustled to the registration office at the crack of dawn and was the first of some 126 young men to make himself available for the service of Uncle Sam.

**The Marcellus Observer
Thursday, October 31, 1940
Local Boys Are Drawn In Draft**

The first of the local boys in Marcellus to be drawn for service in the draft included Dwight Ramsden, Donald Leon Wilson, Robert Dunbar Falkner and Gordan William Hickman . . .

THIRD TERMITES AT WORK

The Marcellus Observer, October 3, 1940

Stone of Marcellus, " . . . six prominent men in the community embracing the Towns of Marcellus, Camillus, Elbridge, Skaneateles and Van Buren, . . . the names of representative citizens to serve on draft board. . . for this vicinity . . . " (MO 9/26/40). Responding to the new law, the young men of the community registered, including Jim Quinn of Reed Street who was first to sign up in Marcellus.

Election

The war also led President Roosevelt to run for an unprecedented 3rd term in November and many in Republican Marcellus, as well as throughout the country, viewed this as a blatant grab for power by FDR, and contrary to precedents set by his predecessors. In spite of a strong challenge by Wendell Willkie, however, FDR was elected to a third term, the people realizing that he was indispensable at the time. What was also important to the voters that November was a plan to create a County Manager plan of government for Onondaga County and the towns were virtually unanimous in their opposition to it. To many in the rural areas, it smacked of another attempt at centralization of power and resentment that people were not able to govern themselves. It would be defeated in that vote and another 20 years would pass before the electorate would approve the reorganization of county government.

Year's End

For people in the community, the events taking place throughout the nation and world were significant in 1940, but so too were those issues which affected normal lives, such as when to put out the garbage, or should the house be decorated for Christmas that year. Neither the pigeons in the Presbyterian Church steeple nor the commendation of the Village Board by the State Comptroller made national headlines that November, but they were important news items locally. The ornamental lights that the Board decided to install in the village center was equally significant. And when the Board ordered the firemen not to go out of town to answer a fire that December, its concern was not only protection for the town, but also an attempt to remain local, detached from that beyond its borders. This isolation would not last.

274

The Marcellus Observer - Thursday, November 7, 1940
Notice - Ash and Garbage Collection

This will be (as near as possible) the winter schedule for ash and garbage collection:
Mondays garbage
Tuesdays   South, Park, Bradley, and West Main
Wednesdays   First, Reed, Orange and East Main.
Thursdays   School, Chrisler and part of North Street from Main to Nine Mile Creek.
Fridays   Scotch hill and Orchard Road.
No ashes will be collected unless in regulation containers (1 bu. metal baskets). When there is snow, paths and outside doorway to cellar must be cleared or no collections will be made.
M. R. Corp

The Marcellus Observer - Thursday, December 12, 1940
Village To Put Up Ornamental Christmas Lights

The Marcellus Observer - Thursday, December 26, 1940
Firemen Not To Go Out Of Town

NOW THAT HE IS HERE, WHAT ARE YOU GOING TO DO WITH HIM?

The Marcellus Observer, Dec 26, 1940

The Marcellus Observer
Thursday, January 16, 1941
Mayor W. S. Spaulding Voted Most Useful Citizen

The Marcellus Observer
Thursday, January 23, 1941
Marcellus Ready To Show Growth

The Marcellus Observer
Thursday, January 23, 1941
Local People Asked To Contribute Guns To British

The Marcellus Observer
Thursday, February 6, 1941
Owners Warned Of Dog Ordinance

1941

With the arrival of 1941, a critical year in our nation's history, many, like the woman depicted in the cartoon by Glen Fellows, agreed with the caption. It was a new year in Marcellus, but there was wonder about what it would bring, other than icy roads, " . . . a serious dampener to the celebration . . . that covered all roads after midnight" (MO 1/2/41).

Parking continued to annoy Main Street merchants, but many agreed that " . . . Marcellus is hardly large enough, nor the problem of sufficient gravity, to make limited parking necessary" (MO 1/2/41). It was, however, an issue that the Village Board would address that summer.

Most Useful Citizen

The head of that board, Mayor William Spaulding, was voted the Most Useful Citizen at the beginning of the year in a poll conducted by the local paper. A popular man with the people, " . . . acquainted with everybody . . . He knows Marcellus as few other men know it. He knows its needs and . . . its faults, and is correcting both as fast as he can. He goes about without fanfare, but his accomplishments for his home village are those of a permanent nature . . . " (MO 1/16/41). The paper also noted that Marcellus was " . . . destined to become a greater village than at present . . . evidenced by the demand for homes made by people now living in the cities . . . improvements of the last few years, and the new faces now seen on our streets and in our stores and churches is an indication of still further growth in the future" (MO 1/23/41).

The War, Dogs and the School

The war was still very much on people's minds, as residents were asked to contribute surplus weapons to the British and Marcellus women " . . .interested in sewing for the Red Cross and Bundles for Britain met . . . This sewing club . . . but one of several in Marcellus which are working faithfully for this splendid cause" (MO 2/6/41).

While some complaints were made about village dogs running loose at night and disturbing the peace, others lamented the demolishing of the old Marcellus School on West Main Street. To many it looked as if their alma mater had been struck by a bomb, a reminder, perhaps, of the on-going war in Europe.

The Pond and Elections

In February, the Village Board received notice from the State that improvements were needed at the village reservoir, and during the summer construction months, fencing and other protection would be installed.

25 Feb 1941 - " . . . communication from the New York State Department of Health regarding the public water supply serving the Village of Marcellus . . . by the proper maintenance of the drainage ditch along the north side of the reservoir, reasonable protection can be furnished and protection against improper use of the adjacent slope can be attained . . . at the time of the inspection, the fence along the road is not particularly good. It would be most desirable to enclose all the property by a man-proof, closely woven type fence . . . recommend that at an early date you give serious consideration to starting such a project by replacing the fence along the road with the idea of eventually enclosing the entire property with a more protective fence."

Mayor Spaulding and Trustee Norris were each renominated for an term and following the March 18th election, the Board reappointed James Woodbridge as Clerk-Treasurer and conducted the annual public hearing on the 1941 budget.

18 Mar 1941 - " . . . total number of ballots cast - 13. For William S. Spaulding, Mayor for two years - 13. For Leonard Norris, Trustee for two years - 13."

7 Apr 1941 - " . . . that J. F. Woodbridge be appointed Clerk and Treasurer for a term of two years, at a salary of $600.00 per year."

The Marcellus Observer
Thursday, March 6, 1941
Club Wants Local Houses Numbered
The members of the Citizens Club of Marcellus, realizing that it is a distinctive disadvantage to our town not to be able to readily locate its residents, have voted their approval and requested the Village Officers to take in consideration having all of the houses in the Village numbered. This would be a step in the right direction to improve our village and will make it much more convenient for the people to locate residents here.

---

28 Apr 1941 - " . . . public hearing on the proposed budget for 1941 was held, Monday evening . . ."

House Numbers and Taxes

The Board also responded favorably to a proposal from the Citizens Club of Marcellus made earlier in the year about having houses in the Village numbered, although it was not as simple as the Club seemed to make it appear. Today's home mail delivery would not be possible without such numbering and, with the advent of the 911 emergency system in recent years, the numbering of houses seems to have become even more essential.

As usual, there were complaints from taxpayers, and following a letter from one resident in the spring of 1941, the Board agreed to adjust that person's water rate. Today this policy is still common with the Board, which often receives requests for rate adjustments. These changes are usually granted when unusual conditions warrant such consideration.

12 May 1941 - " . . . enclosed find costs to cover water taxes to January 1, 1941, except the one for . . . $47.63. I'm not paying this for two reasons:
> I. Lack of funds
> II. Sincerely hoping your Board or you can pare this quite a lot.

Why? It was largely built up last winter when, on account of drought, we had to use a lot of water in the barn up to Feb. We not only had to use some, we had to waste quite a bit in order not to freeze. Since this did us no good and you no harm, I hope you may pare it down a lot. We really don't make any other heavy demands on (the) Village
> I. No gutters to clean
> II. No sidewalks to clean
> III. No ashes to collect

12 May 1941 - " . . . that the water rates for the winter of 1939-40 on the R. W. Stone property be adjusted by deducting $10.00 . . . to allow for water used to keep the pipes from freezing."

Old Home Celebration

Memorial Day again attracted a large crowd to Marcellus and during the July celebration, the old timers were welcomed home, a home that had witnessed much change for those who had not visited in several years.

PROGRAM

MARCELLUS OLD HOME CELEBRATION

Thursday, July 3rd.

7:00 — Siren to blow announcing opening of Celebration
"TO THE COLORS" BLOWN AND FLAG LOWERED FROM LIBERTY POLE
AMATEUR BOXING BOUTS
Held Near Liberty Pole   Refereed by "Babe" Risko
9:00 — DANCE IN ST. FRANCIS HALL

Friday, July 4th.

12:30 — Siren to blow starting parade
1:30 MUSICAL EXHIBITION IN MAIN STREET
With the following Drum Corps participating: Post 41 American Legion, Sons of American Legion Post 41, Valentine Myer Post 311, Jewish War Veterans
BAND CONCERT
On the Bank lawn — Marcellus Central School Band
3:30 — FIREMANIC SPORTS IN MAIN STREET
5:00 — FIVE MILE FOOT RACE
Between John L. Sullivan, Marcellus, and Percy Smoke, Onondaga Reservation
7:00 — WATER FIGHT: Mattydale vs. Mottville

LINE OF MARCH
Parade forms on Reed Parkway. From Reed Parkway to North Street; left on to Maple Street; right to Orange Street; right on to Main Street; left on to South Street to Green Lantern. Counter march to Main Street, right. Marching units will proceed down to the flag pole where the colors and drum corps will be massed, after which the corps will put on an exhibition.

Again, The War

In the midst of celebration, there were again reminders of the war overseas. The "Home Fires Club" was organized by The Marcellus Observer, the purpose of which was to have members " . . . write letters to the boys away from home . . . Local residents urged to send in the names of boys . . . in camp . . . to keep the boys from becoming homesick while they are in the employ of Uncle Sam" (MO 7/3/41). Another reminder was the Marcellus USO Committee, headed by Fred Hyatt, which, together with the Community War Needs Fund, collected " . . . money to take care of any emergency that might come along . . . doled out to worthy causes that have been brought about by the War in Europe" (MO 7/17/41).

> The Marcellus Observer
> Thursday, July 3, 1941
> "Home Fires" Club Open To Everyone
>
> The Marcellus Observer
> Thursday, July 17, 1941
> Big USO Drive To Start In Marcellus Monday

Summer Projects

The summer was also busy for the Village Board, which provided every house in the village with a new number. It also approved new steel fencing for the reservoir, protecting the Village water supply and in answer to an earlier complaint from the State Department of Health. There was, however, another " . . . complaint against the local water . . . from the housewife who does her own washing. The water is hard and much more soap is necessary than if it were softer" (MO 7/17/41). This latter grievance remains a source of contention today and there are many residents who would willingly exchange Village water for that at Otisco Lake, provided by OCWA (Onondaga County Water Authority). In the years to come, this may actually happen because maintaining the reservoir will become too expensive an operation for the Village to continue. New mandates by the State of New York, such as a filtration plant, may force the Village to seek alternatives for its public water, such as OCWA.

In addition, the Board attempted that summer to solve the traffic and parking problem in the village by having the curb on the south side of Main Street removed, allowing cars to park further and widening the highway about ten feet. Doing the same on the north side of Main Street was thought to be too expensive especially for the utility companies that would find it necessary to remove poles and overhead wires. In contrast, today's Village Board believes that curbing is not only essential for traffic safety on Main Street, but also serves to delineate parking as well as to beautify the village center.

Perhaps the most ambitious proposal

> The Marcellus Observer
> Thursday, July 17, 1941
> House Numbers On This Week
>
> The Marcellus Observer
> Thursday, July 17, 1941
> New Fence At Village Reservoir
>
> The Marcellus Observer
> Thursday, July 24, 1941
> Workmen Remove Curb In Main St.
> Widening Project
>
> The local street-widening project, which is expected to alleviate the present traffic problem in the center of the village, began this week with the removal of the curb along the south side of Main Street in front of the stores.
>
> The removal of the curb and the subsequent paving of the extension will make it possible for cars to park ten feet further in towards the sidewalks. This will leave just that much more room for passing cars. It is thought that the plan will go far towards solving the traffic question in Marcellus.
>
> The Marcellus Observer
> Thursday, August 7, 1941
> Zoning Ordinance Is Proposed
> Protection For Property Owners Seen In New Zoning Plan
> Committee Appointed
> Ordinance Will Also Regulate Build of Gas Stations and Business Blocks

that summer was a zoning ordinance that called for the appointment of a committee that would be responsible for a review of all new construction to determine whether or not it was in keeping with the type of buildings already in that area. The proposed law was controversial and following its passage would lead to the creation of a zoning map, clearly defining residential, industrial and business districts in the village

4 Aug 1941 " . . . Resolved that Edward V. Baker, N. Giles Case and Clifford W. Dorchester, all of the incorporated Village of Marcellus . . . be and hereby are appointed . . . as, or and to be a Commission, to be known as the Zoning Commission of the incorporated Village of Marcellus . . . to recommend the boundaries of the original zoning districts to be formed in said Village of Marcellus and appropriate regulations to be enforced therein and to make a preliminary report and to hold public hearings thereon . . . "

As the summer wound down, so too did much of the construction and other activity in the Village. New sidewalks were laid on the south side of Main Street and villagers were requested by the Board " . . . to cut the weeds in the vacant spaces in the village. The weeds . . . not only an aggravation to sufferers from hay fever and asthma, but . . . a fire menace as well" (MO 8/14/41). The Fire Department, using funds earned from the Old Home Celebration, purchased an oxygen inhalator, to help keep the department modernized. By mid September, the main street project was completed and some suggested that the area be beautified by having the old horse trough, which used to stand on the corner of Main and North Streets, be located, set up somewhere in the village and filled with flowers. Apparently the trough could not be located in 1941, but today, the Garden Club of Marcellus provides a wonderful service, filling the village flower boxes each spring with colorful arrangements that do much to "make the valley village beautiful," as one of its former Presidents, Debbie Kelley, used to say.

The Marcellus Observer
Thursday, Sept. 18, 1941
People Asked To Register For Defense

The Marcellus Observer
Thursday, Oct. 23, 1941
"Loan Closet" For Use Of Community
. . . The articles needed to make up the closet are donated or loaned by anyone having them. So that it may be known what to give, the following list will give some idea: wheel chair, crutches, back rest, invalid table, bed pans, hot water bottles, ice bags, sheets, pillow cases, rubber sheeting and any other things which might be useful in cases of sickness . . .

The Marcellus Observer
Thursday, November 6, 1941
Former Marcellus Barber Elected Mayor Of Syracuse

Civil Defense and A Loan Closet

September also saw the registration of people in Marcellus for Civilian Defense, a registration requested by the President so that the nation might be prepared for any eventually. It called for all men and women, with no age limit, to sign up, " . . . to state their abilities . . . and state other activities in which they might be of use in time of emergency" (MO 9/18/41). In addition to this preparation, a health center was established in Marcellus, part of which was to include a loan closet for those who might need particular items in time of illness, a loan closet still in operating sixty years later.

Halloween and Elections

The firemen again sponsored a major carnival for the children of the Village at the end of October and in November, Republicans were again victorious in Town elections. Supervisor Morris Mulroy was cross endorsed by Democrats and Republicans in Marcellus, a tribute not only to his popularity and ability but also another example, perhaps, of the desire of many not to change leadership in troubled times. Another interesting election in 1941 was that of Thomas Kennedy, a former Marcellian, as Mayor of the City of Syracuse, " . . . one of its boys who, like a hero from one of Horatio Alger's books, made good in the big city" (MO 11/6/41).

The Marcellus Observer
Thursday, Dec. 11, 1941
Local Boys In Dangerous War Zone

At least four Marcellus boys are facing the guns and bombs in Hawaii and the Philippines, . . . The lads known to be in the dangerous war zone at present are: Pvt. Stedman Bird, Pvt. William Nightingale, Staff Sgt. John Hainey and Pvt. Louis Macholl. No word has been received concerning any of these boys and no local names have appeared on the first casualty list sent to Washington and published in the daily papers . . .

The Marcellus Observer
Thursday, Dec. 25, 1941
Inquiring Reporter
When Will The War End?

Frank Griffing: In the winter of 1943. It will take a year to lick them. I don't think that Germany can stand another winter.

John Wilson, Salesman: The war will end after the first personal defeat of Hitler as head of the German Army. The U-boat campaign now being waged by the U. S. will also hasten the end.

Harry Burns: In about 2 years. With Japan depending upon the countries she fighting for 80% of her raw materials, it is hard to see how it could last longer than that. . . .

Louis Nightingale: The trouble will continue for 5 years before the countries will be entirely subdued. The fighting may stop before that time, but real peace will not be attained under five years.

WAR!

When the Thursday edition of *The Marcellus Observer* was published and distributed on December 4, 1941, things seemed quite normal in the community. The editor commented that " . . . traffic and parking conditions on Main Street, Marcellus, are improved more than the most optimistic expectation . . . a remarkable change for the better . . . the residents . . . asked to decorate their homes and to help make the village beautiful with Christmas greens and lights . . ." (MO 12/4/41). The following Sunday, however, was anything but normal. Early in the morning of December 7, 1941, the United States was attacked by Japan at Pearl Harbor and the peace that Americans had so desperately craved was shattered. For the people of Marcellus, thousands of miles away from the attack, the concern was very real because some local men were known to have been stationed in the war zone. Things had changed, and so too had priorities. Christmas decorations would not be as common in 1941, as in the past. Local government continued to operate, urging drivers to keep their cars parked off the streets so that plows could clear

them of snow, and again ordered the firemen not to take fire equipment out of town without permission.

8 Dec 1941 - " . . . that the Village Clerk notify the Fire Department that the fire apparatus is not to be taken outside the limits of the Town of Marcellus . . . "

The community also participated in a county-wide blackout in December, a practice that was conducted throughout New York State on December 21st, just two weeks after Pearl Harbor. While that Sunday was the shortest day of the year in 1941, for a number of Marcellus parents, like Mr. Mrs. Harold Nightingale, the days and nights must have been quite long, having received word two days later that their son, William, had been wounded in defense of the Philippines. Their anxiety and that of many others would continue "for the duration," a phrase becoming more commonly used to indicate how long the war would last. That, no one knew.

1942

Throughout 1942, Village Board Meetings were held, but there seemed to be few items of great concern. There was the appointment of residents to a variety of posts and committees, but World War II, fighting it and winning it, occupied the attention of most people, and the Village board minutes primarily reflected the auditing and paying of

Zoning

ORDINANCE

Effective February 1, 1942

●

Village of Marcellus

Onondaga County

New York

municipal bills. One item, early in the year did garner some minutes and discussion and that was a public hearing on the proposed zoning ordinance. Such concerns as the slaughter house on First Street, bowling alleys and pool halls in the Village center, as well as set backs, building permits and the establishment of industrial, business and residential districts in the village were discussed before final adoption at the end of the month. Zoning in the village has been amended since it was first adopted in 1942, but the basic framework remains in place, enforced by the Clerk-Treasurer as well as a codes officer who serve as the Board's representatives.

12 Jan 1942 - " . . . in compliance with the request of William Robinson, Zone Coordinator, William Kilcoyne was appointed to represent the Village on the Mutual Aid Plan . . . Mrs. Adelaide J. Uttley be and is hereby appointed Registrar of Vital Statistics for the term ending December 31, 1945."

19 Jan 1942 - " . . . Public Hearing on the proposed zoning ordinance . . . discussed the question of the slaughter house on First Street . . . the question of Bowling Alleys and Pool Rooms coming under the Residential use district. Also . . . discussed the set back lines as contained in Sec. 3 of Article 4 which provides that the side yard shall be of a width of not less than twelve feet."

21 Jan 1942 - " . . . that the Zoning Ordinance hereto attached be and hereby is duly adopted and the same shall become effective, February 1st . . . the appointment of Vincent Dillon, Leonard Annabel, Edward O'Hara, Kenneth King, Jacob Schneider and Clarence Coon as Fire Police by the Fire Department was duly confirmed by the Board."

MO Jan 29, 1942

The Home Front

Following Pearl Harbor, the nation began to mobilize for war. Not only was there a need for fighting men but also a demand for war materials and the community responded to the request for scrap metals by turning in old license plates, some " . . . dating back to 1917 and 1918, the days of the last war" (MO 1/15/42). The community was also reminded of the young men who enlisted or were drafted into the armed service by a Roll of Honor, the publication of which in *The Marcellus Observer* was regularly updated throughout the war years. The Village Board also found it useful, during these uneasy times, to appoint six men as fire police, whose duties would " . . . consist mainly of directing traffic within the village before the truck leaves and at the scene of the fire, and protect property of both the fire department and the home owner" (MO 1/29/42).

As the federal government amended the Selective Training and Service Act, requiring all men between the ages of 20 and 45 to register, people at home were encouraged to do their part in the war against the Axis powers, particularly by buying war stamps. By March, a committee was" . . . appointed to promote the sale of Defense Bonds and Stamps in the Town of Marcellus, and parts of Onondaga and Otisco . . . hope that every person receiving a monthly or weekly income . . . invest a portion of that income in Bonds or Stamps" (MO 3/12/42). Not only was this an attempt by the government to curb inflation and prevent civilian spending, but an inducement to save for needed purchases after the war.

With the melting snows of March, " . . . flooding waters from Nine Mile Creek went on a rampage . . . causing considerable inconvenience if not property damage . . . tearing out driveways and washing down the gutters . . . " (MO 3/12/42). Marcellians flocked to see the 1941 academy award picture, "How Green Was My Valley," and they may also have wondered, How wet? Another washout a week later on Election Day rushed " . . . down the hills both from the east and the west, the water stopped in the middle of the village" (MO 3/19/42), one reason, perhaps, for the very low voter turnout that reelected Stephen Hunt as Trustee.

17 Mar 1942 - " . . . ten ballots were cast, of which Stephen H. Hunt, received 9 . . . blank - 1"

The Draft, The Farm, The School, The Village

Election day was also the start of the third draft ordered by Washington and the first number in the area drawn in the lottery was that of Robert Gallinger, the son of the paper's editor, who was soon joined by hundreds of other young men. As the spring snows continued to melt, farmers in the area were urged to gather up scrap metal for the war effort. The director of salvage for the county commented that " . . . the scrap iron and steel on American farms would make 139 battleships. From the scrap on Onondaga county farms alone could be made 2,000 tanks or 20,000 bombs. The events of 1942 will decide who will win the war" (MO 3/26/42). The school became very involved in the war effort, promoting the sale of bonds and stamp sales and as the Marcellus community conducted another successful blackout test in early April, it joined with several other villages in a county-wide cleanup week to collect old metal for the war effort. The Board's appointment of Lester Norris as Fire Chief also assured an orderly transition of power from Albert Palen.

> **The Marcellus Observer**
> **Thursday, April 2, 1942**
> **Marcellus Central Does Grand Job In Bond And Stamp Sales**
> A total of $4,876.78 in bonds and stamps is chalked up for Marcellus Central School, according to a report made this week by Principal Chester S. Driver of the school.

> **The Marcellus Observer**
> **Thursday, April 2, 1942**
> **Blackout Is Success Here**
> Marcellus' second test blackout of last Thursday night was pronounced almost 100% successful . . .

> **SELL THAT SCRAP!**
> **Old Metal Will Be Collected The Week of April 13**
>
> **Fourth Registration**
> **New York State Selective Service**
> All male citizens of the United States and other male persons who were born on or after April 28, 1877, and on or before February 16, 1897, are required to register with Selective Service . . .

13 Apr 1942 - " . . . Fire Department submitted the following list of officers duly elected at its annual meeting. Chief - Lester C. Norris, 1st Asst. Chief - Roy Bennett, 2nd Asst. Chief - Harold Freeborn. These officers were approved by the Village Board."

By the end of April, a third blackout and practice air raid in the Village was planned as was a fourth registration for the draft, at the Village Hall, this time for those men in the 45-65 age bracket. This registration was " . . . as important to the government as was the registration of the younger men. There are thousands of men in this age bracket experienced in trades vital to the successful culmination of the war" (MO 4/23/42). In the end, almost 300 men in this age category registered at the village Hall, " . . . some still had their registration cards from the last war" (MO 4/30/42).

The Marcellus Observer
Thursday, April 30, 1942
Householders Must Sign Sugar Ration Cards At School Starting May 4th

---

The Marcellus Observer
Thursday, June 18, 1942
Sugar Rationing Applications Now Available in Town

The Marcellus Observer
Thursday, June 18, 1942
Marcellus Residents Add 500 Pounds Of Scrap Rubber To Nation's Stockpile

The Marcellus Observer
Thursday, July 2, 1942
Town Preps For Old Home Celebration

Victory!!

MO September 17, 1942

More Rationing, Scrap Drives

Beginning in May, the rationing of sugar began, and with it " . . . the biggest registration job ever undertaken in so limited a time in the United States. Within four days, the Nation's 130,000,000 men, women and children . . . registered . . . " (MO 4/30/42) so that they could receive ration books based on the size of the family unit. By the time the first registration was completed on May 7th, almost 4,000 people had been registered in the Marcellus community and this was followed by another registration at the Engine House in June. By that time, rubber was in short supply and that item was now added to the nation's scrap drive. The Boy Scouts were instrumental in collecting hundreds of pounds of surplus rubber, including " . . . a preponderance of tires, along with a good supply of garden hose, old boots, shoes, raincoats, rubber balls, jar rubbers, rubber toys, tubes and many other articles . . . " (MO 6/18/42).

Recruiting, Planning

In addition to this drive, the County Civilian Defense asked the village to recruit at least 30 additional firemen in case of emergency . . . not . . . active firemen nor air raid wardens, . . . the auxiliary force . . . brought into play only in case of an emergency such as a bombing or a fire of an unusually serious nature" (MO 7/2/42). As this was being done, the Marcellus Firemen prepared for the Old Home Celebration in July, an event that would feature a decidedly patriotic theme that year.

It was decided to call off the Six-Town Picnic that August, the first such cancellation in 57 years, " . . . fear that the shortage of fuel and tires would preclude any large attendance . . . " (MO 8/6/42). Plans were made, however for creating a casualty and first aid station in Marcellus and meetings were held at the Village Hall for " . . . men interested in becoming auxiliary policemen . . . to maintain order in case of an air raid, blackout or other emergency" (MO 8/13/42). Boys and girls throughout the county were encouraged to participate in a treasure hunt to collect rubber for the war effort, and the Marcellus Garden Club sponsored a victory garden show, with a number of exhibits, displays and classes conducted at the Grange Hall.

The Fall

That fall, there was some concern in town that the local paper might have to shut down, but the publisher assured readers that he would keep the presses rolling as long as possible, despite a shortage of both advertising and labor. When school opened in September, over 900 students had enrolled and " . . . in keeping with the war-time practice of highlighting physical fitness, students of Marcellus Central . . . given mass exercises in physical education each Friday . . . in addition to the regular physical education classes . . . required of each student" (MO 9/10/42). Most of the school's previous graduates had either gone directly into the service or were on their way, many already in active combat. The school placed an honor roll of its former students " . . . in the lobby of the Marcellus Central School . . . continuously expanded until it carried the names of three hundred forty-eight young man and fourteen young women, serving in some branch of the armed forces" (Heffernan 116). The Village Board appointed fire inspectors for the Village and that of the Fire Chief, Lester Norris, as one of the captains of a "scrap harvest" in the Village, encouraging everyone to search out old metals for the war effort. Even pupils at the school rounded up old keys as part of this new campaign.

> **The Marcellus Observer**
> **Thurs., Sept. 17, 1942**
> **Marcellus Boys See Action At Dieppe And Guadalcanal**
>
> **The Marcellus Observer**
> **Thurs., Sept. 24, 1942**
> **This And That**
> The town is getting bereft of boys. Most of them have either gone or are getting ready to go. We look ahead to the day when our youth will come home again, safe and sound. Those of us who remember the first World War will recall similar conditions at that time, except that the poor fellows were sent across almost as soon as they learned to march. Many of our lads are thousands of miles apart, but we are with them in spirit every day.
>
> **The Marcellus Observer**
> **Thurs., Sept. 24, 1942**
> **New War Plaque At School To Honor Former Students**

14 Sep 1942 - " . . . on recommendation of the Chief of the Fire Department, Harold Freeborn and Kenneth King were duly appointed Fire Inspectors for the Village of Marcellus."

> **The Marcellus Observer - Thursday, October 22, 1942**
> **Marcellus Students Collect 6,201 Keys**
> . . . The drive for keys is widespread and this has been made in many other schools throughout the state. It is estimated that the Marcellus keys will weigh around 400 pounds or more, which is a grand gift to Uncle Sam's army. Local boys and girls would like nothing better than to feel that their keys were being tossed into Japan or on top of Hitler's head . . . if you can't throw a bomb you can at least throw your house key at the Nazis or Japs.
>
> **The Marcellus Observer - Thursday, October 22, 1942**
> **United War Fund On Way Toward Goal**
> . . . The War Fund has set a goal of $1,045,997 and Marcellus will do its share in helping to reach it. The fund will be used on 32 Home Front organizations, including hospitals, Onondaga Health Association, Free Dispensary, homes for the orphaned, aged, blind and handicapped, Boy Scouts, Girl Scouts, Visiting Nurses and many others, as well as for American War Services such as the USO and Army and Navy Relief, and the Allied Relief Services, including Chinese, Russian, British, Polish, Greek and other . . .

By October, gas rationing, which had been in effect in most of the eastern states since May, was becoming more exact, a coupon system of ration books being distributed through the office of the Town Clerk. Non-essential or pleasure driving would be discouraged or banned by limiting coupons to three gallons of gasoline a week. A United War Fund committee was established for the Town of Marcellus, organizing volunteers to solicit funds for a variety of war relief organizations. With " . . . most families . . .

purchasing war bonds, expending up to 10 percent of the family income . . . giving to the Red Cross and other needed organizations . . . " (MO 10/22/42), the committee's goal of $6,000 by October 30th was a big challenge.

Elections

In 1942, Governor Lehman decided not to run for another term and the Republican candidate, the first since 1920 was chosen, Thomas E. Dewey dominating state government in New York for the next twelve years. In Marcellus, a few days after the election, the Village Board, in a gesture of wartime harmony with the Town, agreed to a five-year contract that provided fire protection for residents of the district.

The Marcellus Observer
Thursday, November 19, 1942
Gas Rationing Cut In Effect
November 22

Landlords Must Register Monday

Cots, Blankets Needed For Marcellus Casualty Station

The Marcellus Observer
Thursday, Nov. 26, 1942
New Draft Law Affects 39 Boys In Marcellus
The passing of the teenage draft law, by which two million more men will be brought into the armed service, will immediately affect 39 residents of the Town of Marcellus.

The Marcellus Observer
Thursday, Dec 3, 1942
"Share The Meat" Campaign Now Ready For Launching

---

9 Nov 1942 - " . . . that a contract with the Town Board to furnish fire protection for the Town Fire District, for a term of five years, at an annual charge of $600.00, be approved, subject to the approval of the Fire Department."

Rationing, Rent Control, The Draft

By the end of November, even coffee was being rationed and a cut on gasoline ration books was ordered as well. Landlords were required to register their dwelling units under the government's rent-control program and a request went out for donations of cots and blankets at the new casualty station to be set up at Marcellus Central School. A new draft law would begin to affect 18-year old men and " . . . in a drive to make a complete list of local men in the armed forces, both in the United States and overseas, . . . " (MO 12/3/42), *The Marcellus Observer* began to publish the names of the boys it had on hand, updating that list "for the duration".

Another drive was to salvage silk stockings and nylon hosiery, " . . . silk for the making of powder bags for heavy-caliber guns and nylon for production of other vital war goods" (MO 12/3/42), such as parachutes.   Residents throughout Onondaga County were also urged to participate in a "Share the Meat for Victory" campaign, which called for a voluntary rationing of meat. If all family members restricted their consumption of meat, the Office of Civilian Defense stated, more would be available for the Army, Navy and Lend Lease needs. The Office of Civilian Defense also began to prepare for the salvage of tin cans and by the start of the year, "Tin-Can Saturdays" would be commonplace.

The War By Year's End

On December 14, 1942, the Village fire siren burned out during an air raid drill and no replacements could be found since they were not being manufactured for uses other than the military. Eventually, a siren was located and loaned to the Village by the Office of Civilian Protection but the incident might seem to point out how all encompassing the war had become and how interdependent the country and its citizens. Even the traffic lights on North and South Streets, which were now just flashing and not changing color, were a reminder of the war. Waiting for the light to change was a waste of gasoline, while a flashing amber light meant "proceed with caution", a reminder that the country was at war and of the need to be attentive to danger. The Fire Department urged residents to be particularly cautious during the holiday season, fearful that furnaces and stoves as well as candles on Christmas trees would be left unattended.

The Marcellus Observer - Thurs, December 25, 1942
Residents Warned Of Holiday Fire Hazards
The combination of holiday festivities and severe cold present a major fire hazard and residents of Marcellus are urged by fire chief Norris to use utmost precaution during this holiday season . . .
Every fire today necessitates a waste in time and materials to repair and such a hindrance to the war effort must be guarded against.

Christmas in 1942 was lean for many Americans and there were many reminders. There were not as many gifts around the tree and meals were not as generous as in the past, perhaps even meatless. There were constant reminders that those on the home front, young and old, men, women and children, could help win the war by doing their part. By year's end, history had not recorded much allied success, but there was the conviction that this conflict was only Volume I, the first part of a struggle that would eventually result in victory.

For the Duration	Volume One

MO December 3, 1942	MO December 11, 1942

The Marcellus Observer
Friday Morning, January 8, 1943
Marcellus Flier Shot Down in
North Africa

FIRST WAAC

ELIZABETH SEYMOUR

1943

This was another war year and the conflict continued to dominate both the news and conversation. Little else seemed to matter, as Allied leaders met to plan strategy for the war overseas and the nation continued to mobilize its resources at home. In the village, news of Lt. Emmett Conley being shot down in North Africa and Elizabeth Seymour as the first woman WAC from Marcellus made headlines. The community " . . . staged a War Bond Frolic on the weekend of January 30, 1943 . . . a program of music and comedy . . . followed by a War Bond auction . . . Over five thousand dollars was raised . . . To add to the festivities, twenty-six volunteers drove in to the USO headquarters in Syracuse and brought one hundred service men . . . to Marcellus for the weekend . . . Various families entertained the visitors overnight and for Sunday dinner, and the churches gave them a special welcome on Sunday morning" (Heffernan 117-118).

Entertaining the servicemen was a great success for the community, in sharp contrast to the news that some local boys like Louis Macholl, had been captured or, like John T. Campion, killed on the battlefield. The impact of the war was becoming more pronounced even in small-town America.

Planning Victory

As the American Red Cross planned its biggest drive in history, the community of Marcellus assigned a quota of $5,600, and Marcellus Central School planned a Victory Concert to raise money through the sale of war stamps and bonds, and the Village planned for the re-election of Mayor Spaulding and Trustee Norris.

20 Feb 1943 - " . . . nominated William S. Spaulding to succeed himself as Mayor for a term of two years. There were no other nominations . . . nominated Leonard Norris to succeed himself as Trustee for two years for a term of two years. There were no other nominations."

VICTORY GARDEN PROGRAM—Francis Hyatt, Chairman
(Sample of form to be used in canvassing the village Saturday)

1. Name .... Address ....
2. Number in family ....
3. Do you plan a garden this year? .... Size? ....
4. Would you like additional land? ....
5. Have you land someone else could use? .... Size? ....
    Location? ....
6. Having no garden plot, will you use one provided by Committee?

The Marcellus Victory Garden Committee also met at the Village Hall, presided over by Francis Hyatt, to plan a canvas of the entire village by the Boy Scouts " . . . with a questionnaire aiming to find out what interest each family has in the program . . . Plans . . . under way to have available for families who lack garden space, plots of land from workable tracts scattered thruout (sic) the village . . . " (MO 3/12/43).

Election, 1943

Election day was March 16th, but no vote was recorded in the Village Board minutes, or in the pages of *The Marcellus Observer*. Nevertheless, William S. Spaulding was re-elected as Mayor for another two year term as was Trustee Leonard Norris and at the annual meeting the Board was pleased to note that the county firemen had developed a plan for mutual aid, Marcellus placed in a district with neighboring villages at the head of which was the Marcellus Fire Chief, Lester Norris. The Board not only made its usual appointments but had to cope with the resignation of long-time employee, William Kilcoyne, a man " . . . well versed in village affairs and one of the most efficient of village servants . . . called upon to do all sorts of task around town . . . " (MO 4/9/43), as street superintendent and special policeman.

5 Apr 1943 - " . . . Donald Wing was appointed Street Commissioner for a term of one year at an annual salary of $1800.00. Arthur W. Wilson was appointed Village Attorney for a term of one year at an annual salary of $150.00. Stephen H. Hunt was appointed acting Mayor in the absence

of the Mayor. J. F. Woodbridge was appointed Clerk and Treasurer for a term of two years, at an annual salary of $600.00 per year. The First National Bank was designated official Depository and the Marcellus Observer, the Official Newspaper. The second Monday of each month at 7:30 p.m. was designated as regular meeting nights."

Fresh Air on the Farm and in the Village

At the end of the month, a fresh air committee was " . . . appointed in Marcellus to make an appeal on behalf of the children living in the tenements of New York City asking for two weeks free hospitality in the homes of kindly people for boys and girls from six to twelve years of age" (MO 4/30/43). In addition, farmers were informed that there were " . . . thousands of boys in New York City, ages ranging from 15 to 17 years, . . . anxious to work on farms for their room and board . . . " (MO, 5/7/43), an answer in many cases, to the labor shortage that many upstate farms experienced during the war years. The Board also renewed its labor contract with Mel Corp to collect ashes and garbage in the Village, at a salary that compensated him for a rise in prices and costs.

> **The Marcellus Observer**
> **Friday Morning, May 28, 1943**
> **No Old Home Day This Year**
> Chief Lester Norris of the Marcellus Fire Department has announced the decision of the department to forgo their annual Fourth of July celebration this year, because of the exigencies of war. He emphasized that this is a temporary condition and that the popular Old Home Celebration series will be revived just as soon as conditions will permit.

10 May 1943 - " . . . Bids for the removal of ashes and garbage having been received . . . and the bid of Melville Corp having been found to be lowest, it was resolved that a contract be entered into with the said Melville Corp for a period of one year . . . for the annual sum of $2400.00 to be paid in same monthly installments of $100.00 each."

Memorial Day was held in 1943, saluting the soldier dead of previous wars as well as honoring those of the present conflict. There was no Old Home Day that year however, wartime conditions being blamed for the absence.

> **The Marcellus Observer**
> **Friday Morning, June 4, 1943**
>
> **First Audible Signal**
> 2-minute steady note of siren
> **Lights Out**
> **Homes and Buildings**
> Street and traffic lights on; pedestrians and traffic may move
>
> **Second Audible Signal**
> 2-minute short blasts
> **All Lights Out**
> **Everything stops**
>
> **Third Audible Signal**
> 2-minute steady note of siren
> **Lights Remain Out**
> **Homes and Buildings**
> Street and traffic lights on; pedestrians and traffic resume movement
>
> **Fourth Audible Signal**
> 5-second steady note of siren
> **All Clear**
> Everything returns to normal

A June Bride's Dilemma

OH GOODNESS! HOW MANY POINTS WILL THAT TAKE?

MO June 25, 1943

The War's Presence

The war's presence continued to be evident throughout the community. June, always a month for brides, was also a test for the new air raid signals, published at the request of

Warden Clayton Pilot so that people would know what to do during a practice blackout. There was also a second victory concert sponsored by the school that month to sell war stamps and bonds.

The Village Board also began to refer building permit applications to its Zoning Committee that month, marking its beginning as a citizen entity which today hears appeals and makes decisions regarding zoning and planning issues in the Village.

14 Jun 1943 - " . . . Mr. Frank Ort applied for permission to build a 10 x 14 hen house on the rear of his lot on Second Street. It was decided to refer the petition to the Committee which drafted the Zoning Ordinance for its interpretation of the ordinance. Mr. Baker, Chairman of the Committee, appeared before the Board and upon his statement that it was not the intention to prohibit the construction of small buildings for personal use, the permission was granted."

The Marcellus Observer
Friday Morning, July 16, 1943
Church Group Suggests Curfew As Curb To Mischief

The Marcellus Observer
Friday Morning, July 23, 1943
Harry Long Gives Opinion On Curfew
Says That Community House Is Answer to Problem

Marcellus Central School would graduate fifty-six students that month, many of whom would soon " . . . begin serving their country either in war plants or in the armed services" (MO 6/18/43). While some went off to war, there was concern about other young people in the community whose reckless behavior was viewed as annoying and troublesome. Since the war began, " . . . crime rates across the nation jumped, and some officials claimed that youths were having one last fling before entering the Army" (Carruth 779). This led some in Marcellus to discuss the idea of a curfew as a means of controlling misbehavior in the village, while others promoted the idea of a community playground or recreation center for the young to gather and entertain themselves. *The Marcellus Observer* encouraged this idea, suggesting that " . . . attention be directed to the plot of ground, almost an acre in size, that lies in the center of the square made up by First, Reed, North and Main streets, directly behind the Village Hall. This plot is useless as a building site, as it has no entrance except thru the village lane, and is growing up with weeds . . . this would be ideal as a playground and would make a safe, convenient and pleasant place . . . if properly landscaped and shaded" (MO 7/30/43)

The Marcellus Observer
Friday Morning, July 23, 1943
Marcellus Boy Reported Missing In Action
Donald Kelly Was In Naval Battle

The Marcellus Observer
Friday Morning, July 30, 1943
Marcellus Responds To Simulated Bombing Attack

Always, the War
There was always the war. The Kelly family waited anxiously for word about their son, Donald, missing in action in the Pacific. The community participated in a simulated attack on Marcellus, a realistic encounter that made citizens aware of and the Fire Department busy responding to the necessity of being prepared.

"During these times of curtailment and shortage, local folks . . . kept close at home . . . the front porch . . . the length and breadth of . . . summer travels . . ." (MO 8/13/43). There was also talk of another Village picnic, a diversion from the war and a way for folks to have a little fun in these troubling times.

When school opened that September, there was some concern about a shortage of ration coupons to meet the needs of the school cafeteria, an issue that was " . . . overcome in a large measure by the foresight of Principal Chester S. Driver of Marcellus Central School, who has been directing the canning of over 800 quarts of fresh vegetables at the school during the past month" (MO 9/3/43). Faculty and students had planted a victory garden near the school earlier that year, and were now able to harvest an abundant supply of vegetables for the canning process.

Another bond drive that September would ask local residents " . . . to back the fighting forces of U.S.A. to the very limit of their resources . . . to invest in at least one

Capt. J. Emmett Conley | Pfc. Stedman Bird

extra $100 war bond . . . " (MO 9/3/43), the community responding in typically fine fashion. Two local boys were recognized for their heroism in the war, at a time when good news was needed at home. "Few have seen more action in so short a time than the lad who used to be one of the baseball stars of the town and is now doing his share towards winning the war," said the local editor about Capt. J. Emmett Conley (MO 10/1/43). In the Pacific, " . . . Stedman

Bird . . . a true soldier like his father and uncles, has now hung up a record that will make him outstanding in this war. Marcellus . . . proud to own a son who has such courage and fearlessness" (MO 10/15/43).

MO November 5, 1943

Elections

During the fall, as the Allies continued to make progress in the Italian campaign, elections were held in the Town of Marcellus and included ballots from members of the armed forces serving away from home. A tribute to the fact that even during time of war, Americans possessed and exercised this sacred right, it didn't help the Democrats in Town. The vote again " . . . resulted in a sweeping Republican Victory. Morris Mulroy, Republican candidate for supervisor, won over his opponent, Harry E. Long, Sr., by a heavy majority" (MO 11/5/43). There had also been an attempt to run candidates on a 3rd, or Victory Party earlier in the year, but its petition had been rejected by the Board of Elections because the " . . . pages are not numbered consecutively beginning with number One at

the foot of each page as required . . . " (MO 9/10/43). This seems to have been a simple mistake in 1943 but, as history has noted, it has been repeated in recent elections also.

American Legion

One group in Marcellus, whose efforts were tireless on behalf of the war effort and the service men, was the American Legion. As a successor to the G.A.R. of Civil War days and as an outgrowth of American involvement in World War I, the Ralph Share Post of the American Legion conducted a number of campaigns on behalf of the American serviceman as well as sponsorship of the Memorial Day Parade each year. In November 1943, the American Legion purchased the Coyne Block in Marcellus, one of the oldest buildings in the Village and would remodel it into a modern club for the returning soldiers as well as present members of the Ralph Share Post. Dating back to the 1840s, this building witnessed much of the history of the Village, " . . . at one time . . . the only store in Marcellus . . . the tradition . . . fittingly carried on through the acquisition of this fine old structure by the American Legion" (MO11/26/43).

MO November 26, 1943

MO December 24, 1943

An End To The Year

At the year came to a close, the people of the community, like those throughout the nation were grateful, " . . . in spite of . . . disrupted lives, the loss of hope, and the many vacant chairs at . . . Thanksgiving tables . . . " (MO 11/26/43) as Rev. Charles Fryer of the Methodist Church in Marcellus noted in his holiday message. Christmas would also be celebrated in Marcellus in 1943, and Santa Claus was busy delivering gifts to servicemen in both theaters of war. There was, however, no Village Christmas tree that year -- many people in the community did not feel the Christmas spirit.

The Marcellus Observer - Friday, Dec 24, 1943
No Village Christmas Tree Glows On Snow
Because of War Need
No Municipal Christmas tree will blaze forth in the public square this Christmas season! Conservation of electricity, the grim reality of the war and surprising dearth in the Christmas spirit are some of the reasons given.
S. H. Hunt, one of the members of the village board tells this paper that something appears to be lacking this Christmas
'There is very little inspiration for a tree this year,' said Mr. Hunt. 'Folks just don't feel like they do other years.'

Village government continued to operate, local fire inspectors expressing their concern to the Board, during this holiday season, about several properties that needed immediate attention.

MO December 31, 1943

The editor commented that " . . . It was a war Christmas, and the gifts were largely of war quality. Local people seemed to be in accord that this Christmas was one to be forgotten soon, the real Christmas celebration to be held the first Yuletide following the end of the war . . .. With almost every family saddened by the absence of husband, sons or daughters, Christmas came and left without fanfare or jubilee. Most families had a Christmas dinner, but not like the dinners of the past . . . " (MO 12/31/43). There was still a war on when the community said goodbye to1943 and many looked forward to the dawn of a new year and the hope they thought it might bring.

1944

This year began where the last one left off - with war news and rationing. *The Marcellus Observer* had earlier organized the Home Fires Club, a group " . . . of persons who agreed to write letters to those away from home. Probably, Mrs. Cora Marshfield and Patrick Kelly were the most prolific of the correspondents" (Heffernan 118) and their letters from home throughout this year in particular were most encouraging to the servicemen and women overseas. Mothers were encouraged to save grease and fats from the kitchen and the Boy Scouts continued to collect waste paper. A Fourth War Loan Campaign was organized by some " . . . members of the Onondaga Farm Bureau . . . assisted by County 4-H clubs and other farm organizations . . . to reach every farm in the county" (MO 1/28/44). Tin cans were added to the list of collectibles, as "Tin Can Saturday" became something of a ritual with many youth. For many people, the winter and the war may have become somewhat more tolerable as the Village Board, responding to suggestions by the Citizens Club, authorized the lighting of Coon's Pond for public skating and provided a new and safer sliding area on Reed Parkway.

> **The Marcellus Observer**
> **Friday Morning, January 14, 1944**
> **Scouts To Collect Waste Paper In**
> **Village January 22**
>
> **The Marcellus Observer**
> **Friday Morning, February 18, 1944**
> **Reed Parkway Slide Ready**
> **For Coasting**
> Marcellus children (and possibly some of the grownups) will hail with delight the new sliding place that has been provided by the Village Board on Reed Parkway, and the lighting of Coon's Pond for public skating. The Board has directed that the streets leading to the sliding place should be barricaded so that local children, from the ages of 2 to 92, may romp in complete safety . . .
> Coon's Pond has long been a favorite skating place for Marcellus children . . .

MO January 14, 1944

The Marcellus Observer - Friday Morning, February 18, 1944
Observer Suggests Local Projects As Postwar Program

The time for postwar planning has arrived . . . as a start . . . this editor sets forth a group of ideas that have long been uppermost in his mind . . .It is his desire that the reader will comment . . . and perhaps out of these comments may be born a tangible and worthwhile post war program.

FOR THE COUNTY - . . . a large addition to Marcellus Park to the east . . . could be turned into an athletic field . . . Such a field might have other uses . . . Field days, drills, competitive races and outdoor bazaars . . .

FOR THE VILLAGE - More than anything else Marcellus needs a new postoffice . . . possibly a modern brick building . . . another thing that Marcellus should strive for is curbs on most of the streets, especially the main arteries.

FOR THE GARDEN CLUB - Marcellus should be outstanding. It should attract visitors. Norwich has its roses. Rochester has its lilacs . . . Why not a particular flower for Marcellus? The Garden Club could select a certain flower or shrub . . . could then be cultivated in abundance, grown in the yards, on the laws, and even in public flower beds.

FOR THE GRANGE - . . . The Grange could sponsor a program that would build a new public market in the western part of Syracuse . . . would attract hundreds of people . . . who do not now go to the North side market . . .

All towns and villages of any size or degree of progressivism are thinking of the end of the war and of a program to follow this great event. Marcellus is growing. Our new residents are enthusiastically in love with the village and its conveniences. We have excellent water, a new sewer system, a number of stores, four active churches, good bus service, several manufacturing plants, a picturesque park, efficient physicians, a dentist, a newspaper, a bank, and a school that surpasses anything in the state for a rural centralized school. Marcellus has much to be proud of. It has advantages that few other villages have to offer. It is near to cities, and within ten minutes drive of two beautiful lakes. We should have a postwar program. What other town is better equipped to carry out such a program, and what community has more to work with?

Postwar Programs

Long before the war was over, an editorial in *The Marcellus Observer* suggested that the time for postwar planning had arrived, an idea that some may have thought a bit presumptuous. However, the suggestions that were made in 1944 were not only insightful but in the years since the war have, for the most part, been adopted and promoted by local residents and groups.

Hunt Retires - Case Elected

Having served the village as a Trustee for 16 years, Stephen H. Hunt decided to retire from that position. At the village caucus in mid-February he nominated Newton Giles Case, a member of one of the oldest families in the community. Case, who lived with his wife and two sons on Reed Parkway, would go on to win the election in March, and would be reelected in 1946 and again in 1948.

19 Feb 1944 - " . . . Mr. Giles Case was nominated by Stephen H. Hunt for office of Village Trustee for term of two years . . . There were no further nominations . . . "

Horace M. Stone

Horace M. Stone

In early March, " . . . Marcellus lost its leading citizen. Horace M. Stone, for many years a most colorful force in public affairs . . . passed on" (MO 3/10/44). Born in Marcellus in 1890 and educated locally, he became a prominent attorney, and served as Supervisor of the Town of Marcellus as well as in the State Assembly, the latter for thirteen successive terms. He was fully involved in the life of the community and a tireless worker for the town he loved so well. Stores and other businesses closed on the day of his funeral, which attracted hundreds of people. They listened to and fully appreciated the words of Pastor Frost who stated: "Horace Stone has left the state of New York and the County of Onondaga the poorer for his passing. This beautiful valley of Marcellus, which he preferred to any other place on earth, will be more empty since he no longer walks its familiar ways" (MO 3/17/44).

The War

Meanwhile the war was still raging overseas. There had been some noted success in both the European and Pacific theaters and the battle waged on the home front to both conserve and produce caused the government to relax some of its regulations in 1944. An ease in tension was also reflected in the movies, which " . . . enjoyed their greatest year in box office history, grossing $2,000,000,000 as the European markets began to open in liberated areas" (Carruth 791). For those young men and women overseas, this picture of the Strand theater in Marcellus was printed in March 1944, reminding them of home and of such peaceful pleasures as attending a movie, once the war was over.

Appointments and Approvals

Following elections in March, the new Board met to approve appointments, including that of Lester Norris who was reelected Fire Chief and of William Alford as street commissioner. The Board also authorized a survey for a storm sewer on Reed Avenue and First Street, where water runoff was a major concern for residents. It was not, however, until major drainage work on First and Reed Streets took place in 1999 that residents were able to enjoy dry basements.

24 Apr 1944 - " . . . a survey for a storm sewer on Reed Ave and First Street was authorized."

The Marcellus Observer
Friday Morning, May 12, 1944
Nightingale Mill Burns!

The "Pride of Marcellus"

In May 1944, The Marcellus Observer published a photo of Sgt. Bill MacFarlane standing in front of an airplane, on the side of which were printed the words "Pride of Marcellus". MacFarlane went on to explain that because he talked so much about the great little place in which he lived, the fellows in his crew decided to name the plane after their chief's hometown. Marcellus pride also seemed to shine that spring when the volunteer firemen were called out to fight grass fires on a lazy Sunday afternoon and when a midnight blaze practically destroyed the Nightingale Mill. The Tin Can Drive netted almost a ton of recyclables that spring and victory gardens continued to bud throughout the village.

The Marcellus Observer - Friday, June 9, 1944
Invasion Greeted By Prayer And Silent Acceptance
Marcellus awoke with a sudden start early Tuesday morning when the church bells of the village pealed out the news that the long-awaited invasion of France by the Allied forces had begun. Although the news was not entirely unexpected, it came at an hour, and with a suddenness that was extremely exciting . . .

At five o'clock, just as dawn was breaking, the church bells of Marcellus rang out that momentous news. People awoke suddenly, and realized that the invasion was on. The very air seemed to be charged with expectancy. Every radio in the community was turned on, and men, women, and children, many of them still clad in night-clothes crowded around to get every bit of information available. Many of these families had boys on the invasion front, and interest ran high . . .

During the day a number of people, mostly wives and mothers, went silently to the churches for prayer, meditation and comfort. Others knelt in their homes . . .

Thus, Marcellus passed D-Day, a day that will be remembered in history through all time. School children will remember that they were excused from classes to attend an hour of prayer . . . Pastors will remember that they were called upon to bring comfort to some who were overcome with emotion. The world will remember that this day marked the first real step in the liberation of an enslaved Europe.

Memorial Day and D-Day

The community turned out to honor its soldier dead on Memorial Day, particular respect paid to Pvt. William Nightingale, who, missing for two years in the Philippines, was officially declared dead by the War Department. As the Boy Scouts mounted another paper drive and plans for a 5th War Loan Drive were made in early June, word reached the village that D-Day, the invasion of Europe by Allied forces, had begun on June 6th. Residents were thrilled with the news, but equally concerned about and prayed for Marcellus boys who were located in the invasion zone and for others, like Donald Kelly and Harold Waters, sailors still missing in action.

Village Matters

While war news dominated conversation and the headlines, the Village Board was confronted with the need to fix the village clock -- " . . . the huge weight that regulates the striking mechanism . . . had become disconnected and come down through the floor . . . " (MO 6/9/44) of the Methodist Church steeple. There was also a need to improve the village reservoir by purchasing adjoining land and reforesting the area to protect the watershed. In addition, the Board received a letter from the New York State Department of Labor reminding the Village of the need to enforce building codes as defined by state law -- reminders that while the war continued, so too did the business of government.

12 Jun 1944 - " . . . an expenditure of $500 for the purchase of land adjoining the reservoir was authorized."

19 Jul 1944 - " . . . communication received from New York State Department of Labor, to wit: . . . Your attention is called to the provisions of Section 472 of the Labor Law regarding 'Enforcement and Investigations of Article 17, Public Safety' requiring the Industrial Commissioner to inquire into the administration and enforcement of the provisions of this article by all public officers charge with the duty of enforcement. This law covers such places as theatres, moving picture houses, public halls, dance halls, skating rinks, bowling alleys, dining and dancing places, amusement resorts, etc., where one hundred or more persons may assemble. Your Village has a board or officer charged with the enforcement of building laws or ordinances and shall therefore enforce the provisions of Article 17 of the Labor Law and for such purpose have all the powers of the Industrial Commissioner. Upon receipt of this letter, kindly furnish this office with the name of the designated enforcing official so that we may furnish him with the department forms and certificates and instruct him in work of safety in public assembly."

> **The Marcellus Observer**
> **Friday Morning, August 11, 1944**
> **Hickman's To Open Friday For Business**
> Hickman's Market will reopen Friday morning. This announcement is made by Donald Hickman, who states that for the present the store will sell only unrationed foods, including beef, pork and veal. Lamb is still among the rationed meats. Since closing the store a few weeks ago, the staff has been busy painting and remodeling the interior of the market. The cooler has been remodeled and painted and a new cooling motor installed.

Retail and Other Matters in the Village

In July, the 5th War Loan Campaign in Marcellus closed, exceeding its goal by selling over $91,000 in government bonds, much of the success attributed to " . . . the retail stores who did a splendid job in selling bonds" (MO 7/14/44). In addition, the postoffice block, one of the best business sites in town, was sold to Willis B. Sharp, who intended " . . . to paint it, make needed repairs and wait until after the war before . . . any extensive remodeling" (MO 7/14/44). Also, Hickman's Market, on First Street, was closed " . . . by an OPA order prohibiting the firm from buying or selling products having point values, after July 24" (MO 7/14/44). The market, a retail fixture in the Village for many years, was closed, not because of health violations, but because of " . . . failure to register with the Office of Price Administration . . . " (MO 7/28/44) as a wholesale and retailer of meat. By mid-August, the market reopened along with " . . . a movement . . . to free the market from . . . charges made by the OPA" (MO 8/11/44).

The summer of 1944 was somewhat dry and the Village urged residents, " . . . with Marcellus water supply at an all time low, . . . to curtail the use of water as much as possible . . . " (MO 89/18/44). A concern for health officials in the village was an increase in the number of polio victims. The year would witness the introduction of penicillin and very effective use of DDT as an insecticide, but a vaccine for infantile paralysis was still ten years away.

Labor Day, Halloween, and Election Day

As plans were made for school to reopen in the fall and for war ballots and holiday

> **The Marcellus Observer - Friday, August 25, 1944**
> **Send Holiday Gifts Overseas Next Month**
> **By Jane Conley, Acting P.M.**
> This year the Christmas mailing period for both Army and
> Navy overseas forces is the same - September 15 to October 15.
>
> **The Marcellus Observer - Friday, September 8, 1944**
> **Marcellus Passes Quiet Labor Day**
> One of the calmest Labor Days in the memory of local people
> was observed last Monday, with nearly every service station in
> town out of gas . . .
> Local people . . . , either sat around on the porches or worked
> in the gardens. Few left town except on business. To each one
> that this reporter made the statement, "A pretty quiet Labor
> Day," there came a wistful grin.
> "Wait until next year," was the inevitable answer.

MO August 11, 1944

gifts to be mailed overseas, the community was at rest that Labor Day. Many may have been anticipating the end of the war and the blessed quiet that it might bring. The conflict, however, was not over, and this was brought graphically home to the community when " . . . word was received that Sgt. Edward J. Brown, . . . of Marietta, had been killed on September 19, in the Asiatic theater of the war" (MO 9/29/44).

The Scouts continued to collect papers throughout the fall, and the Marcellus community became involved in another United War Fund campaign in October. The firemen again alerted residents about the importance of fire prevention, noting that " . . . victory over our human enemies is now assured, but not victory over fire" (MO 10/6/44), and they also staged their annual Halloween Carnival and Parade for the kids in town, a celebration that resulted in " . . . little damage done here by Hallowe'eners . . . " (MO 11/3/44). Some thought the biggest scare was the November election,

Booooo!
MO October 27, 1944

> **The Marcellus Observer - Friday, November 10, 1944**
> **What The Voters Wanted**
> The fact the President Roosevelt won by a great majority was
> evidence enough that he was the man the voters wanted. A great
> many of us thought differently, but now that the people have spoken
> we must throw aside party desires and work with the elected
> president to end the war and restore peace to the world. . . . Franklin
> D. Roosevelt is our president. We have often disagreed with his
> policies, and we have often thanked God that we had such a leader in
> time of great national stress. He has been a great war-time president,
> and we of the minority voters are trusting that he will also become an
> equally great peacetime president.

pitting the incumbent President Roosevelt, vying for an unprecedented fourth term, against the popular New York Governor, Thomas Dewey. While some thought that FDR was destroying tradition, others thought him to be indispensable as a war leader. When the votes were tallied, " . . . Marcellus went for Dewey two to one . . ." (MO 11/10/44), but the vote in the nation was clearly for FDR. One of the most remarkable things about November 7, 1944, however, might be the fact that in the midst of the greatest conflict in history, a democratic election took place on that day, the results of which would be almost universally accepted by the voters. The strength of the republic and its citizens was never more evident.

Year's End

That mettle would continue to be tested in Marcellus and the nation as the year came to an end and causalities overseas mounted. Harry Hamacher, Milton Garvey and James

MO Nov 10, 1944

Harry Hamacher

Milton Garvey

James Thompson

Thompson, would make the ultimate sacrifice in the waning months of 1944, giving powerful testimony to the meaning of November 11th. The families of these young men would experience a painful Christmas in 1944, their deaths a reminder of just how precious both life and home were and how costly the price of peace and freedom.

Conclusion

In 1940, Thomas Wolfe's novel, *You Can't Go Home Again*, was published. The novel, while largely autobiographical, tells of an author who returns home, after having written a successful story about himself and his hometown. " When he returns to that town he is shaken by the force of the outrage and hatred that greets him. Family and friends feel naked and exposed by the truths they have seen in his book, and their fury drives him from his home. He begins a worldwide search for his own identity . . . At last . . . returns to America and rediscovers it with love, sorrow, and hope" (New York Times Book Description).

MO December 22, 1944

Throughout the 1940s, Wolfe's novel, which was published two years after he died, was quite successful, especially, it would seem, in small town America -- in places like Marcellus, where a village atmosphere and love of community continues to be renewed by each succeeding generation.

By 1944, the longing to go home was a hunger for hundreds of young servicemen and women from Marcellus. It was a desire shared by their loved ones and helps to explain the overwhelming response of the home front in Marcellus to the war effort. For Marcellians, there was no need to rediscover what they already appreciated. For them, the end of the war meant an end to separation and going home again.

Chapter 15 – Adjusting To Peace

Americans were resolved to win the war in 1945 but the costs would continue to mount before it was over. When the war ended, Americans were relieved, but they were

Our New Year Resolution

MO December 29, 1944

Benjamin A. McClaude   Frederick C. McClaude   James E. McClaude

also anxious about what the postwar years would bring. As the servicemen and women returned home, including the three sons of Mr. Mrs. William McClaude of Howlett Hill Road, their thoughts turned to matters of peace, but it would be a restless time and a period of adjustment for small-town America.

The Marcellus Observer - Friday, January 19, 1945
Marcellus Has Public Rink At Coon Pond

Young Marcellus, and perhaps a few oldsters, have cause to rejoice this week with the announcement that the village is to have a public skating rink. Arrangements have been completed to have "Coon's Pond," a spot dear to several pat generations of Marcellians, set aside as a public rink.

The Marcellus Observer - Friday, January 26, 1945
Worst Snow In Years Silences Old Timers

Snow and more snow! It has long ceased to be funny in the minds of those who have to do battle with it, yet it comes . . . There are homes in the Borodino-Spafford area that have been marooned since the first big deluge a month and a half ago . . . Old timers scratch their heads and say little. Gone are the stories of the snows back in '84 or '97. This snow tops anything the memories of the old fellows can muster in the line of a snow yarn. From this time forth the stories will be of the snow of '45 . . .

The Marcellus Observer - Friday, February 9, 1945
Notice of Snow Removal

A Village Ordinance provides that all property owners shall keep their sidewalks clear of snow and ice. For some time past the Village has, as a public service, taken care of this removal. They find now, however, due to the heavy fall of snow and high winds, that no equipment is available to do this work. If you have a dangerous condition on the sidewalk in front of your property it should be taken care of promptly to avoid accidents.   VILLAGE BOARD

1945 - Winter Woes

Back home, the winter of 1945 was one of the most severe on record, blocking roads, closing schools and causing much difficulty for residents of the Town and Village. While many young people enjoyed the public skating rink at Coon's Pond, others complained about the snow, when " . . . almost every night a new supply is laid over the landscape to take the place of that which might have been shoveled or plowed the day before" (MO 1/26/45). There was also concern in the Village about fire, not only the ability of the volunteers to get to a blaze, but the shortage of water to fight it. To that end, the Board " . . . connected the east side of the village with Otisco Lake water, leaving the remainder of the corporation on the regular village water . . . running two lines of fire hose from the Otisco Lake hydrant in front of the Presbyterian church to a village water hydrant about 100 feet east . . . The growth of the village in the past few years has placed a greater burden on the water resources" (MO 1/26/45). This was a temporary fix, but one which would meet present needs while plans were made to enlarge the reservoir.

The winter storms continued into February, causing a coal shortage emergency and continuing to tax the already overworked highway crews. The Village was also forced to remind residents and property owners that the plowing of sidewalks was no longer possible and that individuals were now obligated to clean their own walks, a law that remains in effect to this day.

Clayton A. Edgerton

The Marcellus Observer
Friday Morning, March 23, 1945
Kenyon Gets Unanimous Vote
Polling 200 out of 205 votes cast, Varnum S. Kenyon was ushered into the mayor's job in Marcellus last Tuesday in one of the largest village elections in the history of the village. Clayton Edgerton received 177 votes, and the former trustee, Leonard Norris, got 20 write-in votes . . .
The election of Mr. Kenyon was unanimous, . . . Five of the ballots were either blank or were wrongly marked.

Village Elections
Early in February, Mayor William S. Spaulding stated that he would not be a candidate for reelection in March and the move was on to find a successor. By the end of the month, there were several candidates and the contest eventually settled around two individuals. Louis Newell, head of the local ration board and proprietor of Newell's Grill, along with Varnum S. Kenyon, a former Village Trustee, would campaign for the nomination. Eventually, " . . . Kenyon was nominated for the post of Mayor, and Clayton A. Edgerton for Trustee . . . at the largest caucus ever held in the Village of Marcellus . . . For the trusteeship . . . Leonard Norris, the present incumbent, was high man in the first ballot, but did not have the required '50% or over' needed. Mr. Edgerton advanced . . . winning the nomination . . . It was a typical neighborhood get-together and everyone was good-natured over the outcome. It was truly the greatest political gathering that village politics has ever attracted" (MO 3/2/45). In the election that followed on March 20, 1945, the nominees were swept into office in one of the largest village elections in its history, a testament to the strength of local democracy in action.

The Marcellus Observer - Friday Morning, March 23, 1945
The Village Beautiful

What does Marcellus have that a thousand other villages lack? About 300 service men and women could rise as one person and say, "It is Home, that's what!"

But it is more than that. Marcellus is pleasantly situated within easy driving distance of two cities, but that doesn't necessarily make it beautiful. It has good clean air, but even that isn't everything. It has over a thousand neighborly people, but no matter what a big item that is, it doesn't adequately describe our town - and our town is beautiful in a lot of ways.

New residents are thrilled the first morning they awaken in a new home in our village, and they continued to be thrilled the longer they live here. Why is it? They enjoy our Saturday afternoon shopping crowd of neighbors. They enjoy calling the storekeepers by their first names. They love the quaint, homelike atmosphere of our village churches. They enjoy the courteous manner in which they are treated by tradesmen, garage men, bankers - everybody. When you live in Marcellus you just get that way, it seems.

Let us keep Marcellus that way. Let us preserve this spirit of neighborliness, this feeling of interest, one in the other. Let us preserve our shaded avenues, our arches of stately trees, our clean and picturesque streets. Let us, above all, preserve our sacred traditions. Let the old Marcellus of yesterday be so entwined with the Marcellus of today that to our new neighbors the historic story of our village may be like the unrolling of a panoramic picture. Let those pioneers who worked to make our village the gorgeous spot it has come to be, be revered and honored.

Let us keep Marcellus The Village Beautiful.

---

20 Mar 1945 - " . . . the results were as follows. The total number of ballots cast were 205. For the Office of Mayor for a term of 2 years, Varnum S. Kenyon received 200 . . . For the Office of Trustee for a term of 2 years, Clayton Edgerton received 177."

Spring, 1945

As the local editor reminded residents of the beauty of the village, and local Boy Scouts began another paper drive, participation in a National Clothing Drive " . . . to

| George R. Arthur | James M. Kelly |

obtain used clothing for destitute people all over the world" (MO 4/6/45) was begun locally. The new officers of the Village Board were sworn in, making several appointments and approvals and the community stopped to honor both George R. Arthur, awarded the Bronze Star for his heroic achievement in combat, as well as mourn the death of another Marcellus soldier, James Kelly, who died in the fight at the Remagen Bridge. The 11th Marcellus soldier to die in the conflict, Kelly was not the last, as the war even claimed the President of the United States in April of 1945, as much a casualty as any soldier. The local paper noted that " . . . Franklin Delano Roosevelt was a great man, whether we voted for him or not, and he will go down in history as one of the great presidents. His death was a distinct shock, not only to America, but to a big world that needs him . . . President Harry S. Truman has been left with a big job . . . Some great philosopher has said that God always raises up a man to lead in time of great need. America trusts that Harry S. Truman is that man" (MO 4/20/45).

2 Apr 1945 – " . . . J. Fred Woodbridge was appointed Clerk and Treasurer at salary of $750.00."

9 Apr 1945 - " . . . James C. Pilot was granted permission to make alterations and erect additions to his property at 15 North Street in accordance with plans filed with the Village Clerk."

The Marcellus Observer
Friday Morning, May 11, 1945
Marcellus Greets V-E With Prayer
And Thanksgiving

Marcellus celebrated V-E Day in a sensible manner.

Everyone with a radio available listened attentively to the presidential proclamation, grateful that the first phase of the war had ended. There was no noise, no loud jubilation, no stoppage of essential work.

At noon the school pupils were dismissed and about three o'clock most of the local stores closed for the remainder of the day. The whole scene was much in contrast with November 11, 1918, when the world went mad with joy, parading and cutting up in a most ridiculous manner.

The opinion of local people appeared to be that the real celebration would come at the end of the Jap war. Most families have sons in the service who have no hope of coming home until the Japs have given up, so the urge to celebrate last Tuesday was dampened. It was, however, observed with a prayerful determination to carry on until the coming of what is now referred to as V-J Day.

V-E DAY

The war, at least part of it, was ending, when President Truman proclaimed May 8, 1945 as V-E Day, for Victory in Europe. Resistance by the Japanese continued in the Pacific, however, causing many in the community to dampen their enthusiasm until that phase of the war ended. The Village Board did approve the lighting of the Village Clock, its illumination having been dimmed during the war years.

Code inspection continued and the Board approved a system for ash and garbage pickup, part of a new setup in village maintenance that consisted of a three-man crew under the direction of a superintendent of streets (including sewers, water, ash and garbage collection) and police work.

14 May 1945 - " . . . it was regularly moved, seconded and carried that the lighting of the Village Clock be restarted . . . Mr. Kenneth King, Fire Inspector, submitted a report on conditions at the Alvord House and the Parsons Block. The Clerk was instructed to notify the owners of these properties to correct the fire hazards mentioned in the report."

The Marcellus Observer - Friday Morning, May 18, 1945
Ash And Garbage Notice
Beginning May 17, the Village truck will pick up ashes and garbage in the village two days each week, Mondays and Thursdays. The village will be entirely covered by the truck on each of those days. Residents are asked to have ashes and garbage at the curb . . . and containers should be set out by 8 o'clock . . . covered tightly . . . No large piles of rubbish will be taken, and newspapers and magazines should be kept until picked up by a local organization or by the village truck.
VILLAGE BOARD, Marcellus, N.Y.

The Marcellus Observer
Friday Morning, May 25, 1945
Committee Asks Bond Buyers To Vote For Local Service Women
Active members of the Wacs, Waves, Marines, Spars, Army and Navy Nurse Corps, and the Red Cross Overseas Field Service are eligible to compete for prizes in connection with the 7th War Loan Campaign, . . . the following women from this area are eligible:

Gwendolyn Bell	Spar
Arlene Burns	Wave
Lillian Chisholm	Wac
Alice Goldych	Wac
Betty Henderson	Wave
Nancy Janet McKenzie	Wave
Catherine P. Moak	Nurse
Phyllis M. Murphy	Wac
Adeline I. Pelchy	Wave
Helen Prosonic	Wave
Margaret Jean Prosonic	Wave
Isabel R. Scott	Wac
Eleanor Seymour	Wac
Elizabeth M. Seymour	Wac

With the surrender of Germany earlier in the month, the Memorial Day celebration was especially meaningful in 1945 and in an attempt to both honor women in the service and promote a 7th War Loan Campaign, any person purchasing a War Bond during the drive became eligible to cast a ballot for their favorite service woman, who were in turn eligible for cash prizes.

Snow, Parking, Dogs and Sidewalks

When June arrived, so too did a letter urging the Village to make application for State aid to pay for the unusual expenses of the previous winter. Response by the State to such disasters has become even more common in recent years, that of the Labor Day storm in 1998 being a prime example.

That summer, the Board was also concerned with a speeding and parking problem in the Village, and to that end hired another officer for part time patrol.

8 Jun 1945 - " . . . a communication received from the Onondaga County Attorney
To Clerks of Town and Village Boards: . . . Chapter 473 of the Laws of 1945 . . . permits application to the State of New York for State aid for extraordinary expenses incurred by your municipality for snow control, commencing November 15, 1944 and ending April 15, 1945. This must be done on or before July 1, 1945."

11 Jun 1945 - " . . . Village Attorney Wilson submitted a draft of an ordinance governing automobile speed and parking . . . and that a public hearing be held, July 2, at 8:00 P.M."

9 Jul 1945 - " . . . that Kenneth King be engaged as patrolman, part-time, for the remainder of the official year at the rate of $100.00 per year, plus additional compensation for special occasions."

There was worry about a growing rabies problem in Onondaga County, and this caused the Board to remind dog owners that a dog quarantine would continue to be strictly enforced in the community. The Board also listened to suggestions that, as part of the new collection system, Village employees carry garbage and ashes from the cellars to the curbs. While this idea was deemed too costly, tax dollars did pay for new sidewalk construction that was thought to be quite necessary.

> **The Marcellus Observer - Friday Morning, July 13, 1945**
> **Lock Up That Dog!**
> Local peace officers wish to urge dog owners to keep all dogs in confinement during the present rabies quarantine . . .
>
> **The Marcellus Observer - Friday Morning, July 20, 1945**
> **Ash Trucking Would Cost $4,000 - Board**
> The additional cost to the village of trucking ashes and garbage from the cellars of Marcellus residents would be around $4000, in the opinion of some of the members of the Village Board when confronted with the suggestion that ashes be carried out by village employees.
>
> **The Marcellus Observer - Friday Morning, July 27, 1945**
> **New Sidewalk Being Laid On Lower North St.**

> **The Marcellus Observer**
> **Friday Morning, August 10, 1945**
> **The Atomic Bomb**
> Mankind has launched out upon an uncertain sea. He has used the very power of life to kill other men. He has harnessed the very force of all nature, not into warmth, or power or for light, but to force the end of the worst war in history.
> It is too bad that this great force, which has been in existence since the world began, has to be first harnessed as an ugly weapon of destruction. It is too bad that its great power had to first be felt as a death dealing bomb. . . .
> Yes, man has set sail in uncharted waters. Where will he fare to? Will his journey destroy him or will it find him a better world in which to live? Only time will tell.

The War Comes To An End

The summer of 1945 continued to witness bloody fighting in the Pacific and another Marcellus soldier died on the battlefield. "Pfc. Harvey W. Leigh, 27, father of four children, was killed in action June 22 on Okinawa, according to notification received by his parents, Mr. and Mrs. Lot Leigh, and his wife, Mrs. Edna Van Epps Leigh of Marcellus" (MO 7/27/45). Harvey Leigh was the 12th soldier from Marcellus to die in the conflict, and it occurred just a few weeks before the United States unleashed its final weapon of destruction on Hiroshima and Nagasaki. With the dropping of the atomic bombs, Japan sued for peace on August 14th, and the worst war in history came to end. Marcellus, along with the rest of the world, could now celebrate V-J Day, a Victory over Japan that was very costly for many American, including Marcellus, families.

> **The Marcellus Observer - Friday Morning, August 17, 1945**
> ## Bells And Sirens Proclaim End Of War As Villagers Dance And Shout With Joy
> V-J Day found Marcellus prepared to celebrate in a fitting manner. When the old bell in the Presbyterian church and the siren began to proclaim the end of the war, shortly after 7 o'clock, the quiet village suddenly came to life.
> While the siren was still blowing and the bell still ringing, local firemen enthusiastically boarded the two fire trucks and sailed noisily up and down the streets and out into the country districts, . . . Within a few minutes the streets were filled with joyous villagers, slapping each other's backs, shaking hands and hugging one another.
> Wednesday morning the crowd gathered at the village postoffice to exchange greetings and to congratulate those to whom the end of the war meant most. Several wives of servicemen wept tears of joy as their friends rejoiced with them over the outcome of the war. It was the most neighborly gathering in the history of the village.
> The community now awaits the returning of the men and women from t services. Only when that is accomplished will the cup of joy and gratitude be completely full.

Postwar Marcellus

As the community awaited the return of its service men and women, life gradually returned to a somewhat normal routine. There was worry throughout the nation that another depression might return and fear that many returning soldiers as well factory workers would be unemployed in postwar America. These concerns did not materialize, however, as Americans eagerly awaited and then bought the many consumer goods that were unavailable during the war. Automobile and appliance manufacturing provided many jobs. In addition, returning soldiers were assisted by passage of the G.I. Bill, enabling them to not only obtain job priority but also educational assistance if they wanted to continue their schooling and financial help if they wished to buy homes, farms and businesses. After the war, there were many building permits issued by the Village for construction of new homes, particularly on lower First Street, Second Street and South Street, as well as permits to remodel older homes and businesses throughout the community. This construction not only provided employment but it also heightened a concern about the Village water supply, promptly the Board to survey the system. With more residents in the Village, not only would the water supply be burdened, but other services such as sewage disposal, garbage pickup, and police and street maintenance as well.

> **The Marcellus Observer**
> **Friday Morning, August 24, 1945**
> **Survey Made To Increase Water Supply**
>
> A survey is being made of the Marcellus water system and facilities with a view of determining the possibilities of getting more water for the village. A competent engineer has been engaged to make the survey and to make tests in the vicinity of Rockwell Springs Reservoir for additional water.
>
> With the village steadily growing the need for more water has been apparent for several years . . . Marcellus water, while known by housewives to be hard, is of a high degree of purity. Some agitation was begun by a group of local housewives, just prior to the war, to persuade the village to install a water-softening plant, but the war halted the plan.

24 Sep 1945 - " . . . public hearing on the application of L. D. Paul for a zone change on his property at 34 and 36 North Street was held on this date. Mr. Paul was present and explained his plans for moving his offices to this location and converting his present office building to residential apartments. A petition against the proposed zone change, signed by owners of nearby property, was presented and there was some discussion of the matter. The Board reserved decision until some future date."

8 Oct 1945 - " . . . that a permit be granted to Mr. Morris to build a two story house and attached garage at 25 First Street, in accordance with plans on file in the Clerk's office."

> **The Marcellus Observer - Friday, Oct 26, 1945**
> **New 1946 Ford Shown Friday**
>
> Friday is V-8 Day!
> An automotive public that has not seen a new car since the war will get the first opportunity to view the 1946 Fords on that day. Bartlett Motors will have one of the new, improved models on display . . .
>
> **The Marcellus Observer - Friday, Nov 9, 1945**
> **Republicans Retain All Offices In Hard-Fought Election**
>
> **The Marcellus Observer - Friday, Nov 16, 1945**
> **State Muddles Village Parking On Main Street**

Halloween, Elections, Parking

The Halloween celebration in 1945 was marked by some thoughtless action on the part of several who defaced windows and cars with obscene markings, as well as an effigy of the Mayor tacked to a telephone pole on Main Street. Most disappointing, however, was a lack of cider and lemonade (shortage of sugar), which canceled the usual Halloween parade and party sponsored by the firemen. There was, however, much anticipation about the arrival of a new automobile in Bartlett's showroom, the first since the war years. There was also interest in the town election results that witnessed another first, a man (Morris Mulroy) running against a woman (Mary Wybron) for the position of Marcellus Town Supervisor.

New parking zones created on Main Street by the State drew much protest from Marcellus merchants in November, their argument that there was now less room for cars in the common center, adversely affecting their businesses.

8 Nov 1945 - " . . . in view of the objections of all of the merchants on both sides of Main Street to the parking lanes as laid out on the pavement by the State Highway Dept. and in view of

the fact that no permission has been granted by the Village Board for marking such parking lanes, the Village Board does hereby protest such action on the part of the State Highway Department and request the Department to show its authority for such action."

Year's End

The year had been a most significant one in the history of the world and in the history of small-town America. Similar to the returning veterans of 1918, those who were welcomed back to Marcellus in 1945 would find a community that was still home, but

> The Marcellus Observer
> Friday Morning, November 16, 1945
> New Banner Of Welcome Flies Over Main Street

one that had been, as they had been, altered by war. Many sacrifices had been made both at home and overseas and there was a longing for quiet, full-time, peacetime pursuits. This generation had seen enough of depression and war and craved the simple pleasures of home, family, and community but they were also realists. As the new year approached, " . . . Tennyson might have been writing of our first postwar Christmas when he said:

'Hope the best, but hold the present fatal daughter of the past,

Shape your heart to front the hour, but dream not that the hour will last.'

The war is over and we can only hope and pray it was the last" (MO 12/28/45).

> The Marcellus Observer
> Friday Morning, January 4, 1946
> New Year Welcomed With Parties, Noise And Merriment
>
> Marcellus ushered in the New Year with joy and merriment. Several parties were held in this vicinity, many for soldiers who had returned. Promptly at midnight the chimes told of the arrival of 1946 and that was a signal for folks all over town to wish one another a Happy New Year. At that moment there was considerable slapping of backs and many good wishes were spread around.
>
> The Marcellus Observer
> Friday Morning, January 11, 1946
> Wrap Garbage In Paper, Say Village Collectors
>
> Garbage collection would be greatly help, and fewer pails would be damaged, if housewives would wrap each meal's garbage in a separate paper and place it in the container . . . In freezing weather, loose garbage freezes to the pail, making it next to impossible to remove it.

1946

While the nation would have to contend with mounting inflation and some bitter labor disputes in 1946, the year began in Marcellus in a festive mood, residents grateful that the war was over and their service men and women were home or on their way. The business of village government continued, with a reminder about garbage collection, and acceptance by the Board of a new street, extending from Slocombe Avenue north to Reed Avenue. Once envisioned as an extension of Second Street, the newly renamed Kelly Avenue would also witness new housing, some of the ranch house variety, increasingly popular in the postwar period.

4 Jan 1946 - " . . . a deed dedicating that part of Second Street south of Reed Ave for Village purposes was received from Lloyd W. and Ruth Cummings. Moved by Mr. Case and carried that the street be accepted and renamed Kelly Avenue."

Clothing Drive and Bike Riding

The community began to participate in the Clothing and Tinned Fruit drive for Overseas Relief early in the year, a reminder that the war, while over, was not fully won yet. The Board also found it necessary, after a rash of " . . . sidewalk-riding bicyclists, bumping into three persons within a week and side-swiping several others . . . " (MO 1/26/46) to remind people of an ordinance prohibiting the riding of bicycles on the sidewalks. It appears that bicyclists and pedestrians have competed for use of the sidewalks in Marcellus as far back as the turn of the century. Even today, this has not changed, as skateboarders have been added to the competition. The Registrar of Vital Statistics did not change either, in 1946, as Mrs. Adelaide Uttley was reappointed to that position for another four-year term.

11 Feb 1946 - " . . . Mrs. Adelaide J. Uttley was reappointed Registrar of Vital Statistics for a term of four years."

Plans, Discharges and Permits

As plans were made for a new band in Town, the three sons and two daughters of Mr. and Mrs. Frank Seymour returned home from the war. It was " . . . quite unusual for a family to have five of its members in the service, and this is one of the few families in town that did . . . Furthermore, all the five sons and daughters were discharged as sergeants or the Naval equivalent" (MO 2/15/46). As many Marcellians looked ahead to the construction season, the Board began to remind residents of the need to obtain building permits. Permits applied not only to new construction but to remodeling as well and sometimes involved a public hearing if construction meant a change in zoning. In the postwar years, there were a number of changes that individuals wanted to make to their properties, both residential and commercial. To help facilitate the evaluation process, the Board in March authorized the creation of the Zoning Board of Appeals, to which would be appointed four, later five, members. This Board acts, even today, independent of the Village Board and its decision is a final judgment on the merits of a zoning issue. The Board also accepted the results of the Village election that month, as N. Giles Case was reelected to succeed himself with the unanimous vote of twenty-three Village residents.

The Marcellus Observer
Friday Morning, February 22, 1946
Necessity Of Permit To Build Stressed
Board's Permission Necessary To Build, Remodel
If you are contemplating building a new home, or even planning to remodel the outside of your present home or place of business, you must consult with the Village Board before doing so. This, of course, if your property is located inside the village limits.

11 Mar 1946 - " . . . Joseph Menapace presented an application, together with a certificate of assent by neighboring property owners, for a permit to alter the building at 20 North Street, making an automobile show room in the north half of the first floor and an apartment in the south half. A public hearing on the application was called for Monday evening, March 26th. An application by Calvin A. Spade for a permit to remodel a barn on the south side of Slocombe Ave into a six room house, was presented. A permit was granted."

19 Mar 1946 - " . . . that Edward V. Baker, Lester C. Norris, Clifford Dorchester and Henry E. Phillips be and hereby are appointed Zoning Board of Appeals."

19 Mar 1946 - " . . . for Trustee, for two years, N. Giles Case received 23 votes."

Teen Club

In this first year of the postwar period, there seemed to be a growing interest in doing something to promote the development of the youth of the community. Even the word " teenager" seems to have become more commonplace in the postwar years and, despite, its

The Marcellus Observer
Friday Morning, March 29, 1946
That "Teen Age Club"
A few weeks ago we wrote in this column that a club for teenagers of this village would be an asset to the community. Since then, we have had much comment on the suggestion - pro and con. The pros are greatly in the majority, and the principal worry of the cons is that a suitable place is not available. Practically all agree that the idea has merit and should be investigated.

bantam size, Marcellus's interest in its young people paralleled that in much larger cities and towns. There are any number of suggestions as to why this interest developed, including the influence of Dr. Benjamin Spock's book, *Baby and Child Care*, published in 1946, which encouraged parents to consider their children's needs before their own. Others have suggested that the young parents of this baby boom generation, deprived of much during the Depression and separated from one another by wartime experiences, wanted to make sure that things were better for their own kids, an attitude that would shape an entire generation and echo into the 21st century as well. Irrespective of this, Marcellus adults in 1946 felt obliged to provide an atmosphere as well as a place that would enable young people to socialize, practice correct behavior and mature into good citizens. A club for teenagers was promoted, some suggesting the school as a community center both year round and around the clock. Others were interested in using the American Legion building as a youth center and by the summer, "Harmony Hangout", as it would be called, became a reality. Recreation committees, as part of Village and Town government would follow and today the Recreation Department's budget ensures a wide variety of services for the community's youth, especially during the summer months.

The Marcellus Observer
Friday Morning, April 12, 1946
Residents Sign Petition Asking
Zoning Change
At a . . . hearing before the Village Board last Monday evening, Joseph Menapace showed evidence of agreement among residents of North Street to his proposal that the former L. D. Paul office be returned to business use as a display room for Kaiser-Fraiser cars.

The Marcellus Observer
Friday Morning, April 19, 1946
""Don't Rake Rubbish Out Into Street!" - Morgan
The raking of rubbish to the curb and leaving it for the trash collectors to pick up has brought stiff criticism from George Morgan, Village Foreman, who claims that such practice is against the rules. All rubbish must be placed in containers if the village truck is to carry it away.

Appointments, Hearings, Reminders

When the Village Board conducted its annual meeting in April, a variety of appointments were made. A public hearing, the first of several that year, was held that month -- an application for change in zoning requiring Board approval. There was also some concern expressed about the condition of the gutters on North and South Streets and the desire of the Board to have the State correct what would continue to be a problem along this State highway. By the end of the month, the State did make some improvement, widening part of North Street, but filling the ditches as well as improving the drainage along this highway would be a continual struggle between the Village and the State for the next sixty years. Another concern, the raking of rubbish into the streets, drew the wrath of the highway foreman and automobile drivers were cautioned about the return of the traffic light on Main Street. "During the war, when tires and gasoline were short, the lights were set on continuous signal, meaning only a momentary stop for caution" (MO 4/19/46).

1 Apr 1946 - " . . . that George W. Morgan be appointed Street Commissioner at a salary of $2800 per year and . . . allowed one week's vacation with pay . . . the salary of the Clerk and Treasurer combined, be increased to $850 per year . . . the wages of John Kelly and Melville Corp

be increased to $1.02 per hour for a 40 hour week, with time and a half for overtime, . . . Martin K. King . . . reappointed policeman at $100 per year . . . "

> **The Marcellus Observer**
> **Friday Morning, April 12, 1946**
> **Watch Stop Signal, Drivers Advised**
> Local drivers are warned that the traffic lights in the center of the village are now directing traffic as they did before the war days, by turning red and green at specified intervals.
>
> **The Marcellus Observer**
> **Friday Morning, April 26, 1946**
> **Section Of North St. Being Widened**
> The widening of the road on North Street, near the common center, was begun this week with men from the State Highway Dept. doing the labor.

8 Apr 1946 - " . . . public hearing on the application of Mr. Joseph Menapace for zone change at 20 North Street . . . Mr. Steadman gave his position in the matter. He said he had hoped that the neighborhood would remain residential, but did not wish to be the only holdout; would agree to the change of zone if assured of protection by written agreement."

8 Apr 1946 - " . . . Clerk was instructed to write to the State Highway Department in regard to the dangerous condition of the gutters on North and South Streets."

Memorial Day

Memorial Day in 1946 was its first peacetime observance in a number of years and in his address, speaking primarily to the veterans of the war just concluded, Martin Sennett reminded all who were listening, of the duties of citizenship, of the reasons why small-town communities like Marcellus are willing to sacrifice -- to insure the survival of the republic. In his speech, he noted: "Those of you who are here, I know are glad to be here. I know too that you, as well as everyone else, are thinking of those fellows who are not here . . . It is about those fellows who are not here, and our duties to them, that I speak. It seems strange, having given up from one to four years of our lives in the service, that we should still owe a duty to anyone. But, we have invested our service, and they have invested their lives, for the principles of democracy. Therefore, it is our duty to them, and to ourselves, to insure that it is a good and lasting investment. Neither we who came back nor the fellows who died, were thinking very much about

> **The Marcellus Observer - Friday, June 7, 1946**
> **First Peacetime Memorial Day Observance Impressive**
> Memorial Day was observed with fitting solemnity in Marcellus, with nearly everyone turning out to pay tribute to those who have given their lives in wars past. The parade started the observance . . . At the monument . . . remarks, followed by a prayer . . . Memorial flowers . . . dedicated to the dead . . . The parade reformed and marched to the park . . . speakers . . . concluding ceremony . . . at the flagpole . . .

principles either then, or now. Regardless of that, however, we did serve, and they did die for those principles on which our country is built . . . " (MO 6/7/46).

With Jobs and Money, Few Complaints

With the lifting of wartime controls and the demand for consumer goods increasing sharply, local companies, such as Allen V. Smith, Crown Mills and Camillus Cutlery, advertised frequently for jobs that summer. In addition, local stores were now stocking items that had once been strictly rationed. Despite rising prices, few complained, since many had saved and sacrificed during the war. Now they wanted to

> **The Marcellus Observer - Friday, July 19, 1946**
> **More Food on Market Shelves**
> The meat situation in Marcellus is getting definitely better. With plenty of beef now in the coolers, local housewives are beginning to hope for larger quantities of pork and lamb. Some are so optimistic as to even hope to see hams again on the vacant hooks. The price of meat has gone higher in keeping with the times but few are complaining too much. It seems so good to be able to obtain meat that, as yet, the hungry populace has given little thought to price . . .
> Butter is once more adorning the shelves of the stores openly . . . Margarine is still on the short list . . . Sugar has taken a considerable jump, but still remains rationed.

spend. The only complaint seemed to come from the local editor, who bemoaned the lack of news in a summer column saying " . . . It's vacation season and people seem to be taking a vacation from doing everything. I'd give a week's pay to look out the office window right now and see a man bite a dog . . . " (MO 7/26/46). With the opening of "Harmony Hangout" as a teen center, even the youngsters had no complaint.

> **The Marcellus Observer**
> **Friday Morning, August 2, 1946**
> **Teen-Age Center To Open Soon**
> With the rooms in the legion building which will house 'Harmony Hangout' rapidly rounding into shape, the committee of teenagers has already prepared a list of 11 chaperones who will be in attendance at the canteen's activities . . .

> **The Marcellus Observer**
> **Friday Morning, September 20, 1946**
> **Village Borrows $15,000**
> A number of current and proposed improvements in the village of Marcellus have caused the board of trustees to negotiate a new bond issue in the amount of $15,000. This new issue, which was successfully bid for by the First National Bank of Marcellus, is repayable over the next five years.

Village Improvements

Improved financial conditions led to the construction of more homes in the southern part of the Village, in an area known as the Wilson Tract, and this was accompanied by the opening and dedication of new streets. The Village Board also found it prudent to pass a bond resolution that would authorize street and sidewalk as well as sewer and water improvements, not only in this new development but in other parts of the Village. The resolution also covered the cost of a fire truck, money well spent and at a time when few taxpayers voiced objection.

19 Aug 1946 - " . . . special meeting . . . an offer to dedicate lands for street purposes . . . being Wilson Drive . . . a proposed street to be known as Dunlap Avenue . . . part of Baker Road . . ."

28 Aug 1946 - " . . . a resolution authorizing the consolidation into one bond issue of $15,000 serial bonds of the Village of Marcellus, New York, the bonds heretofore authorizing this date by separate bond resolutions for street improvements, sidewalk improvements, water improvements, sewer improvement, storm sewer improvements, and for a fire truck."

16 Sep 1946 - " . . . the bid of the said First National Bank of Marcellus be and the same is hereby accepted, and said $15,000 Public Improvement (Serial) Bonds, 1946, bearing interest at the rate of 1.00 per centum per annum are hereby accepted . . ."

> **The Marcellus Observer**
> **Friday Morning, September 20, 1946**
> **Drivers Warned Of School Bus Statute**
> With the opening of the fall school term, a new regulation regarding the passing of school busses has gone into effect. Many, if not most, drivers of automobiles seem unaware of this change. According to the new statute, it is illegal to pass a stationary school bus regardless of the direction from which you approach it unless you are signaled to do so by the bus driver.
> In the past, the rule required that you stop and then proceed with caution. Now you stop and remain stopped until the bus is again under motion or the driver waves you by. All violations of this ruling are required to be reported to Albany . . .

Openings In The Fall

When school started in September, enrollment was an all-time high, fueled in part by veterans hoping to obtain their high school diplomas and then, perhaps, make use of the G.I. Bill to further their education. In addition, as if to anticipate the number of baby boom children that would soon be attending school, a new state law now required motorists to stop for stopped school busses. In a community such as Marcellus, this law became and remains quite significant since the entire school campus lies adjacent to the Village and is serviced by Village streets.

Not only did school open in September, so too did the teen center. "Flocking to the Legion rooms were over 175 teen-agers and guests (twice the crowd that was anticipated) and from all reports the place was really rocking. The record player recently purchased by the Legion . . . given a major workout as the kids kept the music going - some sweet and some hot" (MO 9/27/46). The local Community Chest drive would also get underway, a major focus of which was the prevention of juvenile delinquency in their advertisements.

The Marcellus Observer - Friday Morning, October 11, 1946
What One Town Found Out About JUVENILE DELINQUENCY
This wasn't a crowded city or a factory town. It was a quiet country town that had never had any juvenile crime problem. That is, . . . UNTIL . . . The Boy Scouts, the Girl Scouts, and the Community House shut down. The folks who ran them had gone to fight or into war work. Then a series of crimes broke out . . . traced to children of 'good' families. Investigation showed 'there was just no place for the kids to go for wholesome recreation.' Give . . . for the kids. Give . . . for our town . . . Give . . . because you're wise enough to want our youngsters to grow into citizens you can be proud of.

The Marcellus Observer
Friday Morning, November 1, 1946
Teen-Agers Make Success Of First
Dance; Hall Filled With Local Youth

The Marcellus Observer
Friday Morning, November 8, 1946
Hallowe'en Passes With Little Damage

The Marcellus Observer
Friday Morning, November 22, 1946
Petition To Village Board Asks
Restraint On Garbage Fires

Meats and Treats

In mid October, President Truman announced that " . . . meats were off the controlled list for good. Immediately Marcellus merchants got busy . . . there was beef on their counters the next morning" (MO 10/18/46). In addition, the Fire Department announced that it would resume its "Kiddie Karnival," bringing back the Halloween parade and party that had to be canceled the previous year. For the teens, " . . . the first public dance held by Harmony Hangout, . . . at St. Francis Hall . . . was a decided success" (MO 11/1/46), and Halloween pranks were few in number, with little serious damage.

In November, elections were held and the Marcellus vote enabled the Republicans to take a majority in both houses of Congress. The Village Board also voted to grant building permits to L. D. Paul for new homes on a street that would eventually bear that surname. It was also presented with a petition signed by residents asking that the Board investigate and then ban the burning of garbage in the Village. Today, such practice is not allowed by Village ordinance, but at the time, the burning of trash in backyards and in furnaces was common.

11 Nov 1946 - " . . . that permits be granted to L. D. Paul to erect Cape Cod bungalows on Lots Nos. 4, 5, 7, 8, 9 on a street running in an easterly direction between No. 32 and 34 North Street."

Observer Changes Hands

As the year ended, so did ownership of *The Marcellus Observer* by Roy A. Gallinger. A leader in the community and a gatherer of all sorts of news, he began work at the paper in 1925 and when he left, some local identity seemed to go with him. The new owners of the paper seemed to express that sentiment when they asked for help in gathering local news. "Some people have asked us 'why don't you put more local news in your paper', our answer has always been, 'We aren't well enough acquainted with these good people to write about them'" (MO 12/27/46). The postwar years would mark additional changes in local identity, some of which included building landmarks dating back to the founding of the Village.

1947

When the new year began, Governor Dewey's announcement " . . .that state taxes would not be increased by the 1947 Legislature was praised as far-sighted and in the best interests of the State . . . " (MO 1/3/47). It was a well-received message because rising prices, labor demands, and a housing shortage had led to some restlessness in a nation still trying to convert to a peacetime economy. In Marcellus, these concerns did not seem, now, to be as anxious. The new owners of *The Marcellus Observer*, still trying to become familiar with the community, received a lot of advice from residents and

---

The Marcellus Observer - Friday, Jan 3, 1947
Getting Acquainted

We still think Marcellus is one of the most attractive of all places to live and to work. Going home and coming to work, we find the beauty of the snow interesting beyond belief. I suppose some people condemn it but others can still find enjoyment in it. It was really a picture going home last Friday. The headlights of the car made the snowflakes seem as thousands of diamonds falling from the sky. The boys and girls tell us that skating and skiing have been perfect. Hope to join them soon.

---

dispensed some interesting comment in its weekly column, while praising the beauty of Marcellus that winter.

The Marcellus Observer - Friday, January 17, 1947
The Question In Mind Today is Which Shall It Be? Maiden Lane Or?

Back in the year 1922, there was shown on the map of Marcellus a street which was listed as 'Maid-en Lane'. Later that name was changed. Some of the residents of the village remember that change. To others the name Maiden Lane is new, but nevertheless the ghost of Maiden Lane has returned. The spirits from the past were aroused when inquiries as to the correct spelling of the present name were started.

. . . The poles at both ends of the street hold up signs spelled 'Slocombe'. On further investigation, it was found the Marcellus phone book lists the name as 'Slocum' . . .

How this variety of spelling came about no one seems to know . . . the people of the street prefer it spelled 'Slocum' and in some cases a preference to return it to the original 'Maiden Lane'.

There is a question in the minds of a number of the older residents whether the name was ever officially changed to its present name.

Incorporation, Inspection, Application

The beginning of 1947 was particularly significant for the Marcellus Fire Department, which was allowed by the Village Board to incorporate as a legal entity that year. In addition, fire inspection reports were submitted to the Village Board and orders to remedy were issued. Preparations were also made by the Board to increase the Village water supply, making application to the federal government for financial assistance in the construction of a pumping station and storage tank. The Board also may have discussed an item in the local paper that questioned the correct name for Slocombe Street.

13 Jan 1947 - " . . . that the Fire Department be authorized to incorporate under the laws of the State of New York. The Village Fire Inspectors submitted reports of inspections of property . . . a request that action be taken within one week to carry out the recommendations of the Inspectors. The Mayor and Clerk . . . authorized to execute the necessary papers in . . . application to the Federal Works Agency for an advance for the purpose of preparing plans for a water pumping station and steel storage tank . . . "

Roy A. Gallinger

Gallinger Recognized

No one, however, questioned the American Legion when it presented its Distinguished Citizenship Award to Roy A. Gallinger that year. The former publisher of *The Marcellus Observer* was cited for his record during the war, sending " . . . a copy of *The Observer* to every service man and woman from the community every week while they were in service . . . the equivalent of a letter from home and . . . of no small value in keeping up their morale. In addition to this, the columns of his newspaper . . . always . . . available to assist in any civic enterprise" (MO 2/7/47).

The Marcellus Observer
Friday Morning, March 7, 1947
Storm Breaks 30-Year Record
3-Day Battle Slowly Getting
Traffic Back to Normal
Records of long standing went down under the wave after wave of snowflakes the past week. All branches of traffic, including motor, air and locomotive were stalled throughout the entire State . . . The gorge route out of Marcellus was the only open route traversable . . .

Snow and Elections

March came in like the proverbial lion in 1947, the situation fairly critical at times such as " . . . mothers with young babies marooned as long as three days in isolated spots where even snow-plows found it a difficult task to break through the huge drifts" (MO 3/7/47). By Election Day, however, twelve voters braved the elements to re-elect Varnum Kenyon and Clayton Edgerton as Mayor and Trustee.

18 Mar 1947 - " . . . the results were as follows:
For Mayor   Varnum S. Kenyon   12 Votes
For Trustee, 2 years   Clayton A. Edgerton   12 Votes

Notices and Appointments

The arrival of spring in 1947 seemed to signal, as it does today, the arrival of the construction and lawn season, as business and advertising picked up the momentum that had disappeared during the Depression and War. Insecticides developed and used during the war were now being applied on Village and residential trees; and people who had saved during the war could now buy the new home they had always wanted. The Board also made its appointments and served notice of the fee levied for those who wishing to be connected to Village utilities such as sewer and water.

7 Apr 1947 - " . . . that J. Fred Woodbridge be appointed Clerk and Treasurer at an annual salary of $850."

14 Apr 1947 - " . . . that the Village make a flat charge of $20 each for sewer and water connections to buildings in the Village."

Civic Pride

April also dated the start of the Marcellus Community Council, a civic association that would become the lead agency for promoting youth programs in the community. "The first programs launched were a Youth Canteen and a summer playground, with its swimming program " . . . From its simple offerings, . . . the Council's programs branched into many activities . . . " (Heffernan 254), and today operates as part of the Town of Marcellus Recreation Department.

Another group that became increasingly active after the War was the Ralph Share Post of the American Legion. Returning veterans gradually took over leadership of the

---

The Marcellus Observer - Friday Morning, April 25, 1947
New Civic Organization
Plans Already Started on the M.C.C.

For some time a need has been felt for a civic organization to plan and organize such projects as may be deemed necessary to contribute to the general betterment of the community life.

Plans have already been started to set the wheels in motion for such an organization to be known as the Marcellus Community Council. Foremost in the purpose of this council we find a sponsorship of youth recreational activities to encourage community interest in the activities of the younger set.

The Marcellus Observer - Friday Morning, May 16, 1947
Learn-To-Swim Campaign
Red Cross Swimming Project Ok'd By Community Council

. . . a program begun last summer by the . . . Red Cross will be expanded this year to include all the youth of the community who are interested in swimming. The program was accepted . . . by the Community Council as one of the worthwhile projects to be sponsored during the summer months . . .

The Marcellus Observer - Friday Morning, June 13, 1947
Marcellus Without Water 4 Hours

The Village water supply was cut Wednesday afternoon, to connect in the main to the new tract on South Ave. Work seems to be progressing at a rapid pace on the new tract, which will be known as Wilson Drive.

The Marcellus Observer - Friday Morning, June 20, 1947
Marcellus Topic Of Speech
Geographical Survey of Marcellus Topic of Speech by Bernard Rabin At Citizen Club Meeting

---

group, attracting new members and planning a variety of activities. One of these undertakings was placing a new Memorial Plaque " . . . on the monument in front of the Methodist church. The new marker will contain the names of dead of World War II which will be added to the names and inscription on the original plaque" (MO 4/25/47). On Memorial Day, Post Commander Fred Hyatt " . . . spoke impressively after the unveiling and decorating of the plaque containing the names of the community's dead heroes of W.W. I and W.W. II" (MO 6/6/47).

Progress

By June, an enlargement of the Village was evident in both the powers of the Board and the addition of new housing. As if to underscore this growth, a speech by Bernard Rabin at a meeting of the Citizens Club that month relayed a history of Marcellus, particularly " . . . the influence of geography on the residents of the valley past and present . . . the patterns of settlement, the changes in agriculture and the industries on the Creek" (MO 6/20/47). It was a speech that not only drew much interest in 1947, but remains significant as a source of reference for historians today as well.

9 Jun 1946 - " . . . that the Treasurer be and is hereby authorized to set up a petty cash fund of $200 in accordance with the provisions of the Village law."

Marcellus And The Nation

While Marcellus was enjoying its Old Home Day celebration in July, the first Republican Congress in fifteen years was planning to recess for the summer. Many programs of the 80th Congress had been and continued to be controversial, providing campaign issues for the presidential race in 1948. The Truman plan to aid Greece and Turkey fight the spread of communism was not a source of argument, nor was the Marshall Plan which called for billions of dollars to help Europe recover from the War. When Congress, however, passed the Taft-Hartley Bill in June, over the President's veto, there were frightening predictions of violent clashes between labor and management, none of which occurred in the "dog days of summer."

MO August 29, 1947

Permits and Projects

Neither was there much argument on the Village Board when Frank Seymour, along with others, applied for a zoning permit change and Elizabeth White was appointed Registrar of Vital Statistics, completing the term of Adelaide Uttley who had passed away unexpectedly. The Board also approved the establishment of a Recreation Project, submitting an application to the New York State Youth Commission for funding. The Mayor issued warnings to those who were violating the Village traffic laws that summer and a study was conducted by the local postmaster as to the possibility of having a carrier in the Village.

The Marcellus Observer
Friday Morning, July 11, 1947
Council Project Successful
Playground Program Gets Off To A Good Start With 78 Children
The summer recreation program started by the Community Council got underway July 1, with . . . youngsters taking part in softball, badminton, tennis, ping-pong, volleyball and baseball. The program has been moved to the park for the remainder of the summer.

The Marcellus Observer
Friday Morning, August 22, 1947
Mayor Issues Warning To Traffic Violators
Mayor Varnum S. Kenyon states that the Village intends to bring justice to bear to all traffic violators . . . One of the most frequent infringements is jumping the stop light at the corners of Main and North Sts., and Main and South Sts., which presents a dangerous hazard to both motorists and pedestrians. Exceeding the Village speed limit of 25 miles per hour is another dangerous practice . . .

The Marcellus Observer
Friday Morning, August 22, 1947
Bill Conley Makes Rounds Of The Village
. . . Although Marcellus is far below the needed population quota for a local mail carrier, Mr. Conley has investigated every possibility of providing the Village with this service . . .

---

7 Jul 1947 - " . . . the application of Frank Seymour Jr. to change the zoning on a part of his property on North Street from residential to business, to permit the New York State Water Service Corporation to erect and maintain a pumping station thereon."

14 Jul 1947 - " . . . the intention of the Village of Marcellus to establish a Recreation Project. The Village of Marcellus is about to submit an application for such project to the New York State Youth Commission for its approval . . . Mrs. Elizabeth C. White was appointed Registrar of Vital Statistics to complete the unexpired term of Mrs. Adelaide J. Uttley, deceased."

Expansion

September marked the largest registration in the history of the school as well as an expansion of the activities of the Community Council into the winter season. The expansion of the Allen V. Smith Company, which had purchased another plant in Colorado, gave indications of a prosperous future and added employment for the community as well.

The Marcellus Observer - Friday Morning, September 26, 1947
Council Report Of Activities - Winter Plans - 1947-48
The Council, with the support of the various organizations of the village, proposes to carry out an extensive program of winter activities, not only for the youth of the village but for adults as well. The winter program . . . will include bowling, dancing and supervised games for youngsters of various age groups. Among other adult activities planned are gatherings at which newcomers to the village will have an opportunity to meet their townsfolk. Adult evening craft classes at the school are . . . planned

Responsibilities

Town elections meant registration in October and the local paper urged residents not to " . . . shirk that greatest of honors and privileges! . . . Local elections are just as important as presidential elections, for out of these elections, issues of wider scope are finally influenced" (MO 10/3/47). Nor did the Village Board avoid its responsibility, authorizing improvements to its sewer system and eliminating direct disposal of sewage into Nine Mile Creek. The Board also appointed Harold Leigh " as a patrolman for the Village of Marcellus . . . on duty . . . at various hours . . . especially on guard for speeding motorists. Another main duty . . . to quell any rowdyism such as has been causing disturbance to the peace of our town" (MO 10/24/47). In addition, made aware that building and remodeling was being done without a permit from the Village, the Board reminded residents to complete that responsibility before starting construction. Later in the month, at a special meeting, the Board made residents aware of the plans that were being formalized for improving the water supply in the Village, a project that would take several more years to complete.

13 Oct 1947 - " . . . resolution authorizing the construction of additions to the sewer system in the Village of Marcellus, New York at a maximum estimated cost of $12,000."

The Marcellus Observer
Friday Morning, October 10, 1947
Septic Tank Being Installed on Main St

The new septic tank being installed on lower Main Street to handle the sewage disposal between Orange St. and Nine Mile Creek was recently approved by the Village Board.

Undoubtedly one of the greatest improvements from a healthful standpoint, this has been an issue of long standing both from the residents of the area as well as State officials. Sewage disposal for this area has been drained into Nine Mile Creek creating a more or less unsanitary condition, which will now be eliminated.

The Marcellus Observer
Friday Morning, October 31, 1947
More Water For Village Discussed At Village Board Meeting on Monday

At another special meeting of the Village Board . . . O'Brien and Gere, Consulting Engineers, presented unfinished drawings of the proposed water project to supply Marcellus with more water from Otisco Lake.

Our present system . . . is in excellent condition although nearly 40 years old. But line after line has been added to it until now the Village Board claims that it is not adequate to supply all the families of Marcellus . . . because of the present drought . . . our homes and probably our lives are at stake if the present system should fail . . . the new supply would be cheaper and we would never have to worry about water.

A few years ago, the U.S. government proposed that villages that would like to improve their present supply of water ask and they would supply the necessary money to prepare plans for such a project. Our board being foresighted enough to know that the village was growing and would continue to grow submitted their application and it was accepted.

It so happens that the N.Y. Water service is going to build a pumping station at the end of North Street and at this station the Village will make an emergency connection to the Otisco Lake line and with the installation of a small pump, water can be pumped to a Tank Reservoir which will be located at the top of Reed Parkway . . .

There are today 375 meters in the village of Marcellus and more are being required as time moves on. Our present requirements on the reservoir total about 90,000 gallons a day.

This project will be put to the people for a vote in the near future and it is hoped that everyone might see the good and also the necessity of putting in this supply . . .

Commitment

In November, citizens turned out to vote in the town elections and a request that Village residents, because of a lack of rain in the fall, to be cautious in the use of water, met with a positive response. The Board also responded favorably, on Grievance Day, to requests by disabled veterans for tax exemptions.

18 Nov 1947 - " . . . at Grievance Day, . . . presented an application for the full exemption provided by law on the property of a disabled veteran . . . Exemption in the amount of $5000 was granted."

The commitment of the community, however, was never more evident as the year ended in 1947. Neighbors and friends, young and old, men and women, professionals and

> **The Marcellus Observer**
> **Friday Morning, December 10, 1947**
> **Hilliard Home Completed**

tradesmen spent an entire year donating time, labor and money to build a home for Fred Hilliard. A casualty of the war, Hilliard came home as a paraplegic and the community responded enthusiastically in a drive to " . . . build a specially equipped home for the disabled veteran . . . The completed house at 11 Chrisler Street, was presented to Hilliard and his wife at Christmas, 1947" (Heffernan 118), a fitting a way to mark the season and seemed a fitting parallel to the movie, *Miracle On 34th Street*, being offered at the Strand Theatre uptown.

1948

Throughout the year, President Truman and the Republican Congress would argue furiously over a number of issues, particularly that of loyalty and " . . . the supposed presence of communists in government positions" (Carruth 813). The arrival of 1948 seemed to produce little Marcellus news at the start, a local reporter wishing everyone a Happy New Year, but stating " . . . there is little to write about: of course the weather is always good for a few lines and right now it is about as cold as I've seen it" (MO 1/2/48).

Fire Contract

Within a few days, however, a local issue, which seemed to parallel the fight in Washington emerged, as the Village and Town of Marcellus began to spar over the terms

> **The Marcellus Observer**
> **Friday Morning, January 9, 1948**
> **Fire Protection Contract Discussed At Special Meeting**
>
> **The Marcellus Observer**
> **Friday Morning, January 16, 1948**
> **Public Hearing On Contract**
> . . . The percentage of fires is greater in the rural area than in the village and the department feels that more property could be saved if they had equipment to get to the fires faster and have enough water with them when they arrive.

of a new fire contract, the last one having expired in November 1947. Even the issue of snow plowing affected relations between the two entities. Before purchasing its own plow the previous fall, the Village used to rely on the Town " . . . to handle snow removal problems . . . this proved inadequate since the Town highways were necessarily given first preference to keep main arteries of travel open, and the Village streets serviced after the main highways had been cleaned" (MO 1/9/48). With its own plow, however, the Board now relied on the Village highway crew to keep the streets clean, as much as it relied on Doc Walsh to keep sickness in abeyance that winter. The issue of the fire contract, however, would continue virtually throughout the year, the main argument being the purchase of additional fire apparatus. It was not until October that the question was finally resolved.

5 Jan 1948 - " . . . the Clerk notify the Town Board that unless an agreement is reached on a new Fire District contract by January 15th, this Board would not feel itself obligated to continue to furnish fire protection beyond the Village limits."

12 Jan 1948 – " . . . Dr. Joseph H. Walsh was appointed Health Officer for a term of 4 years beginning as of this date."

Parking and Polio

There was also a fuel shortage that winter, as both businesses and homeowners were urged to conserve fuel oil. In addition, the issue of parking in the Village again gained notoriety and this problem would not be resolved until year's end.

A major scare in the postwar years was the great increase in the number of cases of infantile paralysis, more commonly referred to as polio. In those years, the March of Dimes conducted an annual campaign, and " . . . once again the generosity and consideration of the people of Marcellus was proven . . ." (MO 2/20/48). Within a month, the annual Red Cross campaign began, and the community was told that the need was greater than ever because of the increase in the cost of living and the fact that 1947 set a new record for disaster relief.

> **The Marcellus Observer**
> **Friday Morning, January 30, 1948**
> **Parking Problem Getting To Be Serious in Marcellus**
> One of the subjects discussed . . . many times from the people of Marcellus is the lack of parking space in the downtown section of the village. One of the measures advanced . . . is to have the people working in the stores of the village find a parking place away from the stores and out of the way of the shoppers . . .
> Behind the Engine House was one of the places suggested. In front of the Presbyterian garages was another . . . Another suggestion was the installation of parking meters on the village streets . . .
>
> **The Marcellus Observer**
> **Friday Morning, February 27, 1948**
> **Give To The Red Cross Now**

The winter also seemed like a good time to plan for the summer and, anticipating record crowds at Marcellus Park, County officials made plans to acquire more land and make improvements at this facility. Plans were also begun to " . . . halt use of the Village dump adjacent to the northeastern corner of the park as unsightly and a health menace" (MO 2/27/48), a concern that would start to be addressed the next month.

Election and Protection

N. Giles Case

In March, the Village election drew only nine voters, returning N. Giles Case to office. The Board also announced that the Village Patrolman, Harold Leigh, would be " . . . on call at all times . . . on the alert for . . . parking offenders in an effort to clear up the situation" (MO 3/19/48). The local paper also noted that much progress had been made in extending additional protection for Village residents who crossed the East Hill Bridge. Protection against fire, however, was denied to Town residents. Because the Village, with only one fire truck, might be left without protection and a new fire contract authorizing another truck had not been signed by the Town, the Board ordered

> **The Marcellus Observer - Friday Morning, March 19, 1948**
> **Many Improvements In Village**
> Many of you may have noticed that wire screen is being installed on the bridge at the foot of East Hill. This certainly is a very worthwhile project. Up until now this unscreened bridge invited the opportunity for some inquisitive child to topple through into the creek. Or even a grown-up might have lost their footing and find themselves sliding through the open rails. We are glad to see this danger spot protected. Also the huge elm tree surrounding the old Parson property at the corner of Orange and Main Streets are being removed. These trees have been in need of attention for sometime and their removal is another step toward improvement in the Village.
>
> **The Marcellus Observer - Friday Morning, March 26, 1948**
> **Town Without Protection**
> **Mayor Issues Orders that the Fire Trucks are Not to Leave Village After March 27; Contract Not Signed**

the fire truck not to leave the Village. It was a dangerous situation but one which the Village felt necessary. It would also be repeated almost 50 years later when negotiations between the Village and the Town over an expired fire contract led to a similar order by the Village Board in 1995.

That same month, the Board took steps to provide more health protection for residents, acquiring land for a Village dump. It also voted to discontinue the office of Village Attorney, a decision that would subsequently be reversed in later Board action

16 Mar 1948 - " . . . the total number of ballots cast for the office of Trustee for a term of two years was 9, of which N. Giles Case received 9."

29 Mar 1948 - " . . . was voted to purchase a piece of land from Mrs. Sarah M. Baker for the sum of $1200.00, said land to be used for a Village dump."

5 Apr 1948 - " . . . it was voted to discontinue the office of Village Attorney."

The Marcellus Observer
Friday Morning, April 23, 1948
Litter In The Streets

The appearance of many towns is marred by the habit which some of their people have, of throwing small articles of paper on the streets or sidewalks. This gives an impression of disorder and lack of neatness. Some people seem to think that if they buy something in a paper bag or wrapper, they are entitled to throw the bag or wrapper into the street.

They can make a contribution to the appearance of their home town, if they would throw such bits of paper into a proper receptacle or take it home and dispose of it where it is not open to view . . .

Permits and Police Justice

The spring again brought out a great many building permits as well as approval of the budget by the Village Board. While an editorial in *The Marcellus Observer* urged residents to keep litter off the streets, the Board decided to do something about parking in the streets, discussing the situation in a special meeting as well as appointing Dr. M. W. Sullivan as Police Justice. A local veterinarian, Dr. Sullivan served in this position for ten years, and became responsible for helping to enforce traffic and parking laws in the Village, with stiff penalties.

Dr. M. W. Sullivan
Village Police Justice
1949-1959

12 Apr 1948 " . . . building permits were granted as follows: Richard V. May, Calvin A. Spade, Joe Wheelock, Webb & Orr, Alan Palmer, Arthur L. Waters."

26 Apr 1948 - " . . . A public hearing on the proposed budget for the current fiscal year was held at 8:00 O'clock P.M., . . . No one appeared in opposition . . . motion by Mr. Case, seconded by Mr. Edgerton, the . . . budget was adopted: . . . local assistance estimated to be received from the State of New York by the Village of Marcellus during the fiscal year . . . is $4,336.00."

10 May 1948 - " . . . Building permits were granted to Harry Long, Dudley Hickman and Wendell Ghent . . . Glenn Spencer . . . granted permission to purchase water from the Village . . . that the office of Police Justice be established. "

24 May 1948 - " . . . Dr. M. W. Sullivan was appointed Police Justice to serve for the remainder of the year at a salary of $150."

The Marcellus Observer - Friday Morning, May 28, 1948
Village Board Holds Special Meeting To Discuss Parking Problem; Appoint Doctor M. W. Sullivan New Justice

Sheep in the Cemetery

Another topic of discussion was the condition of the Village Cemetery, the resting place for many of the first settlers of the community as well as the burial ground for many Revolutionary and Civil War Veterans. Stones needed to be righted and the sheep that had been placed there do " . . . a real job of getting the overgrown grass down to normal . . . but it will take work, which takes money, to bring the cemetery up to what it should be as a spot of historic interest . . . " (MO 5/28/48).

Other veterans would be buried that spring including one of the first of the Marcellus boys to give his life in World War II. John T. Campion came home to be buried on the hill as the American Legion and the Veterans of Foreign Wars were making plans for Memorial Day. It would include a parade to be led by another Marcellus veteran, Forrest Vosler, as Parade Marshall. During an air mission over Germany, Vosler had become wounded and risked his own life to save others, and " . . . for his heroism, President Franklin D. Roosevelt pinned the Congressional Medal of Honor on the blouse of Forrest L. Vosler, on August 31, 1944" (Heffernan 119).

Summer, 1948

As the summer of '48 drew near, residents of the community were encouraged to participate in the Fresh Air Campaign, promoted so sharply in the Mauldin cartoon. The

FRESH AIR FUND
A Rare Aroma   by Bill Mauldin

"It's a bottle of fresh air I scooped up in Central Park. I take a whiff from time to time."

MO June 11, 1948

summer also meant another Old Home Day Celebration as the " . . . firemen who were the hosts for the day provided the tremendous crowd with several forms of entertainment . . . The Mutt Show . . . brought out the biggest collection of dogs . . . ever seen at one time" (MO 7/9/48). Marcellus Park lived up to expectations, crowds of people visiting the beauty spot: " . . . on the fourth of July there were over 6,000 people there. The following Sunday that same number or more . . . " (MO 7/16/48). Hundreds of Marcellus youngsters participated in the Red Cross summer swimming program, and many residents spent the summer doing a lot of painting and remodeling, " . . . the Hardware Store having the outside shingled, Ed Bartlett putting in a new surface for the driveway down at the garage, Bud Fisher doing over the Men's Shop and Seymour Parsons remodeling and rewiring our building . . ." (MO 8/13/48). While some were making improvements, others were destroying property, as an August headline in *The Marcellus Observer* screamed " Garden Wrecked by Boys". A rather senseless act, the paper went on to say that " . . . this sort of vandalism can create a bad name for the village . . . has no place in our village and we hope never to print stories on destructive vandalism again" (MO 8/13/48). Perhaps it was in anticipation of such vandalism that requests for State police patrols were requested that summer.

9 Aug 1948 - " . . . John E. Berry was authorized to communicate with the State Police in regard to a patrol for the Village."

> **The Marcellus Observer**
> **Friday Morning, September 10, 1948**
> **New Equipment Ordered**
>
> **he Marcellus Observer**
> **Friday Morning, September 10, 1948**
> **Should Marcellus Have A Full-Time Policeman?**
>
> **The Marcellus Observer**
> **Friday Morning, October 8, 1948**
> **Fire Prevention Week**

New Equipment and Contract

Also in anticipation of a new fire contract, the Village Board authorized the purchase of new equipment and a new alarm system by the Fire Department that August, an air horn that is still sounded and operates on compressed air instead of electric power. By the time school reopened in September, there was talk of a full time policeman for the Village and in early October, the new fire contract, a five-year agreement between the Village and the Town of Marcellus was signed.

30 Aug 1948 - " . . . the purchase of the Sanford-Ford pumper at a cost of approximately $11,000, the Gamewell fire alarm system at a cost of $2,627.50, of which the Fire Department will pay $700, and the tank truck was duly authorized."

11 Oct 1948 - " . . . agreement . . . between the Town Board . . . of Marcellus . . . and the Village Board of . . . Marcellus . . . to furnish fire protection . . . the sum of Four Thousand Dollars ($4,000.00) per year, payable on or before the first day of March of each year . . . This agreement shall continue for a period of five years from the fifth day of November, 1948, and shall terminate on the fourth (4th) day of November, 1953."

MO September 10, 1948

Truman vs. Dewey

In the election of 1948, the Governor of New York, Thomas Dewey, was thought to be a certain winner over President Truman, splits in the Democratic Party virtually assuring a Republican win. In one of the most stunning political upsets in history, however, Truman won the election, with the Democrats winning a majority in Congress as well. Following the election, the local editor urged all citizens to help " . . . our Congressmen as well as our President, in forging the mold for the future peace of the world. Let us all cooperate . . . and may be wish success to the men who were elected in one of the biggest elections of all times" (MO 11/5/48).

Parking Ordinance, Bonds, Rate Hikes

By November, the Board authorized more restrictive parking laws in the Village and at the special hearing informed the two residents in attendance that there would be " . . . the addition of from 3 to 5 dollars added to their assessments when the appointment of a new officer on full time pay is established . . . The purchase of a new car . . . the upkeep and insurance . . . will amount to many thousands of dollars a year" (MO 11/12/48). In December the Board authorized the issuance of bonds to pay for the purchase of fire equipment and by the end of the month, informed residents that an increase in water rates would become effective in January.

9 Nov 1948 - " . . . ordinance to be known as the Parking Ordinance of the Village of Marcellus, be and hereby is adopted and enacted . . . no vehicle shall be parked on any street or public highway in the Village between the hours of 1:00 a.m. and 6:00 a.m. . . . no vehicle shall be parked at any time within the following restricted areas: on the west side of Orange Street; on the north side of Maple Street; on the north side of Main Street at a distance nearer than 140 feet to the east Village line; on the east side of North Street between the north end of the bridge over Nine Mile Creek and the intersection of North Street and Scotch Hill Road . . . "

13 Dec 1948 - " . . . resolution authorizing the issuance of $15,000 serial bonds of the Village of Marcellus for the purchase of fire fighting apparatus and equipment consisting of a fire truck with equipment for the same and a tank truck with equipment for the same."

> **The Marcellus Observer**
> **Friday Morning, November 12, 1948**
> **Two Residents At Hearing**
> **Board Members Go Ahead With**
> **Plans for Village Safety**
>
> **The Marcellus Observer**
> **Friday Morning, December 31, 1948**
> **Water Rates To Be Increased Here;**
> **Hydrants and New Lines Needed**

The Village had grown during the year, expanding beyond the borders that had once defined it but still directed toward the common center. This growth required not only the expenditure of money but also a reevaluation of legislation, the services provided, and the interdependence that expanded between Village and Town. The Village would continue to grow in the years ahead, but the traditional view of pre-war Marcellus would change.

1949

When Harry Truman was inaugurated in January 1949, he confidently dedicated himself to what he called a "Fair Deal" for the American people, looking forward to enactment of policies he long favored. The year, however, would prove to be somewhat anxious as Americans became increasingly alarmed about the spread of communism both at home and overseas and an uneasiness that affected everyday living.

Meet Your Neighbor

Almost as if to relax the worry, the year began with a party in Marcellus - a "Meet Your Neighbor Night" on January 16th in the school gym, sponsored by the Marcellus Community Council. As the community increased in population in the postwar years,

> **The Marcellus Observer - Friday Morning, January 28, 1949**
> **Our Town**
> One of the finest things we know of is living in a small town. So many of the people in Syracuse ask 'How are things going and how do you like it out in the country?' Of course, our reply is always 'swell.' We tell them of the many different organizations it has been our privilege to belong to. We tell them of the neighborliness of the residents, of the Volunteer firemen who give so much. We tell them of the lack of religious discrimination. How the members of one church are always willing and glad to help out their neighbors. We like the fact that when a good project is proposed it doesn't have to be handled by one group, but receives the cooperation of all the local organizations We tell them of the way people help us to gather news by their many phone calls. How the reading of a weekly paper is so different in so far as exciting news is concerned. Rather than read the Atom Bomb that fell on Bikini is now outdated, they prefer to read that Mr. and Mrs. So and so had dinner with their friends on Sunday; or that a dinner will be held on the following Thursday at one of the churches if they would care to drop in on one of these they will enjoy a meal fit for a king and in a supply ample for the stoutest of eaters. Be it in New York State or any State of the Union, for down-right friendliness and the right to speak your piece when you think something is wrong you can't beat the small town. It's a pleasure to see our children going to a school that not one in the city can equal. And it is always a pleasure to tell of the Community Council's wonderful idea of Meet Your Neighbor night. Let's try very hard to keep it that way.

there were many new residents and the gathering was an attempt to welcome them to town, as well as provide " . . . a sort of reunion for people who have lived in the vicinity for many years, but rarely all get together" (MO 1/7/49). Even a list of over fifty available baby sitters was published in the paper so that there would be no excuse for missing the affair. The Board's favorable response to the start of a youth program would also help to ease tension in this last year of the decade.

14 Feb 1949 - " . . . the intention of the Board . . . to establish a Youth Recreation Project . . ."

> **The Marcellus Observer**
> **Friday Morning, February 25, 1949**
> **Newest Truck Delivered February 19th;**
> **Department Is Now Second To None**
> With the acquisition of the new fire truck by the Village for the protection of its people, Marcellus can be proud of its Fire Department for it is second to none in the rural areas . . .
> A series of blasts are being arranged for the new fire horn that will give the firemen the direction of the fire without over burdening the telephone operators, in times of fire . . .

> **The Marcellus Observer**
> **Friday Morning, March 4, 1949**
> **New Fire Signals**
> The new system of the Village Fire Department is the division of the Village and Town into sections by signals . . . as follows:
>
> | Town | Village |
> |------|---------|
> | North 33 | North 23 |
> | South 34 | South 24 |
> | East 35 | East 25 |
> | West 36 | West 26 |
> | Center of Village | |
> | 44 | |

Alarms

February brought news of the arrival of the last of the fire equipment and " . . . the new fire horn booming out every so often. . . . We can't decide if it sounds more like a cow in distress or a plugged horn on the diesel" (MO 2/11/49), thought some. Even today, residents and visitors wonder about and are sometimes startled by the sounds of the horn, which, in 1949 signaled the location of a fire in the Town or Village.

Members of the Citizens Club were also startled at their February meeting by the message of a former FBI agent who " . . . told of the dangers of communism and how easily they infiltrate into the ranks of the unsuspecting . . . a speech so worthwhile it is too bad every single person in town could not be present so they might fully realize the danger of communism and impress their children of the extreme caution with which they must listen and watch" (MO 3/4/49). Even Marcellus, so isolated it first appears from worldly concerns, was emotionally affected by events happening throughout the nation and world.

Incumbents Return

Elections in March produced a significant increase in the number of voters that year, motivated perhaps by the communist scare, which renewed interest in government, or perhaps by complaints being echoed throughout town about the laws and taxes recently enacted. Whatever the reason, there was no change in government as " . . . Mayor Kenyon, Clayton Edgerton and Doctor M. W. Sullivan were elected to office" (MO 3/18/49), followed by the usual appointments at the Board's April meeting.

15 Mar 1949 - " . . . annual election of the Village of Marcellus . . . results were as follows:
Total number of ballots cast was 63. For Mayor (2 years) - Varnum S. Kenyon received 54 votes . . . For Trustee (2 years) - Clayton A. Edgerton received 37 votes; Arden B. Fisher received 23 votes . . . For Police Justice (4 years) - M. Wallace Sullivan received 57 votes . . . "

4 Apr 1949 - " . . . James F. Woodbridge was appointed Village Clerk and Treasurer at a salary of $850.00 per year . . . Arthur W. Wilson . . . as Village Attorney at a salary of $150 per year . . . William Alford was appointed Street Commissioner and Building Inspector at a rate of $1.15 per hour regular time, and $1.725 overtime, and Martin K. King was appointed patrolman part time at an annual salary of $100.00."

**The Marcellus Observer
Friday Morning, April 15, 1949
Ask Residents To Bring Complaints To
Board**

Mayor Kenyon states that if you have any complaints, please bring them to the Village Board meetings where they can be straightened out and corrected. Rather than a lot of talk on the outside of the meetings about what is wrong and how it should or could be corrected, attend the meetings and take part in the Village affairs. IT IS YOUR COMMUNITY.

If you will notify the Village Clerk, any complaints you may have will be heard by the Board . . .

Also, Mayor Kenyon states that if anyone in the Village would like to take over the responsibilities of the administration of the Village affairs, he will be very cooperative and relinquish his office at any time . . .

**The Marcellus Observer
Friday Morning, May 8, 1949
New Officer Appointed By Village To
Apprehend Speeders**

Mayor Kenyon has made arrangements with Frank Pugh, who has made such a notable record in checking the speeding of trucks and cars in Camillus . . . to devote part of his time Marcellus Village. The Village Board feels that this arrangement will make it possible to give our children and residents more protection from speeding . . . Mayor Kenyon would welcome very much any suggestions anyone has to make instead of just criticism.

**The Marcellus Observer
Friday Morning, June 17, 1949
Speeding Cut 40 Percent In Marcellus Under
Frank Pugh and Doc Sullivan Jurisdiction**

. . . We of Marcellus have been blessed with two men who are incorruptible, despite the threats of various parties or people endowed with so much power. To Officer Frank Pugh and Doctor M. W. Sullivan goes the hearty thanks of the Observer for a job well done. Speeding has been cut by 40 percent in the village. Parking violations have decreased with the increased vigilance of Mr. Pugh . . . noticeable lessening of speed by travelers through the Village, who have come before the court of Justice Sullivan, been found guilty and paid their fine regardless of what connections they had . . .

Advice

In the spring, while the Mayor was advising residents of the need to bring their complaints to the Board for resolution, parents were being warned by the National Foundation for Infantile Paralysis that " . . . the 1949 polio season is 'just around the corner,' . . . a list of precautionary measures to be observed by those in charge of children during the epidemic danger period . . . " (MO 4/22/49). Caution and concern seemed to be a dominant theme in 1949 and it would continue.

Resolve

Determined to enforce the speeding laws in the Village, the Board appointed another police officer that Spring and just as unwavering, the Mayor issued a proclamation on May 15th, celebrating "I Am An American Day." The Memorial Day celebration seemed to reinforce that sense of patriotism on May 30th as hundreds viewed the parade and listened to the speeches. In addition, efforts " . . . to insure the safety of children and adults, to insure the safety of all visitors and to make Marcellus a safe place to drive through . . . " (MO 6/17/49) were realized within a month of Officer Frank Pugh's appointment.

Water Problems

The Old Home Day Celebration promised to be bigger than ever in 1949, but one of its most famous participants, John L. Sullivan, the 77-year-old long distance runner was unable to race, not because of his age, but because of rain. His annual five mile sprint against any and all competitors had become an integral part of the celebration, but a back injury and wet pavement led to some disappointment at this year's event. He promised to return in 1950.

A greater disappointment concerned the village reservoir as drought conditions led to a request that residents conserve water. This concern would become even more serious as June moved into July as the hot and dry weather continued. With the supply of water at a low level, bacteria started to grow in Rockwell Pond, causing the Village Health Officer,

> **The Marcellus Observer**
> **Friday Morning, June 24, 1949**
> **Residents Ask To Use Less Water**
> Village and State authorities have asked that a special appeal be sent out to the residents of our town to try and use less water during this serious time.
> It has been reported that our drinking water has been drained four inches in one week. If this rate continues a fire hazard will result. Let's be on the safe side and use less water to sprinkle the garden, having leaky faucets fixed and even doing with a few less baths until the water level again becomes normal . . .
>
> **The Marcellus Observer**
> **Friday Morning, July 1, 1949**
> **Boil Drinking Water Before Using As A Precautionary Measure**
> **Health Officer Asks Boy Scouts To Inform People to Boil Water**
>
> **The Marcellus Observer**
> **Friday Morning, July 8, 1949**
> **Continue To Boil Drinking Water**
> **Progress Slow On Chlorinating Water At Pond**
>
> **The Marcellus Observer**
> **Friday Morning, July 15, 1949**
> **Continue To Boil Drinking Water**
> **Marcellus Park Not Affected By Order**
>
> **The Marcellus Observer**
> **Friday Morning, July 22, 1949**
> **"Boil Water" Edict Order Ended July 18**
> **Possible Epidemic Averted By Order of Health Official**
>
> **The Marcellus Observer**
> **Friday Morning, July 29, 1949**
> **Residents Again Asked To Conserve On Water Here**
> The residents of the Village are asked to conserve on water. The Rockwell Spring Pond, the source of our water supply is at very low ebb due to the extreme heat and lack of rain.

Doc Walsh, to issue a "boil water" edict. When chlorine was added to the water to kill the bacteria, however, it did not have the immediate effect that was hoped for and residents were again told to boil their water before drinking it. Soon after this, a chlorinator was installed, but test results, taking almost another week, prolonged the emergency. While some parts of the Village were on Otisco Lake water, as well as some areas in and around Marcellus Park, the boil-water order would remain in effect for over three weeks that summer, again raising tension and adding to the burden of an already anxious public. At a special meeting of the Village Board on July 20th, the Village Board authorized the reconstruction of the reservoir, the addition of a chlorinating system, pumping unit and supply line, as well as the construction of water distributing mains within the Village and the acquisition of necessary land, the cost of which was to be paid in $45,000

worth of serial bonds. It was an emergency, and an expense in 1949 that is just as significant today as pipes and mains in the Village continue to age and keeping up with Federal and State mandates becomes increasingly difficult each year. In addition, terrorist threats to water systems throughout the country have made the issue of water quality and quantity "the biggest environmental issue that we face in the 21st century," (Christie Whitman, Administrator of the Environmental Protection Agency, *U.S. News & World Report*, August 12, 2002).

20 Jul 1949 - " . . . resolution authorizing the construction of additions to the water supply and distribution system of the Village of Marcellus, New York, at an estimated maximum cost of $45,000 and providing for the issuance of $45,000 serial bonds of said village to pay the cost thereof."

More Health and Safety

As school was getting set to reopen in September, other concerns arose in the community -- that of having children immunized against childhood diseases and the importance of driving with care in a school zone. There was also an increase in the number of schools that started to offer a "Driver Teaching" course, including Marcellus

The Marcellus Observer - Friday Morning, August 26, 1949
Inoculation Stressed For County Children
. . . There is a need for more education of parents to induce them to get their youngsters inoculated against diphtheria, small pox and whooping cough . . . the importance of immunization now or before youngsters enroll or return to school.

The Marcellus Observer - Friday Morning, September 2, 1949
Increase in Number Of Schools Teaching Driving Noted Throughout Nation

The Marcellus Observer - Friday Morning, September 23, 1949
Over 100 Attend Special Meeting Of Board To Discuss Meters

WHEN DRIVING IN A SCHOOL ZONE YOU ALWAYS DRIVE WITH CARE
NEW YORK STATE DIVISION OF SAFETY

MO August 26, 1949

Central. Not only would high school students learn to drive, " . . . on the road instruction . . . given in a dual controlled car furnished by a local dealer to the school" (MO 9/16/49), but adults in evening classes would learn as well.

The Board was also concerned with automobile issues, in particular, parking and speeding in the Village. When the Board proposed the installation of parking meters on the main streets of the Village, a great many residents turned out to attend a Board meeting to discuss the idea. There were arguments that meters would prevent "all day parkers", including some businessmen and workers who parked all day in front of their own businesses, rather than in the village lot behind the fire barn. Others thought that meters would scare business away from the Village while still others voiced their resentment as to the number of tickets that were being issued by the police. A suggestion was made" . . . at the meeting that it might be just as well to erect limited parking signs in the business district" (MO 9/23/49) and a week later, " . . . a committee of local merchants . . . met with the Board to work out a solution . . ." (MO 1017/49).

Don't Forget the Rally Saturday Night at Dillons --- Speeches, Entertainment, Free Coffee and Sandwiches

MO Nov 4, 1949   The Democratic Club of Marcellus, James Quinn, president

Elections & Exemptions
In November, Town elections were hotly contested by the Democratic Club, although, " . . . Marcellus again proved its Republican trend by sweeping into office every candidate on the ticket" (MO 11/11/49). The voter turnout, however, was one of the largest in many years, and it seemed to echo that renewed interest in voting that was evident in the earlier Village elections in March.

On November 11th, the community paused to honor those who died in World War I and a few days later marked Grievance Day granting a number of tax exemptions to the veterans of World War II.

15 Nov 1949 - " . . . Grievance Day, . . . several veterans filed applications for exemptions from tax by reason of the application of pensions and other government payments to the purchase of real estate. Exemption were granted to the following persons in the amount set opposite each name:

Thomas E. Dillon	$1,586.00	James M. Murphy Jr.	$1,064.00
Arden B. Fisher	$550.00	Forrest L. Vosler	$1,367.00
William S. Spaulding Jr.	$632.00	Louis J. Snow Jr.	$710.00

New Solutions and New Problems

December brought news of a parking solution, one-hour signs, in the Village business district as well as the installation of a new chlorinator in the reservoir to improve the Village water supply. Now, however, complaints about conditions at the Village dump would surface, requiring Board action.

12 Dec 1949 - " . . . persons appeared to complain of conditions at the Village Dump."

The Marcellus Observer Friday, December 2, 1949 1-Hour Parking Signs To be Erected Here	The Marcellus Observer Friday, Dec 2, 1949 New Chlorinator Installed In Rockwell Springs	The Marcellus Observer Friday, December 16, 1949 Supreme Court Action To Be Taken on Village To Prevent Dumping; Health Menace

By the end of the month, " . . . in an effort to clean up and avoid any future fires that cannot be extinguished in the village dump, the Village Board . . . asked the people to keep all papers and rubbish that will burn separate from Ashes, Garbage, Bottles and Tins" (MO (12/30/49). Although this solution might be viewed today as environmentally unsound as well as temporary (it was), it also seems to highlight the role of government at the local level -- see a problem and fix it.

The End of the Decade

The 1940s were now at an end and in looking back, the people of this small village in Central New York might have wondered at all that had occurred. A decade that began in economic depression, labored under wartime conditions, and was still adjusting to peace, ended as the Soviets tested their first atomic bomb. Concern over what the future might hold would continue into the 1950s, but so too would the optimism that inspired the "G.I." generation, along with the resolve needed to meet any challenge.

One of this generation was a young man by the name of Frank Kelly. Born in Marcellus in 1921, he was one of eight children born to John Patrick Kelly and Jessie Elizabeth Wilson. He was raised in the Village on what became Kelly Avenue, graduating from Marcellus Central High School in 1939, the salutatorian of his class. Like others of his generation, and in spite of the Depression, he was optimistic, looking ahead to a bright future when Pearl Harbor suddenly threw the United States into World War II. He, along with other Marcellus graduates in the class of '39, went to war. Some, like his brother Donald, whose ship was torpedoed in the Mediterranean Sea, did not return. When the war was over, he returned home, got a job in business, married his wife Doris in the latter part of the decade and raised two sons. He became involved in the life of his community, his church, and a variety of fraternal and other organizations. Decades later, when he retired, he remained active in his community, proud of what had been accomplished and eager to be a civic minded senior citizen. " 'We've done the work of democracy, day by day,' former President George Bush proudly declared of his generation in 1989" (Strauss & Howe 277).

Frank Kelly and others, like George "Popeye" Manahan, Hugh Dawson, Jim and Bernie Reagan, were typical of this "G.I." generation. When these young men returned to Marcellus after the war, they did the work of democracy in their hometown, day by day, every day. Sixty years later, many of this generation are still at work.

Chapter 16 – Concern Amid Celebration

The decade of the 1950s was, for all Americans, somewhat anxious and those living in the community of Marcellus were not immune from this disquiet. They continued to

Parroting the Commie Line

MO July 15, 1949

A Cure-All Cures Nothing

MO November 18, 1949

worry about expansion of communism domestically and overseas, as well as the threats posed by increasing inflation and the spread of polio at home. The peace, so dearly bought in 1945, seemed to be an illusion for many throughout much of the 1950s, as a cold war between the Soviet Union and the United States deepened and a hot war erupted in Korea. The character of the people of the community, however, like that of most Americans did not weaken during this period of tension but in fact became strengthened by the challenges presented. The citizens also found cause to celebrate 100 years of incorporation as a Village, a centenary that honored the past and the legacy that was now theirs.

1950 - Displaced Persons and Youth

In response to this anxiety, the people of Marcellus took an eager interest in a number of community causes. The war had displaced a number of people all over the world and the community, throughout the year, would sponsor a number of families " . . . to come to this country where they could live normally and happily" (MO 1/6/50).

> **The Marcellus Observer**
> **Friday Morning, January 20, 1950**
> **Displaced Persons**
> In allowing the unfortunate displaced persons of Europe to find asylum in America, our nation may be enriched. Among those unhappy people are artists, musicians, scientists, doctors, engineers and many other professions needed in America. Hitler wanted to get rid of this sort of culture and sought to destroy it. We can save it.
> The Irish were once new to our shores. Today a great many of our leaders are the descendants of those poor folks who came to America, lived in shanties and dug our ditches and canals. Next came the Italians, able bodied and willing workers. These, too, after a period of menial labor, became leaders and valued citizens. Now come the displaced persons. We need them just as much as we needed the Irish and Italians before them. Let us welcome them to our shores.

Another project was the formation of a youth center, " . . . someplace, somewhere in Marcellus that kids could call their own. A place parents should be proud to send their children to plan their own activities when they want them; a place adequately supervised" (MO 1/13/50). The people of the community were concerned, not only with the spread of polio among youth, but about the increasing influence of television and the fact that some of the movies were not suitable for young people. Every generation of parents, it seems,

326

has its own concern for youth, reflected today, for example, in AIDS education as well as movie and TV ratings.

The Water Tank

For many other adults of the Village, the erection of a water tower was of even greater concern that year. Responding to the demand for more water as well as a need to increase water pressure, the Board had authorized the building of a tower high above the Village, on the western hill above Reed Parkway, the engineers having selected the least expensive location possible. The site met with considerable objection from some residents,

who preferred not only another location but also a tower that would not be so visible or offensive looking. Throughout the winter, challenges would continue, and would include a public hearing conducted by the New York State Water and Control Commission. After considerable debate, the tower would be built at the site originally selected, yet another example, it seems, of a public need, accompanied by the public response, "not in my back yard." Today, the tower, which stores 250,000 gallons of water, is barely visible as it rises over Highland Drive and Reed Parkway in the Village, many residents not even aware of, but dependent on its existence.

Election Weather

The community experienced some bad weather early in March, zero temperatures and high winds closing roads and schools, and disrupting travel. By Election Day, March 21st, however, the roads were clear and 39 voters showed up at the polls, the vast majority selecting L. Seymour Parsons as Trustee to replace N. Giles Case, who declined to run again. This was the beginning of a long career in village government

L. Seymour Parsons

for Seymour Parsons. A local contractor who had lived in the village most of his life, Parsons' roots in the community stretched all the way back to 1807 when his great grandfather became the first resident pastor of the Presbyterian Church in Marcellus. He knew the community well, knew its people and understood its problems and would become the longest serving Trustee in the history of the Village, retiring because of ill health in 1986.

21 Mar 1950 - no vote was recorded in the board minutes. The Marcellus Observer recorded the vote total as 39, and L. Seymour Parsons received 37 of those votes.

Another name that would become synonymous with village government was that of Lester Norris, who, having served as Fire Chief for the previous eight years, wound up his term in April, " . . . many improvements made during his tenure . . ." (MO 4/7/50).

10 Apr 1950 - " . . . the following newly elected officers of the Fire Department were approved:
Roy Bennett   Chief
Carl Wood   First Asst. Chief
Clarence Coon   Second Asst. Chief

Sheep and Saucers

Spring not only meant a clean up in the Village, but also brought a call for more sheep to pasture in the Village Cemetery, an experiment that proved to be quite effective the previous year. Another interesting development that spring was the news that flying saucers were real, according to reports written in *U.S. News & World Report* magazine. No sightings, however, were reported in Marcellus, nor was the Fire Department called out that spring, the members thanking residents " . . . for their carefulness in burning dry grass and brush" (MO 5/12/50). The veterans' graves were again decorated for Memorial Day in May, the war a little more distant, but the peace still somewhat unstable.

> **The Marcellus Observer**
> **Friday Morning, April 14, 1950**
> **Sheep Needed To Pasture In Village Cemetery**
>
> **The Marcellus Observer**
> **Friday Morning, May 5, 1950**
> **""Flying Saucers" Real Thing Says U.S. News In Authenticated Report**

Building and Remodeling

While clean-up and fix-up continued, including the addition of air conditioning to the Strand Theater uptown, the construction season opened, and a great many building permits were again issued by the Village. Some of these were for new construction while others were for renovation and remodeling of older residences, another sign of Village expansion and development in the new decade.

12 Jun 1950 - " . . . building permits were granted to L. S. Parsons, L. D. Paul, William K, Groeling, Theodore E. Davey and John Gallinger for dwellings and to Joseph Miller for a garage . . . that no Village equipment may be used by a private individual unless a permit for such use has been granted by the Village Board."

Korea and Old Home Day

The Firemen planned for a special Old Home Day celebration in 1950, held for the first time at Marcellus Park, adding fireworks to the program and arranging with the M.

& O.L. Railroad to run an " . . . excursion train from Marcellus Park to Martisco and return . . . the first passenger run since 1915" (MO 6/9/50). Such peaceful plans, however, were rocked on June 25th with news that North Korean forces had launched a surprise invasion of South Korea. Two days later, American forces were ordered to Korea by President Truman. This was another war causing more uneasiness in a decade that was already marked with uncertainty. The outbreak of hostilities in Asia, however, did not dampen enthusiasm in Marcellus as a crowd estimated at 10,000 commemorated one of the largest Old Home Day celebrations in memory on July 3rd and 4th.

> **The Marcellus Observer**
> **Friday, July 14, 1950**
> **Village To Clamp Down On Parking**
> **Violators Here**
> At a meeting of the Village Board, Police officials attended to discuss the one-hour parking limit areas in the village. It was agreed that a crackdown was in order. The many careless offenders who have been disregarding the one-hour limit will find their cars ticketed . . .
> It was also recommended that heavier fines be levied in an effort to impress drivers with the seriousness and cut arrests to a minimum . . .

Sidewalks and Parking and Water

With an increase in building that summer, there was the addition of a new street, Wilson Drive, and an increase in sidewalk construction as well, property owners having to pay for such installation and at the proper grade established by the Village. Today, installation and repair of public sidewalks is a responsibility of the Village, its expense borne by all taxpayers, rather than individual owners. A crackdown on those who disregarded the parking limits in the Village was authorized, as was the usual billing for water and other services.

By August, the Board would award a contract for the construction of the water tank above Reed Parkway, as well as another for the installation of pumps, valves, and mains required to complete the necessary upgrade. This project was long overdue and became even more necessary as the Village increased in population in the postwar years. Since its installation, the water tower has served the community well, having been reconditioned in the early 1970s as well as requiring some surface preparation and repainting in 1990.

10 Jul 1950 - " . . . Arthur W. Wilson present a deed to the street known as Wilson Drive, . . . motion . . . seconded . . . the street was accepted by the Village . . . that property owners who wish sidewalks laid by the Village, be advised that they may pay for same when billed, or in ten equal annual installments, with interest on the unpaid balance, each installment to be due and payable with the Village tax. In no case may sidewalks be built until the proper grade has been established by the Village Board.

14 August 1950 - " . . . Clerk was instructed to bill the Strand Theatre for water service connection in the amount of $20.00 . . . "

23 Aug 1950 - " . . . that Contract No. 2 for the construction of a 200,000 gallon water tank be awarded to Pittsburgh-DesMoines Steel Company for the sum of $10,850.00 and that Contract No. 1, for the construction of a base for the tank, and the furnishing and installing of pump, valves and mains be awarded to Street Bros. Construction Co. Inc. for the sum of $19,800.00"

Korea and Defense

School opened in September amid concerns for those who would graduate and might be drafted into another war, but by mid month the situation in Korea appeared to have brightened, *The Marcellus Observer* commenting " . . . already encouraging signs of improvement . . . reports . . . indicate that the evident military ability of this country to cope with the communists in Korea has impressed the countries of Southeast Asia . . . " (MO 9/15/50).

> **The Marcellus Observer**
> **Friday, September 15, 1950**
> **Civil Defense Program Under Way**
> **In Marcellus**
> Our local defense program is being organized and will be in full operation in time for the first alert which will take place in October . . .
>
> **The Marcellus Observer**
> **Friday, September 15, 1950**
> **Mutual And Moving Up Day To Be Held Tonight; Ask Residents To Cooperate**
>
> **The Marcellus Observer**
> **Friday, September 22, 1950**
> **Meeting For wardens At Legion Rooms Sept. 29th**

As if in reaction to the many alarms that seemed to continuously develop in the postwar period, communities throughout the nation, including Marcellus, decided to organize a civil defense program. The call went out for volunteers, and local groups, including churches and fraternal organizations, responded. Coordinators for the Town and Village were selected and wardens were assigned to direct volunteers in different areas of the town.

In addition, the first Mutual Aid Day for the Western Division Volunteer Fire Companies was held in Marcellus in September. A mock fire and rescue was held and residents were forewarned that such a program was developed " . . . so that in case of extreme emergency, aid could be brought to the stricken area from all companies in the Western Division, and still leave no community without adequate fire protection" (MO 9/15/50).

December 7, 1941 had taught Americans a valuable lesson in preparedness but by June 1950, it seemed to have been forgotten as North Korea staged a surprise attack against its peaceful neighbor. By the end of September, as U.S. forces under General Douglas MacArthur drove the North Koreans back to the 38th parallel, the course of the war had changed. A costly price had been paid, however, for being unprepared and many Americans, for the rest of the decade, would remain ever vigilant, their concern for being prepared paramount. In another September, fifty-one years later, however, American complacency was again shattered as terrorists attacked the United States, causing the death of thousands of civilians and provoking a war that remains on-going today.

Effects of the War

By October, the war in Korea expanded as United Nations Forces crossed into the North, General MacArthur confidently predicting that the troops would be home by Christmas. At home, President Truman had been given " . . . sweeping stand-by controls over the economy - including the authority to impose rationing and wage and price controls" (MO 10/13/50) by Congress and the people in Marcellus joined hundreds of other communities in the State and world in celebrating United Nations Day. They would also participate in the Crusade for Freedom, making contributions and adding their signatures to a Freedom Scroll, " . . . giving unified voice to all people who believe in the freedom of the individual and human dignity" (MO 10//20/50). One of the greatest of those freedoms was expressed at the ballot box in November as voters across the country reaffirmed Democratic control and provided President Truman with a majority in both houses of Congress.

The War Expands

Shortly after Thanksgiving, as the first family of displaced persons was arriving in Marcellus, a violent windstorm caused considerable damage throughout the community. On the next day, just as suddenly as a freak storm, tens of thousands of Chinese soldiers attacked UN forces in Korea, driving MacArthur and his army back to the 38th parallel. Just as suddenly the complexion of the war changed, the conflict widened considerably, and the mood of the country became increasingly solemn. While there were talks of

> **The Marcellus Observer**
> **Friday, November 24, 1950**
> **First Latvian Family To Arrive Saturday, Nov. 25th**
> The Displaced Persons Committee is very happy to announce that the first of the Displaced Persons will arrive in Marcellus on Saturday, November 25th. The Juchimek family consists of 45-year-old Adrezy, the father; Anna, the mother; and their 7-year-old son . . .
>
> **The Marcellus Observer**
> **Friday, December 8, 1950**
> **Many Volunteers Needed To Complete Units Necessary For Civil Defense Here**
>
> **The Marcellus Observer**
> **Friday, December 29, 1950**
> **Transportation Directors To Register All Vehicles**

massive air attacks on China itself, communities began to ready their defenses at home, when a state of national emergency was declared by President Truman: "It is almost impossible to exaggerate the potential seriousness of our military involvement with Chinese Communists," wrote the editor of *The Marcellus Observer* (MO 12/8/50).

Residents of Marcellus enjoyed the Christmas season and such customs as community caroling at the village tree in front of the Methodist church. They also took pride in welcoming the Juchimek family (sometimes referred to as Delayed Pilgrims) from Poland and participated actively in buying both Christmas Seals to eliminate tuberculosis and Christmas trees to help the blind. Just as active, however, was the uneasiness and fear that the new year might not bring peace, but the possibility of another world war.

1951

The confusion and uncertainty of 1950 led, in 1951, to a world that seemed to be preparing for another world war. There was talk of declaring war on China, ending the communist threat in Asia once and for all, and as casualties mounted in Korea, there seemed to be no retreat from the march towards war. Wage and price controls returned and the military began to call up more young men to active duty. When Chinese Communists troops took the South Korean capital on January 1, 1951, Americans probably wondered what difficulties lay in the year ahead.

> **The Marcellus Observer**
> **Friday, January 5, 1951**
> **Jesse Ramsden Heads Dept.**
> Jesse Ramsden has been appointed head of the Village Maintenance and Repair Department . . .
>
> **The Marcellus Observer**
> **Friday, January 5, 1951**
> **Please Keep Cars Off Streets Nights**
>
> **The Marcellus Observer**
> **Friday, January 12, 1951**
> **Civil Defense Organized For Marcellus Area**
> The Civil Defense Project in the Marcellus area has been steadily forging ahead . . .
> . . . official Air Raid Warning Signals and their respective meanings throughout the State . . . are. . .
>   a. Yellow Alert Signal - Attack Likely . . .
>   b. Red Alert Signal - Attack Imminent . . .
>   c. White Alert Signal - All Clear . . .
> . . . Personnel assignments for the Town and Village of Marcellus are: . . .

Preparations

As the year began in Marcellus, the Board appointed a new head of Village maintenance and again urged residents to keep their cars off the streets at night to allow unrestricted plowing by Village crews. Other projects included a strengthening of civil defense programs at home, making people aware of the warning signals that would be used in the event of an air raid, as well as a listing of those responsible for different assignments in the event of attack. Blood donors became even more important that winter, as the Red Cross struggled to meet not only local needs but military requests as well. When the blood drive ended in January, Marcellus residents had donated a record number of units, a testament not only to the donors, but to the many organizers in the community as well.

BE PREPARED

TO SAVE YOUR LIFE IN AN

Atomic Attack

HERE COL. RYCRAFT AD SEE THE MOVIES OF THE BOMBING OF BRITIAN MARCH 15th AT MCS

MO February 23, 1951

By March, the number of soldiers in Korea rose along with the casualties, as the two sides lined up around the 38th parallel. General MacArthur began calling for an attack on China itself and the Office of Civil Defense was calling for added preparation at home.

An Election Challenge

In Village elections that year, an independent write-in candidate challenged the incumbent Mayor, who had been nominated for another two-year term. Carl J. Hoffman conducted a spirited crusade for the office, and in much political advertising, appealed to all residents to exercise their right to vote and to question the action or inaction of the Village Board. The campaign did have a desired effect in that it brought out a great many voters on March 20th, but the results were disappointing for Mr. Hoffman as an overwhelming majority returned Varnum Kenyon to office. Clayton Edgerton, who had served as Trustee for six years, declined to run again, and Earl M. Bush, a local auto dealer, nominated at the February caucus, was elected to a two-year term to replace him.

> 20 Mar 1951 - " . . . annual election . . . the results were as follows:
> Total number of ballots cast was 281
> For Mayor, 2 years   Varnum S. Kenyon   received   238 votes . . .
> For Trustee, 2 years   Earl. M. Bush   received   228 votes . . .

Board Action

When the new Board of Trustees met in April, a decision was made to separate the offices of Clerk and Treasurer as well as make appointments to various positions in Village government and approve members of the Marcellus Fire Department and its Chief, Roy Bennett. The Board would also look favorably on the formation of a ladies auxiliary of the Marcellus Fire Department and by the end of the month approved a Village budget for the fiscal year. As housing increased in the Village, the addition of new streets and sidewalks also required Board action. Before more construction took place, the Trustees passed an ordinance that established regulations for these as well as connections to Village utilities.

> 2 Apr 1951 - " . . . contact Mrs. Florence Potter in regard to taking over the Clerk's works . . . that the offices of Clerk and Treasurer be separated; that J. F. Woodbridge be appointed Treasurer at an annual salary of $850.00, and that he act as Clerk until such time as the Board shall appoint a Clerk."

> 23 Apr 1951 -" . . . members of the Marcellus Fire Department, as of April 23, 1951.

30 Apr 1951 - " . . . public hearing was held . . . there being no objections, the budget was finally adopted and the tax rate set at $30.00 per $1,000.00"

30 Apr 1951 - " . . . all new streets in the Village of Marcellus shall be sixty (60) feet wide, graded, adequately drained, graveled and in good condition, with proper provisions for sidewalks, with VILLAGE APPROVED water and sewer connections to each proposed lot on its respective side of the street and have sufficient dwellings erected thereon . . . "

Being Aware, Being Involved

Mrs. Rhea M. Eckel

Ever present during the year, it seemed, was the need to do something, the need to be involved, to inform -- a legacy perhaps of the uncertainty of the times, and common it seems, when conditions are unsettling. When President Truman relieved General MacArthur of his command in Korea that April, the community, like much of America, was troubled and the need to do something, especially during the spring of the year, was urgent. When the Community Council met to discuss its role in sponsoring youth programs, or the Boys Scouts conducted another successful paper drive, this need was expressed. When the community listened to Mrs. Rhea Eckel speak about preparedness should a bomb fall and when families agreed to host a child in the Fresh Air Program, they were fulfilling human needs consistent with the time.

Even the meetings of the Village Board started to attract some interest on the part of residents. When the Trustees decided to forego the collection of ashes and garbage by village workmen (who were needed on other projects), in favor of a contract by private individuals, interest was especially keen on the bidding process.

14 May 1951 - " . . . Clerk was instructed to obtain rights of way from Clarence M. Woodford and Crown Woolen Mills Corporation for Village employees to cross these properties to take care of the ditch and catch basins carrying the stream that flows between the properties on First Streets . . . that Henry E. Phillips be appointed Village Historian."

In addition, when the Board met to adopt an ordinance governing the acceptance of new streets, a large group of village residents attended, an action applauded by the local editor.

The Marcellus Observer - Friday, May 18, 1951
Village Board Encouragement
At the village board meeting this Monday night a hearing on a proposed ordinance was held. The village board instead of going ahead and having to figure out the ways and means of pleasing everyone, was joined by a number of citizens who were for and against the proposal. It gave them something tangible to work with and we are sure they appreciate it more than we can say. We should be interested in any and all meetings of the board. Not only can our troubles be ironed out, but the board may be able to prevent the same trouble from happening in other places. It is your village. All workings are for you. Take an interest and help the board as they were helped Monday night.

Memorial Day

Mr. George Cregg, the guest speaker at the Memorial Day celebration that year, which had " . . . one of the longest parades and . . . one of the largest crowds . . . asked that all present remember what was being done in Korea at the present time, to remember what our boys were fighting for" (MO 6/1/51). For many in the crowd and throughout the nation on May 30th, the threat of communism was as real as that posed by the Axis powers only a few years before. Unlike World War II, however, there was great debate about how to deal with the threat, further frustrating an already anxious people.

June Decisions

June brought a number of individuals to a special meeting of the Board to discuss the acceptance of new streets -- specifically Reed Parkway, Meadow, and Highland Streets -- by the Village. Many questions were asked, and the Board provided specific requirements to the developer in order to make a street acceptable. Similarly, a developer or builder today must, before construction begins, provide specific information as well as satisfy a detailed list of conditions before the Planning and Village Board give approval.

> **The Marcellus Observer**
> **Friday, June 15, 1951**
> **Discuss Improvements To**
> **Make Streets Acceptable**

> **The Marcellus Observer - Friday, June 15, 1951**
> **A New Service To The People Of Marcellus**
> Starting Monday, June 11th, 1951, the municipal offices in the village hall will be open each day from 9:30 a.m. to 12 noon to receive water rents, which will be collected on a quarterly basis and to file suggestion and complaints which can be brought to the attention of the Board at their regular meetings . . . Mrs. Joseph Morrocco will be in charge of this work and we feel very fortunate in having procured her services . . .

In addition, the Village offices would be open more often beginning that June -- a service that not only was needed but again gave evidence of the expanding role of government at the local level. A group of Marcellus businessmen also decided to enlarge their activity, organizing a Chamber of Commerce to promote local merchants and projects to benefit the entire community.

> **The Marcellus Observer**
> **Friday, June 22, 1951**
> **The Marcellus Chamber Of**
> **Commerce**

By the end of the month, a cease-fire in Korea had been proposed and discussions begun to end the conflict. Those talks, however, would be on going for the next three years. To the graduating class of 1951, the local editor noted: " . . . Things may look very dark to you now, with the threats of another world war in the making, conscription of men for the armed forces, and the possibility of no jobs because you are of military age . . . but we do know that the students of other generations have faced the same problems and the United States is still the grandest country in the world in which to live. Confusion, probably, is gnawing at your minds on what to do. Our only advice is to see your objective in life and keep striving towards it. Come what may, you are of the same blood of the men who have dealt with and licked problems in the past, that were most foreboding . . . " (MO 6/29/51).

Be Alert

July was a busy month for the Village Board, as it asked for resident cooperation when it approved a contract with Jacob Schneider for the collection of garbage and ashes. The Board also appointed Mrs. M. A. Morrocco as Village Clerk, a watchful public servant in that office for the next dozen years. On the 4th, Old Home Day celebrants cheered " . . . one of the biggest parades in years led by Seward Collard and Jack Lovett, . . . returned . . . from the Korean War Theatre" (MO 7/6/51). Then came the rain, but not enough to spoil the fireworks that evening.

2 Jul 1951 - " . . . the contract with Jacob Schneider for the collection of garbage and ashes, twice a week, for one year beginning June 1st, 1951 and ending May 31st, 1952, at $62.75 per week, was presented and signed . . . that Mrs. M. A. Morrocco be appointed Clerk."

> **The Marcellus Observer - Fri, July 6, 1951**
> **Village Board Asks Residents To Cooperate in Regards To Ash Collection**
>
> **The Marcellus Observer - Fri, July 27, 1951**
> **Red Alert Proves Very Successful In Marcellus Area**
> . . . Preparedness is the essence of survival in this atomic age. Help your Civilian Defense Chief and you may save your life.
>
> **The Marcellus Observer - Fri, July 27, 1951**
> **Zoning Ordinance Must Be Complied With Says Board**
> This ordinance was enacted to define the Residential Use, Business Use, Industrial and Manufacturing Use Districts. These three Districts are clearly defined in copies of this Ordinance which are available at the Village Office . . .

Later in the month, several air raid alerts, both yellow and red, were conducted in the Village and Town and Civil Defense officials applauded the cooperation of the residents. The Board also alerted homeowners and businessmen as well as manufacturers and service providers of the need to comply with zoning laws. It also requested that the traffic light at Reed and First be removed in anticipation of installing stop signs and the Fire Department, anticipating the arrival of telephone dial-up service, planned to meet with the Board to discuss appropriate fire alarm signals.

23 Jul 1951 - " . . . public hearing on the application of the Finger Lakes Telephone Corporation for a zone change . . . adjacent to the property of John Wybron, from residential to business use . . . "

9 Aug 1951 - " . . . have the traffic light at the corner of Reed and First Streets removed . . . the Fire Department also asked . . . to meet with the Village Board . . . to discuss the subject of fire alarm signals, when the new dial telephone system goes into effect."

Continued Alert

As the summer wound down and the school year began, the Office of Civilian Defense was still very busy trying to make people aware of the necessity of being prepared in case of emergency. What procedures to follow, what had been done, and what needed to be

> **The Marcellus Observer**
> **Friday, August 24, 1951**
> **Civil Defense**
> **Procedure In Case of Emergency – Marcellus Sector**
>
> **The Marcellus Observer**
> **Friday, August 24, 1951**
> **Civil Defense**
> **Civil Defense In Marcellus Up To Now**
>
> **The Marcellus Observer**
> **Friday, September 14, 1951**
> **Practice Air Raid To Be Held This Saturday By 8 Counties**
> **Procedure In Case of Emergency - Marcellus Sector**
>
> **The Marcellus Observer**
> **Friday, October 19, 1951**
> **Corp. Cronk Killed In Korea**
> Corp. Clifford J. Cronk, 20, son of Mr. and Mrs. Arlington Cronk of Syracuse, RD 2, was killed in action Sept. 24 in Korea, according to word received by his parents recently . . .

A Chinese Puzzle

MO September 21, 1951

done were explained in detail by the local media, and a practice air raid drill across upstate New York was conducted in mid September. A week after the practice drill, Corp. Clifford Cronk became the first Marcellus boy to die in Korea, a conflict that was becoming more and more puzzling to most Americans.

Traffic and Zoning

Board business seemed to center around streets and traffic issues as well as zoning applications in the fall. A Zoning Board of Appeals was set up to handle residents' petitions. Today, the zoning board, now numbering five members appointed by the Mayor for five-year terms, performs the same function.

19 Oct 1951 - " . . . the ownership of Paul Street was discussed, and it was established that the Village did not own it . . . it was decided to place 4 "Stop" signs at the intersection of Reed and First Streets, . . . the following be appointed to serve on the Zoning Board of Appeals for 3 years: Edward V. Baker (chairman), Lester C. Norris, Clifford W. Dorchester, and Henry E. Phillips (as clerk) . . . "

23 Oct 1951 - " . . . that Mr. Clayton Pilot's application for change in zone at 20-25 North Street (from residential use property to business use property) be granted."

29 Oct 1951 - " . . . in the event a sewer becomes stopped between the main sewer and the house, it shall be the responsibility of the property owner."

Community Projects and Election Mood

The local Chamber of Commerce continued to gain momentum that fall, as did the Community Chest drive but the Blood Donor Drive failed to meet its quota, " . . . the prevalence of colds and other minor ailments . . . blamed . . ." (MO 11/2/51). The "Meet Your Neighbor Night" was very successful that November, but the election results for the Democrats were not, as " . . . Marcellus followed the trend of the rest of the country by electing all the Republican candidates to office" (MO 11/9/51). The main issue in the campaign was the proposed County-wide sales tax, opposed by so many voters. This, plus an anti-Washington mood, brought out the vote, and the citizens of Marcellus voted Republican. An opposition mood also seemed to be reflected in a November article sponsored by the local Chamber of Commerce. By drawing people's attention to the fact that these things could happen, the Chamber hoped to convince the Town of Marcellus to consider building and zoning ordinances, similar to those in the Village.

> **The Marcellus Observer**
> **Friday, November 30, 1951**
> **Trailer Camp Planned Across From Marcellus Park!**
>
> **Slaughter House To Be Built Off Reed Parkway!**
>
> **Rendering Plant To Be Built On East Hill!**
>
> **Junk Yard Coming Across From Highland Cemetery!**
>
> **Midget Auto Races Every Sunday In Marcellus!**

End of Year

The sale of Christmas Seals was reported to be very good that season and the second annual tree sale to help the blind of Onondaga County was equally well received by the community. As the year ended, more and more people began to read the novel, *Catcher in the Rye* by J.D. Salanger, published about six months earlier in the year. It is the story of a young man who spends three days around the Christmas holidays trying, as he transitions to adulthood, to understand himself and the world around him. Some adults might have been similarly confused about themselves and the complexity of modern life as 1951 ended. They were also, however, ever hopeful, always determined to find solutions, and 1952 would present that opportunity.

1952

The year would bring about some significant change on the national scene, as Dwight Eisenhower was elected President, the first Republican administration in Washington since Herbert Hoover 20 years previously. The war in Korea would continue to dominate international news, while at home discontent over inflation and a wartime hysteria known as McCarthyism mounted.

Turn on Your Porch Light! to fight POLIO Wed., Jan. 30

Citizens' Concerns

In Marcellus, the first meeting of the Citizens Club that year brought out a good crowd that held a discussion on Village affairs. The erecting of signs at the four entrances as well as speeding in the Village dominated the discussion, and the Trustees commented on the improvements, particularly with the storm and sewer drainage system. The Trustees would also approve appointments that month. That of Carl Wood as Fire Chef, however, was unacceptable because he was not a Village resident, a State requirement at the time that has since been amended.

14 Jan 1952 - " . . . that Dr. J. H. Walsh be reappointed Health Officer for four years, effective January 12, 1952."

22 Jan 1952 - " . . . that the appointment of Carl Wood, submitted by the Volunteer Firemen, as Fire Chief, be rejected since he is not an elector of the Village; that the appointment of Clarence Coon as First Assistant Chief be accepted since he meets with the requirements as stated in . . . Village Law."

For families in Marcellus, the fear of infantile paralysis was more pronounced than ever and the Mothers' March On Polio in January, particularly leaving the porch light on as volunteers made collections, would prove to be very successful. The

Lester C. Norris
Village Mayor
1955-1982

Chamber of Commerce would continue to promote Village merchants as well as safety on the Village streets, having a School Safety Patrol as one of its goals that year. In addition, the February caucus selected Seymour Parsons as Trustee, and in March, the incumbent was re-elected in a light turnout of voters.

18 Mar 1952 - " . . . annual election . . . Total number of ballots cast was 34. For Trustee, 2 years   L. Seymour Parsons   received   33 votes
John Odell   received   1 vote

Resignation and Appointment

Early in April, Earl M. Bush resigned as Trustee due to ill health. To that position, Lester C. Norris was appointed, the beginning of a thirty-year relationship that this distinguished public servant would have in Marcellus Village government. As a partner in the Uttley-Norris Funeral home, and a long-time member and Chief of the Marcellus Fire Department, Norris knew about Village matters and would become very active in his role as a member of the Village Board. The

Board would also approve Clarence Coon as Chief of the Marcellus Fire Department, the painting of the Village offices as well as a salary increase for the Village Clerk.

7 Apr 1952 - " . . . that Mr. Earl M. Bush's resignation as Trustee, as contained in his letter of March 27, 1952, be accepted, with regrets . . . that the appointments made by the Marcellus Fire Department, be accepted, namely: Chief - Clarence Coon . . . that Mr. Lester C. Norris be appointed Trustee to complete the unexpired term of Mr. Earl M. Bush, which vacancy occurred as a result of Mr. Bush's resignation because of ill health . . .. it was decided to have the Village office painted."

30 Apr 1952 - " . . . that the salary of Mrs. Morrocco be raised to $1200.00 per year, effective May 1, 1951."

The Marcellus Observer
Friday, April 11, 1952
Enlargement of Marcellus Park Started
Monday, April 1st; Map On Display Here
Enlargement of Marcellus Park, long planned project of Onondaga County Park Board, got under way Monday. . . . For a number of years while attendance and competition for space at the popular picnic site increased steadily, the Park Board has been seeking a way to overcome the barrier created by the Marcellus and Otisco Railroad tracks, separating the present park from unused county land to the east . . .
In addition to clearing and grading of the railroad area now being done, it calls for more picnic tables and fireplaces, a new 260-car parking area, a park road and paths, toilets, water lines, a new park office and service building, and improvement of the ball diamond. Screen planting of evergreens will be done within the next few weeks . . .

The Marcellus Observer
Friday, May 16, 1952
Notice
The Village Board asks the cooperation of all those living in the Village, in the matter of rubbish disposal. Rather than raking leaves and other rubbish into the gutters, it is asked that such matter be placed in receptacles and left at the curb on the regular ash and garbage collection days, at which time Mr. Schneider will pick them up.

Enlargement

The spring of 1952 was distinguished by some development and expansion. While the Village Board asked residents to cooperate as they completed their yard work, a site would be cleared and graded to enlarge Marcellus Park by over 14 acres, enabling " . . . people to come from miles around to picnic . . . " (MO 5/23/52) and nearby residents to enjoy a facility so close to home. The addition of more evergreen trees to the village reservoir would provide even more protection to the watershed.

27 May 1952 - " . . . Mr. Kenyon called Syracuse University regarding evergreens for the reservoir . . . we can purchase white pine and Norway spruce for $1.00 per hundred . . . plantings are about 6" high."

Reminders and Projects

Memorial Day was another reminder of the sacrifices being made in Korea and as people wondered how many more years would pass before the conflict would end, the local editor urged " . . . a prayer for the boys in Korea and in the many veterans hospitals in the country . . ." (MO 5/30/52).

As the population of school age children mushroomed in the postwar years, there was a need to build an addition to

MO May 30, 1952

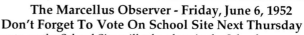

The Marcellus Observer - Friday, June 6, 1952
Don't Forget To Vote On School Site Next Thursday
The vote on the School Site will take place in the School Auditorium from 3:00 p.m. until 8 p.m. Thursday, June 12th.
The site to be voted on is the Stone property which is adjacent to the present grounds now occupied by the school . . .

the school and throughout the year, an advisory committee had sifted through a number of proposed sites. By June, the group had chosen the Stone farm property which was adjacent to the present school and the paper urged voters to cast their ballot for or against the proposed site. The voters approved the site and construction would begin the next year, adding another building to the campus, known today as the K.C. Heffernan Elementary School.

A project begun in Marcellus that summer and financed by local businesses was the

> **The Marcellus Observer – Fri, June 13, 1952**
> **Welcome Wagon Services Inaugurated Here**
> The Welcome Wagon service officially got under way in this community Tuesday, June 10th, as Mrs. Ethel J. Reynolds, hostess paid visits to two newly arrived families . . .

Welcome Wagon service. Small gifts provided by local merchants were presented to families and individuals in the community, conveying " . . . the good wishes of the townspeople to . . . newcomers, mothers of new babies, engaged girls, those celebrating the sixteenth birthday and to those moving from one home to another within the community . . . " (MO 6/13/52). The "Fresh Air" Program was another summer project in which local residents again found much satisfaction, providing a country vacation for New York City boys and girls. Children of the community were also able to participate in a summer swimming program, the Marcellus Community Council having secured Jordan Pool for this purpose, as well as planning a variety of other recreational activities.

Permits and Deeds

June was also the start of the building season and a great many permits were issued by the Village Board. Deeds to Austindale and Paul Streets were requested so that they could become dedicated streets of the Village, and the Board also implemented some recommendations that would improve record keeping by the Village Clerk and Treasurer. Such counsel is even more common today, the Office of the State Comptroller providing not only a regular audit of Village finances but advice that helps to streamline Village governmental operations.

24 Jun 1952 - " . . . applications for building permits were presented. Clerk was directed to write Mr. Louis Austin that the Board would like a deed to 200 feet of Austindale Ave., so that the Village can complete construction work on the street . . . that the deed to Paul Street be accepted . . . that the bill for . . . setting out trees at the reservoir be paid."

30 Jun 1952 - " . . . that the recommendations of Mr. Herbert Kraus (regarding the keeping of records - cash receipts, cash payment, tax roll, water consumers' account, Treasurer's and Clerk's duties, accounting records and reports) be put into effect immediately."

Sullivan Retires Amid Fireworks

July began with the Old Home Day Celebration, but without John L. Sullivan, the legendary long distance runner who competed in so many celebrations in the past. At the age of 80 and having raced for 66 years, Sullivan was forced to retire because of age and health conditions. Nonetheless, the show did go on, including " . . . one of the biggest parades . . . with over 33 separate units . . . led by the Skaneateles School Band, . . . offering their services for the support given by the Marcellus Fire Department in February when their school was destroyed by fire . . . In the evening, the greatest display of fireworks ever given in Marcellus" (MO 7/4/52).

Summer Agendas

For the Village Board, fire inspections and speeding, as well as accepting new streets in the Village, monopolized the summer agendas. In August, as New York State Gas & Electric Company was celebrating its 100th birthday, negotiations with the Village over a new contract for street lighting began -- a contract which dated back many years and had been renewed continuously up to the present time. For some businesses in the Village, a special phone service was put in place that summer, anticipating the installation of the

The Marcellus Observer - Friday, July 25, 1952
Speeding Again
Since we who live in Marcellus are the ones who must contend with speeding motorists both of local origin and transients, we think the Village Board could be approached to have an officer on duty during the day and in the evening. Enough people at this time are aroused so that a petition may be tendered . . .

The Marcellus Observer - Friday, August 8, 1952
Special Phone Service For Businessmen
With the installation of the new telephone system in the very near future and the elimination of the operators at the local switchboard, the problem arose of how to handle calls for the Doctors, Undertakers, etc., when there was no one at home to take the call. A system has been worked out whereby one individual in the village, already hired will handle all such calls . . . a name and number in the phone book to read 'if no answer call - -' . . .

The Marcellus Observer - Friday, August 22, 1952
Residents Of Town Of Skaneateles Petition For Fire Protection From Marcellus

The Marcellus Observer - Friday, Sept 5, 1952
Skaneateles Town Board O.K. 's New Fire District For Marcellus Dept.

new system being planned for later in the year. Better communications would enable the volunteers to respond more quickly to mutual aid fire calls that summer, and would also lead to a request by some residents in the Town of Skaneateles, for fire protection from the Marcellus Fire Department. By September, the new fire district of Shepard Settlement was created and a contract for fire protection with the Marcellus Fire Department was negotiated. The contract has been formally validated every year since by both governing bodies.

14 Jul 1952 - " . . . that Wm. B. Armstrong and Carl Wood be appointed Fire Inspectors for the Village . . . that the deed to Upper Reed Parkway be accepted . . . that the deed to Austindale Avenue be accepted."

11 Aug 1952 - " . . . discuss the acceptance of a portion of Highland Drive by the Village . . . New York State Electric & Gas Corporation, was present to discuss a new contract for street lighting . . . "

8 Sep 1952 - " . . . Fire Inspectors' reports were reviewed, and Clerk was directed to write property owners regarding fire hazards found on their premises."

The Marcellus Observer - Friday, Sept 12, 1952
Heavy Registration At MCS This Year
This year marks the greatest registration at Marcellus Central School. 1281 pupils registered September 3rd as compared with 1219 in 1951.
To help alleviate crowded conditions at the school, St. John's Parish Hall is being used to take care of 95 children, 56 of them being in the kindergarten and 37 in the First Grade . . .

The Marcellus Observer - Friday, Sept 26, 1952
Speed Watch Purchased By Village; Here Soon

School Reopens
A special concern for the Village Board as school reopened that fall was the amount of speeding that was occurring in the Village and in an open letter that was printed in the paper, notified residents that it had " . . . purchased a Speed Watch, which will cut down the speeding, if not entirely eliminate it" (MO 9/26/52). Once the speed timing device was in place, the Board would then authorize its use in the Village by police officers and other officials, and the posting of speed limits at all entrances to the Village as well.

13 Oct 1952 - " . . . that the Police Officer or any other officials may operate at any time anywhere within the incorporated limits of the Village of Marcellus a Speed Watch or other registered official electric timing device for regulating speed, and that all main entrances to the Village shall be properly posted."

Autumn Activities
The Community Chest conducted its annual fund drive that fall, and the Firemen held their annual Halloween party as well. The major news item, however, was the presidential election campaign being waged across the country. Korea, communism and

340

corruption had led to much dissatisfaction with the Truman administration and in the election that November, the Democrats led by Adlai Stevenson, would be defeated. In a landslide victory, Dwight Eisenhower won the Presidency, and together with Richard Nixon, would soon take over the reigns of government in Washington.

> **The Marcellus Observer**
> **Friday, November 14, 1952**
> **D-Day This Sunday - 12:01 A.M.**
> D-Day' for Marcellus telephone users will be at 12:01 a.m. on Sunday, November 16. That is the date and hour set for the changeover to dial service and the introduction of toll-free calling between here and Syracuse . . .

> **The Marcellus Observer**
> **Friday, November 14, 1952**
> **Marcellus Residents Will Have 24-Hr. Station For Calls**
> In the event of a Fire - Dial 68-2111. Keep cool; give your name and exact location

Dial Service and Other Utilities

An historic day in Marcellus history would follow on the heels of the election and that was the elimination of local switchboard operators and the changeover to telephone dial service. One of the initial concerns with this conversion was calling to report a fire, but this was addressed by having " . . . but one number - 68-2111 - . . . in the event you have a Fire to report" (MO 11/14/52). An invitation was extended to the Village Board to be present for the conversion. At the same meeting, the Trustees decided to raise water rates for those inside and outside the Village and grant building permits only on those streets that had been accepted by the Village. Resolutions accepting new streets, approving the Shepard Settlement fire contract, purchasing new fire fighting apparatus as well as constructing sewers, sidewalks, curbs, and gutters were approved by the Board late in the year.

· 10 Nov 1952 - " . . . an invitation was read from the Finger Lakes Telephone Corporation, to be present at the conversion to the dial system, Saturday evening, November 15, 1952 . . . decided to raise the water rents as follows . . . no building permits will be granted for the construction of any building unless or until the street on which it is to be built, has been accepted by the Village."

18 Nov 1952 - " . . . resolution authorizing the issuance of $5,000.00 serial bonds of the Village of Marcellus for the purchase of fire fighting apparatus and equipment . . . the Village shall, upon receipt of proper deed . . . accept the balance of Second Street, south to the intersection of Meadow Street, and Meadow Street from First Street to the intersection of Second Street."

8 Dec 1952 - " . . . resolution adopted, authorizing the signing of a contract covering fire protection for Sheppard Settlement . . . resolution authorizing the . . . construction of storm sewers on Reed Parkway, . . . the construction of sidewalks, curbing and gutters on certain streets, . . . the construction of sewer improvements, . . . the purchase of a sewer cleaning machine . . . "

> **The Marcellus Observer**
> **Friday, December 12, 1952**
> **Construction Of School O.K.'d By Voters Of District**
> Despite rain which continued all through the voting, 214 people went to the school on Wednesday to express their opinion as to whether the new primary school should be built. The voting was 295 - yes, or in favor of erecting the building, 7-no and 2 ballots were marked incorrectly . . void . . .

School Vote

As 1952 came to an end, voters in the community were asked once again to decide about the proposed primary school building that was to be built next to the high school. An informational meeting in early December was followed a week late by a vote authorizing construction, bids for which would be taken in early spring, 1953. The decision to build a new school, as well as the increase in new home construction gave evidence of a vigorous population growth in Marcellus. In addition, the efforts of the Citizens Club and Chamber of Commerce promoted an expanding economy and an increase in the services provided by both volunteers and government labeled Marcellus as a progressive community. This expansion, however, was changing Marcellus from a country town and the changes would become more apparent as the Village celebrated its centennial in 1953.

1953

Many were glad that the old year was over and that the new one would bring a fresh start.

May He Do a Better Job

MO January 2, 1953

The year would be significant for the Village of Marcellus in many ways, particularly as it celebrated its centennial birthday. The year would also mark the death of Joseph Stalin, the signing of a Korean War armistice and the announcement by Dr. Jonas Salk that he had discovered a vaccine for poliomyelitis, all of which would be welcome news to a people that had struggled with uncertainty and anxiety since 1945. There was also a new administration in Washington and " . . . when Dwight Eisenhower became President, he may have been the most widely admired new Chief Executive since George Washington" (Graff 706). People admired "Ike" as a hero of World War II and just as he had helped win that conflict, the nation looked to this even-tempered and fatherly man to settle the peace that seemed to have so far eluded the G.I. generation.

The Marcellus Observer
Friday, January 2, 1953
Village Purchases Salt Spreading Machine

The Village . . . has recently purchased a salt-spreading machine to be used in combating icy conditions of the streets . . . Salt will be used on the streets from now on, in the place of sand or cinders. The use of this . . . machine is going to save much time and labor . . . the streets will be in better condition all winter, and in the Spring, it will do away with the necessity of having to remove tons of cinders from the storm sewers and also the streets . . .

The Marcellus Observer
Friday, January 16, 1953
Speeders Clocked With Stop Watch By Officer Frank Pugh

Village Matters

For the Board of Trustees, the year began with the purchase and use of a salt spreading machine to improve driving conditions and continued use of the Speed Watch to slow down speeders in the Village. It also published notices to residents about building permits and water shut-offs, an attempt to control unplanned construction in the corporation as well as head off problems from developing in the future.

12 Jan 1953 - " . . . the following notices published in the Marcellus Observer: . . . that building permits will not be granted for any buildings to be erected on streets which have not been accepted by the Village . . . . no one has any right to turn the water shut-offs without authority from the Village maintenance men . . . ."

The most serious issue at the time, however, was that of ash and garbage collection. When bids were received for such collection, the Board decided to reject them and to remove such collection from its jurisdiction, proposing that each individual homeowner make his own arrangements with local truckers. The Board would keep the Village Dump open for residents to use, but argued that the cost of ash and garbage collection was too expensive for the Village Budget. The Board went on to argue that some individuals did not need the service and yet are taxed for it and others with tax exemptions received the service but did not pay for it. The decision would set off a storm of protest and controversy and heated discussions at the Village Caucus in February.

9 Feb 1953 - " . . . bids for ash and garbage collection were received, as follows:
Carl Riggall, Jr.   twice per week Monday & Thursday @ $77.50 per week
                       once per week Monday & Thursday @ $70.00 per week
Jacob R. Schneider   twice per week Monday & Thursday @ $80.00 per week

The Marcellus Observer
Friday, February 27, 1953
Edgar Bartlett Nominated For Mayor At
Village Caucus Tues

The Marcellus Observer
Friday, March 6, 1953
Bartlett Accepts Nomination
Kenyon Will Accept Office on Write-in Vote

Village Caucus

On February 24th, at Village Caucus a heated exchange took place over the garbage collection issue. Two candidates for Mayor were nominated, including the incumbent, Varnum S. Kenyon and a challenger, Edgar Bartlett. In the vote that followed, Mr. Bartlett received 67 of the ballots cast and Mr. Kenyon received 31, a clear admonishment of the incumbent, whose vote on the garbage collection issue had angered many residents. While the two men would face each other in the March 17th election, Lester C. Norris received the only nomination for Trustee, to succeed himself, as did M. W. Sullivan, renominated to succeed himself as Police Justice. The caucus produced a large turnout, but " . . . with over 100 people present, on the second story of a frame building, with only one stairway and no curb on smoking of any kind, an outbreak of fire could have been a disaster" (MO 2/27/53). This was an unpleasant reminder by the local editor and one that needed to be addressed.

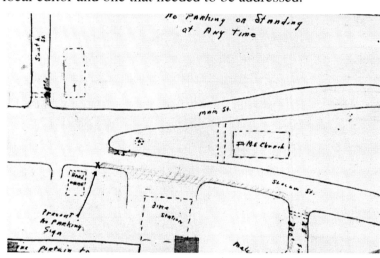

Village Parking

While discussion went on about the issue of garbage collection, and the Mayor tried to explain the reasons for the Board action, the concern about parking near the Engine House again developed. On recommendation of the Fire Department, an ordinance was passed which restricted parking and/or standing at certain points. The map, while plainly drawn in 1953, depicts those parking restrictions as they apply to this day.

9 Mar 1953 - " . . . ordinance pertaining to parking . . . duly adopted . . . Resolved that there shall be absolutely no car parking or standing at any time in the following designated areas:

1. West side of South Street, for a distance of 25 feet from the intersection of West Main and South

2. South side of Slocum Street, for a distance of 25 feet from the point in front of the Methodist Church

3. North side of Slocum Street, from present No Parking Sign in front of Marcellus Hardware, to the intersection of Slocum and First

4. East side of First Street, for a distance of 300 feet from the intersection of Slocum and First, to Joseph Malcolm's driveway

5. West side of First Street for a distance of 25 feet from the intersection of Slocum and First.

All of the above parking restrictions were adopted on recommendation of the Marcellus Fire Department, in the interests of safety and speedy maneuvering of fire equipment in answering fire alarms."

Village Election

On March 17th, Village elections were held, the largest voter turnout in the corporation's history. The issue in the election was the decision of the Village Board to end Village jurisdiction over the collection of ashes and garbage and let individuals make their own arrangements for such collection. The incumbent, Varnum S. Kenyon, who was seeking his 5th term as Mayor, having been first elected in 1945, was denied that office by the residents of the Village, and it was a stunning rebuke to a man who had been in public service for the Village since 1914.

The Marcellus Observer
Friday, March 20, 1953
Record Breaking Vote Sweeps
Bartlett Into Office
Over Half Marcellus Voters Elect Ed Bartlett To Office

The largest vote ever recorded in Marcellus swept Edgar M. Bartlett into office as Mayor by the large margin of 348 for Bartlett and 109 for Mayor Varnum S. Kenyon, who ran on a write-in ticket . . .

The election really stirred up all residents of the village who were aroused over the collection of ashes and garbage. The manner of payments was to be taken off the budget and left to the individual to take care of the necessary financial arrangements of disposing of his own trash. This is the main cause of why Mayor Kenyon was replaced at the caucus and defeated at the polls. We sincerely wish the new Mayor loads of luck in his new undertaking and hope the Villages show as much enthusiasm in giving a helping hand after he takes office as they have shown in electing him

17 Mar 1953 - " . . . total number of ballots cast was 465

For Mayor For 2 Years

Edgar Bartlett	received	348 votes
Varnum S. Kenyon	received	109 votes
Spoiled	7	
Blank	1	
Total	465	

Edgar M. Bartlett
Village Mayor
1953-1955

For Trustee For 2 Years
Lester C. Norris . . . 385 votes

For Police Justice For 4 Years
M. W. Sullivan . . . 414 votes

Village Youth

Another shock for Village residents that month was the disorderly conduct of some Marcellus teenagers, which caused them to be " . . . expelled from places of entertainment or have these places closed by their owners because of the undisciplined act of these children" (MO 3/27/53). A week later, a number of parents and young people met " . . . to discuss with the eleven members of the Community Council the issue of a Youth Center in Marcellus" (MO 4/3/53). While the unruly acts of young people at this time were no different from that of a century earlier, there was, it seems, an undercurrent of boredom with many teenagers in the 1950s and many adults felt obliged to entertain and keep the young occupied.

A New Village Board

With the annual meeting in April, the Bartlett administration made a number of appointments and discussed the budget, the Mayor stating " . . . that he is becoming acquainted with the financial status of the Village and its problems and will endeavor to cut expenses in every way possible" (MO 4/10/53). The most important issue was, however, that of garbage collection and at its April 13th meeting, the Board invited proposals for furnishing this service. By the end of the month, bids had been received and the Board accepted that of Carl Riggal Jr. The issue was resolved, once again indicating, it seems, that "all politics is local" and that service in a small town is paramount.

6 Apr 1953 - " . . . Mr. Parsons be designated as Acting Mayor . . . Mrs. M. A. Morrocco be appointed clerk, at the same salary . . . "

13 Apr 1953 - " . . . that Mr. Thomas H. Dyer be appointed Village Attorney . . . at a salary of $150.00 per year . . ."

28 Apr 1953 - " . . . sealed bids for garbage and ash collection, . . . awarded to Carl Riggal Jr., . . . weekly, $71.95, for the year, $3,741.40"

New Town Supervisor

The end of April also brought news of the death of Morris H. Mulroy, Supervisor of the Town of Marcellus for the previous sixteen years, his passing quite sudden and unexpected. He had played a major role in promoting his hometown as Supervisor, and was well respected by political leaders as well as by friends, neighbors and fellow farmers. Justice of the Peace Walter B. Marquis was appointed to fill the vacancy left by the death of Mr. Mulroy.

New School and Flag Pole

Other items of news that spring included the building of a new elementary school near the Village, now known as the Katherine C. Heffernan Elementary School. Although outside the limits of the corporation, the school applied for permission to use Village utilities, water and sewer. This was granted by Board action with the stipulation that the school provides all labor and material in its construction and that the Village highway crew supervise the connection.

The Board also was interested in having the community flagpole removed from its present site in front of the Alvord House to a site on the Methodist Church lawn. By the end of the month, the pole was removed to its new location and Ed Bartlett, now the Mayor, gave it a new coat of paint, just as he had done many years before.

11 May 1953 - " . . . permission to make a connection to the Village water system for the new school to be built soon . . . Clerk was directed to write Mr. Stanley Munro regarding permission to move the flag pole to a place on the Methodist Church lawn, which will be satisfactory to the Church, Village and Veterans."

Sheep and Busses

The community celebrated Memorial Day in typical fashion that year, but some visitors, while putting flowers on relatives' graves, " . . . were shocked to find sheep in the Village Cemetery . . . " (MO 6/5/53). Some residents were equally upset with the news that they might be denied bus service because the Cayuga Bus Company was in the process of disbanding and the new company would eliminate the route over East Hill. While the Auburn Bus Company would be granted a franchise to operate through the Village, " . . . residents of W. Seneca Turnpike and Onondaga Hill voiced their objections of granting a franchise to the company unless they included in it the continued operation of a bus line called the Onondaga Hill Route" (MO 6/12/53). Following a public hearing, both the Village and Town Boards decided to defer action until after a hearing was conducted by the Public Service Commission, a process that would not be resolved until November.

9 Jun 1953 - " . . . resolution . . . granting a franchise to the Auburn Bus Company to operate motor buses through the Village of Marcellus under certain conditions, was adopted."

MARCELLUS - - 1853
CENTENNIAL - - 1953

This year marked the 100th anniversary of the founding of the Village of Marcellus, and while the actual incorporation date was early in June, the community observed the

occasion in connection with the Old Home Day and Fourth of July festivities. Decorated with flags and bunting, residents celebrated with speeches and prizes, a parade, games and rides, a fitting commemoration of that day, June 4, 1853 when forty-one men voted to incorporate as a Village.

**The Marcellus Observer
Friday, June 19, 1953
Village Girds For 100th
Anniversary Celebration**

**The Marcellus Observer
Friday, June 26, 1953
Brief Resume Of The Past
One Hundred Years For
Village of Marcellus
1853-1953**

**The Marcellus Observer
Friday, July 3, 1953
Old Home Day – Centennial
Program Opens Tonight**

The Marcellus Observer - Friday, July 10, 1953
Biggest Crowd In Years Help Marcellus To Celebrate Its Centennial And Old Home Day
Saturday morning, July 4, 1953 found the Village of Marcellus celebrating its One Hundredth Birthday with ceremonies, parade and festivities appropriate for the occasion.
Opening the program at 9: 00 a.m., Mayor Ed Bartlett . . . introduced Miss Lucy Sweet, who gave what is known as a 'Rambling History of Marcellus'. Following this the Mayor introduced past mayors: . . . Then came the honored guests of the Centennial, being Marcellus' oldest and finest. The Oldest Woman living in Marcellus was Mrs. Fanny Gay, 91, . . . The Oldest Man living in Marcellus was Charles Curtin, 91, . . . The youngest resident of Marcellus went to the son of Mr. and Mrs. Wm. Groeling who was born June 27, 1953, at 11:00 a.m. Following the awards, . . . the Honorable Searles Schultz, N.Y. State Assemblyman, . . . covered the growth and progress of the village. Upon completion of the . . . Ceremony, the Firemen's Old Home Day Parade . . . proceeded to the Marcellus Park site where the rides and concessions kept many busy for the rest of the day.

The Village Dump

One of the issues confronting the men who voted to incorporate in 1853 would continue to perplex those who sat on the Village Board in 1953 - that of accumulating debris and what to do with it. For those in 1953, however, more scrap was being gathered and the Village dump was no longer capable of handling that of its residents and those outside the corporation who used the dump but paid nothing for its support. Therefore, when the Board decided to close the dump to all except those living in the Village, this action would bring on another Village-Town controversy that would only be resolved when both Boards met to discuss what was really a community-wide concern.

16 Jul 1953 - " . . . after Monday, July 27th, the Village of Marcellus Dump be closed to everyone except people living in the Village of Marcellus."

The Marcellus Observer - Friday, July 24, 1953
The Village Dump
Into the limelight of Marcellus again creeps the unsuspecting menace of the Village Dump.
It has caused much dissension in the past. It will cause dissension in the future, unless SOMETHING IS DONE ABOUT IT NOW! . . . May we suggest a public hearing with both Boards present to iron it out . . .

The Marcellus Observer
Friday, August 7, 1953
The Korean Truce At Long Last
. . . a comment on the war that was not a war. The Korean Truce which caused the cessation of bloodshed, has caused joy and happiness in many hones all over the country . . .

Armistice

The end of July brought news of a Korean War armistice but not before news of another Marcellus casualty. Cpl. Daniel Welch was reported missing following an attack by Chinese Communist troops on the post he was defending north of the 38th parallel. A young man of twenty-two at the time, the body of Cpl. Welch was not recovered and returned for several years. The armistice had brought hope, but not all of the boys would be home soon. In addition, " . . . warned of the still critical need for blood in spite of the Korean armistice . . . many soldiers . . . wounded in the last days of the fighting . . ." (MO 8/21/53), the Ladies Auxiliary of the Marcellus Fire Department sponsored a Red Cross unit to receive blood donors from the community. In addition, the Community Chest campaigned in the fall for increased donations to help worthy causes, " . . . among which is the USO whose program must be stepped up because of the Korean Truce. The problem of maintaining morale among the troops is acute . . . " (MO 8/28/53).

Safety Patrol

As the kids went back to school in September, the Citizens Club pursued its project of securing volunteers for a School Safety Patrol and was able to put it into operation by mid-October. Supervised by mothers who volunteered their time each day, the main streets of the Village were patrolled and children would have help in crossing the busy corners. With Village Board approval, every adult participating would also " . . . be deputized, . . . provided with her own patrol belt and whistle . . . " (MO 10/16/53), along with the full power of regulating traffic and issuing tickets if necessary. The Village Board also authorized the purchase of an electric timer for the floodlights at the Village Hall, an added safety feature and mischief deterrent at Halloween time.

MO September 11, 1953

12 Oct 1953 - " . . . the persons whose names appear on the attached list, be accepted as members of the Marcellus Adult Safety Patrol . . . that the Village buy an electric timer clock and have it installed in the wiring of the two flood lights at the Village Hall."

> **The Marcellus Observer**
> **Friday, November 6, 1953**
> All Republican Candidates Elected; Director Plan Defeated In Marcellus
>
> **The Marcellus Observer**
> **Friday, November 6, 1953**
> **Onondaga Coach Corp., Granted Franchise**

November Elections

In November, Ben Marquis was elected Supervisor along with other Republican candidates for Town office and the voters also helped the rest of the County defeat a County Director Plan. Such a plan would have replaced the Board of Supervisors as the governing agency of the County with a director acting as chief executive and many towns outside the City of Syracuse viewed this as a form of one-man dictatorship which would be costly to the taxpayers. The idea of a County Executive would eventually develop, but not for another decade. Interestingly the first County Executive, in 1962, would be a Marcellian, John H. Mulroy, son of the long time Town Supervisor, Morris Mulroy. The bus situation in Marcellus would also be resolved that month as the Onondaga Coach Corporation was allowed by the Public Service Commission to operate from Auburn to Syracuse, on both routes, providing uninterrupted service to residents, the Board endorsing the franchise after a public hearing in December.

8 Dec 1953 - " . . .application has been made to the Board of Trustees . . . by Onondaga Coach Corp. for consent to operate an omnibus route on and along certain highways through the Village of Marcellus . . .."

A Grateful Community

As the year came to an end, the people of the community found much for which to be grateful at Thanksgiving and again as the Christmas season arrived. The firemen bought blue lights for their cars that November, a color that for many signifies hope for the help that is on the way. The color finds much use during the Christmas season as well, a symbol of light and peace, of hope for the future, a soft glow to combat anxious nights.

> **The Marcellus Observer**
> **Friday, November 13, 1953**
> **Let Us Give Thanks**
> Marcellians have a lot to we thankful for in 1953. We have our churches, schools and wonderful neighbors. Our town is small, neat and quiet. Many people who have come here to live have remarked how much better they feel, and strongly recommend to their friends to move here. We have just celebrated our Centennial. 100 years of fine living, religious freedom and prosperity . . .
>
> **The Marcellus Observer**
> **Friday, November 27, 1953**
> **Firemen Buy Blue Lights For Cars**
> . . . to facilitate firemen reaching the firehouse to man the trucks, or in reaching the scene of the fire, or in controlling traffic . . .

MO December 25, 1953

Conclusion

The early 1950s, while anxious, had seen much success, particularly over polio and communist expansion in Asia and at home. The years ahead would continue to be uneasy and there were additional crises that increased cold war tension between the United States and the Soviet Union. The rest of the decade, however, was also marked by business expansion, unprecedented prosperity and signs of patriotism everywhere, in major cities and in small-town America. It was a happy time for many, a time of rest and relaxation, when people sought security and enjoyed simple pleasures. For the time being, the crusades had been fought and reform was suspended.

Christmas in Marcellus

The works of Norman Rockwell seemed to typify the aspirations of many people in small-town America at the time. The picture above, drawn at the end of the decade and displayed in the Village Office at present, is not that of Rockwell, but it does seem to illustrate the hopes and thoughts of many who sought quiet and peace in the 1950s as well as the straight lines and balance of a Rockwell painting. It was a time that would be challenged by the turbulence of the next decade.

EPILOGUE
End of the First 100 Years

From 1853 to 1953, the Village of Marcellus changed, and yet, it remained the same. Nestled at the bottom of a valley and surrounded by limestone hills, the sleepy hamlet in 1853, was a trading center for local farmers and a crossroads for itinerant travelers on their way west. By 1953, it was still a center of the local farm trade, but also a home for hundreds who worked in the manufacture of agriculture-related products. Its economy had changed but not dramatically.

What had once been a small homogeneous village of about 350 people, similar in background and customs, had become by 1953, a diverse community of almost 1,400 residents from many different lifestyles. The community was much larger, but the people were still one, now out of many.

When it became a Village in 1853, a major concern for the elected Trustees was the animals that roamed the dirt streets that often turned to mud. By 1953, their concern was about the automobiles that clogged the macadamized streets that needed constant repair. Village government had become more complex, yet the problems remained quite similar in nature.

In the years that followed incorporation, the Village experienced many changes and the residents found it necessary to react to many changes. However, many times it was a reworking, a revision, or a modification – usually an improvement on what had been.

The Next Fifty Years (1953-2003)

In 1941, Roy Gallinger, the editor of *The Marcellus Observer*, captured the history of the Village of Marcellus and the spirit of its people in a poem that he quoted and is as valid today as it was over sixty years ago. Entitled the Bridge Builder, it sums up the role that individuals and families play as they face the challenges and decisions of their own generation and prepare for those that will follow.

In the next fifty years, the Village of Marcellus would adjust. "The traditional picture of Marcellus as basically an agricultural and milling community gradually changed. While farming continued to hold its place in the economy, one by one most of the locally operated mills, which had given employment to so many people for so many years, began to bow in the face of changing markets, rising costs, and competition from large corporations utilizing modern technologies" (Heffernan 120).

In the next fifty years, many old homes and buildings in the Village would fall to the wrecker's ball, while many other landmarks would remain intact, often remodeled by businessmen or homeowners to a former glory. "While new structures were

The Marcellus Observer
Thursday, June 26, 1941
The Bridge Builder
An Old man traveling a lone highway,
Came at evening cold and gray
To a chasm vast and deep and wide
Through which flowed a sullen tide.

The old man crossed in the twilight dim,
The sullen stream had no fears for him;
But he turned when safe on the other side,
And built a bridge to span the tide.

"Old man," said a pilgrim standing near,
You're losing strength in building here.
Your journey ends with the ending day,
You never again will pass this way.

"You have safely crossed the chasm wide,
Why build this bridge at eventide?"

"Good friend, in the path I've come today,
There follows a youth who must pass this way."

The chasm that's been naught to me
To that fair youth may a pitfall be.
He, too, must cross in the twilight dim;
Good friend, I build this bridge for him."

appearing in the central village, many of the old business blocks continued to house various types of retail and service establishments" (Heffernan 127).

In the next fifty years, there would be a continued increase in the population as more and more people moved to the suburbs, dramatically changing the make-up of the native population. "However, unlike many fast-growing suburban areas, Marcellus has been able to maintain a strong community spirit while capitalizing on the talents and interests of the newcomers and, at the same time, integrating them into the established groups and institutions" (Heffernan 162).

In the next fifty years, the role of government in the Village would also change. More and more services would be added and an aging infrastructure required continuous consideration by the elected representatives of Village residents.

The next fifty years will also see the emergence of a new generation and it, too, would build bridges to the 21ˢᵗ century – ones that their own children will follow.

A Welcome Home

As the Village began its second century, its residents, like those who first settled the community, exhibited an optimism that was reflected in their daily lives and is common in many small towns "where everybody knows your name," to quote the lines of a 1990s

TV show. The people worked hard at their jobs and they worked energetically on volunteer projects that promoted the best interests of their community. They raised their children to be God-fearing and expected good behavior from them. They insisted on good schools for their children and were willing to pay the expense that was involved in providing such opportunity. They practiced the faith of their fathers and they lived it. They expected to triumph over adversity as had their forefathers and they would convey this attitude to their offspring. They took pride in their homes and their community and as the next year arrived, would renew the commitment and resolve that was their legacy.

"The writer of the play, *Our Town*, Thornton Wilder, once said, 'I am interested in those things that repeat and repeat and repeat in the lives of the millions.' In this play, Wilder explores those things that repeat and repeat and repeat. Birth, love, disappointment and death are the themes that ripple through the drama as well as through the lives of people in 1901, in 1801, and in 2001 . . . Attending a performance of *Our Town* is like spending an evening with friends and neighbors . . . that is why *Our Town* has endured and is still one of the most widely produced American plays" (Boorstin & Kelley 156). Marcellus is our town and every town in small-town America. It has endured because each generation has made it possible for the next to assume the responsibilities that are expected of them. It also endured because it is made up of families and friends and neighbors who view their town as a welcome home – a place that, from the top of East Hill or West Hill welcomes them home each night.

BIBLIOGAPHY

352

Amerman, George L. <u>Historical Sketch of the Town of Marcellus</u>. Marcellus: 1914.

Boorstin, Daniel J and Kelley, Brooks Mather. <u>A History of the United States: The Humanities Supplement</u>. Englewood Clifs, NJ. Prentice Hall, Inc. 1991

Bruce, Dwight. <u>Onondaga's Centennial. Gleanings of a Century</u>. Vol. I & II. Boston: The Boston History Company. 1896.

Cambell, Wallace H. <u>Historic Marcellus and Vicinity</u>. Finger Lakes Telephone Corporation, 1963.

Carruth, Gorton. <u>What Happened When. A Chronology of Life and Events in America</u>. New York: Harper & Row, Publishers, Inc., 1989

<u>Census of the Village of Marcellus, 1898</u>. Unpublished Record.

Clark, Joshua V.H., A.M. <u>Onondaga: or Reminiscences of Earlier Times</u>. Vol. 11. Syracuse: Stoddard and Babcock. 1849.

Clayton, Prof. W.W. <u>History of Onondaga County, 1615-1878</u>. New York. Syracuse: D. Mason & Co. 1878.

Davenport, Mary K. <u>Marcellus in the World War</u>.

Elliot, Katherine. <u>Building Structure Inventory of the Village of Marcellus</u>. Prepared by the Division For Historic Preservation, New York State Parks and Recreation Department, Albany, NY, 1989. Unpublished Inventory.

Foley, Jasena Rapplaye. <u>The Night the Rock Blew Up</u>. Syracuse: Onondaga Historical Society. 1973

Graff, Henry F. <u>America, The Glorious Republic</u>. Boston: Houghton Mifflin Company, 1985

Griffing, Frank. "Memories of Marcellus." Series in <u>The Marcellus Observer</u>. Marcellus: 1950's.

Heffernan, Kathryn C. <u>Nine Mile Country. The History of the Town of Marcellus, N.Y</u>. Visual Artis Publications, Inc., 1978.

Heffernan, Kathryn C. <u>The Parish of Saint Francis Xavier, Marcellus, New York, 1873-1973</u>. Marcellus, 1973

<u>Historic Buildings of The Village of Marcellus</u>. Prepared by the Landmarks Association of Central New York, 1979. Unpublished Survey.

<u>Marcellus and Otisco Lake Railway</u>. National Railway Historical Society, Syracuse Chapter, 1950.

Marcellus Methodist Church, 1816-1966. Sesquicentennial Publication. Marcellus: 1966.

Marcellus Township. Clipping Files, Onondaga Historical Association, Syracuse.

Marcellus Village Directory. 1899.

Maslyn, David. History of the Marcellus Free Library. Unpublished manuscript.
McKee, Harley J. et al. Architecture Worth Saving in Onondaga County. Syracuse: New
    York State Council on the Arts and Syracuse University School of Architecture.
    1964.

Minutes of the Board of Trustees, Village of Marcellus., 1853-1953. Unpublished
    Records.

New York State Census of 1855, 1865, 1875, 1892, 1905, 1915, 1925

175 Years 1801-1976. First Presbyterian Church. Marcellus: 1976.

 Onondaga County Directory, 1868 -1869.

Palmer, Richard F. Gone But Not Forgotten. The Marcellus and Otisco Lake Railway.
    Marcellus: Central New York Chapter National Railway Historical Society, Inc.
    1966.

Parsons, Israel, M.D. The Centennial History of the Town of Marcellus. Marcellus:
    Reed's Printing House. 1878.

Phillips, Henry E. Marcellus History 1794-1939. Old Home Day Celebration. Marcellus:
    1939.

Population Schedules of the United States: Census of 1850, 1860, 1870, 1880, 1900,
    1910, 1920, 1930

Rabin, Bernard. The Influence of Geography Upon the Settlement Patterns and Way of
    Life of the Marcellus Valley. Syracuse: 1947. Unpublished manuscript.

Roe, Rev. Andrew. "In Times Gone By. Brief Sketches of Earlier and Later Times in
    Marcellus." The Marcellus Observer. Marcellus: Weekly Series 1894-1895.

St. John's Church, 1824-1974. Anniversary Publication. Marcellus: 1974.

Smith, Rev. George R. Presbyterian Church, Memorial History. Canandaigua: Ontario
    County Times Steam Printing House. 1883.

Strauss, William and Howe, Neil. Generations. The History of America's Future, 1584 to
    2069. New York: William Morrow and Company, Inc., 1991.

Sweet, Homer D. L. Sweet's Atlas of Onondaga County, New York. New York: Walker
    Brothers and Co. 1874.

354

The Marcellus Observer, 1979-1953

Town of Marcellus. Clerk 's Records, 1830-1976. Unpublished Records

Village of Marcellus. Village Center Design Guidelines. Prepared by SUNY College of
Environmental Science and Forestry, 1998. Unpublished Document.

Woodford, Mrs. Clarence M. The First Church of Marcellus, New York, 1801-1936.
Skaneateles: Skaneateles Press. 1936.

ILLUSTRATIONS

Most of the images are from The Marcellus Historical Society Museum Collection or from copies of The Marcellus Observer, 1879-1953. Another recognition of the generosity of these organizations is also warranted.

INDEX

APPENDIX

Officers of the Village of Marcellus - 1853-2003

Year	President (Mayor)	Trustee	Trustee	Trustee
1853	Machan, William J.	Rowley, Elijah	Soules, Isaac N.	Bradley, Isaac
1854	Aiken, Edmund	Soules, Isaac N.	Bradley, Isaac	White, J. G. B.
1855	Tefft, Luke I.	Gasper, Caleb	Phillips, Joseph	Mills, Myron S.
1856	Cobb, Stephen	McGonegal, H. G.	Mills, Myron S.	Cowles, John H.
1857	Cobb, Stephen	Coon, Daniel G.	Smith, John L.	Cowles, John H.
1858	Coon, Daniel G.	Cobb, Stephen	Chrysler, Cornell	Warner, Seymour
1859	Crysler, Cornell	Wellington, William	Machan, William J.	Sarr, James
1860	William Wellington	Coon, Daniel G.	Moses, Chester	Parsons, Bishop N.
1861	Moses, Chester	Coon, Daniel G.	Wellington, William	DeCoudres, Thomas
1862	Cowles, John H.	Moses, Benjamin F.	Smith, John L.	Nickerson, J. May
1863	Cowles, John H.	Coon, Daniel G.	Platt, Joseph B.	Smith, John L.
1864	Howe, E. R.	Coon, Daniel G.	Platt, Joseph B.	Smith, John L.
1865	Moses, Chester	Moses, Irving	Walker, Thomas	Cobb, Stephen
1866	Moses, Chester	Moses, Irving	Coon, Daniel G.	Cobb, Stephen
1867	Bush, Ira	Sayre, James C.	Dada, Samuel	Hemingway, Seneca
1868	Moses, Chester	Coon, Daniel G.	Smith, John L.	Cowles, John H.
1868***	Moses, Chester	Machan, William J.	Sprague, Harvey	Beach, Lauren
1869	Moses, Chester	Dada, Samuel	Sprague, Harvey	Bishop, Ira
1870	Rhodes, Thomas	Bishop, Ira	Dada, Samuel	Bronson, Hiram
1871	Rhoades, Thomas	Hooper, Samuel	Coon, Daniel G.	Bronson, Hiram
1871***	Moses, Lucius*	Curtis, Albert	Hunt, Jasper	Hooper, Samuel
	Brown, Oscar J. **			
1872	Brown, Oscar J.	Curtis, Albert	Hunt, Jasper	VanVranken, John B.
1873	Case, Newton G.	Curtis, Albert	Hunt, Jasper	VanVranken, John B.
1874	Coon, Daniel G.	Johnston, James	Woodbridge, Joseph	Hooper, Samuel
1875	Sherman, Isaac N.	North, Robert F.	Dunlap, James M.	Alvord, R. Warren
1876	Sherman, Isaac N.	Sayre, James C.	North, Robert F.	VanVranken, John B.
1877	Sherman, Isaac N.	Curtis, Albert	Sayre, James C.	Axton, James
1878	Coon, Daniel G.	Johnston, James	Stocking, George	Hunt, Jasper
1879	Coon, Daniel G.	Johnston, James	Woodbridge, Joseph*	Hunt, Jasper
			Axton, James**	
1880	Sherman, Isaac N.	Axton, James	Bronson, Selah	DeCoudres, Charles H.
			Hunt, Jasper*	
			Banks, Franklin**	
1881	Case, Newton G.	Stocking, George	Curtis, Albert**	Dodd, Simon Jr.
1882	Case, Newton G.	Stocking, George	Curtis, Albert	Dodd, Simon Jr.
1883	Sherman, Isaac N.*	Mogg, S. N.*	Bronson, Selah M.*	Keefe, John*
1883***	Case, Newton G.	Stocking, George	Curtis, Albert*	Dodd, Simon Jr.
			Slocombe, Sidney**	
1884	Gallup, William H.	VanVranken, John B. (2)	Reed, Edmund (2)	Newton, Eli (1)
1885	Whiting, Myron M.			Julia, R. Almon (2)*
1886	Gallup, William H.	Dunlap, James M. (2)	Case, Charles (2)*	Whiting, Myron M. **
1887	Whiting, Myron M.		Gallup, W. H. (2)	Wells, Harvey (1)
1888	Whiting, Myron M.	VanVranken, John B. (2)		Wells, Harvey (2)
1889	Dodd, Simon Jr.		Gallup, W. H. (2)	
1890	Bronson, Selah M.	Griffin, John E. (2)		Sherman, Isaac N. (2)
1891	Gallup, William H.		Bronson, Selah M. (2)	

Officers of the Village of Marcellus - 1853-2003

Year	Trustee	Collector	Treasurer	Clerk
1853	Coon, Daniel G.	Taylor, Joseph	Kennedy, George N.	Kennedy, Henry T.
1854	Hoyt, Nathan G.	Taylor, Joseph	Kennedy, George N.	Kennedy, Henry T.
1855	Herring, James W.	Wilson, Amery	Cowles, John H.	Kennedy, Henry T.
1856	Smith, John L.	Wilson, Amery	White, Jeremiah G. B.	Chrysler, Cornell*
				Wilson, Amery**
1857	Rockwell, Alfred	Cobb, Belus S.	White, Jeremiah G. B.	Wilson, Amery
1858	Venzia, Alfred	Wilson, Amery	White, Jeremiah G. B.	Wilson, Amery
1859	North, John	Cobb, Belus S.	Cowles, John H.	Wilson, Amery
1860	DeCoudres, Thomas	Cobb, Stephen	Cowles, John H.	Wilson, Amery
1861	Chrysler, Cornell	Cobb, Stephen	Cowles, John H.	Wilson, Amery
1862	Lyman, Frederick A.	Cobb, Stephen	Cowles, John H.	Wilson, Amery
1863	Reed, Hiram	Wilson, Amery	Lyman, Frederick A.	Wilson, Amery
1864	Cowles, John H.	Cobb, Belus S.	Cowles, John H.	Wilson, Amery
1865	Alvord, Calvin G.	Cobb, Stephen	Lyman, Frederick A.	Wilson, Amery
1866	Walker, Thomas	Cobb, Stephen	Lyman, Frederick A.	Wilson, Amery
1867	Walker, Thomas	Cobb, Stephen	Wilson, Amery	Wilson, Amery
1868	Reed, Hiram	Cobb, Stephen	Wilson, Amery	Wilson, Amery
1868***	Dada, Samuel	Cobb, Stephen	Wilson, Amery	Wilson, Amery
1869	Walker, Thomas	Cobb, Stephen	Wilson, Amery	Wilson, Amery
1870	Hooper, Samuel	Cobb, Stephen	Wilson, Amery	Wilson, Amery
1871	Beach, Lauren	Cobb, Stephen	Wilson, Amery	Wilson, Amery
1871***	-	Griffin, Stores M.	Moses, Irving	Wilson, Amery**
1872	-	Dada, Samuel	White, William B.	DeCoudres, Charles H.
1873	-	Dada, Samuel	White, William B.	DeCoudres, Charles H.
1874	-	Dada, Samuel	White, William B.	DeCoudres, Charles H.
1875	-	Dada, Samuel	White, William B.	DeCoudres, Charles H.
1876	-	Dada, Samuel	White, William B.	DeCoudres, Charles H.
1877	-	Johnston, James	White, William B.	Walker, Thomas
1878	-	Reed, Edmond J.	White, William B.	VanVranken, J. B.
1879	-	Reed, Edmond J.	White, William B.	VanVranken, J. B.
1880	-	Hunt, Jasper	White, William B.	VanVranken, J. B.
1881	-	Dada, Samuel	White, William B.	Seymour, John M.
1882	-	Dada, Samuel	White, William B.	Seymour, John M.
1883	-	Dada, Samuel	Case, Newton G.	Seymour, John M.
1883***	-	Dada, Samuel	Case, Willis T.	Seymour, John M.
1884	-	Dada, Samuel	Case, Willis T.	Seymour, John M.
1885	-	Johnston, James	Case, Willis T.	Seymour, John M.
1886	-	Walker, Thomas	Case, Newton G.	Seymour, John M.
1887	-	DeCoudres, J. Fred	Case, Newton G.	Seymour, John M.
1888	-	DeCoudres, J. Fred	Case, Newton G.	Seymour, John M.
1889	-	Stearns, John N.	Case, Newton G.	Seymour, John M.
1890	-	Stearns, John N.	White, William B.*	Seymour, John M.*
			DeCoudres, J. Fred**	Roe, Cary A.**
1891	-	Evans, John Jr.	DeCoudres, J. Fred	Roe, Cary A.

Officers of the Village of Marcellus - 1853-2003

Year	President (Mayor)	Trustee	Trustee	Trustee
1892	Moir, Edward	Griffin, John E. (2)		Woodbridge, Jas E. (2)
1893	Moir, Edward		Bronson, Selah M. (2)	
1894	Griffin, John E.*	Whiting, Myron M. (2)		Anderson, James (2)*
	Roe, Cary A.**			Coon, D.D.F.**
1895	Reed, Edmund		Jones, Henry S. (1)	Brown, Charles J. (2)
1896	Reed, Edmund	Coon, D. D. F. (2)	Newton, Eli A. (2)	
1897	Sarr, James			Brown, Charles J. (2)
1898	Slocombe, Sidney	Drake, Arthur E. (1)	Scott, John W. (2)	
1899	Slocombe, Sidney	Drake, Arthur E. (2)		-
1900	Slocombe, Sidney		Scott, John W. (2)	-
1901	Sherman, Isaac N.	Share, Isaac A. (2)		-
1902	Sherman, Isaac N.		Brown, Charles J. (2)	-
1903	Scott, John W.	Newton, Eli A. (2)		-
1904	Scott, John W.		Brown, Charles J. (2)	-
1905	Moir, Edward	Dillon, Charles (2)		-
1906	Moir, Edward		Brown, Charles J. (2)	-
1907	Moir, Edward	Dillon, Charles (2)		-
1908	Moir, Edward		Brown, Charles J. (2)	-
1909	Slocombe, Sidney	Dillon, Charles (2)		-
1910	Thompson, Fred A		Schoonmaker, F. T. (2)	-
1911	Thompson, Fred A.	Gillette, Frank H. (2)		-
1912	Thompson, Fred A.		Woodbridge, James E. (2)	-
1913	Thompson, Fred A.	Reed, Edmund (2)		-
1914	Gillette, Frank H.		Coville, E. W. (2)	-
1915	Thompson, Fred A	Reed, Edmund (2)		-
1916	Clark, Elmer P.		Coville, E. W. (2)	-
1917	Clark, Elmer P.	Curtis, Ward R. (2)		-
1918	Baker, Edward V.*		Scott, L. W. (2)*	-
	Jones, Charles E.**		Clark, Howard I.**	
1919	Jones, Charles E.	Curtis, Ward R. (2)		-
1920	Jones, Charles E.		Clark, Howard I. (2)	-
1921	Slocombe, Sidney	Kilcoyne, Patrick J. (2)		
1922	Jones, Charles, E.		Clark, Howard I. (2)	-
1923	McNair, James G.	Spaulding, John (2)*		-
		Parsons, James B.**		
1924	McNair, James G.		Kenyon, Varnum S. (2)	-
1925	McNair, James G.	Parsons, James B. (2)		-
1926	McNair, James G.		Kenyon, Varnum S. (2)	-
1927	McNair, James G. (2)	Parsons, James B. (2)		-
1928			Kenyon, Varnum S. (2)	Gillett, Frank H. (2)
1929	McNair, James G. (2)	(no successor)		
1930		Kenyon, Varnum S. (1)	Hunt, Stephen H. (2)	-
1931	Thornton, Michael J. (2)	Kenyon, Varnum S. (2)		-
1932			Hunt, Stephen H. (2)	-
1933	Thornton, Michael J. (2)	Kenyon, Varnum S. (2)		-
1934			Hunt, Stephen H. (2)	-

Officers of the Village of Marcellus - 1853-2003

Year	Trustee	Collector	Treasurer	Clerk
1892	-	Hellganz, J. George	DeCoudres, J. Fred	Roe, Cary A.
1893	-	Hellganz, J. George	Stearns, John N.	Roe, Cary A.
1894	-	Dada, Samuel	Stearns, John N.	Knapp, Frank W.
1895	-	Peck, Cassius A.	Stearns, John N.	Knapp, Frank W.
1896	-	Peck, Cassius A.	Stearns, John N.	Knapp, Frank W.
1897	-	Peck, Cassius A.	Stearns, John N.	Knapp, Frank W.
1898	-	Jones, Charles E.	Stearns, John N.	Knapp, Frank W.
1899	-	Peck, Cassius A.	Stearns, John N.	Knapp, Frank W.
1900	-	Beach, Andrew W.	Stearns, John N.	Knapp, Frank W.
1901	-	Beach, Andrew W.	Woodbridge, Jas E.	Knapp, Frank W.
1902	-	Beach, Andrew W.	Woodbridge, Jas E.	Knapp, Frank W.
1903	-	Beach, Andrew W.	Woodbridge, Jas E.	Knapp, Frank W.
1904	-	Beach, Andrew W.	Woodbridge, Jas E.	Knapp, Frank W.
1905	-	Beach, Andrew W.	Woodbridge, Jas E.	Knapp, Frank W.
1906	-	Beach, Andrew W.	Woodbridge, Jas E.	Knapp, Frank W.
1907	-	Olley, James H.	Woodbridge, Jas E.	Knapp, Frank W.
1908	-	Woodford, Clarence	Woodbridge, Jas E.	Knapp, Frank W.
1909	-	Woodford, Clarence	Woodbridge, Jas E.	Jones, Charles E.
1910	-	Woodford, Clarence	Woodbridge, Jas E.	Jones, Charles E.
1911	-	Woodford, Clarence	Woodbridge, Jas E.	Jones, Charles E.
1912	-	Woodford, Clarence	Marble, Austin C.	Jones, Charles E.
1913	-	Woodford, Clarence	Marble, Austin C.	White, Howard
1914	-	Woodford, Clarence	Marble, Austin C.*	White, Howard
			Kenyon, Varnum S. **	
1915	-	Woodford, Clarence	Kenyon, Varnum S.	White, Howard
1916	-	Woodford, Clarence	Kenyon, Varnum S.	White, Howard
1917	-	Woodford, Clarence	Kenyon, Varnum S.	White, Howard
1918	-	Woodford, Clarence	Kenyon, Varnum S.	White, Howard
1919	-	Woodford, Clarence	Kenyon, Varnum S.	White, Howard
1920	-	Woodford, Clarence	Kenyon, Varnum S.	Clark Elmer P.
1921	-	Woodford, Minnie	Kenyon, Varnum S.	Clark Elmer P.
1922	-	Wright, Alice M.	Austin, Helen L.*	Clark Elmer P.
			Woodbridge, J. Fred**	
1923	-	Wright, Alice M.	Woodbridge, J. Fred	Dillon, Charles
1924	-	Wright, Alice M.	Woodbridge, J. Fred	Dillon, Charles
1925	-	Wright, Alice M.	Woodbridge, J. Fred	Dillon, Charles
1926	-	Wright, Alice M.	Woodbridge, J. Fred	Dillon, Charles
1927	-	Wright, Alice M.	Woodbridge, J. Fred	Dillon, Charles
1928	Weidman, John H. (1)	-	Woodbridge, J. Fred*	Dillon, Charles *
	(no successor)			Jones, Charles E. **
1929		-	Woodbridge, J. Fred	Jones, Charles E.
1930	-	-	Woodbridge, J. Fred	Jones, Charles E.
1931	-	-	Woodbridge, J. Fred	Jones, Charles E.
1932	-	-	Woodbridge, J. Fred	Jones, Charles E.
1933	-	-	Woodbridge, J. Fred	Jones, Charles E.
1934	-	-	Woodbridge, J. Fred	Jones, Charles E.

Year	President (Mayor)	Trustee	Trustee	Trustee
1935	Thornton, Michael J. (2)	Kenyon, Varnum S. (2)		-
1936			Hunt, Stephen H. (2)	-
1937	Thornton, Michael J. (2)	Norris, Leonard (2)		-
1938			Hunt, Stephen H. (2)	-
1939	Spaulding, William S. (2)	Norris, Leonard (2)		-
1940			Hunt, Stephen H. (2)	-
1941	Spaulding, William S. (2)	Norris, Leonard (2)		-
1942			Hunt, Stephen H. (2)	-
1943	Spaulding, William S. (2)	Norris, Leonard (2)		-
1944			Case, Newton Giles (2)	-
1945	Kenyon, Varnum S. (2)	Edgerton, Clayton A. (2)		-
1946			Case, Newton Giles (2)	-
1947	Kenyon, Varnum S. (2)	Edgerton, Clayton A. (2)		-
1948			Case, Newton Giles (2)	-
1949	Kenyon, Varnum S. (2)	Edgerton, Clayton A. (2)		-
1950			Parsons, L. Seymour (2)	-
1951	Kenyon, Varnum S. (2)	Bush, Earl M. (2)*		-
1952		Norris, Lester C.**	Parsons, L. Seymour (2)	-
1953	Bartlett, Edgar M. (2)	Norris, Lester C. (2)		-
1954			Parsons, L. Seymour (2)	-
1955	Norris, Lester C. (2)	Paul, Donald A. (2)		-
1956			Parsons, L. Seymour (2)	-
1957	Norris, Lester C. (2)	Paul, Donald A. (2)		-
1958			Parsons, L. Seymour (2)	-
1959	Norris, Lester C. (2)	Paul, Donald A. (2)		-
1960			Barry, Charles C. (2)	-
1961	Norris, Lester C. (2)	Paul, Donald A. (2)		-
1962			Barry, Charles C. (2)	-
1963	Norris, Lester C. (2)	Paul, Donald A. (2)		-
1964			Barry, Charles C. (2)	-
1965	Norris, Lester C. (2)	Paul, Donald A. (2)		-
1966			Barry, Charles C. (2)	-
1967	Norris, Lester C. (2)	Paul, Donald A. (2)		-
1968			Rollin A. Wilson (4)*	-
1969	Norris, Lester C. (5)	Paul, Donald A. (5)		-
1970				-
1971			Parsons, L. Seymour**	-
1972			Parsons, L. Seymour (4)	-
1973				-
1974	Norris, Lester C. (4)	Paul, Donald A. (4)*		-
1975				-
1976		Snyder, Garth**	Parsons, L. Seymour (4)	-
1977		Snyder, Garth (1)		
1978	Norris, Lester C. (4)	Snyder, Garth (4)		-
1979				-
1980			Parsons, L. Seymour (4)	-

Officers of the Village of Marcellus - 1853-2003

Year	Trustee	Collector	Treasurer	Clerk
1935	-	-	Woodbridge, J. Fred	Jones, Charles E.*
				Woodbridge, J. Fred**
1936	-	-	Woodbridge, J. Fred	Woodbridge, J. Fred
1937	-	-	Woodbridge, J. Fred	Woodbridge, J. Fred
1938	-	-	Woodbridge, J. Fred (1)	Woodbridge, J. Fred (1)
1939	-	-	Woodbridge, J. Fred (2)	Woodbridge, J. Fred (2)
1940	-			
1941	-	-	Woodbridge, J. Fred (2)	Woodbridge, J. Fred (2)
1942	-	-		
1943	-	-	Woodbridge, J. Fred (2)	Woodbridge, J. Fred (2)
1944	-	-		
1945	-	-	Woodbridge, J. Fred (2)	Woodbridge, J. Fred (2)
1946	-	-		
1947	-	-	Woodbridge, J. Fred (2)	Woodbridge, J. Fred (2)
1948	Police Justice	-		
1949	Sullivan, M. W. (4)		Woodbridge, J. Fred (2)	Woodbridge, J. Fred (2)
1950				
1951			Woodbridge, J. Fred (2)	Morrocco, M. A. (2)
1952				
1953	Sullivan, M. W. (4)		Woodbridge, J. Fred (2)	Morrocco, M. A. (2)
1954				
1955			Woodbridge, J. Fred (2)	Morrocco, M. A. (2)
1956				
1957	Sullivan, M. W. (4)		Woodbridge, J. Fred (2)	Morrocco, M. A. (2)
1958				
1959			Woodbridge, J. Fred (2)	Morrocco, M. A. (2)
1960	Reagan, Bernard L. (1)			
1961	Reagan, Bernard L. (4)		Woodbridge, J. Fred (2)	Morrocco, M. A. (2)
1962				
			Woodbridge, J. Fred (2)*	
1963			Morrocco, M. A. **	Morrocco, M. A. (2)
			Morrocco, M. A.*	Morrocco, M. A.*
1964			Palen, Shirley **	Palen, Shirley **
1965	Reagan, Bernard L. (4)		Palen, Shirley (2)	Palen, Shirley (2)
1966				
1967			Palen, Shirley (2)	Palen, Shirley (2)
1968				
1969	Reagan, Bernard L. (4)		Palen, Shirley (2)	Palen, Shirley (2)
1970				
1971			Palen, Shirley (2)	Palen, Shirley (2)
1972				
1973	-		Palen, Shirley (?)	Palen, Shirley (?)
1974	-			
1975	-		Palen, Shirley (2)	Palen, Shirley (2)
1976	-			
1977	-		Palen, Shirley (2)	Palen, Shirley (2)
1978	-			
1979	-		Palen, Shirley (2)	Palen, Shirley (2)
1980	-			

Officers of the Village of Marcellus - 1853-2003

Year	President (Mayor)	Trustee	Trustee	Trustee
1981				-
1982	Norris, Lester C. (4)*	Snyder, Garth (4)*		-
	Snyder, Garth**	Tuthill, Sidney P.**		
1983	Snyder, Garth (3)	Tuthill, Sidney P. (3)		-
1984			Parsons, L. Seymour (4)*	-
1985				-
1986	Sennett, Martin (4)	Hall, Hugh (4)	Lollis, Raymond**	-
1987			Lollis, Raymond (1)	-
1988			Lollis, Raymond (4)	-
1989				-
1990	Sennett, Martin (4)	Bishop, Barbara (4)		-
1991				-
1992			Grant, Edwin H. (4)	-
1993				-
1994	Eisenberg, Frederic B. (4)	Warrender, Richard (4)*		-
1995		Curtin, John P.**		-
1996		Curtin, John P. (4)	Wilson, Robert J. (2)	-
1997				-
1998	Eisenberg, Frederic B. (4)		Wilson, Robert J. (4)	-
1999				-
2000		Curtin, John P. (4)		-
2001				-
2002	Eisenberg, Frederic B. (4)		Wilson, Robert J. (4)	-
2003				

*died or resigned   **appointed   ***special election   (1) = years elected or appointed

Officers of the Village of Marcellus - 1853-2003

Year	Trustee	Collector	Treasurer	Clerk
1981	-		Palen, Shirley (2)	Palen, Shirley (2)
1982	-			
1983	-		Palen, Shirley (2)	Palen, Shirley (2)
1984	-			
1985	-		Palen, Shirley (2)	Palen, Shirley (2)
1986	-			
1987	-		Palen, Shirley (2)*	Palen, Shirley (2)*
			March, Gary L.**	March, Gary L.**
1988	-		March, Gary L. (4)	March, Gary L. (4)
1989	-			
1990	-			
1991	-			
1992	-		March, Gary L. (4)	March, Gary L. (4)
1993	-			
1994	-			
1995	-			
1996	-		March, Gary L. (4)	March, Gary L. (4)
1997	-			
1998	-			
1999	-		March, Gary L. (3)	March, Gary L. (3)
2000	-			
2001	-			
2002	-		March, Gary L. (4)	March, Gary L. (4)
2003				

*died or resigned   **appointed   ***special election   (1) = years elected or appointed

ISBN 155395738-5

9 781553 957386